ARBITRATION AND
LABOR RELATIONS

ARBITRATION AND LABOR RELATIONS

(Third Edition of ARBITRATION OF LABOR DISPUTES)

by

CLARENCE M. UPDEGRAFF

*Professor of Law, Hastings College
of the Law*

THE BUREAU OF NATIONAL AFFAIRS, INC. • WASHINGTON, D.C.

Printed in the United States of America
Library of Congress Catalog Card Number: 72-96798
Standard Book Number 87179-098-X

13

Dedicated to my son
Dr. Clarence M. Updegraff, Jr., M.D.

FOREWORD TO FIRST EDITION

In the many decades of bargaining between employers and employees, pressures of numerous sorts have been devised and brought into use by the respective parties.

On the side of the employers, the lockout, the discriminatory discharge, reduction in rank, docking of pay, transfer from desirable to less desirable work, and almost innumerable other disciplinary actions have been at times used to discourage employee demands whether made individually or collectively. On the side of employees, pressures have taken the form of strikes, picketing, slowdowns, hot-cargoing, sabotage, arbitrary limitations on production, and several others. These are all more or less dramatic incidents and all in a sense involve "self-help."

Generally speaking, the law abhors a breach of the peace and has in most fields restricted self-help to the minimum for that reason. In the areas of labor disputes wasteful conflicts have remained unfortunately common even in our times, and the means by which they can be reduced or eliminated are current subjects of thought and study.

The economic losses involved in any of the above pressure methods of bringing the opposing parties to agreement are often very great. Prior to the legal recognition of the strike, peaceful picketing and collective bargaining, only the employer was, in all probability, able to bear the expense of protracted economic pressure. Even in that period, however, virtually all concerted actions by employees were criminally punishable as conspiracies. On the other hand, employers were left virtually free to deny employees their livelihoods by lockouts or discharges of men who were persistent either individually or collectively in demanding better working conditions, or increased compensation.

In this day of legally permitted strikes and picketing, and statutorily established rights to collective bargaining, labor groups have come to be as strong as and, in many instances, stronger than employers. Under their leadership more employees now can be caused to cease work simultaneously for pressure purposes and to slow down production than in former times. All instances of application of economic pressure by employers to employees or vice versa are economically wasteful in character. It, therefore, becomes more and more evident, as the great powers of the contending parties are equalized and recognized, that the welfare of the state as a whole must be sought through a means of reduction of general economic losses incident to the bargaining competition between the parties to labor disputes.

Arbitration appears to be an effective and practical means of disposing of disputes as a substitute for wasteful interruptions of production. There are indications that the number of instances of arbitration and the significance of arbitrational awards will continue to grow as rapidly for some time in the future as they have in the immediate past. Court action, as a rule, is too slow and too technical to offer a sufficiently prompt or adaptable solution for labor disputes. Courts are not always in session and, when they are, they are not equipped with adequate tools and rules to enable them to solve many controversies which daily arise in the fields of ethics and general employer-employee relationships.

Hundreds of arbitrations of labor controversies have been held in recent years. If those who have had experience with a substantial number of these pool the results of their observations and studies and by publication make them available for study and use by others, some measure of forward progress may result. Other arbitrators considering subsequent issues may turn to such work for guidance and suggestions. Some employer organizations and employers engaged in disputes may turn to the resulting pages to discover conclusions to be drawn from previous arbitrations, and in the light of the same, arrive at agreements without either wasteful interruption of production or arbitration. A set of labor arbitration reports may be a development of the not far distant future.

This work is intended to furnish in the present volume a general survey of arbitration in relation to labor disputes. It is clearly recognized that some of the decisions and awards referred to largely depend upon the particular terms of the contracts involved in them or the peculiar relationship of the parties, so that as precedents they may not have the same measure of validity when cited in later arbitrations as reported court decisions usually have in subsequent legal controversies under the *stare decisis* doctrine. Equally with reports, however, these arbitrational decisions and awards, when more completely collected, may furnish a fund of information and illustrate a technique of approach to problems which should make them as useful logically to arbitrators and bargaining parties involved in the processes of labor relations decisions as are the law reports to judges and lawyers concerned about questions which confront them.

The text matter presented does not cover fully and exhaustively all the details of the law of arbitration as found in statutes and court decisions involving the validity of arbitration proceedings and awards in general. These have been amply covered in various texts, law review articles, and encyclopedias. Labor arbitrations, unlike commercial arbitrations, seldom reach the courts. They are resorted to by the parties because of a conviction that it is less costly to lose an arbitration case than to engage in the industrial conflict that is often the only alternative; the same conviction generally leads the losing party to accept and abide by the award.

Hence, the aim of the present work has been to present, as briefly as is consistent with a sufficient degree of thoroughness, a description of labor arbitration as it exists in practice, with only sufficient reference to the statutes and court decisions as may enable its users to make at least an initial step in further studying any disputed question.

The purpose of the present work is to set forth fully a special and important procedural method by means of which the rights and privileges of the employers and employees are declared and protected.

. . . .

It will be noted that the authors have, with some misgivings, undertaken the rather ambitious task of attempting, in one work, to accomplish two objectives: (1) an exposition of the law of arbitration, as applied particularly to labor disputes, with citations to the authorities, to serve as a useful reference work for lawyers; and (2) a practical and not-too-technical guide for the layman who may be called upon to conduct an arbitration without benefit of legal counsel. The authors are aware that they have not fully accomplished these objects. It is inevitable that certain portions, which may be quite useful to the lawyer, will be very heavy reading for the layman; and conversely, other portions, which may appear "light" to the lawyer, will be useful and informative to the layman.

. . . .

In spite of our misgivings, we entertain the hope that the generous reader, whether lawyer or layman, may find in these pages something that will be helpful in a practical way to him, in a field that has as much practical importance to the layman as to the lawyer. If this volume helps in some measure to furnish the manager of industrial relations, the business agent, or the lawyer engaged in assisting in the maintenance of amicable labor relations, with a practical guide to the proper conduct of a hearing before an arbitrator, it will have served its purpose.

CLARENCE M. UPDEGRAFF
WHITLEY P. MCCOY

FOREWORD TO SECOND EDITION

Practically all that was written in the foreword of the first edition of this work has remained valid through the intervening years. The first edition was published in 1946. It suggested in the foreword that "A set of labor arbitration reports may be a development in the not far distant future." It is an interesting coincidence that in that same year the first volume of the BNA *Labor Arbitration Reports* appeared. This coverage of arbitration decisions and awards has given excellent service to all parties interested in Labor Arbitration since that date, and it continues to expand in character and usefulness to those active in the field of labor relations.

Meanwhile, the field of labor arbitration has developed tremendously in activity and in common acceptance. Acts of legislatures and decisions of the highest courts have shown approval and contributed to its increasing prestige. Apparently this growth is even now continuing at an accelerating pace.

As the preemption doctrine, unionization, and the practice of collective bargaining have increased the importance of labor relations, the use of arbitration has been correspondingly extended. The Lincoln Mills arbitration enforcement decision added an aspect of increased importance to agreements to arbitrate which could only have been supplied by the United States Supreme Court.

In preparing the second edition the objectives have been fourfold:

First, to eliminate a few parts of the first edition which now may be called obsolete;

Second, to comment upon what appear to be the important recently developing trends and beliefs, practices, and results of labor arbitration considered as a whole;

Third, to present analyses of recent statutes, decisions of boards, and courts, which appear destined to affect the expansion and directions of development of labor arbitration in the immediate future; and

Fourth, to bring the text of this book generally and the annotations into line with present beliefs, practices, and laws.

Three new chapters have been included, new sections have been added to several of the old chapters, and all the text has been revised.

The three new chapters are devoted to the titles "Summary of Labor Laws and Policy," "Arbitration and Various Areas of Employment," and "The Legal Rules of Evidence — Their Function in Relation to Arbitration." The chapter on "Observations Concerning Several of the Types of Disputes More Commonly Arbitrated," has been very considerably increased in scope.

The chapter on Labor Laws and Policy is not offered as exhaustive so as to be a search reference but rather for general informational use. The new part of the book devoted to legal rules of evidence was thought to be desirable not because court-enforced rules of evidence should be applied in governing the presentation and receipt of testimony at an arbitration hearing, but because they are not. The rules and principles of legal evidence and the reasoning on which they rest should be fully understood by every person who undertakes to weigh evidence and to present or decide controverted matters. When these rules are not used to determine the admissability of testimony, it must be recognized by all conscientious parties that some of them are very important in weighing the evidence. A brief review of this area of the law will inevitably aid both those who have no legal training and those who have had some previous legal training as they undertake to prepare, present, or ponder the testimony on the basis of which the decision must rest.

CLARENCE M. UPDEGRAFF

August 1960

FOREWORD TO THIRD EDITION

The first edition of this book was in some degree the joint work of W. P. McCoy and the present author. It was so entitled. Mr. McCoy sold his interest in the copyright to the undersigned and did not participate in the work of the second edition. It has been decided to omit his name from the present, third edition to avoid possibly misleading indications of responsibility in respect to it, and to change the title.

In effect, however, this is a third edition of the book above designated.

In the approximately nine years since the last edition appeared, many developments directly or indirectly affecting labor arbitration have occurred. These cannot be briefly or easily summarized. It seems well, however, to mention in this foreword some of the leading matters which have contributed to important changes in the labor relations area. Most of the subjects, noted only briefly here, are more fully developed in the following text at the parts where they are relevant.

Broadly speaking, authorities commenting on the field of labor arbitration may be said to have viewed the expanding scope of arbitration and arbitrability as generally requiring holding in favor of a party seeking to obtain such proceeding unless it can be said with positive assurance that the dispute in question is clearly excluded by the arbitration clause concerned. Doubts are to be resolved in favor of arbitration.[1]

The federal courts, speaking on arbitration since the year of the last edition (1961), have been inclined to hold that an action to

---

[1] For excellent treatments of the subject, see W. Willard Wirtz, "Due Process of Arbitration," The Arbitrator and the Parties, Proceedings of the Eleventh Annual Meeting, National Academy of Arbitrators (Washington: BNA Books, 1958), pp. 1-36, and Arnold Ordman and Robert G. Howlett, "The Arbitrator and the NLRB," The Arbitrator, the NLRB, and the Courts, Proceedings of the Twentieth Annual Meeting, National Academy of Arbitrators (Washington: BNA Books, 1967), pp. 47-111. For a well-reasoned judicial opinion, see Textile Workers Union of America v. Cone Mills Corporation, 188 F. Supp. 728, 47 LRRM 2111 (1960).

require arbitration may be brought under the U. S. Arbitration Act, as well as under the Labor Management Relations Act (Sec. 141 of Title 29) where the complaint does not present any matters inconsistent with the latter statute.[2]

Since the second edition of this work (1961) the NLRB has much extended its treatment of jurisdictional disputes and thus has shown the way for arbitrational determinations for parties who have turned to grievance procedure instead of to the unfair labor practice charge solutions of such questions.[3] The many-faceted cases of *Fibreboard*,[4] *Wiley*,[5] *Darlington*,[6] *American Ship Building*,[7] and *NLRB* v. *Brown*[8] have added their impact and influences and for labor arbitrators have extended the area of rules and principles to be studied, distinguished, and applied to the constantly varying fact situations that arise to require decisions. As would be assumed, these are later herein treated in some detail.

The *Spielberg*[9] decision has been increasingly commented on since its appearance. It is recognition by the National Labor Relations Board that awards of arbitrators shall be recognized as effective if the proceedings "have been fair and regular, all parties had agreed to be bound, and the decision of the arbitration panel is not clearly repugnant to the purposes and policies of the Act." That decision, however, was foreshadowed much earlier by the Board's words in *Consolidated Aircraft Corporation*.[10] Since its decision *Spielberg* has been endorsed by the *Steelworkers* trilogy[11] and by a 1964 amendment to the Labor Management Relations Act.[12] Thus it may be observed that the great increase in labor arbitration in recent years appears to be unanimously approved

---

2 Western Automatic Machine Screw Company v. International Union, United Automobile, Aircraft and Agricultural Workers of America, 335 F. 2d 103, 56 LRRM 2978 (1964).

3 See 20th New York University Conference on Labor; § 10(k), 61 Stat. 149 (1947), 29 U.S.C. § 160(k) (1964); NLRB v. Radio and Television Broadcast Engineers, 364 U. S. 573, 47 LRRM 2332 (1961).

4 379 U. S. 203, 57 LRRM 2609 (1964).

5 376 U. S. 543, 55 LRRM 2769 (1964).

6 380 U. S. 263, 58 LRRM 2657 (1965).

7 380 U. S. 300, 58 LRRM 2672 (1965).

8 380 U. S. 278, 58 LRRM 2663 (1965).

9 112 NLRB 1080, 36 LRRM 1152 (1955) . See *supra* No. 1.

10 47 NLRB 694, 12 LRRM 44 (1943) enforced in 144 F. 2d 785, 14 LRRM 553 (1944).

11 363 U. S. 564, 46 LRRM 2414 (1960) and 593, 46 LRRM 2423 (1960).

12 29 U.S.C. 173(d).

and encouraged by the U. S. Supreme Court, the Congress, and the NLRB. It is clear that popular opinion also supports arbitration as a valued, perhaps indispensable, medium for solution of labor differences and promotion of good labor relations.

The *Spielberg* bases for approval of awards by the NLRB, however, were no surprise to people informed in the labor field. Since time immemorial the tests of a valid award have been the mutual agreement of the parties to be bound by it, and "fair and regular procedure." Obviously any court or other authoritative reviewing tribunal must always have been expected to deny effect to any award "clearly repugnant" to the properly applicable law. Indeed it is difficult to perceive any logic by which a result contrary to *Spielberg* could be sustained.

On another tack, the *Avco*[13] decision of March 8, 1968, gives rise to some interesting questions. In that case a state court was denied jurisdiction to enjoin a strike by a union that had refused to arbitrate promotion eligibility though it had contracted to submit all grievances to binding arbitration and to refrain from any strike during the term of the agreement. *Avco* came down on March 8, 1968. On January 26, 1968, the Fifth Circuit had handed down its decision in *New Orleans Steamship Assn.* v. *General Longshore Workers I.L.A., Local Union #1418*,[14] issuing a mandatory injunction to enforce an arbitration award ordering discontinuance of a violation of a no-strike clause. In that case the effect of the decree was to enforce an award. In the opinion the court said,

> "The question presented now is the power of the District Court to enforce the award of an arbitrator in a setting where the arbitrator, in the exercise of undisputed contractual jurisdiction, has ordered an end to work stoppages. The union has refused to abide by his order and asserts that the court is without jurisdiction to remedy the breach. Practically, this is the ultimate or last step in the arbitration process. The agreement between the parties is valid and the authority of the arbitrator over the subject matter and to enter a desist order is not disputed. We can assume, arguendo, that the employer agreed to arbitrate grievances in return for the no work stoppage clause. Does Sinclair foreclose relief to the employer? We hold that it does not.

---

[13] Avco Corp. v. Machinists Aero Lodge #735, 390 U. S. 557, #445, 4-8-68, 67 LRRM 2881 (1968).
[14] 67 LRRM 2430 (5th Cir. 1968).

"Justice Douglas, concurring in part and dissenting in part in that case, forecast the problem which the Sinclair holding poses in the situation here present where we must accommodate, if possible, two national policies: The proscription of Norris-LaGuardia in labor disputes and the use of arbitration to avoid labor disputes. He considered Sinclair, where there had been no arbitration, distinguishable from a case where the arbitration award, as here, is frustrated through a refusal to abide by the decision of the arbitrator. Our approach is to distinguish Sinclair on this same basis and on the more than semantical ground that there is a real difference between an ordinary injunction and an order enforcing the award of an arbitrator although the end result is the same.

"In this case the parties agreed to the remedy of a desist order by the arbitrator. Such an order was entered and breached. The court in enforcing such order or award, although injunctive in nature, would be doing no more than enforcing the agreement of the parties. This not unusual action on the part of a court will lie unless the court has been deprived of jurisdiction by the Norris-LaGuardia Act.

"Norris-LaGuardia is limited to labor disputes and we consider the instant controversy to be outside the scope of a labor dispute as such. We have before us a contract wherein the parties have ceded their remedy of self-help in a labor dispute to arbitration even to the point of permitting the arbitrator to grant a desist order. Once the arbitration was completed, the matter became ripe for specific performance and fell outside the scope of Norris-LaGuardia."

Earlier cases had been decided on the principle that arbitration awards were enforceable in federal district courts under Section 301 (a) .[15] But the *Avco* opinion does not mention the *New Orleans Steamship Assn.* decision; hence it does not necessarily approve the distinction there made at least by implication, between an injunction to stop a strike in resistance to arbitration and a strike to avoid performance of an award after the arbitrational procedure. The distinction seems to be a desirable one, but some might argue that the strike to resist the effect of an award is still a labor dispute, as in some sense it arguably is.

Work on this third edition has not required adding a new complete chapter, since the developments that have followed the former edition have been treated under the same chapter headings. Some new sections have been included, and extensive additions have been made to the text.

February 1970   CLARENCE M. UPDEGRAFF

---

15 See Lee v. Olin Mathieson Chemical Corp., 271 F. Supp. 635 (W.D. Va. 1967) and other cases mentioned in the *Avco* opinion, and the dissent therein.

ACKNOWLEDGEMENTS

The author and publishers acknowledge with appreciation the courtesy of *The Hastings Law Journal,* which has kindly permitted use of parts of the text of an article published therein by the author of this work. Its title is "Preemption, Predictability and Progress in Labor Law," 17 *Hastings Law Journal* 473.

Valued assistance in the detail work of the present edition was given by the following persons:

Griffith L. Humphrey, a member of the San Francisco Bar, formerly a member of the Editorial Board of THE HASTINGS LAW JOURNAL, and a member of the Order of the Coif.

· · · · · · ·

James A. Fonda, Peter M. Jacobs, Stephen M. L'Heureux, and Walter C. Sellers.

These men were members of the labor law class during the year 1968-1969. James Fonda was a graduate engineer and was doing part-time personnel work for the U. S. Government; the others all had done advanced work in labor relations prior to attending law school.

TABLE OF CONTENTS

CHAPTER I

GENERAL NATURE OF
ARBITRATION — BACKGROUNDS

SECTION 1

Introduction — Definitions — Historical Backgrounds — Scope
of Arbitration — Voluntary and "Compulsory" Arbitration
— Arbitration and Conciliation

Introduction — Despite some differences as to the role of law
in labor arbitration among those who act as labor arbitrators, it
cannot be doubted that when legal rules are clearly concerned
they must be applied. Otherwise the award can be defeated by a
reviewing court. Today law-trained men are carrying an ever-
increasing load of the work of solving differences between employers and unions. Many of them are active in disputes having
to do with union recognition, contract negotiations, the numerous
disputes which arise in interpretation, grievances, and the various
forms of litigation and arbitration that arise in relation to such
matters. At times objectors to awards and to arbitrators denounce
them as being "too legalistic." [1] It has been suggested by some
that in case of a conflict, the contract of the parties should be
given full effect and, if need be, the law disregarded. As above
indicated, such an award would be of no value if taken into court
by the disappointed party, as it almost surely would be.

Hence the labor arbitrator must have and apply adequate, relevant legal rules and principles. The law generally and the *Spiel-*

---

[1] See "The Role of Lawyers in Arbitration," in Arbitration and Public Policy,
Proceedings of the Fourteenth Annual Meeting, National Academy of Arbitrators
(Washington: BNA Books, 1961); Benjamin Aaron, "Labor Arbitration and its
Critics," 10 Labor Law Journal 605 (1959); and Robert Levitt, "Lawyers, Legalism
and Labor Arbitration," 6 New York Forum 379 (1960).

For an excellent discussion of the place of labor arbitrations in the area of labor
relations generally, see Arnold Ordman in The Arbitrator, the NLRB, and the
Courts, Proceedings of the Twentieth Annual Meeting, National Academy of Arbitrators (Washington: BNA Books, 1967). pp. 47-110.

berg policy of the NLRB require that he know the nature of a
fair hearing and how to conduct one, and that he can write an
award within the authority delegated to him by the agreement to
arbitrate with results non-repugnant to the "purposes and policies" of the national labor relations statutes.

Innumerable disputes go to arbitration that do not require
interpretation or application of law in the findings or writing of
the award. Many of these, however, require some knowledge of
procedure, evidence, or labor relations at some point in the hearing. Many otherwise valid awards have been rendered illegal by
errors affecting such matters. It is to be remembered that the
ambit within which the award in any case may fall must be within
the terms of the submission agreement.

Those concerned with labor disputes have constantly made expanding use of arbitration in recent years for their solution. This
is true both in respect to numbers of cases and as to variety of
types of questions submitted. Almost all types of controversies
and all subjects of collective bargaining are frequently entrusted
to the process of arbitration. Many unions and employers who, a
few years ago, were adamant against submission to arbitration
now accept that process as not only a suitable and final step in
the settlement of grievances, but also as available as an aid to the
completion of collectively bargained labor contracts in almost all
details. It may be assumed that if high integrity, understanding,
and strict impartiality, coupled with adequate knowledge of labor
law and economics, characterize the actions of the great majority
of persons selected to act as arbitrators during coming years, the
resulting confidence that interested parties will repose in the
arbitrational process may continue to reduce the waste and bitterness incident to strikes, lockouts, and similar pressure steps, which
in the past have affected dealings between organizations of employees and employers.

There can be little doubt that the present importance of arbitration received great impetus from World War II conditions
which, for practical purposes, originated in 1940. The "no-strike,
no-lockout" pledge,[2] which had as its purpose the furnishing of a

---

2 See Updegraff, "War-Time Arbitration of Labor Disputes," 29 Iowa L. Rev. 328
(1944).

foundation for virtually universal arbitration by the National War Labor Board, furnished also a strong impetus toward arbitration of controversies other than those submitted to the Board, its agencies, or appointees. Collective bargaining thus took a long stride forward. Demands of employees and refusals of employers were not to be buttressed by strikes and lockouts in which economic force would be likely to prevail irrespective of fairness and logic.[3] The nation at war needed production and human services of all kinds. With economic warfare foresworn for the war period, parties unable to agree turned naturally to the step of seeking a decision upon the subject in dispute from impartial but adequately informed third persons. In short, imposition of arbitrary demands or refusals by means of expensive and wasteful exchange of economic blows and losses gave way to logical solutions of a relatively inexpensive and orderly character.

Definitions — Arbitration may be said to be the hearing and determination of a cause between parties in controversy by a person or persons chosen by the parties, or appointed under statutory authority, instead of by a judicial tribunal as ordinarily provided by law.[4]

The agreement to submit an existing dispute to arbitration is usually known as a *submission*. By this contract the parties undertake to submit to and be bound by the award of one, two, or more arbitrators in relation to the matter which may be in dispute between them.

The decision of an arbitrator is commonly called an *award*. The term *decision*, however, is not uncommonly used to refer to the entire document in which an arbitrator or a board of arbitrators summarizes, weighs, and discusses the evidence and the applicable laws as they progress toward the award.

The term *umpire* is sometimes used to designate a presiding arbitrator or an arbitrator selected by other arbitrators who have

---

3 Murphy, "Current Trends in Labor Arbitration," 11 N.Y. U. Conf. on Labor, 231 (1958); L. J. Carey, "Arbitration, Its Place in Today's Disputes," 5 University of Detroit Law Jour., 180-8 (1942). See and compare Brennan v. Brennan, 164 Ohio St. 29, 128 N.E. 2d 89 (1955); Re Curtis & Castle, 64 Conn. 501, 30 A 769 (1894); Martin v. Vansant, 99 Wash. 106, 168 P. 990 (1917).

4 Omaha v. Omaha Water Company, 218 U. S. 180, 54 L. Ed. 991, 30 S. Ct. 615 (1909) ; Perry v. Cobb, 88 Me. 435, 34 Atl. 278 (1896) ; Deal v. Thompson, 51 Okla. 256, 151 P. 856 (1915) ; Annotation 47 L.R.A. (N.S.) 341.

been directly appointed by the parties in dispute. It is supposed that the *umpire,* not having been selected directly by the parties, or either of them, will bring to the deliberations of the board an impartiality and a detachment of view somewhat greater than that which may be found to characterize the treatment of the subject in dispute by an arbitrator directly appointed by the disputants. More correctly, it should designate a person selected to make a sole decision despite nonconcurrence of others acting as co-arbitrators.[5] In somewhat frequent instances, the designation *umpire* is used to refer to a semipermanently selected arbitrator who, by mutual advance appointment by the parties, is available to be called in to make awards upon any disputed matters that they may be unable to solve during the life of their agreement.[6]

Historical Backgrounds — In many parts of the world, early records show a tendency to discard tribal warfare, the blood feud, and other forms of violence for something in the nature of arbitration.[7] The settlement of disputes in accordance with an ordeal or by appealing to the judgment of more or less impartial third persons appears to be procedure that; in the nature of things, would antedate a true and mature legal system.[8]

In all systems of primitive law, three elements of social control invariably seem to make early appearances. In the Roman law, these social controls were designated as *fas, boni mores,* and *lex.* The weakest of these in the beginning of the historical period was *lex,* or law. In all legal systems that truly develop to maturity it comes to be the dominant factor, but *fas,* the ethical or religious teaching, and *boni mores,* public opinion, always remain important factors. The judge comes to deal almost entirely with law. At any rate, it dominates his technique of decision. The arbitrator, however, deals with all three.

---

5 See Haven v. Winnisimmet Co., 93 Mass. (11 Allen) 377, 87 Am. Dec. 723 (1865); Cravens v. Estes, 144 Ky. 511, 139 S. W. 761 (1911); Lesser v. Pallay, 96 Ore. 142, 188 P. 718 (1920); Tyler v. Webb, 49 Ky. (10 B Mon.) 123 (1850).
6 See Collective Bargaining Negotiations and Contracts (Washington: The Bureau of National Affairs, Inc.).
7 See Wolaver, "The Historical Background of Commercial Arbitration," 83 University of Pennsylvania Law Review, 132-146 (1934); Cf. Plucknett, A Concise History of the Common Law, pp. 108-114 (Rochester: Lawyer's Coop. Pub. Co., 1936).
8 See Plucknett, A Concise History of the Common Law, (5 ed.) pp. 83 *et seq.* (Boston: Little, Brown & Co., 1956), and Pound and Plucknett, Readings on the History, etc. of the Common Law, (3 Ed.) pp. 134 *et seq.* (Rochester: Lawyer's Coop. Pub. Co., 1927).

There is, perhaps, a deep underlying instinct that through the centuries has caused men at the first step away from settlement of disputes through violence to prefer voluntary arbitration rather than submission to authority.[9] Nevertheless, the authoritarian idea arose. This, no doubt, is because violence is likely to spread so as to involve many who originally had no interest in the dispute and perhaps to engulf them and their security in the conflict. Apparently there has been an element consisting of the older, more responsible, and clearer minded folk in every age of society who opposed use of force and advocated settlement of controversies through the application of logic and a study of the developed principles and practices of custom, ethics and law, and public opinion based upon them, such as they were at that particular time and place.[10]

Thus, when one attempts to comment upon the history of arbitration, he is commenting upon a feature of society that antedates the establishment of a legal order. In fact, it antedates history. But at times it seems almost to disappear by reason of having been superseded by a system of law that involves the compulsory submission of disputes to authority, rather than the voluntary selection of and submission to an arbitrator.

This background gives a clue to the reason why arbitration seems to be much preferred to actions in the courts in some areas and in relation to certain types of disputes.[11] As formerly indicated, judges are, in the main, expected to apply and to emphasize legal principles, the element of social control designated by the Romans as *lex*. Arbitrators are expected to apply not only the law, but also ethical concepts and precepts of behavior resting upon custom or public opinion.[12] It should be noted, however, that the authority or jurisdiction of the arbitrator may be sharply limited by the form of submission under which he is acting. If that narrowly restricts him to

---

9 See Wolaver, *op. cit.,* p. 132.

10 Cf. Phillips, "A General Introduction," 83 Uni. Pa. Law Rev., p. 119 *et seq.* (1934) and Jones, "Historical Development of Commercial Arbitration in the United States," 12 Minn. Law Rev., 240-262 (1927).

11 See Milwaukee American Ass'n v. Landis, 49 Fed. (2nd) 298 (1931); Black v. Woodruff, 193 Ala. 237, 69 So. 97 (1915); Nelson v. Atlantic Coast Line R. Co., 157 N. C. 194, 72 S. E. 998 (1911); Myers v. Jenkins, 63 Ohio St. 101, 57 N. E. 1089 (1900); Martin v. Vansant, 99 Wash. 106, 168 P. 990 (1917).

12 See J. H. Leavenworth and Son v. Kimble, 157 Miss. 462, 128 So. 354 (1930); Fuerst v. Eichberger, 224 Ala. 31, 138 So. 409 (1931).

strict legal interpretation of a contract or a statute, he may not, with any binding effect, proceed into wider fields.[13]

While arbitration seems historically to have preceded the law, it must always have been ineffective unless the parties in good faith accepted, regarded themselves bound by, and performed the awards, or unless behind the award some strong sanction existed that virtually imposed it. This may well have been a divine sanction, a strong public opinion, or the fear of displeasure of the arbitrator in any instance where the latter was a powerful neighbor or overlord. In historical times, however, the arbitrational award takes its sanction from its legal validity and comes to rest upon the law and upon ultimate court enforcement.[14] Thus, we become concerned with the type of arbitration and the breadth and character of the awards that the courts regard as valid and suitable for judicial enforcement if a party fails to perform his promise to be bound by and to perform as the arbitrator shall decide.[15]

In Statham's *Abridgement of the Law* are listed three cases where the courts speak of "arbitrement." In a footnote to this material, Klinglesmith notes that "there was an early custom for litigants, or prospective litigants to agree to arbitrate the matters in dispute between them," as "shown by some very early cases." Bracton's *Note Book* reports one case in the year 1231 (S. 649), another in 1233 (S. 732), and a third in 1224 (S. 983). These cases in no way indicate there was anything novel about them. They are relatively incomplete as to any indication of procedure, but they do state it was necessary to prove the "conventions," or submission, or agreement by which they "put themselves upon an arbitrement." The translator states: "The third case is an entirely different proceeding (N. B. 984) in which the final agreement seems to be put

---

13 Refinery Employees' Union v. Continental Oil Co., 268 F.2d 447 (1959); Milwaukee American Ass'n v. Landis, 49 Fed. (2nd) 298 (1931); Mead-Morrison Mfg. Co. v. Marchant, 51 S. Ct. 104, 282, U. S. 808, 75 L. Ed. 725 (1930).

14 Conger v. Dean, 3 Iowa 463, 66 Am. Dec. 93 (1856); Whitcher v. Whitcher, 49 N. H. 176, 6 Am. Rep. 486 (1870); and see Textile Workers' Union v. Lincoln Mills of Alabama, 353 U. S. 448, 40 LRRM 2113 (1957).

15 United States v. Gleason, 175 U. S. 588, 44 L. Ed. 284, 20 S. Ct. 228 (1900); Burchell v. Marsh, 17 How. (U. S.) 344, 15 L. Ed. 96 (1854); McJimsey v. Traverse, 1 Stew. (Ala.) 244, 18 Am. Dec. 43 (1830); Bumpass v. Webb, 4 Port. (Ala.) 65, 29 Am. Dec. 274 (1835); Hynes v. Wright, 62 Conn. 323, 26 A. 642, 36 Am. St. Rep. 344 (1893). See text and cases cited herein, Chapters VIII and X.

into the hands of arbitrators two of whom were justices sitting on the case."

In 1609 Lord Coke held that an agreement to submit a dispute to an arbitrator could be revoked at the will of either party.[16] This was clearly but a dictum, since the arbitrational proceeding had been completed and an award given. Nevertheless, it was accepted as a correct statement of law by the judges of the court. Apparently, the learned judge was thinking of agency, where the power of revocation is ordinarily inherent in the person creating the power. It is altogether likely that he was influenced also by the fact that he did not like the idea of decision of disputes outside of the courts. This attitude of judicial hostility toward arbitration became more evident in later times.

The majority of the court in *Scott* v. *Avery*[17] held in an opinion by Lord Campbell that an agreement to refer any dispute to arbitration is binding and that no action can be maintained on the dispute until an award has been made by the arbitrator. But Barons Bramwell and Martin urged the minority view that such contracts were ousting the courts of jurisdiction and were therefore against public policy. The majority opinion finally was accepted by the American courts. In *U. S. Asphalt Refining Company* v. *Trinidad Lake Petroleum Company*,[18] Judge Hough stated it to be his belief that, "No reason for the simple statement that arbitration agreements are against such policy has ever been advanced, except that it must be against such policy to oust the courts of jurisdiction." In making this statement, he was criticizing previous decisions of the Supreme Court of the United States and while he bowed to them in that case, his criticisms gave much support to the trend of legal thought that resulted in statutes legalizing arbitration, even in cases that are clearly subject to jurisdiction of the courts, and where the work of a judge is in fact being done by an arbitrator or arbitrational board.

A considerable number of court decisions and federal and state statutes in force today clearly recognize and further establish the legality of arbitration procedure, put the sanctions of law behind

---

16 Vynior's Case, 4 Coke 302, Trinity Term, 7 Jac. 1 (1609).
17 5 H. L. C. 811, 25 L. J. (Exch.) 308 (1855).
18 222 Federal 1006 (S D. N. Y., 1915).

awards, and expressly provide for their enforcement through court procedure where necessary.[19] The view is generally taken that the statutes do not create an entirely new system of arbitrational rights, privileges, and procedures, but rather supplement the same as they previously existed and were recognized by the common law prior to the passage of the statutes.[20]

Scope of Arbitration — It is now the prevailing view that disputes of all kinds, excepting those involving criminal questions, properly may be submitted to arbitration.[21] Both questions of law and fact may be arbitrated,[22] and it is not required that the subject matter be one on which a suit might be brought in the courts.[23] The construction of the arbitration agreement itself is arbitrable and, where the dispute involves both civil and criminal questions, it may be construed as divisible so that the civil question may be subject to arbitration. The fact that an arbitrator may make an erroneous application or construction of the law does not impair the validity of the agreement to submit to arbitration.[24]

The breadth of the arbitrational field is not restricted by arbitrary classifications of law. Torts, contracts, and property questions, including future as well as past damages, may be submitted for an

19 Of great importance in respect to labor disputes is the decision of Textile Workers' Union v. Lincoln Mills of Alabama, 353 U. S. 448, 77 S. Ct. 912, 40 LRRM 2113, 28 LA 519 (1957). See Local 1912, International Assoc. of Machinists v. U. S. Potash Co., 270 F.2d 496, 33 LA 127 (1959). See Appendix D, *infra*. for a table of state arbitration statutes. For their effect upon the common law, see Shanferoke Coal & Supply Corp. v. Westchester Serv. Corp., 293 U. S. 449, 79 L. Ed. 583, 55 S. Ct. 313 (1935); Marine Transit Corp. v. Dreyfus, 284 U. S. 263, 76 L. Ed. 282, 52 S. Ct. 166 (1932); Glidden Co. v. Retail Hardware Mutual F. Ins. Co., 181 Minn. 518, 233 N. W. 310, 77 A. L. R. 616 (1930); Nippon Ki-Ito Kaisha v. Ewing-Thomas Corp., 313 Pa. 442, 170 A. 286 (1934).
20 Black v. Woodruff, 193 Ala. 327, 69 So. 97 (1915); Lilley v. Tuttle, 52 Colo. 121, 117 P. 896 (1911); Rankin, 36 Ill. 293, 87 Am. Dec. 205 (1865); Powers v. Douglass, 53 Vt. 471, 38 Am. Rep. 699 (1881); Winnie v. Eldeckin, 2 Pinney (Wisc.) 248, 1 Chad. 219 (1849).
21 An Arbitration clause in a contract which violates the federal antitrust laws cannot be a subject of a controversy in a state court. Fox Films Corp. v. Muller, 296 U. S. 207, 56 S. Ct. 183 (1935); Deshon v. Scott, 202 Ky. 575, 260 S. W. 355 (1924).
22 Deshon v. Scott, 202 Ky. 575, 260 S. W. 355 (1924); Johnson v. Noble, 13 N. H. 286, 38 Am. Dec. 485 (1847).
23 Deshon v. Scott, 202 Ky. 575, 260 S. W. 355 (1924); Annotation 58 L. R. A. 181; 47 L. R. A. (N.S.) 380 *et seq.*, 443.
24 Franks v. Battles, 147 Ark. 169, 227, S. W. 32 (1921); Annotation 58 L. R. A. 181 (1903); 47 L. R. A. (N.S.) 346 (1914); Johnson v. Noble 13 N.H. 286, 38 Am. Dec. 485 (1847); Willesford v. Watson, 42 L.J. Ch. N.S. 447 (1873).

award.[25] Even rights in land may be submitted to arbitration in some jurisdictions and the final award becomes binding upon the parties, despite the fact that the arbitrator could not officially pass upon the title.[26] In such real estate questions, however, it is ordinarily required that the submission be in writing.[27] Some states require it to be executed in the same manner as is required to validate a deed.[28]

With this great breadth of possible decisions open to arbitration, it is not surprising that the scope of its use has been broadening in recent years. The motion picture industry has found it peculiarly effective because of its speed and flexibility on the matter of adjusting disputes of all kinds, but particularly in the matter of distribution of films.

In the United States there exist several thousand commercial or industrial trading associations. Hundreds of these have made their own rules on arbitration;[29] in many instances they have acted quite independently of statutes. They have made a notable contribution toward maintaining good relations among their members who have been parties to disputes. In the field of foreign trade, many parties have long since discovered that arbitration operates much more effectively and quickly than would the courts of any country with possible jurisdiction of their disputes, while the submission or standing agreement to arbitrate in such instances may give much aid in settling what might otherwise be a hotly contested question — the proper jurisdiction for trial.[30] Real estate boundary line ar-

---

[25] Tenn. Coal, Iron & R. Co. v. Roussell, 155 Ala. 435, 46 So. 866 (1908); Lund v. Johnson Fare Box Co., 9 N.Y.S. (2nd) 638, 256 App. Div. 267 (1939); Cueroni v. Coburnville Garage Co., 315 Mass. 135, 52 N. E. (2nd) 16 (1944).

[26] Davy's Executor v. Faw, 7 Cranch (U. S.) 171, 3 L. Ed. 305 (1813); Lilley v. Tuttle, 52 Colo. 121, 117 P. 896 (1911); Cady v. Walker, 62 Mich. 157, 28 N.W. 805 (1886); Deal v. Thompson, 51 Okla. 256, 151 P. 856 (1915); Brown v. Wheeler, 17 Conn. 345, 44 Am. Dec. 550 (1847); Cox v. Heuseman, 124 Va. 159, 97 S. E. 778 (1919).

[27] Davy's Executor v. Faw, 7 Cranch (U. S.) 171, 3 L. Ed. 305 (1813); Walden v. McKinnon, 157 Ala. 291, 47 So. 874 (1908); Bunnell v. Reynolds, 205 Mo. App. 653, 226 S. W. 614 (1920); Galbraith v. Lunsford, 87 Tenn. 89, 9 S. W. 365 (1888); Stewart v. Cass, 16 Vt. 663, 42 Am. Dec. 534 (1844).

[28] Miller v. Graham, 1 Brev. (S. C.) 448 (1849); French v. New, 28 N. Y. 147, 2 Abb. Dec. 209, reversing 20 Barb. 481 (1865).

[29] See 5 Arbitration Journal, pp. 10, 119, 313 (1941) and 6 Arbitration Journal, p. 271 et seq. (1942).

[30] See Great Western Ins. Co. v. United States, 112 U. S. 193, 28 L. Ed. 687, 5 S. Ct. 99 (1884); Marine Transit Corp. v. Dreyfus, 284 U. S. 263, 76 L. Ed. 282, 52 S. Ct. 166 (1932); Red Cross Line v. Atlantic Fruit Co., 264 U. S. 109, 68 L. Ed. 582, 44 S. Ct. 274 (1924).

bitrations and appraisals have been submitted many times in the immediate past to arbitration or to arbitrational appraisers,[31] but probably no field mentioned above has expanded comparably with that involving labor disputes in the number of matters submitted to arbitrations in recent years.[32]

There are, for obvious reasons, no statistics concerning the total number of matters submitted to private arbitrators. Information received from the General Counsel of the Federal Mediation and Conciliation Service, who also acts as Chief of the Arbitration Division, shows the trend. The figures following indicate the number of cases in which arbitrators were appointed by that authority in the years shown. A memorandum received from the American Arbitration Association indicated its volume of arbitrational appointments to have been as set forth below.

YEAR	FEDERAL MEDIATION AND CONCILIATION SERVICE (Totals From Panels and Direct)	AMERICAN ARBITRATION ASSOCIATION
1948	646	1,324
1949	630	1,426
1950	601	1,250
1951	540	1,353
1952	656	1,372
1953	683	1,835
1954	999	2,123
1955	986	2,017
1956	1,099	2,175
1957	1,270	2,598
1958	1,755	2,758
1959	1,810	2,816
1960	2,090	3,231
1961	2,277	3,942
1962	2,607	3,842
1963	2,795	4,074
1964	3,222	3,932
1965	3,380	4,097
1966	3,474	4,007
1967	3,995	4,437
1968	4,247	4,931

31 Davis v. Havard, 15 Serg. & R. (Pa.) 165, 16 Am. Dec. 537 (1827); Brown v. Wheeler, 17 Conn. 345, 44 Am. Dec. 550 (1847); Shackleford v. Purket, 2 A. K. Marsh (Ky.) 316, 12 Am. Dec. 422 (1819); Cox v. Jagger, 2 Cow. (N.Y.) 638, 14

Voluntary and "Compulsory" Arbitration — Arbitration in the true sense is voluntary.[33] While it may be and usually is compulsory that the parties to arbitration respect and obey the award that terminates the proceedings, it is not compulsory that the parties enter into an arbitrational agreement. The agreement to arbitrate, however, may be of rather sweeping nature, and cover all future disputes arising between the parties in respect to certain subjects for a specified length of time. Such contracts, as previously stated, were largely subject to unilateral repudiation at common law. Where such a "contract" exists and is held valid, it might be said that the arbitration is compulsory under the "contract." [34] However, it is important to remember that entry into the "contract" itself was voluntary.

The above is subject to the qualification that during the World War II period, the National War Labor Board on numerous occasions by directive order established "contracts" between the parties that contained provisions for arbitration and ordered arbitration of various disputes.[35] This practice, like the National War Labor Board, may properly be regarded as having been a feature of the temporary war economy and social regulation, and not one of per-

---

Am. Dec. 522 (1824) ; Calhoun v. Dunning, 4 Dall. (U. S.) 109, L. Ed. 767 (1792) ; Cox v. Heuseman, 124 Va. 159, 97 S. E. 788 (1919) .

32 A letter from a former Chief of the Arbitration Division stated: "It is true that arbitration is on the increase. I believe the fact so many companies and unions during the periods of war have obtained satisfactory results by resorting to arbitration instead of strikes and lockouts indicates that arbitration will continue to play a permanent part in the settlement of labor disputes." Experience has well supported his forecast.
See Braun, The Settlement of Industrial Disputes (Philadelphia: Blakiston Co., 1944) p. 148.

33 See Kellor, Arbitration in Action (New York: Harper & Bros., 1941) p. 7; Smith v. Morse, 9 Wall. (U. S.) 76, 19 L. Ed. 597 (1859) ; Stewart v. Cass. 16 Vt. 663, 42 Am. Dec. 534 (1844) ; Robinson v. Bickley, 30 Pa. 384 (1892) ; Whitcher v. Whitcher, 49 N. H. 176, 6 Am. Rep. 486 (1870) ; Houston Saengerbund v. Dunn, 41 Tex. Civ. App. 376, 92 S. W. 429 (1906) .

34 For examples of such clauses in actual labor contracts, see Collective Bargaining Negotiations and Contracts (Washington: The Bureau of National Affairs, Inc.) and Union Agreement Provisions (Washington: U. S. Dept. of Labor, 1942) p. 154 *et seq.*

35 For a number of specific instances, see Nat. Labor Relations Act, 29 U. S. C. A. Sec. 151 *et seq.;* Goldberg v. Rialto Retailers, 43 N. Y. Supp. (2nd) 432 (1944) ; Ensley v. Associated Terminals, 8 N.W. (2nd) 161, 304 Mich. 522, 12 LRRM 581 (1943) ; City Bank Farmers Trust Company v. O'Donnell, 39 N. Y. Supp. (2nd) 842, 179 Misc. 770 (1943) .

manent character. However, such procedure could arise again should the conditions that brought it about recur.

All supposed jurisdiction of the National War Labor Board carried back to the idea that the War Labor Board itself was the result of a theoretically voluntary agreement between industry and labor embodied in the no-lockout, no-strike pledges made when the Board was conceived. This in turn was intended to amount to an undertaking that disputes between the parties would not be carried to the length of economic combat in the form of strike or lockout, but rather made the subject of Board decisions.[36] In other words, the no-strike, no-lockout agreement was in somewhat abstract theory treated as a sweeping nationwide compact between industry and labor to the effect that all disputes arising during the war period, including not only those that existed when the Board was founded but also those to arise thereafter, were, by the effect of such agreement, submitted en masse to arbitrational decision by the National War Labor Board.

Since it is quite obvious that under our legal system there were no representatives nor organizations authorized to speak for all of industry on this matter, industry may not be regarded as having been contractually bound to arbitrate. If that be true, it would seem to follow that labor, even though competently and legally represented by international officers, would not have been bound by the agreement since the supposed other party, industry, may not be regarded as having been competently, legally bound by the theoretical undertaking. The whole setup, therefore, appears to have involved an imposition of virtually compulsory arbitration operating under executive order of the President, and, at least in some degree, under congressional authority subsequently expressed in the Stabilization Act[37] and the Smith-Connally Act. Under both of these laws, certain powers and authorities were assumed by the National War Labor Board to the exclusion of authority previously regarded as vested in the several states.[38]

---

[36] Employers Group of Motor Freight Carriers v. Nat. War Labor Board, 143 Fed (2nd) 145, 14 LRRM 705 (1944). See: Executive Orders 9017 and 9250; tit. 3, Sec. 1, 2, 50 U. S. C. A. Appendix, Sec. 1507 note, 901 note; Glen Alden Coal Co. v. Nat. Labor Relations Board, 141 Fed. (2nd) 47, 13 LRRM 759 (1944).

[37] Chap. 325, Tit. II, 58 Stat. 643 (Tit. 50, U.S. C. A. App., Secs. 961 note, 963, 964, 966).

[38] Chap. 144, 57 Stat. 163, (Tit. II, Sec. 251; Tit. 50 App., Secs. 309, 1501 *et seq.*). See In re Matter of Creager, et al., 323 Ill. App. 594, 15 LRRM 566 (1944).

Other efforts have been made from time to time to impose "compulsory arbitration" by statute. Where the effect of such acts has been to require parties to arbitrate without agreement on their part, they have been declared unconstitutional several times.[39] It is said that if the law attempts to compel a party to submit a dispute to arbitration and to deny him access to the courts, it violates due process of law.[40] An interesting exception appears to have been made in connection with the exercise of the power of eminent domain where property is to be taken for public use and in connection with which statutes have provided that certain facts shall be ascertained by a proceeding on the pattern of arbitration.[41] It may be well to note this and its relation to questions arising in the labor field, because of the undisputed public interest in the latter since that characteristic in some instances has furnished an argument for requiring arbitration in connection with labor disputes. Indeed the United States Supreme Court has so construed Section 301 (a) of the Labor Management Relations Act as to make agreements to arbitrate certain labor disputes specifically enforceable.[42] Again, it

---

[39] See Simpson, "Constitutional Limitations on Compulsory and Industrial Arbitrations," 38 Harv. Law Rev. 668 (1925) and Cutler v. Richley, 151 Pa. 195, 25 A. 96 (1892) ; Wolff Packing Co. v. Court of Industrial Relations, 262 U. S. 522 (1923) ; Lehman v. Ostrovsky, 264 N.Y. 130, 190 N. E. 208 (1934) ; Sobey 1. Thomas, 37 Wis. 568 (1875) ; Goerke Kirch Co. v. Goerke Kirch Holding Co., 118 N. J. Eq 1, 176 Atl 902 (1935) , Re Smith, 381 Pa. 223, 112 A2d 625, App. dismd. 350 U. S. 858 (1955) .

Under the Norris-LaGuardia Act, an employer is not bound to seek arbitration when a union has resorted to threats or violence. Cater Construction Co. v. Nischwitz et al., 111 Fed. (2d) 971 (1940) .

[40] See note 39 *supra* and Philadelphia Housing Authority v. Turner Construction Company, 343 Pa. 512, 23 Atl (2nd) 126 (1942) ; Stevenson v. King, 243 Ala. 551, 10 So (2nd) 825 (1943) .

[41] North Laramie Land Co. v. Hoffman, 268 U. S. 276, 69 L. Ed. 953, 45 S. Ct, 491 (1915) ; Bragg v. Weaver, 251 U. S. 57, 64 L. Ed. 135, 40 S. Ct. 62 (1919) ; Bedford Quarries Co. v. Chicago I. & L.R. Co., 175 Ind. 303, 94 N. E. 326, 35 L. R. A. (N.S.) 641 (1912) .

[42] Textile Workers' Union v. Lincoln Mills of Alabama, 353 U. S. 448, 1 L. Ed. (2d) 972, 77 S. Ct. 912, 40 LRRM 2113, 28 LA 519 (1957) . It had been held that an employer's refusal to arbitrate according to a labor agreement improperly interfered with collective bargaining and violated the Wagner Act. Consolidated Aircraft Corp. v. NLRB, 141 Fed. (2nd) 785, 14 LRRM 553 (1944) .

See State v. Howat, 109 Kan. 376, 198 Pac. 686 (1921) . But see, Dorchy v. Kansas, 264 U. S. 286 (1924) ; and cf: Marine Transit Corp. v. Dreyfus, 284 U. S. 263, 76 L. Ed. 282 (1932) ; Atchison T. & S. F. Ry. v. Brotherhood of Locomotive Firemen & Engineers, 26 Fed. (2nd) 413 (1928) ; Hoboken Manufacturers Ry. Co. v. Hoboken Railroad Warehouse & Steamship Connecting Co., 132 N. J. Eq. 111, 27 A. (2nd) 150 (1943) ; Philadelphia Housing Authority v. Turner Construction Co., 343 Pa. 512, 23 A. (2nd) 426 (1942) ; Upington v. Commonwealth Insurance Co. of New York, 298 Ky. 210, 182 S. W. (2nd) 648 (1944) .

should be observed that the original entry into the agreement to arbitrate was entirely voluntary.

In this connection the federal laws applicable to adjustment of labor disputes in the railroad industry[43] are interesting as well as important. In most of the disputed cases, the National Railroad Adjustment Board, which consists of 36 members (half selected by the employee organizations and half by the employers), has failed to agree upon a referee or arbitrator.[44] In such instances it is required by statute to call upon the National Mediation Board to make such appointments. Great care has been taken by the latter in making selections of its appointees, but nevertheless serious issues have arisen as to the fitness of some to serve.[45] The statutes provide that the awards are "final and binding." They are certified to the appropriate district court which is given authority to enforce or to set them aside. Neither party may appeal from an adverse award of the Adjustment Board. Hence some criticism has arisen, with suggestions that an amendment should be passed providing for appeals by parties against whom awards may be made and for imposition of penalties for nonobedience to an award where no appeal has been taken within a specified time.[46]

Perhaps much of the strain in the area in question has arisen because of the virtually compulsory type of arbitration provided.[47] In the essential field of national transportation, however, the need to provide effectually against interruptions of service by strikes or

---

43 44 U. S. Statutes at Large, 577 as amended by 48 Stat. 1185, 49 Stat. 1189, 1921 and 54 Stat. 785; 45 U. S. Code Annotated, Sec. 151 *et seq*. For an interesting discussion, see Long, et al. v. Van Osdale, et al, 218 Ind. 483, 29 N.E. 2d 953 (1940). In relation to this subject generally see contents of Chapter IV, Section 4, *infra*.

44 The National Mediation Board had to select 30 out of 40 referees during the first five years of its operation. The Railway Labor Act and the National Mediation Board, p. 21 (Washington: Government Printing Office, 1940).

45 See Spencer, The National Railroad Adjustment Board, VIII, Studies in Business Admin. No. 3, p. 24 (Chicago: The University of Chicago Press, 1938).

46 Kaltenborn, Governmental Adjustment of Labor Disputes, pp. 55-58, 252 (Chicago: Foundation Press, 1943). See Chapter IV, Section 4, *infra,* and cases there cited.

47 The policy declared by the statutes requires that the carrier employers and employees "settle all disputes," so as to "avoid any interruption of commerce" or "the operation of any carrier and the employees thereof." 44 Stat. 577, Sec. 2. Some students have concluded that the Railway Labor Act in fact provides "genuine compulsory arbitration." Braun, The Settlement of Industrial Disputes, pp. 124, 160 (Philadelphia: Blakiston Co., 1944). This view is supported by the result in Delaware and Hudson R. R., et al. v. Williams, et al., 129 Fed. (2nd) 11 (1942) and in Brotherhood of Railroad Trainmen v. Toledo, Peoria & Western R.R., 64 Sup. Ct. Rep. 413, 13 LRRM 725 (U. S. Sup. Ct., 1944).

lockouts seems to be commonly accepted. The general opinion rather clearly indicates adoption of the view that the boards in question have been able and effective and that the general pattern of the statute is desirable, with perhaps need for its change only in the details above stated.[48]

Some statutes, while providing for enforcement of arbitration contracts, have provided a direct right of appeal to the courts, and upon review, certain of these statutes have been sustained upon the ground that they contain no denial of due process, since provision is expressly made for judicial review of any award or decision made by the arbitrator.[49]

An imposition of arbitration has been sustained in connection with public works contracts, where statutes provide that those who become contractors for such jobs must agree to arbitrate certain possible disputes in respect to losses or failure to perform work in compliance with specifications.[50] It is to be noted that in these situations, the original entry into the agreement to arbitrate or submit future disputes to arbitration is not compulsory, since the contractor is not bound in any way to undertake the work excepting as he may wish to do so. In some workmen's compensation statutes, provision is made for arbitration of disputes by those who elect to come under their provisions.[51] Here such election may be thought of as furnishing the voluntary step of the parties upon which rests the entire arbitrational proceeding. It may be repeated that in a true sense arbitration must be voluntarily agreed upon and that so-called "involuntary arbitration" has not generally been accepted. Where it is imposed and does survive, it must, in all logic, be regarded as litigation in the usual sense, even though heard before a special court or tribunal.

The Labor-Courts Proposal

"Labor courts," as they are designated and maintained in other countries, have been suggested from time to time with the implica-

---

[48] See Kaltenborn, *op cit.*, p. 252 and Braun, *op. cit.*, p. 154 *et seq.* Cf. the creation, difficult functioning, and later restriction of the operation of the Maritime Labor Board. Kaltenborn, *op. cit.*, pp. 73-83.

[49] Isaac v. Donegal & Conroy Mut. Fire Ins. Co., 301 Pa. 351, 152 A. 95 (1930); White Eagle Laundry Co. v. Slawek, 296 Ill. 240, 129 N. E. 753 (1921); Alexander v. Fletcher, 175 S.W. (2nd) 196 (1944).

[50] See Wood v. Seattle, 23 Wash. 1, 62 P. 135 (1900).

[51] Hunter v. Colfax Consol. Coal Co., 175 Iowa 245, 154 N. W. 1037 (1916); Deibeikis v. Link-Belt Co., 261 Ill. 454, 104 N. E. 211 (1914).

tion that they are and can be maintained in a substantial degree different from a compulsory arbitration system.[52] Their advocates appear to believe they will be more acceptable to unions and employers than compulsory arbitration.[53] There is, in the last analysis, no essential difference. Under each one the parties are expected to submit their disputes to official authority and to obey the official decision.

True, the last few years have witnessed many paralyzing strikes in our country. Among other industries they have affected steel, city transit, docks, airlines, newspapers, the oil industry, and others. There appears to be no reason to believe that the creation of labor courts would have prevented these or could prevent similar stoppages in the future. Some of them were carried on in defiance of injunctions. It would seem, however, that Congress is becoming concerned about a study of all industries with a view to determining what businesses and services are so essential that the public must not even briefly be deprived of them. If for these there is provided a non-work-stoppage way of solving labor disputes that cannot be settled by collective bargaining, the method or official body by which it is conducted and applied may be called a "labor court," an "emergency labor disputes board," an "essential industries labor commission," or otherwise. The name by which it is designated will not disguise its purpose or make it any the more or less acceptable to the parties to be affected by it. Several state efforts to maintain uninterrupted service in the public utility industries have been defeated by decisions of the U. S. Supreme Court.[54] In recent years growing union organization of public employees has pointed to the probability of legislative action to preserve unbroken the functioning of certain public services that are indispensable for maintenance of health, safety, and the general welfare. Congress has several times considered this problem without action, but the

---

[52] Fleming, "The Presidential Address: The Labor Court Idea," The Arbitrator, the NLRB, and the Courts, Proceedings of the Twentieth Annual Meeting, National Academy of Arbitrators (Washington: BNA Books, 1967), pp. 229-249.

[53] Professor Sprague Holden, p. 84, U. S. News & World Report, February 10, 1969.

[54] Amalgamated Assn. of Street, Elect. Ry. and Motor Coach Employees of America v. Wisconsin Employment Relations Board, 430 U. S. 383, 27 LRRM 2385 (1951); Amalgamated Ass'n of Street Elect. Ry. & Motor Coach Employees v. Missouri, 374 U. S. 74, 53 LRRM 2394 (1963).

subject is clearly one which must be confronted and acted on in the not far distant future.[55]

Arbitration and Conciliation — Among labor negotiators of limited experience there sometimes is found to be some confusion of the process of conciliation with that of arbitration. Conciliation may be regarded as an extension of a voluntary negotiation of the parties by which they are seeking to adjust the matters in which they have found themselves at odds.[56] The conciliator is, or should be, a completely neutral third person, either selected by the parties or appointed by competent authority[57] to assist them in their negotiations by persuading one side or the other that, in view of economic, social, or political conditions, it should yield its contentions, or by suggesting and urging compromises as between the parties with the hope that some solution may be found upon which they may voluntarily agree. The conciliator makes no decision or award.[58] He makes only compromise proposals or arguments by which he seeks to educate or persuade the parties into an agreement at which they themselves arrive.

In many instances, the services of the conciliator are of great value. This may be said particularly of the widely experienced men employed by the Federal Mediation and Conciliation Service.[59] Spending months at full time, these men, working first with

---

55 See also text herein at Chap. V, Secs. 3, 4 and 5.

56 It is not a regular practice in the United States for parties to a dispute to select a conciliator or mediator by joint action, though that practice is by no means uncommon. When an impasse is recognized to exist, the third party, if invited to intervene by the parties acting together, is more likely to be requested to function as an arbitrator. At times services of well-liked federal commissioners of conciliation in whom both parties have confidence will be expressly requested by joint action of a union and a company. Generally speaking, the conciliator enters the case by official appointment upon the request of one rather than both parties. Neither will be bound to accept his suggestions, however, even if both have joined the request for the appointment.

57 Most requests are directed now to the Federal Mediation and Conciliation Service which maintains a large staff of extraordinarily well-qualified commissioners well located throughout the country to render prompt and effective cooperation in aiding the parties to reach an agreement. Labor departments of several of the states will also, on request, furnish similar aid.

58 See Updegraff, "War-Time Arbitration of Labor Disputes," 29 Iowa L. Rev. 328, 338 (1944).

59 For description see Handbook of Federal Legislation, Bulletin No. 39, Part II, p. 57 (Washington: U. S. Dept. of Labor, Division of Labor Standards, 1941) and Management Rights and the Arbitration Process, Proceedings of the Ninth Annual Meeting, National Academy of Arbitrators (Washington: BNA Books, 1956), pp. 96-101.

one company, then another, and working with all unions, are ordinarily well informed as to the general conditions in all lines of business. They know what concessions have been made by others in the same business and situation, and are competent to advise as to what concessions can be made without loss of competitive position. Their wide experience and broad general information as to what unions have demanded and what concessions they have received in various localities and lines of human activity permit them to judge whether a union in a given case is asking more than it may reasonably expect will be conceded or asking more than it can be fairly supposed the employer is in a position to grant. Thus the conciliator brings to the conference a breadth of experience not likely to be duplicated by that of any of the parties representing one of the two sides of the controversy. Furthermore, he is likely to bring into the discussion a fresh point of view and an impartiality that may help them to solve disputes.

The long experience of the United States Conciliation Service, dating from 1913, plus that of the Federal Mediation and Conciliation Service which succeeded it under the Taft-Hartley Act in 1947, has caused most employers and employee organizations to have a considerable confidence in the commissioners. On the basis of this confidence, even the most difficult and flatly formed issues are many times liquidated.

Where conciliation has definitely failed, however, the conciliator has one last and always available suggestion to make. It is that the parties agree to submit their dispute to impartial arbitration. In contrast with the conciliation process, arbitration implies that the dispute will be submitted to the final decision of the arbitrator or umpire and that the parties, even though completely disappointed, will respect and abide by the decision.[60]

At a conciliation table, there is usually a great deal of "give and take," discussion, and proposals. At the arbitration hearing, this stage has been left behind. The parties are no longer trading. Each one is intent upon persuading the arbitrator that the demand or

---

[60] See United States v. Gleason, 175 U. S. 588, 44 L. Ed. 284, 20 S. Ct. 228 (1899) ; Burchel v. Marsh, 17 How. (U. S.) 344, 15 L. Ed. 96 (1854) ; Livingston Woodworth, 15 How. (U. S.) 546, 14 L. Ed. 809 (1853) ; Chambers v. Crook, 42 Ala. 171, 94 Am. Dec. 637 (1868) ; Curley v. Dean, 4 Conn. 259, 10 Am. Dec. 140 (1822) ; Stose v. Heissler, 120 Ill. 433, 11 N. E. 161 (1887) .

the refusal that he represents is legally and ethically correct or expedient and that in fairness and as a result of impartial and honest judgment between the parties, the award should be consistent with the same. It is true that sometimes it happens that the parties in an arbitration hearing may again be started upon the bargaining and trading process that will lead them to agreement.[61] This, however, is unusual; ordinarily the parties have assumed positions from which they will not voluntarily yield further, and in the end the arbitrator must decide between them.

Obviously, the award will sometimes take the form of a decision entirely consistent with the contentions of one and against the other. There are times, however, when an arbitrator may find himself happily able to give the parties an award that represent a fair and, to them, mutually satisfactory compromise.

SECTION 2

The Functional Field of Arbitration—Advantages of Arbitration Over Litigation in Various Types of Controversies—Economic Losses in Strikes, Lockouts, and Slowdowns Contrasted With Relative Speed and Economy of Arbitration

The Functional Field of Arbitration — As earlier suggested, the process of arbitration is applicable to virtually every type of dispute, whether involving legal rights or conflicting interests, ethical questions or others. Parties have used it in connection with agreements to purchase and sell, barter, to renew leases, and to fix prices or rentals.[62] Arbitrators have been called in to ascertain the amount of loss or damage to property in respect to which one party may be liable to the other in tort or under a contract.[63] In many instances, insurance policies in their appraisal clauses provide for arbitration.[64] Again, what is essentially arbitration has been used for the

---

61 Exceptions appear at times, especially when one of the parties is surprised or disappointed by its own witnesses or discovers facts at the hearing not earlier considered.

62 Davis v. Havard, 15 Serg. & R. (Pa.) 165, 16 Am. Dec. 537 (1827) ; Bunnell v. Reynolds, 205 Mo. App. 653, 226 S. W. 614 (1920) .

63 Tennessee Coal, Iron & R. Co. v. Roussell, 155 Ala. 435, 46 So. 866 (1908) .

64 Seyk v. Millers National Insurance Company, 74 Wis. 67, 41 N. W. 443, 3 L. R. A. 523 (1889) .

purpose of fixing boundary lines,[65] to eject from land,[66] to ascertain a balance of debt due,[67] to verify the performance of a contract,[68] to determine the efficiency of mechanical appliances,[69] and to ascertain the quality or classification of goods.[70] It has been known to apply in connection with right to organization membership,[71] rights in respect to the estates of deceased persons,[72] and to fix the amounts of compensation to be paid for invasions of patent rights, copyrights, and good will.[73]

Its functional value in connection with labor bargaining is particularly prominent. In many instances, employees make a demand for a concession in respect to hours, compensation, direct or indirect, and working conditions, which previously has not been made, and which the employer is under no legal obligation or compulsion to make.[74] In such cases the arbitrator is not dealing with legal rights, but rather with social, economic, or ethical expediency.[75] In other words, in this very rapidly growing field of labor arbitration, there is, as often as not, pending between the parties a dispute in respect to which no court may be said to have jurisdiction under any conception of law or equity.

---

[65] Turner v. Spicer, 198 Ky. 739, 249 S. W. 1038 (1923); Burnett v. Miller, 174 Ky. 91, 191 S. W. 659 (1917); Spencer v. Winselman, 42 Cal. 479 (1872); Davis v. Havard, 15 Serg. & R. (Pa.) 165, 16 Am. Dec. 537 (1827).

[66] Wilson v. Manson, 17 Pa. Dist. 938 (1908).

[67] French v. Richardson, 5 Cush. (Mass.) 450 (1850); Palmer v. Davis 28 N. Y. 242 (1863).

[68] Deshon v. Scott, 202 Ky. 576, 260 S.W. 355 (1924); Smith v. Becker, 2 Ch. (Eng.) 86, 8 B. R. C. 432 (1916); Wilesford v. Watson, 42 L. J. Ch. N. S. 447, 3 Eng. Rul. Cas. 374 (1913).

[69] In re Lower Baraboo River Drainage District, 225 N.W. 331, 199 Wisc. 230, 63 A.L.R. 1165 (1929).

[70] See Kellor, Arbitration in Action, pp. 54, 80 (New York: Harper & Bros., 1941).

[71] See American Jurisprudence, Titles, "Societies and Clubs" and "Mutual Benefit Societies"; 19 R.C.L. pp. 1224 et seq. and 25 R.C.L. pp. 57 et seq.

[72] Konigmacher v. Kimmel, 1 Penrose & W. (Pa.) 207, 21 Am. Dec. 374 (1829).

[73] See Callaghan v. Myers, 128 U. S. 617, 32 L. Ed. 547, 9 S. Ct. 177 (1888); Paramount Famous Lasky Corp. v. U. S., 282 U. S. 30, 75 L. Ed. 145 (1930).

[74] Many arbitrations have dealt with seniority rights, holidays, vacations, classification of workers, union security clauses, etc.

[75] See The Profession of Labor Arbitration, Selected Papers From the First Seven Annual Meetings, National Academy of Arbitrators (Washington: BNA Books, 1957), particularly articles on pp. 66 and 76. The issue at times is whether the concession requested by the union is customary or usual in the industry or area, a factor which the employer, so far as law is concerned, is in normal times entitled to disregard if he feels it expedient to do so. Many National War Labor Board directives, however, were based upon such considerations under the wage stabilization rules during World War II.

Advantages of Arbitration Over Litigation in Various Types of Controversies — While arbitrational procedure is more fully discussed in a following chapter, it is well to note at this point that arbitration has a marked advantage over litigation, because of the procedure.[76] The arbitrator may proceed to the scene of dispute, he may observe the operation of a machine, the location of the place, the chemical tests of goods where quality is in dispute; he may examine the account books that may be relevant to a question before him; he may accept information from informal sources without regard to the sometimes hampering technicalities of the law of evidence; and he may ordinarily proceed promptly to the decision of the matter in controversy without the need of postponing decisions in favor of other matters pending on a long docket, as might be the case with the judge if the matter were to be considered in court.[77] In many instances arbitrators are appointed from the ranks of skilled men in a particular profession, known to have peculiar or professional knowledge of the technical matter in dispute.[78] The selection of similarly qualified judges under similar circumstances is, of course, impossible.

Another feature of arbitration, as contrasted with litigation, is found in the fact that the parties to a dispute are usually able to proceed throughout arbitration proceedings to an award and performance of the award without the rancor and harshness of dealings which too often follow in the wake of court adjudication of their rights. In labor cases, the arbitrator with wide knowledge of labor unions and the terms active in the adjustment of labor disputes obviously enjoys a technical advantage over any but the most exceptional judge in the weighing of labor and industry rights,

---

[76] Gonzalez v. Gonzales, 174 Cal. 588, 163 P. 993 (1917) ; Franks v. Franks 1 N.E. (2nd) 14 (1936) ; Dworkin v. Caledonian Ins. Co., 285 Mo. 342, 226 S.W. 846 (1920).

[77] See Milwaukee American Ass'n v. Landis, 49 Fed. (2nd) 298 (1931) ; Wabash Ry. Co. v. American Refrigerator Transit Co., 7 Fed. (2nd) 335 (1925) ; Franks v. Battles, 147 Ark. 169, 227 S.W. 32 (1921).

[78] The American Arbitration Association through its various "panels" constantly tries to supply men of suitable education and experience where technical qualifications may be important. The same may be said of the Federal Mediation and Conciliation Service. Arbitrators are appointed on the basis of experience in relation to labor disputes and assignments are often made because the appointee is well informed in respect to the industry or area concerned in the particular controversy.

See also "Automation and Job Evaluation Techniques," Labor Arbitration and Industrial Change, Proceedings of the Sixteenth Annual Meeting, National Academy of Arbitrators (Washington: BNA Books, 1963), pp. 238-265.

even in those instances where the matter in dispute between the parties might properly be also a subject of litigation.

Economic Losses in Strikes, Lockouts, and Slowdowns, Contrasted With Speed and Economy of Arbitration — The strikes and lockouts that have tied up entire industries, interfered with transportation, education, public utilities, and even public safety, are too fresh in the memory of all to require description or elaboration. The "sit-down strike" is easily remembered.[79] The effects of slowdowns and strikes, few as they have been comparatively speaking, are clearly within the recollections of all who have observed developing factors in the labor field.[80]

With no elaboration concerning them, therefore, it is well to note that by comparison arbitration furnishes a means of resolving labor disputes that is relatively so inexpensive as to be of negligible cost, as compared with that caused by impairment of production likely to occur when the parties to a labor dispute have reached an impasse that formerly was regarded as soluble only by major economic pressures.[81] The amount of money involved through loss of earnings, loss of production, deterioration of products, loss of profit through failure to deliver goods, and other related causes ordinarily amounts to thousands of dollars in even the relatively small lockouts and strikes. In the big, industry-wide work interruptions, such as have taken place in coal, steel, air transportation, city transit, newspaper, and at times the railroads, the losses have quickly mounted just as easily into the millions.[82] The public inconvenience, never measurable in dollars and cents, is a factor as important as the losses to the immediate parties.[83]

Where the dispute is referred to arbitration, the parties continue at work, no wages are lost, no production is foregone, no

---

[79] See Spangenberg, "Legal Status of the Sit Down Strike, Equitable Remedies," 35 Mich. Law Rev. 1330 (1937) ; 52 Harv. Law Rev. 1017 (1939) .

[80] See Kaltenborn, Governmental Adjustments of Labor Disputes, pp. 12-13 (Chicago: Foundation Press, 1943) .

[81] See Frankfurter and Greene, The Labor Injunction, Ch. I (New York: The Macmillan Co., 1930) .

[82] Kaltenborn, Governmental Adjustments of Labor Disputes, pp. 1-14 (Chicago: Foundation Press, 1943) .

[83] Note 23 *supra.*

public disturbance is created to bring criticism upon either side.[84] The procedure may be prompt, the result relatively soon known, and in many instances where pay increases have been granted, the award is made retroactive so that its advantages may extend back to the time of the beginning of the controversy, as well as to the period following the proceedings. Thus, arbitration makes it unnecessary for the union to maintain a "war chest" and at the same time it is likely to eliminate employer losses from idleness of plant, interference with deliveries, and similar results of work stoppages. It may be well said that in many instances the most adverse course of decision open to the arbitrator in respect to either party will be less costly than the effects of a strike or lockout. The actual arbitrational expense itself is usually relatively small. It will ordinarily consist of a small travel charge with perhaps hotel and hearing room expenses added, plus a professional fee which will range from a very nominal to a fair professional per diem charge, the latter being ordinarily governed by the financial capacity of the parties to pay and the relative importance and difficulty as well as number of the issues to be determined. Scrutiny and standards published by the Federal Mediation and Conciliation Service and by the American Arbitration Association tend to keep such charges on a reasonable level.

SECTION 3

Arbitration of Labor Disputes at Common Law — Recent State Statutes — The Federal Statutes

At Common Law — In the early common law, labor organizations were regarded as criminal conspiracies and any demands made by such groups were regarded as unlawful and criminal attempts at extortion.[85] In such an atmosphere, therefore, it is not surprising that there is virtually no evidence of arbitration of

---

84 Braun, The Settlement of Industrial Disputes, pp. 130-135 (Philadelphia: Blakiston Co., 1944).

85 See "Historical Introduction," Landis and Manoff, Cases on Labor Law (2 Ed.), pp. 1-40 (Chicago: Foundation Press, 1942); Truax v. Corrigan, 257 U. S. 312, 66 L. Ed. 254, 42 S. Ct. 124 (1922); American Federation of Labor v. Buck's Stove and Range Co., 219 U. S. 581, L. Ed. 345, 31 S. Ct. 472 (1910); National Protective Ass'n v. Cumming, 170 N.Y. 315, 63 N.E. 369 (1902).

An excellent discussion of this subject is found in "The Role of the Law in Arbitration," Arbitration and the Law, Proceedings of the Twelfth Annual Meeting, National Academy of Arbitrators (Washington: BNA Books, 1959), pp. 68-69.

what might properly be called in modern terminology a labor dispute.[86] Arbitrations as such, however, were long ago given some recognition in statutes as suitable means of settling various controversies.[87] Since early times the courts have adhered to the view that parties may not by private agreement deprive courts of jurisdiction given them by law.[88] Hence, the agreement to arbitrate must be legally complete as a contract, and must conform to law, else the result of performing the contract to the stage of hearing and award will have no valid and binding effect. While arbitration is not a court proceeding, it ultimately depends upon the law and the courts for enforcement of awards. Obviously, if the parties respect and abide by an award after it is made, their dispute is solved. But if the award were to have no effect other than merely a persuasive one, it would be of little value. Hence this question has always been present. What must be the preliminary steps to arbitration so that awards resulting from it will have such validity as will bring about their recognition and enforcement in the courts if such step becomes necessary?

In a sense it may be said that modern arbitration law rests upon contract law, but laws pertaining to arbitration have been considerably modified in modern times by statutes specifying the subjects of,[89] the conditions of,[90] and the agreements upon which[91] valid arbitrational steps may be taken so as to condition the awards emerging therefrom, in the end, to be enforced in the courts if

---

86 Cf. Trade Disputes and Trade Unions Act, 1927, 17 & 18 Geo. V. Chap. 22.

87 Stat. 9-10 William III, Ch. 15; 2 & 3 Edw. VI, Chap. 15; 7 Geo. I, Chap. 13. Cf. British Trade Disputes Act, 1906, 6 Edw. VII, Chap. 47, L. R. Gen. Stat. 44 (1906), pp. 246.

88 Sanford, et al. v. Boston Edison Co., 316 Mass. 631, 14 LRRM 880 (1944); Home Ins. Co. v. Morse, 20 Wall. 445, 22 L. Ed. 365 (1874); Lewis v. Brotherhood Accident Co., 194 Mass. 1, 79 N.E. 802 (1907); First Nat. Bank v. White, 220 Mo. 717, 120 S.W. 36 (1909); Hartford Fire Ins. Co. v. Hon, 66 Nebr. 555, 92 N.W. 746 (1902).

89 Tennessee Coal, Iron & R. Co. v. Roussell, 155 Ala. 435, 46 So. 866, 130 Am. St. Rep. 56 (1908); Deshon v. Scott's Administrator, 202 Ky. 575, 260 S. W. 335 (1924); Hall v. Kimmer, 61 Mich. 269, 28 N. W. 96 (1890); Murphy v. Greenberg, 246 Pa. 387, 92 A. 511 (1914).

90 Wilkinson v. Prichard, 145 Iowa 65, 123 N. W. 964 (1909); Hooper v. Fromm, 92 Kan. 142, 141 Pac. 175 (1914).

91 Adinolfi v. Hazlett, 242 Pa. 25, 88 A. 869 (1913); Red Cross Line v. Atlantic Fruit Co., 264 U. S. 109, 68 L. Ed. 582, 44 S. Ct. 274 (1923); Marine Transit Corp. v. Dreyfus, 284 U. S. 263, 76 L. Ed. 282, 52 S. Ct. 166 (1932).

adherence and obedience to them does not follow the agreement of the parties.[92]

State Statutes — As might well be assumed, the statutes of the several states differ considerably among themselves and from the United States Arbitration Act.[93] Some state statutes merely codify the common law.[94] Some of them go further than the common law and seek to aid arbitration by providing that an award of arbitrators may be given effect as a verdict by a jury, so that judgment may be entered upon it on the basis of simple proof that the procedure preceding the award complied with all relevant laws.[95] Some statutes limit the common-law right of a party to a submission agreement to withdraw therefrom before an award is made, while others provide that such agreements are enforceable in the courts.[96] Roughly classified, the results of the statutes may be stated as follows: (1) some merely restate the common law on arbitration;[97] (2) some provide that agreement of the parties in effect makes the submission a rule of court so that awards may be enforced and judgments entered on them as on jury verdicts;[98] (3) some provide that the courts shall compel specific performance of a valid arbitration agreement and give enforcement to awards

---

[92] Frank v. Battles, 147 Ark. 169, 227 S. W. 32 (1921); Deerfield v. Arms, 20 Pick. (Mass.) 480, 32 Am. Dec. 228 (1838).

[93] For a list of citations to state statutes, see Appendix D, *infra*. For further data on the same see Labor Arbitration under State Statutes (Washington: U. S. Department of Labor, 1943) and Sturges, Commercial Arbitrations and Awards, pp. 88-116, 957-987 (Kansas City: Vernon Law Book Co., 1930); Goerke Kirch Co. v. Goerke Kirch Holding Co., 118 N. J. Eq 1, 176 A. 902 (1935); Gilbert v. Burnstine, 225 N. Y. 348, 174 N. E. 706, 73 A. L. R. 1453 (1931); State ex rel. Fancher v. Everett, 144 Wash. 592, 258 Pac. 486 (1927).

[94] See Paine v. Kentucky Ref. 159 Ky. 270, 167 S. W. 375 (1914); Parker v. Providence & S. S. B. Co., 17 R. I. 376, 22 A. 284, 33 Am. St. Rep. 869 (1891).

[95] But in such cases the award must fully satisfy the statutory requirements. Sandford Laundry, Inc. Simon, et al., 255 N. Y. 488 (1941).

See Re Curtis & Castle Arbitration, 64 Conn. 501, 30 A. 769, 42 Am. St. Rep. 200 (1894); Morville v. American Tract Soc., 123 Mass. 129, 25 Am. Rep. 40 (1877); Renaud v. State Ct. of Mediation and Arbitration, 124 Mich. 648, 83 N. W. 620, 83 Am. St. Rep. 346 (1900); Murphy v. Greenberg, 246 Pa. 387, 92 A. 511 (1914).

[96] Levy as Vice-Pres. of International Ladies Garment Workers Union v. Superior Ct., 15 Cal. 2d. 692, 104 P. 2d. 770 (1940). See Glidden Co. v. Retail Hardware Mut. Fire Ins. Co., 181 Minn. 518, 233, N. W. 310, 77 A. L. R. 616 (1930); Finsilver, Still, & Moss v. Goldberg, Maas & Co., 253 N. Y. 382, 171 N. E. 579, A. L. R. 809 (1930); Nippon Ki-Ito Kaisha v. Ewing-Thomas Corp. 313 Pa. 442, 170 A. 286, 93 A. L. R. 1067 (1933).

[97] See Paine v. Kentucky Ref. Co., 159 Ky. 270, 167 S. W. 375 (1914); Parker v. Providence & S. S. B. Co., 17 R. I. 376, 22 A. 284, 33 Am. St. Rep. 869 (1891).

[98] See Zehner v. Lehigh Coal & Nav. Co., 187 Pa. 487, 41 A. 464, 67 Am. St. Rep. 586 (1898).

made thereunder;[99] (4) some provide that parties to a pending
action in court may refer their controversy to an arbitrator and
obtain judgment by the court entered upon his award.[100]

The Federal Statutes—The United States Arbitration Act makes
"valid, irrevocable and enforceable" agreements to arbitrate in
relation to maritime transactions involving commerce." It has
been held applicable to a dispute concerning wages alleged to
have been due under the Fair Labor Standards Act, despite a provision in Section 1 that "nothing herein contained shall apply
to contracts of employment of seamen, railroad employees, or any
other class of workers engaged in foreign or interstate commerce."
However, it now seems unlikely this statue will have much importance in relation to arbitration of labor issues.[101]

The Norris-LaGuardia Anti-Injunction Act provides in Section
8 that "No restraining order or injunctive relief shall be granted
to any complainant who has failed to . . . make every reasonable
effort to settle such dispute either by negotiation or with the aid

---

[99] See Marine Transit Corp. v. Dreyfus, 284 U. S. 263, 76 L. Ed. 282, 52 S. Ct.
166 (1932) ; Shanferoke Coal & Supply Corp. v. Westchester Serv. Corp. 293 U. S.
449, 79 L. Ed. 583, 55 S. Ct. 313 (1934). The much-discussed decision of Textile
Workers Union v. Lincoln Mills of Alabama, 353 U. S. 448, 77 S. Ct. 912, 40 LRRM
2113, 28 LA 519 (1957) decreed specific performance under a statute which certainly did not expressly provide for such relief. See Section 4 *infra,* this chapter.

[100] See Murphy v. Greenberg, 246 Pa. 387, 92 A. 511 (1914).

[101] The decision of some federal courts indicate that the United States Arbi-
tration Act may apply to labor disputes not clearly within the definition of "commerce" in section 2 of the statute. Donahue v. Susquehanna Collieries Co., 138
Fed. (2d) 3 (1943) ; Watkins et al. v. Hudson Coal Co., 54 F. Supp. 953 (1944).
But see Gatliff Coal Co. v. Cox, 142 Fed. (2d) 876, 14 LRRM 782 (1941) ; Agostini
Bros. Bldg. Corp. v. U. S. etc., 142 Fed. (2d) 854 (1944) ; and Bernhardt v. Polygraphic Co., 350 U. S. 198, 76 S. Ct. 273, 25 LA 693 (1956) . Since Textile Workers
Union v. Lincoln Mills of Alabama, 353 U. S. 448; 1 L. Ed. 2d 972, 77 S. Ct. 912,
40 LRRM 2113, 28 LA 519 (1957) , it seems unlikely the United States Arbitration
Act will be held to apply to labor arbitrations generally. The attitude of the highest
court in ignoring that statute was one of eloquent silence.

On this act generally see Sturges and Murphy, "Some Confusing Matters Relating
to Arbitration Under the United States Arbitration Act" (1952) , 17 Law and Con-
temporary Problems, 580, and Burstein, "The U. S. Arbitration Act — A Re-
evaluation," 3 Villanova Law Jour. 125 (1958) .

See "The Proposed Uniform Arbitration Act: a Panel Discussion," Critical Issues
in Labor Arbitration, Proceedings of the Tenth Annual Meeting, National Academy
of Arbitrators (Washington: BNA Books, 1957) pp. 112-143. A recent court decision
holds that invocation of the U. S. Arbitration Act does not broaden a court's review of a labor arbitration which sustained a discharge. Block Pontiac v. Candando,
274 F. Supp. 1014, 66 LRRM 2371 (E.D. Pa., 1967) .

of any available governmental machinery of mediation or voluntary arbitration."[102]

In the preamble (Section 1) of the Labor Management Relations (Taft-Hartley) Act, it is declared to be the "purpose and policy" of the Act to provide "orderly and peaceful procedures for preventing interference" by either employees or employers with the legitimate rights of the others. Section 203 (c) of the same Act requires the Director of the Federal Mediation and Conciliation Service, if he fails to bring parties to a labor dispute to agreement by conciliation, to "seek to induce the parties voluntarily to seek other means of settling the dispute without resort to strike, lockout or other coercion" . . . Moreover it provides in section 203 (d) that "Final adjustment by a method agreed upon by the parties is hereby declared to be the desirable method for settlement of grievance disputes arising over the application or interpretation of an existing collective-bargaining agreement." Consistent with such policy, the Act also provides for board-of-inquiry hearings in cases of national emergencies.[103]

The 60-day notice or cooling-off period provision and the requirement that the Federal Mediation and Conciliation Service be notified 30 days after the 60-day notice is given in the National Labor Relations Act are a part of the same apparent policy.[104]

All of these statutory provisions, while they provide no procedural machinery for arbitration, clearly contemplate that arbitration, a familiar, often-used means of resolving labor disputes, was and is to be encouraged and expanded in use. Taken together, they furnish a clear background of federal governmental approval of arbitration. In fact, though the above statutes were not all expressly relied on in the majority opinion of the United States Supreme Court in the *Lincoln Mills* case,[105] they must be con-

---

[102] 47 Stat. 72, 29 U. S. Code, Sec. 108.

Enforcement of an award by directing a union to desist from a strike in defiance of it and intended to defeat it is not prohibited by the Norris-LaGuardia Act. New Orleans Steamship Assn. v. I.L.A., Local 1418, 67 LRRM 2430 (5th Cir., 1968) .

[103] 29 U. S. C. A. §§ 206-207; and see Beatty, "Arbitration of Unfair Labor Practice Disputes." 14 Arbitration Journal 180 (1959) .

[104] NLRA § 8 (d) .

[105] 353 U. S. 448, 1 L. Ed. 2d 972, 77 S. Ct. 912, 40 LRRM 2113, 28 1080 (1955) . See "Arbitration and/or the N.L.R.B.," Labor Arbitration and Industrial Change, Proceedings of the Sixteenth Annual Meeting, National Academy of Arbitrators (Washington: BNA Books, 1963) , pp. 175-191, 28 LA 519 (1957) . Spielberg Manufacturing Company, 112 NLRB 1080, 36 LRRM 1152 (1955) .

sidered as clear components of the policy and the atmosphere in which the far-reaching and important decision in that case was made and announced. The *"Spielberg* policy" of the NLRB is to honor an arbitration award if the parties agreed to honor it, the hearing procedure was fair, and the award is not repugnant to the policy of the National Labor Relations Act.

The discussion of the *Lincoln Mills* decision should be prefaced by an account of the decision handed down by the U. S. Supreme Court in 1954 in the wage suit brought by the Association of Westinghouse Employees against the Westinghouse Electric Corporation.[106] There was no majority opinion, the Court splitting four ways. But the judgment of the Court was that Section 301 did not confer jurisdiction over such a suit on the federal district courts.

The basic disagreement related to the congressional intent in Section 301. According to one view, Section 301 was merely a procedural provision designed to open the federal courts to suits under collective bargaining agreements; it did not create any substantive federal law to apply in such suits. But according to another view, Congress intended the federal courts to fashion substantive rules for interpreting and enforcing collective bargaining agreements.

In an opinion in which Justices Burton and Minton joined, Mr. Justice Frankfurter took the view that Section 301 was merely procedural, that "all it does is to give procedural directions to the federal courts." So construed, he said, Section 301 does not give the federal courts jurisdiction over the wage claims involved in the *Westinghouse* case. But Frankfurter then went on to state that if Section 301 should be construed as giving the federal courts power to fashion a body of substantive law to apply in these suits, it then would be subject to constitutional objections since it does not explicitly provide or define the new substantive rights created.

In a brief concurring opinion, Chief Justice Warren and Mr. Justice Clark agreed that the federal court did not have jurisdiction of the case, stating that Section 301 was not intended "to authorize a union to enforce in a federal court the uniquely per-

---

106 Association of Westinghouse Salaried Employees v. Westinghouse Electric Corp., 348 U. S. 437, 99 L. ed. 510, 35 LRRM 2643 (1954).

sonal right of an employee for whom it had bargained to receive compensation for services rendered his employer." They did not consider it necessary to raise the constitutional issues posed by Mr. Justice Frankfurter.

Concurring separately, Mr. Justice Reed also agreed that the federal court did not have jurisdiction of the *Westinghouse* case. But he disagreed with Mr. Justice Frankfurter on the intent of Section 301. He viewed Section 301 as giving the federal courts authority to fashion substantive law, drawing on both federal and state statutes, and he did not regard the section as subject to constitutional objections as so construed. The fact that the federal courts might be required to apply a considerable amount of state law in these suits did not make Section 301 unconstitutional, in his opinion.[107]

In dissenting, Justices Douglas and Black agreed with Mr. Justice Reed's views as to the intent and constitutionality of Section 301. But in disagreement with all of the other seven justices, they took the position that Section 301 gave the federal court jurisdiction of the *Westinghouse* case.

In 1957, the U. S. Supreme Court handed down its landmark decision in *Textile Workers' Union* v. *Lincoln Mills of Alabama*.[108] The union was suing for specific performance of a contract to arbitrate as it had negotiated with the employer. The majority of the court held that Section 301 (a) of the LMRA conferred upon federal district courts full jurisdiction over suits concerning labor contracts in interstate commerce. It decided that this section of the Act amounts to a mandate to the federal courts to make, create, or judicially enact a body of federal law for application to such agreements and by means of which to test their

107 Previous decisions consistent with this view are found in Hamilton Foundry and Machine Co. v. International Moulders and Foundry Workers Union, 193 F. 2d 209, 29 LRRM 2223 (1951); Textile Workers Union of America, C. I. O. v. Aleo Manufacturing Co., 94 F. Supp. 626, 27 LRRM 2164, 15 LA 726 (1950); United Electrical and Radio Machine Workers of America v. Oliver Corp., 205 F. 2d 376, 32 LRRM 2270 (1953); Textile Workers Union, C. I. O. v. Berryton Mill, 20 Labor Cases, Par. 6659, 28 LRRM 2540 (D.C. Georgia, 1951).

108 353 U. S. 448, 1 L. ed 2d 972, 77 S. Ct. 912, 40 LRRM 2113, 28 LA 519 (1957). Companion decisions were Goodall-Sanford, Inc., v. United Textile Workers, 353 U. S. 550, 40 LRRM 2118, 2120 (1957) and General Electric Co. v. Local 205, United Electrical Radio & Machine Workers, 353 U. S. 547, 40 LRRM 2119, 28 LA 520 (1957).

validity. The decision asserted that such courts received, under
the section concerned, jurisdiction to order specific performance
of agreements to arbitrate disputes arising under such labor
contracts.

The majority opinion stated that:

> ". . . the substantive law to apply in suits under Section 301 (a)
> is federal law which the courts must fashion from the policy of our
> national labor laws. Federal interpretation of federal law will gov-
> ern, not state law. But state law, if compatible with Section 301 (a),
> may be resorted to in order to find the rule that will best effectuate
> the federal policy. Any state law applied, however, will be absorbed
> as federal law and will not be an independent source of private
> rights."[109]

Common law, statutes, and decisions prior to the *Lincoln Mills*
case are still important. Some courts have held that *Lincoln Mills*
did not divest the state courts of their jurisdiction.[110] The California Supreme Court, for example, has declared that the *Lincoln
Mills* decision merely held that an action for breach of a labor
agreement may be brought in the federal courts.[111] It concludes
that at present there is concurrent state and federal jurisdiction
over such suits. It would seem clear, however, that state courts
are now bound to apply federal law concerning collective bargaining agreements.[112]

In the *Lincoln Mills* case, the court resolved a considerable
question as to the power of the courts to grant specific performance of agreements to arbitrate since the Norris-LaGuardia Act.
It asserted that the Norris-LaGuardia Act never was intended to
prohibit such decrees.[113] Although the decision evoked a long and
persuasive dissenting opinion from the pen of Mr. Justice Frank-

---

109 353 U. S. at p. 457, 40 LRRM 2119, 28 LA 520.
110 Bull S. S. Co. v. National Marine Engineers' Beneficial Ass'n. 41 LRRM 2121,
2126 (2d Cir., 1957); McCarroll v. Los Angeles Dist. Council of Carpenters, 315
P. 2d 322, 40 LRRM 2709 (Cal., 1957); Anchor Motor Freight Corp. v. International Brotherhood of Teamsters, 34 Lab. Cas. par. 71, 225 (N.Y. 1958); Potoker
v. Brooklyn Eagle, Inc., 2 N.Y. 2d 553, 141 N.E. 2d 841, 28 LA 344, *cert. denied*,
355 U. S. 883, 29 LA 434 (1957) (enforcement of arbitration provisions in the
contract can be had in either state or federal court); Artcraft Specialty Co. v.
UMW, 33 Lab. Cas. par. 71, 211 (Pa., 1957).
111 See McCarroll v. Los Angeles County Dist. Council of Carpenters, 40 LRRM
2709 (1957), *aff'd*, 41 LRRM 2431, *cert. denied*, U. S. Sup. Ct. (1958).
112 See *idem* at p. 330.
113 353 U. S. 448, 40 LRRM 2113, 28 LA 519 (1957). See U. S. Steel Workers v.

furter, it must now be taken to express the law of the land to the extent that it can be understood and applied. But it leaves many questions of state and of concurrent state and federal jurisdiction unanswered. Recent developments are discussed herein in Chapters II, VIII, and X.

Most of all it leaves a great uncertainty in a constitutional area. The courts have accepted the congressional mandate to fashion or make laws applicable to the contracts concerned. What are the limitations, if any, upon this judicial power to legislate? May the Congress from now on delegate its legislative power to the courts? If so, to what extent? However, this much is clear: Agreements of parties to labor contracts to arbitrate as the final step in a grievance procedure have a sanction to support their validity and to encourage their performance such as never before existed. Employees and employers engaged in businesses that bring them under the federal labor statutes no longer may point to the now obsolete common-law decisions holding contracts to arbitrate future disputes unenforceable. They must perform them and abide by the resulting awards. Moreover, the extent of the application of the preemption doctrine in expressing the federal jurisdiction stated and applied in the *Lincoln Mills* case serves to emphasize the importance of scrupulous observance by arbitrators of all applicable federal laws in considering the claims of the parties to labor controversies.

SECTION 4

The Issue of Arbitrability — The *Lincoln Mills* and the *Cutler-Hammer* Decisions

The Lincoln Mills Decision — As will be obvious from the discussion above, the U. S. Supreme Court, in reaching the *Lincoln Mills* result, was confronted by a common law which long had been unreceptive toward arbitration. Executory agreements to arbitrate were not enforceable in the federal courts until the

---

Galland Henning Mfg. Co., 241 F. 2d 323, 325, 27 LA 855 (7 Cir. 1957); Engineers Ass'n v. Sperry Gyroscope, 148 F. Supp. 521, 28 LA 93 (S.D. N.Y., 1957).

In a suit by employees and union members against an employer and a union to enforce an arbitrational award under § 301, the court observed that unless it granted a remedy, there would be none. Lee v. Olin Mathieson Chemical Company, 271 F. Supp. 635 (W.D. Va., 1967).

passage of the U. S. Arbitration Act and, as observed above, this statute excludes from its applicability all "contracts of employment" of "workers engaged in foreign or interstate commerce." [114] Moreover, the full meaning of Section 301 (a) of the Taft-Hartley Act has yet to be clarified.[115] It most certainly is true that the text of Section 301 does not point clearly to the result reached by the court in the *Lincoln Mills* decision. "The statute does not expressly state what law shall be applied to determine the rights of the parties or their remedies.[116] Mr. Justice Douglas stated in his majority opinion that the legislative history was "cloudy and confusing."

None may dispute, however, that it was the purpose of Congress to attain industrial peace as far as possible, and this requires collective bargaining and resulting enforceable agreements. Hence the majority wrote: "The agreement to arbitrate grievance disputes is the *quid pro quo* for the agreement not to strike." The court thus perceived in Section 301 a congressional intent to reverse the common-law rule and to declare the federal law to be that executory agreements to arbitrate grievances are not voidable, but are firm and binding obligations. The majority opinion found no impediment to its result in the Norris-LaGuardia Act. On the contrary it stated that the Norris-LaGuardia Act itself exhibited "a policy toward settlement of labor disputes by arbitration." It is notable that the United States Arbitration Act was not mentioned in the majority opinion.

Much remains undecided among the issues raised by the *Lincoln Mills* decision. The respective parts to be played by state and federal laws remain to be resolved. The state laws apparently when approved by judicial alchemy become federal laws. However that may be, it now is clear that a party to an arbitration agreement involved in interstate commerce no longer may disavow the undertaking by coolly pointing out that at common law such agreements, while executory, are unenforceable. Whether an employer or a union, the unwilling party must now proceed to ar-

---

114 9 U.S.C. Sec. 1 *et seq:* see Sec. 3 *supra*, under "The Federal Statutes," Note 101.
115 Mendelsohn, "Enforceability of Arbitration Agreements under Taft-Hartley, Section 301," 66 Yale L.J. 167 (1956).
116 Judge Wyzanski in Textile Workers Union v. American Thread Co., 113 F. Supp. 137, 32 LRRM 2205 (1953).

bitration. In the past in many states, either party might have notified the other that it deemed the subject matter in dispute to be nonarbitrable and in this way, excepting for possible economic repercussions, ended the matter.

Reluctant to incur the ill will or economic pressures of the other party, some parties have submitted to arbitrators the preliminary question whether the main dispute was arbitrable.[117] This step now appears to be obligatory in many situations where, until the *Lincoln-Mills* decision, it was thought to be more or less elective.

The Cutler-Hammer Doctrine — Long prior to the *Lincoln Mills* decision, statutes of several states had changed the common-law rules by making agreements to arbitrate legally enforceable, provided they involved certain specified types of disputes and were in due, legally prescribed form. Hence the suit to enforce arbitration has long been familiar in the American legal scene. In 1947 an interesting development in this area was presented by a view expressed in a New York state court decision that became known as the *"Cutler-Hammer* doctrine." [118] The core of controversy arising from that decision is found in the following words of the court: "If the meaning of the provision of the contract sought to be arbitrated is beyond dispute, there cannot be anything to arbitrate and the contract cannot be said to provide for arbitration."

The dispute was over a bonus which had gone through a collective bargaining stage and had then been the subject of discussion by representatives of the parties with the result that the union spokesmen had felt confidence enough in their claim to take it to court. The court denied that this controversy had sufficient substance to be the subject of arbitration. It is well known that, while the text of a written contract cannot generally be altered by parol evidence, the latter may always be considered in relation to a writing to prove, for example, that the cloudy or ambiguous words were supplied by one party to take advantage of the other. Or

---

117 See Franks v. Battles, 147 Ark. 169, 227 S.W. 32 (1921); Annotation 58 LRA 181 (1903); 47 LRA (NS) 346 (1914); Twin Coach Co., 1 LA 59 (1944); Pan American Airways, 5 LA 590 (1946); Illinois Bell Tel. Co., 15 LA 274 (1950); See General Electric Co., 31 LA 924 (1958).

118 Local 402, Int. Ass'n of Machinists v. Cutler-Hammer, Inc. 271 Opp. Div. 917, 67 N.Y.S. 2d 317, 19 LRRM 2232 (1st Dept., 1947), Affd. 297 N.Y. 519, 74 N.E. 2d 464, 20 LRRM 2445 7 LA 959, (1947). See Scoles, "Review of Labor Arbitration Awards on Jurisdictional Grounds," 17 U. Chi. Law Rev. 616 (1950).

oral proof of duress or fraud or sharp dealings in bargaining may be shown to have impaired the bargaining.[119] Waiver or estoppel may be proved by oral evidence to have followed the writing.[120] The union and the company in the *Cutler-Hammer* case apparently had agreed that such a dispute should go through arbitration. It was unfortunate that the court usurped the matter of decision by taking merely a superficial look at the text of the contract. Certainly it would not have denied but would rather have secured justice by referring the matter to an arbitrator as agreed by the parties. There can have been no reason to suppose that if, after all the evidence was in, the claims of the union appeared to have no merit, an arbitrator would not have so found and awarded.

The principal vice of the now fortunately discredited and repealed *Cutler-Hammer* decision appears to have been that it substituted as the decisional voice between parties to a labor dispute that of a judge elected or appointed politically for that of an arbitrator selected by them as they had agreed. With all due respect for the American judiciary, it may be observed that many of them have had little or nothing to do with labor law, labor economics, or the great field of human relations, involved in the contacts of management and labor. The parties to labor disputes know this and, when they have agreed to submit a dispute to a person of their own selection or a person to be named by the American Arbitration Association, the Federal Mediation and Conciliation Service, or some other agency, they must be understood to desire the services of a tried and experienced labor arbitrator. True, there may be later a court review of the award. In such case, the court should proceed not by considering the issue *de novo,* but only by ascertaining that the arbitration proceedings were regular, the findings sustained by the evidence, and the award complete and not in excess of the submission terms.

Another vice of the *Cutler-Hammer* decision was that it offered a weak, but apparent, excuse for other courts, purporting to follow that court decision, under the doctrine of *stare decisis,* to stretch its effect to even more unfortunate extremes than occurred in the

---

119 See Chapter VI, Secs. 5, 15, and 16 *infra.*
120 See Chapter VI, Sec. 16, *infra.*

leading case. In the *Botany Mills, Inc.,* case[121], for example, the New Jersey Supreme Court ruled that the claims of the union in respect to vacation pay were nonarbitrable as wholly without merit, even after a respected and experienced arbitrator had made an interim award supporting the claims.

The parties might well improve such situations by expressly agreeing that all disputes as to arbitrability should themselves be arbitrable. It is submitted, however, that even without such an express agreement, the issue of arbitrability is itself, logically a dispute between the parties within the usual terms of the grievance provisions of labor agreements and should, therefore, be treated as a preliminary question to be considered and decided, at least in the first instance, by the arbitrator.

When the *Lincoln Mills* decision and the *Cutler-Hammer* doctrine are considered together, a clearly possible injury to labor arbitration as it should be becomes apparent. Ill-advised judicial action is envisioned in any matter in which a judge first decides, under *Lincoln Mills,* that a dispute is within the scope of the arbitration agreement of the parties and so within the jurisdiction of the court for possible enforcement, then concludes that the contentions of one party have no merit, and finally decides the matter consistently with that view.[122] As earlier stated, this could greatly harm arbitration generally and would deny agreed arbitrational procedure to the party desiring it. It would give the parties exactly what they agreed against — a judicial decision rather than an arbitrator's hearing and award.[123]

It is to be observed, however, that opinions of the federal circuit courts very largely restricted the scope of judicial inquiries to matters which necessarily require court decision as preliminary to any conclusion whether an agreement to arbitrate existed when asserted by the party asking an enforcement order. In the *Local No. 149* case[124] the First Circuit court stated it found "nothing in

---

121 Botany Mills, Inc. v. Textile Workers Union of America, 27 LA 165 (1956); permanent stay 28 LA 315 (1957); 50 N.J. Super. 18, 30 LA 479 (1958). Petition for certification granted June 16, 1958, 27 N.J. 320 (1958).

122 Refinery Employees' Union v. Continental Oil Co., 268 F. 2d 447 (1959).

123 See Plant, "Arbitrability under the Standard Labor Arbitration Clause," 14 Arbitration Journal 51 (1959).

124 Technical Engineers, Local No. 149, Etc. v. General Electric Company, 250 F. 2d 922 (1957) (1st Circuit).

the terms of the . . . arbitration agreement to warrant the conclusion that the employer had agreed to arbitrate the question of arbitrability of the grievance stated in the petition." It affirmed a judgment refusing a decree of specific performance.

In a later matter before the Seventh Circuit court,[125] the opinion observed that the defendant had agreed to arbitrate various disputes only if requests were made by the union in writing within 10 days after the receipt of the employer's final answer. The request in the case was not delivered until 13 days after the employer's refusal. Hence the court concluded there could be no obligation to arbitrate the matter which had been in dispute in the grievance procedure.

Criticism of the *Cutler-Hammer* doctrine cannot be carried so far as to suggest that the mere, wholly unfounded request of any party for arbitration should exclude the court from ascertaining whether there exists any ground for asking enforcement of such procedure. The foregoing criticism of that doctrine is aimed rather at the idea that when a court is asked to order enforcement of a clear agreement to arbitrate, it should first determine whether the plaintiff's contentions as to the issue to be arbitrated have substantial merits or no merits. This position indicates that the court, without full hearing on the merits of the issue to be arbitrated, should refuse a decree for performance if it concludes that plaintiff's contentions to be arbitrated on their merits are baseless, frivolous, or wholly without merit. Thus the question that should be arbitrated, as above stated, is exposed to the possibility of being decided superficially by the court. Even if the court holds a hearing on the merits of such issues, it will then be decided by a court rather than by an arbitrator contrarily to the agreement of the parties.

A recent decision by the Second Circuit court appears to have been very well reasoned.[126] In that matter the parties had broadly agreed to arbitrate virtually all disputes that might arise under a contract to sell and deliver merchandise. The court held they were

---

125 Brass & Copper Workers Federal Labor Union No. 19322, A.F.L.-C.I.O. (Ptf.) v. American Brass Co., 272 F. 2d 849 (1959) (7th Circuit).

126 Robert Lawrence Co. v. Devonshire Fabrics, Inc., 271 F. 2d 402 (1959) (2d Circuit). But see Engineer's Association v. Sperry-Gyroscope, 251 F. 2d 133 (1957) (2d Circuit).

bound to arbitrate a charge of fraud in relation to such contract excepting only the question whether the agreement to arbitrate, itself, had been induced by fraud. That question the court resolved, then referred the matter back for a stay until arbitration on the merits could be carried out as agreed.

The U. S. Supreme Court, itself, in three companion cases, was more positive. In the case of *Steelworkers* v. *American Manufacturing Company*[127] it stated that the *Cutler-Hammer* decision "could only have a crippling effect on grievance arbitration." There it also expressed the view that,

> "The function of the court is very limited when the parties have agreed to submit all questions of contract interpretation to the arbitrator. It is then confined to ascertaining whether the party seeking arbitration is making a claim which on its face is governed by the contract. Whether the moving party is right or wrong is a question of contract interpretation for the arbitrator. In these circumstances the moving party should not be deprived of the arbitrator's judgment, when it was his judgment and all that it connotes that was bargained for."

In the *Enterprise Wheel and Car Company* case[128] the Court declared that the federal policy favoring arbitration of labor disputes would be undermined if courts had the final say on the merits of awards. The *Warrior and Gulf Navigation Company*[129] opinion expresses the positive position that:

> "In the commercial case, arbitration is the substitute for litigation. Here arbitration is the substitute for industrial strife. Since arbitration of labor disputes has quite different functions from arbitration under an ordinary commercial agreement, the hostility evinced by courts toward arbitration of commercial agreements has no place here. For arbitration of labor disputes under collective bargaining agreements is part and parcel of the collective bargaining process itself."

Then the Court reemphasizes its view by writing that,

> "Arbitration is the means of solving the unforeseeable by molding a system of private law for all the problems which may arise and to provide for their solution in a way which will generally accord with the variant needs and desires of the parties. The processing of dis-

---

127 80 S. Ct. 1343; 46 LRRM, 2414 (1960).
128 80 S. Ct. 1358; 46 LRRM 2423 (1960). See Steelworkers Local 4936 v. Sharon Tube Co., 67 LRRM 2079 (W.D. Pa., 1967).
129 80 S. Ct. 1347; 46 LRRM 2416 (1960).

putes through the grievance machinery is actually a vehicle by which meaning and content is given to the collective bargaining agreement."

In 1963, Section 7501 appeared in the Civil Practice Law and Rules of the State of New York. It reads as follows: "A written agreement to submit any controversy to arbitration is enforceable without regard to the justiciable character of the controversy and confers jurisdiction on the courts of the state to enforce it and to enter judgment on an award. In determining any matter arising under this article, the court shall not consider whether the claim with respect to which arbitration is sought is tenable or otherwise pass upon the merits of the dispute." [130]

This enactment no doubt will erase the unfortunate effect of *Cutler-Hammer* in the state where it was announced. It remains for lawyers elsewhere to be watchful and alert that its effects do not survive in other states where it was favorably regarded between the date of the decision and the curative legislation.

---

[130] Book 7B, McKinney's Consolidated Laws of New York Annotated, Art. 75, Sec. 7501.

CHAPTER II
SUMMARY OF LABOR LAWS AND POLICY
SECTION 1
Background Summary of Common Law and Policy*

Since this is a book on labor arbitration, rather than on labor law as a whole, it makes no effort to cover the latter great and important subject in detail. It is obvious, however, that those who undertake to deal with labor disputes should have ready access at least to brief information concerning the general nature of labor law and policy. Essentially, this should include some descriptive materials on the milestone federal statutes and the preemption doctrine which, as declared by the U. S. Supreme Court, has largely siphoned the more important labor matters away from jurisdiction of the states and into the hands of federal authorities.

The brief treatment that follows is intended to furnish the general background that is adequate for common reference and to guide one who must do further research to his point of beginning. The arbitrators, personnel executives, and union representatives without legal training who may use this book should find the materials in this chapter of particular interest.

When the common-law rules which preceded all federal legislation and the long series of statutes are studied, they seem to sustain the generalization that the course Congress has followed has been fairly consistent regardless of who was tenant of the White House at the time, or which party was in the majority on Capitol Hill.

For the purpose of this discussion, the following subheadings will be briefly considered:

    1. Labor Law Prior to the Sherman Act.

    2. The Sherman Act.

---

* Some materials in this section were used by the author in an address at the University of Minnesota on January 8, 1960. Use here is authorized.

3. The Clayton Act.

4. The Eight-hour Day Laws.

5. The Prevailing Wage Laws (the Davis-Bacon Act, the Walsh-Healey Act, and various other statutory standards established where federal expenditures are involved).

6. The Railway Labor Act.

7. The Norris-LaGuardia Anti-Injunction Act.

8. The Wagner Act. (National Labor Relations Act.)

9. The Fair Labor Standards Act. (The Wage and Hour Act.)

10. The Taft-Hartley Act. (The Labor Management Relations Act.)

11. The Landrum-Griffin Act. (The Labor Management Reporting and Disclosure Act of 1959.)

---

1. *Labor Law Prior to the Sherman Act* — From the slavery and serfdom of ancient and medieval times, there emerged through the Black Death of 1348 a pattern of English legislation repressive upon freedom of the laboring classes. One-fourth to one-half of the English population died in that year. This scarcity of working people created competition for the services of those who survived. The various statutes of laborers were intended to restore the previous obligations and limitations upon earnings of workers. Generally speaking, these statutes were not effective. Labor was too scarce; the competition for it was too great. There was widespread disregard of the law. But from this atmosphere emerged the concept that organization of labor and collective demands on behalf of any labor group were criminal conspiracies and as such should be sharply suppressed. This pattern continued in the Anglo-American system of law into early times on this continent. The *Philadelphia Cordwainers* case of 1806 established the pattern for early judicial treatment of organized labor in this country. These cordwainers, or shoemakers, were united in a club. The club presented to their employers a concerted demand for increases of compensation for production of fancy straps and trimmings of shoes. The employers appealed to the public prosecutor and

through his activities a grand jury indicted the journeymen cord-wainers for "contriving and intending unjustly to increase their compensation." The trial before Recorder Levy resulted in con-demnation of the club, or union, members for conspiracy.[1] A num-ber of similar decisions followed in Pennsylvania and elsewhere.[2]

In the case of *Commonwealth* v. *Hunt,* in 1842,[3] Chief Justice Shaw, though probably an opponent of labor unions, sustained the right to strike, apparently because he had knowledge at the time that an opposite result would result in a disastrous work stoppage and a costly series of criminal prosecutions in and around Boston. His purpose was not so much a broad-minded, liberal objective, sympathetic to workers, as one to save investments of people of his class in a considerable number of newly built mills in the area of Boston. Since that date, however, the right of or-ganized workers to quit concertedly, that is to say, to strike, has been generally recognized. Modifications of this right have re-quired that the strike be for legally approved objectives, but the right itself has not been unqualifiedly denied since the Shaw de-cision. Since then the strike has been generally regarded as legal if its primary objective is to improve the condition of the working people in the organization.

It will be remembered that the early strikes were considered to be concerted quittings of work. This must be contrasted with the present established view that workers who have struck a plant are deemed to be "striking employees." A few decades ago, the striking worker ceased all relations to the employer; he lost sen-iority and all job rights. Today, he retains all seniority and job rights and may even be entitled to be ordered back to work by the National Labor Relations Board against the will of the em-ployer, if the Board concludes an unfair labor practice of the employer caused the strike.

---

1 Gregory, Labor and the Law, p. 24.
2 See Com. v. Carlisle, Brightly, 36 Penn. N.P. (1821); People v. Melvin, 2 Wheeler (N.Y.) Crim. Cases 262 (1810).
Documentary History of American Industrial Society, pp. 36-59.
3 4 Metcalf (Mass., 1842).
Picketing came into extensive use soon after the Commonwealth v. Hunt deci-sion. Peaceful picketing was assumed to be lawful and was in 1940 identified with freedom of speech. Thornhill v. Alabama, 310 U.S. 88, 60 S. Ct. 736, 6 LRRM 697 (1940). It is now, however, subject to reasonable state controls. See Car-penters and Joiners Union v. Ritter's Cafe, 315 U.S. 722, 62 S. Ct. 807, 10 LRRM 511 (1942).

In the period prior to 1890, the practice developed of requiring employees to sign agreements that they were not union members and that they would not join any union while employed by the employers requiring the signature. These were known as "yellow-dog contracts" and they were universally denounced by labor unions. Their legality, however, was sustained in the case of *Hitchman Coal and Coke Co. v. Mitchell.*[4] Some employers continued the practice of fighting union organizations by means of yellow-dog contracts and injunctions up to 1932, the time of the Norris-LaGuardia Act.[5] This was true despite the fact that Congress had previously tried to outlaw the yellow-dog contract, as also did the State of Kansas. These statutes were held unconstitutional in the decisions of *United States* v. *Adair*[6] and *Coppage* v. *Kansas.*[7]

2. *The Sherman Act* — Meanwhile, the Sherman Antitrust Act had become law on July 2, 1890.[8] It seems highly unlikely that Congress was preoccupied with labor at the time that statute was finally determined and the Act was passed and signed. Fairly soon after its passage, however, the famous *Danbury Hatters'* case arose. The case grew out of work stoppages and widespread boycotts by organized labor to force the manufacturers of hats in Danbury to come to terms. In the case of *Loewe* v. *Lawlor,*[9] the organized activities of the labor unions were held to violate the Sherman Act. After extended litigation, the judgment against the union was finally settled for a total of somewhat more than $235,000, of which it is said the American Federation of Labor furnished approximately $216,000. This case was twice tried by a jury, was four times in the United States Circuit Court of Appeals, and three times before the United States Supreme Court. A number of cases thereafter followed and applied the holding.[10]

---

4 245 U. S. 229, 38 S. Ct. 65 (1917).

5 Act of March 23, 1932, Tit. 18 U. S. Code § 3692 and Tit. 29 U.S. Code § 101 and ff.

6 208 U. S. 161, 28 S. Ct. 277 (1908).

7 236 U. S. 1, 35 S. Ct. 240 (1914).

8 Tit. 15 U. S. Code § 1 and ff, July 2, 1890.

9 208 U. S. 274, 28 S. Ct. 301 (1908); s.c. 235 U. S. 522, 35 S. Ct. 170 (1915).

10 See Coronado Coal Co. v. United Mine Workers of America, 268 U. S. 295, 45 S. Ct. 551 (1924) and other cases cited later herein under the Clayton Act discussion.

3. The Clayton Act — There would appear to be no doubt that certain parts of the Clayton Antitrust Act of October 15, 1914,[11] were written and urged upon Congress by friends of Labor. Section 6 of the Clayton Act declares that "the labor of a human being is not a commodity or article of commerce." It expressly goes on to state that nothing contained in the antitrust laws shall be construed to forbid the existence and operation of labor, agriculural or horticultural organizations, instituted for the purposes of mutual health, etc.

Section 20 of that Act expressly provides that no restraining order or injunction shall be granted by any court of the United States or a judge or judges thereof in any case between an employer and employees "in any matters involving disputes about conditions of employment unless necessary to prevent irreparable injury to property and where there is no adequate remedy at law." It expressly states that no restraining order shall prohibit any person or persons acting singly or in concert from attending any lawful meeting for the purpose of peacefully obtaining or communicating information or peacefully persuading any person to work or refrain from working.

These provisions of the Clayton Act were hailed as labor's Magna Charta or "Bill of Rights," but in a series of decisions, the United States Supreme Court virtually nullified the advantages organized labor had assumed would be reaped from the passage of the Act. The decision in *Duplex Printing Co.* v. *Deering*[12] was one of several holding that, since the statute approved only peaceful and legitimate methods and objectives of labor and since apparently certain union methods and economic pressures were regarded as illegitimate and improper by the courts, these activities would be enjoined despite the provisions of the Clayton Act. The text of the Act clearly shows that Congress itself intended to protect legitimate and proper organizations of working people and their legitimate and lawful use of their collective strength as means

---

11 Tit. 15 U. S. Code § 12 *et sequitur,* Tit. 28 U. S. Code § 381 *et sequitur* and Tit. 29 U. S. Code § 52.

12 254 U. S. 443, 41 S. Ct. 172 (1921). Similar results were reached in Bedford Cut Stone Co. v. Journeymen Stonecutters' Assn., 274 U. S. 37, 47 S. Ct. 522 (1927), and a number of other matters before the U. S. Supreme Court.

of obtaining reasonable adjustments of working hours, working conditions, and compensation.[13]

4. *The Eight-hour Laws* — The sympathetic interest of Congress in working men and women as a class is shown also by the federal Eight-hour Laws, a group of laws adopted between 1892 and 1940. Prior to 1940, these laws limited the number of hours that could be worked by laborers and mechanics to eight a day. Since 1940, however, these employees may be worked more than eight hours a day, provided they are paid time and one-half for the overtime hours.

On June 25, 1938, Congress passed the Fair Labor Standards Act that requires payment of time and one-half for work in excess of 40 hours a week to employees engaged in commerce or the production of goods for commerce.[14] Another group of laws required payment of time and one-half for work above eight hours a day on government construction or production contracts.[15]

5. *The Prevailing Wage Laws* (the Davis-Bacon Act, the Walsh-Healey Act, and various other statutes providing standards of working conditions and compensation where federal expenditures are involved) — The Davis-Bacon Act, which requires payment of prevailing wage rates on federally financed construction or public works, was enacted in March of 1931.[16] The 1936 Walsh-Healey Act is similar in its objectives, though it goes further than the earlier Davis-Bacon Act. The Walsh-Healey Act applies to government supply contracts for amounts exceeding $10,000.[17] It requires that the minimum wage or wages to be paid shall be the prevailing minimum rate or rates in the industry involved, as determined by the Secretary of Labor. It requires also that time and one-half shall be paid for all hours worked in excess of eight in one day or 40 in one week, whichever is greater. It forbids labor of male employees under 16 and girls under 18. It prohibits the use of convict labor, and it specifies that no government sup-

---

13 For much later rationalization on this subject, see U.S. v. Hutcheson, 312 U. S. 219, 61 S. Ct. 463, 7 LRRM 267 (1941).

14 Tit. 29 U. S. Code § 201 *et seq.*, and see Mitchell v. Southwest Engineering Co., 271 F. 2d 427, 14 WH Cases 344 (1959).

15 See Maritime Commission, Tit. 46 U. S. Code § 1111 *et seq.*, Public Act No. 831 and Public Works Acts, Public Act No. 849; Tit. 40 U. S. Code § § 321-326.

16 Tit. 40 U. S. Code § 2762.

17 Tit. 41 U. S. Code § § 35-45.

plies shall be manufactured under working conditions that are dangerous or unsanitary. Similar provisions appear in statutes applying to the bituminous coal industry,[18] the statutes governing leases of government mineral lands,[19] the Merchant Marine Act,[20] and statutes establishing labor standards on federally aided road construction.[21]

6. *The Railway Labor Act* — The Railway Labor Act of 1926[22] created the National Railroad Adjustment Board and the National Mediation Board. The Adjustment Board, upon submission by a complaint by either a railroad or an organization of employees, will take jurisdiction over "disputes between an employee, a group of employees and a carrier or carriers growing out of grievances or out of the interpretation or application of agreements concerning rates of pay, rules, or working conditions . . ." The disputes, however, first must have been "handled in the usual manner up to and including the chief operating officer of the carrier designated to handle such disputes." Questions involving "changes in rates of pay, rules or working conditions not adjusted by the parties in conferences" and other disputes "not referable to the National Railroad Adjustment Board and not adjusted in conference between the parties or where conferences are refused" go to the National Mediation Board.

It is the purpose of the Adjustment Board to interpret and apply collective agreements and not to add to, detract from, or modify them. On the other hand, the Mediation Board was created to help the parties, through mediation, to reach agreement on terms of collective bargaining contracts and, upon the parties' failure to complete a contract, to induce them to submit their dispute to voluntary arbitration.[23]

It is not consistent with the purposes of this chapter to dwell too long upon collective bargaining or arbitration under the Rail-

---

18 Tit. 15 U.S. Code § 828.
19 Tit. 30 U.S. Code § 187.
20 Tit. 46 U.S. Code § 1101 *et seq.*
21 Act Nov. 9, 1921 (23 U.S. Code). Similar statutory standards have been established to apply in public works programs, Tit. 5 U.S. Code c. 16; to housing projects, Act of Sept. 1, 1937, Tit. 42 U.S. Code c. 8; to rural electrification projects, Tit. 7 U.S. Code § 901 and various others, Act of July 22, 1937, Tit. 7 U.S. Code § 1000 *et sequitur.*
22 Tit. 45 U.S. Code § § 151-163, 181-188. See Chapter V, Section 4 *infra.*
23 See Jones, Handling of Railroad Disputes 1888-1940 (1941).

way Labor Act. It suffices to say at this time that the obvious purpose of the Railway Labor Act was to reduce, or eliminate, work stoppages affecting the railroads. These are the great veins and arteries of commerce without which virtually none of the other industries of the country could prosper, if they could indeed even continue to exist. Railroad strikes stop the flow of food, fuel, and clothing and the movement of raw materials. They prevent shipment of finished goods and all but stop the travel of sales, purchasing, and government representatives. This can bring about a paralysis of government and stoppage of indispensable economic movement that the Congress considered intolerable. Hence it moved to provide special and thoughtful legislation in this area.

It will be noted, however, that this legislation is written and established on the assumption that railroad workers must be given full and fair opportunities to bargain collectively and to attain their fair share of the fruits of industry. At the same time, neither such employees nor the unions that represent them are to be accorded all the full freedoms of bargaining and the right to apply coercive strike pressures available as weapons of aggression and defense to labor unions representing workers in other industries. Strikes in the railroad business are not prohibited. But they are rendered unlikely and have come to be very infrequent because of the statutory procedures made available and the cooling-off periods required as conditions precedent to interruptions of railway service.

In view of the present doctrine of national emergencies, it seems pertinent to ask: Will similar federal legislation be supplied for other essential industries?

7. *The Norris-LaGuardia Anti-Injunction Act* — The Norris-LaGuardia Act,[24] which was signed by President Hoover on March 23, 1932, was designed and intended to prevent the defeat of collective bargaining by means of labor injunctions. It will be recalled that previous mention was made of the yellow-dog contract and its recognition as establishing certain legal contractual and property rights on behalf of employers in the decision of the *Hitchman Coal and Coke Company* case.[25]

---

[24] Tit. 18 U. S. Code § 3692 and Tit. 29 U. S. Code § § 101-115.
[25] 245 U. S. 229, 38 S. Ct. 65 (1917), n. 4 *supra*.

As stated previously, two earlier efforts to outlaw the yellow-dog contract were defeated by decisions of the United States Supreme Court in *Coppage* v. *Kansas*,[26] and *Adair* v. *United States*.[27] Nevertheless, Congress moved against this type of labor repression again and outlawed the yellow-dog contract. It also expressly limited the kind and number of union activities that could be enjoined by the federal courts. It required that hearing procedure should precede the issuance of even the limited injunction permitted under that statute. And it also provided that such injunctions as continued to be permissible should issue only after definite and clear establishment of jurisdictional facts before the court, including commission of unlawful acts, irreparable injury to the complainant's property, proof that greater injury would be inflicted upon the complainant by denial of relief than inflicted upon the defendants by granting it, proof the complainant had no adequate remedy at law, and proof that public officers charged with the duty to protect the complainant's property were either unwilling or unable to furnish such protection.

It is not the intention to cover here all details of the Norris-LaGuardia Act. It suffices for the present purpose to say that this statute has made the suit for a labor injunction a rarity in federal courts, rather than a common form of procedure. That was what it was intended to do. Again, Congress appears to have been concerned to protect the common rank-and-file working man to see that his rights and opportunities to bargain collectively for a fair share of the fruits of industry should not be defeated and to protect from technical obstructions the labor unions legitimately representing rank-and-file workers for these approved objectives. This act has been applied to preclude courts from issuing injunctions against strikes in breach of contracts.[28] But, again, it may be asserted that Congress, in the Norris-LaGuardia Act, moved only to terminate employer tactics that were deemed to be unfairly destructive of reasonable collective bargaining. There was no indication in this statute that government would not move equally to stop unfair tactics from the labor side of the economic arena. Still less was there reason to suppose that Congress was abdicating its

---

26 236 U. S. 1, 35 S. Ct. 240 (1914).
27 208 U. S. 161, 28 S. Ct. 277 (1908).
28 Avco Corp. v. Aero Lodge No. 735, 390 U. S. 557, 67 LRRM 2881 (1968).

power and duty to protect the national, economic well-being from both sides should there arise need for such a move.

8. *The Wagner Act* — The National Industry Recovery Act of 1933, which was declared unconstitutional in *Schechter Poultry Corporation* v. *United States*,[29] contained as its Section 7 (a) a provision that all employees should have the right to organize and to bargain collectively through representatives of their own choosing, to be free from interference, restraints, or coercion of employers of labor in matters of organization, and should be free to reject yellow-dog contract proposals as conditions of employment. When this Act was held unconstitutional in the *Schechter* case in 1935, the Wagner Act, also known as the National Labor Relations Act, was promptly introduced, passed by Congress, and became law.[30] It had one focal purpose. That was to require employers in the United States to recognize legitimate labor organizations and to bargain with them collectively. To this end, it prohibited any interference with union organization and prohibited certain defined, unfair labor practices. The unfair labor practices were popularly thought of as falling into three groups: (1) refusal to bargain; (2) discrimination to hire, discharge, or take other action against any employee because of union membership or activity; and (3) fostering, recognizing, or continuing to bargain with a company-dominated union. The Wagner Act was held to be constitutional in *National Labor Relations Board* v. *Jones and Laughlin Steel Corporation*.[31]

Early enforcement of the Wagner Act brought about violent employer condemnation and protest. It was denounced as a biased and one-sided class of legislation. It was blamed for a number of disorders at various industrial plants over the country. Many of these were involved in hearings before the National Labor Relations Board and the courts as enforcement of the statute progressed. The Act remained virtually as originally passed for a period of 12 years. During this time, the labor unions greatly strengthened themselves in membership, organization, and financing. Numerous

---

29 295 U. S. 495 (1935).

30 The Wagner Act (1935), Tit. 29 U. S. Code § § 151 *et seq.*

31 301 U. S. 1 (1937). For historical background see p. 1 and following in The Arbitrator, the NLRB, and the Courts, Proceedings of the Twentieth Annual Meeting, National Academy of Arbitrators (Washington: BNA Books, 1967) and Forkosch, A Treatise on Labor Law, p. 575 *et seq.* (Bobbs Merrill, Indianapolis, 1953.)

employers who theretofore had consistently refused to bargain collectively were constrained to change their positions after their attitude had been made unlawful by the statute.[32]

9. *The Fair Labor Standards Act* — While the industry of the United States was adjusting itself to collective bargaining as required and in many instances imposed and regulated by the Wagner Act, the Fair Labor Standards Act was enacted on June 25, 1938.[33] The background of previous federal regulation of wages and hours was not extensive. An act had been passed in 1918 to regulate minimum wages for women in the District of Columbia. This had been held unconstitutional.[34] Subsequently, the United States Supreme Court had reversed its position on the subject in the case of *West Coast Hotel Company* v. *Parrish*.[35] In some respects the latter decision opened the way to passage of the Fair Labor Standards Act, otherwise known as the "Wage and Hour Act." [36]

The Fair Labor Standards Act established the 40-hour basic work-week and required that time and one-half be paid for all hours over 40. It originally established a minimum wage of 25 cents per hour, to be increased to 30 cents an hour in 1939, and to 40 cents an hour in 1945. The 40-cent minimum was achieved in many industries before 1945 under industry wage orders. The minimum was raised to 75 cents an hour in 1950 and to $1.00 an hour in 1956. The Fair Labor Standards Act was amended by the Portal-to-Portal Act of 1947[37] which, broadly speaking, limited the time to be paid for to that customary in the industry, and by extensive amendments adopted in 1949.

It should suffice to say concerning this law, at this time, that it further evidences an objective of the members of the Congress and

---

[32] See Millis and Brown, From the Wagner Act to Taft-Hartley (1950); also Millis and Montgomery, Organized Labor (1948); and Wolman, Ebb and Flow in Trade Unionism (1936).

[33] Tit. 29 U. S. Code § 201 *et seq.* For recent interpretations of the act, see Mitchell v. S. W. Engineering Co., 271 F. 2d 427, 14 WH Cases 344 (1959); Mitchell v. Tune, 178 F. Supp. 138, 14 WH Cases 348 (1959); and Hogue v. Wilcox and Ziegler, Inc., 178 F. Supp. 180, 14 WH Cases 341 (1959).

[34] Adkins v. Children's Hospital, 261 U. S. 525, 43 S. Ct. 394 (1923).

[35] 300 U. S. 379, 57 S. Ct. 578, 1 LRRM 754 (1937).

[36] Phelps, The Legislative Background of the Fair Labor Standards Act (1939); Stitt and Angus, U. S. Department of Labor, Bureau of Labor Standards, Handbook of Labor Statistics, Bulletin No. 694, Vol. 2, pp. 400-403 (1942).

[37] Tit. 29 U. S. Code §§ 216, 251-262.

of the Executive Branch of the Government to provide opportunities of employment at living wages.

An apparent purpose was to provide more jobs for workers. It was intended to benefit all wage earners whether they had joined or been affected by labor union organizations or not. The unions were not referred to in the Act as enforcement agencies, though many have since used the Fair Labor Standards provisions as terms in their agreements with employers.[38]

10. *The Taft-Hartley Act* — American industry had been adjusting itself more and more to collective bargaining and to federal regulation of employer and employee relations from the passage of the Wagner Act of 1935 to the passage of the Taft-Hartley Act of 1947. During this 12 years, despite considerable economic and social frictions, innumerable board hearings and court cases, the new and greatly extended pattern of collective bargaining had been gradually forged and recognized throughout the United States. However, a number of criticisms of conditions under the Wagner Act had appeared. Some of these criticisms had little merit. These disappeared. But others appeared to have justification and became increasingly strong. The result was the Taft-Hartley Act, or Labor Management Relations Act.[39]

Upon thoughtful and careful analysis, it appears that those who passed the Taft-Hartley Act proceeded upon certain basic presuppositions. One of these was that some dominating figures in labor unions had become dictatorial to employers and were not engaging in true collective bargaining. Another presupposition was that the protection of the labor statutes was intended for the rank-and-file workers as such and not for labor unions as organizations or for labor union bosses who would exploit or misrepresent the rank-and-file worker-union members. Hence, the Taft-Hartley provisions were designed to preserve and protect the rights of rank-and-file workers and for that purpose to curb and restrict certain tendencies discovered among irresponsible union leadership. In

---

38 The Fair Labor Standards Act was held constitutional in U. S. v. Darby, 312 U. S. 100, 61 S. Ct. 451 (1941) . The industry wage order procedure was sustained in Opp Cotton Mills v. Administrator, 312 U. S. 126, 61 S. Ct. 524 (1941) .

39 Tit. 29 U. S. Code § 141 *et seq.;* Act of June 23, 1947, Public Law 101, 80th Congress, 1st Session, Amended by Public Law 902, 80th Cong., 2nd Session.

doing this, the statute established several new rights, privileges, and immunities for workers:

A. The Right to Work. The Taft-Hartley Act outlaws the closed shop. It continues as valid the union shop but expressly validates state statutes that prohibit all forms of so-called union security agreements. Nineteen states now have such statutes. These are generally referred to as "right-to-work laws."

B. Protection from Union Coercion. Employees are protected in the right to organize, as in the Wagner Act, but they also are protected in the right to refrain from any and all union activities if they so desire. In other words, the rank-and-file worker, at least theoretically, has a full freedom of choice to become or not to become a union member and to be active in and support union affairs.

C. Termination of Union Representation. The Wagner Act provided voting procedure to obtain certification of a union. This was continued under the Taft-Hartley law, but Taft-Hartley provided also a procedure by which those wishing to do away with representation by a given union may file a petition with the board, obtain an election upon the subject, and by a majority of their ballots terminate the same.

D. Reasonable Initiation Fees. Prior to the Taft-Hartley Act there was no regulation of initiation fees. Some unions desiring to restrict membership and to create artificial scarcity of available, member-employees had put initiation fees at high figures. Under the Taft-Hartley Act, if the union is to enjoy the privilege of a union shop, it must not charge the prospective member a "fee in an amount which the Board finds excessive or discriminatory under all the circumstances."

E. Compulsory Checkoff Banned. Under the Taft-Hartley Act, the consent of the individual member is required. This must be in writing and it must be revocable after a year.

F. Opportunity of Individual to Present Grievances. Under the Wagner Act, the individual workman was often forgotten when his own grievance was presented to or settled with the employer. In the Taft-Hartley Act, it is provided that "any individual employee or a group of employees shall have the right at any time to present grievances to their employer and to have such grievances adjusted, without the intervention of the bargaining representative as long as this adjustment is not inconsistent with the terms of a collective-bargaining contract or agreement then in effect; Provided further, that the bargaining representative has been given opportunity to be present at such agreement."

G. Jurisdictional Strikes and Secondary Boycotts Banned. Jurisdictional strikes and boycotts have always been unpopular with rank-and-file workers. Sometimes, however, these disputes involved wasteful stoppages which seemed expedient to union leadership. These strikes sometimes really involve competition between union leaders for recognition and support of dues-paying members. Sometimes the rank-and-file workers, the employer, and the public are all losers. The Taft-Hartley Act, in effect, requires that such disputes be submitted to the National Labor Relations Board for peaceful determination. The use of secondary boycotts also is prohibited by the Act under Section 8 (b). These provisions are too long and complex for coverage in the limited scope of the present work.[40]

H. Craft-Unit Bargaining. Under the Wagner Act, the Board often ruled that all production and maintenance employees in a given plant should be represented by a single union. Thus the skilled workers in well-defined crafts were sometimes forced into being represented by a union that also included semi-skilled and unskilled workers. In many instances, such unions did not take into account nor emphasize what the skilled workers deemed to be fair and proper wage differentials favorable to them.

Under Section 9 (b) of the Taft-Hartley Act, it is possible for craft unions to take over representation of such skilled men unless they vote against separate representation.

I. Independent Union. From the beginning of enforcement of the Wagner Act in 1935, the National Labor Relations Board favored local unions that were parts of the internationals. Those in turn were affiliated with the AFL or the CIO. Under the Taft-Hartley Act, it is expressly required that even small independent unions that are affiliated with no others be given equal treat-

---

40 See National Labor Relations, § 8 (b).

ment with unions affiliated with national organizations or with other unions.

J. Communist Control Terminates. Between 1935 and 1947, it developed that several local unions and, indeed, some national unions had come to be Communist-dominated. The Taft-Hartley Act denied the privileges, protection, and assistance of the National Labor Relations Board to labor unions unless their officers filed affidavits with the National Labor Relations Board stating that they were not members of the Communist Party nor affiliated with such Party. The affiant was also required to state formally that he did not believe in and was not a member or supporter of any organization that believed in or taught the overthrow of the United States Government by force or by any illegal or unconstitutional method.

Nearly all of the unions regarded as recognized and established labor organizations soon had these affidavits on file. A few never filed them. The provisions of the Labor-Management Reporting and Disclosure Act of 1959, discussed *infra*, should be considered in relation to this section. A substituted provision in that act prohibiting Communists from holding labor union offices has been held unconstitutional as being in effect a bill of attainder. (See note 43 *infra*, this chapter.)

K. Financial Information of Unions Made Available. Between 1935 and 1947, it became evident that there were questionable and mysterious manipulations of the financial affairs of several large unions. It was thought that such improprieties might be reduced, if not eliminated, by giving rank-and-file members more information about their unions' financial affairs. Hence, it was provided that the Secretary of Labor and all union members should be given annual reports showing all receipts of all kinds and the sources of such receipts. Unions were required to report total assets and liabilities to the end of the last fiscal year and to report all disbursements, including purposes for which they were made. The penalty for failure to comply was loss of access to the procedures of the NLRB. Most of the unions which are regarded as established and respected representatives of rank-and-file workers in America soon complied with this requirement, although there were some notable exceptions. Political use of union funds was prohibited.

L. Personal Liability of Individual Member. The Taft-Hartley Act expressly provides, as had the Norris-LaGuardia Act, that the rank-and-file membership should not be held liable for activities of labor unions and the officers thereof "excepting upon clear proof of actual participation, or actual authorization of" unlawful acts or ratification of the same. The Taft-Hartley Act makes labor unions, as such, suable in the federal courts but it does not increase the personal liability of rank-and-file union members which was earlier limited, in 1932, by the Norris-LaGuardia Act.

M. Voting Rights of Strikers, Replacements. The Act provides that workers who have been permanently employed to replace economic strikers may vote in an election to choose a bargaining agent and that the permanently replaced economic strikers may not vote. However, the strikers who have not been permanently replaced by new, regular employees may vote in such an election. (See Section 9 (c) (3) of the Taft-Hartley Act and the amending Section 702 in the Labor-Management Reporting and Disclosure Act of 1959.)

N. Security of Health and Welfare Funds. The Taft-Hartley Act undertook to give protection to the individual member against improper tampering with health and welfare funds. These were required to be set up in separate trusts and limited to the declared uses of paying pensions or annuities and the like. It was required that the employer and the union both be represented on the board of trustees administering the trusts. This was an added protection to rank-and-file employees against improper uses or risks of these funds for political or other purposes.

11. *The Landrum-Griffin Act.* The wide-spread violent denunciation of the Taft-Hartley Law that was heard just before and immediately after its passage mainly emanated from labor unions and labor union members who had been guilty of engaging in the prohibited practices. The statute remained a part of the labor law of the United States with relatively minor changes for 12 years, and much criticism of the Act disappeared. Meanwhile, however, certain unfortunate characteristics were discovered among a minority of labor union leaders, management spokesmen, and others. These called for further correction. The number of wrong-doing labor

union leaders and employers involved was small, but some of them had prominent positions in large and economically important organizations. Evil and harmful practices by even a minority of labor and management exploiters so situated are unfortunate and damaging to the entire American economy. It was only natural that, sooner or later, these practices would engage the attention of Congress. When they did, the result was adoption of the Labor-Management Reporting and Disclosure Act of 1959, or as it is more often called, the Landrum-Griffin Act.[41] Understanding of this law requires a brief glance at its background, which is here briefly summarized.

A. After some two years of investigation and hearings, the so-called McClellan Committee, more officially known as the "Senate Select Committee on Improper Activities in the Labor or Management Fields," made a report that covered in very substantial detail and volume the following points:

(i) There had developed a significant, definite lack of democratic procedures in a number of labor unions; constitutions had been perverted; one man dictatorships had thrived and fear, intimidation, and violence had robbed some memberships of participation in union affairs.

(ii) Certain international unions had flagrantly abused their powers over local unions by putting some in trusteeships for no valid reason and had continued these trusteeships unjustifiably. In doing this, they had curbed rank-and-file membership, sometimes with violence and intimidation. Some locals had been plundered financially and many had been used as pawns in political battles.

(iii) The Committee pointed out that certain managements had been in collusion with unions. Some had paid bribes to be allowed to continue substandard working conditions, and had conspired with some unions to organize their employees to the exclusion of other unions. Some companies had granted business concessions and loans to union leaders.

(iv) The Committee reported widespread misuse of union funds. It pointed out that financial safeguards were lacking.

41 Public Law 86-257, signed Sept. 14, 1959.

There was great irresponsibility concerning disbursements. There were extensive "borrowings" of union funds by union officers. There had been destruction of financial records and of cancelled checks. There were numerous "flat expense allowances" for which the officers were not required to account.

(v) The McClellan Committee reported also on many instances of violence in labor and management disputes. Some of these involved top officials of unions, who had hired goons and thugs for acts of assault or battery.

(vi) The Committee reported that some managements and union agents had engaged in a regular program of activities that were illegal and improper under the Wagner Act as amended by Taft-Hartley. These involved failure to bargain collectively in any true sense and resulted in illegal discrimination and company-dominated unions.

(vii) There were also reports that recognition or organizational picketing had been abused by some unions for the purpose of extorting funds from management and for the purpose of imposing membership upon employees of some picketed plants before any of them had indicated a desire to join the union. Some such unions had ignored the NLRB processes entirely instead of submitting to them and taking lawful steps for peaceful organizing.

(viii) The Committee also commented on the "no man's land" created by the National Labor Relations Board's limitation of its exercise of jurisdiction and the exclusion of the states from these areas of jurisdiction. In the Guss case, the U. S. Supreme Court held that states could not take cases within the NLRB's statutory jurisdiction even though the NLRB declined to handle the cases.[42] This, the Committee reported, had made exploitation of workers and circumvention of labor organizations possible because unions and employers had no recourse to any governmental protection in such excluded situations.

(ix) It was also reported by the Committee that law enforcement officers had been lax in investigating and prosecuting acts of violence resulting from labor-management dis-

---

[42] Guss v. Utah Labor Relations Board, 353 U. S. 1, 39 LRRM 2567 (1957).

putes. In some areas, it was declared, this had resulted in ramp-
ant violence without any action by law enforcement agents.

(x)   The report also stated that some members of the legal
profession, having been retained as counsel for an entire
union, had in fact protected only the interests of certain officials even though these interests conflicted with those of the
membership. In so doing, such persons were said to have in-
dulged in various unethical practices debasing to the standards
of their profession.

As would be assumed from the foregoing, this report brought
Congress to the conclusion that the law was in need of substantial
strengthening and improvement. It is not intended to attempt here
a full and detailed study and discussion of all of the provisions of
the recent act. In fact, available space permits only a bare outline
or sketch of some of its most important and prominent features for
the purpose of indicating its general nature.

B.   Title I of the statute has been called the "Bill of Rights" of
union members:

(i)   This part of the Act is devoted to recognizing and improving the rights of union members. It contemplates that
each union shall have a democratic administration and that
there shall be equality of rights concerning the nomination of
candidates, voting in elections, and having a voice in business
transactions. The statute undertakes to provide for freedom of
speech and assembly in union meetings and business discussions. It provides for balloting on increases in dues and fees
and on assessment levies. It provides the right of suing and
testifying in judicial and agency proceedings, subject to exclusion of employer aid and exhaustion of reasonable union hearing procedures (not exceeding four months in duration) . The
Act undertakes safeguards against unjustified union disciplinary action or expulsion from union membership. Individual
members are entitled to inspect copies of union contracts and
to bring suits to recover misappropriated union assets in situations where the union itself neglects to do so. (Law, Sections
101-105, 201, 301, 501, 609.)

(ii)   Election procedures are set up in respect to dues, fees,
and assessments which are intended to give the rank-and-file

membership of unions ultimate control of these basic matters. (Law, Section 101.)

(iii) Protection in the right to freedom from violent interference with rights provided in the statute is offered in Section 610 by making violations subject to fines up to $1,000.00 and to imprisonment up to one year, or both.

(iv) It will be important that since a recognized union represents all employees in the unit even though they are not members of the union, the nonunion members in the unit are given protection of their basic rights by having access to the contracts affecting them and being entitled to enforcement of such individual rights as they have. (Law, Section 104.)

(v) Extensive provisions in Title II of the statute require union reports. Labor organizations are required to adopt constitutions and bylaws and to file these with the Secretary of Labor. They must also report on their finances and report in full concerning trusteeships of local unions. (Law, Section 201.)

(vi) Unions are required to report with respect to their administrative policies in considerable detail. They must make available to all members and to the Secretary of Labor the name and the address of the union, the names and titles of the officers, the rates of dues, fees, and assessments, the qualifications for membership, the amount and kind of insurance coverage, authorizations for disbursements, provisions for financial auditing, provisions for calling of meetings, provisions for officers, stewards, and representatives, disciplinary matters, authorization for bargaining demands, ratification of contract terms, authorization for strikes, and all matters pertaining to issuing work permits. (Law, Section 201.)

(vii) The required full financial reports when properly made will indicate the condition of the union to the members and to the Secretary of Labor. These union reports and documents are to be open to public inspection. The requirement that they be correctly made and filed is supported by a provision for a fine of $10,000 and imprisonment for one year for falsification or improper concealment or destruction of union records. (Law, Sections 205, 209.)

C. The foregoing "rights" are implemented in part and supplemented by the provisions described in the following:

(i) Under Title II of this statute, union officers and employees are also required to report situations or relationships involving identification of such officers or employees with management or ownership. These reports are to cover direct or indirect holding of securities of the employer company, business transactions with the employer, and all payments involved in the labor-management relationship which the reporting party receives as a consultant. (Law, Section 202.)

(ii) Employer expenditures and arrangements are required to be reported when they involve loans, direct or indirect payments or expenditures or agreements with respect to any of these or which appear to involve subsidization of any labor organization or officer, agent, steward, or other representative. Each covered payment, loan, promise, or agreement must be reported in detail giving the names of the parties immediately concerned, together with a full explanation of the circumstances. (Law, Section 203.)

(iii) Labor relations "consultants" who, according to evidence before the Committee, acted in some instances as go-betweens, collecting money from one side and paying it to the other by way of direct or indirect bribes, must now report fully all receipts from both sides and payments out of funds to both sides, if any are made. (Law, Section 203.)

(iv) Trusteeships directed or authorized by international or parent unions, which take over the business affairs and assets of local unions, are now restricted in Title III of the Act. Their legitimate objectives are defined in the statutes as those of correcting corruption, correcting financial malpractices, assuring the performance of union contracts, assuring performance of bargaining representatives' duties, restoring democratic procedures and carrying out the legitimate objects of the labor organizations. All unions are required to report within 30 days the establishment of trusteeships and the financial moves which follow thereafter, as well as the termination of the trusteeship when its legitimate purpose has been accomplished. A trusteeship properly established is presumed valid for 18 months and thereafter is presumed invalid. Criminal prosecutions are authorized for willful violations of the trusteeship requirements. Fines up to $10,000 and imprisonment up to one year, or both, are possible penalties. (Law, Sections 301-306.)

(v) The Act provides for adoption of democratic procedures in the election of union officers, requiring that these be elected by members in good standing by secret ballot. The maximum terms of office and the minimum frequencies of elections are established in the Act. Provisions are made requiring democratic processes in the nomination of the candidates, the preservation of records of elections, and the removal of elected officers who are guilty of misconduct. (Law, Sections 401-404.)

(vi) Misappropriation of union funds is made a federal crime. The statute expressly provides that no union shall have authority to free any of its personnel from liability for breach of trust in such instances. It also provides that embezzlement such as here described shall be punished by a fine up to $10,000 and imprisonment up to five years. The federal law does not limit state authority to prosecute for these offenses under applicable state criminal laws. (Law, Sections 501, 604.)

(vii) The statute provides a ban against Communists and convicts holding union offices or holding any employment by unions other than clerical or custodial. (The provision against Communists holding labor union offices has been held unconstitutional as in effect a bill of attainder.) [43] The criminals excluded are those who have been convicted of robbery, extortion, embezzlement, larceny, burglary, arson, and certain other listed crimes of violence. These persons are excluded from serving in active labor relations capacities until five years after termination of the Communist party membership or after conviction of or imprisonment for the crimes named. However, if the convict has had his citizenship rights restored, the ban against him is nullified. He may also be restored to qualifica-

---

[43] United States v. Archie Brown, dba Brown Food Store, 380 U.S. 278, 58 LRRM 2663 (1965). See generally on this subject D. Saposs, Communism in American Unions (1959).

tion by favorable action of the Federal Board of Parole. (Law, Section 504.)

(viii) Extortion picketing is outlawed. Personal profit derived from pressures of picketing are prohibited and the receipt of such profit is punishable by a fine up to $10,000 and imprisonment up to 20 years. (Law, Section 602.)

(ix) The statute is given strength by a provision that the Secretary of Labor shall make investigations to discover violations of the law and by giving him authority to bring civil action for appropriate relief. Whenever evidence comes to the hands of the Secretary that in his opinion will warrant a criminal prosecution, he is authorized and directed to certify it to the Attorney General for action. (Law, Sections 104, 606, 607.)

(x) The new Act also provides that the "no man's land" that arises under the restrictions of jurisdiction by the NLRB and the *Guss* decision is overruled by ceding jurisdiction back to the states over all matters rejected by the NLRB under its jurisdictional standards of August 1, 1959. It is provided, however, that the Board may not increase this exclusion of cases in the future. (Law, Section 701, see Chapter II, Section 3 *infra*.)

(xi) A number of other Labor Management Relations Act changes were brought about by the statute under discussion. Very briefly stated these may be described as follows:

(a) A new Section 8 (b) (7) inserted in the Act makes it an unfair labor practice for a union to picket for recognition or organizational purposes where (A) another union has been lawfully recognized by the employer and no representation issue may be raised, (B) a valid election has been conducted by the NLRB within the past 12 months, or (C) the picketing continues for a reasonable period of time (not to exceed 30 days) and no election petition is filed. There is an exception to the last prohibition for informational picketing that does not stop deliveries of performance of services by employees of other employees. Another proviso to this prohibition (C) requires that when an election petition is filed, the NLRB shall forthwith direct

and conduct an election without regard to the usual hearing or showing-of-interest requirements. (Law, Section 704.)

(b) Voting rights have been granted to replace economic strikers in elections conducted within 12 months of the beginning of the strike. Section 9 (c) (3) of the Taft-Hartley Act, which denied voting rights to such strikers, is amended. (Law, Section 702.)

(c) As would be supposed certain parts of the National Labor Relations Act were amended in respect to the new reports required under the Act of 1959. Part of Section 8 (a) (3) and Section 9, subsections (f), (g), and (h), requiring union officers to file affidavits denying membership in a Communist organization or devotion to Communistic teachings were repealed. (Law, Section 201.)

(d) Section 8 (e) of the National Labor Relations Act has been added to make it an unfair labor practice for unions and employers to enter into "hot-cargo" agreements and to make such agreements void whether executed before or after the amendment takes effect. This is subject to some exceptions affecting the construction and apparel industries. (Law, Section 704.)

(e) The secondary-boycott provisions in Section 8 (b) (4) of the Taft-Hartley Act were amended to close certain loopholes by making it unlawful for a union to effect a boycott of a struck employer by (1) inducing individual employees of neutral employers to stop work, (2) inducing exempt employees or employees of exempt employers (railroads, municipalities, etc.) to stop work, and threatening, coercing, or restraining neutral employers to get them to stop doing business with a struck employer. There is an exemption for certain subcontracting situations in the garment industry. (Law, Section 704.) There also is an exception for union publicity for the purpose of truthfully advising the public, consumers, and union members that goods are produced by an employer with whom the union has a primary dispute and are distributed by another employer. In exercising this privilege, however, the union may not picket neutral establishments and the publicity must not induce employees of neutral employers to refuse to pick up, deliver, or transport goods, or to refuse to perform any services at the distributor's establishment. This amendment appears as a new proviso to Section 8 (b) (4) . (Law, Section 704.)

(f) Section 8 (f) of the National Labor Relations Act was amended to permit pre-hire and seven-day union-security contracts in the building and construction industry subject to a number of specific restrictions. (Law, Section 705.)

(g) Subsections (a) , (b) , and (c) of Section 302 of the Labor Management Relations Act limiting payments that may be made by employers to employee representatives have been amended to outlaw loans and requests for loans to employee representatives. As amended, Section 302 also makes it illegal for union officers or agents to demand or accept unloading fees from motor carriers. However, it exempts employer contributions to qualified trust funds for pooled vacations, holiday pay, and similar benefits. (Law, Section 505.)

The Congressional Policy

When the essential characteristics of the Reporting and Disclosure Act of 1959 are considered, together with characteristics of previous major federal labor statutes, it appears that Congress has followed a consistent policy at least since the Clayton Act was passed in 1914. Each of the statutes examined indicates concern of Congress for the health, safety, and general welfare of all people and a purpose to attain fair compensation and proper working conditions for the rank-and-file workers in American industry. To the extent that labor unions have been encouraged and strengthened they have been given support upon the theory that they could and would function lawfully to assist in obtaining fair wages and working conditions for industrial workers through collective bargaining.

In 1947, when the provisions of the Taft-Hartley Act were before Congress, the majority was apparently moved by the thought that certain protections for rank-and-file workers in American industry were required. The Taft-Hartley Act, as previously observed, was mainly directed to restrain and limit activities of labor union leadership in the interest of securing fair, full, and honest consideration for the rights of each rank-and-file worker whether a member of a union or otherwise.

It seems that similar considerations moved the majority of Congress as the votes were taken on the Reporting and Disclosure Act of 1959. A study of that statute, from beginning to end, indicates concern of the majority in Congress for the welfare of American industry as a whole and for the welfare and the protection of the rank-and-file workers in American industry in particular.

It is only fair to emphasize that the improprieties uncovered and emphasized in the McClellan Committee reports indicated that while there was great corruption in a few places, there was no corruption or impropriety in the great and overwhelming majority of local and national unions nor in the great AFL-CIO *Federation*.

SECTION 2

The Preemption Doctrine*
A Resumé of Its Implementation

The great majority of labor disputes that find their way to arbitration involve some common law or statutory legal background. Many of them require knowledge of law and a considerable number confront the arbitrator with the duty of deciding what the law is, or which of two or more possibly applicable laws should control in the particular case. This makes it indispensable that the arbitrator of labor disputes have some knowledge of the preemption doctrine as it has developed in respect to the supremacy of federal laws and the consequential reduction of importance of state laws in respect to labor involved in commerce or in the production of goods for commerce. The doctrine of federal preemption relates both to applicable substantive law and to the forum in which enforcement of that law is sought. In summary, the preemption doctrine may be stated thus: When an activity is arguably subject to those portions of the National Labor Relations Act, as amended, that define unfair labor practices and certain protected activities, the states as

---

* While preparing this third edition, the author contributed much of this section as an article in the Hastings Law Journal. Its use herein is fully approved.

well as the federal courts must defer to the exclusive authority of the National Labor Relations Board and are, therefore, ousted of jurisdiction to proceed unless either (1) the Board declines to assert jurisdiction, or (2) it is established by the party seeking to invoke a state ruling that the Board would decline to assert jurisdiction if application were made to it.[44]

Background

At the turn of the century, it appeared that all commerce (like all Gaul when Caesar wrote) was divided into three parts. These were:

1. Local or intrastate commerce.
2. Interstate commerce: local aspects.
3. Interstate commerce: national aspects.

The belief, then, was that all matters of local or intrastate commerce were exclusively within the control of the affected sovereign states and would so remain. Matters in the class of local aspects of interstate commerce were, if Congress had taken no action in respect to them, subject to state control until Congress decided otherwise and took action (preemption). Matters in the area of national aspects of interstate commerce were beyond the reach of the states and exclusively in the federal area. Silence of Congress implied its conclusion that these were to be left unregulated by laws; it did not open them to state control.[45]

For several decades certain labor relations problems — aspects of commerce — were apparently considered only under the contracts clause of the Constitution, and their character as factors of commerce was ignored. Thus legislation against the "yellow dog" contract was held unconstitutional when enacted by the U. S. Congress[46] and by a state.[47] However, when the pressure against the

---

44 San Diego Bldg. Trades Council v. Garmon, 359 U. S. 236, 43 LRRM 2838 (1959); Consolidated Theatres, Inc. v. Theatrical Stage Employees Union, 69 Cal. 2d 713 (1968).

45 Sonneborn v. Cureton, 262 U. S. 506 (1922); Houston, E. & W. Tex. Ry. v. United States, 234 U. S. 342 (1914); Minnesota Rate Cases, 230 U. S. 352 (1913); New York Cent. R.R. v. Hudson County, 227 U. S. 248 (1912); Leisy v. Hardin, 135 U. S. 100 (1890); Bownan v. Chicago Ry., 125 U. S. 465 (1887); Coe v. Errol, 116 U. S. 517 (1886); Brown v. Houston, 114 U. S. 622 (1884); Cooley v. Port Wardens, 53 U. S. (12 How.) 299 (1851).

46 Adair v. United States, 208 U. S. 161 (1908).

47 Coppage v. Kansas, 236 U. S. 1 (1914).

enforcement of such agreements, and against the employer organizations that had supported and made them effective, gained decisive strength, the Norris-LaGuardia Anti-Injunction Act[48] was passed and signed by President Hoover. This statute must be regarded as a forerunner of the National Labor Relations Act (Wagner Act),[49] and of the Fair Labor Standards Act;[50] the latter statutes are now sustained under the commerce clause.

The Supreme Court upheld the Wagner Act in 1937.[51] In so doing, it "rediscovered" the broader aspects of the national commerce power.[52] From that time to the present there has been a marked trend, in the Supreme Court, in the Congress, and in the White House, away from statism and toward nationalism in over-all labor policy. It is evidently the Washington view that the national welfare requires federal supremacy in the labor area because the decentralized and sometimes conflicting views of the several states might permit, if indeed they did not earlier create, chaos injurious to the national welfare.

Recent Trends

In *Construction Workers* v. *Laburnum Constr. Corp.*,[53] the Supreme Court upheld a Virginia state court common law tort decision indicating that Congress had not given the National Labor Relations Board exclusive jurisdiction over the type of action concerned therein. The Court apparently approved the thesis that if a state did impose a heavy damage liability, such liability would strongly inhibit the disputed conduct in subsequent incidents. To this extent, the decision then gave the state courts co-jurisdiction with the National Labor Relations Board to determine the legality or illegality of borderline conduct that might or might not be an unfair labor practice in the opinion of the Board.[54] In *Weber* v. *Anheuser-Busch Brewing Co.*[55] a state undertook to enforce its an-

---

48 47 Stat. 70 (1932), as amended, 29 U.S.C. § § 101-11, 113-15 (1964); see Loeb, "Accommodation of the Norris-LaGuardia Act to other Federal Statutes," 11 Lab. L.J. 473 (1960).

49 49 Stat. 449 (1935), as amended, 29 U.S.C. § § 151-66 (1964).

50 52 Stat. 1060 (1938), 29 U.S.C. § § 201-19 (1964).

51 Jones and Laughlin Steel Corporation v. NLRB, 301 U. S. 1, 1 LRRM 703 (1937).

52 Compare Gibbons v. Ogden, 9 Wheat. 1 (1824).

53 347 U. S. 656, 34 LRRM 2229 (1954).

54 *Id.* at 668-69; see *id.* at 670-71 (dissenting opinion).

55 348 U. S. 468, 35 LRRM 2637 (1955).

titrust laws, and the Supreme Court denied the authority of the state, asserting that even though "no unfair labor practices were involved, it would not necessarily follow that the State was free to issue its injunction. If this conduct does not fall within the prohibition of Section 8 of the Taft-Hartley Act, it may fall within the protection of Section 7 . . . ." [56] The Court added for emphasis that "the areas that have been pre-empted by federal authority and thereby withdrawn from state power are not susceptible of delimitation by fixed metes and bounds." [57] In this connection, the Court quoted from *Garner* v. *Teamsters Union*: [58] "the Labor Management Relations Act leaves much to the states, though Congress has refrained from telling us how much." [59] This penumbral area, it added, "can be rendered progressively clear only by the course of litigation." [60]

In another incident where a lower state court had issued an injunction, the Nebraska Supreme Court stated: "[T]he union shop agreement violates the First Amendment in that it deprives the employees of their freedom of association and violates the Fifth Amendment in that it requires the members to pay for many things besides the costs of collective bargaining." [61] The U. S. Supreme Court discussed the Railway Labor Act and declared, "we pass narrowly on § 2, Eleventh of the Railway Labor Act. We only hold that the requirement for financial support for the collective-bargaining agency by all who receive the benefits of its work is within the power of Congress under the Commerce Clause and does not violate either the First or the Fifth Amendments." [62] The Nebraska Supreme Court's decision was reversed.

In the atmosphere of this period, in 1950, the NLRB promulgated certain criteria to be applied in rejection or acceptance of jurisdiction of labor disputes. These criteria indicated that only the larger and more important matters and parties would be heard by the Board. The limiting criteria were amended in 1954 and in 1958. State boards and state officials in some locations assumed that

---

[56] *Id.* at 478-79.
[57] *Id.* at 480.
[58] 346 U. S. 485, 33 LRRM 2218 (1953).
[59] 348 U. S. at 480, quoting 346 U. S. at 488.
[60] 348 U. S. at 480-81; see 346 U. S. at 488.
[61] Railway Employees Dep't v. Hanson, 351 U. S. 225, 230, 38 LRRM 2099 (1956).
[62] *Id.* at 238.

the disputes rejected by the NLRB were thereby automatically returned to the jurisdiction of the states, might be treated as "local
aspects" of interstate commerce, and therefore were under concurrent jurisdiction of the states and the United States. The Supreme
Court, however, quite positively indicated that even though the
NLRB was rejecting jurisdiction of a number of such disputes,
they were not returned to the jurisdiction of the states because the
federal government had established a policy, expressed in the Wagner and Taft-Hartley Acts,[63] vesting exclusive jurisdiction over
such matters in the federal Board and the federal courts.[64] Hence a
"no man's land" was created in which certain comparatively minor
labor disputes (though probably extremely important to the
parties concerned) would not be considered by the NLRB and
could not be heard by any other tribunal. This holding was in
effect reversed by Section 701 of the Labor-Management Reporting
and Disclosure Act of 1959[65] which provides a subsection (c) to
be added to Section 14 of the Taft-Hartley Act providing that
states do have jurisdiction to decide cases which may arise under
any section of the National Labor Relations Act of which the
NLRB declines to take jurisdiction. It adds further that the Board
shall not refer back to the states any class of case over which it
would have taken jurisdiction as of August 1, 1959. This legislation, however, neither qualifies nor undermines the view that the
nationalistic labor policy excludes state authority except where the
state is permitted to have or retain jurisdiction at the sufferance
of Congress or under "interpretations" of the Supreme Court.

This is nowhere better illustrated than under Section 14 (b) of
the National Labor Relations Act,[66] as amended by the Taft-
Hartley Act which provides that union shops shall be valid in any
part of the United States where not expressly prohibited by the
state. Some 19 states have "right to work" laws containing such
prohibitions. A much-publicized issue kept alive before Congress
by the unions is whether Congress should repeal Section 14 (b),

---

63 49 Stat. 449 (1935), as amended, 29 U.S.C. § § 151-66 (1964); 61 Stat. 136
(1947) as amended, 29 U.S.C. § § 153-87 (1964).

64 Guss v. Utah Labor Relations Bd., 352 U. S. 817, 39 LRRM 2567. For further
treatment of the jurisdictional standards of 1959, see Chap. II, Sec. 3 and note 162
infra.

65 73 Stat. 519 (1959), 29 U.S.C. § § 153, 158-60, 164, 186-87, 401-531 (1964).

66 61 Stat. 151 (1947), 29 U.S.C. § 164 (b).

thereby striking down all of the statutes of the 19 states that have prohibited union shops.

The atmosphere created by the labor preemption decisions had so pervaded the jurisdictional question that a California court declared in 1957 that "whatever doubt there may have been . . . as to the jurisdiction of the State courts following a refusal of the Federal Board to assume jurisdiction in the first instance was completely set at rest by the recent decisions of the Supreme Court of the United States in the *Guss, Fairlawn* and *Garmon* cases . . . . As long as the facts of a given case fall within the jurisdiction of the National Labor Relations Board, the Congress has completely displaced the power of the courts of this state to deal with the matter even though those same facts might otherwise give our courts jurisdiction under the Jurisdictional Strike Act."[67] The California court refused to award damages for losses brought about by certain picketing and refused to apply the result of the *Laburnum* decision. It distinguished the latter by noting that there the peace of the state was threatened; apparently it was not under the California facts, for no violence was charged.[68]

In 1957, and no doubt partly as a result of the same developing atmosphere of sweeping preemption, the Supreme Court handed down a revolutionary and far-reaching decision in *Textile Workers Union* v. *Lincoln Mills.*[69] The opinion, by Mr. Justice Douglas, held that Section 301 (a) of the Labor Management Relations Act, 1947[70] (Taft-Hartley Act) "is more than jurisdictional — that *it*

---

[67] McKenzie, Inc. v. International Ass'n of Machinists, 39 LRRM 2757 (Cal. Super. Ct., 1957) at p. 2759.

The federal preemption doctrine was, no doubt, a factor in the California Attorney General's opinion Local Regulation of Professional Strikebreakers, 45 Ops. Cal. Att'y Gen. 140-45 (1965).

[68] McKenzie, Inc. v. International Ass'n of Machinists, note 67, *supra,* at p. 2761. Full understanding of the significance of this opinion requires calling to mind both of the U. S. Supreme Court opinions in San Diego Bldg. Trades Council v. Garmon, 353 U. S. 951, 39 LRRM 2574 (1957) and 359 U. S. 236, 43 LRRM 2838 (1959). Recent California cases appear to require, before state jurisdiction may be invoked, a showing by the party urging such jurisdiction, that either the NLRB has declined jurisdiction or that it would do so if the matter were brought before it. Musicians Union v. Superior Court, 69 Cal. 2d 695 (1968).

For a very good study of Garmon and surviving state powers, see Michelman, State Power to Govern Concerted Employee Activities, 74 Harv. L. Rev. 641 (1961).

[69] Textile Workers Union v. Lincoln Mills, 353 U. S. 448, 40 LRRM 2113 (1957).

[70] 61 Stat. 136 (1947), as amended, 29 U.S.C. § § 153-87 (1964).

authorizes federal courts to fashion a body of federal law for the enforcement of these collective bargaining agreements *and includes
within that federal law specific performance of promises to arbitrate* grievances under collective bargaining agreements."[71] In a
later part of the opinion the Justice states: "We conclude that the
substantive law to apply in suits under § 301 (a)   is federal law,
which the courts must fashion from the policy of our national
labor laws."[72] He indicated that "federal interpretation of the federal law will govern, not state law. . . . But state law, if compatible
with the purpose of Section 301, may be resorted to in order to find
the rule that will best effectuate the federal policy."[73] He explained
that any state law applied, however, would be absorbed as federal
law and would not be an independent source of private rights.[74]

It is important to remember that while the courts have traditionally "found" or "declared" legal rules, filling the hiatuses of statutes, and have thus contributed to the growth of law under the
aegis of *stare decisis,* the federal courts have not previously in this
manner openly asserted authority to join Congress in law "fashioning" or legislating.

Preemption Plus Judicial Legislation

Appreciation of the full impact of the *Lincoln Mills* opinion requires briefly calling to mind some historical background concerning arbitration. In the year 1609 Lord Coke had held in *Vynior's
Case*[75] that since it was against public policy that any man who desired to litigate be excluded from the King's courts and the opportunity to start an action at law, he could not, even by his promise
to arbitrate a possible future dispute, be debarred from appealing
to the courts. Hence he could refuse to arbitrate, and litigate
though he had agreed not to do so.

This decision stood as an anomalous concept through many
years. The arbitration contract has been a prominent example of

---

71 Textile Workers Union v. Lincoln Mills, 353 U. S. 448, 451-52, 40 LRRM 2113
(1957) . (Emphasis added.)

72 *Id.* at 456.

73 *Id.* at 457. Here the court cites Jerome v. United States, 318 U. S. 101, 104
(1943) .

74 353 U. S. at 456. In this connection he refers to Board of Comm'rs v. United
States, 308 U. S. 343, 351 (1939) .

75 4 Coke 302, Trinity Term, 7 Jac. 1 (1609) . See Chap. I, Sec. 1, *supra.*

a situation in which parties could enter into a solemn, clearly prov-
able agreement (to arbitrate a future dispute) and yet where
either of them could completely repudiate the agreement (and litigate instead). Some states have largely reversed the consequences
of *Vynior's Case* by statute, but it is still effective in a few localities
in fields not governed by the *Lincoln Mills* decision, which is to
say in disputes not in the labor area. But insofar as contracts to
arbitrate labor disputes are concerned the U. S. Supreme Court
has overruled Lord Coke without the direction of statute.

Some two years before *Lincoln Mills,* Mr. Justice Frankfurter
had written in *Weber* v. *Anheuser-Busch Brewing Co.,*[76]

"By the Taft-Hartley Act, Congress did not exhaust the full sweep
of legislative power over industrial relations given by the Commerce
Clause. Congress formulated a code whereby it outlawed some
aspects of labor activities and left others free for the operation of
economic forces. As to both categories, the areas that have been preempted by federal authority and thereby withdrawn from state
power are not susceptible of delimitation by fixed metes and bounds.
Obvious conflict, actual or potential, leads to easy judicial exclusion
of state action. Such was the situation in *Garner* v. *Teamsters Union.*
. . . But as the opinion in that case recalled, the Labor Management
Relations Act 'leaves much to the states, though Congress has refrained from telling us how much. . . .'

"This penumbral area can be rendered progressively clear only by
the course of litigation. Regarding the conduct here in controversy,
Congress has sufficiently expressed its purpose to bring it within
federal oversight to exclude state prohibition, even though that with
which the federal law is concerned as a matter of labor relations be
related by the State to the more inclusive area of restraint of trade."[77]

Since *Garmon*[78] came down, in 1959, if the issue to be determined
is conceived by a court as one which appears *arguably* to involve
Section 7 or Section 8 of the National Labor Relations Act[79] or in

76 348 U. S. 468, 480, 35 LRRM 2637 (1955).
77 *Id.* at 480-81.
78 359 U. S. 236, 43 LRRM 2838 (1959), 353 U. S. 951, 39 LRRM 2574 (1957).
79 A few recent examples are Musicians Union v. Superior Court, 69 Cal. 2d 695
(1968); Continental Slip Form Builders, Inc. v. Brotherhood of Constr. & Gen.
Labor, 193 Kan. 459, 408 P.2d 620 (1965); Hutchby v. District Court, 406 P.2d 70
(Nev., 1965); Retail Clerks v. Christiansen, 52 CCH Lab. Cas. ¶ 51,404 (Wash.,
1965). Some courts in parallel situations proceed to decision apparently at the risk
of reversal in some fact situations. See Farmington Cleaners, Inc. v. Connecticut State
Labor Relations Bd., 52 CCH Lab. Cas. ¶ 51,395 (Conn. Super. Ct., 1965); Pavillion
Nursing Home v. Litto, 47 Misc. 2d 161, 261 N.Y.S.2d 620 (Sup. Ct., 1965), *rev'd as
to money damages but injunction allowed,* 48 Misc. 2d 775, 265 N.Y.S.2d 695 (1965);

fact *arguably* to involve any unfair labor practice, though perhaps a very doubtful, borderline case, it is the established view that the court should refuse decision on the merits and reject jurisdiction. The National Labor Relations Board must be accorded a prior right and authority to decide matters arguably within its jurisdiction. Should the Board, too, decline jurisdiction, the matter goes to "no man's land."

The fact seems to be, however, that the word *arguably* is of such uncertain meaning that it cannot logically be used as a test of jurisdiction. Virtually every case which goes to any court is *arguable,* or it would not be in litigation. When the doctrine of preemption and consequently the application of the supremacy clause are made to depend upon a word of such cornucopian content, prompt, thorough congressional study and action are indicated.

Preemption, Judicial Legislation, and Labor Arbitration

When the *Lincoln Mills* case came to the Supreme Court there was no federal statute applicable to general jurisdiction over and the handling of labor dispute arbitration and there is none today. But the "fashioning" of federal law by the Court to fill this need is just as far reaching as if the *Lincoln Mills* result had been enacted by Congress. Without judicial legislation or the "fashioning" of a federal rule or principle of law and making it retroactive, there was no basis upon which the Court could say that the parties had agreed to arbitrate and hence could be required to do so by a federal court decree.

It is not impossible that the attitude of the Supreme Court in relation to arbitration was in some degree affected by its knowledge that the lower federal courts and the National Labor Relations Board were confronted by an extremely great caseload of labor problems. One obvious solution to the dilemma was vastly to expand the scope of arbitration and thereby reduce the burden falling upon the federal courts and the NLRB.

Braun's Buns v. Pennsylvania Labor Relations Bd., 52 CCH Lab. Cas. ¶ 51,400 (Pa. County Ct., 1965). Compare Buscarello v. Guglielmelli, 44 Misc. 2d 1041, 255 N.Y.S.2d 615 (Sup. Ct., 1965). State courts have no jurisdiction to decide matters arguably within the jurisdiction of the NLRB, Continental Slip Form Builders v. Brotherhood of Constr. & Gen. Labor, *supra.* If any labor relations in dispute are arguably within the jurisdiction of the NLRB, state courts should not undertake to control them by injunction. Mitcham v. Ark-La Constr. Co., 397 S.W.2d 789 (Ark., 1965).

Thus to avoid one consequence of nationalist preemption — a tremendous overload on the National Labor Relations Board — the Court held that agreements to arbitrate labor disputes were specifically enforceable under "fashioned" rules of federal common law. In this way the preemption doctrine was extended to provide some means of deciding the great federal caseload of disputes that it caused.

However, as stated in numerous instances, since *Garmon,* the plaintiffs who sought enforcement of an arbitration agreement have been refused relief on the basis that the question to be resolved was *arguably* a matter requiring decision by the National Labor Relations Board. Yet the Court, in the so-called *"trilogy"* cases,[80] fortified the view that arbitration of labor disputes should be encouraged and that the decisional authority of arbitrators should not be diluted or defeated by substitution of judges' conclusions for arbitrational awards when questions of arbitrability are taken into the courts for enforcement or rejection. In *United Steelworkers* v. *Enterprise Wheel and Car Co.*[81] the Court emphasized the view that arbitration of labor disputes is favored as a matter of federal policy and that this policy would be impaired if the courts undertook to substitute their decisions for the awards of arbitrators.[82] In *United Steelworkers* v. *Warrior & Gulf Navigation Co.*[83] the Court declared that arbitration "is the substitute for in-

80 See herein Chap. I, Sec. 4, *supra* United Steelworkers v. Enterprise Wheel & Car Co., 363 U.S. 593, 46 LRRM 2423 (1960) ; United Steelworkers v. Warrior & Gulf Navigation Co., 363 U.S. 574, 46 LRRM 2416 (1960) ; United Steelworkers v. American Mfg. Co., 363 U.S. 564, 46 LRRM 2414 (1960). And see Torrington Co. v. Metal Prods. Workers, 347 F.2d 93, 59 LRRM 2588 (2d Cir. 1965); Long Island Lumber Co. v. Martin, 15 N.Y.2d 380, 207 N.E.2d 190, 259 N.Y.S.2d 142, 59 LRRM 2237 (1965).

81 363 U.S. 593, 46 LRRM 2423 (1960).

82 *Id.* at 598 (1960). The courts have deferred to a congressionally created Board. Brotherhood of R.R. Trainmen v. Certain Carriers, 349 F.2d 207, 59 LRRM 2576 (D.C. Cir., 1965).

If the contract does not provide for arbitration, the court has jurisdiction to decide the grievance. International Bhd. of Tel. Workers v. New England Tel. & Tel. Co., 240 F. Supp. 426 (D. Mass., 1965). For ambiguity or defective procedure, awards should be remanded to the arbitrator. Smith v. Union Carbide Corp., 231 F. Supp. 980 (E.D. Tenn., 1964), *rev'd,* 350 F.2d 258, 60 LRRM 2110 (6th Cir., 1965); *In re* Certain Carriers, 349 F.2d 207, 59 LRRM 2576 (C.A. D.C., 1965).

83 363 U.S. 574, 46 LRRM 2416 (1960). It has been held that a dispute litigable under § 303(b) of the Taft-Hartley Act must be arbitrated if the parties have so agreed. Old Dutch Farms, Inc. v. Milk Drivers Union, 243 F. Supp. 246, 59 LRRM 2745 (E.D.N.Y., 1965). It has also been held that the propriety of a lockout was arbitrable where it was not expressly excluded. IBEW v. Hearst Corp., 352 F.2d

dustrial strife." [84] It went on to assert that "since arbitration of labor disputes has quite different functions from arbitrations under an ordinary commercial agreement, the hostility evinced by courts toward arbitration of commercial agreements has no place here. For arbitration of labor disputes under collective bargaining agreements is part and parcel of the collective bargaining process itself." [85]

In this case the Court also stated that "arbitration is the means of solving the unforeseeable by molding a system of private law for all the problems that may arise and to provide for their solution in a way which will generally accord with the variant needs and desires of the parties. The processing of disputes through the grievance machinery is actually a vehicle by which meaning and content are given to the collective bargaining agreement." [86]

Preemption, Judicial Law Making, and the Individual

In the case of *Smith* v. *Evening News Ass'n*,[87] the Supreme Court held that individual employees have the right to maintain suits under Section 301 of the Labor Management Relations Act. Two years later, in 1964, it held in *Humphrey* v. *Moore*[88] that individual employees can maintain an action to enjoin enforcement of a joint union-employer agreement if it violates the union's duty of fair representation.

The courts have generally emphasized the long-established rule that the individual claimant must exhaust contractual grievance and intraunion remedial procedures before bringing suit in court for establishment of his rights.[89] It has been held that a claimant's failure to comply with the time limitations prescribed by griev-

---

957, 57 LRRM 2052, 2625 (4th Cir., 1965); see Brewery Workers Union v. Adolph Coors Co., 239 F. Supp. 279, 59 LRRM 2947, 2950 (D. Colo., 1964), *aff'd*, 344 F.2d 702, 60 LRRM 2176 (10th Cir., 1965).

84 363 U. S. at 578.

85 *Ibid.*

86 *Id.* at p. 581.

87 371 U. S. 195, 51 LRRM 2646 (1962). The opinion relies heavily on a broad interpretation of § 301 of the Taft-Hartley Act and Lincoln Mills. The action was held not preempted under the Garmon rule as "arguably" a matter for NLRB decision. See Martin v. Ethyl Corp., 341 F.2d 1, 58 LRRM 2275 (5th Cir., 1965) (husband may maintain action for wife in community property state).

88 375 U. S. 335, 55 LRRM 2031 (1964). But the court held there was no violation of fair representation; the Lincoln Mills opinion was explained and followed.

89 Desrosiers v. American Cyanamid Co., 51 CCH Lab. Cas. ¶ 19,500 (D. Conn., 1965); Verbiscus v. Marine & Shipbuilding Workers, 238 F. Supp. 848, 58 LRRM 2029 (E.D. Mich., 1964) (union officer required to file complaint with Secretary

ance procedure will be fatal to his claims even if he did not know about them.[90]

The burden is upon the individual employee to show that the union failed to represent him properly, and in such case he must proceed within union rules even in cases where the union completely omitted to process his grievance.[91] The burden is similarly upon the individual when he charges that the union and the employer have entered into a settlement unfavorable to his rights.[92] It has been held generally that the individual employee, not being technically a party to the collectively bargained agreement under which the arbitration was carried out, has no right or standing to attack the award in court.[93] However, the individual employee's

---

of Labor). Even a suit brought by the Secretary of Labor to set aside a union election at the request of a defeated candidate was dismissed because of failure to show that the party had exhausted all remedies available under the union constitution. Wirtz v. United Steelworkers, 52 CH Lab. Cas. ¶ 16,815 (N. D. Ala., 1965). See also Boeing Airplane Co. v. UAW, 349 F.2d 412, 59 LRRM 2988 (3rd Cir., 1965) (employer who could not initiate arbitration not barred from court for failure to do so) ; Smith v. General Elec. Co., 63 Wash. 2d 624, 388 P.2d 550, 55 LRRM 2474 (1964) (aggrieved party not union member but bound to follow grievance procedure). Exhaustion of unduly restricted remedies is not required. Thommen v. Consolidated Freightways, 234 F. Supp. 472, 57 LRRM 2292 (D. Ore., 1964) (contract procedure created only union organizational remedies, hence did not bar action by individual claimant).

90 But timeliness is an issue to be decided by the arbitrator. The court should not stay arbitration when this is in question, but should refer the matter to arbitration. Metropolitan Opera Ass'n v. American Guild of Musical Artists, 52 CCH Lab. Cas. ¶ 51,398 (N.Y. Sup. Ct., 1965) ; Smith v. General Elec. Co., note 89 *supra.*

91 Kennedy v. UAW, 52 CCH Lab. Cas. ¶ 16,578 (1965). But see Archibald v. Local 57, International Union of Operating Eng'rs, 52 CCH Lab. Cas. ¶ 16,516 (D.R.I., 1964).

92 Zeaner v. Highway Truck Drivers Union, 234 F. Supp. 901 (E.D. Pa., 1964) (individual bound by union's adverse action if taken in good faith and in fair representation) ; Cortez v. California Motor Express Co., 226 Cal. App. 2d 257, 38 Cal. Rptr. 29 (1964) (decision of joint labor-management committee that employee be dropped for disability binding in absence of showing of unfair representation). See Sherman, Union's Duty of Fair Representation and the Civil Rights Act of 1964, 49 Minn. L. Rev. 771 (1965).

93 Corbin v. Friendly Frost Stores, Inc., 49 CCH Lab. Cas. ¶ 51,090 (N.Y. Sup. Ct., 1964) (petitioner had fully participated in hearing and both parties had agreed on the issue) ; Pernice v. Burns Bros., 50 CCH Lab. Cas. ¶ 51,187 (N.Y. Sup. Ct., 1964) (court held plaintiff not proper party to seek nullification of award; also rejected jurisdiction on ground that there was "arguably" a union unfair labor practice question involved and hence there would be federal preemption) ; New York Joint Bd., Amalgamated Clothing Workers v. Rogers Peet Co., 50 CCH Lab. Cas. ¶ 51,144 (N.Y. Sup. Ct., 1964) (member not formal "party" to arbitration contract).

It is for the arbitrator to decide whether the employee has lost his right to have his grievance considered in arbitration. Kociuba v. Stubnitz Greene Corp., 52 CCH Lab. Cas. ¶ 51,388 (Pa. C.P., 1964).

duty to exhaust remedies, and the other procedural rules which usually restrict his rights, are likely to be excused where he can show that the union was guilty of a breach of duty of fair representation or that the union and the employer have entered into an improper agreement to limit or destroy his rights.[94] It is clearly the duty of a union to show fairness and good faith whenever called upon to enforce the personal rights of their members under the labor agreements and under Section 301.[95] This means that the unions' responsibilities in the area of preserving employees' rights may be much greater than they were before *Lincoln Mills*.[96]

Jurisdictions — Federal, State, and Concurrent

In the *Smith* case,[97] the preemption doctrine was interpreted to mean that the state courts have jurisdiction over suits by individual employees against their employers and that Section 301 of the Labor Management Relations Act, creating federal jurisdiction for suits between unions and employers without regard to amount or citizenship, does not exclude the individual's right of action. This

---

94 Fuller v. Highway Truck Drivers Union, 233 F. Supp. 115, 57 LRRM 2065 (E.D. Pa., 1964) (employees may maintain suit where unfair representation alleged); Tully v. Fred Olson Motor Serv. Co., 50 CCH Lab. Cas. ¶ 19,198 (Wis. Cir. Ct., 1964) (matter "arguably" concerned unfair labor practice, hence federal preemption controlled and six-month limitation on filing unfair labor practices charges applied by state court).

Courts require evidence of unfair representation such as bad faith, arbitrary action, or fraud by the union to excuse a member from being bound by the contracted duty to arbitrate and to allow recovery against the union or the employer. See Kennedy v. Bell Tel. Co., 52 CCH Lab. Cas. ¶ 16,639 (S.D. Cal., 1965); Deacon v. International Union of Operating Eng'rs, 52 CCH Lab. Cas. ¶ 16,605 (S.D. Cal., 1965); Desrosiers v. American Cyanamid Co., 51 CCH Lab. Cas. ¶ 19,500 (D. Conn., 1965) (union shown to have refused to represent claimant); Thompson v. Brotherhood of Sleeping Car Porters, 243 F. Supp. 261, 60 LRRM 2194 (E.D.S.C., 1965) (member claimed union unfairly failed to protect his seniority rights). Compare Addeo v. Dairymen's League, 262 N.Y.S.2d 771, 47 Misc. 2d 426, 60 LRRM 2235 (1965) (allegation of conspiracy against plaintiff gives state court jurisdiction even though "arguably" unfair labor practice charge appears).

95 However, where a member has failed to act with diligence on his own behalf he will not be heard to charge his union for the consequences of his neglect. Steen v. UAW, 52 CCH Lab. Cas. ¶ 16,588 (E.D. Mich., 1965). See UAW v. Hoosier Cardinal Corp., 235 F. Supp. 183 (S.D. Ind., 1964) (state statute barred recovery); United Steelworkers v. Copperweld Steel Co., 230 F. Supp. 383, 56 LRRM 2364 (W.D. Pa., 1964).

96 See Vaca v. Sipes, Administrator, 386 U.S. 171, 64 LRRM 2369 (1967) and Balowski v. UAW, 372 F. 2d 829, 64 LRRM 2397 (CA 6. 1967). Cf. NLRB v. Miranda Fuel Co., 326 F. 2d 172, 54 LRRM 2716 (1963).

97 Smith v. Evening News Ass'n, 371 U.S. 195, 51 LRRM 2646 (1962).

is held to be true even though the conduct involved might also be an unfair labor practice or "arguably" so.[98]

In the case of *Carey v. Westinghouse Elec. Corp.*,[99] the Court discussed concurrent jurisdiction of arbitrators and courts over disputes arising from collective bargaining. In that litigation it held that the availability of a Section 10 (k) [100] proceeding (to settle work rights or jurisdiction) before the NLRB would not bar a union from compelling arbitration of a work assignment dispute where the same was within the terms of the collective bargain. The federal and state courts have several times declared that the fact that a grievance is within, or "arguably" within, the jurisdiction of the National Labor Relations Board will not prevent either arbitration or enforcement of an arbitrational award.[101] It has been recognized that proceedings before the NLRB and before an arbitrator proceed on the bases of different rights and issues, but both rest squarely upon the preemption doctrine. The Board proceedings were provided by statute to safeguard the employees' statutory rights. Arbitration rights are of contractual creation, now resting upon Section 301 as interpreted by *Lincoln Mills*, for the enforcement of rights created by the labor agreements. They exist concurrently with statutory rights arising from unfair labor practices.[102] In one situation a trial examiner had found that a union with a

---

98 Fuller v. Highway Truck Drivers Union, 233 F. Supp. 115, 57 LRRM 2065 (E.D. Pa., 1964).

99 375 U.S. 261, 55 LRRM 2042 (1964).

100 61 Stat. 149 (1947), 29 U.S.C. 160 (1964), directing the NLRB to hear and decide jurisdictional disputes.

101 United Steelworkers v. American Int'l Aluminum Corp., 334 F.2d 147, 56 LRRM 2682 (5th Cir., 1964) (employer had repudiated contract charging slowdown). *Cf.* Todd Shipyards Corp. v. Industrial Union of Marine Workers, 344 F.2d 107, 58 LRRM 2826 (2d Cir., 1965), where the question was whether a clause in the contract was proper and legal work protection or an illegal "hot-cargo" clause. See also Amalgamated Ass'n of Street Employees v. Trailways, Inc., 232 F. Supp. 608, 56 LRRM 2186 (D. Mass., 1964) (duty to arbitrate exists through matter in dispute may be unfair labor practice); Westchester, Putnam & So. Dutchess Employers Material Yards Ass'n v. Operating Eng'rs, 52 CCH Lab. Cas. ¶ 51,360 (N.Y. Sup. Ct., 1965).

102 Todd Shipyards Corp. v. Marine and Shipbuilding Workers, 344 F.2d 107, 58 LRRM 2826 (2d Cir., 1965). See also Local 499, IBEW v. Iowa Power & Light Co., 49 CCH Lab. Cas. ¶ 18,818 (S.D. Iowa, 1964). Litigants of labor dispute questions in federal courts are not required to meet either the diversity requirement or the amount in controversy requirement. See Martin v. Ethyl Corp., 341 F.2d 1, 58 LRRM 2275 (5th Cir., 1965). But diversity of citizenship continues to be required for removal of a suit against an unincorporated union from a state court to a federal court, and such unions may be sued in any states in which they have business locations. United Steelworkers v. Bouligny, Inc., 382 U.S. 145, 60 LRRM 2393 (1965).

union shop agreement had violated the National Labor Relations
Act by excluding replacement employees hired during a strike
from becoming members. On these facts a district court granted
the employer a stay of arbitration, holding that the findings of the
trial examiner should not be ignored.[103] Similarly it was held that
when a representation question was pending before the National
Labor Relations Board, arbitration should not be ordered until
the Board could act since the arbitrator's award would necessarily
have to be consistent with the Board's determination.[104]

In another case a federal district court enjoined a union from
arbitrating[105] a grievance to enforce a hot-cargo clause. The court
reached the conclusion that the matter was not arbitrable because
the National Labor Relations Board might hold the contract clause
itself to be invalid. The court ignored the fact that this result could
also have been reached by the arbitrator. The court emphasized
the fact that this was not a suit under Section 301 (a) but one
under Section 10[106] wherein the Board was seeking to enjoin arbitration.

One rather unusual recent case involved a refusal by a federal
district court to remand to a state court a suit to enjoin arbitration. The employer contended that because of duress no valid collective bargaining agreement was made and that the federal court
was, therefore, without jurisdiction. That court held that it had
jurisdiction under Section 301 since a contract had been signed. It
also indicated that the Connecticut State Mediation Board, which
was named as arbitrator in the purported contract, was not a proper
party to the removal proceedings, and therefore the federal court
retained jurisdiction. The probable next step in this regard might
well be a decision as to whether the conduct of which the employer
complained was such an unfair labor practice as to invalidate the
contract; this could *arguably* put the matter into the hands of the
National Labor Relations Board.[107]

---

103 Kentile, Inc. v. United Rubber Workers, 228 F. Supp. 541, 55 LRRM 3011
(D.C.N.Y., 1964). On the exercise of judicial discretion, compare Omaha Beef Co. v.
Amalgamated Meat Cutters, 51 CCH Lab. Cas. ¶ 19,769 (D. Conn., 1965).
104 B D Markets, Inc. v. Meat Cutters, 51 CCH Lab. Cas. ¶ 19,499 (E.D. Pa.,
1965).
105 McLeod v. American Fed'n of Television Artists, 234 F. Supp. 832, 56 LRRM
2615 (S.D.N.Y., 1964), aff'd, 351 F.2d 310, 60 LRRM 2304 (2d Cir., 1965).
106 61 Stat. 149 (1947), 29 U.S.C. 160 (1964).
107 Omaha Beef Co. v. Amalgamated Meat Cutters, 51 CCH Lab. Cas. ¶ 19,769
(D. Conn., 1965).

In another case a federal circuit court considered a dispute between two unions concerning violation of a non-raiding agreement. The National Labor Relations Board had certified the respective units to be represented. An interpretation of the Board's ruling was made by an arbitrator and enforced by the court.[108]

A New York supreme court case held that an NLRB decision that an employer removed his plant in good faith, and for sound economic reasons after a contract expiration, would bar the union from obtaining arbitration of issues inconsistent with such findings.[109] A strike to force concession of an arbitrable grievance is a contract violation even in the absence of an express no-strike clause. State and federal courts share jurisdiction in these matters under Section 301 of the Labor Management Relations Act.[110] It is established that the NLRB does not commit error by dismissing a complaint upon being advised the matter at issue has been decided by an arbitrator.[111]

In an unusually interesting case, the Board was overruled after it ordered reinstatement of two employees. A trial examiner found that the employer had used a "wildcat" work stoppage led by the two discharged women as a false pretext for their discharge. In rejecting the Board's conclusion the court relied upon an arbitrator's award upholding the discharges.[112]

The Wisconsin Supreme Court has held that termination by retirement of 38 employees between the ages of 60 and 65 with sub-

---

108 International Bhd. of Firemen & Oilers v. International Ass'n of Machinists, 338 F.2d 176, 57 LRRM 2459 (5th Cir., 1964). See Pernice v. Burns Bros., 50 CCH Lab. Cas. ¶ 51,187 (N.Y. Sup. Ct., 1964).

109 Blue Bird Knitwear Co. v. Livingston, 49 CCH Lab. Cas. ¶ 51,070 (N.Y. Sup. Ct., 1964) (whether there remained arbitrable issues after decision of NLRB left to arbitrator).

110 In cases of concurrent jurisdiction the state courts are required to apply federal law. Local 174, Teamsters Union v. Lucas Flour Co., 369 U.S. 95, 49 LRRM 2717 (1962). See Independent Oil Workers v. Mobil Oil Co., 85 N.J. Super. 453, 205 A.2d 78 (1965) (federal courts defer to state courts on matters primarily concerning state laws).

111 Ramsey v. NLRB, 327 F.2d 784, 55 LRRM 2441 (7th Cir., 1964) (employee not given notice of the "arbitration proceeding" but made no claim of irregularity or fraud). After arbitration procedure has been initiated the NLRB has discretionary authority to issue a complaint or defer the same until an award has been made. NLRB v. Thor Power Tool Co., 351 F.2d 584, 60 LRRM 2237 (7th Cir., 1965); and see Kracoff v. Retail Clerks, 244 F. Supp. 38, 59 LRRM 2942 (E.D. Pa., 1965).

112 Raytheon Co. v. NLRB, 326 F.2d 471, 55 LRRM 2101 (1st Cir., 1964) (court stated NLRB trial examiner made findings against employer's good faith on a bare assumption).

stantial pensions as agreed by their labor union was not *arguably* an unfair labor practice so as to exclude it from jurisdiction. The court stated that the union had bargained for the labor agreement and that the terminations were consistent with it. The court noted that the retirements did not violate the Wisconsin Fair Employment Act and that the pension plan was approved by the United States Internal Revenue Service as complying with its regulations.[113] Obviously, however, had one or more of the men filed a charge with the General Counsel of the NLRB alleging a conspiracy to remove them from employment, or had they charged unfair representation before the NLRB, as they appear to have charged before the Wisconsin Industrial Commission, the Board could properly have taken jurisdiction.

The NLRB asserts its authority to act on an unfair labor practice complaint even when the matter falls within the contractual grievance procedure that may lead to arbitration.[114] The Board will refuse to defer to arbitration in situations where the employer has refused to perform a statutory duty to furnish information to the union and has resisted arbitration.[115] The Board's policy is to honor a "fair and regular" award made in grievance procedure.[116] It will not, however, give force and effect to the disposition of a grievance indicated to have been made "final" at a step in the grievance procedure prior to formal and proper arbitration even though the grievance was "abandoned" by failure to pursue it within the contracted time limitation.[117]

Preemption — States' Authority — Protection of Operations

It has long been established that some union pressure tactics, such as sit-down strikes, slowdowns, the calling of union meetings during working hours, and practices involving violence, are not "protected" under the National Labor Relations Act. The process

---

113 Walker Mfg. Co. v. Industrial Comm'n of Wis., 135 N.W.2d 307, 59 LRRM 2454 (Wis., 1965). *Cf.* Westchester, Putnam and So. Ass'n v. Operating Eng'rs, 52 CCH Lab. Cas. ¶ 51,360 (N.Y. Sup. Ct., 1965).

114 Thor Power Tool Co., 148 NLRB 1379, 57 LRRM 1161 (1964). This conclusion of the Board was sustained, NLRB v. Thor Power Tool Co., 351 F.2d 584, 60 LRRM 2237 (7th Cir., 1965).

115 Puerto Rico Tel. Co., 149 NLRB 110 (1964).

116 See Spielberg Corporation, 112 NLRB 1080, 36 LRRM 1152 (1955); Modern Motor Express, 149 NLRB 1507, 58 LRRM 1005 (1964).

117 Electric Motors and Specialties, Inc., 149 NLRB 131, 57 LRRM 1258 (1964).

of examining all the various types of union activities that have appeared (and that may yet appear), and concluding whether each one or the manner or objective of its execution is "protected" or not, is likely to extend well into the future. As far as past experience and litigation have clarified this scene, however, some generalizations may be ventured.

Despite the preemption doctrine and the "law fashioning" by the Supreme Court under the *Textile Workers* v. *Lincoln Mills* decision, the Wisconsin Employment Peace Act[118] and similar state enactments appear to have continued validity to the extent that they do not invade present federal rules. The Wisconsin courts had held that a union that caused several intermittent work stoppages was guilty of an unfair labor practice under the Act that prohibited any interference with production except leaving the premises of the employer in an orderly manner for the purpose of going on strike. The Supreme Court affirmed this holding in *International Union, UAW* v. *Wisconsin Labor Relations Bd.*[119] In reaching this conclusion the Court observed that the state act did not forbid any conduct permitted under the federal statutes. In contrast the NLRB can forbid a strike when its purpose is one of those made illegal by the federal statute, but it has not been given power to forbid a work stoppage because of illegal method.

Under the New York act, however, union conduct was apparently deemed by a state court to be "protected" when it had caused eight noon-day work stoppages in two months, thus disrupting the normal activities of the employer, a dining-club. This characterization as "protected" resulted in a narrow holding by the New York State Labor Relations Board that the act of the employer in discharging some men for this conduct was discriminatory and hence an unfair labor practice.[120]

---

118 Wis. Stat. 1947, c. 111, 11.06 (2).

119 336 U.S. 245, 23 LRRM 2361 (1949). But this result was held inapplicable where there was a single stoppage during working hours. UAW v. Wisconsin Employment Relations Bd., 336 U.S. 245, 23 LRRM 2361 (1949); Wisconsin Employment Relations Bd. v. Algoma Plywood & Veneer Co., 252 Wis. 549, 32 N.W.2d 417, 22 LRRM 2148 (1948), aff'd, 336 U.S. 301, 23 LRRM 2402 (1949), and see Smith, Putting the Wisconsin Employment Peace Act into Effect, 46 Marq. L. Rev. 263 (1963).

120 New York State Labor Relations Bd. v. Union Club, 295 N.Y. 917, 68 N.E.2d 29, 18 LRRM 2083 (1946). But union's right to meet with commissioners of marine department was lost by work stoppage and picketing since this conduct shows bad faith. Donaldson v. Brown, 24 App. Div. 2d 714, 263 N.Y.S.2d 431 (1965).

In a fairly recent case it was held by the state court that the Wisconsin Fair Employment Act was not totally preempted by any federal statute and that the Wisconsin court has jurisdiction to enforce it.[121] On the other hand an action for damages and for injunctive relief against an allegedly closed union under the California statute was denied by the state court on the ground of federal preemption; the court held the matter to be "arguably" one for NLRB decision.[122]

The Supreme Court has held that federal statutes do not license unionized employees to harass the employer by "sit-down strikes" nor to defy the authority of the employer to manage his business while remaining in his service.[123] Nor may the NLRB reinstate men who have been terminated for advocating a slowdown.[124] Under the guidance of these last decisions the NLRB apparently must now follow the view that the states, authorized state agencies, and arbitrators share authority to prevent interference with production by employee groups engaging in harassment other than those protected actions that are taken for a declared and legitimate objective.[125]

In 1950 the Third Circuit held that a single more or less spontaneous work stoppage would not justify discharges or penalties for those who participated in it or led it since it was concluded by the court to be a suitable, concerted activity for the purpose of collective bargaining and protected by Section 7 of the National Labor Relations Act.[126]

On the other hand, it has long been held that refusal to work scheduled overtime is not "protected." However, such conduct

---

121 Walker Mfg. Co. v. Industrial Comm'n, 27 Wis. 2d 669, 135 N.W.2d 307, 59 LRRM 2454 (1965).

122 Directors Guild of America, Inc. v. Superior Court, 64 Cal. 2d 42, 48 Cal. Rptr. 710, 409 P.2d 934, 66 LRRM 2255 (1966).

123 NLRB v. Fansteel Metallurgical Corp., 306 U.S. 240, 4 LRRM 515 (1939).

124 Superior Engraving Co. v. NLRB, 183 F.2d 783, 26 LRRM 2351, 2534 (7th Cir., 1950), cert. denied, 340 U.S. 930, 27 LRRM 2418 (1951); Wyman, Gordon Co. v. NLRB, 153 F.2d 480, 17 LRRM 781 (7th Cir., 1946).

125 See NLRB v. Montgomery Ward & Co., 157 F.2d 486, 19 LRRM 2008 (8th Cir., 1946); The Supreme Court, 1963 Term, 78 Harv. L. Rev. 282-92 (1964), and cases therein cited; cf. Elk Lumber Co., 91 NLRB 333 (1950); Phelps Dodge Corp. 101 NLRB 360, 31 LRRM 1072 (1952). Here it was held that the employer was not under a duty to bargain during a slowdown.

126 NLRB v. Kennametal, Inc., 182 F.2d 817, 26 LRRM 2203 (3d Cir., 1950).

apparently does not relieve the employer from the statutorily imposed obligation to bargain collectively.[127]

A brief study of the unfair labor practice disputes decided by the NLRB in recent years under Section 8 (b) (as recorded in the *NLRB Digest*) confirms the thought that the majority of the practices involved may also be in contention in cases where damages, injunctions, or decrees directing arbitration are sought in state courts under state statutes. Many will, therefore, be "arguably" within the jurisdiction of the NLRB. Hence certain state courts will hold that they do not have jurisdiction, and others will undertake to decide the disputes that come to them concerning interference with production. Some of these latter decisions will be reversed.

The 1959 amendments to Section 8 (b) (4) of the National Labor Relations Act, forbidding unions to cause any person to refuse to handle the products of any other producer and providing against "hot-cargo" contracts and secondary boycotts, have widened the potential scope of federal action against unfair labor practices by unions. It would seem that this widening is likely to create more situations in which it may be "arguable" that the state will be without jurisdiction because of the need for prior NLRB decision. The confusion which may well continue to result from this, with expense and delay, is illustrated by *Hanna Mining Co.* v. *District 2, Marine Engineers Association*.[128] In that case the NLRB had refused to order a representation election, the regional director had refused to issue a complaint asserting illegal picketing, and the General Counsel had sustained such action.[129] All this was based on the assumed fact that the workers concerned were supervisors and hence not within the decisional competence of the Board. The Wisconsin Supreme Court nevertheless expressed the opinion that the picketing conduct of the Engineers' Association was *arguably* an unfair labor practice within the juris-

---

127 See Superior Engraving Co. v. NLRB, 183 F.2d 783, 26 LRRM 2351, 2534 (7th Cir., 1950) , *cert. denied*, 340 U.S. 930, 27 LRRM 2418 (1951) ; NLRB v. Mt. Clemens Pottery Co., 147 F.2d 262, 16 LRRM 502 (6th Cir., 1945) ; E. G. Conn., Ltd. v. NLRB, 108 F.2d 390, 5 LRRM 806 (1st Cir., 1939) . See also Dow Chemical Co., 152 NLRB 1150, 59 LRRM 1279 (1965) .

128 Hanna Mining Company et al v. Dist. #2 Marine Engineers' Beneficial Association, AFL-CIO et al, 382 U.S. 181, 86 S.Ct. 327, 60 LRRM 2473 (1965) .

129 Hanna Mining Company, same case in 127 N.W. 2d 393, 56 LRRM 2189 (1964) .

diction of the NLRB, and hence preempted from the authority of the state court.[130] The U. S. Supreme Court held that the actions of the NLRB, above stated, amounted to a ruling by the Board that it did not have jurisdiction, and remanded the case to the Supreme Court of Wisconsin.[131] That court sent it back to the state circuit court with directions for further proceedings "not inconsistent with the Opinion of the Supreme Court of the United States." [132] Though the power of the state court was declared by the Supreme Court not to be preempted, the question was certainly one "arguably" for the NLRB. (A good number of responsible men must have thought so.) In such a case, *Garmon* indicates there remains only the limbo of "no man's land."

Preemption — States' Authority — Picketing

While picketing seems to have long been subject to state and even local authority,[133] peaceful picketing, deemed to be within the protection of the National Labor Relations Act, may not be unduly prohibited by a state court even though such picketing is contrary to state law.[134] In *Garmon* the Supreme Court held that the California state court was preempted of jurisdiction to enjoin peaceful picketing or to assess damages against a union. The reason was that such picketing was "arguably" within the protection of Sections 7 or 8 of the National Labor Relations Act, and hence the character of the picketing must be determined by the NLRB. The majority indicated that if the Board decided that the activity was neither protected nor prohibited, or even if the Board declined jurisdiction, the states were not free to regulate such matters. Mr. Justice Frankfurter, in the minority opinion, repeated a statement which he had made in a former decision, that the

---

130 *Idem.*

131 Case cited in note 128 *supra.*

132 The Hanna Mining Co. et al v. Dist #2 Marine Engineers' Beneficial Association, AFL-CIO (1966) , 139 N.W.2d, 553 (1966) .

133 Thornhill v. Alabama, 310 U. S. 88, 6 LRRM 697 (1940) ; Senn v. Tile Layers Union, 301 U. S. 468 (1937) .

134 San Diego Bldg. Trades Council v. Garmon, 359 U. S. 236, 43 LRRM 2838 (1959) ; Garner v. Teamsters Union, 346 U. S. 485, 33 LRRM 2218 (1953) .

In one recent matter a federal court declined jurisdiction to enjoin enforcement of a city ordinance restricting distribution of handbills and requiring a license to distribute them. It required a showing of exhaustion of state court remedies before application of federal court aid. This view puts the dilemma of what to do with the "arguable" cases directly into the hands of the state courts in the first instance. United Steelworkers v. Bagwell, 239 F. Supp. 626 (W.D. N.C., 1965) .

statutory definition of what authority had been taken from the
states was "of Delphic nature" and required to be made concrete
by "the process of litigating elucidation." [135] A concurring opinion
indicated that four members of the Court would not agree that
the states should be powerless when the union activities are
"neither protected nor prohibited" by the federal Act. If such was
to be the law, they stated, "then indeed state power to redress
wrongful acts in the labor field will be reduced to the vanishing
point." [136] It may now be suggested, in view of numerous recent
cases in which state courts have refused to act because a question
was "arguably" for decision by the NLRB, that we may be approaching the vanishing point.

If violence becomes an element it seems to be the present rule
that the state has authority to award damages and to protect the
public peace.[137] Though it has been made clear that the federal
courts will generally protect peaceful picketing from unreasonable
or extreme state restrictions,[138] it was held in the case of *Carpenters*

---

[135] 359 U. S. at 241. "Delphic nature" imputes obscurity and ambiguity. Ancient
learning, from which the term derives (as well Mr. Justice Frankfurter must have
known) had the Delphic oracles uttered by a priestess (Pythia) who was seated on
a tripod above a chasm from which arose foul and noxious vapors. Inspired by
these vapors she uttered the confused-sounding oracles which required especially
trained prophets for their interpretation or translation.
All can agree the federal labor laws, taken as a whole today, are obscure and
ambiguous. They need clarification. However, legislation rather than "litigating
elucidation" would obviously get the task done sooner and better.
The previous use of this simile was in International Ass'n of Machinists v.
Gonzales, 356 U. S. 617, 619, 42 LRRM 2135 (1958).

[136] 359 U. S. at 254.

[137] See cases cited *supra* note 101. See also UAW v. Russell, 356 U. S. 634, 42
LRRM 2142 (1958); UAW v. Wisconsin Labor Relations Bd., 351 U. S. 266, 38
LRRM 2165 (1956); United Constr. Workers v. Laburnum Constr. Co., 347 U. S.
656, 34 LRRM 2229 (1954); Kohn v. Wagner, 52 CCH Lab. Cas. ¶ 51,354 (N.Y. Sup.
Ct., 1965); K & B Foam Products Co. v. Wagner, 52 CCH Lab. Cas. ¶ 51,362 (N.Y.
Sup. Ct., 1965).

[138] Thornhill v. Alabama, 310 U. S. 88, 6 LRRM 697 (1940); International
Ladies Garment Workers Union v. Hendrix, 52 CCH Lab. Cas. ¶ 51,375 (D. Ala.,
1965). But recent decisions show reluctance of state courts to act where the matter
is arguably a labor dispute within the federally preempted area of authority.
Operating Eng'rs v. Meekins, Inc., 175 So. 2d 59, 59 LRRM 2597 (Fla., 1965); Baltimore Bldg. Trades Council v. Maryland Port Authority, 238 Md. 232, 208 A.2d 564
(1965).
An Illinois court reversed a trial court which had granted an injunction against
picketing a construction job and causing secondary boycott activity, on the ground
the matter arguably required an NLRB decision. Larson & Sons, Inc. v. Radio &
Television Broadcast Eng'rs, 52 CCH Lab. ¶ 16,842 (Ill., 1965). See also Smith v.
Pittsburgh Gage & Supply Co., 245 F. Supp. 864 (W.D. Pa., 1965).

& Joiners Union v. *Ritter's Cafe*[139] that specific state statutes which
undertake to restrict peaceful picketing to the area in dispute
do not involve the use of powers preempted by the federal government. The state law of Texas was upheld. However, the nonstatutory policy of the State of Illinois to prohibit peaceful non-
employee (or "stranger") picketing was denied enforcement
because the Supreme Court concluded that elimination of such
pickets would unduly restrict "free communication." [140] Moreover,
while peaceful picketing has repeatedly been held immune from
injunctions, the immunity terminates where the picketing is preceded by a "context of violence." [141]

In the case of *Giboney* v. *Empire Storage & Ice Co.*,[142] the Supreme Court upheld the validity of state-imposed picketing bans,
apparently on the theory that a state policy against monopolistic
dominance of business should take precedence over freedom of
speech. Injunctions imposed under state laws against peaceful
picketing have been sustained where the purpose of the picketing
was the attainment of objectives not sanctioned by state policy.
Representative cases upholding state injunctions have involved
picketing to impose a system of racial quota employment,[143] to
compel self-employed persons to work only during union working
hours,[144] to obtain a union shop contract regardless of the employees' wishes,[145] and to compel an employer to put only union
members on his payroll in violation of a state right-to-work law.[146]

It seems to be sound to generalize, then, that states may enjoin:
mass picketing, threats of bodily injury or property damage, and

---

139 315 U. S. 722, 10 LRRM 511 (1942). See also Thomas v. Collins, 323 U. S. 516
(1945).
140 AFL v. Swing, 312 U. S. 321, 326, 7 LRRM 307 (1941).
One recent state decision, apparently relying in part on *Vogt*, declared broadly
that peaceful picketing may be enjoined if its purpose is to defeat a reasonable
state policy. Delaware River and Bay Authority v. Int'l Org. of Masters, Mates and
Pilots, 211 A.2d 789, 795 (N.J., 1965).
141 Milk Wagon Drivers Union v. Meadowmoor Dairies, Inc., 312 U. S. 287, 7
LRRM 310 (1941).
142 336 U. S. 490, 23 LRRM 2505 (1949).
143 Hughes v. Superior Court, 339 U. S. 460, 26 LRRM 2072 (1950). For a recent
case of similar nature see Petition of Curtis, 52 CCH Lab. Cas. ¶ 51,351 (E.D. Mo.,
1965).
144 International Bhd. of Teamsters v. Hanke, 339 U. S. 470, 26 LRRM 2076
(1950).
145 Building Service Employees v. Gazzam, 339 U. S. 532, 26 LRRM 2068 (1950).
146 Local 10, United Ass'n of Journeymen Plumbers v. Graham, 345 U. S. 192, 31
LRRM 2444 (1953).

obstruction of public ways, gates of factories, and employees' homes. They may also enjoin recurrent unannounced work stoppages and probably any picketing intended to implement them. *Milk Wagon Drivers Union* v. *Meadowmoor Dairies, Inc.*[147] expressly authorizes state injunctions against peaceful picketing after a "context of violence" has been created, and state statutes may reasonably limit picketing within an area of dispute.[148] But neither state common law nor nonstatutory policy may be enforced to exclude peaceful picketing by nonemployees, ("strangers"), in the absence of a dispute between an employer and his employees.[149] It must also be recognized that if in any of these cases, normally within the "states' authority," a contention, or perhaps even a mere suggestion, appears that an unfair labor practice may "arguably" be involved, the court may conclude, that even though state protection of the same state policy was approved in a prior case, it will now be struck down.[150] It may conclude that the primary privilege of the NLRB to decide some unfair labor concept must be preserved, even though such concept has been heretofore unknown and hence unannounced. The fact that the Board's opinions are "not wholly consistent on the meaning" of the statutes (as stated by Mr. Justice Frankfurter in the quotation above) creates a situation which invites prompt congressional clarification. This need is particularly acute since the General Counsel of the Board may refuse to accept jurisdiction and refuse to issue complaints, while at the same time state courts are frequently refusing to take substantive action upon disputes which they conclude (rightly or wrongly) are "arguably" for decision by the Board.

Mr. Justice Frankfurter, in *Teamsters Union* v. *Vogt, Inc.*,[151] sought to illuminate this area. He explained that a series of then recent cases had established that a "State, in enforcing some public

---

147 312 U. S. 287, 7 LRRM 310 (1941).

148 Carpenters Union v. Ritter's Cafe, 315 U. S. 722, 10 LRRM 511 (1942).

149 AFL v. Swing, 312 U. S., 321, 7 LRRM 307 (1941) ; Musicians' Union v. Superior Court, 64 Cal. 2nd 695 (1968), advance citation 69 A.C. 724.

150 See Weber v. Anheuser-Busch Brewing Co., 348 U. S. 468, 35 LRRM 2637 (1955), and compare Giboney v. Empire Storage and Ice Co., 336 U. S. 490, 23 LRRM 2505 (1949).

151 354 U. S. 284, 40 LRRM 2208 (1957). Some courts have refused to enjoin picketing to obtain union security contracts on the basis that their jurisdiction is restricted to consideration only of the results of execution of such agreements and putting them into effect. Kitchens v. Doe, 172 So. 2d 896 (Fla., 1965) ; Painters Union v. Joyce Floors, Inc., 398 P.2d 245 (Nev., 1965). See also Retail Clerks v.

policy, whether of its criminal or its civil law, and whether announced by its legislature or its courts, could constitutionally enjoin peaceful picketing aimed at preventing effectuation of that policy." [152] It is difficult to reconcile this statement with the facts and his statements in *Weber,* particularly when the antecedent *Giboney* opinion is called to mind. Three dissenting justices in *Vogt* seem to approve *Giboney,* but with unusual emphasis they state that after the *Vogt* opinion "state courts and state legislatures are free to decide whether to permit or suppress any particular picket line for any reason other than a blanket policy against all picketing." Neither the expressed hope of the *Vogt* majority that the law be clarified nor the feared result forecast by the minority seem to have come about in the decisions in the 12 years since the publication of *Vogt.* But the more recent *Avco,* which combined preemption and Norris-LaGuardia to exclude a state court from enjoining a strike in breach of no-strike agreement, casts doubt upon this line of decisions as to jurisdiction of the state courts.[153]

The *Garmon* opinions, delivered on April 20, 1959, do not discuss *Vogt,* which was then only two years old. They give no explanation as to whether *Garmon* is to restrict or limit whatever state authority is inferrable from *Vogt.* It is submitted that such an explanation would have been an excellent place for some of Mr. Justice Frankfurter's "litigating elucidation" since he wrote the majority opinion in both cases and was also author of *Weber* (which went unmentioned in *Vogt*).

Schermerhorn, 375 U. S. 96, 54 LRRM 2612 (1963) where the holding ignores the fact that under a right-to-work law and § 14 (b) of Taft-Hartley, the picketing could be putting pressure on the employer to enter into an agreement which would be a clear violation of both state and federal law. It does not seem to be necessary to make a concession which is itself wrong as the only means of testing an obviously unlawful demand. The legal test could be had in an appeal from an injunction which *prima facie* would be sound and that procedure would maintain matters in status quo until a final judgment could be had. If the demanded clause is of doubtful validity in its nature, the injunction should not issue.

    A number of cases, without stressing the matter of state policy involved, have held that if a union activity in question appears not to be arguably within the jurisdiction of the NLRB, it may be enjoined by the state courts. See Operating Eng'rs v. Meekins, Inc., 175 So. 2d 59 (Fla., 1960). See also *Ex parte* Ford, 236 F. Supp. 831 (E.D. Mo., 1964); Dugdale Constr. Co. v. Operative Plasterers Ass'n, 135 N.W.2d 656 (Iowa, 1965)

    152 354 U. S. at 293.

    153 Avco Corp. v. Machinists Aero Lodge #735, 390 U. S. 557, 67 LRRM 2881 (1968).

It is to be noted that the majority and the minority opinions in *Garmon* both indicated that as a result of the majority view the state courts are deprived of jurisdiction whenever it appears that a matter is "arguably" one requiring primary NLRB determination. Thus they recognize that another semi-"no man's land" is created. Even in the "arguable" case where the NLRB after consideration declines jurisdiction, the court relief that might have been available if prompt action had been possible will have been dissipated by the need to delay decision until it was determined whether the court's authority had been preempted. There exists, then, on this theory, no competent jurisdiction decision and no remedy, though a clearly defined state policy may be defeated by the challenged activity.

There may be a few instances since *Vogt* and *Garmon* where state courts have felt more confident in issuing labor injunctions, but the *Hanna Mining* case[154] may be used to show the perplexity into which the use of "arguably" leads as a test of jurisdiction. It will be remembered that in *Hanna* the matter was before the NLRB and in the courts some three years — long enough to defeat all efforts to obtain prompt relief.[155] In the *Hanna Mining Company* opinions both the state court in its apparent error and the U. S. Supreme Court in reversing, cited and apparently approved *Vogt*. The concurring opinion suggests that in many such future cases, the parties may have to visit the Supreme Court to learn whether the "aspects" of the picketing for which an injunction is sought are "primary" or "secondary," since the states may regulate only the former and have been "preempted as to the latter."

Aside from picketing, the present perplexities clouding the limits of state and federal jurisdiction are illustrated by a recent action of a Texas state court in refusing to accept jurisdiction of a suit by union members against their union for causing their discharge in that the union ordered a plant shut down contrary to the employer's orders.[156] The Texas court concluded that it was

---

154 Hanna Mining Co. v. District #2 Marine Engineers' Assn., 382 U. S. 181, 60 LRRM 2473 (1965). See note 128 *supra* this section.

155 See Hanna Mining Co. et al v. District #2 Marine Engineers' AFL-CIO 139 N.W.2d 553 (1966).

156 International Union of Operating Eng'rs v. Casida, 376 S.W.2d 814, 55 LRRM 2383 (Tex. Civ. App., 1964), *cert. denied*, 380 U. S. 955, 58 LRRM 2720 (1965).

"reasonably arguable" that the issue in question was within the jurisdiction of the NLRB. Hence the court decided it had no jurisdiction. Another state court, one judge dissenting, accepted jurisdiction over a libel suit brought by campaigners for one union against another union involved in an NLRB representation election.[157] Contrarily, and further illustrating the present unpredictability of application of law in this area, another state court held it could not decide a damage suit by a member against his own union for failure to prosecute a grievance for him.[158] The writer of the majority opinion was apparently yielding (while still in doubt) to what he felt was the somewhat obscure result of the Supreme Court's conclusions. A dissenting judge stated,

> "While this matter of federal preemption in the field of labor relations remains cloudy, I do not believe that a state court should deny its own jurisdiction where it is unable to point out a logical argument showing that the fact situation is "arguably" within the jurisdiction of the National Labor Relations Board as constituting activity which is protected or prohibited by sections 7 and 8 of the Act."[159]

There appears to have been no substantial judicial treatment of the question as to whether states have power to enjoin organizational and recognition picketing in violation of Section 8 (b) (7) of the National Labor Relations Act.[160] It seems to be a fair assumption, however, that litigants will normally seek a federal court ruling on such matters, as being "arguably" within the scope

---

157 Meyer v. Joint Council 53, Teamsters Union, 416 Pa. 401, 206 A.2d 382 (1965). The dissenting judge indicated that, in his opinion, all doubtful tort actions should be rejected as within the scope of primary NLRB authority. In Linn v. United Plant Guard Workers, 382 U. S. 912 (No. 45), 61 LRRM 2345 (1966) a district court had held against entertaining a common law suit brought by an employer against a union organizer on the ground the matter was arguably within the jurisdiction of the NLRB. The Supreme Court, by a margin of five to four, reversed and indicated that the tort libel action is one of the matters which the National Labor Relations Act left "to the states" when Congress "refrained from telling how much" else was omitted from federal preemption. The dissenters were vigorous in their condemnation, with Mr. Justice Black asserting, "this new Court-made law tosses a monkey wrench into the collective bargaining machinery Congress has set up to try to settle labor disputes. . . ." *Id.* at 665.

May one not ask if this is not in fact a court-made partial repeal of court-made law set up under *Lincoln Mills?*

158 Owens v. Vaca, 59 LRRM 2165 (Mo. App., 1965).

159 *Ibid.* (dissenting opinion). (Emphasis added.)

160 Pennsylvania state courts refused to enjoin some peaceful picketing at construction sites where the union's conduct was "arguably" protected or prohibited under the federal statutes as the NLRB might decide. Seifert & Son, Inc. v. Local 229, IBEW, 52 CCH Lab. Cas. ¶ 16,640 (Pa. C.P., 1965).

of preempted powers, though a state injunction would likely be sustained in a "context of violence" or in any situation so clearly "unprotected" conduct and an unfair labor practice that recourse to the NLRB for decision would seem to be obviously unnecessary.[161]

SECTION 3

The *Guss* Case and No Man's Land

It was of course obvious that many earlier views and supposedly well-established rules and concepts were terminated when the Wagner Act was held constitutional.[162] But even the long and revolutionary opinion in the *Jones & Laughlin* case did not forecast the full extent of change of attitude in respect to control over interstate commerce and production of goods for commerce that has evolved by way of interpretations of the Wagner Act as amended by Taft-Hartley and Landrum-Griffin.[163] In the *Jones & Laughlin* opinion, however, a number of unanswered questions appeared that may be said to have cast their shadows before them by way of presaging coming events.

In 1950 the U. S. Supreme Court held that by occupying the field of legislation to limit and control collective bargaining, and strikes in relation thereto, Congress had closed the field to state regulation and hence held that a Michigan statute inconsistent with the federal law must be declared inoperative.[164]

The wording of Section 10 (a) of the National Labor Relations Act is important. It reads as follows:

"Sec. 10 (a) The Board is empowered, as hereinafter provided, to prevent any person from engaging in any unfair labor practice (listed in Section 8) affecting commerce. This power shall not be affected by any other means of adjustment or prevention that has been or

---

161 The California Supreme Court recently vacated an order of a trial court enjoining picketing. This court indicated it would not assume authority to sustain this decree in the absence of a showing that the NLRB had specifically declined to accept jurisdiction. Russell v. IBEW, 64 Cal.2d 22, 48 Cal. Rptr. 702, 409 P.2d 926 (1966) ; see also 80 Harvard Law Review 1600.

162 NLRB v. Jones & Laughlin Steel Corp., 301 U. S. 1, 81 L. ed 893, 1 LRRM 703 (1937).

163 101. 80th Cong., 1st Sess., as amended by Public Law 902, 80th Cong., 2nd Sess. and Act of Sept. 14, 1959, P.L. 86-257, 86th Cong., 1st Sess.

164 Automobile Workers v. O'Brien, 339 U. S. 154, 26 LRRM 2082 (1950).

may be established by agreement, law, or otherwise: Provided, that
the Board is empowered by agreement with any agency of any State
or Territory to cede to such agency jurisdiction over any cases in any
industry (other than mining, manufacturing, communications, and
transportation except where predominantly local in character) even
though such cases may involve labor disputes affecting commerce,
unless the provision of the State or Territorial statute applicable to
the determination of such cases by such agency is inconsistent therewith."[165]

In 1950 the NLRB announced criteria on the basis of which it
would accept jurisdiction of labor disputes. In 1954 and in 1958
these criteria were substantially changed in amounts. The standards as of August 1, 1959, are summarized in a footnote.[166]

The U. S. Supreme Court had held in 1946 that the New York
State Labor Relations Board, operating under a state statute, was

---

[165] 49 Stat. 453, 29 U. S. Code, Sec. 160 (a) , as amended by P.L. 101, 80th Cong.,
1st Sess.

[166] The 1958 NLRB jurisdictional criteria. The August 1, 1959, NLRB Jurisdictional Standards (See LRX p. 310a) .
The jurisdictional yardstick under which the Board was operating on August 1,
1959. Under the Labor-Management Reporting and Disclosure Act of 1959, Sec. 701,
the NLRB may not refuse cases meeting these "yardsticks" — states have jurisdiction
over all cases not measuring up to NLRB tests.
GENERAL NON-RETAIL BUSINESSES—
Jurisdiction will be asserted if the yearly outflow or inflow, direct or indirect, is
$50,000 or more.
  Direct outflow, i.e., goods shipped or services furnished by employer outside
the state.
  Indirect outflow, i.e., sales within the state to users meeting jurisdictional
standards, except the indirect inflow or indirect outflow standard.
  Direct inflow, i.e., goods or services furnished directly to employer from outside
the state.
  Indirect inflow, i.e., purchase of goods or services which originated outside
employer's state, but purchased from seller within the state.
  Direct and indirect outflow can be combined to meet the $50,000 requirement.
  Direct and indirect inflow can be combined to meet the $50,000 requirement.
  Outflow and inflow cannot be combined to meet the $50,000 requirement.
OFFICE BUILDINGS —
Jurisdiction will be asserted if —
  (1) Gross yearly revenue is $100,000, provided
  (2) $25,000 of the revenue is derived from organizations which meet the juris-
dictional yardsticks, except the $50,000 indirect outflow and indirect inflow tests.
RETAIL CONCERNS —
Jurisdiction will be taken if gross yearly volume of business exceeds $500,000.
INSTRUMENTALITIES OF INTERSTATE COMMERCE —
Jurisdiction will be assumed if —
  (1) $50,000 yearly revenue is derived from interstate part of the enterprise,
or if
  (2) $50,000 yearly revenue is derived from services performed for employers
meeting jurisdictional yardsticks, except the $50,000 indirect outflow and indirect
inflow tests for non-retail businesses.

without authority to regulate any conduct within the scope of authority assumed by express words or implication in the National Labor Relations Act.[167] In this lengthy and apparently fully considered decision, the Court concluded that state action was excluded from the nature of the federal legislation and the subject matter concerned, even though the statute involved contained no express nullification of the state's authority. This view has been adhered to in subsequent decisions.[168]

With these opinions already known to the legal profession, the Garner case cannot have come as a surprise to lawyers active in the labor law field when it came down.[169] For the purpose of organizing employees of an interstate trucking company, the Teamsters Union had been picketing its loading area. No strike was involved. Drivers employed by others refused to cross the picket line and caused a considerable reduction in the business of the trucking company. The state trial court enjoined the picketing as an attempt to coerce the company to compel its employees to become members of the union. The applicable Pennsylvania statute made it an unfair labor practice for the employer to encourage or discourage membership in any labor organization by

PUBLIC UTILITIES —
  Jurisdiction will be assumed if —
    (1) Gross yearly volume of business is $250,000, or if
    (2) Yearly inflow or outflow, direct or indirect, exceeds $50,000.
TRANSIT SYSTEMS, EXCEPT TAXICABS —
  Jurisdiction assumed if gross annual business exceeds $250,000.
TAXICAB FIRMS —
  Jurisdiction assumed if the test for retail concerns is met, i.e., annual business exceeds $500,000.
NEWSPAPERS —
  Jurisdiction assumed if annual gross business exceeds $200,000.
COMMUNICATION SYSTEMS (RADIO, TELEVISION, TELEGRAPH AND TELEPHONE) —
  Jurisdiction assumed if annual gross business exceeds $100,000.
NATIONAL DEFENSE —
  Jurisdiction assumed if there is found to be a substantial impact on national defense.
HOTELS AND MOTELS, OTHER THAN RESIDENTIAL —
  Jurisdiction assumed if annual gross business exceeds $500,000. If at least 75 percent of guests have resided in hotel or motel for a month or more during the preceding year, it is deemed to be residential.

167 Bethlehem Steel Co. v. New York State Labor Relations Board, 330 U. S. 767, 19 LRRM 2499 (1946).

168 Plankington Packing Co. v. Wisconsin Employment Relations Board, 338 U. S. 953, 25 LRRM 2395 (1950).

169 Garner v. Teamster's Union, 346 U. S. 485, 33 LRRM 2218 (1953).

its hiring or tenure of employment policies. Reviewing the trial court's holding, the Supreme Court of Pennsylvania reversed and held that the issue was exclusively within the authority of the NLRB. In a unanimous opinion, the U. S. Supreme Court affirmed and agreed with the Supreme Court of Pennsylvania that the states no longer had jurisdiction in the field in question.

The *Laburnum*[170] decision was another significant one on this subject. Here the U. S. Supreme Court held that the Virginia state court had jurisdiction of a common-law tort action by an employer to recover damages from unions that took coercive action to obtain recognition, despite the fact such conduct was also an unfair labor practice under the Labor Management Relations Act. The Court explained the result by observing that Congress had not given the National Labor Relations Board exclusive jurisdiction over the type of question here concerned, since it did not provide or suggest any substitute for the common-law, traditional assessment of damages caused by tortious conduct.

In a subsequent case, an interstate railroad which engaged in hauling loaded truck trailers (piggy-back) brought an action in the Superior Court of Suffolk County Massachusetts to enjoin a labor union from conduct which interfered with such operations and which allegedly violated the Labor Management Relations Act. Employees of motor carriers with which the union had collective bargaining agreements had been persuaded by agents of the union to refrain from delivering loaded trailers to the railroad for piggy-backing. The union was not concerned in any way with the railroad's labor policy nor was there any claim that the union interfered in any manner with the railroad's employees. The Superior Court granted a permanent injunction against the Teamster's Union and the Massachusetts Supreme Judicial Court affirmed the decision. The United States Supreme Court held that the case was within the exclusive jurisdiction of the NLRB and that the railroad might seek any remedy it might have before the NLRB under the Labor Management Relations Act. It concluded that the state court had no authority to enjoin the union's conduct and reversed the judgment of the Massachusetts court.[171]

---

170 Construction Workers v. Laburnum Construction Corp., 347 U. S. 656, 34 LRRM 2229 (1954).

171 Teamster's Union v. New York, New Haven and Hartford R.R., 350 U. S. 155, 37 LRRM 2271 (1956).

In another matter bearing upon general jurisdiction, the action was brought in a Nebraska state court by employees of the Union Pacific Railroad Co. against the company and labor organizations. Plaintiffs were not members of any of the defendant labor organizations and did not desire to join. They claimed that the union-shop agreement violated the right-to-work provision of the Nebraska Constitution.[172]

The answer denied that the Nebraska Constitution and laws controlled, and alleged that the union-shop agreement was authorized by Section 2, Eleventh, of the Railway Labor Act, as amended, which provides that notwithstanding the law of "any state," a carrier and a labor organization may make an agreement requiring all employees within a stated time to become a member of the labor organization, provided there is no discrimination against any employee and provided that membership is not denied or terminated "for any reason other than the failure of the employee to tender the periodic dues, initiation fees, and assessments (not including fines and penalties) uniformly required as a condition of acquiring or obtaining membership."

The Nebraska trial court issued an injunction and the Nebraska Supreme Court affirmed. It stated: "That the union-shop agreement violates the First Amendment in that it deprives employees of their freedom of association and violates the Fifth Amendment in that it requires the members to pay for many things besides the costs of collective bargaining." The Nebraska Supreme Court, therefore, held that there is no valid federal law to supersede the "right-to-work" provision of the Nebraska Constitution. The case went to the Supreme Court of the United States on appeal. After discussing the history of the Railway Labor Act, the Supreme Court stated: "We pass narrowly on Section 2, Eleventh, of the Railway Labor Act. We only hold that the requirement for financial support for the collective bargaining agency by all who receive the benefits of its work is within the power of Congress under the Commerce Clause and does not violate either the First or

---

172 Art. XV, Sec. 13 provides: "No person shall be denied employment because of membership in or affiliation with, or resignation or expulsion from a labor organization or because of refusal to join or affiliate with a labor organization; nor shall any individual or corporation or association of any kind enter into any contract, written or oral, to exclude persons from employment because of membership in a labor organization."

Fifth Amendments. We express no opinion on the use of other conditions to secure or maintain membership in a labor organization operating under a union or closed-shop agreement." Thus, the U. S. Supreme Court reversed the decision of the Nebraska Supreme Court.[173]

Despite the foregoing decisions and numerous others emphasizing the extent of federal preemption in the labor relations field, a number of writers had apparently taken the view that if the NLRB administratively determined an area of dispute was not important enough to be given its time and attention, it should be treated as a "local aspect" of interstate commerce and should be subject to the "concurrent jurisdiction" of the states and federal authority.[174] Some states, despite the cases above mentioned, had by this time assumed that the criteria by which the NLRB rejected jurisdiction over a considerable area of comparatively minor cases, might be held to have left jurisdiction over such questions to the states.[175]

It was inevitable that the Supreme Court should sometime clearly decide whether matters rejected by the Board reverted into state jurisdiction. It did so in *Guss* v. *Utah Labor Relations Board.*[176] In this case a union had filed unfair labor practice charges against an employer and the NLRB had declined to take jurisdiction. The Utah State Labor Board undertook to grant the relief sought by the union and this action was affirmed by the state Supreme Court. The decision of the U. S. Supreme Court, however, reversed the Utah Supreme Court and emphasized that the National Labor Relations Act, Sec. 10 (a) expressly authorizes the NLRB to delegate some of its jurisdiction to agencies of the states that have labor laws in harmony with the apparent con-

---

173 Railway Employees Department v. Hanson, 351 U. S. 225, 38 LRRM 2099 (1956).

174 See Feldblum, "Jurisdictional 'Tidelands' in Labor Relations," 3 Labor L.J. 114, 116, (1952); Roumell and Schlesinger, "The Preemption Dilemma in Labor Relations," 18 University of Detroit Law Journal, 135, 141, (1954); 50 Northwestern University Law Review, 190, 204, 211 (1955).

175 Dallas General Drivers v. Jax Beer Co., 278 S.W. 2d 384, 36 LRRM 2188 (Texas 1955).

176 Guss v. Utah Labor Relations Board, 352 U. S. 817, 77 S.Ct. 65, 39 LRRM 2567 (1957); in San Diego Building Trades Council v. Garmon, 353 U. S. 951, 39 LRRM 2574 (1957), the California court had assumed jurisdiction after the NLRB had declined to act, but the U. S. Supreme Court held that exclusive jurisdiction was vested in the NLRB despite its prior ruling.

gressional policy as expressed by provisions in the Taft-Hartley Act. The Supreme Court noted that under this provision no cession of authority had been made to the Utah Labor Relations Board. Hence, it concluded Utah had no authority to act in the case at hand. In reaching its conclusion, the Court emphasized that this provision for cession of authority under a proviso added to Section 10 (a) of the National Labor Relations Act in 1947, was "the exclusive means whereby states may be enabled to act concerning the matters which Congress has intrusted to the National Labor Relations Board." The difficulty created by this decision was apparently fully appreciated by the Court, which recognized its decision would "create a vast no man's land subject to the regulation by no agency or court." It concluded, however, that this was a consequence of the statute and was a question that would have to be solved by amendment of the statute. In other words, the unfortunate situation was one created by Congress and Congress would have to remedy it. This Congress undertook to do in Section 701 of the Labor-Management Reporting and Disclosure Act of 1959.

In the *Guss* opinion, the Court expressed the view that the NLRB might considerably reduce this "area of no man's land" either by reasserting its jurisdiction more fully or by ceding jurisdiction to states where the states have labor laws in harmony with the policy of the federal statutes. However, it is significant and interesting that, while the Board did expand its acceptance of jurisdiction somewhat, it has not ceded authority to the states, and as the process for its doing this is studied, grave doubts appear as to its practicability. Who is to appraise, interpret, and apply the effect of all state statutes and decisions? Who will police these rules, principles, and standards of law so that in case they change in the future so as not to be in harmony with federal statutes, the ceded power can be withdrawn? Must the states have labor relations boards? Will it be required that every last detail of the state legislative policy be in harmony with the federal labor laws to justify this cession of authority? Must the cession be piecemeal as various cases arise? These and numerous other questions are, without doubt, thought-provoking.

A companion case decided with the *Guss* case was *Amalgamated Meat Cutters* v. *Fairlawn Meats, Inc.*[177] Here there was clearly enough activity in interstate commerce to bring the case within the jurisdiction of the NLRB. The Supreme Court held that in such a situation the district court had no authority to enjoin. It said: "It is urged in this case and its companions, however, that state action should be permitted within the area of commerce which the National Board has elected not to enter when such action is consistent with the policy of the National Act. We stated our belief in *Guss* v. *Utah Labor Relations Board* that 'Congress has expressed its judgment in favor of uniformity.' We add that Congress did not leave it to state labor agencies, state courts or to this court to decide how consistent with federal policy state law must be. The power to make that decision in the first instance was given to the National Labor Relations Board, guided by the language of the proviso to Section 10 (a). This case is an excellent example of one of the reasons why, it may be, Congress was specific in its requirement of uniformity. Petitioners here contend respondent was guilty of what would be unfair labor practices under the National Act and the outcome of proceedings before the National Board would, for that reason have been entirely different from the outcome of the proceedings in the state courts."

The NLRB, in exercising its discretion to determine the cases it will accept or decline, has never asserted its jurisdiction to the full limits. It is important that the Supreme Court in the *Guss* case and its companion decisions excluded the power of the states to assume jurisdiction in labor disputes even in the instances where the NLRB has rejected jurisdiction. There is probably no doubt that the states still have considerable authority to decide matters pertaining to disputes and disorders, torts, and criminal acts arising in connection with labor disputes. The Taft-Hartley Act expressly gives the states authority to pass and to enforce the right-to-work acts, which apparently may exclude all usual forms and degrees of union-security contracts.[178] It seems to be clear that the states may still exercise police powers to prevent offenses against the peace and dignity of the state and they may enjoin

---

177 Amalgamated Meat Cutters v. Fairlawn Meats, Inc., 353 U. S. 948, 39 LRRM 2571 (1957).
178 See Taft-Hartley Act § 14 (d).

violence, mass picketing, intimidation, and threats against employees, peaceful picketing of homes, and obstruction of factory entrances, and the like.[179] Probably the states can also enjoin sit-down strikes and strikes that assume a pattern of violence. There seems to be no doubt that the states still continue to have jurisdiction to award damages in tort cases for violent picketing, destruction of property, and the like.[180]

After the decision in the *Guss* case came down, the Illinois Circuit Court held in *Puckett Buick Co.* v. *Teamster's Union*,[181] that under the effect of the *Guss* and the *Fairlawn* cases, the state has no further jurisdiction of any action brought by an interstate employer to enjoin picketing for the apparent object of obtaining a union contract from the employer, since all questions as to whether such picketing would constitute an unfair labor practice would have to be resolved by the NLRB under the Taft-Hartley Act. The judge said: "It is my opinion from a reading of these cases that the entire field is preempted by Congress; it is preempted and the state court lacks jurisdiction. I think that the National Labor Management Act provides a comprehensive system for dealing with labor relations and dealing with unfair labor practices affecting interstate commerce."

The California Superior Court held in *McKenzie* v. *International Association of Machinists*[182] that it had no authority in a case where the company sought to enjoin the Machinists union from picketing a place of business and otherwise applying economic pressure to obtain recognition and bargaining rights. In bringing its action, the company relied upon the California law applicable to jurisdictional strikes. The court expressed its position as follows: "Whatever doubt there may have been . . . as to the jurisdiction of the State courts following the refusal of the Federal Board to assume jurisdiction 'in the first instance' was completely set at rest by the recent decisions of the Supreme Court of the United States in the Guss, Fairlawn, and Garmon cases . . . As long as the facts of a given case fall within the jurisdiction of the

---

179 See United Auto Workers v. Wis. Employment Rd. Bd., 351 U. S. 266, 38 LRRM 2165 (1956).

180 United Construction Workers v. Laburnum Corp. 347 U. S. 656, 34 LRRM 2229 (1954).

181 Puckett Buick Co. v. Teamster's Union, 39 LRRM 2753 (1957).

182 McKenzie v. International Association of Machinists, 39 LRRM 2757 (1957).

National Labor Relations Board, the Congress has completely displaced the power of the courts of this state to deal with the matter even though those same facts might otherwise give our courts jurisdiction under the jurisdictional strike act." The California court rejected the argument that it should recognize authority to award damages for losses brought about by the picketing and refused to apply the result of the *Laburnum* decision. It distinguished the latter by noting that the acts that supported the jurisdiction in respect to damages in *Laburnum* were threats to the peace of the state. This involved violent conduct and the damages were awarded under rules of torts normally applicable thereto. In this case, the court stressed the fact that the acts involved did not include violence or coercion.

Virtually all activities today involve some aspect of interstate commerce. Very few transactions of even the smallest business can be said to have no flavor at all of interstate business. In theory, the NLRB potentially would seem to have authority even over the minute interstate details of commercial flow of activity within the country. In one case the Supreme Court of the United States wrote: "It has been well settled by repeated decisions of this Court that an employer may be subject to the National Labor Relations Act although not himself engaged in commerce . . . Long before the enactment of the National Labor Relations Act it had been many times held by this court that the power of Congress extends to the protection of interstate commerce from interference or injury due to activities which are wholly intrastate."[183] Consistently with this statement in the *Fainblatt* case, a number of other decisions have expressed or assumed the federal board's authority over comparatively small local businesses.[184]

The Labor-Management Reporting and Disclosure Act of 1959 contained in the section numbered 701 a subsection (C) to be added to Section 14 of the Taft-Hartley Act which provides in effect that states shall have jurisdiction to decide cases that may arise under that section of which the NLRB declines to take jurisdiction. It also provides the Board shall not refer back to authority of

---

183 NLRB v. Fainblatt, 306 U. S. 601, 4 LRRM 535 (1938).
184 NLRB v. Gulf Public Service Co., 116 F. 2d 852, 7 LRRM 438 (1941); NLRB v. New Madrid Mfg. Co., 215 F. 2d 908, 34 LRRM 2844 (CA 8, 1954); Bogalusa Motors Co., Inc., 107 NLRB 97, 33 LRRM 1067, (1953); and Goff-McNair Motor Co., 110 NLRB 104, 35 LRRM 1104 (1954).

the states any class of cases over which it would have taken jurisdiction as of August 1, 1959.[185] To some extent, this reoccupies the
no man's land. Most states, however, do not have labor relations
boards or other official bodies to decide the issues so returned to
their jurisdiction. It may, therefore, be assumed that the state
courts will have jurisdiction over such labor questions as reach
them and that some of the disputes rejected by the Board may be
the subjects of arbitration.

---

[185] For a summary of the criteria in effect on August 1, 1959, see note 166 *supra*.

CHAPTER III

SELECTION OF ARBITRATORS — THEIR QUALIFICATIONS, JURISDICTION, AND COMPENSATION

SECTION 1

Selection of Arbitrators

Parties to labor disputes have followed numerous methods in the selection of arbitrators, arbitrational boards, and umpires. Some of the most commonly used and frequently satisfactory methods are described below.

1. Agreement in an annual or long-term contract that a certain named person shall act as arbitrator or umpire if the parties find themselves in dispute in connection with any question arising under the contract during its term of effectiveness. Arbitrators or umpires so appointed are often, somewhat misleadingly, called "permanent arbitrators" or "permanent umpires." In this situation, the parties should obtain, as far as possible, knowledge concerning the honesty, ability, impartiality, and availability of the party named to act. A check should be made to ascertain whether he has personal connections or obligations that are likely, in any case, to sway his judgment to favor one of the parties, even in circumstances in which his honesty is not questioned, but where his unconscious prejudices may in some way affect his conclusions.[1]

---

[1] See Wolff, Crane, and Cole, "The Chrysler-U.A.W. Umpire System," at p. 111 in The Arbitrator and the Parties, Proceedings of the Eleventh Annual Meeting, National Academy of Arbitrators, (Washington: BNA Books, 1958), and Alexander, "Impartial Umpireships: The G.M.-U.A.W. Experience" at p. 108 in Arbitration and the Law, Proceedings of the Twelfth Annual Meeting, National Academy of Arbitrators (Washington: BNA Books, 1959).

As all know, it is difficult for a man to rule against his preconceptions or self-interest. It is even harder for a man identified as a union leader to hold against a union, or an industry spokesman to decide against an employer. In such cases, to the pressures of probably established beliefs concerning equities in the economic struggle are added fears of being suspected of disloyalty to persons who in general have similar interests and objectives. Obviously, this furnished the reason for having "public" members on the National War Labor Board and on its numerous panels during World War II. See note 4, *infra.*

There have been a considerable number of instances where a neutral permanent umpire has been selected for an entire industry or for a group of related industries.[2] This process is usually satisfactory for a time, assuming the impartiality, honesty, and ability of the arbitrator or umpire. Experience clearly indicates that there is a considerable recurrence of various types of disputes in relation to a given industry and even in relation to individual manufacturing plants or other mercantile establishments. A permanent umpire or arbitrator, if maintained in office for a substantial period of time, has an opportunity to become intimately acquainted with all of the pros and cons of such disputes, and in the light of experience, is more likely to produce logical, convincing, and satisfactory results than the *ad hoc* arbitrator whose experience may be limited to unrelated and scattered cases.[3]

2. *Agreement by the parties to submit an existing dispute to a named arbitrator or umpire for an award.* Persons designated to act on a single issue are likely to be referred to as *ad hoc* arbitrators. Here, obviously, the same precautions should be taken as in paragraph 1 above, but the importance of the investigation of the proposed arbitrator may perhaps be somewhat less extensive since he is to act only in the single dispute or hearing in respect to which he is named.

3. *An agreement in an annual or term contract that in case any dispute passes through all the grievance stages and requires arbitration, a certain designated party, such as the Director of the Federal Mediation and Conciliation Service,[4] the American Arbitration Association, a judge, or some other presumably neutral third person, shall name the arbitrator or furnish a list from which the*

---

2 This practice seems to be increasing. It is now found in some relatively small firms' labor contracts. See Arbitration Provisions in Union Agreements, Bulletin No. 780 (Washington: U. S. Dept. of Labor, 1944). For illustrations, see Collective Bargaining Negotiations and Contracts (Washington: The Bureau of National Affairs, Inc.). For an employer's view, see Hill and Hook, Management at the Bargaining Table, pp. 73-87 (New York: McGraw-Hill Book Co., 1945).

3 See Alexander, "Impartial Umpireships," at p. 108, Arbitration and the Law, Proceedings of the Twelfth Annual Meeting, National Academy of Arbitrators (Washington: BNA Books, 1959); Fredman, "Umpire System — A High Court for Grievances," 44 Commerce Magazine (1948).

4 When appointment of an impartial arbitrator is requested, letters may be addressed to the Director of the Federal Mediation and Conciliation Service, U. S. Department of Labor, Washington, D. C., or to the General Counsel of that Service, who is also Chief of the Arbitration Division.

arbitrator shall be chosen by the parties. If the parties agree that a United States district judge, the mayor, or other prominent official shall appoint the arbitrator, they will almost certainly obtain inexperienced arbitrators, chosen from the ranks of local lawyers, school teachers, or preachers. For the settlement of minor controversies, where no great feeling has been aroused, this can turn out to be satisfactory; but when an important or difficult issue develops, with perhaps the future welfare of the entire community dependent upon a sound and wise solution made in the light of a thorough knowledge of the difficult field of labor relations, the result could be disastrous. Today, the principal appointing agencies are the Federal Mediation and Conciliation Service and the American Arbitration Association. During World War II it was a common practice for arbitrators to be appointed by the National War Labor Board and the various regional war labor boards. All of these agencies prepared lists of names of men of proven ability and experience, and endeavored to make unbiased appointments; all were generally successful in satisfying the parties,[5] but occasionally they were unsuccessful. Where the parties cannot agree on any active agency as the appointing power, they usually request one of them to furnish a list of available men; the arbitrator is then chosen by the parties from that list. Central clearing files of information concerning available men most often named by these agencies are understood to be maintained by various employer and employee organizations such as the National Association of Manufacturers, state merchants' and manufacturers' associations, the AFL-CIO, various international unions, and some firms that offer a "service" of such information. If these organizations keep such lists on complete and impartial bases, they can be very useful. But if, as may be the tendency, reports are made only to register complaints, and never satisfaction, the results must be worthless, for no arbitrator can avoid, at some time or other, complaint from a losing party.

4. An agreement in a special submission of a single issue or dispute that a certain designated party such as the Director of the Federal Mediation and Conciliation Service or the American Arbitration Association shall name the arbitrator or furnish a list from

---

[5] See Braun, The Settlement of Industrial Disputes, pp. 147-148 (Philadelphia: Blakiston Co., 1944).

which the arbitrator shall be chosen by the parties.[6] Here again, for the reasons stated above, the experience and a knowledge of competent men possessed by the appointing officer are relied upon because of the confidence of the parties that that official will furnish a well-informed and impartial person who will be satisfactory to them.

5. *A provision in a contract that each party will name one (or two or three) to a board of arbitration, and that the arbitrators named by the parties will elect an additional neutral person, usually to act as chairman, and sometimes to act as "umpire."* These provisions usually do, and in all cases should, provide that if the arbitrators named by the parties cannot in a specified length of time agree upon the additional neutral member, either party shall have authority to call upon the Director of the Federal Mediation and Conciliation Service, the American Arbitration Association, or some other neutral agency for the appointment of the additional member or for a list from which the parties may make a selection. In the absence of this latter provision, it is entirely possible for the designated arbitrators themselves to become dead-locked upon the selection of the odd or neutral member.[7]

The term "umpire" is sometimes used to designate a party who is selected under the authority of the submission to decide the dispute when the board of arbitrators are unable to agree or are evenly divided.[8] In a sense, he may become the sole arbitrator of the issue originally submitted, and be bound to act accordingly. It is not necessary that any of the original arbitrators concur with him to make his decision valid and binding.[9]

In some instances, the men whom the parties have appointed as "arbitrators" according to their custom and understanding are not expected to decide anything or to participate in the decision or

---

6 See Rule 12, Voluntary Labor Arbitration Rules of the American Arbitration Association, reprinted in Appendix E of this book.

7 See Allen-Bradley Co. v. Anderson & Nelson Distilleries Co., 99 Ky. 311, 35 S.W. 1123 (1896) ; Day v. Hammond, 57 N.Y. 479, 15 Am. Rep. 522 (1874) ; Chandos v. American Fire Ins. Co., 84 Wis. 184, 54 N.W. 390, 19 L.R.A. 321 (1893).

8 Day v. Hammond, 57 N.Y. 479, 15 Am. Rep. 522 (1874) ; Chandos v. American Fire Ins. Co., 84 Wis. 184 N.W. 390 (1893).

9 Hartford Fire Ins. Co. v. Bonner Mercantile Co. (C.C.), 44 Fed. 151, 11 L.R.A. 623 (1890) ; Haven v. Winnisimmet Co., 11 Allen (Mass.) 377, 87 Am. Dec. 723 (1865) ; Day v. Hammond, 57 N.Y. 479, 15 Am. Rep. 522 (1874).

award.[10] When the chairman or impartial arbitrator is appointed, these so-called "arbitrators" appear before him as attorneys or spokesmen for their respective constituents and, through presentation of evidence and arguments to him, seek to obtain his adherence to the view of the side that made their appointments. It is a misnomer to call their parties "arbitrators." Such designation somewhat unnecessarily complicates the procedure. It would greatly simplify the proceedings in such cases to recognize them as representatives in arbitration or call them by some other title, to acknowledge throughout the proceedings that the matter in dispute is to be submitted to the impartial party appointed independently of the contending parties, and to proceed upon the agreement that he is to act as sole arbitrator.

This avoids the requirement that the award shall be supported by a majority of the arbitrators to be final and binding. And in the type of situation above described, it may well occur that the so-called arbitrators appointed by the respective sides will be adamant in their adherence to the contentions of their respective constituents.[11] In such case, the impartial arbitrator is relatively helpless to select a course not dictated by the extreme view of either the one side or the other. It is perhaps best, if the parties insist upon calling their respective appointees arbitrators, to make it clear that the impartial member to be selected by them, or appointed by an outside authority, shall act as "umpire," or that the members of the board appointed by the parties are not "arbitrators" in the proper sense of the term.

6. *Sometimes the agreement provides that in case the necessity for arbitration of the controversy arises, each party shall furnish to the other a list of proposed arbitrators from which the other shall be entitled to strike out names until a person is discovered who is mutually satisfactory.* This process is often unproductive

---

10 See p. 143 *et seq.*, The Profession of Labor Arbitration, Selected Papers From the First Seven Annual Meetings, National Aacademy of Arbitrators' (Washington: BNA Books, 1957) ; this is particularly obvious when a union or company appoints one of its own officers or its legal adviser as frequently occurs.

11 Such appointees are often frank in stating that they have been appointed to vote for certain result and will do so regardless of any adverse evidence or arguments that may be presented at the hearing. Some of the state statutes provide that all abitrators shall be "disinterested" or "unbiased." The presence on an arbitration board of one who does not comply with such an act certainly impairs the validity of the entire proceeding where such a statute applies.

because of the likelihood that each party in constructing a list to furnish to the other is somewhat too likely to make careful selection of those prejudiced to the side of the writer of the list. In all probability, these prejudices are known to the other party, and cause him to strike out all names. Where this method is used, it should be supplemented by an additional provision to the effect that if, after the submission of names, no agreement has been reached within a stipulated time, either party shall be authorized to call upon a neutral official source such as the Director of the Federal Mediation and Conciliation Service or the American Arbitration Association to designate an arbitrator whom both parties shall be bound to accept or to furnish a short list from which the parties may make a choice by the well-known process of alternately striking names until all unacceptable names are off or only one remains.[12]

SECTION 2
Qualifications of Arbitrators

Arbitrators may be said to fall into two general classes: professional (or semiprofessional), and amateur. Though arbitration of labor disputes has only in recent years come into wide use, a rather large body of part-time and full-time professional labor arbitrators is now available. They are to be found in all the large centers of population and many are scattered among smaller cities and towns from coast to coast. Some of these have acquired such experience that they may truly be termed "professional," to distinguish them from those whose experience has been limited to only a few, occasional matters.

The field of labor relations, with its deep and illuminating historical background, its complexities in modern industrial society, its deep-seated animosities, and its own peculiar terminology, is so vast a study in itself and so great a mystery to the average citizen that the finding of a *competent* amateur is next to impossible. The very words which roll so easily off the tongues of personnel directors and union men, *e.g.*, checkoff, Dobie, preferential shop, Chinese overtime, split shift, stretch-out, night-shift differential, spare hand, posting and bidding, maintenance of membership, and escape clause, are meaningless to the uninitiated. The amateur arbi-

---

12 Many existing contracts so provide. At times, parties request the Federal Mediation and Conciliation Service to appoint a specified arbitrator, if available.

trator who has a sufficient familiarity with the subject to be of real value to the parties will almost inevitably be a social worker or minister who has labored with factory employees, a lawyer who has represented industry or labor in contract negotiations or disputes, or a retired industrial relations manager. Regardless of how fair, honest, or competent such men may be, their backgrounds may be viewed by one party or the other as disqualifying them.

A particular issue in dispute may be so simple that the parties will consider it unnecessary to have an arbitrator who is familiar with the field of labor problems. In such cases they may pick an amateur from outside the classes suggested above, and in some cases he may do a creditable job. But companies and unions which engage in frequent arbitration have come to rely chiefly on the professional arbitrators. In the long run, they obtain more satisfactory results from the experienced service thus procured.

Most professional and semiprofessional arbitrators are lawyers or men with considerable legal training, though there are a few notable exceptions — men who have had no legal experience beyond that gained in holding arbitration proceedings where the parties are represented by attorneys. The past experiences of union negotiators with lawyers employed by companies for the purpose of blocking negotiations, rather than of consummating them, have given rise to a certain amount of distrust of the profession. While it can hardly be denied that legal training is advantageous to a man who is to be responsible for settling important controversies in a manner that will not be open to legal attack, it cannot be denied that the wrong type of lawyer makes a poor arbitrator. The man who is so concerned with technical rules of procedure and evidence that he cannot permit the parties to present to him a complete picture of the background and underlying cause of a bitter dispute may render an award that will be not only technically perfect but also a logical resolution of the immediate controversy. But he is not likely to take fully into account the desirability of rendering an award based on gradually developing social convictions as well as legal concepts — that is, one calculated to cure those underlying animosities that precipitated the specific dispute. In so far as he fails to do so, within the limits of the facts and justice of the specific issue, he will fail to render the complete service that could have been given by one not hidebound by outmoded concepts.

One experienced arbitrator, a judge, has said that there is nothing more to arbitrating than to judging; that it calls for the same sort of expertise; and that only those qualified to be judges are qualified to be arbitrators.[13] Other scholars experienced both in jurisprudence and labor arbitration have taken issue with this statement.[14] Mr. Justice Douglas in the majority opinion in *Steelworkers* v. *Warrior & Gulf Navigation Co.* said:

> "The labor arbitrator is usually chosen because of the parties' confidence in his knowledge of the common law of the shop and their trust in his personal judgment to bring to bear considerations which are not expressed in the contract as criteria for judgment. The parties expect that his judgment of a particular grievance will reflect not only what the contract says but, insofar as the collective bargaining agreement permits, such factors as the effect upon productivity of a certain result, its consequences to the morale of the shop, his judgment whether tensions will be heightened or diminished. . . . The ablest judge cannot be expected to bring the same expertise and competence to bear upon the determination of a grievance, because he cannot be similarly informed."[15]

On the other hand, if the arbitrator is possessed of good common sense, a basic knowledge of the problems of labor and of management, and sound judgment, a knowledge of law will often enable him to find legal and logical bases to justify an award that is demanded by practical as well as ethical considerations.[16]

What has been said above is not to be taken as an attempt to justify any disregard of the clear legal rights of the parties. Where the parties have executed a contract, the meaning of a clause is in dispute, and such clause can in fact and in law have only one meaning, the arbitrator is bound so to hold, regardless of how unjust to a particular individual such holding may appear or how illadvised the agreement may have been. A frequent complaint made of lawyers as arbitrators is that they fail to take into account the "human element" — the developing social concepts previously referred to. Perhaps such criticism is sometimes justified. But too

13 Wallen, Saul, Arbitrators and Judges . . . Dispelling the Hays' Haze (1965).
14 Fuller, Lon L., Collective Bargaining and the Arbitrator, Collective Bargaining and the Arbitrator's Role, Proceedings of the Fifteenth Annual Meeting, National Academy of Arbitrators, (Washington: BNA Books, 1962), p. 17.
15 United Steelworkers of America v. Warrior and Gulf Navigation Co., 363 U. S. 574, 581, 80 S.Ct. 1347, 46 LRRM 2416 (1960).
16 Garrett, Sylvester, The Role of Lawyers in Arbitration, Arbitration and Public Policy, Proceedings of the Fourteenth Annual Meeting, National Academy of Arbitrators, (Washington: BNA Books, 1961) p. 102.

often that criticism is merely the result of an award that gives effect only to contract obligations voluntarily assumed by the parties. No arbitrator has a legal or moral right to alter or ignore the contract that the parties have themselves made. An amateur, especially if he has no legal training, is rather too prone to commit that fault and to attempt some unauthorized pioneering in respect to what he may deem to be an idealistic relationship of the parties — a sure way to court disaster.

It is always assumed that the parties selected shall act without partisanship or bias.[17] If it transpires, therefore, that an arbitrator has a selfish interest in the question in respect to which he undertook to act, or if he was previously committed to support the contentions of one of the parties, he is disqualified. However, mere knowledge of the subject upon which he is to pass, assuming that his mind is open, will not impair the validity of his award.[18] Friendship, previous business associations, or even the status of being a creditor[19] of one of the parties, will not necessarily disqualify an arbitrator, provided there is no question of fraud or misconduct, interest, or bias in his reaching his award.[20] A warning should be given at this point, however, that if a party with full knowledge that a person nominated to be arbitrator is an employee of the other, agrees that such nominee shall act as arbitrator,[21] he will be bound by the award, despite a later claim of prejudice based upon the relationship of which he had previous knowledge. Thus, if a labor organization should agree that the personnel manager of the employer, the president of the company, or the chairman of the

---

[17] Morville v. American Tract Soc., 123 Mass. 129, 25 Am. Rep. 40 (1877); Kelly v. Trimont Lodge, 154 N.C. 97, 69 S.E. 764 (1910); Brodhead-Garrett Co. v. Davis Lumber Co., 97 W.Va. 165, 124 S.E. 600 (1924).

[18] Morville v. American Tract Soc., 123 Mass. 129, 25 Am. Rep. 40 (1877); Brush v. Fisher, 70 Mich. 46., 38 N.W. 446, 14 Am. St. Rep. 510 (1888); Martin v. Vansant, 99 Wash. 106, 168 Pac. 990 (1917).

[19] Ross v. German Alliance Ins. Co., 86 Kans. 145, 352, 119 Pac. 366 (1911); Continental Ins. Co. v. Vallandingham, 116 Ky. 287, 76 S.W. 22, 105 Am. St. Rep. 218 (1903); Morville v. American Tract Soc., 123 Mass. 129, 25 Am. Rep. 40 (1877); Goodrich v. Hulbert, 123 Mass. 190, 25 Am. Rep. 60 (1877).

[20] Texas Eastern Transmision Co. v. Barnard, 177 Fed. Supp. 123 (1959); National Fire Ins. Co. v. O'Bryan, 75 Ark. 198, 87 S.W. 129 (1905); Rand v. Redington, 13 N.H. 72, 38 Am. Dec. 475 (1847); Longshoremen (ILWU), Local 13 v. Pacific Maritime Association, 278 F.Supp. 755 (D.C. Cal., 1967); Arrow Lacquer Corporation v. Zitolo, 159 N.Y.L.J. 2 (1968).

[21] Williams v. Chicago. S.F. & C. R. Co., 112 Mo. 463, 20 S.W. 631, 34 Am. St. Rep. 403 (1892); Nelson v. Atlantic Coast Line R. Co., 157 N.C. 194, 72 S.E. 998 (1911).

board of directors, should be authorized to take final action upon a grievance as "arbitrator," it would find itself bound by his decision in many states, despite his known interest and bias in respect to some of the matters which might be in dispute.

The parties by their submission agreement have full authority in most jurisdictions to designate the qualifications of arbitrators to be appointed.[22] Thus, if they authorize some party in an official position to appoint a person of a given profession or of specified experience, an appointee who does not meet the required qualifications will not have authority to act.[23] Where statutory qualifications are provided, such as residence within the state, disinterestedness, or membership in a stated profession, no person lacking such qualifications can make a binding award in a proceeding under the statutes.[24]

SECTION 3

Limitations Upon the Arbitrator's Authority

The authority of arbitrators must be found in the submission agreement.[25] They must conform to it, and they have no authority to go beyond its terms or to consider matters not clearly embraced within it.[26] This fact sometimes makes it necessary for an arbitrator to scan carefully the limits of the submission agreement and the collective bargaining contract under which he is acting so as to ascertain the validity of his own appointment and the scope of

---

[22] Western Assur. Co. v. Hall, 120 Ala. 547, 24 So. 936, 74 Am. St. Rep. 48 (1898); Continental Ins. Co. v. Vallandingham, 116 Ky. 287, 76 S.W. 22, 105 Am. St. Rep. 218 (1903); Martin v. Vansant, 99 Wash. 106, 168 Pac. 990 (1917).

[23] American Cent. Ins. Co. v. District Ct., 125 Minn. 374, 147 N.W. 242 (1914).

[24] Produce Refrigerating Co. v. Norwich Union Fire Ins. Soc., 91 Minn. 210, 97 N.W. 875 (1903).

[25] Steinberg v. D. L. Horowitz, Inc., 25 N.Y.S. (2d) 630 (1941); Platt v. Aetna Ins. Co., 153 Ill. 113, 38 N.E. 580, 46 Am. St. Rep. 877 (1894); Swisher v. Dunn, 89 Kans. 412, 131 Pac. 571 (1913); Brescia Constr. Co. v. Walart Constr. Co., 264 N.Y. 260, 190 N.E. 484 (1934); Graham v. Graham, 9 Pa. 254, 49 Am. Dec. 557 (1848); Sley System Garages v. Transport Workers, Local 700, 406 Pa. 370, 178 A.2d 560 (1962).

[26] Amsterdam Dispatch, Inc., et al. v. Devery, 5 N.Y.S. (2d) 427, 2 LRRM 806 (1938); Hemingway v. Stansell, 106 U. S. 399, 27 L.Ed. 245, 1 S.Ct. 473, 10 L.R.A. 826 (1882); Dunton v. Westchester Fire Ins. Co., 104 Me. 372, 71 A. 1037 (1909); Electrical Workers, Local 791 v. Magnavox Co., 286 F.2d 465, 47 LRRM 2296, 2571 (1960); Textile Workers, Local 1386 v. American Thread Co., 291 F. 2d 894, 48 LRRM 2534 (1961); Local 295, International Union of Operating Engineers v. Koldrite Corporation, 53 LRRM 2053 (1963); Lee v. Olin Mathieson Chemical Corp., 271 F.Supp. 635 (W.D. Va., 1967).

his own authority. In the last analysis, however, the arbitrator's decision upon these matters may not be final.[27] The award upon one of these questions may be challenged by either of the parties in court and the interpretation of the submission agreement made by a judge.[28] The U. S. Supreme Court in three companion arbitration cases,[29] placed limits upon the power of the courts by stating that they are not to get into the merits of the dispute; that they are not to substitute their judgment for that of the arbitrator; and that they are not to refuse to order the parties to arbitrate because in their opinion a claim is frivolous or baseless. But the Court did not extend the authority of the arbitrator beyond its well-established limits. In the *Enterprise* case the Court stated:

> "Nevertheless an arbitrator is confined to interpretation and application of the collective bargaining agreement; he does not sit to dispense his own brand of industrial justice. He may of course look for guidance from many sources, yet his award is legitimate only so long as it derives its essence from the collective bargaining agreement."[30]

From the foregoing, it becomes obvious that a shrewd trader bargaining at the time when the submission agreement is being drawn up may cause it to be so phrased that the arbitrator will have great difficulty in finding against his contentions. For example, if the question submitted is whether a certain group of incentive wages was fixed "in accordance with sound business practices" and "after proper time studies," the arbitrator is likely to find himself limited to either affirmation or negation of that question, with little or no discretion in which to make an award in respect to the ultimate fairness of the wage system in operation. Again, if the

---

27 Joseph Goldstein v. International Ladies Garment Workers' Union, 328 Pa. 385, 1-A LRRM 728 (Pa. Sup. Ct., E. District, 1938) ; Colombia v. Cauca Co., 190 U. S. 524, 47 L.Ed. 1159, 23 S.Ct. 704 (1902) ; Swisher v. Dunn, 89 Kans. 412, 131 Pac. 571 (1913) ; Halstead v. Seaman, 82 N.Y. 27 Am. Rep. 536 (1880) ; Underwood Corp. v. Electrical Workers, Local 267, 183 F.Supp. 205, 46 LRRM 3031 (D.C. Conn., 1960) .

28 Towne v. Jaquith, 6 Mass. 46, 4 Am. Dec. 84 (1809) ; Sweet v. Morrison, 116 N.Y. 19, 22 N.E. 276, 15 Am. St. Rep. 376 (1889) ; Hunn v. Pennsylvania Inst., 221 Pa. 403, 70 A. 812 (1908) ; Electrical Workers (IBEW) , Local 2130 v. Bally Case and Cooler, Inc., 232 F.Supp. 394, 56 LRRM 2831 (D.C. Pa., 1964) .

29 United Steelworkers of America v. American Manufacturing Co., 363 U. S. 564, 80 S.Ct. 1343, 46 LRRM 2414 (1960) ; United Steelworkers of America v. Warrior and Gulf Navigation Co., 363 U. S. 574, 80 S.Ct. 1347, 46 LRRM 2416 (1960) ; United Steelworkers of America v. Enterprise Wheel and Car Corp., 363 U. S. 593, 80 S.Ct. 1358, 46 LRRM 2423 (1960) .

30 United Steelworkers of America v. Enterprise Wheel and Car Corp., 363 U. S. 593, 597, 80 S.Ct. 1358, 46 LRRM 2423 (1960) .

question is put to the arbitrator, "Can the employer afford to grant a two weeks' paid vacation to his employees?", the arbitrator is restricted to an analysis of the financial condition of the employer and to the vague question of what he can "afford." He has no authority to pass upon other important questions bearing upon vacation rights. Nor has he authority to determine that, while the employer cannot afford a two-week paid vacation, he can perhaps afford one week or a shorter period of paid vacation. Likewise, if the question submitted was, "Did John Doe's conduct constitute insubordination on the occasion of his discharge?", the arbitrator may pass only upon the conduct and words spoken at the time, and he may have no authority in respect to giving fair and judicial consideration to the antecedent surrounding circumstances. It sometimes happens that the parties in dispute over wages fail to authorize the arbitrator to give retroactive effect to the wage award. Without express authority to take that step, the arbitrator is exceeding his powers if he attempts to award "back wages."

The above are but a few of the situations in which the too-restricted submission eliminates possibility of effective arbitration from the beginning. It should be added that during the course of arbitration the parties by mutual agreement may amend a submission to give the arbitrator more extensive authority, or, on the other hand, they may by mutual agreement restrict the authority to eliminate the possibility of the arbitrator passing upon one of the points originally submitted or handing down an award which amounts to a compromise between the two parties.[31] Such modifications often occur at the beginning of labor arbitrational hearings.

If the submission provides that the arbitrator shall hear and consider only a limited type of evidence, he is restricted to such procedure.[32] In the case of a broad and general submission, however, arbitrators have broad and general authority and are likely to act more effectively in the interest of all parties than where narrow restrictions are imposed.[33] The arbitrators may decide whether

[31] Wilkinson v. Prichard, 145 Iowa 65, 123 N.W. 964 (1909); Graham v. Graham, 9 Pa. 254, 49 Am. Dec. 557 (1848).

[32] Galbraith v. Lunsford, 87 Tenn. 89, 9 S.W. 365 (1888).

[33] Jacob v. Pacific Export Lumber Co., 136 Or. 622, 297 Pac. 848 (1931); Brodhead-Garrett Co. v. Davis Lumber Co., 97 W.Va. 165, 124 S.E. 600 (1924); Chandos v. American Fire Ins. Co., 84 Wis. 184, 54 N.W. 390 (1893).

particular evidence shall be admitted or excluded, and may give all evidence considered such weight as in their honest judgment it is entitled to have.[34] They are not bound by technical court rules in respect to procedure, and they have wide discretionary powers as to the order in which evidence shall be received, the manner in which it may be presented, the question whether the hearing shall be held at the scene of the operation that may be in question, etc.[35]

While the authority of the arbitrator is limited by the submission agreement, it is also subject to other limitations or restrictions, such as during World War II, when under the Stabilization Act an increase in compensation awarded was not binding until approved by the National War Labor Board. In the same period an award interpreting Executive Order 9240 was required to conform to the rulings made by the Secretary of Labor. Clearly, the parties selecting an arbitrator or an umpire could not confer upon him any authority to fix wages or working conditions beyond their own powers to fix by contract.[36] It is incumbent upon the arbitrators, however, to exercise as fully as possible all of the authority granted to them in the sense that they should attempt to take final and complete action upon all matters submitted and leave no conclusions in hypothetical, conditional, or unfinished form.[37]

---

[34] Re Curtis & Castle, 64 Conn. 501, 30 A. 769, 42 Am. St. Rep. 200 (1894); Roberts v. Consumers Can Co., 102 Md. 362, 62 A. 585, 111 Am. St. Rep. 377 (1905); Hollingsworth v. Leiper, 1 Dall. (U. S.) 161, 1 L.Ed. 82 (1786); Electrical, Radio and Machine Workers, Local 116 v. Minneapolis-Honeywell Regulator Co., 48 CCH Lab. Cas. No. 18, 708 (D.C. Pa., 1963).

[35] Sturges, Commercial Arbitrations and Awards, p. 381 (Kansas City: Vernon Law Book Co., 1930); Kellor, Arbitration in Action, pp. 22, 30 et seq. (New York Harper & Bros., 1941); Harvey Aluminum, Inc. v. Steelworkers, 263 F.Supp. 488, 64 LRRM 2580 (D.C. Cal., 1967).

[36] Braun, The Settlement of Industrial Disputes, p. 193 (Philadelphia: Blakiston Co., 1944). An arbitration agreement cannot divest the National Labor Relations Board of jurisdiction. Newspaper Enterprises v. Stern, 105 N.Y. L. J. 2850, 8 LRRM 1082 (1941). The parties could not authorize an arbitrator to set a wage in violation of the Fair Labor Standards Act. Voutrey, et al. v. General Baking Co., 39 F.Supp. 974, 1 WH Cases 616 (1941); Bailey v. Karolyna Co. Ltd., 50 F.Supp. 142, 3 WH Cases 257 (U. S. Dist. Ct., N.Y., 1943). Nor could they confer upon an umpire authority to order a union security clause except in compliance with statutory and constitutional provisions concerning the same. E.g., Wis. Employment Relations Act (1941), Sec. 111.06 (c), and see Kearney v. Washtenaw Mutual Fire Ins. Co., 126 Mich. 246, 85 N.W. 733 (1901), Avco Corp. v. Preteska, 43 CCH Lab. Cas. No. 17,261 (Super.Ct. Conn., 1961). (See 37 LA 320.)

[37] Johnson v. Noble, 13 N.H. 286, 38 Am. Dec. 485 (1847); Murphy v. Greenberg, 246 Pa. 387, 92 A. 511 (1914); Smith v. Potter, 27 Vt. 304, 65 Am. Dec. 198 (1855); Lee Co. v. New Haven Printing Pressmen, Local 74, 248 F.Supp. 289, 61

The submission agreement may expressly require that the arbitrator set forth the reasons for awards, or that the arbitrators furnish full and complete findings of facts. Where such specifications exist, they must be observed.[38]

Another limitation upon the power of the arbitrator is found in the fact that according to common law, as observed in Chapter I hereof, his authority to act may be terminated by the parties at any time before the award is made.[39] This, however, does not mean that the authority may be revoked by one party under the statutory laws of all states without concurrence of the other, contrarily to a collectively bargained agreement, except upon such penalties as are suitable for breach of contract.[40] It sometimes happens that without revocation, or where for some other reason the parties are legally bound to proceed with arbitration, one party will fail to participate in a hearing.[41] In such case, the arbitrator may proceed to hold an *ex parte* hearing, taking the evidence of the parties who appear, and make an award accordingly.[42] Before proceeding to hold an *ex parte* hearing, it is highly important for the arbitrator to be sure that his appointment is valid and in accordance with the collective bargaining agreement,[43] that due notice of the time and place of hearing has been given both parties,[44] and that an *ex parte* proceeding is within the scope

---

LRRM 2009 (D.C. Conn., 1965); Marine and Shipbuilding Workers v. American Dredging Co., 43 CCH Lab.Cas. No. 17, 240 (D.C. Pa., 1961); Overall v. Delta Refining Co., 40 CCH Lab. Cas. No. 66,486 (Tenn., 1960); Burns International Detective Agency v. New Jersey Guards Union, 64 N.J. Super. 301, 165 A. 2d 844 (1960). (See 35 LA 882.)

38 William H. Low Estate Co. v. Lederer Realty Corp., 35 R.I. 352, 86 A. 881 (1913).

39 Paulsen v. Manske, 126 Ill. 72, 18 N.E. 275, 9 Am. St. Rep. 532 (1888); Oskaloosa Sav. Bank v. Mahaska County State Bank, 205 Iowa 1351, 219 N.W. 530 (1928); Williams v. Branning Mfg. Co., 153 N.C. 7, 68 S.E. 902, 138 Am. St. Rep. 637 (1910).

40 Red Cross Line v. Atlantic Fruit Co., 264 U. S. 109, 68 L.Ed. 582, 44 S.Ct. 274 (1924); Read v. State Ins. Co., 103 Iowa 307, 72 N.W. 665, 64 Am. St. Rep. 180 (1897); Mentz v. Armenia Fire Ins. Co., 79 Pa. 478, 21 Am. Rep. 80 (1875); Martin v. Vansant, 99 Wash. 106, 168 Pac. 990 (1917).

41 See Edmunson v. Wilson, 108 Ala. 118, 19 So. 367 (1896); Harbison-Walker Refractories Co. v. Brick and Clay Workers, Local 702, 339 S.W. 2d 933, 47 LRRM 2077 (Ky., 1960).

42 See Sturges, Commercial Arbitrations and Awards, pp. 442 *et seq.* (Kansas City: Vernon Law Book Co., 1930); Garment Workers v. Senco, Inc., 69 LRRM 2142 (D.C. Mass., 1968).

43 Amalgamated Meat Cutters, Etc. v. Penobscot Poultry Co., 200 F.Supp. 879, 49 LRRM 2241 (D.C. Maine, 1961); Steelworkers v. Danville Foundry Corp., 52 LRRM 2584 (D.C. Pa., 1963).

44 Farkash v. Brach, 52 LRRM 2334 (N.Y. S.Ct., 1963).

of the arbitration agreement of the parties.[45] Otherwise, the arbitrator's award will be ineffective.[46]

While arbitrators in some sense act as judges, often with results as important to the parties as any that could be adjudicated by a court, they do not, except under statutes, have authority to subpoena witnesses, to administer oaths to them, or to order the production of written evidence.[47] In this connection, emphasis must be placed upon the propriety of avoiding identification of the arbitrator with the referee with whom he is sometimes confused.[48] The referee is an officer of the court and frequently has powers in respect to hearings that have not been legally given to arbitrators, except in some states, by statutes.[49] It has been held that an arbitrator has immunity from suit by a dissatisfied party.[50]

The authority and jurisdiction of arbitrators are entirely terminated by the completion and delivery of an award.[51] They have thereafter no power to recall the same, to order a rehearing, to amend, or to "interpret" in such manner as may be regarded as authoritative.[52] But they may correct clerical mistakes or obvious errors of arithmetical computation.[53] It has been held that if arbitrators discover that by mistake they have not considered a part

---

[45] Battle v. General Cellulose Co., 129 A.2d 865 (1957); Local 149, Boot and Shoe Workers Union v. Faith Shoe Co., 201 F.Supp. 234, 49 LRRM 2424 (D.C. Pa., 1962); Ulene v. La Vida Sportswear Co., 220 Cal. App. 2d 335, 34 Cal. Rptr. 36 (1963).

[46] Sturges, Commercial Arbitrations and Awards, (Kansas City: Vernon Law Book Co., 1930) at pp. 444, 923; Graham v. Graham, 9 Pa. 254, 49 Am. Dec. 557 (1848); Masters, Mates and Pilots v. Tiger S.S. Ltd., 52 LRRM 2392 (1963); Fuller v. Pepsi-Cola Bottling Co., 63 LRRM 2220 (Ky., 1966).

[47] Knaus v. Jenkins, 40 N.J.L. 288, 29 Am. Rep. 237 (1878); Pepin v. Societe St. Jean Baptiste, 23 R.I. 81, 49 A. 387, 91 Am. St. Rep. 620 (1901).

[48] State ex rel. Wright v. McQuillin, 252 Mo. 334, 158 S.W. 652 (1913); Johnson v. Noble, 13 N.H. 286, 38 Am. Dec. 485 (1847).

[49] State ex rel. Wright v. McQuillin, 252 Mo. 334, 158 S.W. 652 (1913).

[50] Babylon Milk and Cream Co. v. Horvitz, 151 N.Y.S. 2d 221, 26 LA 121 (N.Y. Sup. Ct. 1956).

[51] Black v. Woodruff, 193 Ala. 327, 69 So. 97 (1915); Goerke Kirch Co. v. Goerke Kirch Holding Co., 118 N.J. Eq. 1, 176 A. 902 (1935); Frederick v. Margworth, 221 Pa. 418, 70 A. 797 (1908); Byars v. Thompson, 12 Leigh (Va.) 550, 37 Am. Dec. 680 (1841).

[52] Bayne v. Morris, 1 Wall. (U.S.) 97, 17 L.Ed. 495 (1863); Woodbury v. Northy, 3 Greenleaf (Me.) 85, 14 Am. Dec. 214 (1824); Robinson-Rea Mfg. Co. v. Mellon, 139 Pa., 257, 21 A. 91, 23 Am. St. Rep. 186 (1891); Indigo Spring, Inc., v. N.Y. Hotel Trades Council, 59 LRRM 3024 (1965).

[53] Robinson-Rea Mfg. Co. v. Mellon, 139 Pa. 257, 21 A. 91, 23 Am. St. Rep. 186 (1891); Byars v. Thompson, 12 Lehigh (Va.) 550, 37 Am. Dec. 680 (1841). Hartley v. Henderson, 189 Pa. 277, 42 Atl. 198 (1899); Goodell v. Raymond, 27 Vt. 241 (1855); see also anno. 104 A.L.R. 710, 717.

of the question submitted to them they may again convene and award in respect to the same.[54]

Some statutes provide that arbitrators shall operate under the jurisdiction of a specified court that is expressly given power to order a rehearing by the arbitrators, or, if the court sets aside or requires a substantial change in an award, it may recall the arbitrators and resubmit the same to them.[55]

SECTION 4
Compensation of Umpires, Arbitrators, and Boards

It should be assumed by all parties that persons acting as arbitrators or umpires should be reasonably compensated.[56] Their fees are either fixed by agreement between the parties or, if the parties have not come to an express understanding, the arbitrators may within reasonable limits fix their own fees.[57] The overwhelming majority of contracts providing for arbitration contain a provision to the effect that the fees and expenses shall be equally divided between the parties. This, on its face, appears to be fair and proper. As a practical matter, however, it would seem to be desirable, at least in some instances, to provide that the arbitrator may award as to the proportion of the fee to be borne by each of the respective parties. This would make it possible for arbitrators to follow an equitable course in assessment of their charges for services. It has been charged at times that a financially strong company assumes a stubborn and tenacious position in respect to matters in dispute, unnecessarily pressing the issues to arbitration. In such instances, the company that is wrong should pay the major part of the expense that it has caused. It likewise may happen that a financially strong union organization may be equally at fault in pressing an unmeritorious demand against a financially weak employer. There are occasions when even the party that is right in its contentions at the hearing, and that wins the award, should equitably pay most of the compensation for the services leading to the decision. If the submission agreement carries a stipu-

---

54 Frederick v. Margworth, 221 Pa. 418, 70 A. 797 (1908).
55 American Guaranty Co. v. Caldwell, (C.C.A. 9th), 72 F. (2d) 209 (1934); Nippon Ki-Ito Kaisha v. Ewing-Thomas Corp., 313 Pa. 442, 170 A. 286 (1934); McCann v. Alaska Lumber Co., 71 Wash. 331, 128 Pac. 663 (1912).
56 Paine v. Kentucky Ref. Co., 159 Ky. 270, 167 S.W. 375 (1914); Kelly v. Lynchburg & D.R.Co., 110 N.C. 431, 15 S.E. 200 (1892).
57 Everett v. Erie County, 266 N.Y.S. 299, 148 Misc. 778 (1933).

lation to the effect that the expense and costs of arbitration shall be borne by the parties in proportions to be determined by the arbitrator and that he may award concerning them, the equities regarding such expenses may be fully and fairly considered. Such a provision would be entirely valid under decisions of the courts.[58] The parties are protected by the fact that if the amount charged by the arbitrator is excessive it may be reduced by the court in case, under any subsequent proceedings, it comes under judicial review.[59] Under some state arbitration statutes, fees are fixed, but the parties may, by agreement, increase the compensation of the arbitrator if they see fit.[60] If the parties or one of them can establish that there was any fraud or misconduct on the part of the arbitrator, the entire fee charge is invalidated,[61] though this will not be the case if the arbitrators are prevented from reaching an award by action of the parties.[62] It has long been settled that an arbitrator has a lien for the total of his reasonable charges upon the award itself,[63] and this probably includes any documents in his hands pertaining to the case.

It has sometimes been suggested that arbitrators should act without charge. Without doubt, men who have made a profession or quasi-profession of arbitration have acted and will act from time to time without compensation in circumstances where the parties are financially unable to pay for services. It should be generally assumed, however, that "the laborer is worthy of his hire." Those who, with ability to pay, seek free arbitration are unlikely to obtain the services of arbitrators having the knowledge and experience that furnish the foundation for competently carrying through a hearing, considering the evidence, and making a proper and sound decision. Uncompensated services are dangerously likely to be worth no more than their cost.

It should be stated that for some years a limited amount of high grade arbitrational service was furnished without cost by

---

58 Republic Iron & Steel Co. v. Norris, 25 Ga. App. 809, 104 S.E 921 (1959); Tri-State Transp. Co. v. Stearns Bros., 195 N.C. 720, 143 S.E. 473 (1928).

59 See authorities cited, notes 50 and 51 *supra.*

60 Paine v. Kentucky Ref. Co., 159 Ky. 270, 167 S.W. 375 (1914).

61 Kelly v. Lynchburg, & D.R. Co., 110 N.C. 431, 15 S.E. 200 (1892).

62 Davis v. Bradford, 58 N.H. 476 (1878).

63 Russell v. Page, 147 Mass. 282, 17 N.E. 536 (1888); Clement v. Comstock, 2 Mich. 359 (1852); New York Lumber, etc. Co. v. Schnieder, 119 N.Y. 475, 24 N.E. 4 (1890).

arbitrators of experience and skill on the payroll of the old United States Conciliation Service.[64] This was discontinued, partly because of the fact that many parties who used it found it increasingly difficult to terminate any dispute at an earlier grievance procedure step. The financial burden to all concerned appeared to have been greatly increasing when the free arbitration service was discontinued.

The liability of the parties to an arbitration for the fees of the arbitrator is generally held to be joint and several,[65] even though they are regarded as equally liable for payment of the arbitrator's fees in the absence of a provision that the arbitrator may award the proportions in which the same shall be paid by the parties. Thus, though the parties have each agreed to pay half of the expenses and fees, either may be held liable for the entire amount, with the obligation to apportion the cost between themselves, and without that agreement in any way qualifying the arbitrator's right to collect the full amount from either party.[66] One who voluntarily pays the compensation for which another party is liable, is not always recognized as having a right of action against that party to recover the amount so paid.[67] It has been held, however, that a party who pays the entire fee is not necessarily a "volunteer," and that it may have a right to enforce contribution from the other.[68] If the amount of the fee was not expressly agreed upon, the parties will be held liable for a reasonable fee, which is generally a matter of fact to be determined by a jury or by the court.[69] It will, of course, be determined by the character of the service rendered, the complexity of the matters studied, the length of time reasonably expended on the hearing, the conference of arbitrators, the studies necessitated outside of the hearing, and the amount of time reasonably devoted to writing the decision and award.[70]

---

[64] See Braun, The Settlement of Industrial Disputes, pp. 142, 145 (Philadelphia: Blakiston Co., 1944).

[65] Paine v. Kentucky Ref. Co., 159 Ky. 270, 167 S.W. 375 (1914).

[66] Young v. Starkey, 1 Cal. 426 (1851); Holcomb v. Tiffany, 38 Conn. 271 (1871).

[67] See Paine v. Kentucky Refining Co., 159 Ky. 270, 167 S.W. 375 (1914); American Ann. Cases 1915D, 398.

[68] Russell v. Page, 147 Mass. 282, 17 N.E. 536 (1888); Paine v. Kentucky Ref. Co., 159 Ky. 270, 167 S.W. 375 (1914); Shaw v. Gwin, 154 S. 392 (La. App. 1934).

[69] James v. Southern Lumber Co., 153 Mass. 361, 26 N.E. 995 (1891).

[70] Paine v. Kentucky Ref. Co., 159 Ky. 270, 167 S.W. 375 (1914); Davis v. Bradford, 58 N.H. 476 (1878); Giddings v. Hadaway, 28 Vt. 342 (1856).

CHAPTER IV

THE AGREEMENT TO ARBITRATE
AND THE SUBMISSION

SECTION 1

Agreement to Arbitrate — In General

Today, the most commonly employed method of enforcing collective bargaining agreements is to use the procedure upon which the parties have agreed. Usually this consists of processing the grievance up through the formal channels, with final decision, if needed, to be reached by arbitration. This method of settlement has been endorsed by the United States Supreme Court in the *Lincoln Mills* and *"Steelworkers* trilogy" decisions.[1] However, the authority and jurisdiction of arbitrators are always limited to the questions properly embraced in the agreement to arbitrate[2] and the submission, and these agreements must deal with legally arbitrable matters to be valid.[3] Otherwise, the entire arbitration proceeding and the award will be null and void.[4] In general, questions dealing with crimes have been held by the courts not to be

---

[1] Textile Workers Union of America v. Lincoln Mills of Alabama, 353 U. S. 448, 77 S.Ct. 912, 1 L.Ed. 2d 972, 40 LRRM 2113 (1957); United Steelworkers of America v. American Manufacturing Co., 363 U. S. 564, 80 S.Ct. 1343, 4 L.Ed. 2d 1403 (1960); United Steelworkers of America v. Warrior & Gulf Navigation Co., 363 U. S. 574, 80 S.Ct. 1347, 4 L.Ed. 2d 1409, 46 LRRM 2416 (1960); United Steelworkers of America v. Enterprise Wheel & Car Co., 363 U.S. 593, 80 S.Ct. 1358, 4 L.Ed. 2d 1424, 46 LRRM 2423 (1960).

[2] Atkinson v. Sinclair Refining Co., 370 U.S. 238, 82 S.Ct. 1318, 8 L.Ed. 2d 462, 50 LRRM 2433 (1962); Sturiale v. Cliffcorn Answering Service Inc., 22 App. Div. 2d 819, 254 N.Y.S. 2d 859, 58 LRRM 2030 (1964); I.B.E.W. v. Wadsworth Electric Manufacturing Co., 240 F.Supp. 292, 58 LRRM 2861 (E.D. Ky., 1965).

[3] See Cox, "The Place of Law in Labor Arbitration," at p. 76 in The Profession of Labor Arbitration, Selections from the First Seven Annual Meetings, National Academy of Arbitrators (Washington: BNA Books, 1957); and People v. Lindsey, 86 Colo. 458, 283 Pac. 539 (1929); California Lima Bean Grower's Ass'n v. Mankowitz, 9 N.J. Misc. 362, 154 A. 532 (1931); In re Fang, 237 N.Y.S. 366, 227 App. Div. 766 (1929); Ball-Thrash Co. v. McCormick, 172 N.C. 677, 90 S.E. 916 (1916).

[4] Capitol Airways Inc. v. Airline Pilots Association International, 237 F.Supp. 373, 54 LRRM 2326 (M.D. Tenn., 1963).

arbitrable.[5] On the other hand, it is not required that a legal right of action be involved.[6] Questions of both fact[7] and law[8] may be arbitrated, even including the interpretation of the arbitration agreement itself.[9] The parties may voluntarily agree, however, to submit the issue of arbitrability to an arbitrator providing there is a "clear demonstration" that he is to determine the issue of arbitrability.[10] But the courts have made it very clear that when the question is whether the parties have agreed to submit a given dispute to arbitration or not, it is a question to be decided solely by the courts.[11] Therefore, when a case covers both arbitrable and nonarbitrable issues, the arbitrable issues must be severed and tried by the arbitrator, leaving those that are not arbitrable to the courts.[12] The fact that the arbitrator conceivably might make an erroneous decision in respect to a question of law is not a legal ground for a refusal to continue in an arbitration proceeding or to respect an award.[13] Where a criminal question is involved, along with noncriminal issues, the latter may be segregated by the arbitrators and validly made the subject of an award. In many cases, employers and unions have arbitrated discharges for acts that were crimes as well as reasons for termination of em-

---

5 Franks v. Battles, 147 Ark. 169, 227 S.W. 32 (1921); Deshon v. Scott, 202 Ky. 575, 260 S.W. 355 (1924).

6 Milhollin v. Milhollin, 71 Ind. App. 477, 125 N.E. 217 (1919); Dugan v. Phillips, 77 Cal. App. 268, 246 Pac. 566 (1926); Deshon v. Scott, 202 Ky. 275, 260 S.W. 355 (1924).

7 Deshon v. Scott, 202 Ky. 275, 260 S.W. 355 (1924); Johnson v. Noble, 13 N.H. 286, 38 Am. Dec. 485 (1869); J.P. Greathouse Steel Erectors, Inc. v. Blount Brothers Construction Co., 374 F. 2d 324 (D.C. Cir., 1967).

8 Houston Saengerbund v. Dunn, 41 Tex. Civ. App. 376, 92 S.W. 429 (1906); Masonic Temple Ass'n v. Farrar, 422 S.W. 2d 95 (Mo. Ct. App., 1967); Prima Paint Corp. v. Flood & Conklin Mfg. Co., 388 U. S. 395, 87 S.Ct. 1801, 18 L.Ed. 2d 1270 (1967).

9 Goodwing v. Miller, 32 Ind. 419 (1869); School District No. 46 v. Del Bianco, 68 Ill. App. 2d 145, 154, 215 N.E. 2d 25, 29-30 (1966); Butchers' Union Local 229 v. Cudahy Packing Co., 59 Cal. Rptr. 713, 428 P. 2d 849 (1967); Oil, Chemical & Atomic Workers International Union v. Southern Gas Co., 379 F.2d 774, 65 LRRM 2685 (5th Cir., 1967).

10 United Steelworkers of America v. Warrior & Gulf Navigation Co., 363 U. S. 574, 80 S.Ct. 1347, 4 L.Ed. 2d 1409, 46 LRRM 2416 (1960).

11 Atkinson v. Sinclair Refining Co., 370 U. S. 238, 241, 50 LRRM 2433, 82 S.Ct. 1318, 1320, 8 L.Ed. 2d 462, 465 (1962).

12 Younker Brothers, Inc. v. Standard Construction Co., 241 F.Supp. 17 (S.D. Iowa, 1965).

13 Johnson v. Noble, 13 N.H. 286, 36 Am. Dec. 485 (1847); Marcy Lee Mfg. Co. v. Cortley Fabrics Co., 354 F. 2d 281 (2d Cir., 1963); Newark Stereotypers' Union No. 18 v. Newark Morning Ledger Co., 261 F.Supp. 832, 64 LRRM 2024 (D. N.J., 1966); Saxis Steamship Co. v. Multifacs International Traders, Inc., 375 F. 2d 577 (2d Cir., 1967).

ployment.[14] No action by an arbitrator can give legality to an objective of the parties that is itself illegal under common law or by statute.[15] Thus, an unlawful promise by an employer to grant an increase during World War II by a means constituting an evasion of the Stabilization Act would have been no more valid if supported by an award than it would have been otherwise. An award of a wage rate below the minimum set by the Fair Labor Standards Act would not give the substandard wage validity. Nor would an award providing for a union-security clause be valid where the clause is prohibited by a valid statute or state constitutional provision.[16]

Under standard arbitration clauses every grievance, unless specifically excluded, is deemed to be included within the proper scope of arbitration.[17] These would include rates of pay, hours of work, seniority rights, vacation rights, furlough rights, promotion rights, rights to bid in or select type of work, right to reinstatement after discharge, right to reclassification, union security rights and other related similar rights or claims of many sorts.[18]

Even where the controversy constituting the subject of arbitration has become the subject of other proceedings prior to the

14 Jenkins Brothers v. Local 5623, United Steelworkers of America, 341 F. 2d 987, 58 LRRM 2542 (2d Cir., 1965), cert denied, 382 U. S. 819, 86 S.Ct. 45, 15 L.Ed. 2d 66, 60 LRRM 2233 (1965). But see: Local 453 International Union of Electrical, Radio & Machine Workers, AFL-CIO v. Otis Elevator Co., 206 F.Supp. 853, 855, 50 LRRM 2689 (S.D. N.Y. 1962), rev'd on other grounds, 314 F. 2d 25, 52 LRRM 2543 (2d Cir., 1963); Marlin Rockwell Corp., 24 LA 728 (1955); Kroger Co., 25 LA 906 (1955).

15 Benton v. Singleton, 114 Ga. 548, 40 S.E. 811 (1902): Hall v. Kimmer, 61 Mich. 269, 28 N.W. 96, 1 Am. St. Rep. 575 (1886): Smith v. Gladney (Tex. Civ. App.) 70 S.W. (2d) 342 (1934). In the latter case, recovery was allowed, however, on an award which emerged from a contract which, of itself, would not have supported an action.

16 See Wis. Employment Relations Act (1941) Sec. 111.06 (c), and Automobile Workers, Local 283, etc. v. Wisconsin Emp. Rel. Bd., 14 N.W. (2d) 872, 14 LRRM 771 (Wis., 1944). Cf. Hall v. Kimmer, 61 Mich. 269, 28 N.W. 96, 1 Am. St. Rep. 575 (1886).

17 Procter & Gamble Independent Union of Port Ivory v. Procter & Gamble Mfg. Co., 298 F. 2d 647, 49 LRRM 2557 (2d Cir., 1962), citing United Steelworkers v. Warrior & Gulf Navigation Co., 363 U. S. at 582-583 (1960).

18 See: Textile Workers Union of America v. Lincoln Mills, 353 U. S. 448, 77 S.Ct. 912, 1 L.Ed. 2d 972, 40 LRRM 2113 (1957) (pay, hours of work, wrongful discharge); General Electric v. Local 205, U.E.W., 353 U. S. 547, 77 S.Ct. 921, 1 L.Ed. 2d 1028, 40 LRRM 2119 (1957) (pay, etc.); United Steelworkers of America v. Enterprise Wheel & Car Co., 363 U. S. 593, 80 S.Ct. 1358, 4 L.Ed. 2d 1424, 46 LRRM 2423 (1960) (reinstatement and back pay); Charles Dowd Box Co. v. Courtney, 368 U. S. 502, 82 S.Ct. 519, 7 L.Ed. 2d 483, 49 LRRM 2619 (1962) (wage increase).

entrance into the submission agreement, such as before a state labor relations board, the National Labor Relations Board, or the courts, it would seem that the matter ordinarily might be considered a proper subject of arbitration, and the rights of the parties fixed by an award, unless a statute provides otherwise.[19] During World War II, wage increases were required to have War Labor Board approval under the Stabilization Act. The Fair Labor Standards Act expressly fixes certain definite standards of wages and hours, and under the Walsh-Healey Act the Secretary of Labor must determine the minimum wage. There are a considerable number of other comparable instances to be found in state and federal acts where arbitration could not affect rights clearly defined by law. While the pendency of an action in court concerning a subject in dispute is not usually held to be a bar to its also becoming the subject of an arbitrational proceeding,[20] some state courts have held otherwise.[21] In most jurisdictions, the arbitration statutes expressly provide that the subject matter of the suit pending in court may be submitted to arbitration either with or without a rule of court.[22] There are a few statutes, however, that have been so construed that the agreement on arbitration, after litigation in court has started, results in a termination of the court

---

19 Marino v. Axel Roffman Associates, 53 LRRM 2997 (N.Y. Sup.Ct., 1963); United Steelworkers of America v. American International Aluminum Corp., 334 F. 2d 147, 56 LRRM 2682 (5th Cir., 1964), cert. denied, 379 U. S. 991, 58 LRRM 2256 (1965). See Murphy v. Greenberg, 246 Pa. 387, 92 A. 511, Ann Cas. 1916A, 354; 42 A.L.R. 728 et seq. Under Section 10 of the National Labor Relations Act, however, it has been held that the jurisdiction of the National Labor Relations Board is exclusive, and an order of the Supreme Court of New York, entered under the N.Y. Civil Practice Act, affirming an arbitrator's award, was set aside. Matter of Benedict, 39 N.Y.S. (2d) 852, 12 LRRM 577 (1943). However, it is thought that where the arbitration is under a state statute or under common law principles the award, while not precluding the National Labor Relations Board from proceeding, should be held binding under an adequate submission agreement covering a question excluded from jurisdiction by the criteria of the NLRB and revested into state jurisdiction by Section 701 of the 1959 amendments to the Labor Management Relations Act. Cf. NLRB v. Reed & Prince Mfg. Co., 118 F. (2d) 874, 885, 8 LRRM 478 (1941); NLRB v. Eclipse Moulded Products Co., 126 F. (2d) 576, 578, 10 LRRM 360 (1942); NLRB v. Algoma Net Co. 124 F. (2d) 730, 9 LRRM 531 (1941).

20 Nettleton v. Gridley, 21 Conn. 531, 56 Am. Dec. 378 (1852); Murphy v. Greenburg, 246 Pa. 387, 92 A. 511 (1914).

21 Magaziner v. Consumers Banking Co., 254 Mass. 4, 149 N.E. 547 (1925).

22 State ex rel. Watkins v. North American Land & Timber Co., 106 La. 621, 31 So. 172 (1902); State, Knaus, Prosecutor v. Jenkins, 40 N.J.L. 288, 29 Am. Rep. 237 (1878); Zehner v. Lehigh Coal & Nav. Co., 187 Pa. 487, 41 A. 464, 67 Am. St. Rep. 586 (1898).

proceedings.[23] In some jurisdictions, the statutes have made specific provisions for the arbitration of matters upon which court action has been started.[24]

SECTION 2

Agreements to Arbitrate and Submission Agreements Distinguished — Effect of the *Lincoln Mills* Decision

Since the arbitrational procedure is founded upon an agreement or contract to arbitrate, it is necessary that there be a valid contract between the parties to arbitrate and to abide by the award.[25] While the very agreement to arbitrate implies that the parties will respect and perform the award,[26] a much better practice is to include an express undertaking that they will do so.

Agreements for the arbitration of a controversy fall into two primary classifications: One is an agreement to submit a presently existing controversy to arbitration.[27] This is known as an "agreement to arbitrate," and it may even include the arbitration of actions presently pending before a court.[28] The second is an agreement to arbitrate controversies that may arise in the future.[29] This latter type of agreement may be found in several situations: (1) as a specific clause in a contract providing that disputed issues arising under the contract, which go through the grievance procedure without a settlement having been reached, will be submitted to arbitration;[30] (2) in a contract with a clause providing that

---

23 Reith v. Wynhoff, 28 Wis. 2d Wis. 2d 336, 137 N.W. 2d 33 (1965). See Ft. Dodge Lumber Co. v. Rogosch, 175 Iowa 475, 157 N.W. 189 (1916); Wertheim v. Burns Bros., 12 N.J. Misc. 676, 174 A. 238 (1935); Decker v. Ladish-Stoppenback Co., 203 Wis. 285, 234 N.W. 355 (1931).

24 See Davis v. Badders, 95 Ala. 348, 10 So. 422 (1891); Pettit v. Wingate, 25 Pa. 74 (1855); McGinnis v. Curry, 13 W.Va. 29 (1879).

25 In re Arbitration between Victor Klinger et al. and J. S. Krum, Inc., 19 N.Y.S. (2d) 193 (1940); Nutt v. United States, 125 U. S. 650, 31 L.Ed. 821, 8. S.Ct. 997 (1887); Gordon v. United States, 7 Wall (U. S.) 188, 19 L.Ed. 35 (1868).

26 Masonic Temple Association of St. Louis v. Farrar, 422 S.W. 2d 95 (Mo. Ct. App., 1967).

27 White Eagle Laundry Co. v. Slawek, 296 Ill. 240, 129 N.E. 753 (1921); Nelley v. Mayor & City Council of Baltimore City, 224 Md. 1, 166 A. 2d 234 (1960).

28 Young v. Crescent Developing Co., 240 N.Y. 244, 148 N.E. 510 (1925); Lebel v. Cyr, 140 Me. 98, 34 A. 2d 201 (1943); Pick Industries v. Gebhard-Berghammer, Inc., 262 Wis. 498, 56 N.W. 2d 97 (1952).

29 Fore v. Berry, 94 S.C. 71, 78 S.E. 706 (1913); McKenna Process Co. v. Blatchford Corp., 304 Ill. App. 101, 25 N.E. 2d 916 (1940).

30 Hughes v. National Fuel Co., 121 W.Va. 329, 3 S.E. 2d 621 (1939); Spence, Bryson, Inc. v. China Products Co., 308 Mass. 81, 30 N.E. 2d 885 (1941).

future disputes arising out of certain business dealings shall be arbitrable;[31] (3) clauses in the bylaws of corporations or associations that provide for the arbitration of disputes arising thereunder. These clauses are normally construed as agreements on behalf of the shareholders or members to arbitrate matters thus arising, and to be bound by the decision;[32] (4) many annual contracts existing today between employers and unions include a blanket provision that the parties will arbitrate all disputed or controverted matters that, after exhausting the grievance procedure, remain unsettled. All of these types of agreements may be referred to as agreements "to submit to arbitration." A specific contract or agreement between the parties stating the exact existing question and agreeing to submit the dispute stated to arbitrators, and to perform the award may properly be referred to as a "submission," or as a "submission agreement." [33] The agreement to submit to arbitration, looking toward a possible future dispute, now appears to be as effective to entitle the parties to enforce arbitration in some jurisdictions as a submission, but a distinction between the two may sometimes be quite important in respect to legal rights that may arise because of a breach of the agreement to arbitrate, on the one hand, or a failure to participate in a hearing and to respect the award, on the other.[34] Evidence dealing with the measure of damages may be quite clear if the matter has reached the state of being a "submission" and an award has been made.[35] On the other hand, damages may be refused for an alleged breach of agreement to arbitrate a dispute that arose after the contract was made because the evidence or

---

[31] In re Kramer & Uchitelle, Inc., 288 N.Y. 467, 43 N.E. 2d 493 (1942); Brotherhood of R. & S.S. Clerks v. Norfolk S.R. Co., 143 F. 2d 1015, 14 LRRM 905 (4th Cir., 1944); Tas-T-Nut Co. v. Continental Nut Co., 125 Cal. App. 2d 351, 270 P. 2d 43 (1953).

[32] Glasner v. Bressler, 218 N.Y. 218, 22 N.E. 2d 347 (1939); In re Toynton-Brown Co., 308 Mich. 727, 14 N.W. 2d 550 (1944).

[33] District of Columbia v. Bailey, 171 U. S. 161, 43 L. Ed. 118, 18 S.Ct. 868 (1897); Whitcher v. Whitcher, 49 N.H. 176, 6 Am. Rep. 486 (1870); Millsaps v. Estes, 137 N.C. 535, 50 S.E. 227.

[34] Norwich Union Fire Ins. Soc. v. Cohn (CCA 10th) 68 F.2d 42 (1933); W. H. Blodgett Co. v. Bebe Co., 190 Cal. 665, 214 Pac. 38 (1923); Coles v. Peck, 96 Ind. 333, 49 Am. Rep. 161 (1884); Crescent Stave Co. v. Brown, 181 Ky. 787, 205 S.W. 937 (1918).

[35] Bullock v. Mason, 194 Ala. 663, 69 So. 882 (1915); Pond v. Harris, 113 Mass. 114 (1873).

theory upon which the amount of damages is calculated is hypothetical or uncertain and speculative.[36]

The continued applicability of the above distinction has been severely limited by the United States Supreme Court in three important decisions. As was discussed in Chapter 1, Section 4, *supra,* the *Lincoln Mills* decision overruled *Westinghouse Electric Corp.,*[37] which had done much to contribute to the foregoing distinction, and stated that if the industry is involved in interstate commerce, the agreements to arbitrate are specifically enforceable in federal courts. The Court felt that Congress, in Section 301 of the LMRA, intended that arbitration should be substituted for industrial strife. In so deciding, the Court in effect authorized the lower federal courts to cooperate with it in fashioning from the policies of the national labor laws a body of federal law for the enforcement of collective bargaining contracts falling within Section 301. ". . . [S]tate law, may be resorted to in order to find the rule that will best effectuate the federal policy," but "[a]ny state law applied . . . will be absorbed as federal law and will not be an independent source of private rights." [38]

This statement decided the question of whether federal law has preempted state law in this area.[39] The Court stated that Section 301 was designed to expand, not to limit, the forums available to the parties for the enforcement of arbitration agreements.[40] However, when the state courts enforce an arbitration agreement ". . . incompatible doctrines of local law *must* give way to principles of federal labor law. . . ." [41] (Emphasis added). Therefore, the substantive principles of federal labor law must be paramount in cases coming within Section 301 because ". . . Congress

---

36 Electrical Research Products v. Vitaphone Corp., 20 Del. Ch. 417, 171 A. 738 (1934) ; Munson v. Straits of Dover Steamship Co., 43 CCA 57, 102 F. 926 (1900) .

37 Association of Westinghouse Salaried Employees v. Westinghouse Electric Corp., 348 U. S. 437, 75 S.Ct. 488, 99 L.Ed. 510, 35 LRRM 2643 (1954) .

38 Textile Workers Union v. Lincoln Mills of Alabama, 353 U. S. 448, 457, 77 S.Ct. 912, 918, 1 L.Ed. 2d 972, 981, 40 LRRM 2113 (1957) .

39 Charles Dowd Box Co. v. Courtney, 368 U. S. 502, 508, 82 S.Ct. 519, 532, 7 L.Ed. 2d 483, 488, 49 LRRM 2619 (1962) .

40 See Chap. II, Sec. 2, *supra.*

41 Local 174, Teamsters, Chauffers, Warehousemen & Helpers of America v. Lucas Flour Co., 369 U. S. 95, 102, 82 S.Ct. 571, 576, 7 L.Ed. 2d 593, 598, 49 LRRM 2717 (1962) ; and see Avco Corporation v. Machinists Aero Lodge 735, 390 U. S. 557, 67 LRRM 2881 (1968) .

intended doctrines of federal labor law uniformly to prevail over inconsistent local rules." [42]

Because most labor contracts negotiated today involve industries in interstate commerce, and are therefore within Section 301, it would seem that the distinction between an agreement to arbitrate and a submission agreement is one of limited applicability. Since the Supreme Court has evidenced in *Lincoln Mills*, the *"Steelworkers* trilogy," and *Charles Dowd Box* the intent to apply federal law in the enforcement of such agreements, one can expect major differences between these two types of arbitration agreements virtually to disappear.

SECTION 3

Capacity of Parties to Enter Into Arbitration Agreements

Generally speaking, any officer of an employer company entrusted with general authority to deal with and adjust labor relations will be held to have adequate authority to enter into an agreement to arbitrate or a submission.[43] It does not follow, however, that an agreement made by anyone having authority under the company, such as a foreman or other supervisory employee ordinarily not having contractual authority, will bind the company in respect to an arbitrational proceeding.[44]

By the same token, it must not be assumed that every union officer has authority to bind the organization by agreeing to an unusual agreement to arbitrate or by entering into a special submission agreement.[45] Some union constitutions and bylaws require that their contracts be submitted to the entire membership at an

---

42 *Id.*, 369 U. S. at 104, 82 S.Ct. at 577, 7 L.Ed. 2d at 600.

43 See Richards v. Attleborough Nat. Bank, 148 Mass. 187, 19 N.E. 353 (1889).

44 See Huber v. Zimmerman, 21 Ala. 488, 56 Am. Dec. 255 (1852); Trout v. Emmons, 29 Ill. 433, 81 Am. Dec. 326 (1862); Pope v. Wheatley (Tex. Civ. App.) 54 S.W.2d 846 (1932).

45 It would seem unlikely, for example, that a department steward or even a "bargaining committee" appointed to negotiate an annual contract would have the power in question though they now probably would have power to include a general arbitration clause as the terminating step of the grievance procedure. It would clearly seem to be valid to bind the local union in such cases only after ratification by the membership at a union meeting. The president or an international representative should be able to bind the union on such a contract, particularly if his action is consistent with usage and is not known to require ratification from the international heads of the organization.

open meeting for approval. Under such a union constitution, a contract including an agreement to arbitrate would be of doubtful validity without such approval unless, knowing that it had not been so approved, the membership had, by implication, tacitly adopted and approved it by acting under it so as to have become estopped to deny its validity. In other instances, though the contract may include an agreement to arbitrate all controversies that may arise during a certain period, that clause may be so phrased as to require that each dispute to be submitted to arbitration be the subject of a separate and distinctly negotiated "submission agreement," bargained and executed after the controversy has arisen. In such situations, the question would naturally arise as to which officer or officers, if any, of the union would be authorized to agree to the terms of the submission and to execute the same as indicating the consent of the organization to be bound thereby. If some unauthorized officer or member assumes to enter into such an undertaking, it would have no binding effect upon the organization unless the organization, by acting upon it, waives the lack of authority of the agent, or ratifies his action, or has so held him out as authorized to bind it that it is later estopped to deny his capacity to act for it.[46] Even the *Lincoln Mills* decision would give no validity to a noncompleted negotiation; nor would it nullify a waiver, estoppel, or ratification.

Questions also arise as to the authority of a union, as the employee's exclusive bargaining agent, to bind the individual member of the union by an agreement to arbitrate or by a submission stipulation. The matter in controversy may be whether an individual member has been unjustly or unlawfully discharged and is entitled to be reinstated in his employment with back pay. The Supreme Court has said that if an employee wishes to assert a grievance he must first attempt to use the formal grievance procedure provided for by the contract before he may resort to the state courts.[47] If the rule were otherwise, the employer and the

---

[46] Smith v. Morse, 9 Wall. (U.S.) 76, 19 L.Ed. 597 (1859) ; Wheeler & W. Mfg. Co. v. Aughey, 144 Pa. 398, 22 A. 667, 27 Am. St. Rep. 638 (1891) ; Wharton v. Tierney-Toner Co., 126 Wash. 216, 217 Pac. 998 (1923) ; Warrior Constructors, Inc. v. International Union of Operating Engineers, Local 926, 383 F. 2d 700, 62 LRRM 2313 (5th Cir., 1967) .

[47] Republic Steel Corp. v. Maddox, 379 U. S. 650, 85 S.Ct. 614, 13 L.Ed. 2d 580, 58 LRRM 2193 (1965) .

union would be deprived of the ability to establish a uniform and exclusive method for the orderly settlement of contract grievances. This would then frustrate the basic holding of the *Lincoln Mills* decision that seeks to make contractual arbitration the accepted method of settling industrial disputes. It would also exert a disruptive influence upon both the negotiation and the enforcement of collective agreements. Unless the contract expressly so allows, the aggrieved employee may not sue in the state courts without having first given the union an opportunity to act in his behalf. If, however, such a person participates in the arbitrational proceeding to which the union has agreed, attends the hearing, and awaits the award with the evident intention of abiding thereby, it would seem to be properly inferable that the union has authority to represent him, or that he had waived any defect in that authority that technically had existed. It is obviously good practice, therefore, in cases involving individual members' rights, to be sure that the individual members are consenting and fully informed parties to the agreement to arbitrate and to the submission.

The individual rights of employees in subjects in dispute that reach arbitration have been the subjects of numerous discussions, decisions, and juristic writings. The accepted view today is that to permit the individual employee to take a position opposing that of his collective bargaining representative in the grievance procedure including arbitration "would create an unstable and chaotic condition not conducive to industrial harmony." [48] The usual successive steps of grievance procedure are intended as often as possible to settle the disputes on the basis of agreement between the employer and the union prior to reaching the arbitration step. However, if the union arbitrarily refuses to press his claim, or where it is only done perfunctorily, the employee may then sue in the state courts.[49] While he does not have an absolute right to have his grievance arbitrated, the union does owe him a duty of fair representation in considering his claim.[50] Barring a showing by the employee of discrimination or lack of good faith by the

---

[48] Cox v. R. H. Macy Co., 27 LA 243 (N.Y. Sup. Ct., 1956).

[49] Vaca v. Sipes, 386 U. S. 171, 87 S.Ct. 903, 17 L.Ed. 2d 842, 64 LRRM 2369 (1967).

[50] Humphrey v. Moore, 375 U. S. 335, 84 S.Ct. 363, 11 L.Ed. 2d 370, 55 LRRM 2031 (1964).

union in prosecuting or settling his grievance,[51] he will be precluded from suing in the state courts unless such action is expressly allowed by the contract.[52]

In some instances, the employee has brought suit in an effort to compel arbitration. The decisions generally hold that the right to require arbitration rests upon the agreement to arbitrate and hence can be enforced by only one of the contracting parties, the union, or the employer.[53]

Suppose, however, the employee decides to assert his claim by bringing a law suit against the employer, despite the fact that the matter has been settled as between the employer and the union. May he collect damages? Here again, most courts have held that the action is barred by the arbitration provision, and have stated that the individual's rights under the agreement must be resolved consistently with the remedies and procedure provided within it.[54] A California district court of appeals held that suit by the individual complainant was barred against both the company and the union, where the union has expressly declined to arbitrate.[55]

In some instances an employee may desire to assert a position in conflict with that officially taken by the union. For example, he may be asking a rate of pay or a promotion based on an interpretation of seniority that will be favorable to him but will operate unfavorably to other union members. If such an individual employee has the right to participate in an individual way, all other interested individual members would seem to have the same right to do so. Thus, considerable complexity and conflict might occur in recognizing the right of numerous individual em-

---

[51] Miranda Fuel Co., 140 NLRB 181, 51 LRRM 1584 (1962), enforcement denied, 326 F. 2d 172 (2d Cir., 1963); Vaca v. Sipes, 386 U. S. 171, 87 S.Ct. 903, 17 L.Ed. 2d 842, 64 LRRM 2369 (1967); Comment, Administrative Enforcement of the Right to Fair Representation: The Miranda Case, 112 University of Pennsylvania Law Review, 711 (1963).

[52] Republic Steel Corp. v. Maddox, 379 U. S. 650, 85 S.Ct. 614, 13 L.Ed. 2d 580, 58 LRRM 2193 (1965).

[53] Doyle v. Lasorda, 26 LA 464, rearg. den. 26 LA 556 (N.Y. Sup. Ct., 1956); Curet v. Landriscina, 26 LA 582 (N.Y. Sup. Ct., 1956); Terrell v. Local Lodge 758, IAM, 28 LA 419 (Cal. Dist. Ct. App., 1957); Black-Clawson Co. v. I.A.M. Lodge 355, 313 F. 2d 179, 52 LRRM 2038 (2d Cir., 1962); White v. General Baking Co., 263 F.Supp. 264 (D.C. N.J., 1964).

[54] Jenkins v. Atlas Powder Co., 27 LA 779 (Tenn., 1956); Brandt v. United States Lines, Inc., 246 F.Supp. 982, 55 LRRM 2665 (S.D. N.Y., 1964).

[55] Terrell v. Local Lodge 758, IAM, 26 LA 579 (Cal. Dist. Ct. App., 1957); and Terrell v. Local Lodge 758, 28 LA 419 (Cal. Dist. Ct. App., 1957).

ployees to participate in arbitration or in a suit with conflicting claims. It would be more consistent with the contract and the objectives of both parties to it to hold that individual members may not intervene in the proceeding contrarily to the union's desire and that they are not proper parties to obtain a modification or vacation of an award or to enforce it.[56]

Vaca v. *Sipes* and *Republic Steel* v. *Maddox* do much to strengthen this position, for they require that the employee recognize the union's duty of representing him in grievance matters arising under the contract.[57] While the union can not arbitrarily refuse to press a grievance, it may select those it wishes to arbitrate,[58] and, barring a showing of bad faith on the part of the union, the employee is precluded from seeking redress against the employer in a state court. Any honest settlement within the grievance procedure is, therefore, binding on the employee and is an adjudication of all of his rights in the issue.

Therefore, the arbitration process should be controlled by the employer and the collective bargaining agent of the employees without interference from even interested individual members of the latter in assertion of particular and personal claims inconsistent with, or contrary to, the position taken by the union. The union is under a clear legal obligation to represent all members fairly and the National Labor Relations Act provides for the decertification of a union with which a sufficient number of employees are dissatisfied. Moreover, the individual union member, or a nonunion man, if not given fair representation by the organization, may well be recognized to have his right of action in the state courts,[59] and in some instances it may appear proper to

---

[56] Lammonds v. Aleo Mfg. Co., 26 LA 351 (N. Car. Sup. Ct., 1956); But see Di Rienzo v. Farrand Optical Co., 26 LA 375 (N.Y. Mun. Ct., 1956); Trimarchi v. Sheffield Farms, Inc., 26 LA 741 (N.Y. Sup. Ct., 1956); In re Wall Street Club, Inc., 27 LA 633 (N.Y. Sup. Ct., 1956); Spilkewitz v. Pepper, 27 LA 715 (N.Y. Sup. Ct., 1957); Donnelly v. United Fruit Co., 28 LA 64 (N.Y. Sup. Ct., 1957); Soto v. Lenscraft Optical Corporation, 28 LA 279 (N.Y. Sup. Ct., 1957).

[57] Republic Steel Corp. v. Maddox, 379 U. S. 650, 85 S.Ct. 614, 13 L.Ed. 2d 580, 58 LRRM 2193 (1965); Vaca v. Sipes, 386 U. S. 171, 87 S.Ct. 903, 17 L.Ed. 2d 842, 64 LRRM 2369 (1967).

[58] Vaca v. Sipes, *Id.*, citing Humphrey v. Moore, 375 U. S. 335, 84 S.Ct. 363, 11 L.Ed. 2d 370, 55 LRRM 2031 (1964).

[59] See O'Brien v. Dada, 18 N.J. 457, 114 A. 2d 266, 36 LRRM 2172 (1955); Donato v. American Locomotive Co., 111 N.Y.S. 2d 434, 279 App. Div. 545 (1952). Compare Terrell v. Local Lodge 758 IAM, 28 LA 419 (Calif. Dist. Ct. App. 1957); Vaca v. Sipes, 386 U. S. 171, 87 S.Ct. 903, 17 L.Ed. 2d 842, 64 LRRM 2369 (1967).

allow him relief under Sections 9 or 301 of the National Labor Relations Act.[60]

These views protect the arbitration procedure itself from individual or third-party interference and protect the employer from becoming involved in a controversy between the union and its members or other employees. Moreover, they sustain the security of settlements and awards made at any step in the grievance procedure. Such views will adequately protect the individual employee by giving him a right of action in the cases where the union as his agent has acted tortiously or disloyally in respect to his interests.[61]

Some attention should be given to the fact that many union members are under 21 years of age and therefore are classified legally as "infants." The contract of the infant at common law was ordinarily voidable at his option.[62] It remains so today though statutes have in some degree affected the subject by various provisions.[63] Some of these provide that the infant is bound unless within a specified time after coming of age he disavows the contract.[64] For that reason, it has been held that where an infant has become a party to a submission, and the arbitrators have made their award, the whole matter is voidable at the election of the infant.[65] A few state supreme courts have taken the position that such an arbitrational proceeding is absolutely void.[66]

If the court treats the proceeding as entirely void, and not voidable, it would follow that neither party is bound, even though the arbitrational matter has gone through all of the steps from submission to award.[67] If, however, the contract of the infant in the

---

[60] See Steele v. Louisville & Nashville Railroad, 323 U. S. 192, 15 LRRM 708 (1944) ; Trunstall v. Bro. Locomotive Firemen, 323 U. S. 210, 15 LRRM 715 (1944) .

[61] Vaca v. Sipes, 386 U. S. 171, 87 S.Ct. 903, 17 L.Ed. 2d 824, 64 LRRM 2369 (1967) . See dissenting opinions of Mr. Justice Frankfurter, in Elgin, Joliet & Eastern Railway v. Burley, 325 U. S. 711, 749, 16 LRRM 749 (1945) and on reargument, 327 U. S. 661, 667, 17 LRRM 899 (1946) .

[62] Millsaps v. Estes, 137 N.C. 535, 50 S.E. 227, 107 Am. St. Rep. 496 (1905) ; Webb v. Harris, 32 Okla. 491, 121 Pac. 1082 (1912) ; Dickert v. Aetna L. Ins. Co., 176 S.C. 476, 180 S.E. 462 (1935) : Strother v. Lynchburg Trust & Sav. Bank, 155 Va. 826, 156 S.E. 426 (1931) .

[63] Grissom v. Beidleman, 35 Okla., 343, 129 Pac. 853 (1913) .

[64] Re Willmott, 211 Iowa 34, 230 N.W. 330 (1930) .

[65] Millsaps v. Estes, 137 N.C. 535, 50 S.E. 227, 107 Am. St. Rep. 496 (1905) .

[66] Jones v. Payne, 41 Ga. 23 (1870) ; Handy v. Cobb, 44 Miss. 699 (1870) .

[67] District of Columbia v. Bailey, 171 U. S. 161, 43 L.Ed. 118, 18 S.Ct. 868 (1897) .

above-described situation is treated by the courts of the jurisdiction as voidable, then clearly he may ratify it when he comes of age, and he will be held to have done so if he receives the benefit or enters upon performance of the obligations of the award, or does any other act clearly implying his consent and approval thereof after coming of age.[68]

Some of the same considerations applying to the contracts of infants to arbitrate and to submissions executed by them or on their behalf by a union organization or other person must be considered also to apply in respect to mentally incompetent persons.

Again, many union organizations have among their memberships married women. At common law a married woman was not legally competent to contract to arbitrate or to enter into a submission agreement, and she did not have authority to delegate power to take such steps on her behalf to any other person.[69] Under the married women's separate property acts, however, many of these disabilities have been removed, and a married woman may generally bind herself by contract and by ratification in respect to matters regarded as within her separate estate.[70] Thus, if she is a party to an arbitration dealing with a question whether she is entitled to back pay, under most modern statutes she would have full power to contract or to appoint a union to act as her agent or representative.[71]

Where a claim is being made on behalf of a deceased person, whether for back pay or for compensation because of death or otherwise, the courts are inclined generally to hold that an executor, administrator, or trustee will have power to submit to arbitration any matter that he would have authority to settle out of

---

68 Baker v. Lovett, 6 Mass. 78, 4 Am. Dec. 88 (1809).

69 Sutton v. Tyrrell, 10 Vt. 91 (1838); Morrison Department Store Co. v. Lewis, 96 W.Va. 277, 122 S.E. 747 (1924).

70 Hoste v. Dalton, 137 Mich. 522, 100 N.W. 750 (1904); Brusha v. Board of Education, 41 Okla., 595, 139 Pac. 298 (1914); Bolyard v. Bolyard, 79 W.Va. 554, 91 S.E. 529 (1917).

71 Althen v. Tarbox, 48 Minn. 18, 50 N.W. 1018, 31 Am. St. Rep. 616 (1892); Re Badger, 286 Mo. 139, 226 S.W. 936 (1920); Burwell v. South Carolina Tax Comm., 130 S.C. 199, 126 S.E. 29 (1924); Board of Trade v. Hayden, 4 Wash. 263, 32 Pac. 224 (1892).

court.[72] Thus, a person acting in such fiduciary capacity would have authority to participate in an arbitrational proceeding arranged by a union in respect to rights of a deceased member.[73] A union so acting, however, should take care to receive full specific approval of, and signature upon, the arbitrational submission by such representative of the estate before proceeding on behalf of the deceased. While the executor may submit to arbitration, it is doubtful indeed whether he may delegate to the union the power to act as agent and so to bind the estate.[74] If the union fails to obtain adequate authority or concurrence of such personal representative of a deceased person, the entire proceeding as far as the estate is concerned may be held vulnerable and any award terminating the same unenforceable.[75]

When dealing with an employer's labor relations association, unions should always make a special effort to see that some fully authorized contracting officer of the company signs the agreement to arbitrate or the submission as the case may be. Many agents, even those having power themselves to bind the principal by contract, do not also have authority to agree that someone else, such as an arbitrator or umpire, may do so.[76] This is a matter to be given special consideration when the party agreeing to the submission agreement is a plant production manager or other agent at a factory or other place of business far distant from the general offices of the company where the contracting officers ordinarily transact their business. In respect to the cautions just stated, however, it should be added that ordinarily a fully authorized contracting officer of an employer corporation will have authority to ratify and so to validate an agreement to arbitrate or a submission agreement entered into by some other representative of

72 Hutchins v. Johnson, 12 Conn. 376, 30 Am. Dec. 622 (1837) ; Parker v. Providence & S. S. B. Co., 17 R. I. 376, 22 A. 284, 33 Am. St. Rep. 869 (1891) ; Powers v. Douglass, 53 Vt. 471, 38 Am. Rep. 699 (1881) .
73 Konigmacher v. Kimmel, 1 Penr. & W. (Pa.) 207, 21 Am. Dec. 374 (1829) ; Powers v. Douglass, 53 Vt. 471, 38 Am. Rep. 699 (1881) .
74 Crum v. Moore, 14 N.J. Eq. 436, 82 Am. Dec. 262 (1862) ; Murray v. Blatchford, 1 Wend. (N.Y.) 583, 19 Am. Dec. 537 (1828) ; Parker v. Providence & S. S. B. Co., 17 R. I. 376, 22 A. 284, 33 Am. St. Rep. 869 (1891) .
75 Bailey v. Dilworth, 10 Smedes & M. (Miss.) 404, 48 Am. Dec. 760 (1848) ; Bankers Surety Co. v. Meyer, 205 N.Y. 219, 98 N.E. 399 (1912) ; Konigmacher v. Kimmel, 1 Penr. & W. (Pa.) 207, 21 Am. Dec. 374 (1829) .
76 De Camp v. Grawpner, 157 Ark. 578, 249 S.W. 6 (1923) ; Doggett v. Greene, 254 Ill. 134, 98 N.E. 219 (1912) ; Kinkead v. Hartley, 161 Iowa 613, 143 N.W. 591 (1913) ; Kohl v. Beach, 107 Wis. 409, 83 N.W. 657 (1900) .

the company technically lacking in authority.[77] Where a doubt as to such authority exists, it is well to insist upon the approval indicated by the signature of an agent or officer having full authority to so act.

An attorney is ordinarily held to have authority to submit a client's claims to arbitration even without the client's knowledge or express consent, since the attorney usually has authority to prosecute or defend the client's interests by all suitable and established procedures, and arbitration is one of the commonly used methods of settling controversies.[78] Of course if the client has no capacity to enter into a submission, as in the case of the married woman at common law or the infant or in case the client is mentally incompetent, the agreement by the attorney will be subject to the same incapacity as would have affected the action of the client.[79]

Some employers are partners rather than individual owners of a corporation. In such instances all partners should be required to sign the agreement to arbitrate and the submission, or in some manner expressly authorize the same.[80] It has been held that no partner can bind his co-partners to an arbitrational submission since that type of proceeding is not within the usual course of partnership business.[81] If all do not evidence their agreement, only the partners who have agreed to the arbitrational proceedings are bound.[82] The award will be valid as against those who negotiated the agreement to arbitrate and those who consented to it.[83] Obviously, the other partners may later bind themselves by ratifying the agreement to arbitrate or the submission.[84]

Where the employer is a corporation, it must be noted that with respect to some subjects the corporation may be bound only by acts

[77] Richards v. Attleborough Nat. Bank, 148 Mass. 187, 19 N.E. 353 (1889); Williams v. Christian Female College, 29 Mo. 250, 77 Am. Dec. 569 (1860).
[78] Bank of Glade Spring v. McEwen, 160 N.C. 414, 76 S.E. 222 (1912); Maroulas v. State Industrial Accid. Comm., 117 Or. 406, 244 Pac. 317 (1926); Swartz v. Morgan, 163 Pa. 195, 29 A. 974, 43 Am. St. Rep. 786 (1894).
[79] Bank of Glade Spring v. McEwen, 160 N.C. 414, 76 S.E. 222 (1912).
[80] Hall v. Lanning, 91 U. S. 160, 23 L.Ed. 271 (1875); Karthaus v. Yllas Y Ferrer, 1 Pet. (U. S.) 222, 7 L.Ed. 121 (1828).
[81] Hall v. Lanning, 91 U. S. 160, 23 L.Ed. 271 (1875); Buchanan v. Curry, 19 Johns. (N.Y.) 137, 10 Am. Dec. 200 (1821).
[82] Karthaus v. Yllas Y. Ferrer, 1 Pet. (U. S.) 222, 7 L.Ed. 121 (1828); Jones v. Bailey, 5 Cal. 345 (1855).
[83] Karthaus v. Yllas Y. Ferrer, 1 Pet. (U. S.) 222, 7 L.Ed. 121 (1828).
[84] Buchanan v. Curry, 19 Johns (N.Y.) 137, 10 Am. Dec. 200 (1821).

of certain specifically designated officers.[85] In some important matters, an action of the Board of Directors is required.[86] In general, however, where the subject matter of the arbitration is within the routine of matters entrusted to a given officer or agent of the corporation and where he has authority to settle such matters, he will be held to have adequate authority to represent and bind the corporation on an arbitrational submission.[87] In the case of the municipal corporation, however, while such organizations under general statutes are "persons" and may thereby submit matters to arbitration, it is always well to ascertain whether the corporation is authorized to act upon the subject of the arbitration.[88] In general, however, cities, towns, and other subdivisions of government, including school districts, have some limited authority to submit questions to arbitration.[89] This is inferred from their power and capacity to contract and to prosecute and defend suits in respect to matters entrusted to their authority and within their expressly delegated powers.[90] It is the likelihood of finding restrictions and limitations upon those delegated powers that must be watched.[91] An award granting increased wages, vacations, or retirement rights would be futile if the corporation had no power to grant them because of a statutory or constitutional restriction, or if the power to do so were not delegated to the municipal corporation concerned.[92]

---

[85] Huber v. Zimmerman, 21 Ala. 488, 56 Am. Dec. 255 (1852) ; Trout v. Emmons, 29 Ill. 433, 81 Am. Dec. 326 (1862) ; Richards v. Attleborough Nat. Bank, 148 Mass. 187, 19 N.E. 353 (1889) .

[86] Richards v. Attleborough Nat. Bank, 148 Mass. 187, 19 N.E. 353 (1889) .

[87] Henderson Bridge Co. v. McGrath, 134 U. S. 260, 33 L.Ed. 934, 10 S.Ct. 730 (1889) ; Caddy Oil Co. v. Sommer, 186 Ky. 843, 218 S.W. 288 (1920) ; Moorhead v. Minneapolis Seed Co., 139 Minn. 117, 165 N.W. 484 (1917) ; Medley v. Trenton Invest. Co., 205 Wis. 30, 236 N.W. 713 (1931) .

[88] District of Columbia v. Bailey, 171 U. S. 161, 43 L.Ed. 118, 18 S.Ct. 868 (1897) ; Carter v. Krueger, 175 Ky. 399, 194 S.W. 553 (1917) ; Re Lower Baraboo River Drainage Dist., 199 Wis. 230, 255 N.W. 331 (1929) .

[89] See Chapter V, Section 3 infra, and Hine v. Stephens, 33 Conn. 497, 89 Am. Dec. 217 (1866) ; Hewitt v. Reed City, 124 Mich. 6, 82 Am. Dec. 616 (1900) ; West v. Coos County, 115 Ore. 409, 237 Pac. 961 (1925) ; Re Lower Baraboo River Drainage Dist., 199 Wis. 230, 225 N.W. 331 (1929) .

[90] Maroulas v. State Industrial Accid. Comm., 117 Or. 406, 244 Pac. 317 (1926) ; Chapline v. Overseers, 7 Leigh (Va.) 231, 30 Am. Dec. 504 (1836) ; Re Lower Baraboo River Drainage Dist. 199 Wis. 230, 225 N.W. 331 (1929) .

[91] Hine v. Stephens, 33 Conn. 497, 89 Am. Dec. 217 (1866) ; Trout v. Emmons, 29 Ill. 433, 81 Am. Dec. 326 (1862) .

[92] Carter v. Krueger, 175 Ky. 399, 194 S.W. 553 (1917) .

SECTION 4

Grievance Procedure and Arbitration

Innumerable contracts between unions and employers today contain a considerable section devoted to grievance procedure. With slight variations, nearly all of these conform to a certain pattern.[93] The individual member, having a grievance, reports the same to his foreman or to the steward of his union in the department in which he is employed. If the steward is called in, he takes the matter up with the immediate superior of the complainant. This may be known as the "first step." If they fail to dispose of the dispute to the satisfaction of all parties, the matter goes into the "second step" which ordinarily will involve a higher officer of the company and a higher union official. This may be the chief steward or business agent of the union taking up the matter with the departmental foreman or possibly with an assistant superintendent. If the matter is still unsettled after these parties have tried to dispose of it, it will then proceed to a "third step" which usually means that it goes before a meeting of a shop committee representing the union and certain officers of the company designated to meet regularly with them. If no solution is found at such a meeting, the matter may proceed further to a conference between the top regional officers of the union and the general manager or president of the company. If this fails, the next step is generally arbitration.[94]

For full flexibility it should be provided by the contract between the parties that as the final step in the procedure the full substance of the grievance goes to arbitration and that either party shall be fully authorized to initiate action of the arbitrational machinery. That is to say, if the contract provides that the arbitrator or umpire is permanent, either party should at that stage be entitled to call upon him to set a date for a hearing. If, on the other hand, the

---

[93] See Braun. The Settlement of Industrial Disputes, p. 252 (Philadelphia: Blakiston Co., 1944) ; Collective Bargaining Negotiations and Contracts (Washington: The Bureau of National Affairs, Inc.) ; Union Agreement Provisions, p. 145 et seq. (Washington: U.S. Dept. of Labor, Bulletin No. 686, 1942) ; Settling Plant Grievances (Washington: U. S. Dept. of Labor, Bulletin No. 60, Division of Labor Standards, 1943).

[94] See Arbitration Provisions in Union Agreements, pp. 1, 12 (Washington: U. S. Department of Labor, Bulletin No. 780, 1944) ; Settling Plant Grievances, supra, at p. 24 et seq; Major Collective Bargaining Agreements: Grievance Procedures (Washington: Bureau of Labor Statistics Bulletin No. 1425-1 (1965)).

contract calls for appointment of an arbitrator by some neutral third person, either of the parties to the dispute should then be fully authorized to request such an appointment within a specified time.[95]

This contract should provide that the arbitrator shall then have complete authority to hear the evidence and make an award fully disposing of the subject of the controversy. At this stage, it is ordinarily very important to know just what the limits of the demand have been and in every detail the extent of the dispute. This emphasizes the desirability of having a written grievance filed at the very beginning or "first step" in the grievance procedure, and the importance of having that writing fully and carefully worked out. It may be observed that many unions and employers proceed too far without written records, and that in many instances poorly drawn or inadequately worded statements of grievances cause substantial difficulties.[96] It is strongly recommended that both parties see to it that accurately worded written statements of all grievances are prepared early, so that they will have records definitely showing what the difficulty was, how it was disposed of, by whom, and upon what grounds. It is not an unjustly suspicious demand on the side of either party to a labor contract to demand that full written records be prepared and preserved. It is rather a sensible and logical recognition of the unreliability of human memories.

It often happens that a carefully stated "grievance" is virtually all that is necessary as the substance of a submission agreement. If the contract to arbitrate is sufficient and well stated, each grievance may become automatically, as filed, an adequate statement of the question to be submitted to arbitration. Many arbitrational hearings and awards proceed to final performance without adding a formal submission agreement to the contract to arbitrate and the grievance statement. It often happens that the parties, having a standard agreement to arbitrate all disputes arising between them, proceed to submit to arbitration on the basis of the written griev-

---

95 See Arbitration Provisions in Union Agreements, p. 6 *supra*.

96 This is not unlikely to lead to a prolonged dispute at the arbitration hearing stage at which it is necessary that the issue be defined as an indispensable guide for and limitation upon the umpire or arbitrator. If considerable time has elapsed after the initiation of the grievance, memories may have dimmed, witnesses may be scattered, and collateral issues may have arisen to interfere with the exact statement of the controversy.

ance alone, without supplementing the agreement to arbitrate with a submission contract made immediately preceding the arbitrational hearing. This procedure is sufficient when a general contract has been written and then construed to exclude the need for a formal submission agreement since the entire arbitrational proceeding may sometimes be jeopardized at the start by a tenacious dispute as to just what the question is upon which the arbitrator or umpire shall have authority to make an award. Obviously this question is fundamental since, as herein before indicated, the arbitrator has no authority to make an award in excess of the dispute or controversy submitted to him under the agreement of the parties.

SECTION 5

The Submission Agreement and Grievance Charges and Responses Compared With Court Pleadings

As lawyers all know, the modern court pleadings usually consist of a petition (or complaint), an answer and a reply. Their purpose is to inform the court as to the exact nature of the issue or subject of dispute between the litigating parties. After each of these written documents is filed in court it is subject to attack by various forms of motions or by demurrer, if the opposing party thinks it is obscure or inadequate. The court, usually assisted by argument, will consider the pleading after the motion or demurrer has been filed, and decide whether it is legally adequate and in suitable form. Only when the parties have reached an issue after such preliminary procedure, will the case be put on the calendar for trial on its merits.

In some respects, the written grievance, the responses and the discussions in the several steps of the grievance procedure, when recorded with reasonable accuracy, may be relied upon to serve the arbitrator as the pleadings serve the judge. Hence, when the parties propose that the question to be submitted to the arbitrator shall be, "Shall grievance number so-and-so be sustained or dismissed?", the matter at issue may be clearly ascertainable from the record of the earlier grievance procedure. At this stage the arbitrator may well request the parties to show him in a preliminary way what the record on the grievance is. If he is satisfied that he clearly perceives the full nature of the question or questions that he must decide from that record, he should proceed with the hearing. Otherwise he should request that the parties give him such further data as he may require. In complex situations he should be sure to get this in writing and signed by the authorized representatives of both parties.

Among the companies employing the so-called "permanent arbitrators," it has long been commonplace to omit the negotiation of a formal "submission" in relation to such matters, and to expect the arbitrator or umpire to proceed upon the informal assumption that his job is to hear the evidence and to clear the grievance docket without separate agreements upon specified issues for arbitration as final steps in the grievance procedure.

Therefore, as the multistep grievance procedure becomes an increasingly familiar and routine activity throughout industry, the records that are made should become more complete, clear, and reliable. It is, therefore, possible to predict that the future will see a greater number of arbitrations turn upon a brief submission of evidence to the arbitrator on the relevant facts of a given dispute.

SECTION 6

Formal Requisites — Future Controversies

At common law, there were no formal requirements for either a submission agreement or an agreement to arbitrate, except when the subject matter in controversy, such as title to realty, was such as to require a written or sealed instrument. It was only necessary that the ordinary legal contractual requirements be satisfied, and that they show an undertaking by the parties that the disputed matter should be arbitrated. Many of the present statutes, however, impose formal requisites, such as that the agreement be stated in writing, setting forth both the dispute and the names of the arbitrators.[97] In some instances the enacted law requires that a formal

---

[97] For a detailed study of state statutes and their relation to labor arbitrations see, Labor Arbitration under State Statutes, a report prepared by David Ziskind, (Washington: U. S. Department of Labor, 1943). For a complete and scholarly study of arbitration statutes generally and their relation to commercial disputes see Sturges, Commercial Arbitrations and Awards, (Kansas City: Vernon Law Book Co., 1930). See, Conger v. Dean, 3 Iowa 463, 66 Am. Dec. 93 (1856); Winne v. Elderkin, 2 Pinney (Wis.) 248, 52 Am. Dec. 159 (1849).

acknowledgement be made by the parties, and that they agree upon and set forth the name of the court by which judgment on the award may be entered.[98] It is not unusual that the parties are also required to set forth the time and place of hearing, and to designate the time within which an award must be made.[99]

It is generally adequate that the above-enumerated essentials be set forth in an original general agreement to submit certain types of disputes to arbitration, but if such essentials do not appear therein, a submission agreement providing them will be indispensable.

Where the matters submitted to arbitration are such that an oral agreement regarding them would be valid and enforceable, such an agreement is also usually held to be legally adequate to provide for the arbitration.[100] If, however, the parties cannot competently act upon the subject matter except in writing, the provision for arbitration must likewise be written.[101] Thus, as previously set forth, an arbitration involving title to land would have to be in writing so as to satisfy the Statute of Frauds.[102] It follows that matters pertaining to land that do not involve the title or any transfer thereof, such as value, price, etc., may be submitted by parol agreement to arbitration, but the agreement of the parties alone is not necessarily final if the court in examining the transaction subsequently determines that the title of land was actually involved and the parties have not dealt with the matter in writing as required by law.[103] Real estate questions, of course, are not likely to appear in connection with labor relations. Their occurrence is not entirely impossible, however, and disputes involving other sections of the Statute of Frauds, such as an undertaking to answer for the debt of

---

[98] See, Sturges, *op cit., supra,* pp. 281, 725, and Wilkinson v. Prichard, 145 Iowa 65, 123 N.W. 964 (1909).

[99] Wilkinson v. Prichard, 145 Iowa 65, 123 N.W. 964 (1909); Hopper v. Fromm, 92 Kan. 142, 141 Pac. 175 (1914).

[100] Walden v. McKinnon, 157 Ala. 291, 47 So. 874 (1908); Lilley v. Tuttle, 52 Colo. 121, 117 Pac. 896 (1912); Cady v. Walker, 62 Mich. 157, 28 N.W. 805 (1886); Deal v. Thompson, 51 Okla., 256, 151 Pac. 856 (1915).

[101] District of Columbia v. Bailey, 171 U. S. 161, 43 L.Ed. 118, 18 S.Ct. 868 (1897); Bunnell v. Reynolds, 205 Mo. App. 653, 226 S.W. 614 (1920).

[102] Walden v. McKinnon, 157 Ala. 291, 47 So. 874 (1908); Philbrick v. Preble, 18 Me. 255, 36 Am. Dec. 718 (1841); Galbraith v. Lunsford, 87 Tenn. 89, 9 S.W. 365 (1888); Stewart v. Cass, 16 Vt. 663, 42 Am. Dec. 534 (1844).

[103] Walden v. McKinnon, 157 Ala. 291, 47 So. 874 (1908); Lilley v. Tuttle, 52 Colo. 121, 117 Pac. 896 (1911).

another by an employer who has succeeded to the interests of a predecessor employer by purchase of a going business, are not uncommon.[104]

At common law, it was long held that parties could not enter into a valid agreement to arbitrate disputes arising in the future.[105] It was not denied, however, that after a right once accrued or a controversy actually came into existence, the parties might by agreement legally bind themselves to arbitration and thereby renounce their right to submit the matter primarily to a court for adjudication.[106] The agreement to arbitrate in such cases was regarded as valid and was given full support.[107] Furthermore, by many state courts. it was also established that if the parties had performed an agreement to arbitrate, which in its inception might have been technically defective, their duty to perform the award became binding upon them, and they were not permitted to renounce action taken in obedience to it.[108]

It is not unusual to find in labor contracts limitations upon the agreement to arbitrate; for example, it may be stated that the terms of the annual contract itself may not be modified by arbitration.[109] Or it may be that arbitration is provided for only in a limited number of cases, such as where it is charged that an employee was unjustly or improperly discharged, improperly classified, inadequately paid, or denied seniority or vacation rights. In such instances, it is incumbent upon the parties to consult the contract carefully to determine whether the matter which the parties propose to submit to arbitration is in fact within the terms of the general arbitra-

---

104 Bunnell v. Reynolds, 205 Mo. App. 653, 226 S.W. 614 (1920) .

105 W. H. Blodgett Co. v. Bebe Co., 190 Cal. 665, 214 Pac. 38 (1923) ; Indianapolis Northern Traction Co. v. Brennan, 174 Ind. 1, 87 N.E. 215 (1910) ; Oskaloosa Sav. Bank v. Mahaska County State Bank, 205 Iowa 1351, 219 N.W. 530 (1928) ; First Nat. Bank v. White, 220 Mo. 717, 120 S.W. 36, 132 Am. St. Rep. 612 (1909) .

106 Pacaud v. Waite, 218 Ill. 138, 75 N.E. 779 (1905) ; Cushing v. Babcock, 38 Me. 452 (1853) ; Houston Saengerbund v. Dunn. 41 Tex. Civ. App. 376, 92 S.W. 429 (1906) .

107 Red Cross Line v. Atlantic Fruit Co., 264 U. S. 109, 68 L.Ed. 582, 44 S.Ct. 274 (1924) ; Goerke Kirch Co. v. Goerke Kirch Holding Co., 118 N.J. Eq. 1, 176 A. 902 (1935) ; Martin v. Vansant, 99 Wash. 106, 168 Pac. 990 (1917) ; Kinney v. Baltimore & O. Employees' Relief Assoc., 35 W.Va. 385, 14 S.E. 8 (1891) .

108 Whitcher v. Whitcher, 49 N.H. 176, 6 Am. Rep. 486 (1870) ; Nelson v. Atlantic Coast Line R. Co., 157 N.C. 194, 72 S.E. 998 (1911) ; Williams v. Branning Mfg. Co., 153 N.C. 7, 68 S.E. 902, 138 Am. St. Rep. 637 (1910) .

109 Collective Bargaining Negotiations and Contracts (Washington: Bureau of National Affairs, Inc.) .

tion agreement.[110] If it is not, a special submission agreement must be executed to sustain an arbitration.

As previously noted, at one time the courts generally held, and some courts still maintain, that contracts to arbitrate future disputes incorporated into a general contract are void. Many labor contract arbitration clauses are of this type.[111] This judicial view has led to the question whether or not the fact that such part of the agreement was void necessarily impaired or nullified the rest of the contract.[112] In general, courts examining this question have agreed that the arbitration clause under such circumstances may be treated as a separate or separable undertaking, and that it will not necessarily impair the entire contract unless it is essential to, and a substantial condition of, the entire agreement.[113] It is ordinarily held to be collateral and severable. Some contracts provide that no court action may be maintained by either party for breach of contract, excepting after, and upon an award of an arbitrator.[114] In such instances, the courts which void a clause to arbitrate future disputes are inclined to hold that the presence of such a clause invalidates the entire contract, on the basis that it is against public policy for the parties to exclude themselves from the jurisdiction of the courts.[115] Under such circumstances, it is obviously essential that a submission agreement be entered into after the dispute has arisen, since the general agreement to arbitrate made prior to the occurrence of the controversy can have no binding effect.[116] Parties dealing with labor disputes should be watchful of state laws upon

---

110 *Idem.*

111 Nearly all arbitrational clauses terminating grievance procedure provisions of labor agreements would be vulnerable in this respect. In fact, the majority of arbitration provisions in such agreements look toward controversies arising after the time the agreements are made.

112 Read v. State Ins. Co., 103 Iowa 307, 72 N.W. 665, 64 Am. St. Rep. 180 (1897); Fox Film Corp. v. Ogden Theatre Co., 82 Utah 279, 17 Pac. (2nd) 294 (1933).

113 St. Louis I. M. & S. R. Co. v. Matthews, 64 Ark. 398, 42 S.W. 902 (1897); Read v. State Ins. Co., 103 Iowa 307, 72 N.W. 665, 64 Am. St. Rep. 180 (1897); Fox Film Corp. v. Ogden Theatre Co., 82 Utah 279, 17 Pac. 2d 294 (1933).

114 United States v. Gleason, 175 U. S. 588, 44 L.Ed. 284, 20 S.Ct. 288 (1899); Hamilton v. Home Ins. Co., 137 U. S. 370, 34 L.Ed. 708, 11 S.Ct. 133 (1890); W. H. Blodgett Co. v. Bebe, 190 Cal., 665 214 Pac. 38 (1923); Commercial Union Assur. Co. v. Hocking, 115 Pa. 407, 8 A. 589, 2 Am. St. Rep. 562 (1886).

115 Manchester Fire Assur. Co. v. Koerner, 13 Ind. App. 372, 40 N.E. 1110 (1895); Goerke Kirch Co. v. Goerke Kirch Holding Co., 118 N.J. Eq. 1, 176 A. 902 (1935).

116 Williams v. Branning Mfg. Co., 153 N.C. 7, 68 S.E. 902, 138 Am. St. Rep. 637 (1910); Kelly v. Trimont Lodge, 154 N.C. 97, 69 S.E. 764 (1910).

this phase of arbitration if they would assure themselves that they proceed upon firm legal bases. As set forth in Chapter I, Section 4, *supra,* the *Lincoln Mills* decision and modern statutes have now largely eliminated this difficulty in respect to matters under federal jurisdiction. As to the questions returned to state jurisdiction under Section 701 of the Labor-Management Reporting and Disclosure Act of 1959, there seems to be some minor likelihood of resurgence of state law importance. At this time, however, these matters are far from clear, as indicated herein at Chapter II, Section 3.

Even in the states where an agreement to arbitrate future disputes has been held invalid, the legal defects may be cured by the actual execution of a submission contract by the parties after the controversy has arisen.[117] Furthermore, if they have proceeded upon the agreement as if it were valid, submitted the matter in dispute to arbitrators, and received a proper award, the courts are inclined to hold that the parties are bound, unless of course the award is invalid for some other reason, such as the furtherance of a criminal objective[118] or the attainment of some unlawful restraint of trade.[119]

The unperformed agreement, or "executory contract," for arbitration of a dispute arising in the future, however, is still regarded in some states as void, or voidable at the will of either party, and entirely unenforceable by the courts against the election of either party to disavow the agreement.[120] While many judges were inclined to refer to such agreements as "void" and "illegal," some courts at the same time supported a right to recover damages in case of

---

117 Red Cross Line v. Atlantic Fruit Co., 264 U. S. 109, 68 L.Ed. 582, 44 S.Ct. 274 (1924) ; Oskaloosa Sav. Bank v. Mahaska County State Bank, 205 Iowa 1351, 219 N.W. 530 (1928) ; Whitcher v. Whitcher, 49 N.H. 176, 6 Am. Rep. 486 (1870) ; Nelson v. Atlantic Coast Line R. Co., 157 N.C. 194, 72 S.E. 998 (1911) ; Wilson v. Gregg, 208 Okl. 291, 255 P. 2d 517 (1953) ; 5 Am. Jur. 2d, Arbitration and Award § 36.

118 Franks v. Battles, 147 Ark. 169, 227 S.W. 32 (1921).

119 Paramount Famous Lasky Corp. v. United States, 282 U. S. 30, 75 L.Ed. 145, 51 S.Ct. 42 (1930) ; Fox Film Corp. v. Ogden Theatre Co., 82 Utah 279, 17 Pac. (2nd) 294 (1933).

120 Niagara F. Ins. Co. v. Bishop, 154 Ill. 9, 39 N.E. 1102, 45 Am. St. Rep. 105 (1894) ; Continental Ins. Co. v. Vallandingham, 116 Ky. 287, 76 S.W. 22, 105 Am. St. Rep. 218 (1903) ; First Nat. Bank v. White, 220 Mo. 717, 120 S.W. 36, 132 Am. St. Rep. 612 (1909) ; Kelly v. Trimont Lodge, 154 N.C. 97, 69 S.E. 764 (1910) ; Wilson v. Gregg, 208 Okl. 291, 255 P. 2d 517 (1953) ; Thompson v. Phillips Pipe Line Co., 200 Kan. 669, 438 P. 2d 146 (1968).

breach.[121] The modern tendency under the influence of legislation, however, is to favor broadening and deepening the field of arbitration rather than to restrict it as was formerly the case when courts commonly held against the validity of undertakings to arbitrate future controversies.[122] As noted, this is now reinforced by state statutes, the federal labor statutes, the preemption doctrine, and the *Lincoln Mills* decision.

Statutes in a few jurisdictions provide that all agreements precluding resort to the courts are void.[123] These have been said to imply that any agreement providing for arbitration of subsequently arising disputes will be ineffective. This is founded upon the obsolete idea that it is against public policy to deny access of any party to the courts. However, if the agreement is made a rule of court in such jurisdictions the reason for its invalidity disappears, and as a rule of court, it becomes valid and binding.[124] Hence, in some states the aid of the court seems to be necessary to furnish an initial, technical step in getting a legal, statutory arbitration soundly started, unless the dispute clearly antedated the agreement to arbitrate.[125]

It is not unusual to find provisions in union constitutions, by-laws, or other local or general union rules, to the effect that all controversies that arise between individuals who are members of the union in respect to a union matter, or a dispute between a member and the union, be submitted to either a committee or an arbitrational board of the organization.[126] There seems to be ample

---

121 Red Cross Line v. Atlantic Fruit Co., 264 U. S. 109, 68 L.Ed. 582, 44 S.Ct. Rep. 274 (1924); California Prune & Apricot Growers' Assoc. v. Catz American Co., (CCA 9th) 60 F.2d 788 (1932); Campbell v. American Popular L. Ins. Co., 1 MacArth. (D.C.) 246, 29 Am. Rep. 591 (1873).

122 See Braun, The Settlement of Industrial Disputes, pp. 148, 227 (Philadelphia: Blakiston Co., 1944); Sturges, Commercial Arbitrations and Awards, pp. 82, 85, 88 (Kansas City: Vernon Law Book Co., 1930).

123 See Dunton v. Westchester F. Ins. Co., 104 Me. 372, 71 1037 (1909); Baldwin v. Fraternal Acci. Assoc., 21 Misc. 124, 46 N.Y.S. 1016 (1897); Fox v. Masons' Fraternal Acci. Assoc., 96 Wis. 390, 71 N.W. 363 (1897).

124 United States v. Farragut, 22 Wall. (U. S.) 406, 22 L.Ed. 879 (1874); Hecker v. Fowler, 2 Wall. (U. S.) 123, 17 L.Ed. 759 (1864).

125 Marine Transit Corp. v. Dreyfus, 284 U. S. 263, 76 L.Ed. 282, 52 S.Ct. 166 (1932); Hunter v. Colfax Consol. Coal Co., 175 Iowa 245, 157 N.W. 145 (1916); Gilbert v. Burnstine, 255 N.Y. 348, 174 N.E. 706 (1931); State ex rel. Francher v. Everett, 144 Wash. 592, 258 Pac. 486 (1927).

126 Future controversies of this kind will be affected by the Labor-Management etc. Act of 1959. See Chapter II *supra*; and Ryan v. Cudahy, 157 Ill. 108, 41 N.E. 760, 48 Am. St. Rep. 305 (1895); Nelson v. Atlantic Coast Line R. Co., 157 N.C. 194, 72 S.E. 998 (1911).

authority upon which such provisions may be sustained, particularly in so far as they refer to matters of internal discipline.[127] When property rights become involved, however, there appears a tendency to hold that the rights of the parties must be legally adjudicated, and that a member's right to membership or to property rights in the existence of, or assets of, the local union cannot be taken from him except by properly supported procedure in a court of competent jurisdiction.[128]

The question has at times arisen whether it would be legally sound for a union and an employer to agree that no action might be brought for underpayment of wages, excepting after the dispute was submitted to arbitration.[129] Under some statutes, similar contracts have been sustained.[130] As previously indicated, the modern tendency is to hold such agreements not as illegal attempts to defeat the "jurisdiction of the courts," but rather, as agreements that all wage claims will be supported by a certain kind of evidence.[131]

Under this view of the law, agreements requiring arbitration as a condition precedent to the maintenance of a law suit should be held valid when they refer to back pay, wages payable, hours of employment, vacation rights, working conditions, and other similar questions of fact.[132] An arbitration upon such subjects would partake of the character of an appraisal, and would amount to a fixing of an exact amount of damages for which the aggrieved party might assume the role of plaintiff before a court if a suit upon the

---

127 Pacaud v. Waite, 218 Ill. 138, 75 N.E. 779 (1905).

128 Nelson v. Atlantic Coast Line R. Co., notes 108 and 126 *supra*.

129 United States v. Gleason, 175 U. S. 588, 44 L.Ed. 284, 20 S.Ct. 228 (1899); Arnold v. Bournique, 144 Ill. 132, 33 N.E. 530, 36 Am. St. Rep. 419 (1893); Hood v. Harshorn, 100 Mass. 117, 1 Am. St. Rep. 89 (1868); Jones v. Enoree Power Co., 92 S.C. 263, 75 S.E. 452 (1912).

130 See Sec. 4 *supra*, this Chapter, and Hamilton v. Home Insurance Co., 137 U. S. 370, 34 L. 708, 11 S.Ct. 133 (1890); Kohlsaat v. Main Island Creek Coal Co., 90 W.Va. 656, 112 S.E. 213 (1922); *Re* Lower Baraboo River Drainage District, 199 Wis. 230, 225 N.W. 331 (1929).

131 Mercantile Trust Co. v. Hensey, 205 U. S. 298, 51 L.Ed. 811, 27 S.Ct. 535 (1906); United States v. Gleason, note 129 *supra*; Continental Insurance Co. v. Vallandingham, 116 Ky. 287, 76 S.W. 22, 105 Am. St. Rep. 218 (1903); Sweet v. Morrison, 116 N.Y. 19, 22 N.E. 276 (1889).

132 Compare Norwich Union Fire Ins. Soc. v. Cohn (CCA 10th), 68 Fed. 2d 42 (1933); West v. Coos County, 115 Oregon 409, 237 Pac. 961 (1925); Grady v. Home Fire Ins. Co., 27 R. I. 435, 63 A. 173 (1906); Jones v. Enoree Power Co., 92 S.C. 263, 75 S.E. 452 (1912).

award becomes necessary.[133] It will be noted that in such instances the entire subject is not submitted to the arbitrator, but rather the question, how much was the amount of the back pay due, or, how great was the value of the vacation right denied, etc.[134]

It is interesting to note that some states, such as Nebraska, have held repeatedly that agreements to arbitrate future disputes generally have no validity, and will not be enforced even though they deal with matters merely preliminary and incidental, such as ascertainment of facts.[135] This they hold to be true whether or not the parties have agreed that arbitration procedure shall be a condition precedent to recovery in a law suit.[136] In the State of Pennsylvania the courts have ruled that if an agreement to arbitrate future disputes specifies the arbitrators, it is valid and binding, though unperformed.[137] This is the rule in that jurisdiction whether the subject of the dispute amounts to preliminary and incidental factfinding, or is to be determinative of the main issues or substance of the controversy between the parties.

As it has been previously indicated, submission agreements must make full provision to give the arbitrator authority over the parties, and over the subject matter in dispute and to authorize him to make a final determination of the controversy.[138] The parties may by their submission, however, give the arbitrator as much or as little power as they desire him to have, subject only to legal restrictions.[139] In drawing either an agreement to arbitrate or a sub-

---

133 See Glidden Co. v. Retail Hardware Mutual Fire Ins. Co., 181 Minn. 518, 233 N.W. 310 (1930); Stevenson v. Hazard, 152 Wash. 104, 277 Pac. 450 (1929).
134 Omaha v. Omaha Water Co., 218 U. S. 180, 54 L.Ed. 991, 30 S.C. 615 (1909); Chicago Auditorium Association v. Fine Arts Building, 244 Ill. 532, 91 N.E. 665 (1910); West v. Coos County, note 132 supra.
135 Hartford Fire Insurance Co. v. Hon, 66 Neb. 555, 92 N.W. 746, 103 Am. St. Rep. 725 (1902); Home Fire Insurance Co. v. Kennedy, 47 Neb. 138, 66 N.W. 278, 53 Am. St. Rep. 521 (1896).
136 Hartford Fire Insurance Co. v. Hon, note 135 supra and Home Fire Insurance Co. v. Kennedy, note 135 supra.
137 Penn Plate Glass Co. v. Spring Garden Insurance Co., 189 Pa. 255, 42 A. 138, 69 Am. St. Rep. 810 (1899); Commercial Union Assur. Co. v. Hocking, 115 Pa. 407, 8 A. 589, 2 Am. St. Rep. 562 (1886).
138 Swisher v. Dunn, 89 Kan. 412, 131 Pac. 571 (1913); Brescia Construction Co. v. Walart Construction Co., 264 N.Y. 260, 190 N.E. 484 (1934); Mead v. Owen, 80 Vt. 273, 67 A. 722 (1907); Bailey v. Triplett, 83 W.Va. 169, 98 S.E. 166 (1919); Fagani v. Integrity Finance Corp., 53 Del. 193, 167 A. 2d 67 (1960); Masonic Temple Ass'n of St. Louis v. Farrar, 422 S.W. 2d 95 (Mo. Ct. App., 1967); Campbell v. Farmers Insurance Exchange, 260 A.C.A. 113, 67 Cal. Rptr. 175 (1968).
139 Leavenworth v. Kimble, 157 Miss. 462, 128 So. 354 (1930); Johnson v. Noble, 13 N.H. 286, 38 Am. Dec. 485 (1847); Galbraith v. Lunsford, 87 Tenn. 89, 9 S.W. 365 (1888); Morris v. Zucherman, 262 A.C.A. 485, 68 Cal. Rptr. 913 (1968).

mission agreement, it is important to consider whether common law or statutory arbitration is contemplated,[140] for under statutory arbitration the formalities required are usually greater. But the contract to arbitrate and the submission itself, so far as their contractual validity is concerned, may be tested either by the common law or under the statutes.[141] As elsewhere noted herein, such agreements may be made orally unless they are required by statute to be reduced to writing.[142] They must be made by persons legally capable of contracting and they must be supported by adequate consideration.[143] This element is generally supplied by the reciprocal promises of the parties to abide by the award. It is also of primary importance that the agreement contain a sufficiently definite statement of the matter to be decided and to be made the subject of an award by the arbitrator, so that the extent of the arbitration action can be clearly ascertained.[144] The parties should expressly or by implication agree to respect, abide by, and perform the award.[145] If the state in which the contract is made has any statute providing other formalities, these should be observed.[146]

Excepting where applicable statutes specifically provide the details of arbitrational proceedings, it is possible for the parties to limit the questions submitted, to require the arbitrators to follow legal rules of evidence, to ascertain only the facts, or to find and

---

140 Brown v. Fletcher, 146 Mich. 401, 109 N.W. 686, 123 Am. St. Rep. 233 (1906); Goerke Kirch Co. v. Goerke Kirch Holding Co., 118 N.J. Eq. 1, 176 A. 902 (1935); Millsaps v. Estes, 137 N.C. 535, 50 S.E. 227, 107 Am. St. Rep. 496 (1905).

141 District of Columbia v. Bailey, 171 U. S. 161, 43 L.Ed. 118, 18 S.Ct. 868 (1897); Black v. Woodruff, 193 Ala. 327, 69 So. 97 (1915); Millsaps v. Estes, *supra*, note 5.

142 District of Columbia v. Bailey, note 141 *supra*. Lilley v. Tuttle, 52 Colo. 121, 117 Pac. 896 (1911); Bunnell v. Reynolds, 205 Mo. App. 653, 226 S.W. 614 (1920); Deal v. Thompson, 51 Okla. 256, 151 Pac. 856 (1915).

143 Brown v. Fletcher, note 140 *supra*; Millsaps v. Estes, notes 140 and 121 *supra*; People ex rel. Union Insurance Co. v. Nash, 111 N.Y. 310, 18 N.E. 630, 7 Am. St. Rep. 747 (1888).

144 Tennessee Coal, Iron & Railroad Co. v. Roussell, 155 Ala. 435, 46 So. 866, 130 Am. St. Rep. 56 (1908); Shackleford v. Purket, 2 A. K. Marsh (Ky.) 435, 12 Am. Dec. 422 (1819); Ulene v. Murray Millman of California, Inc., 175 Cal. App. 2d 655, 346 P. 2d 494 (1959).

145 Nutt v. United States, 125 U. S. 650, 31 L.Ed. 821, 8 S.Ct. 997 (1887); Gordon v. United States, 7 Wall (U. S.) 188, 19 L.Ed. 35 (1868); Whitcher v. Whitcher, 49 N.H. 176, 6 Am. Rep. 486 (1870); King v. Beale, 198 Va. 802, 96 S.E. 2d 765 (1957); General Construction Co. v. Hering Realty Co., 201 F.Supp. 487 (E.D. S.C., 1962). See also: Col. Rules of Civil Procedure, Rule 109 (b); Iowa Code Anno., § 90.5.

146 Wilkinson v. Prichard, 145 Iowa 65, 123 N.W. 964 (1909); Inslee v. Flagg, 26 N.J.L. 368, 69 Am. Dec. 580 (1857); Winne v. Elderkin, 2 Pinney (Wis.) 248, 52 Am. Dec. 159 (1847).

apply both the law and the facts.[147] They may, if they wish to do so, submit the controversy without restrictions and give the arbitrators full authority to proceed as they see fit in arriving at an award.[148] In some states, the number of arbitrators required to make a valid award is fixed by statute.[149] If the parties agree so to do, however, they might require that the award be unanimous,[150] or that if the arbitrators disagree, the entire matter shall be decided by a specified member as a single umpire.[151] This course is strongly favored by most parties to labor disputes since it eliminates the chance of a complete deadlock. If the arbitrational proceeding is conducted on the basis of a submission agreement, it must conform to the provisions of the previously made contract to arbitrate, unless the submission clearly shows a mutual agreement of the parties to broaden or to narrow their earlier agreement to arbitrate, by means of the submission agreement, in setting forth the specific issues that arose after and under the general contract.[152]

Where a matter has been pending in court, the parties may generally provide that the court action shall be terminated as a result of entering into the arbitration agreement.[153] On the other hand, they may stipulate that certain disputed matters are to be settled by arbitration rather than adjudication and that judgment shall be entered upon the award.[154] Statutes frequently pro-

---

[147] Leavenworth v. Kimble, 157 Miss. 462, 128 So. 354 (1930); Johnson v. Noble, 13 N.H. 286, 38 Am. Dec. 485 (1847); Galbraith v. Lunsford, note 139, supra; Continental Materials Corp. v. Gaddis Mining Co., 306 F. 2d 952 (10th Cir., 1962).

[148] Re Curtis & Castle, 64 Conn. 501, 30 A. 769, 42 Am. St. Rep. 200 (1894); Galbraith v. Lunsford, notes 139 and 147, supra; Oinoussian S.S. Corp. of Panama v. Sabre Shipping Corp., 224 F.Supp. 807 (S.D. N.Y., 1963).

[149] Marine Transit Corporation v. Dreyfus, 284 U. S. 263 (1932).

[150] Rhodes v. Folmar, 208 Ala. 595, 94 So. 745 (1922); Towne v. Jaquith, 6 Mass. 46, 4 Am. Dec. 84 (1809); Sutcliffe v. Pawtucket Amusement Co., 51 R.I. 493, 155 A. 578 (1931).

[151] King v. Cook, 1 T.U.P. Charit, (Ga.) 286, 4 Am. Dec. 715 (1810); Day v. Hammond, 57 N.Y. 479, 15 Am. Rep. 522 (1874); Chandos v. American Fire Insurance Co., 84 Wis. 184, 54 N.W. 390 (1893).

[152] Wilkinson v. Prichard, note 146, supra; Bank of Monroe v. Widner, 11 Paige (N.Y.) 529, 43 Am. Dec. 768 (1845); Ulene v. Murray Millman of California, Inc., 175 Cal. App. 2d 655, 346 P. 2d 494 (1959).

[153] Alameda County Water District v. Spring Valley Water District, 67 Cal. App. 533, 227 Pac. 953 (1924); Ensign v. St. Louis & S. F. R. Co., 62 How. (N.Y.) 123 (1881); Brendlinger v. Yeagley, 53 Pa. 464 (1866); Reith v. Wynhoff, 28 Wis. 2d 336, 137 N.W. 2d 33 (1965).

[154] Burrell v. United States, 77 C.C.A. 308, 147 F. 44 (1906); Peele v. North & South Carolina R. Co., 159 N.C. 60, 74 S.E. 592 (1912); Neff v. Talbot, 1 Va. Cas. 140 (1803); Hills v. Passage, 21 Wis. 294 (1867).

vide that submission of a pending controversy to arbitration in lieu of a pending suit may be made by a rule of court.[155] In such instances, the submission agreement should be drawn accordingly, though in some cases the courts have decided that consent to the rule may be inferred from an agreement to submit to arbitration while a case is pending in court, and that the parties need not expressly stipulate for such a result.[156]

SECTION 7

Contract Terms Concerning Arbitration — Some Features of Contract Bargaining — Interpretation of Agreements and Submissions

Agreements to arbitrate, which are now specifically enforceable in the federal courts under the *Lincoln Mills* doctrine, are found in practically every collectively bargained contract negotiated today. However, it is necessary to remember that both the court and the arbitrator must find in such contracts the obligation to arbitrate and also full authority over the extent and scope of the matters to be arbitrated. The latter is often more difficult to ascertain than the former. It is therefore relevant to this area of thought to observe answers to the questions: What is collective bargaining? What kind of people do it? How do they work? What kind of documents result?

Collective bargaining is now familiar to all who will likely have occasion to open a book on arbitration of labor disputes. For immediate purpose it is important only to observe the fact that it concerns bargaining about working conditions and terms of employment between an employer or a group of employers on the one hand, and a union (an independent, a local, or an international) on the other.

---

155 Marine Transit Corporation v. Dreyfus, note 149, *supra*; Murphy v. Greenberg, 246 Pa. 387, 92 A. 511 (1914) ; Zehner v. Lehigh Coal and Nav. Co., 187 Pa. 487, 41 A. 464 (1898) . See also: Conn. General Statutes Anno. 52-409; Kentucky Revised Statutes 417.020; New Jersey Statutes Anno. 2A:24-1, 2A:24-2; Ohio Revised Code Anno. 2711.02; 5 Purdon's Pennsylvania Statutes Anno. §§ 1, 2; Virginia Code Anno. § 8-503.

156 Murphy v. Greenberg, note 155 *supra;* Shisler v. Keavy, 75 Pa. 79 (1874) ; Summy v. Heistand, 65 Pa. 300 (1870) .

What kind of people participate? In some instances, a well-educated staff of law-trained men and economists is active on each side. In some other instances, the actual bargaining agents on one side are very well-educated, experienced, and skillful, while on the other side very average people appear. In other instances, the actual bargaining group, union or employer, may be at a great disadvantage because of lack of experience and education as compared to that of their opponents.

This is not to criticize collective bargaining. It is only to point to the practical source of the agreements to arbitrate, to the men who write them, and hence to the atmosphere in which an arbitrator, or court, must seek to interpret and fairly to apply them. It is a common human failing for a writer of words to assume that the reader will draw from them the meaning that the writer intends. Common experience teaches that this unfortunately is often not the case.

When the fortunes of collective bargaining have resulted in the presence of men of limited education and uncertain vocabularies on a bargaining team, words may be poorly selected and sentence structure and punctuation may create ambiguities and thereby invite interpretations which may not be satisfying to at least one of the parties. To some extent an experienced arbitrator may seek to ascribe an orthodox meaning to unusual terms, but he cannot ignore the text of the contract in seeking what he determines to be a sound result. After all, his authority springs from the agreement to arbitrate certain specified disputes as indicated in the writing. Unless a reviewing court can find a firm foundation of authority in the agreement of the parties for the award, it is unlikely to sustain it.

How do collective bargaining representatives work? As a rule, these spokesmen start with a former contract of the same parties, if there was one, and amend it by changing a few words here and there, and by adding or cutting out paragraphs, etc. If there was no prior agreement between the same parties, one side or both are likely to obtain contracts of other parties in the same industry and try to alter the same to satisfy their needs.

What results from this type of work? In both of the foregoing cases, the result is a "piecemeal construction" job that may be defective in that some words were introduced into, or deleted from, one part of the agreement that was in some way dependent upon another part that also should have been amended but was not. The result may weaken both parts as well as related areas of the resulting agreement.

The method of amending agreements is not condemned here. It probably is the most practical way for the parties to work. It is urged, however, that utmost care be taken in such rephrasing. This matter is discussed here to point out again the complexities involved in deciding arbitrability in some connections, and to reemphasize to all concerned the need for a full and careful study of the contractural arbitration provisions, their background, meaning, and application.

Generally speaking, the arbitrator's interpretation of a contract to arbitrate or of a submission may not be regarded as conclusive.[157] If this were not true, the arbitrator would be free to interpret the submission as including matters clearly not embraced within it, or as excluding matters that it was his duty to consider and decide.[158] The matter of such interpretation, therefore, necessarily falls ultimately upon a reviewing court when a controversy arises as to whether the action of the arbitrator was too broad or, on the other hand, inadequate.[159] In general, the courts attempt to find and to give effect to the intentions of the parties when questions of interpretation of arbitrational agreements or submissions come before them.[160] The language of the submission will be taken in its natural, usual sense, unless the context or evidence indicates that a technical or unusual meaning was in-

---

157 Joseph Goldstein, et al. v. International Ladies Garment Workers' Union, 328 Pa. 385, 196 Atl. 43, 1-A LRRM 728 (1938); Columbia v. Cauca Co., 190 U. S. 524, 47 L.Ed. 1159, 23 S.Ct. 704 (1902); Swisher v. Dunn, note 138 *supra*; Holstead v. Seaman, 82 N.Y. 27, 37 Am. Rep. 536 (1880).

158 Boston Store v. Schleuter, 88 Ark. 213, 114 S.W. 242 (1908); Aetna Indemnity Co. v. Waters, 110 Md. 673, 73 A. 712 (1909); Ruch v. York City, 233 Pa. 35, 81 A. 891 (1911); Galveston v. Devlin, 84 Texas 319, 19 S.W. 395 (1892); Local 453, International Union of Electrical, Radio & Machine Workers, AFL-CIO, v. Otis Elevator Co., 201 F.Supp. 213, 49 LRRM 2595 (S.D. N.Y. 1962).

159 McAvoy v. Long, 13 Ill. 147 (1851); Galveston, H. & S. A. R. Co. v. Henry & Dilley, 65 Tex. 685 (1886); Sloan v. Journal Publishing Co., 213 Ore. 324, 324 P. 2d 449 (1957); Amicizia Societa Navegazione v. Chilean Nitrate & Iodine Sales Corp., 184 F.Supp. 116 (S.D. N.Y., 1964).

160 Burchell v. Marsh, 17 How. (U. S.) 344, 15 L.Ed. 96 (1854); Towne v. Jaquith, note 150 *supra*; Hunn v. Pennsylvania Inst., 221 Pa. 403, 70 A. 812 (1908).

tended by the parties.[161] The agreement is considered as a whole, and no one part may be lifted from the document.[162] This disposition by the courts does not permit them to include matters within the arbitrational submission that were clearly excluded, or to exclude therefrom as irrelevant and improper, matters that the parties according to their language have clearly submitted to the arbitrators.[163] The courts will not review an arbitration award on its merits,[164] especially when it states that the parties agree to be bound by the decision of the arbitrator.[165]

It is characteristic of many arbitration agreements in labor disputes that the matter or matters in controversy are stated very broadly, and now and then with downright vagueness and uncertainty.[166] In such instances, if the parties proceed through a hearing, submit their evidence, and await the award without making objections to the uncertainty of the agreement to arbitrate, it is likely that the courts will sustain the award, and hold it effective as an adjudication of all of the rights of the parties and persons in privity with them.[167] But the effect of such a submission agreement while executory, that is, while as yet entirely unperformed, is somewhat doubtful. Whether it will be sustained will depend upon the effects of the common law rules, the state statutes, and in some instances or jurisdictions, upon an applicable rule of court. How it would fare in a federal court since the *Lincoln Mills* decision can be only a field of speculation.

---

161 Columbia v. Cauca Co., note 157 *supra;* Carnochan v. Christie, 11 Wheat. (U. S.) 446, 6 L.Ed. 516 (1826) ; William H. Low Estate Co. v. Lederer Realty Corporation, 35 R.I. 352, 86 A.881 (1913) .

162 Carnochan v. Christi, note 161 *supra;* Richards v. Smith, 33 Utah 8, 91 Pac. 683 (1907) .

163 Hemingway v. Stansell, 106 U. S. 399, 27 L.Ed. 245, 1 S.Ct. 473 (1882) ; Swisher v. Dunn, notes 138 and 157 *supra;* Brescia Construction Co. v. Walart Construction Co., note 138 *supra;* Bailey v. Triplett, 83 W.Va. 169, 98 S.E. 166 (1919) .

164 Straws v. North Hollywood Hospital, Inc., 150 Cal. App. 2d 306, 309 P. 2d 541 (1957) ; Brotherhood of Railroad Trainmen v. Chicago, M., St. P & P. R. Co., 237 F.Supp. 404 (D. D.C., 1964) .

165 New Bedford Defense Products Division of the Firestone Tire & Rubber Co. v. Local No. 1113 of the International Union, United Automobile, Aircraft & Agriculture Implement Workers of America, 160 F. Supp. 103, 41 LRRM 2850 (D. Mass., 1958) , *aff'd.* 258 F. 2d 522, 42 LRRM 2518 (1st Cir., 1958) .

166 See this Chapter, sections 1-2, *supra.*

167 W. H. Blodgett Co. v. Bebe Co., 190 Cal. 665, 214 Pac. 38 (1923) ; Whitcher v. Whitcher, note 22 *supra;* Williams v. Branning Mfg. Co., 153 N.C. 7, 68 S.E. 902 (1910) .

Where the parties have already become parties to a litigation, a submission agreement is ordinarily construed as involving only the matters that were pending before the court as shown by the pleadings, unless the parties expressly add thereto certain other relevant issues to be considered at the same time and made the subject of an award by the arbitrators.[168]

Since at common law the parties were unable to exclude themselves from admission to the courts by an unperformed agreement to arbitrate, neither the submission contract, or the agreement to arbitrate future differences would bar a suit either at law or in equity on the subject matter. In some states, statutes have changed this rule.[169] But where the agreement makes arbitration of some preliminary incidental question of fact a condition precedent to maintenance of a law suit, the parties are held in some jurisdictions to be excluded from proceeding in court until such matter has been arbitrated.[170]

Where an agreement to arbitrate future disputes is not binding until performed, it may be revoked at any time.[171] The party opposing the revocation has been recognized by some courts, however, as having a right of action for damages resulting from breach of the agreement.[172] It follows, also, in such jurisdictions, that even though there is an express stipulation that a suit may not be maintained until the arbitration has been completed, the right of

---

168 York & C. R. Co. v. Myers, 18 How. (U. S.) 246, 15 L.Ed. 380 (1855) ; Alexandria Canal Co. v. Swann, 5 How. (U. S.) 83, 12 L.Ed. 60 (1847) ; Wilkinson v. Prichard, notes 146 and 152 *supra*.

169 Hamilton v. Home Ins. Co., 137 U. S. 370, 34 L.Ed. 708, 11 S.Ct. 133 (1890) note 130 *supra*; Western Assur. Co. v. Hall, 120 Ala. 547, 24 So. 936, 74 Am. St. Rep. 48 (1898) ; First National Bank v. White, 220 Mo. 717, 120 S.W. 36, 132 Am. St. Rep. 612 (1909) ; Pepin v. Societe St. Jean Baptiste, 23 R.I. 81, 49 A. 387, 91 Am. St. Rep. 620 (1901) .

170 Red Cross Line v. Atlantic Fruit Co., 264 U. S. 109, 68 L.Ed. 582, 44 S.Ct. 274 (1924) ; W. H. Blodgett Co. v. Bebe Co., 190 Cal. 665, 214 Pac. 38 (1923) ; Lawrence v. White, 131 Ga. 840, 63 S.E. 631 (1909) ; Read v. State Insurance Co., 103 Iowa 307, 72 N.W. 665, 64 Am. St. Rep. 180 (1897) .

171 Insurance Co. of N. A. v. Kempner, 132 Ark. 215, 200 S.W. 986 (1918) ; Oskaloosa Savings Bank v. Mahaska County State Bank, 205 Iowa 1351, 219 N.W. 530 (1928) ; Williams v. Branning Mfg. Co., note 167 *supra*; Martin v. Vansant, 99 Wash. 106, 168 Pac. 990 (1917) . Register v. Herrin, 110 Ga. App. 736, 140 S.E. 2d 82 (1964) ; Poray v. Royal Globe Insurance Co. 90 N.J. Super. 454, 217 A. 2d 916 (1966) .

172 Red Cross Line v. Atlantic Fruit Co., *supra*, note 170. Hartford Fire Ins. Co. v. Hon, notes 135 and 136 *supra*; Goerke Kirch Co. v. Goerke Kirch Holding Co., note 140 *supra*; Jones v. Enoree Power Co., 92 S.C. 263, 75 S.E. 452 (1912) ; Tejas Development Co. v. McGough Bros., 165 F. 2d 276 (6th Cir., 1947) .

action itself is complete without going through the agreed procedure before an arbitrator.[173]

In the courts of several of the states,[174] as in the federal courts,[175] the applicable statutes have been construed so as to broaden the effects of certain classes of arbitrational agreements. The result has been that an agreement to arbitrate future disputes generally has been made irrevocable, and therefore an effective bar to a suit until the arbitration proceeding has been completed. Such an agreement is specifically enforceable in equity,[176] and no action may be maintained in a court until the arbitration has been completed.[177] Wherever state courts so hold, labor contract grievance procedures that terminate in arbitration, which contain provisions to arbitrate future disputes, appear to be enforceable though they might be so questionable in other states so as to require the execution of a submission after each controversy has arisen. The effect of the U. S. Supreme Court decision in the *Lincoln Mills* case in this area is discussed in Chapter I, Section 4, and this chapter, Section 2, *supra*.

The tendency in framing recent legislation has been to provide that written agreements to submit existing controversies to arbitration is effective to bar a suit upon the dispute until after arbitration.[178] Modern statutes which provide that a submission to arbitration may be established by the parties as a condition precedent to suit have considerably broadened the legal view upon this

---

173 W. H. Blodgett Co. v. Bebe Co., note 170 *supra*; Meachem v. Jamestown, F. & C. R. Co., 211 N.Y. 346, 105 N.E. 653 (1914); Mentz v. Armenia Fire Insurance Co., 70 Pa. 478, 21 Am. Rep. 80 (1875).

174 Gilbert v. Burnstine, 255 N.Y. 348, 174 N.E. 706 (1931); Nippon Ki-Ito Kaisha v. Ewing-Thomas Corp., 313 Pa. 442, 170 A. 286 (1934); State ex rel. Fancher v. Everett, 144 Wash. 592, 258 Pac. 486 (1927).

175 Marine Transit Corp. v. Dreyfus, notes 149 and 155 *supra;* Red Cross Line v. Atlantic Fruit Co., *supra*, notes 170 and 172; Standard Magnesium Corp. v. Fuchs, 251 F. 2d 455 (10th Cir., 1957). Notes 18 and 19 *supra*, and related text.

176 Goerke Kirch Co. v. Goerke Kirch Holding Co., notes 140 and 172 *supra*; State ex rel. Fancher v. Everett, *supra*, note 174; Thorgaard Plumbing & Heating Co. v. County of Kings, 71 D. 2d 122, 426 P. 2d 828 (Washington, 1967).

177 Shanferoke Coal and Supply Corp. v. Westchester Service Corp., 293 U. S. 449, 79 L.Ed. 583, 55 S.Ct. 313 (1935); Gilbert v. Burnstine, note 174 *supra;* Nippon Ki-Ito Kaisha v. Ewing-Thomas Corp., note 174 *supra*.
See: Minn. Statutes Anno. § 527.09 (d).

178 Shanferoke Coal & Supply Corporation v. Westchester Service Corporation, 293 U. S. 449, 79 L.Ed. 583, 55 S.Ct. 313 (1934); Marine Transit Corporation v. Dreyfus, 284 U. S. 263, 76 L.Ed. 282, 52 S.Ct. 166 (1932); Gilbert v. Burnstine, 255 N.Y. 348, 174 N.E. 706 (1931); State ex rel. Fancher v. Everett, 144 Wash. 592, 258 Pac. 486 (1927).

point.[179] In the absence of statute, however, in a few jurisdictions it appears possible for the parties to make a submission to arbitration an effective condition precedent to maintenance of any action in court.[180] This is true, even though the arbitrational proceeding is directed only to the ascertainment of certain facts by appraisers or arbitrators.[181] The judicial approach to such contracts, however, indicates a reluctance on the part of some judges to sustain such agreements so as to exclude the parties from the jurisdiction of the courts until after performances of the condition precedent — arbitration.[182] Where a contract may be so construed, it provides a situation in which either party, by insisting on the arbitration, may block an action in court by the other.[183] In this connection, even though the agreement to arbitrate is clear and the parties have obviously agreed that arbitration is to be a condition precedent to any law suit, if the parties have been vague or uncertain as to the selection of nomination of an arbitrator, the courts have construed the arbitration clause as ineffective. This has then permitted the maintenance of a suit without requiring the condition of arbitration be performed.[184]

179 Red Cross Line v. Atlantic Fruit Co., 264 U. S. 109, 68 L.Ed. 582, 44 S.Ct. 274 (1924) ; Hunter v. Colfax Consolidated Coal Co., 175 Iowa 245, 154 N.W. 1037, 157 N.W. 145 (1916) ; Glidden Co. v. Retail Hardware Mutual Fire Insurance Co., 181 Minn. 518, 233 N.W. 310 (1930) ; Gilbert v. Burnstine, 255 N.Y. 348, 174 N.E. 706 (1931) .

180 W. H. Blodgett Co. v. Bebe Co., 190 Cal. 665, 214 Pac. 38 (1923) ; Pennsylvania Co. v. Reager, 152 Ky. 824, 154 S.W. 412 (1913) ; Second Soc. of Universalists v. Royal Insurance Co., 221 Mass. 518, 109 N.E. 384 (1915) ; Nelson v. Atlantic Coast Line Railroad Co., 157 N.C. 194, 72 S.E. 998 (1911) ; Williams v. Pacific Electric Railway Co., 147 C.A. 2d 1, 304 P. 2d 715 (1957) ; Grunwald-Marx v. L.A. Amalgamated Clothing Workers of America, 192 C.A. 2d 268, 13 Cal. Rptr. 446 (1961) .

181 United States v. Gleason, 175 U. S. 588, 44 L.Ed. 284, 20 S.Ct. 228 (1899) ; Dunton v. Westchester Fire Insurance Co., 104 Me. 372, 71 A. 1037 (1909) ; Chadwick v. Phoenix Accident & Sick Benefit Association, 143 Mich. 481, 106 N.W. 1122 (1906) ; Commercial Union Assurance Co. v. Hocking, 115 Pa. 407, 8 A. 589, 2 Am. St. Rep. 562 (1886) .

182 The Cutler-Hammer decision offers an example of this attitude. See Chapter I, Sec. 4, supra; Western Assurance Co. v. Hall, 120 Ala. 547, 24 So. 936 74 Am. St. Rep. 48 (1898) ; Lawrence v. White, 131 Ga. 840, 63 S.E. 631 (1909) ; Read v. State Insurance Company, 103 Iowa 307, 72 N.W. 665, 64 Am. St. Rep. 180 (1897) ; Fox Film Corporation v. Ogden Theatre Company, 82 Utah 279 (1933) .

183 Continental Insurance Co. v. Wilson, 45 Kansas 250, 25 P. 629, 23 Am. St. Rep. 720 (1891) ; Dunton v. Westchester Fire Insurance Co., 104 Maine 372, 71 A. 1037 (1909) .

184 Aetna Insurance Co. v. McLead, 57 Kansas 95, 45 P. 73, 57 Am. St. Rep. 320 (1896) ; Home Fire Insurance Co. v. Kennedy, 47 Neb. 138, 66 N.W. 278, 53 Am. St. Rep. 521 (1896) .

Many labor agreements provide that arbitration is to proceed only upon the condition that a certain grievance procedure has been followed, or that notice has been served upon one party by the other that it desires to reopen negotiations concerning some feature of the contract.[185] Under some contracts, it also is optional for either one party or the other to demand arbitration following certain preliminary negotiations with regard to the matter in dispute.[186] Here, the courts have been inclined to regard the arbitrational clause as dormant and ineffective until the condition precedent to the right to demand arbitration has been performed.[187] In such cases, therefore, the existence of the arbitration clause would not bar a law suit, even though it might constitute a matter of defense in some respects. It seems very unrealistic to hold, however, as in one Massachusetts case, that where the contract provided that arbitration should be a condition precedent to an action, the condition had been performed by holding the arbitration hearing though there had been no valid award made following it.[188]

Many labor agreements are drawn so as to bind only a local union, and, at times, a local company that is a subsidiary of a holding company. In some instances, labor contracts are drawn so as to affect the local union, the parent union, the local operating employer company, and its parent company. This latter practice is

---

185 See Collective Bargaining Negotiations and Contracts (Washington: The Bureau of National Affairs, Inc.); Union Agreement Provisions, pp. 154, 155, 158 (Washington, U. S. Department of Labor, Bulletin No. 686, 1942); Braun, The Settlement of Labor Disputes, p. 121 Philadelphia, Blakiston Co., 1944); Hill & Hook, Management at the Bargaining Table, pp. 85, 216 (New York, McGraw-Hill Book Co., 1945); Big Apple Supermarkets, Inc. v. Meat Cutters, 52 LRRM 2631 (N.Y. Sup. Ct. 1963).

See also; C.C.H. Labor Law Reporter, Specimen Union Contracts:
59,917 (B.F. Goodrich Co.),
59,920 (Consolidated Edison),
59,923 (Ford Motor Co.),
59,938 (Pittsburgh Plate Glass Co.).

186 Randall v. American Fire Insurance Co., 10 Mont. 340, 25 P. 953, 24 Am. St. Rep. 50 (1891); Chainless Cycle Mfg. Co. v. Security Insurance Co., 169 N.Y. 304, 62 N.E. 392 (1901).

187 Hamilton v. Liverpool & London & Globe Insurance Co., 136 U. S. 242, 34 L.Ed. 419, 10 S.Ct. 945 (1899); German-American Insurance Company v. Steiger, 109 Ill. 254 (1884); Garretson v. Merchants' & Bankers' Fire Insurance Co., 114 Iowa 17, 86 N.W. 32 (1901); Nurney v. Firemen's Fund Insurance Co., 63 Mich. 633, 30 N.W. 350, 6 Am. St. Rep. 338 (1886).

188 Second Soc. of Universalists v. Royal Ins. Co., 221 Mass. 518, 109 N.E. 384 (1915).

better, for while, under some circumstances, it might be held
that the action of the local concern or union would be binding
upon the parent organization, there seems to be good reason to
believe that persons who are not parties to an arbitration agreement, or to a principal contract concerning an arbitration clause
are not bound thereby. In such a case, arbitration would not be
a condition precedent to the maintenance of a law suit, or to the
pursuance of some other avenue of action such as before the National Labor Relations Board or otherwise.[189] There would seem
to be little or no doubt that action by a union would clearly bind
the members thereof.[190] But there is considerable uncertainty as
to whether a union contract providing for arbitration will be regarded as binding upon nonunion employees, even in the instances where the union is clearly the legally established, sole
bargaining agent for all workers in an open-shop or maintenance-
of-membership institution.[191] In such situations, prudence would
seem to dictate that at or before the beginning of the arbitrational
hearing, a submission agreement should be obtained bearing the
signatures of all interested parties, particularly if they were not
parties to the original agreement to arbitrate future controversies.[192]

Occasionally, the parties to a controversy will recognize that one
dispute is typical of many and informally agree that one of them
is to be arbitrated and that the result of the proceeding or award
will be applicable to all of the pending disputed matters.[193] Where
the dispute has to do with a number of individual employees'
claims for overtime, reclassification, vacation rights, or other demands, the submission should clearly so indicate, so that the award
may be authoritative in respect to each one; otherwise, it may be

---

[189] Carpenters' Union v. Citizens Committee, 333 Ill. 225, 164 N.E. 393 (1929);
Brescia Construction Co. v. Walart Construction Co., 264 N.Y. 260, 190 N.E. 484
(1934); Columbus, H. Valley & T. R. Co. v. Burke, 54 Ohio St. 98, 43 N.E. 282
(1896).
[190] Andrews v. Local Union No. 13, Journeymen Plumbers, Gas & Steamfitters,
and Sprinkler Fitters, of Rochester, N.Y., 234 N.Y.S. 208, 133 Misc. 899 (1929).
[191] See this Chapter, Section 3, *supra*. Cone v. Dunham, 59 Conn. 145, 20 A. 311
(1890); Carpenters' Union v. Citizens Committee, 333 Ill. 225, 164 N.E. 393 (1929);
Brescia Construction Co. v. Walart Construction Co., 264 N.Y. 260, 190 N.E. 484
(1934).
[192] Brescia Construction Co. v. Walart Construction Co., 264 N.Y. 260, 190 N.E.
484 (1934); Columbus, H. Valley & I. R. Co. v. Burke, 54 Ohio St. 98, 43 N.E. 282
(1896).
[193] Louis Michel v. Whitecourt Construction Co., 264 N.Y. 23, 189 N.E. 767 (1934).

uncertain as to whether the award in the one case is actually binding as to the several similarly disputed questions.[194] The use of the "test case" type of arbitration is not recommended, however, nor does it appear to be in any way advantageous in view of the simple and relatively informal steps that may be taken, and that, if taken, will make the award definitely applicable to all parties having similar claims or controversies under the contract.

Under the statutes of most states, employees in certain situations are entitled to enjoyment of the right of a mechanic's lien.[195] If a union of such employees enters into an agreement by which arbitration shall be a condition precedent to any suit, it is questionable whether such employees may thereafter assert the mechanic's lien.[196] Some courts have held that the lien is not so waived,[197] but others have held that the submission of the dispute to arbitration results in a waiver of the lien by the arbitrating parties.[198] There is considerable technical doubt and difficulty upon this point and caution would seem to dictate that the parties expressly state, unless they intend the contrary, that the agreement to arbitrate shall not in any case nor any way constitute a waiver of the mechanic's lien, nor a waiver of the right to take any step necessary to secure such lien at any time.[199]

Where there has been a legal submission to arbitration culminating in an award, the award takes the place of the original claim.[200] Thereafter, the remedy in the courts is restricted to the

---

194 This will usually consist of merely adding a short descriptive paragraph to the submission at the beginning of a hearing. If either party objects to such step, it would seem to be helpful to all others concerned, to learn its attitude at that stage rather than at a later time.

195 Tice v. Moore, 82 Conn. 244, 73 A. 133 (1909); Prince v. Neal-Millard Co., 124 Ga. 884, 53 S.E. 761 (1906); Weeter Lumber Co. v. Fales, 20 Idaho 255, 118 Pac. 289 (1911); Spengler v. Stiles-Tull Lumber Co., 94 Miss. 780, 48 So. 966 (1910).

196 Sorg v. Crandall, 233 Ill. 79, 84 N.E. 181 (1908); Brescia Construction Co. v. Walart Construction Co., 264 N.Y. 260, 190 N.E. 484 (1934); New York Lumber & Woodworking Co. v. Schneider, 15 Daly 15, 1 N.Y.S. 441 (1888).

197 Paulsen v. Manske, 126 Ill. 72, 18 N.E. 275, 9 Am. St. Rep. 532 (1888).

198 New York Lumber & Woodworking Co. v. Schneider, 15 Daly 15, 1 N.Y.S. 441 (1888).

199 Such a statement would serve to evidence the mutual intention of the parties which should be determinative on the question whether waiver was agreed on by them or otherwise. See Brescia Constr. Co. v. Walart Constr. Co., 264 N.Y. 260, 190 N.E. 484, 93 A.L.R. 1148 (1934).

200 Dunn v. Sutliff, 1 Mich. 24 (1847); Callanan v. Port Huron & N. W. R. Co., 61 Mich. 15, 27 N.W. 718 (1886); Albert v. Albert, 391 S.W. 2d 186 (Texas Ct. of Civil Appeals, 1965).

enforcement of the award.[201] Unless it is agreed that a judgment may be entered in conformity with the award, the submission and award may be treated as a complete defense to the further maintenance of any suit involving the same subject matter between the parties.[202] Entry of judgment on awards is sometimes provided for by statutes.[203] The parties by their agreement may ordinarily control the question of whether the court is to enter a judgment automatically upon the award, or is to dismiss any pending suit, and thereby regard the award itself as having been selected by the parties as a complete and full alternative to a proceeding before the court.[204] Where the intentions of the parties remain uncertain under the contract, the court may either enter a judgment upon the award, or, it may to do as justice would seem to require. Some statutes, however, expressly regulate for the outcome of a pending suit where the subject matter has also been submitted to arbitration. Obviously, in such instances, the statutes control. Most such statutes provide that the submission to arbitration shall be under a rule of court,[205] but other statutes do not preclude the possibility that the parties may, by their arbitration contract, obtain the same effect as by an ordinary, common-law submission.[206] Under some state acts, arbitration has sometimes been declared to be a method of trial, and the award has been given virtually the effect of a judgment.[207] The matters in arbitration

---

201 Van Derhoof v. Dean, 1 Mich. 463 (1847) ; Houston & T. C. R. Co. v. Newman, 2 Tex. App. Civ. Cas. (Willson) 303 (1884) .

202 Bank of Monroe v. Widner, 11 Paige (N.Y.) 529, 43 Am. Dec. 768 (1845) ; McNulty v. Solley, 95 N.Y. 242 (1884) ; Jones v. Thomas, 120 Wis. 274, 97 N.W. 950 (1904) ; Travelers' Insurance Co. v. Pierce Engine Co., 141 Wis. 103, 123 N.W. 643 (1909) ; Fraizer v. Ford Motor Co., UAW., 364 Mich. 648, 112 N.W. 2d 80 (1961) ; Albert v. Albert, 391 S.W. 2d 186 (Texas Ct. of Civil Appeals, 1965) .

203 Callanan v. Port Huron & N. W. R. Co., 61 Mich. 15, 27 N.W. 718 (1886) ; Bowen v. Lazalere, 44 Mo. 383 (1869) .

204 Black v. Woodruff, 193 Ala. 327, 69 So. 97 (1915) ; Wilkinson v. Prichard, 145 Iowa 65, 123 N.W. 964 (1909) ; Bank of Monroe v. Widner, 11 Paige (N.Y.) 529, 43 Am. Dec. 768 (1845) .

205 See Marine Transit Corp. v. Dreyfus, 284 U. S. 263, 76 Fed. 282, 52 S.Ct. 166 (1932) ; Red Cross Line v. Atlantic Fruit Co., 264 U. S. 109, 68 L.Ed. 582, 44 S.Ct. 274 (1924) ; Murphy v. Greenberg, 246 Pa. 387, 92 A. 511 (1914) .

206 Black v. Woodruff, 193 Ala. 327, 69 So. 97 (1915) ; Modern System Bakery v. Salisburg, 215 Ky. 230, 284 S.W. 994 (1926) ; Bunnell v. Reynolds, 205 Mo. App. 653, 226 S.W. 614 (1920) ; Jones v. Enoree Power Co., 92 S.C. 263, 75 S.E. 452 (1912) .

207 Hecker v. Fowler, 2 Wall. (U. S.) 123, 17 L.Ed. 759 (1864) ; Alexandria Canal Co. v. Swann, 5 How. (U. S.) 33, 12 L.Ed. 60 (1874) ; Murphy v. Greenberg, 246 Pa. 387, 92 A. 511 (1914) .

are started in court, and then remain on the court docket until awards are returned and entered upon them. In many jurisdictions, the judicial view is that if the parties show a mutual intention to terminate a matter that is pending in court by the adoption of an arbitrational proceeding, such an intention will prevail. The suit may then be discontinued, even though a judgment has been entered and it is then pending on appeal, or otherwise remains in controversy in the court.[208] In the jurisdictions which take this view, some courts have insisted upon this result even though arbitrators have refused to act, or the submission agreement has been discovered to be invalid.[209] An unexecuted submission, however, usually does not extinguish the cause of action or bar maintenance of a new suit, if the arbitrational procedure is for any reason defeated or terminated before completion.[210] By proceeding with the trial, on the other hand, the parties may waive the ground for a discontinuance furnished by the agreement to arbitrate during the pendency of the suit in court.[211]

SECTION 8

Subsequent Modification — Waiver — Rescission and
Amendment — Revocation

The conduct of a party to an agreement to arbitrate, after the completion of the agreement, may indicate its bad faith or fraud during the original negotiation.[212] This makes the contract voidable at the option of the other party.[213] However, even in the ab-

---

208 Mooers v. Allen, 35 Maine 276, 58 Am. Dec. 700 (1853); Bank of Monroe v. Widner, 11 Paige (N.Y.) 529, 43 Am. Dec. 768 (1845); Muckey v. Pierce, 3 Wis. 307 (1854).

209 Reeve v. Mitchell, 15 Ill. 297 (1853); Thompson v. Turney Bros., 114 Mo. App. 697, 89 S.W. 897 (1905); McNulty v. Solley, 95 N.Y. 242 (1884); Saffle v. Cox, 9 Humph. (Tenn.) 142 (1848).

210 Ross v. Nesbitt, 2 Ill. 252 (1845); Smith v. Barse, 2 Hill (N.Y.) 387 (1842); Muckey v. Pierce, 3 Wis. 307 (1854).

211 Snively v. Hill, 46 Kan. 494, 26 Pac. 1024 (1891); Smith v. Barse, 2 Hill (N.Y.) 387 (1842); Long v. Fitzgerald, 97 N.C. 39, 1 S.E. 844 (1887); Babcock v. School District, 35 Vt. 250 (1862).

212 Bernhard v. Rochester German Insurance Co., 79 Conn. 388, 65 Atl. 134 (1906); Shawnee Fire Insurance Co. v. Pontfield, 110 Md. 353, 132 Am. St. Rep. 449 (1909); Bradshaw v. Agricultural Insurance Co., 137 N.Y. 137, 32 N.E. 1055 (1893).

213 Western Assur. Co. v. Hall, 120 Ala. 547, 24 So. 936, 74 Am. St. Rep. 48 (1898); Bishop v. Agricultural Insurance Co., 130 N.Y. 488, 29 N.E. 844 (1892); Wynne v. Greenleaf-Johnson Lumber Co., 179 N.C. 320, 102 S.E. 403 (1920).

sence of fraud, a party to an arbitration contract may waive its rights thereunder by proceeding with the arbitration or by other conduct implying that it will not assert its rights.[214] It may also conduct itself so that the other party, in reliance upon the evidence of such conduct, may be led to believe that the arbitration is not to be carried out, and in reliance on that belief change its position to its detriment. Thereafter, the party that induced such a conclusion and so caused the other party to alter its position may be estopped to insist upon the arbitration.[215] Because of deceptive or misleading conduct, the guilty party is refused judicial aid [216] to obtain what otherwise would be its right under the contract.[217] Waiver includes at least some of the elements of an agreement, either expressed or implied, by which the right or contract is waived, rescinded or modified by the parties.[218] On the other hand, estoppel is more closely related to tort law, and relief is given against the party that has misled the other because of the wrong that either has resulted or that may result if the wrongdoer is not estopped.[219]

The misconduct of an arbitrator who has wrongfully interfered so as to virtually prevent arbitration, or who has conducted him-

---

[214] Farnum v. Phoenix Insurance Co., 83 Cal. 246, 23 Pac. 869, 17 Am. St. Rep. 233 (1890) ; Hutchinson v. Liverpool & London & Globe Ins. Co., 153 Mass. 143, 26 N.E. 439 (1891) ; Hickerson v. German-American Ins. Co., 96 Tenn. 193, 33 S.W. 1041 (1895) ; Librascope Inc. v. Precision Lodge No. 1600, I.A.M., 189 Cal. App. 2d 71, 10 Cal. Rptr. 795 (1961) ; In re Rugby Nursing Home, 50 LRRM 2955 (N.Y. Sup. Ct., 1962).

[215] Case v. Manufacturers' Fire & M. Ins. Co., 82 Cal. 263, 21 Pac. 843 (1889) ; Ball v. Royal Insurance Co., 129 Mo. App. 34, 107 S.W. 1097 (1908) ; Chainless Cycle Manufacturing Co. v. Security Insurance Co., 169 N.Y. 304, 62 N.E. 392 (1901) ; Hickerson v. German-American Ins. Co., 96 Tenn. 193, 33 S.W. 1041 (1896).

[216] Manchester Fire Assur. Co. v. Koerner, 13 Ind. App. 372, 40 N.E. 1110, 55 Am. St. Rep. 231 (1895) ; Hutchinson v. Liverpool & London & Globe Insurance Co., 153 Mass. 143, 26 N.E. 439 (1891) ; Gnau v. Mason's Fraternal Accident Association, 109 Mich. 527, 67 N.W. 546 (1896) ; American Cent. Ins. Co. v. Bass Bros., 90 Texas 380, 38 S.W. 1119 (1897).

[217] Western Assur. Co. v. Hall, 120 Ala. 547, 24 So. 936, 74 Am. St. Rep. 48 (1898) ; Niagara Falls Ins. Co. v. Bishop, 154 Ill. 9, 39 N.E. 1102, 45 Am. St. Rep. 105 (1894) ; Read v. State Ins. Co., 103 Iowa 307, 72 N.W. 665, 64 Am. St. Rep. 180 (1897) ; Cole Mfg. Co. v. Collier, 91 Tenn. 525, 19 S.W. 672, 30 Am. St. Rep. 898 (1892).

[218] Niagara Falls Insurance Co. v. Bishop, 154 Ill. 9, 39 N.E. 1102, 45 Am. St. Rep. 105 (1894) ; Continental Insurance Co. v. Wilson, 45 Kan. 250, 25 Pac. 629, 72 A. 835, 132 Am. St. Rep. 449 (1909) ; Penn. Plate Glass Co. v. Spring Garden Ins. Co., 189 Pa. 255, 42 A. 138, 69 Am. St. Rep. 810 (1899).

[219] Arizona ex rel. Gaines v. Copper Queen Consol. Min. Co., 233 U. S. 87, 58 L.Ed. 863, 34 S.Ct. 546 (1913) ; Kirk v. Hamilton, 102 U. S. 68, 26 L.Ed. 79 (1880) ; Dickerson v. Colgrove, 100 U. S. 578, 25 L.Ed. 618 (1879) ; Illinois Standard Mortgage Corp. v. Collins, 187 Ark. 902, 63 S.W. (2d) 342 (1933).

self with such bias and prejudice as to impair the possibility of fair and impartial arbitration, may likewise excuse the party not responsible for the appointment of such arbitrator from proceeding with the arbitration and performance of the award.[220] It is obvious that if a sole arbitrator, or if a member of an arbitration board in a situation where all must participate in the award in order to render it valid, arbitrarily refuses to issue an award, that conduct should not be permitted to impair the rights of any party to the arbitration with whom such an arbitrator is not in collusion.[221]

A party to an arbitrational contract who seeks to question its validity, or to have it set aside on the basis of waiver or estoppel does not thereby necessarily forfeit his own right to insist upon arbitrational proceedings, if the court holds against his contention and concludes that he has acted in good faith and that the arbitrational procedure may be and should be validly pursued.[222] Such conduct, however, may be held to have precluded the party so acting from thereafter insisting on arbitration if it manifests his intention to refuse such procedure.[223]

It is perhaps proper to say that agreements to arbitrate are contracts *uberrimae fidei,* that is to say, contracts requiring the utmost good faith of the parties.[224] Any evidence of bad faith calculated to defeat the object of the arbitration will absolve the other party from abiding by the arbitration. It is consistent with long-established principles of law that a party, who by his bad faith prevents the normal performance of an arbitration contract, may be precluded from entry into the courts where, for example, the arbitrational agreement is one by which the parties have made a suit in court conditional upon the previous observance

---

220 Niagara Falls Insurance Co. v. Bishop, 154 Ill. 9, 39 N.E. 1102, 45 Am. St. Rep. 105 (1894) ; Chism v. Schipper, 51 N.J.L. 1, 16 A. 316, 14 Am. St. Rep. 668 (1888) ; Chapman v. Rockford Ins. Co., 89 Wis. 572, 62 N.W. 422 (1895) .

221 Chism v. Schipper, 51 N.J.L. 1, 16 A. 316, 14 Am. St. Rep. 668 (1888) ; Thomas v. Fleury, 26 N.Y. 26 (1862) .

222 See Bristol v. Bristol & Warren Waterworks, 19 R.I. 413, 34 A. 359, 32 L.R.A. 740 (1869) .

223 See Morse, Arbitration and Award, p. 173 (Boston, Little Brown & Co., 1872) .

224 Western Assur. Co. v. Hall, 120 Ala. 547, 24 So. 936, 74 Am. St. Rep. 48 (1898) ; Read v. State Ins. Co., 103 Iowa 307, 72 N.W. 665, 64 Am. St. Rep. 180 (1897) ; Shawnee Fire Insurance Co. v. Pontfield, 110 Md. 353, 72 A. 835, 132 Am. St. Rep. 449 (1909) .

of the arbitrational procedure.[225] Generally, a person is not permitted to profit by his wrongdoing. Furthermore, one who has willfully defeated arbitrational proceedings may not later set up the fact that the contract between the parties made such procedure a condition precedent to suit, when the innocent party has appealed to a court for enforcement of the contract without being able to establish that the arbitrational procedure was carried through.[226]

It is quite consistent with the rights of the parties, in the absence of statutes, to recognize that by express mutual agreement they may modify their agreement to arbitrate by repudiating or rescinding that agreement. They may also obtain the same result by conduct implying that both parties intend to omit the arbitrational proceedings.[227] At common law, however, even if the arbitration failed, either by a repudiation by one party, or without the fault of either, the doors of the courts were generally open to either party despite the fact that the arbitrational procedure was meant by contract to be a condition precedent to action in court.[228] Some jurisdictions, however, required that any party before entering into the courts, even in such a case, must have taken all reasonable and suitable steps to obtain an award. They have even required that the parties proceed with a new arbitration if it could be arranged.[229] A party, however, who asserted rights under an invalid award has been held to have no right to

---

225 Wainer v. Milford Mutual Fire Ins. Co., 153 Mass. 335, 26 N.E. 877 (1891); Home Fire Ins. Co. v. Kennedy, 47 Nebr. 138, 66 N.W. 278, 53 Am. St. Rep. 521 (1896); Penn. Plate Glass Co. v. Spring Garden Ins. Co., 189 Pa. 255, 42 A. 138 69 Am. St. Rep. 810 (1899).

226 Continental Ins. Co. v. Vallandingham, 116 Ky. 287, 76 S.W. 22, 105 Am. St. Rep. 218 (1903); Hutchinson v. Liverpool & London & Globe Ins. Co., 153 Mass. 143, 26 N.E. 439 (1891); Penn. Plate Glass Co. v. Spring Garden Ins. Co., 189 Pa. 255, 42 A. 138, 69 Am. St. Rep. 810 (1899); Cole Mfg. Co. v. Collier, 91 Tenn. 525, 19 S.W. 672, 30 Am. St. Rep. 898 (1892).

227 Wilkinson v. Prichard, 145 Iowa 65, 123 N.W. 964 (1909); Bangor Sav. Bank v. Niagara Fire Ins. Co., 85 Me. 68, 26 A. 991, 35 Am. St. Rep. 341 (1892); Palm Springs Homes, Inc. v. Western Desert Inc., 215 Cal. App, 2d 270, 30 Cal. Rptr. 34 (1963).

228 Providence Washington Ins. Co. v. Wolf, 168 Ind. 690, 80 N.E. 26, 120 Am. St. Rep. 395 (1907); Continental Ins. Co. v. Vallandingham, 116 Ky. 287, 76 S.W. 22, 105 Am. St. Rep. 218 (1903); People v. Nash, 111 N.Y. 310, 18 N.E. 630, 7 Am. St. Rep. 747 (1888); Friedrich v. Fergen, 15 S.D. 541, 91 N.W. 328 (1902).

229 Fisher v. Merchants Ins. Co., 95 Me. 486, 50 A. 282, 85 Am. St. Rep. 428 (1901); Second Soc. of Universalists v. Royal Ins. Co., 221 Mass. 518, 109 N.E. 384 (1915); Early v. Providence & Washington Ins. Co., 31 R.I. 225, 76 A. 753, 140 Am. St. Rep. 750 (1910).

have the matter again arbitrated when the award was later set aside; the other party in such a case may appeal to the court without showing the condition precedent of a completed arbitrational proceeding and an award.[230]

Waiver and Estoppel — In many connections it has been stated that waiver depends upon intent, and that the intent of the party or parties must be ascertained from an analysis of the facts of the particular case.[231] Some courts have indicated that waiver is virtually a contractual step by which the parties mutually modify a previous agreement to arbitrate by means of a new agreement.[232] This new agreement, however, is almost necessarily one in which the later, mutual intention of the parties would have to be discovered from their original contract and through the process of implication and inference from subsequent conduct, rather than through a new express agreement. Of course, if an express new agreement exists, the courts do not usually speak of "waiver," but refer to a "rescission" of the arbitrational agreement by express subsequent understanding of the parties. Thus, it appears that waiver, if contractual, is based upon a finding from the conduct of the parties of a mutual intent that is inconsistent with an earlier expressed intention to arbitrate, or from words that are repugnant to the agreement to arbitrate.[233] It has even been held that an express agreement that arbitration shall not be waived does not prevent waiver if the facts are strong enough to support the conclusion that one has taken place.[234]

When a union first requests arbitration, the employer company at times may flatly refuse, or it may take the position that

---

230 Levine v. Lancashire Ins. Co., 66 Minn. 138, 68 N.W. 855 (1896); Coffin v. German Fire Ins. Co., 142 Mo. App. 295, 126 S.W. 253 (1910); Aetna Ins. Co. v. Jester, 37 Okla. 413, 132 Pac. 130 (1913); American Fire Ins. Co. v. Bell, 33 Tex. Civ. App. 11, 75 S.W. 319 (1903).

231 Young v. Crescent Development Co., 240 N.Y. 244, 148 N.E. 510 (1925); George L. Hiltl Co. v. Bishoff, 205 App. Div. 856, 198 N.Y.S. 915 (1923).

232 Hutchinson v. Liverpool & London & Globe Ins. Co., 153 Mass. 143, 26 N.E. 439 (1891); Hickerson v. German-American Ins. Co., 96 Tenn. 193, 33 S.W. 1041 (1896); Chandos v. American Fire Ins. Co., 84 Wis. 184, 54 N.W. 390 (1893).

233 Farnum v. Phoenix Ins. Co., 83 Cal. 246, 23 Pac. 869, 17 Am. St. Rep. 233 (1890); Hickerson v. German-American Ins. Co., 96 Tenn. 193, 33 S.W. 1041 (1896); Northern Assur. Co. v. Samuels, 11 Tex. Civ. App. 417, 33 S.W. 239 (1895).

234 Insurance Co. v. Norton, 96 U. S. 234 (1877); Farnum v. Phoenix Ins. Co., 83 Cal. 246, 23 Pac. 869, 17 Am. St. Rep. 233 (1890); Steen v. Niagara Fire Insurance Co., 89 N.Y. 315 (1882).

the matter is not one subject to arbitration under the contract.[235]
From time to time this position has been taken by the unions.
The company's position is likely to be based on either the idea
that the matter involved is one which so intimately concerns
managerial prerogative or company policy that it cannot and
will not be submitted to arbitration. The other position may be
that the contract provides for arbitration only of a narrow or limited type of dispute, and the type of case with which the parties are
immediately concerned is not one of those which they had agreed
to arbitrate.[236] On the other hand, unions have sometimes refused
to arbitrate on the ground that the question involved is a matter
of internal union policy, or that the question before the parties
is one which so affects the union's inherent rights that it cannot
be left to a third person for decision.[237] In either of these cases,
the party refusing to arbitrate may be held to have waived his
right to arbitration, may be said to be estopped from claiming
arbitration if the other party, in reliance upon the position first
assumed by the opposing party, has changed its position to its
detriment. It would be inequitable to allow the party that had
refused to arbitrate later to insist upon the arbitration.[238] It has
also been held that the right to arbitration may be waived by the
participation in some other proceeding designed to settle a controversy, i.e., such as proceedings before a court,[239] the National
Labor Relations Board, or a similar state organization or department. The waiver may also originate in a failure to request arbitration within a reasonable time or within the contractual period

235 Many contracts limit the arbitrational provisions to specific types of controversies. See Braun, The Settlement of Industrial Disputes, p. 123 (Philadelphia,
Blakiston Co., 1944).

236 Cf. Hill & Hook, Management at the Bargaining Table, pp. 85, 224 (New
York, McGraw-Hill Book Co., 1945).

237 Manifestations of this attitude have several times appeared in instances in
which employers have requested that use of certain employees as stewards or other
officers be discontinued. The employer's suggestion of arbitration has been coun-
tered by the claim that the union cannot submit its vital, internal affairs to any
outsider, even to a mutually selected arbitrator or umpire.

238 Wainer v. Milford Mut. Fire Ins. Co., 153 Mass. 335, 26 N.E. 877 (1891);
Penn. Plate Glass Co. v. Spring Garden Ins. Co., 189 Pa. 255, 42 A. 138, 69
Am. St. Rep. 810 (1899); Bristol v. Bristol & Warren Waterworks, 19 R.I. 413,
34 A. 359 (1869); Corbin v. Adams, 76 Va. 58 (1881).

239 Trubowitch v. Riverbank Canning Co., 30 Cal. 2d 335, 182 P. 2d 182 (1947);
Lawton v. Cain, 172 So. 2d 734 (La. App., 1964).

for the same, as set forth in the agreement between the parties.[240] A party who repudiates an entire contract on any ground, may thereafter be held to have waived the arbitration provisions contained therein.[241] But mere inaction or silence, however, ordinarily does not effect a waiver unless it is unduly prolonged.[242]

It sometimes happens that the earlier steps in a grievance procedure ultimately ending in arbitration are waived by one party or the other, and this leads to the question of whether or not the waiver of such steps does not also waive the right under the contract to set up the arbitrational procedure. It is likely to be so held if the arbitrational step is so interrelated with the previous steps of the grievance procedure that the arbitration must necessarily rest upon the former, or upon some determination resulting from the same.[243] If a party intends to insist upon arbitration the only course would seem to be that of carefully following all of the antecedent steps of the grievance procedure, or having the other party join in a special agreement to submit the ultimate controversy to arbitration, if the earlier steps of the grievance procedure have been omitted.[244] The effect of a completed waiver is to bar that party from later claiming any arbitrational right with respect to the grievance.[245] Under a continuing contract, a waiver of arbitration as to one grievance will not necessarily result in waiver of arbitrations in connection with subsequently arising controversies.[246]

---

240 Richardson v. Emmert, 44 Kan. 262, 24 Pac. 478 (1890); Crescent Stave Co. v. Brown, 181 Ky. 787, 205 S.W. 937 (1918); Thomas W. Finucane Co. v. Board of Education, 190 N.Y. 76, 82 N.E. 737 (1907); Cole Mfg. Co. v. Collier, 91 Tenn. 525, 19 S.W. 672, 30 Am. St. Rep. 898 (1892).

241 Farnum v. Phoenix Ins. Co., 83 Cal. 246, 23 Pac. 869, 17 Am. St. Rep. 233 (1890); Wainer v. Milford Mut. Fire Ins. Co., 153 Mass. 335, 26 N.E. 877 (1891); Moore v. Sun Ins. Office, 100 Minn. 374, 111 N.W. 260 (1907); Hickerson v. German-American Ins. Co., 96 Tenn. 193, 33 S.W. 1041 (1896).

242 Chippewa Lumber Co. v. Phoenix Ins. Co., 80 Mich. 116, 44 N.W. 1055 (1890); McNees v. Southern Ins. Co., 61 Mo. App. 335 (1895).

243 Ball v. Royal Ins. Co., 129 Mo. App. 34, 107 S.W. 1097 (1908); Hickerson v. German-American Ins. Co., 96 Tenn. 193, 33 S.W. 1041 (1896).

244 See Hickerson v. German-American Ins. Co., 96 Tenn. 193, 33 S.W. 1041, 32 L.R.A. 172 (1896); 93 A.L.R. 1153.

245 Western Assur. Co. v. Hall, 120 Ala. 547, 24 So. 936, 74 Am. St. Rep. 48 (1898); Providence Washington Ins. Co. v. Wolf, 168 Ind. 690, 80 N.E. 26, 120 Am. St. Rep. 395 (1907); Wainer v. Milford Mut. Fire Ins. Co., 153 Mass. 335, 26 N.E. 877 (1891); Home Fire Ins. Co. v. Kennedy, 47 Nebr. 138, 66 N.W. 278, 53 Am. St. Rep. 521 (1896).

246 Hutchinson v. Liverpool & London & Globe Ins. Co., 153 Mass. 143, 26 N.E. 439 (1891); Penn. Plate Glass Co. v. Spring Garden Ins. Co., 189 Pa. 255,

The construction of some contracts leads to the conclusion that the arbitration clause was inserted more for the protection of one party, or group of parties, than for the other.[247] For example, some contracts provide only for the arbitration of discharged workers. The purpose of such a clause is to provide the discharged workers with a relatively quick and ready means of restoring them to employment with back pay if they are entitled to it. In such cases, only the party for whose protection the arbitration clause was inserted will be in a position to waive it or lose by estoppel.[248]

Thus, if the contract provides that arbitration shall be completed before either party may maintain a legal action upon the contract, or for a breach thereof, then only the party that is entitled to the arbitration may waive it. But he may not, by prolonged procrastination, preclude the other party from the use of the courts.[249] For example, suppose a worker is discharged and he and the union are entitled to have the discharge arbitrated. Instead of doing so they bring about a sit-down strike and demand the workers' return to employment as a condition of terminating the strike. The employer, feeling that under the circumstances he can satisfy the conditions of the Norris-LaGuardia Anti-Injunction Act[250] or a similar state statute, takes the case into court. It would seem that under these circumstances he could not be barred from going into court by reason of the fact that the discharge was not arbitrated, unless it could be established by the union (contrary to our hypothesis) that the union requested arbitration and its request was defeated or frustrated by improper conduct of the

42 A. 138, 69 Am. St. Rep. 810 (1899); Cole Mfg. Co. v. Collier, 91 Tenn. 525, 19 S.W. 672, 30 Am. St. Rep. 898 (1892).

247 Manchester Fire Assur. Co. v. Koerner, 13 Ind. App. 372, 40 N.E. 1110, 41 N.E. 848, 55 Am. St. Rep. 231 (1895); Continental Ins. Co. v. Vallandingham, 116 Ky. 287, 76 S.W. 22, 105 Am. St. Rep. 218 (1903); Chainless Cycle Mfg. Co. v. Security Ins. Co., 169 N.Y. 304, 62 N.E. 392 (1901); Hickerson v. German-American Ins. Co., 96 Tenn. 193, 33 S.W. 1041 (1896); McDonough Construction Co. of Florida v. Hanner, 232 F.Supp. 887, (M.D. N.C., 1964).

248 Continental Ins. Co. v. Vallandingham, 116 Ky. 287, 76 S.W. 22, 105 Am. St. Rep. 218 (1903); Shawnee Fire Ins. Co. v. Pontfield, 110 Ind. 353, 72 A. 835, 132 Am. St. Rep. 449 (1909); Ball v. Royal Ins. Co., 129 Mo. App. 34, 107 S.W. 1097 (1908); Patrick v. Farmers' Ins. Co., 43 N.H. 621, 80 Am. Dec. 197 (1862).

249 Continental Ins. Co. v. Vallandingham, 116 Ky. 287, 76 S.W. 22, 105 Am. St. Rep. 218 (1903); Connecticut Fire Ins. Co. v. Cohen, 97 Ind. 294, 55 A. 675, 99 Am. St. Rep. 445 (1903); Sykes v. Royal Casualty Co., 111 Miss. 746, 72 So. 147 (1916); Cole Mfg. Co. v. Collier, 91 Tenn. 525, 19 S.W. 672, 30 Am. St. Rep. 898 (1892).

250 49 United States Code 301 et seq. (1932).

employer.[251] If the union, on the other hand, having the primary right to demand arbitration in a discharge case, has refused to demand it, but instead seeks to appeal directly to the National Labor Relations Board, or to the court, on the ground that the discharge was discriminatory or in some other way a violation of law, it would seem that under a contract expressly making an arbitration a condition precedent, a court might refuse jurisdiction until the arbitrational proceedings have been completed, though the NLRB would not be as likely to do so.[252]

Rescission and Amendment — It is the general nature of all contracts that they may be rescinded, or "called off," by the parties through a subsequent mutual agreement. This is true both of agreements to arbitrate and of submission contracts, and it has been held that in the absence of a controlling statute, even a formal agreement to arbitrate, stated in writing, may be modified by a subsequent oral understanding of the parties. The only difficulty in this situation lies in the element of proof. Obviously, it is a much better practice, where the parties have agreed to modify the contract to arbitrate, that they do so in writing so as to preserve the exact understanding at which they arrive. The parties that are authorized as the agents to make the original submission agreement or the general agreement to arbitrate future disputes ordinarily have authority to modify the same, and their principals likewise have authority to rescind or amend the agreement.[253] It would not follow, however, that where the top contracting officers of a union and company have entered into an arbitrational agreement, the agreement could be set aside by subordinate representatives. It has been held that an attorney authorized to repre-

---

251 Wainer v. Milford Mut. Fire Ins. Co., 153 Mass. 335, 26 N.E. 877 (1891); Home Fire Ins. Co. v. Kennedy, 47 Nebr. 138, 66 N.W. 278, 53 Am. St. Rep. 521 (1896); Hickerson v. German-American Ins. Co., 96 Tenn. 193, 33 S.W. 1041 (1896).

252 The NLRB is not bound by an arbitrational award, Wertheimer Stores Corp., 107 NLRB 1434, 33 LRRM 1398 (1954); Nettleton Co. v. United Shoe Workers of America, 24 L.A. 339 (N.Y. Sup. Ct. 1955); McAmis v. Panhandle Eastern Pipe Line Co., 23 L.A. 570 (K. C. Mo. Ct. of App., 1954); Western Assur. Co. v. Hall, 120 Ala. 547, 24 So. 936 (1898); Southern Home Ins. Co. v. Faulkner, 57 Fla. 194, 49 So. 542 (1909); Shawnee Fire Ins. Co. v. Pontfield, 110 Ind. 353, 72 A. 835 (1909). But see Chap. X Section I *infra*.

See Beatty, "Arbitration of Unfair Labor Practice Disputes," 14 Arbitration Journal 180 (1959); Wollett, "The Interpretation of Collective Bargaining Agreements," 10 Labor Law J. 477 (1959).

253 Wilkinson v. Prichard, 145 Iowa 65, 123 N.W. 964 (1909); Bangor Sav. Bank v. Niagara Fire Ins. Co., 85 Me. 68, 26 A. 991, 35 Am. St. Rep. 341 (1892); Nashua Railroad Corp. v. Boston Railroad Corp., 157 Mass. 268, 31 N.E. 1060 (1892).

sent a party in arbitration proceedings does not have authority to execute a contract rescinding the agreement or substantially modifying the same.[254] His authority is simply to represent his client in connection with the proceeding, as originally established by contract.[255]

Revocation — As stated earlier, the authority of the arbitrator to act was held at common law to be subject to revocation by either party at any time before the submission was actually consummated by the completion and delivery of an award.[256] It has been so held even though the parties had solemnly agreed against revocation. The view of the courts has been that the validity of the arbitrational proceedings, and of the award rests upon the continuing consent of the parties.[257] After an award has been made and delivered to the parties, it is too late for a revocation of the authority of the arbitrator.[258] If the arbitration procedure was regularly set up and properly followed, and there was no fraud, corruption, or misconduct, the parties are bound by the award.[259] This should be further qualified by repeating that no award can be valid if it furthers a criminal objective, or defies positive law, whether in the form of a common-law rule or principle, or in the form of a statute.[260]

254 Daniels v. New London, 58 Conn. 156, 19 A. 573 (1889); Jenkins v. Gillespie, 10 Smedes & M. (Miss.) 31, 48 Am. Dec. 732 (1848); McLaughlin v. Monaghan, 290 Pa. 74, 138 A. 79 (1927).

255 Daniels v. New London, 58 Conn. 156, 19 A. 573 (1889); Jenkins v. Gillespie, 10 Smedes & M. (Miss.) 31, 48 Am. Dec. 732 (1848).

256 Oskaloosa Sav. Bank v. Mahaska County State Bank, 205 Iowa 1351, 219 N.W. 530 (1928); Jones v. Jones, 229 Ky. 71, 16 S.W. (2d) 503 (1929); Goerke Kirch Co. v. Goerke Kirch Holding Co., 118 N.J. Eq. 1, 176 A. 902 (1935); Martin v. Vansant, 99 Wash. 106, 168 Pac. 990 (1917); Thompson v. Phillips Pipe Line Co., 200 Kar. 669, 438 P. 2d 146 (1968).

257 People v. Nash, 111 N.Y. 310, 18 N.E. 630, 7 Am. St. Rep. 747 (1888); Zehner v. Lehigh Coal & Navigation Co., 187 Pa. 487, 41 A. 464, 67 Am. St. Rep. 586 (1898); Sartwell v. Sowles, 72 Vt. 270, 48 A. 11, 82 Am. St. Rep. 943 (1900). Gerard v. Salter, 146 Cal. App. 2d 840, 304 P. 2d 237 (1956); Machine Products Co. v. Prairie Local Lodge No. 1538, I.A.M., 230 Mis. 809, 94 So. 2d 344 (1957).

258 Williams v. Branning Mfg. Co., 153 N.C. 7, 68 S.E. 902, 138 Am. St. Rep. 637 (1910); Isaac v. Donegal & Conoy Mut. Fire Ins. Co., 301 Pa. 351, 152 A. 95 (1930); Friedrich v. Fergen, 15 S.D. 541, 91 N.W. 328 (1902); Levy v. Scottish Union & Nat. Ins. Co., 58 W.Va. 546, 52 S.E. 449 (1906).

259 United States v. Gleason, 175 U. S. 588, 44 L.Ed. 284, 20 S.Ct. 228 (1899); W. H. Blodgett Co. v. Bebe Co., 190 Cal. 665, 214 Pac. 38 (1923); Re Lower Baraboo River Drainage Dist., 199 Wis. 230, 225 N.W. 331 (1929).

260 Benton v. Singleton, 114 Ga. 548, 40 S.E. 811 (1902); Hall v. Kimmer, 61 Mich. 269, 28 N.W. 96, 1 Am. St. Rep. 575 (1886); Smith v. Gladney (Tex. Civ. App.) 70 S.W. (2d) 342 (1934).

The Pennsylvania courts hold, as mentioned above in Section 6 of this chapter, that where the arbitration agreement specifically names the arbitrators, the agreement to arbitrate is not revocable.[261] In other jurisdictions, it has been held that the agreement to arbitrate, or submit to the judgment of a third person, is not revocable where a right of action for breach of contract has been conditioned upon a previous appraisal or decision by an arbitrator, umpire, architect, or some other third person in an agreed authoritative position.[262]

In many jurisdictions, the fact that the contract to arbitrate or the submission is supported by a consideration of mutual promises or other valuable consideration, does not prevent either party from withdrawing therefrom, and thereby defeating the arbitrational proceedings.[263] It is true that a party so acting might be liable for breach of contract to the extent of whatever damages the other party could prove were suffered because of the breach.[264] As noted above, the Pennsylvania courts appear to dissent from this view and hold that when a contract to arbitrate is supported by adequate consideration and the arbitrator is designated or identified, it is irrevocable prior to the hearing and award.[265] Many union contracts with employers are made for a term of years or from year to year and provide that they may be reopened by either party upon giving 30, 60, and sometimes 90 days' notice of a desire to renegotiate some feature of the contract. If one of the parties is entitled to arbitration of an existing dispute under such contract,

---

261 Mentz v. Armenia Fire Ins. Co., 79 Pa. 478, 21 Am. Rep. 80 (1875); Commercial Union Assur. Co. v. Hocking, 115 Pa. 407, 8 A. 589, 2 Am. St. Rep. 562 (1886); Yost v. McKee, 179 Pa. 381, 36 A. 317, 57 Am. St. Rep. 604 (1897); Frederick v. Margworth, 221 Pa. 418, 70 A. 797 (1908). Capecci v. Joseph Capecci, 392 Pa. 2d 32, 139 A. 2d 563 (1958).

262 Jones v. Enoree Power Co., 92 S.C. 263, 75 S.E. 452 (1912); Martin v. Vansant, 99 Wash. 106, 168 Pac. 990 (1917); Chapman v. Rockford Ins. Co., 89 Wis. 572, 62 N.W. 422 (1895).

263 Colombia v. Cauca Co., 190 U. S. 524, 47 L.Ed. 1159, 23 S.Ct. 704 (1902); Jones v. Harris, 59 Miss. 214 (1881); People v. Nash, 111 N.Y. 310, 18 N.E. 630, 7 Am. St. Rep. 747 (1888).

264 Red Cross Line v. Atlantic Fruit Co., 264 U. S. 109, 68 L.Ed. 582, 44 S.Ct. 274 (1924); Goerke Kirch Co. v. Goerke Kirch Holding Co., 118 N.J. Eq. 1, 176 A. 902 (1935); Martin v. Vansant, 99 Wash. 106, 168 Pac. 990 (1917); Kahn v. Traders Ins. Co., 4 Wyo. 419, 34 Pac. 1059, 62 Am. St. Rep. 47 (1893). Thompson v. Phillips Pipe Line Co., 200 Kan. 669, 438 P. 2d 146 (1968).

265 Mentz v. Armenia Fire Ins. Co., 79 Pa. 478, 21 Am. St. Rep. 80 (1875); McKenna v. Lyle, 155 Pa. 599, 26 A. 777, 35 Am. St. Rep. 910 (1893); Zehner v. Lehigh Coal and Navigation Co., 187 Pa. 487, 41 A. 464, 67 Am. St. Rep. 586 (1898); Frederick v. Margworth, 221 Pa. 418, 70 A. 797 (1908).

it would seem to be questionable whether the other party could thereafter defeat the right to arbitrate by giving the agreed notice, with the purpose of eliminating the arbitrational clause by further negotiation.[266] If the common law rules are applied, the revocation of the authority to arbitrate is effective, but the party so acting, while defeating the arbitration, would appear to be liable in such a jurisdiction for damages proved to result from its refusal to arbitrate.[267]

On the other hand, under some of the statutes noted earlier, the parties would be bound to arbitrate, particularly if the arbitration were directed to the ascertainment of facts, or subsidiary questions prior to litigation.[268] In Pennsylvania, it would seem that under such a contract, if the arbitrator or umpire is specifically designated, the attempt to rescind the arbitration clause would be legally ineffective.[269] It would appear to be entirely possible for the parties to phrase an arbitration clause in such manner that the arbitration provision would be "of the essence" of the contract, and arbitration would then be an absolute condition precedent to any suit thereon by either party. In such case, of course, a party refusing to participate in the arbitration should be subject to defeat, on the ground of his failure to perform an essential condition precedent, if he seeks to sue upon any feature of the contract.[270]

Here again, however, we become involved with implications and legal inferences. It is not necessary that a revocation be in express

266 See Castle Creek Water Co. v. Aspen (C.C.A. 8th), 146 F. 8 (1906); Coles v. Peck, 96 Ind. 333, 49 Am. Rep. 161 (1884); Cooke v. Miller, 25 R.I. 92, 54 A. 927 (1903).
267 Red Cross Line v. Atlantic Fruit Co., 264 U. S. 109, 68 L.Ed. 582, 44 S.Ct. 274 (1924); Hamilton v. Home Ins. Co., 137 U. S. 370, 34 L.Ed. 708, 11 S.Ct. 133 (1890); Hartford Fire Ins. Co. v. Hon, 66 Nebr. 555, 92 N.W. 746, 103 Am. St. Rep. 725 (1902); Goerke Kirch Co. v. Goerke Kirch Holding Co., 118 N.J. Eq. 1, 176 A. 902 (1935). Thompson v. Phillips Pipe Line Co., 200 Kan. 669, 438 P. 2d 146 (1968).
268 Mentz v. Armenia Fire Ins. Co., 79 Pa. 478, 21 Am. Rep. 80 (1875); McKenna v. Lyle, 155 Pa. 599, 26 A. 777, 35 Am. St. Rep. 910 (1893); Zehner v. Lehigh Coal & Navigation Co., 187 Pa. 487, 41 A. 464, 67 Am. St. Rep. 586 (1898); Frederick v. Margworth, 221 Pa. 418, 70 A. 797 (1908).
269 Mentz v. Armenia Fire Ins. Co., 79 Pa. 478, 21 Am. Rep. 80 (1875); Commercial Union Assur. Co. v. Hocking, 115 Pa. 407, 8 A. 589, 2 Am. St. Rep. 562 (1886); Yost v. McKee, 179 Pa. 381, 36 A. 317, 57 Am. St. Rep. 604 (1897); Frederick v. Margworth, 221 Pa. 418, 70 A. 797 (1908). Capecci v. Joseph Capecci, 392 Pa. 2d 32, 139 A. 2d 563 (1958).
270 Jones v. Enoree Power Co., 92 S.C. 263, 75 S.E. 452 (1912); Martin v. Vansant, 99 Wash. 106, 168 Pac. 990 (1917); Chapman v. Rockford Ins. Co. 89 Wis. 572, 62 N.W. 422 (1895).

words in order to be effective;[271] it may be implied. [272] Conduct directly inconsistent with the arbitrational provision of a contract has frequently been held sufficient to operate as a revocation.[273] It has been said that the revocation must be made in the same manner as the original agreement to arbitrate.[274] That is, if the original agreement was by formal contract, the revocation must be equally formal.[275] This, however, has not always been the case.[276] And certainly it is not the case where the court concludes from evidence entirely outside the contract that one of the parties has waived his right to arbitrate, or has become estopped from insisting upon his arbitrational rights. In a certain sense, both waiver and estoppel may operate to terminate arbitrational authority. In some instances where the parties have expressly provided that the arbitrators shall deliver the award within a certain specified time after the hearing and the arbitrators have failed to reach an award, the courts have held that the arbitrational provisions of the contract are satisfied and have spoken of this situation as "revoking" the provisions.[277] Arbitrational proceedings may be terminated by death of one of the parties,[278] the death of an umpire[279] or of an agreed arbitra-

---

[271] Mason v. Bullock, 6 Ala. App. 141, 60 So. 432 (1912) ; Dolman v. Board of Commissioners of Kingman County, 116 Kan. 201, 226 Pac. 240 (1924) ; Williams v. Branning Mfg. Co., 153 N.C. 7, 68 S.E. 902, 138 Am. St. Rep. 637 (1910) ; Morrison Department Store Co. v. Lewis, 96 W.Va. 277, 122 S.E. 747 (1924).

[272] State, Knaus, Prosecutor v. Jenkins, 40 N.J.L. 288, 29 Am. Rep. 237 (1878) ; Williams v. Branning Mfg. Co., 153 N.C. 7, 68 S.E. 902, 138 Am. St. Rep. 637 (1910) ; Morrison Department Store Co. v. Lewis, 96 W.Va. 277, 122 S.E. 747 (1924). Thompson v. Phillips Pipe Line Co., 200 Kan. 669, 438 P. 2d 146 (1968).

[273] Whitfield v. Whitfield, 30 N.C. (8 Ired. L.) 163, 47 Am. Dec. 350 (1847); Williams v. Branning Mfg. Co., 153 N.C. 7, 68 S.E. 902, 138 Am. St. Rep. 637 (1910) ; Bailey v. Stewart, 3 Watts & S. (Pa.) 560, 39 Am. Dec 50 (1842). Thompson v. Phillips Pipe Line Co., 200 Kan. 669, 438 P. 2d 146 (1968).

[274] Insurance Co. of North America v. Kempner, 132 Ark. 215, 200 S.W. 986 (1918) ; Williams v. Branning Mfg. Co., 153 N.C. 7, 68 S.E. 902, 138 Am. St. Rep. 637 (1910) ; Lesser v. Pallay, 96 Ore. 142, 188 Pac. 718 (1920) ; Morrison Department Store Co. v. Lewis, 96 W.Va. 277, 122 S.E. 747 (1924).

[275] Insurance Co. of North America v. Kempner, 132 Ark. 215, 200 S.W. 986 (1918) ; State, Knaus, Prosecutor v. Jenkins, 40 N.J.L. 288, 29 Am. Rep. 237 (1878) ; Lesser v. Pallay, 96 Ore. 142, 188 Pac. 718 (1920) ; Morrison Department Store Co. v. Lewis, 96 W.Va. 277, 122 S.E. 747 (1924).

[276] Whitfield v. Whitfield, 30 N.C. (8 Ired. L.) 163, 47 Am. Dec. 350 (1847); Williams v. Branning Mfg. Co., 153 N.C. 7, 68 S.E. 902, 138 Am. St. Rep. 637 (1910); Bailey v. Stewart, 3 Watts & S. (Pa.) 560, 39 Am. Dec. 50 (1842) ; Sutton v. Tyrrell, 10 Vt. 91 (1838).

[277] Bent v. Erie Telegraph & Telephone Co., 144 Mass. 165, 10 N.E. 778 (1887); Goerke Kirch Co. v. Goerke Kirch Holding Co., 118 N.J. Eq. 1, 176 A. 902 (1935) ; Johnson v. Crawford, 212 Pa. 502, 61 A. 1103 (1905).

[278] Aldrich v. Aldrich, 260 Ill. App. 333 (1931) ; Gregory v. Pike, 94 Me. 27, 46

tor.[280] It has also been held that an arbitration agreement entered into by an unmarried woman becomes void upon her marriage prior to the award.[281] This, however, is apparently not true under the present married women's acts.[282] There is also authority to the effect that bankruptcy or mental incapacity suffered after an agreement to arbitrate was entered into, but before an award was reached, will operate to terminate arbitrational proceedings and the rights of the parties thereunder.[283]

In some jurisdictions a party may revoke the authority to arbitrate a disputed matter by starting a law suit covering the same subject and involving the same parties, and by so doing ignoring the arbitrational procedure.[284] There is some authority, however, to the effect that this does not necessarily operate as a revocation of the authority to arbitrate.[285] In other jurisdictions, this situation is governed by statutes that prevent such a revocation.[286] It is possible that the law will operate to nullify an agreement to arbitrate. This could occur, for example, where the question to be arbitrated is whether there is to be a union shop or check-off, and a statute prohibiting the result demanded by one party is passed while the arbitrational proceedings are pending; or, if the parties contemplate arbitration of certain health or sanitary conditions in the plant, and inspectors under state authority, prior to the comple-

---

A. 793 (1900); Sutton v. Tyrrell, 10 Vt. 91 (1938). King v. Beale, 198 Va. 802, 96 S.E. 2d 765 (1957).

[279] Backus-Brooks Co. v. Northern Pacific Railway Co. (C.C.A. Minn.), 21 F. (2d) 4 (1927); Mooers v. Allen, 35 Me. 276, 58 Am. Dec. 700 (1853); Sutton v. Tyrrell, 10 Vt. 91 (1838).

[280] Backus-Brooks Co. v. Northern Pac. Railway Co. (C.C.A. Minn.), 21 F. (2d) 4 (1927); State, Knaus, Prosecutor v. Jenkins, 40 N.J.L. 288, 29 Am. Rep. 237 (1878); Williams v. Branning Mfg. Co., 153 N.C. 7, 68 S.E. 902, 138 Am. St. Rep. 637 (1910). King v. Beale, 198 Va. 802, 96 S.E. 2d 765 (1957).

[281] State, Knaus, Prosecutor v. Jenkins, 40 N.J.L. 288, 29 Am. Rep. 237 (1878); Williams v. Branning Mfg. Co., 153 N.C. 7, 68 S.F. 902, 138 Am. St. Rep. 637 (1910); Morrison Department Store Co. v. Lewis, 96 W.Va. 277, 122 S.E. 747 (1924).

[282] Husband v. Epling, 81 Ill. 172, 25 Am. Rep. 273 (1896).

[283] State, Knaus, Prosecutor v. Jenkins, 40 N.J.L. 288, 29 Am. Rep. 237 (1878); Williams v. Branning Mfg. Co., 153 N.C. 7, 68 S.E. 902, 138 Am. St. Rep. 637 (1910); Sutton v. Tyrrell, 10 Vt. 91 (1838).

[284] Bullock v. Mason, 194 Ala. 663, 69 So. 882 (1915); Jones v. Jones, 229 Ky. 71, 16 S.W. (2d) 503 (1929); Nurney v. Fireman's Fund Ins. Co., 63 Mich. 633, 30 N.W. 350, 6 Am. St. Rep. 338 (1886); Williams v. Branning Mfg. Co., 153 N.C. 7, 68 S.E. 902, 138 Am. St. Rep. 637 (1910).

[285] State, Knaus, Prosecutor v. Jenkins, 40 N.J.L. 288, 29 Am. Rep. 237 (1878); Sutton v. Tyrrell, 10 Vt. 91 (1838).

[286] New York Lumber & Woodworking Co. v. Schneider, 1 N.Y.S. 441 (1888); Everett v. Brown, 198 N.Y.S. 462, 120 Misc. 349 (1923).

tion of arbitration, investigate the conditions and issue valid orders under state factory statutes that eliminate any possible significance of the proposed arbitration.

The effect of revocation is to place the parties in the same position they occupied prior to the making of the arbitration agreement. Their respective rights against each other are restored as nearly as possible consistent with the fact that the arbitration agreement no longer exists.[287] However, if a person who is party to an arbitration agreement revokes the authority of the arbitrator to proceed, the opposing party has acquiesced in such revocation, and the arbitrator has discontinued his consideration of the matter; thereafter, the revoking party cannot renounce his previous revocation and insist upon rights in connection with the arbitration.[288] However, there have been some cases before the courts where a party, having revoked the arbitrational authority, has then proceeded inconsistently with the revocation, and so has been said to waive the revocation in such sense as to become bound by the arbitrational proceeding and award.[289] This might occur through the act of the party, that having stated it would not proceed with the arbitration, and having attempted to revoke the same, nevertheless attends the hearing, tenders evidence, and so conducts itself as to lead to the inference that it has abandoned its purpose to revoke. Again, it may surrender its position of having revoked the authority of the arbitrator by accepting benefits under the award and assuming the position that it will insist upon it and its effects as against the other party.[290]

In the absence of statutes so requiring, some courts will not decree specific performance of an arbitration contract.[291] Where the refusal to abide by the arbitration agreement will result in irrep-

---

287 Goerke Kirch Co. v. Goerke Kirch Holding Co., 118 N.J. Eq. 1, 176 A. 902 (1935) ; People ex rel. Union Ins. Co. v. Nash, Ill. N.Y. 310, 18 N.E. 630, 7 Am. St. Rep. 747 (1888) ; McKenna v. Lyle, 155 Pa. 599, 26 A. 777, 35 Am. St. Rep. 910 (1893) ; Sartwell v. Sowles, 72 Vt. 270, 48 A. 11, 82 Am. St. Rep. 943 (1900) .

288 Key v. Norrod, 124 Tenn. 146, 136 S.W. 991 (1910) ; Hawley v. Hodge, 7 Vt. 237 (1835) .

289 Harrell v. Terrell, 125 Ga. 379, 54 S.E. 116 (1906) ; Seely v. Pelton, 63 Ill. 101 (1872) .

290 Harrell v. Terrell and Seely v. Pelton, note 289 supra.

291 Red Cross Line v. Atlantic Fruit Co., 264 U. S. 109, 68 L.Ed. 582, 44 S.Ct. 274 (1924) ; Goerke Kirch Co. v. Goerke Kirch Holding Co., 118 N.J. Eq. 1, 176 A. 902 (1935) ; Kaufmann v. Liggett, 209 Pa. 87, 58 A. 129, 103 Am. St. Rep. 988 (1904) ; Pepin v. Societe St. Jean Baptiste, 23 R.I. 81, 49 A. 387, 91 Am. St. Rep. 620 (1901) . But see Chapter one, Section 4 supra for the results of the Lincoln Mills decision.

arable injury, courts have ordered the arbitration carried out even without the aid of statute.[292] Today, the *Lincoln Mills* decision gives the court the power to decree specific performance of arbitration contracts affecting interstate commerce. A similar result has also been reached where the arbitration contract, as is usually the case in the labor agreement, is incidental to a partly performed principal contract of which the arbitration clause is but a subordinate factor.[293] In some instances, courts have held that the attitude of one party in announcing its repudiation of the arbitration agreement has been justified by prior misconduct of the opposing party, and that in such case the repudiating party incurs no penalty and does not waive rights to the arbitration provision.[294]

While the arbitration procedure in labor disputes has not frequently been under an order of court, such procedure appears to be applicable under some state statutes. It should be noted, therefore, that when the parties are engaged in arbitration under a rule or order of court, neither party is free to repudiate or to revoke the authority of the arbitrator, since in such case the authority flows from the court, rather than from the parties.[295] It follows, however, that if the court, upon request of a party and upon a sufficient cause therefor, sees fit to vacate the order for the arbitration, it is ordinarily permissible for such action to be taken.[296] In some instances, parties have agreed to arbitrate subject to a rule of court; in those cases it may be said that neither party is free to withdraw and defeat the arbitration prior to an order of the court.[297] In other

---

292 See Lincoln Mills decision discussion, Chapter I, Section 4 *supra* and Chapter X, Section 1 *infra*. Castle Creek Water Co. v. Aspen (C.C.A. 8th), 146 F. 8 (1906) ; Mutual Life Ins. Co. v. Stephens, 214 N.Y. 448, 108 N.E. 856 (1915) ; Kaufmann v. Liggett, 209 Pa. 87, 58 A. 129, 103 Am. St. Rep. 988 (1904) ; Martin v. Vansant, 99 Wash. 106, Pac. 990 (1917) .

293 March v. Eastern Railroad Co., 40 N.H. 548, 77 Am. Dec. 732 (1860) ; Goerke Kirch Co. v. Goerke Kirch Holding Co., 118 N.J. Eq. 1, 176 A. 902 (1935) ; Mutual Life Ins. Co. v. Stephens, 214 N.Y. 488, 108 N.E. 856 (1915) ; Lake Shore Power Co. v. Edgerton, 43 Ohio App. 545, 184 N.E. 37 (1932) .

294 Chambers v. Crook, 42 Ala. 171 (1868) ; Wynne v. Greenleaf-Johnson Lumber Co., 179 N.C. 320, 102 S.E. 403 (1920) ; Emerson v. Udall, 13 Vt. 477 (1841) .

295 Brown v. Fletcher's Estate, 146 Mich. 401, 109 N.W. 686, 123 Am. St. Rep. 233 (1906) ; Zehner v. Lehigh Coal & Navigation Co., 187 Pa. 487, 41 A. 464, 67 Am. St. Rep. 586 (1898) ; McCann Alaska Lumber Co., 71 Wash. 331, 128 Pac. 663 (1912) ; Lovinger v. Hix Green Buick Co., 110 Ga. App. 736, 140 S.E. 2d 83 (1964) .

296 Tyson v. Robinson, 25 N.C. 333 (1843) ; Zehner v. Lehigh Coal & Navigation Co., 187 Pa. 487, 41 A. 464, 67 Am. St. Rep. 586 (1898) ; McCann v. Alaska Lumber Co., 71 Wash. 331, 128 Pac. 663 (1912) .

297 Frink v. Ryan, 3 Ill. 322 (1841) ; Ivins v. Ivins, 77 N.J.L. 368, 72 A. 94 (1909) ; Huston v. Clark, 12 Phila. 383 (1878) .

jurisdictions, however, the party attempting to withdraw might find a statutory impediment to his doing so.[298] In any case, withdrawal, under the common law, would subject the party so doing to liability for damages to the extent they might be proved by the opposite party as flowing from the revocation.[299] As previously stated, however, statutes in numerous states now supplant common-law rules for revocation. It is usually held that a statute merely supplements the common law, but if the statute is inconsistent with the common law, it will control and the common law is regarded as superseded.[300] Ordinarily, under a statutory proceeding, neither party is free to revoke and withdraw without permission of the court having jurisdiction of the matter. Where a statute makes revocation impossible under a statutory proceeding, however, it does not necessarily have that effect if the parties have contracted, and are proceeding not under the statute but under ordinary and long-established common-law rights.[301] Some statutes clearly apply only to written contracts to arbitrate, and make them irrevocable excepting upon grounds that may exist in equity or at law.[302] The irrevocability of a contract under the statute may be equally applicable to contracts to arbitrate future disputes and to submission agreements. The primary problem in any jurisdiction with an arbitration statute is to ascertain to what extent the statute has nullified or abrogated the common law.[303] In most jurisdictions, however, the statutes are regarded as supplemental to, rather than sub-

---

[298] Hecker v. Fowler, 2 Wall. (U. S.) 123, 17 L.Ed. 759 (1864); Alexandria Canal Co. v. Swann, 5 How. (U. S.) 83, 12 L.Ed. 60 (1847); Murphy v. Greenberg, 246 Pa. 387, 92 A. 511 (1914).

[299] Red Cross Line v. Atlantic Fruit Co., 264 U. S. 109, 68 L.Ed. 582, 44 S.Ct. 274 (1925); Goerke Kirch Co. v. Goerke Kirch Holding Co., 118 N.J. Eq. 1, 176 A. 902 (1935); Jones v. Enoree Power Co., 92 S.C. 263, 75 S.E. 452 (1912); Martin v. Vansant, 99 Wash. 106, 168 Pac. 990 (1917); Thompson v. Phillips Pipe Line Co., 200 Kan. 669, 438 P. 2d 146 (1968).

[300] Cocalis v. Nazlides, 308 Ill. 152, 139 N.E. 95 (1923); In re Ames-Farmer Canning Co., 190 Iowa 1259, 179 N.W. 105 (1921); Dickie Mfg. Co. v. Sound Construction & Engineering Co., 92 Wash. 316, 159 Pac. 129 (1916).

[301] Black v. Woodruff, 193 Ala. 327, 69 So. 97 (1915); Conger v. Dean, 3 Iowa 463, 66 Am. Dec. 93 (1856); Modern System Bakery v. Salisbury, 215 Ky. 230, 284 S.W. 994 (1926); Bunnell v. Reynolds, 205 Mo. App. 653, 226 S.W. 614 (1920).

[302] Red Cross Line v. Atlantic Fruit Co., 264 U. S. 109, 68 L.Ed. 582, 44 S.Ct. 274 (1923); Goerke Kirch Co. v. Goerke Kirch Holding Co., 118 N.J. Eq. 1, 176 A. 902 (1935); Gilbert v. Burnstine, 255 N.Y. 348, 174 N.E. 706 (1931).

[303] Marine Transit Corp. v. Dreyfus, 284 U. S. 263, 76 L.Ed. 282, 52 S.Ct. 166 (1932); California Prune and Apricot Growers' Assoc. v. Catz American Co. (C.C.A. 9th), 60 F. (2d) 788 (1932); Gilbert v. Burnstine, 255 N.Y. 348, 174 N.E. 706 (1931).

stituted for, the common-law rules and principles in the arbitrational field.[304]

It seems to be assumed by all who are active in labor dispute arbitration that the *Lincoln Mills* decision, coupled with the concept of federal preemption of jurisdiction over labor matters, has resulted in making most agreements to arbitrate disputes irrevocable and judicially enforceable.[305] Even disputes on matters returned to state jurisdiction by the Labor-Management Reporting and Disclosure Act of 1959, Section 701, by amending Section 14 of the National Labor Relations Act would seem to be in a large degree so affected.[306] As long as there is even a limited area of labor disputes not fully within federal jurisdiction but within the states' area of authority, however, the state statutes will continue to require study and application.

---

304 Utah Construction Co. v. Western Pac. Ry. Co., 174 Cal. 156, 162 Pac. 631 (1916); Ezell v. Rocky Mountain Bean & Elevator Co., 76 Colo. 409, 232 Pac. 680 (1925); Bunnell v. Reynolds, 205 Mo. App. 653, 226 S.W. 614 (1920); Isaac v. Donegal & Conoy Mutual Fire Ins. Co., 301 Pa. 351, 152 A. 95 (1930).

305 Updegraff, Clarence M., "Preemption, Predictability and Progress in Labor Law," 17 Hastings Law Journal, 473 (1967).

306 See Chapter I, Section 4 and Chapter II, Section 1, *supra* for discussion.

CHAPTER V

ARBITRATION AND VARIOUS AREAS OF EMPLOYMENT

SECTION 1

Scope and Purpose of This Chapter

Five sections constitute the contents of this chapter. The subject of the first appears above. The second observes the growing and generally satisfactory use of arbitration in the solution of labor disputes in the majority of ordinary areas of industrial employment. The third section indicates the restrictions upon and some arguments for collective bargaining and arbitration in public or governmental areas. The fourth briefly describes the federal legislation undertaken for the purpose of reducing to the minimum interruptions of work in the railroad and airline transportation industries and of settling labor disputes that otherwise might have the potential to interrupt commerce. The fifth and longest section undertakes to present a study of the present laws and the special need for legislative attention to public utilities other than those under the Railway Labor Act. Its object is to point out the contradictions and pitfalls that hamper arbitration, now inherent in the public utilities area, and to emphasize the desirability of both federal and state legislation in relation to public utilities' labor relations.

In this respect the character and the measure of success of the Railway Labor Act in reducing work stoppages cannot make it an entirely applicable pattern since it rests in part on the commerce clause of the Constitution. However, many public utility employers are sufficiently engaged in commerce today to validate a pattern of legislation similar to that of the Railway Labor Act. Other, smaller utilities' disputes could very well continue to be the subjects of state legislation. Thorough study, however, offers the con-

179

clusion that the better type of legislation in this area would return the entire field of labor legislation in respect to public utilities (other than transportation) to the states for local regulation. This should be qualified to retain some reviewing jurisdiction in a federal board or in the courts to insure that no state action would get out of line with federal labor policy.

SECTION 2

Manufacturing — Construction — Services — Wholesale Trade — Transportation — Retail Trade — Mining — and Miscellaneous

As indicated by statistics elsewhere shown herein, labor arbitration has been increasing regularly during recent years. This is due in part to increased confidence in arbitration as a process or procedure for settlement of labor disputes. It is also due in part, however, to the spread of unionism into virtually all of the more common areas of employment. While there apparently are no reliable statistical figures indicating the proportional numbers of arbitration cases in the various industries, it seems reasonable to assume that they will not be greatly disproportionate to the total number of disputed matters that have been the subject of assistance given to parties by the Federal Mediation and Conciliation Service in recent years. The numbers of these cases given in the 21st Annual (1968) Report of that service are as follows:[1]

Manufacturing	5,157
Retail, Wholesale and Service Industries	1,208
Public Utilities, Communication and Transportation	522
Construction	514
Mining, Agriculture and Finance	75
Government — Federal and State	9

It should not be overlooked that while many important disputes concerning terms of labor agreements go to arbitration, numerous relatively less important grievance matters also are arbitrated. Issues of the latter sort are unlikely to get into major disputes on contract terms and the like, which mainly concern the Federal Me-

---

[1] Federal Mediation and Conciliation Service, 21st Annual Report, 1968.

diation and Conciliation Service. It seems correct to infer that arbitration has become increasingly acceptable to virtually all who become engaged from time to time in the types of disputes that normally go to mediation and later to arbitration.[2] One may, therefore, venture the generalization that the scope of activity in arbitration has come to be as broad as unionization and as broad as the scope of work of the Federal Mediation and Conciliation Service.

Thus, in manufacturing, construction, rendition of service, wholesale and retail trade, mining and miscellaneous industrial activities, arbitration functions smoothly. Normally it should be acceptable to the parties as superior to economic pressures. However, there is no doubt that employees in most areas of employment have the right to impose economic pressures. Employers in the majority of nonpublic service industries have the right to lockout employees if they so desire in relation to labor disputes. They also have certain other means of giving economic emphasis to their contentions. As elsewhere observed, arbitration should in most areas be regarded as voluntary. If parties become engaged in a dispute they cannot settle by the normal means of negotiation, they have, and should have, freedom of choice either to engage in economic pressure or to enter into voluntary arbitration. The universality with which arbitration has been accepted and the similarity of its functioning in the various areas make it quite unnecessary to offer specific statistics of its operation and results in any of the above-mentioned industries.

There have been a few instances of unions temporarily adopting an absolute policy against arbitration, but it is believed that none of the international unions at present, whether affiliated with the AFL-CIO, or otherwise, refuses as a fixed policy to enter into arbitration as a means of terminating disputes.

SECTION 3

Public Employees — In General

It clearly is arguable that in certain areas in which the public is immediately and vitally interested, there should be no work stop-

---

2 Murphy, "The Foreman's Role in Arbitration," 13 Arbitration Journal 98 (1958). This author states (p. 99), "Approximately 95 per cent of the 125,000 collective bargaining agreements in existence contain arbitration clauses, and each year the volume of arbitration seems to increase."

pages or lockouts. In some of these areas, it is difficult to perceive how arbitration could take the place of political or official decision in more than a most limited manner, if at all.

While men who enter nonpublic employments, which have no well-known restrictions and hazards, are recognized as having the right to bargain collectively to improve the conditions of their employment so as to make it more desirable, the welfare of the state and of society as a whole must always be sustained and held to be more important than the rights, privileges, and immunities of any individuals or groups of individuals within the society or state. Any organization that undertakes to dominate, to obstruct, or to dictate to lawful government may logically be thought of as seditious if not anarchical. It is the function of those elected or appointed to govern in our society to maintain stability in the interest of the public and, among other things, to provide for police protection, fire protection, education, and many other well-known governmental services.

Under our laws, organized labor groups normally have the right to bargain collectively and to put economic pressures in the form of work stoppages and peaceful picketing behind their requests or demands. A work stoppage by policemen, however, could leave the public without protection against lawless people. A strong weight of legal, social, and economic opinion opposes this right to strike. Some, therefore, argue that it necessarily follows that policemen have no right to unionize, since that step may involve individual obligations and loyalties inconsistent with normal police duties.[3]

In 1919 Calvin Coolidge, at that time Governor of Massachusetts, called the Boston police strike "a desertion of duty." His position was that no citizen has the right to strike against the sovereign state at any time. President Woodrow Wilson referred to the Boston police strike as, "an intolerable crime against civilization." Samuel Gompers, when President of the American Federation of Labor, stated: "When policemen accept charters from the A.F.L.,

---

[3] Herbert W. Cornell, "Collective Bargaining by Public Employee Groups," 107 Univ. of Penn. L. Rev. 46-64 (1958); Murray Seasongood and Roscoe L. Barrow, "Unionization of Public Employees," 21 U. of Cincinnati L. Rev. 327 (1952); Vogel, "What About the Rights of the Public Employee?", Labor Law Journal 604 (1950); a comment "Union Labor and Municipal Employer," 45 Ill. L. Rev. 374 (1950).

it is with the distinct understanding that strike action will not be resorted to and no obligation is assumed which in any way conflicts with their oaths or duty."[4]

President Franklin D. Roosevelt at one time expressed himself thus: "Since their own services have to do with the functioning of the government, the strike of public employees manifests nothing less than an intent on their part to prevent or obstruct the operations of government until their demands are satisfied. Such action, looking toward the paralysis of government by those who have sworn to support it, is unthinkable and intolerable."[5]

Despite the foregoing arguments, the fact remains that in recent years unions have much increased their organizational activity in the public sector. In view of the statistics that over one million public employees are now union members, it must be admitted that public employee unions have been reasonably successful in terms of demonstrating to the nonunion work force the positive benefits that can accrue from union membership.[6] The fear that union activity in the public sector spells loss of employment[7] has been allayed by the willingness of governmental units to implement procedures by which public employees participate with management in the formation of labor policies. This development is exemplified by Executive Order 10988 in which President Kennedy created procedures for union recognition and collective bargaining in federal employment.[8]

The New York experience of 1968,[9] the St. Louis firemen's strike,[10] and the Detroit teachers' strike[11] are significant examples that demonstrate all too clearly the undesirable consequences of public service work stoppages. Yet, as one commentator has ob-

---

[4] See Christian Science Monitor, issues of Sept. 1, through Oct. 31, 1919; Ziskind, One Thousand Strikes of Government Employees, pp. 39-51 (1940).

[5] Letter to Luther C. Steward, President, National Federation of Federal Employees, August 16, 1937.

[6] See Anderson, "Labor Relations in the Public Service," 1961 Wis. L. Rev. 601.

[7] People v. Chicago, 278 Ill. App. 318, 116 N.E. 158 (1917).

[8] See Weisenfeld, "Collective Bargaining by Public Employees," 89 Monthly Labor Review, June 1966, p. 610.

[9] See N.Y. Times, Jan. 9, 1969, at 18. Annual Message of Governor Rockefeller to the New York Legislature.

[10] See Mo. Rev. Stat. §§ 105.500-.530 (1966). Public employees in the state may engage in negotiations, but firemen are excluded.

[11] Detroit Free Press, June 6, 1966, at 3, col. 7.

served, these disruptions may be only a preview of future problems that may develop as unionization of public employees continues to expand.[12] It is thus imperative that existing and proposed means of circumventing public employee strikes must be thoroughly explored and brought into the mainstream of public life. Of these, binding arbitration is the frontier area.

The question that remains unanswered with respect to legislative approval of binding arbitration is what subjects may be arbitrated without undermining our democratic form of government.[13] Neither officers of states nor those of municipalities may bargain away sovereign powers, and it is obvious that the powers entrusted by voters to mayors and councilmen or to other governmental officers must be exercised by them and may not be delegated. In some sense, it would seem to follow that no state or municipal government may accept either dictation or collective bargaining that would amount to subjecting the municipalities, as such, to pressure concerning policemen's wages, working conditions, or tenure. It is arguable, however, that public officers with authority to act in an area of substantial discretion should be able to appoint a referee, an appraiser, or an arbitrator to hear evidence and to reach a conclusion within that range of discretion with the advance understanding that necessary, subsequent official action would be taken consistently with it. Thus, a governing body could apparently validly exercise its authority and make use of the knowledge of an experienced labor arbitrator should it be disposed to do so. Somewhat like men in the armed services, policemen find themselves in an area of employment in which, by entering it, they have sacrificed their right to strike. It need not follow, however, that they have also surrendered their right to join collective bargaining organizations and to participate in the normal activities of the latter. Views differ upon the latter point. Some authorities insist that the policeman is normally in a situation where, since he cannot have both, he must choose either employment of the type he has

---

12 See "A New Frontier in Collective Bargaining: Public Workers and Citizen Bosses." Remarks of Sam Zagoria, Member, NLRB, at the Labor Law Inst. for layman sponsored by Fed. Bar., Columbus Chapter at Ohio State Univ., Columbus, 1968.

13 See Everett Fire Fighters v. Johnson, 35 LRRM 2434 (Wash. Sup. Ct., 1960), where a form of binding arbitration was held invalid because adequate standards were not formulated for the arbitrator; cf. Transit Union Div. 85 v. Port Authority, 417 Pa. 299, 208 A. 2d 271 (1965).

or the right to belong to a union and to participate in the usual union activities.[14]

State Statutes — A number of states have enacted labor relations acts more or less on the pattern of the National Labor Relations Act. These are intended to guarantee and to regulate collective bargaining. None of these statutes, however, appears to apply to public employment and most of them, like the NLRA, exclude state and political subdivisions from the definition of "employer." In the case of *Railway Mail Association* v. *Corsi*,[15] it was held that it was not a denial of equal protection of the laws for a state statute to provide for collective bargaining for private employees and to exclude from it organizations of public employees. There appears to have been no judicial determination of the question whether the legislative branch of the government, which is theoretically coordinate with, and not superior to, the executive branch, has authority to require the executive branch to bargain collectively with public employees. There now seems to be no doubt, however, that the legislative branch of the government may exercise its own sovereign discretion to exclude public employees from the right to collective bargaining provided by a statute applicable only to private employees. Currently the right of public employees to organize and join a union has been recognized in 13 states.[16] The right to unionize is a sham unless the public employee can enter into and enforce a collective bargaining agreement. Over one third of the states recognize the proprietory nature of a governmental authority in its capacity as an employer and allow collective bargaining. Courts of several states have prohibited unionization of public employees in essential occupations such as law enforcement[17] and fire fighting.[18] These decisions are based on the theory that the uninterrupted performance of certain public services is so essential to the public welfare that it overrides the employees' right to organize.

---

[14] Rhyne, Labor Unions and Municipal Employee Law, National Institute of Municipal Law Officers, Washington, D.C., pp. 26, 28, 79, 100, 310, 343, 362.

[15] 267 App. Div. 417, 293 N.Y. 315, 56 N.E. 2d 721, 326 U.S. 86, 16 LRRM 813 (1945).

[16] See, e.g. Fla. Stat. Ann. § 839.221 (1965); Mass. Gen Laws Ann. ch. 149, § 178 (1965).

[17] Perez v. Board of Police Commr's., 78 Cal. App. 2d 638, 178 P. 2d 537 (1947).

[18] Hutchinson v. Magee, 278 Pa. 119, 122 A. 234 (1923).

The right to strike has been denied most public employees.[19] The states of California, Connecticut, Florida, Georgia, Hawaii, Maine, Massachusetts, Michigan, Minnesota, Nebraska, New York, Ohio, Pennsylvania, Texas, Virginia, and Wisconsin have enacted legislation making public employee strikes unlawful.[20] Public employee strikes have been declared unlawful by court decision in other states.[21]

Other Statutes — The National Labor Relations Act provides that "the term 'employer' includes any person acting as an agent of an employer, directly or indirectly, but shall not include the United States, or any wholly owned Government corporation, or any Federal Reserve Bank, or any State or political subdivision thereof," or any person subject to the Railway Labor Act or any labor organization (other than when acting as an employer), or anyone acting in the capacity of officer or agent of such labor organization.[22] The Fair Labor Standards Act also excludes from its coverage employees of the United States as well as those of the states and political subdivisions of any of the same.[23]

The District of Columbia, which is governed by federal legislation, is subject to statutes that expressly prohibit members of the police from affiliating with any organization that claims and uses the right to strike. It also prohibits members of the fire department from directly or indirectly engaging in any strike.[24]

Union Views — As previously indicated, there have been substantial differences of opinion on the matters discussed in the foregoing. Numerous able attorneys representing employee organizations have contended that municipalities should be recognized to have the inherent and implied power to enter into labor union contracts without such action being expressly authorized by statute. They submit that these municipal labor contracts do not neces-

---

19 See Board of Educ. v. Reading, 32 Ill. App. 2d 567, 207 N.E. 2d 427 (1965).
20 See, e.g., Cal. Labor Code §§ 1960-63c (West Supp. 1966); N.Y. Civ. Serv. § 210 (McKinney Supp. 1967); Ohio Rev. Code §§ 4117.01-.05 (1965).
21 See, e.g., Board of Educ. v. Local 63, Public School Employees, 233 Minn. 144, 45 N.W. 2d 797 (1951); New Jersey Turnpike Authority v. Local 1611, State Employees, 83 N.J. Super. 389, 200 A. 2d 134 (ch. 1964); Alcoa v. Local 760, IBEW, 203 Tenn. 12, 308 S.W. 2d 477 (1957).
22 Wagner Act, 29 U. S. Code Ann. § 152 (1941). NLRA as amended, Sec. 2 (2) and (3) and see LMRA (Taft-Hartley Act) § 305.
23 Wage and Hour Act, 29 U. S. Code Ann. § 203 (1941).
24 D.C. Code (1940) § 4-125 and § 4-407.

sarily mean that municipal employees shall have the right to strike or otherwise withdraw from or impair public law enforcement and protection.[25] In fact, many authorities assert that the right to organize and join a union in which the public employee can participate in the decision-making process is the most significant method of minimizing the possibility of a public employee strike.

It is the union view that municipal labor contracts involve no surrender or unlawful delegation of authority. The public officials are exercising their delegated authority to decide questions relating to the status of public employees by entering into the usual type of employer-union contract rather than by some type of council action such as an ordinance or resolution. Moreover, by entering into labor agreements and permitting public employees to organize and to bargain collectively, it is asserted, public officers are merely according to public employees the constitutional right of equal protection of the laws.[26]

Labor spokesmen usually complete their contentions upon this subject by asserting that the normal and usual constitutional and statutory provisions granting authority to elected and appointed officials to act on behalf of states and municipalities can be and should be construed to authorize them to act either by a formal statute or resolution or by contract with a labor union of public employees if deemed suitable. They then point out that formal action may be taken finally by resolution or otherwise after the contract details, such as fixing wages, hours, and working conditions, have been informally worked out in collective bargaining, possibly with the aid of a referee or arbitrator.

Since most public employees cannot strike, a union view has developed that unions do not have the requisite economic power to enforce their demands when bargaining with a public employer.[27] For this reason employee unions have not been entirely successful in terms of bargaining results.

---

[25] Paper by Jos. A. Padway, Gen. Counsel, Am. F. of L., 11 Lawyers Guild Review 1-7 (1942); Paper by Lee Pressman, Gen. Counsel, C.I.O. (1942), reprinted in full in Rhyne, *op. cit. supra* at pp. 532-44.

[26] Here they rely on the general principle expressed in Labor Board v. Jones & Laughlin, 301 U. S. 1 (1937).

[27] See Moderly, "The Strike and Its Alternatives In Public Employment." 1966 Wisconsin Law Review, Spring, 1966. p. 549.

Several alternative methods have been used to prevent public strikes. Mediation[28] and factfinding[29] have been used with some degree of success. A tribunal that is authorized to make binding decisions in disputes under collective bargaining agreements[30] has been set up in one state.

Arbitration — Legislation allowing public employees to bind themselves voluntarily to the results of arbitration has not been enacted until recently.[31] In Minnesota, municipal, county, state, and university hospital employees may utilize arbitration in disputes over maximum work hours and minimum hourly wages. If mediation does not resolve the dispute, the parties must submit to binding arbitration. Moreover, this statute provided that both the terms of a proposed collective bargaining contract and the terms of an existing contract are arbitrable issues. Rhode Island legislation allows public employers to enter voluntarily into binding arbitration with labor organizations representing teachers. A Wisconsin statute is probably the broadest enacted on voluntary arbitration to date. The act gives public employers the right to enter into an agreement to arbitrate disputes arising under a collective bargaining agreement but covers only state employees. The violation of an arbitration agreement of this type is made a prohibited practice that may be enjoined by the Wisconsin Employment Relations Board. Orders of the Board are enforceable in the state courts.

Though the United States Supreme Court seems to have clearly rejected compulsory binding arbitration in the case of *Amalgamated Ass'n of Street, Electric Ry. and Motor Coach Employees Div. 1287* v. *Missouri*,[32] it has been upheld by a state where adequate guidelines for the arbitrator and reasonable restrictions on his authority were specified by the legislature.[33] Compulsory binding arbitration has received some legislative approval.[34] These laws

---

[28] See, e.g. Ore. Rev. Stat. § 243.750 (1965).

[29] See Krinsky, "Public Employment Fact Finding In Fourteen States," 17 Labor Law Journal, 532-540 (1966).

[30] See Neb. Rev. Stat. §§ 48-801 (1960).

[31] See Minn. Stat. § 179.35 (1961); Wis. Stat. §§ 111.80, .94 (Supp. 1967); R.I. Gen Law Ann. §§ 28-9.3-1 to 3-16 (Supp. 1966).

[32] 374 U. S. 74, 53 LRRM 2394 (1963).

[33] See Transit Union Div. 85 v. Port Authority, 417 Pa. 299, 208 A. 2d 271 (1965).

[34] See, e.g. Cal. Pub. Util. § 95650 (West Supp. 1966); Mass. Gen. Laws Ann. ch 465 § 24 (1967); Pa. Stat. Ann. Tit. 55, § 563.2 (1964).

are restricted to publicly owned authorities. Some authorities still have serious doubts as to the legality of this type of legislation.[35] These same authorities are of the opinion that legislation of this type is detrimental to the development of effective negotiations and the process of collective bargaining since the temptation in such situations could be to simply disagree and let the arbitrator decide. In the case of public utilities the necessity of settlement may override this problem, but in other areas of the public sector, the fear of inequities of compulsory arbitration will probably discourage its acceptance.

As previously indicated, an important question remains as to what subject may be arbitrated without undermining our democratic form of government. In this connection, it is axiomatic that a delegated power normally may not be redelegated. When the public duty to make a decision in respect to public employees' wages or working conditions has been given to a highway commission, a city council, or a school board, it normally may not redelegate that power to another board or person for final action. A few subjects that cannot be reasonably delegated to an arbitrator because of this important impediment would be those provided for by the rules of civil service: promotions, layoffs, position classifications, compensation and fringe benefits, examinations, discipline, and merit salary determinations.[36] On the other hand the following matters could possibly be delegated to an arbitrator for a binding decision under an existing contract: grievance matters, applications for seniority rights, work schedules relating to assigned hours and days of the week and shift assignments, scheduling of vacations and other time off, use of sick leave, application and interpretation of established work rules, health and safety practices, and interdepartmental tranfers.[37] Then too, public authorities often act through, or upon the conclusions of, appraisers, referees, expert engineering firms, accountants, and others. It would seem equally logical and suitable for city councils, school boards, and the like to refer disputes to experienced labor arbitrators with an understanding that whatever official action may be required would later be taken in

---

[35] See Shenton, "Compulsory Arbitration In The Public Service," 17 Labor Law Journal, 138 (1966).

[36] See Wis. Stat. Ann. §111.91 (2) (Supp. 1967).

[37] Compare Wis. Stat. Ann. §111.91 (1) (Supp. 1967).

pursuance of the report or award.[38] It would be only a step of common sense for an arbitrator requested to act in such a relationship to review carefully the applicable laws under which he is directed to proceed and to ascertain with some care the extreme limits of his authority and that of the employer. Constitutions and statutes of some states will be found to authorize arbitrational procedure in respect to certain matters concerning public employees where similar provisions may not be found in other states. Moreover, the party to whom the holding of a hearing and the weighing of evidence is referred may wisely term his conclusions a "Report and Recommendation" in some areas even though they would be thought of as an award if written in relation to a private employment relationship.

SECTION 4

The Railway Labor Act — Air Transport Industry

The Railway Labor Act of 1926, as amended in 1934, contains a statement of policy and purposes. The latter are: (1) To avoid any interruption to commerce or to the operation of any carrier engaged therein; (2) to forbid any limitation upon freedom of association among employees or any denial, as a condition of employment or otherwise, of the right of employees to join a labor organization; (3) to provide for the complete independence of carriers and of employees in the matter of self-organization; (4) to provide for the prompt and orderly settlement of all disputes concerning rates of pay, rules, or working conditions; (5) to provide for the prompt and orderly settlement of all disputes growing out of grievances or out of the interpretation or application of agreements covering rates of pay, rules, or working conditions.[39]

Those who wrote the Act desired to eliminate interruptions of railway service and to protect the rights of employees to organize

---

38 See Killingsworth, "Grievance Adjudication in Public Employment," p. 149 in The Arbitrator and the Parties, Proceedings of the Eleventh Annual Meeting, National Academy of Arbitrators (Washington: BNA Books, 1958) ; and Christie v. Port of Olympia, 27 Wash. 2d 534, 179 P. 2d 294 (1947) ; Norwalk Teachers' Assn. v. Board of Education, 138 Conn. 269, 83 A. 2d 482 (1951) .

39 45 U.S.C. §§ 151-163, 181-188. For an excellent short study of the Act, see Carroll R. Daugherty, "Arbitration by the National Railroad Adjustment Board," Chapter V, Arbitration Today, Proceedings of the Eighth Annual Meeting, National Academy of Arbitrators (Washington: BNA Books, 1955) , pp. 93-126.

in associations of their choice. They intended to provide a peaceful means for management and labor in the railway industry to settle all differences.[40] The Act itself provides the machinery for the solution of disputes. Interference with the workings of this machinery by either side is unlawful.[41]

"Major" and "Minor" Disputes — The Railway Labor Act sets up different procedures for major disputes, on the one hand, and minor disputes, on the other. Demands for new collective bargaining agreements or for changes in existing ones give rise to "major" disputes. Any dispute of a major nature is to be settled by the National Mediation Board. If settlement is impossible and the parties will not submit to arbitration, the President has power to appoint an emergency board. The latter then makes an additional attempt to settle the dispute.

"Minor" disputes typically are grievances of individual employees over alleged violations of their rights under an existing agreement. Jurisdiction to settle minor disputes is conferred by the Act upon the National Railroad Adjustment Board. The legislative history of the Act indicates that the statutory provisions dealing with that Board and with special, system, group, or regional boards of adjustment that may take its place, are to be considered as compulsory arbitration in this limited field.[42] The awards handed down by these boards are final and binding upon the parties and are enforceable by a court action. Courts in which proceedings for either enforcement or review of such awards are brought have no power to review them on the merits. Specific provision is made in the Act that such awards may be set aside or remanded by a court only (1) because of board failure to comply with the requirements of the Act, (2) for failure of the award to conform, or confine itself, to matters within the scope of the board's jurisdiction, or (3) because of fraud or corruption by a member of the board that handed down the award. Board awards are void if parties adversely affected were denied the due process of law guaranteed under the federal Constitution.

---

40 Elgin, Joliet & Eastern R.R. Co. v. Burley, 325 U. S. 711, 16 LRRM 749 (1945).
41 45 U. S. Code § 151-152; Baltimore and Ohio Ry. Co. v. United Railroad Workers, 271 F. 2d 87, 44 LRRM 2974 (1959).
42 See, Railroad Trainmen v. Chicago River & Indiana R.R. Co., 353 U. S. 30, 39 LRRM 2578 (1957).

The headquarters of the Railroad Ajustment Board is in Chicago, Illinois. The Board consists of 18 representatives of carriers and a like number from national labor organizations. It is set up in four divisions. The first has jurisdiction over grievances and arbitrations of train and yard service employees. The second deals with disputes of shop employees. The third is responsible for issues of sleeping car conductors and other sleeping car and dining car employees, train dispatchers, telegraphers, clerks, freight and express handlers, signalmen, and maintenance-of-way employees. The fourth division considers disputes involving employees in water transportation, guards, and all other employees not within the responsibilities of the other divisions. The caseloads, the attitudes, and even some of the details of procedure are considerably different as among the various divisions.[43]

The NRAB's jurisdiction does not extend to minor disputes in the airline industry. Minor disputes in that industry are settled by an air system, group, or regional board of adjustment. The awards handed down by these boards in minor disputes in the airline industry have the same status and effect as similar awards settling minor disputes in the railroad industry.[44]

"Major" disputes — disputes over proposed new agreements or proposed changes in existing ones — are handled by the National Mediation Board, as stated above. It handles both railroad and airline disputes. No provision for compulsory arbitration is made by the Act insofar as major disputes are concerned. In its mediation provisions, the Act provides "cooling-off" periods which are intended to eliminate or, at least to postpone, serious interruptions of service of any carrier. The operation of these features is briefly as follows:

(1) Assume a party desires changes in its working agreement. The initiating party must give the other party 30 days' notice. Within 10 days of receipt of this notice the parties must agree upon a time and place for conference to discuss the request or demand. This conference must be held within 30 days after notice.

(2) The parties then conduct the conference. There is no time limit as to when this conference may terminate. If no agreement is

---

43 See, Carroll R. Daugherty, *op. cit. supra.* pp. 97-109.
44 Machinists v. Central Airlines, Inc., 372 U. S. 682, 52 LRRM 2803 (1963).

reached through this conference, the law provides that the *status quo* shall be maintained for 10 days after the conference has terminated.

(3) At this time intervention by the National Mediation Board is provided. The Board will attempt to bring the parties to a settlement. If no agreement can then be reached the Board undertakes to "induce" the parties to refer the matter to arbitration. If arbitration is rejected by the parties, the Board must promptly notify the parties in writing that mediation has failed. It also may notify the President. The parties are then required to leave matters in *status quo* for an additional 30 days.

(4) A possible step here is an agreed arbitration. If so, the parties select one or two arbitrators each, who then acting together select one or two impartial members bringing the board to membership of three or six.

(5) In the third phase above, a possible strike date may be set and the President may appoint an emergency board that will try to settle the dispute.[45] This board reports in writing to the President, and he usually makes the reports public.

Parties to a major dispute are under no duty to accept suggestions of the NMB (including suggestions that the parties submit their controversies to arbitration). On the other hand, if carriers and their employees elect to proceed under merger or acquisition arrangements containing compulsory arbitration provisions required by the Interstate Commerce Commission, then they are bound by the arbitration provisions. According to federal appellate courts they accepted the agreements to arbitrate by accepting the arrangements.[46]

Employers Covered — The Railway Labor Act covers all interstate railways and air transport companies. It does not cover city transit companies or suburban electric lines unless they are part of an interstate system.[47] The Interstate Commerce Commission determines the status of carriers for purposes of the Railway Labor

---

45 Jacob J. Kaufman, "Emergency Boards Under The Railway Labor Act," 9 Labor Law Journal 910 (1958).

46 New Orleans & Northeastern R.R. Co. v. Bozemon, 52 LRRM 2322 (1963); Batts v. Louisville & Nashville R.R. Co. 316 F. 2d 22, 52 LRRM 2895 (CA, 6, 1963).

47 Chicago, S.S. & S.B.R.R. v. Fleming, 109 Fed. 2d 419 (1940).

Act.[48] Such a determination by the Commission is conclusive upon the courts if supported by substantial evidence.[49] Carriers that bring themselves into this carrier-classification for purposes of bankruptcy may not deny this classification for labor adjustment purposes.[50] Those railways that operate entirely within the boundaries of a state are included under the provisions of the Act if they are engaged in interstate commerce. This is true even if the road is operated by a sovereign state.[51]

Employees Covered — Employees not in supervisory capacities and some lower rank supervisory employees are covered. This latter classification is determined by the Interstate Commerce Commission.[52] Included in these groups are such employees as auditors, claims agents, foremen, supervisors, road masters, train dispatchers, technical engineers, yard masters, storekeepers, etc.[53] The Act applies only to people designated as within its coverage.[54] The Railway Labor Act covers only the classifications of defined, admitted wage earners when they are engaged and employed by a defined, admitted carrier.[55]

A 1951 amendment to the Act allows wage earners in the proper classifications to enter into union-shop or maintenance-of-membership agreements with their managements. This amendment has been held to have superseded the state right-to-work laws.[56]

Air Transport Coverage — The Railway Labor Act was amended to cover labor relations in the air transport industry in 1936. The entire Act applies to the industry with the exception of Section 3, which deals with and provides for the National Board of Adjustment. The "cooling-off" provisions, as before described, apply generally to the air transport industry. The Interstate Commerce Com-

---

48 Shields v. Utah I.C.R.R., 305 U. S. 177, 3 LRRM 669 (1938); Hudson & Manhattan R.R. v. Hardy, 103 Fed. 2d 327, 4 LRRM 796 (1939).
49 Note 47 *supra*.
50 See 70 Harv. L. Rev. 739 (1957).
51 Taylor v. Fee, 233 Fed. 2d 251, 38 LRRM 2117 (1956); See Bernard Schwartz, "Administrative Law," 27 N.Y.U. L. Rev. 928, 935 (1952); Sprague v. Woll, 122 Fed. 2d 128, 8 LRRM 1041 (1941).
52 45 U. S. Code § 151.
53 Lundburg v. Chicago Great Western Ry. Co., 76 F. Supp. 61, 21 LRRM 2293 (1948).
54 *Supra*, note 1.
55 Locomotive Firemen v. I.C.C., 147 Fed. 2d 312, 15 LRRM 816 (1945).
56 Railway Employees Dept., AFL v. Hanson, 351 U. S. 225, 38 LRRM 2099 (1956).

mission determines the classification of air carriers for purposes of the Act.[57] A recent case determined before the National Mediation Board ruled that a national airline was covered by the Act, including even its guided missile range division that operated under contract with the United States Air Force.[58]

In the air transport area, the Act covers the same types of employees as in the railway industry. These include clerical and office employees, store employees, fleet service employees, communication employees, mechanics, plant maintenance personnel, and the like.[59]

Some writers have expressed the view that applications of the Act to air transportation is a misfit. They emphasize the difference between rail and air transportation industries and stress the fact that when the Railway Labor Act was enacted and made applicable to the railway industry there were, already in existence, mature unions which could readily fit into the pattern for which the legislation was designed. They also point out that in the air transport industry the only union of any stature is the Air Line Pilots' Association. They conclude that the air transport industry is not yet stabilized and that the Act, rather than aiding stabilization, tends to hamper it. They urge the passage of new and modern legislation expressly designed for the air transport business.[60]

Voluntary Arbitration — The Railway Labor Act provides also that the parties to a dispute may, by mutual agreement, submit the dispute to a private board of arbitration that is subject to specified procedures and is authorized to make an award having the same binding effect as an award of the NRAB or of a special system, group, or regional board of adjustment. A special arbitration board may also be established by a strike settlement agreement solely for the purpose of settling disputes arising out of the strike. In the case that such strike settlement agreement does not conform to the RLA provisions governing voluntary arbitration, the procedures before such special board would be governed by the principles of common law.

---

57 See N.M.B. Cases Numbers R-1706, 18, 19, 20, 21, 29, and 35 (January 31, 1947).
58 N.M.B. Case No. C-2505, November 9, 1956.
59 Note 32, *supra*.
60 See Malcolm A. MacIntyre, "The Railway Labor Act — A Misfit For The Airlines," 19 Journal Air Law & Comm. 274 (1952).

When a board of arbitration that is constituted in conformity with the RLA provisions governing voluntary arbitration has handed down its award, the board does not lose jurisdiction to interpret the award after the terms of the award have been incorporated into a collective bargaining agreement. In the agreement to arbitrate, a period can be fixed during which the award shall continue in force, but the award does not expire by the mere fact that its terms are incorporated into a collective bargaining agreement. Therefore, a dispute over the meaning and application of an award that has been incorporated into a collective bargaining agreement may be referred back to the board of arbitration, since the award remains in effect and the board of arbitration has jurisdiction to pass on its meaning and application. Under the voluntary arbitration provisions of the Act, any question concerning the meaning or application of an award may be referred back to the board of arbitrators that made the original award. But the jurisdiction of the board extends only to the interpretation and application of the original award, and any amendment or modification of the award would be invalid.[61]

The authority granted a board of arbitration by the Railway Labor Act to interpret an award made by it does not empower the board to make a new award. Consequently, an interpretation by the board that is inconsistent with the award and with the questions submitted to the board exceeds the board's authority to review and interpret its awards and amounts, in effect, to an entirely new award. Under such circumstances the award may be impeached and set aside as being beyond the authority of the board.[62]

Compulsory Arbitration — Until 1963, compulsory arbitration had been resorted to only in wartime. But in order to meet national emergencies arising out of threats of nationwide railroad strikes, Congress has twice enacted special laws virtually providing for compulsory arbitration of major disputes. In order to avert a strike in the so-called "work rules" dispute, Congress passed a special law requiring the railroads and the unions to arbitrate the two main issues. The law was upheld by the courts as constitu-

---

61 Railroad Telegraphers v. New York Central R.R. Co., 181 F. 2d 113, 25 LRRM 2604 (CA 2, 1950).

62 Mid-Continent Airlines v. Railway & Steamship Clerks, 15 LC Para 64, 723 (DC, Mo., 1948).

tional, and the award of the arbitration panel was enforced.[63] The U. S. Supreme Court held, however, that neither the special law nor awards made under it was intended to supersede state "full-crew" laws.[64] A second special law was enacted in 1967 in a dispute between the major railroads and six shopcraft unions. It extended the no-strike period under the Railway Labor Act, provided for a special five-man board to mediate the dispute, and authorized binding settlement by that board if mediation failed.

Court Action — The courts have been slow to issue injunctive relief for breach of legal duties under the statute unless there appeared to be some possibility that violence would occur.[65] The view has been taken that, while the Railway Labor Act does not generally restrict application of the Norris-LaGuardia Act, injunctive relief in railroad cases should be allowed when necessary to carry out the specific provisions of the Railway Labor Act.[66] Peaceful strikes and picketing may be enjoined when intended to defeat the jurisdiction of the Board under this statute.[67]

In the case decided by the U. S. Supreme Court in 1960, a railroad argued that where a union makes a bargaining demand that is unlawful under the Railway Labor Act, the controversy is removed from the Norris-LaGuardia Act's definition of a "labor dispute," and a strike to enforce the demand becomes enjoinable in the federal courts. A majority of the Court found it unnecessary to rule on this contention, since the union's request for a job freeze was a bargainable demand under the Railway Labor Act. It rejected contentions that the demand was an attempt to usurp legitimate managerial prerogatives and that it violated the Interstate Commerce Act by going against the congressional intent to foster an efficient railroad system.[68]

---

63 Locomotive Firemen & Engineers v. Certain Carriers, 331 F. 2d 1020, 55 LRRM 2517 (CA D.C.; 1964) *cert. denied.* 377 U. S. 918, 56 LRRM 2064.

64 Locomotive Engineers v. Chicago, Rock Island & Pacific R.R. Co., 382 U. S. 423, 61 LRRM 2209 (1966).

65 See Chicago R. & Ind. R.R. v. Brotherhood of R.R. Trainmen, 229 Fed. 2d 926, 37 LRRM 2523, *cert. granted,* 352 U. S. 865 (1956).

66 See Virginia Ry v. System Federation No. 40, Ry. Employees Dept. AFL, 300 U. S. 515 LRRM 743 (1937) where the court allowed injunctive relief.

67 See note 41, *supra.*

68 Railroad Telegraphers v. C. & N.W.R. Co., 362 U. S. 330, 45 LRRM 3109 (1960).

The view is favored by some that the jurisdiction of the Railroad Adjustment Board is exclusive and should not be usurped
nor shared by the courts, and that the latter should have authority to review only where it is charged there has been unauthorized
action, corruption, or the like.[69]

Conclusion — The Railway Labor Act has apparently had a
strong stabilizing influence in the transportation industry. Its application in the air transport area has been unsatisfactory in some
respects. However, the Act, both praised and criticized as are most
man-created institutions, must be considered as a whole a valuable
aid toward eliminating interruption of service in the transportation industry and hence valuable to all the public. This statute and
experience with it, though in some respects imperfect, must always be considered when there appears to be need for legislation
to reduce strike frequency and severity and to substitute arbitration for economic pressures in other industries.

SECTION 5

Public Utilities Other Than Those Under the Railway Labor Act

In approaching this topic, one must assume with more emphasis
than in other connections that the welfare of society as a whole
must be set above the claims or demands of any included, lesser
group. This principle seems to apply with strong logic and force
to the functions and services of public utilities and to apply to ownership as well as to employee organizations. Over the country today
in all communities, large and small, all people and all activities of
all people are so dependent upon the various public utility services
that great dangers, hardships, inconveniences, and losses invariably
are widely suffered when any one of such services is interrupted.

For a few examples, the stoppage of electric service today will
leave innumerable homes in any community without light and
without heat for household warmth or cooking. All household ap-

---

[69] George Rose, "The Railway Labor Act and the Jurisdiction of the Courts,"
8 Labor Law Journal 9 (1957). This article discusses all contentions, pro and con.
See Gainey v. Brotherhood of Ry. and Steam Clerks, Etc., 177 F. Supp. 421, 44
LRRM 2807 (1959) holding that the relations between railroads and unions under
the Railway Labor Act are not subject to being policed by the federal courts.

pliances will be useless. Discontinuance of water service in any community will bring about great danger of fire and menace health and life in case the public is suddenly put to the necessity of using such waters as may be obtained from nearby streams, ponds, lakes, or wells. Stoppage of gas service will prevent cooking and heating in innumerable homes, as well as activities in industrial establishments. Interruption of telephone service will virtually paralyze normal social and commercial activities. Discontinuance of city transit in public vehicles will promptly fill the streets with added private automobiles so that the next result will be to immobilize great numbers of them in downtown traffic jams.

The foregoing observations deal with well-known facts. Indeed, much comment concerning them had been published during the first half of the present century, pointing to the need for as much legal assurance as possible against interruption of these vital services. Several states enacted legislation providing for public intervention into labor-management disputes concerning public utilities. Compulsory arbitration was provided for in the statutes of California, Florida, Indiana, Maryland, Massachusetts, Missouri, Nebraska, New Jersey, Pennsylvania, and Wisconsin. The New Jersey and Virginia laws provided for state seizure and operation of utilities where continuous service was endangered by a labor dispute.

On February 26, 1951, the United States Supreme Court decided the case of *Amalgamated Association of Street, Electric Railway and Motor Coach Employees of America* v. *Wisconsin Employment Relations Board*.[70] It held the Wisconsin law to be unconstitutional on the ground that by the enactment of the National Labor Relations Act, Congress had undertaken to regulate labor relations to the full extent of its constitutional power and thus by preemption had eliminated the power to regulate labor dispute matters which otherwise might have been held to inhere in the sovereign states. The Court clearly put its position to be that a state statute that requires collective bargaining until an impasse is reached and thereafter requires arbitration, must be held invalid because federal labor legislation contemplates that the employer and employees shall continue to bargain collectively even after a strike is started.

---

[70] 340 U. S. 383, 27 LRRM 2385 (1951).

A steadfast friend of labor, Mr. Justice Frankfurter, dissented from the decision that declared the Wisconsin public utility anti-strike statute ineffective because of federal preemption and stated:

"But the careful consideration given to the problem of meeting nation-wide emergencies and the failure to provide for emergencies other than those affecting the Nation as a whole do not imply paralysis of State police power. Rather, they imply that the States retain the power to protect the public interest in emergencies economically and practically confined within a state. It is not reasonable to impute to Congress the desire to leave States helpless in meeting local situations when Congress restricted national intervention to national emergencies."[71]

Despite the decision of the United States Supreme Court concerning the Wisconsin statute, the state acts concerning public utility collective bargaining and possible work stoppages have continued on the statute books. But local enforcement of such statutes has been timid and uncertain. Since the U. S. Supreme Court held the Wisconsin statute to be unenforceable, several proposals have been made to amend the National Labor Relations Act so as to return full authority in the vital public utilities labor relations area to the states.

A bill was introduced in the Congress by Senator Spessard L. Holland in 1959 to alleviate the situation described by Mr. Justice Frankfurter. The bill did not pass and the states are still without authority to protect continuity of service of privately owned public utilities. In fact the situation has been compounded by a later decision of the Supreme Court holding a Missouri statute to be ineffective because of the federal preemption of authority over labor relations with the included express preservation of the right to strike.[72] This 1963 case is one of the most recent decisions by the Supreme Court in this area. Unlike the Wisconsin legislation, which provided for compulsory settlement of labor disputes in public utilities, the Missouri legislation provided for seizure of the utility by the governor in the event of labor-created emergencies. Refusing to accept the state's characterization of the statute as

---

[71] Amalgamated Ass'n of St., Elec. Ry. & Motor Coach Employees v. Wisconsin Employment Relations Bd., 340 U. S. 383, 406-07, 27 LRRM 2395 (1951).

See C. M. Updegraff, "Preemption, Predictability and Progress in Labor Law," 17 Hastings Law Journal 509-516 (1966).

[72] Amalgamated Ass'n of St., Elec. Ry & Motor Coach Employees v. Missouri, 374 U. S. 74, 53 LRRM 2394 (1963).

emergency legislation, the Court held that the state legislation could not deny the rights guaranteed to employees by Section 7 of the NLRA. Congress itself had imposed such restrictions only in the case of national emergencies. Although the labor relations of state-owned and state-operated public utilities were by definition excluded from the operation of the NLRA, the mere seizure of a utility under these circumstances did not make the utility either state-owned or state-operated.

Application of Federal Preemption to Public Utilities — Prior to 1950 the NLRB decided whether to exercise jurisdiction over a particular controversy on a case-by-case basis, determining in each instance whether the operation of a particular enterprise affected interstate commerce within the meaning of the Act. Then in 1950 the Board formulated jurisdictional yardsticks for various industries.[73] Applying these standards, which were revised in 1954, the Board would exercise jurisdiction over labor controversies only if the enterprise involved did a certain dollar value of business, enterprises in various industries being assigned differing dollar volumes.[74]

Subsequently, in *Guss* v. *Utah Labor Relations Bd.*,[75] the Court created a "no man's land" with regard to the exercise of jurisdiction over labor disputes affecting commerce. The Court said that Congress, in granting the NLRB jurisdiction over such disputes, had removed entirely the power of the states to deal with them if the Board declined to cede jurisdiction to a state tribunal by the method set forth in the NLRA.

In order to narrow the no man's land that the decision in *Guss* created, the Board's jurisdictional yardsticks were revised downward in 1958.[76] In addition, the NLRA was amended in 1959 to give the Board the option to refuse jurisdiction in case of "any labor dispute involving any class or category of employers," if the labor dispute does not substantially affect commerce.[77] The Board was also authorized to refuse jurisdiction by means of rule or de-

---

[73] See 26 LRRM (1950). For more complete discussion of these criteria see Chap. II, Sec. 3, *supra*.
[74] See Decisions of Courts and Administrative Agencies, 5 L. 6 L.J. 571-72 (1954).
[75] Guss v. Utah Labor Relations Bd., 353 U. S. 1, 39 LRRM 2567 (1957).
[76] See 42 LRRM 96 (1958). These appear herein at note 162 in Chapter II, Sec. 3.
[77] 73 Stat. 541 (1959).

cision or by publication of rules in accordance with the provisions of the Administrative Procedures Act. However, this authorization applies only if the Board had not asserted jurisdiction over the particular industrial classification prior to the adoption of the 1958 standards. If the Board had asserted jurisdiction over an industrial group prior to August 1, 1959, such exercise of jurisdiction cannot be withdrawn. Therefore, it seems with regard to all businesses, including public utilities, only the Board may exercise jurisdiction over labor controversies if its jurisdictional standards are met. Since almost all public utilities meet these standards, the states have been precluded from regulating most labor disputes in the public utility industry.

Currently the doctrine of federal preemption is applied dogmatically in labor relations preventing the balancing of state and federal interests. Once the federal government has acted it is said to have preempted state legislation directly affecting the subject.[78] Yet, even under the preemption doctrine, state legislation, otherwise valid, should not be rendered invalid because of a conflict unless the repugnancy or the congressional interest to preempt is readily apparent. Both state and federal regulations should be permitted to operate if both can be accommodated within the concept of federal supremacy.[79] The latest major holding on federal preemption in labor relations appeared in *San Diego Building Trades v. Garmon*:[80] "When an activity is arguably subject to §7 or §8 of the Act, the States as well as the federal courts must defer to the exclusive competence of the National Labor Relations Board if the danger of state interference with national policy is to be averted."[81] The court noted two exceptions to the rule. One is "where the activity regulated was a merely peripheral concern of the Labor Management Relations Act."[82] The second limitation is "where the regulated conduct touched interests so deeply rooted in local feeling and responsibility that . . . [the court] could not infer that Congress had deprived the states of the power to act."[83]

---

78 See, e.g., Sears, Roebuck & Co. v. Stiffel Co., 376 U. S. 225 (1964).

79 See, Hood v. New Mexico B. of Examiners, 374 U. S. 424 (1967); Florida Lime and Avocado Growers Inc. v. Paul, 373 U. S. 132 (1963).

80 359 U. S. 236, 43 LRRM 2838 (1959). See Chapter II, Sec. 2, *supra* for discussion.

81 Id. at 245.

82 359 U. S. at 243.

83 359 U. S. at 244.

Effectuating the State Interest — In view of the foregoing, it seems obvious that the states have a valid interest in the consequences of local public utility service stoppages and should be allowed to exercise their police power to protect the public from the unreasonably disruptive and possibly extremely dangerous effects of such disputes. Because the Supreme Court has never had the opportunity to pass on the validity of state legislation which has actually been confined to true emergency situations, it would appear that a remnant of the police power is still available to the states. In *Division 1287, Amalgamated Ass'n of St. Ry. Employees* v. *Missouri,* the Court concluded that "nothing we have said even remotely affects . . . the right or duty of the chief executive or legislature of a state to deal with emergency conditions of public danger, violence or disaster under appropriate provisions of the state's organic or statutory law."[84] Although this statement was dictum in 1963, it was implicit in the holding in *Amalgamated Ass'n of St. Ry. Employees* v. *Wisconsin Employment Relations Bd.*[85] where the Court also had before it a comprehensive code. It is clear from both these cases that a code providing for comprehensive state regulation of labor disputes in public utilities, regardless of careful application to true emergency situations, must fall. But state legislation utilizing a narrow definition of labor dispute consistent with the public's interest in the continued operation of a public utility will, when combined with a restrictive definition of public utility, have a greatly improved chance of surviving constitutional challenges.

There are, however, additional limitations on the ability of the states to act even in the case of local emergencies. The Supreme Court has indicated that it will not allow the state governments to regulate the area of local emergencies to a greater extent than the federal government has regulated the area of national emergencies.[86] The federal laws do not, however, contain compulsory settlement provisions, such as mandatory submission of the dispute to binding arbitration. Thus, proposed state legislation must also stop short of providing binding methods for settlement and must concentrate on temporarily abating the emergency by enjoin-

---

84 374 U. S. at 83.
85 340 U. S. 383, 27 LRRM 2385 (1951).
86 374 U. S. 74 (1963) ; 340 U. S. 383, 27 LRRM 2385 (1951).

ing the work stoppage. This is an unfortunate result with respect to some public utilities where there may be a necessity to employ compulsory arbitration or where it would be more effective to all concerned than an injunction that offers no lasting solution. Also, it is clear that this strict limitation of the police power to emergencies deprives the states of normally exercised sovereign powers and obtains a dubious result in leaving primary jurisdiction over public utility pressure conduct by unions and employers in the NLRB.

Operating Costs — Numerous working rules have expanded the costs of operations for all utilities from the biggest steamship and rail lines to the smallest municipal utility operations.[87] While utilities commissions have discussed rate bases (present fair value or prudent investment), reproduction costs, and rates of returns, they have had some tendency to overlook the rapid changes that have been taking place in operating costs. It is not meant that the commissions have completely failed to have these factors in mind as they dealt with estimates of "fair return." But they have shown some tendency to assume such costs to be something more or less stable, whereas the truth is they have been changing so rapidly recently in all departments — labor, equipment, and consumable supplies — that a public utility rate can scarcely be considered and established before the whole picture of gross income, net income, and consequential rate of return has been altered.[88]

While labor union officials often recognize the necessity of unfailing public service in their utterances, it is common knowledge that strikes and threats of strikes have occurred affecting electric utilities, gas services, telephones, street railways, bus lines, and railroads. In other words, when the union demands are not met, the unions are likely to treat the public utility much as they would treat any private employer and cause the public utility service to be interrupted, whatever inconvenience that may entail. The fact that there is a public interest in the continuity of service becomes

87 See Simpson, "Possible Labor Difficulties in the Utility Field," 38 P.U. Fort. 345 (1946); also Editorial, "Cleveland Demand," 43 Mass Trans. 478 (1947); and Sussna, "Compulsory Arbitration for Utilities — a Reappraisal," 61 Public Utilities Fortnightly 433 (1958).

88 Updegraff, "Present Value the Iowa Rate Base for Public Utilities — the Recent Fort Dodge Decision." 43 Iowa Law Review 317 (1958); McDiarmid, "The Utilities Face a Big Financial Problem," 41 P.U. Fort. 3 (1948); Ely, "Financial News and Comment," 39 P.U. Fort. 108 (1947).

secondary to the employer's contentions on the one hand and to the attainment of the union's demands on the other. The concern of public utility managements that service be constant has been said to have caused them to concede more and to yield more readily in recent years than has been the case with private employers.[89] For this reason, labor costs are proportionally more burdensome to public utilities in many places than to many private employers. It has been asserted that union demands for wages tend to put unskilled and semiskilled employees of the utility field in the higher-paid compensation brackets that formerly were available only to truly skilled workers who had served long apprenticeships.[90] It has been charged that in addition to direct and indirect wage demands affecting the hourly rates of pay and hence total labor costs, employee organizations have also increasingly demanded of utility companies "working conditions" which often amount to "feather-bedding."[91]

It appears to have been a basic assumption of some union spokesmen that the inability of the utility to pay is not a material factor to be considered in relation to a wage dispute.[92] They frequently have asserted that utility employees must have their wage demands met regardless of the fact that the expense involved in doing so will put the public utility company so deeply into the red that a receivership may be inevitable. Labor organizations urge that utility employees are entitled to live in accordance with generally accepted or theoretically advocated "standards of living," and that unless wages are paid accordingly, utility companies should discontinue operations or become parties to some arrangement for liquidation, public subsidization, or public ownership. In other words, whether right or wrong, union leaders have put pressure upon private ownership that must tend to force public takeover or subsidization to attain wage increases and employment condition advantages.[93]

---

89 See Heiges, "State Labor Legislation for Public Utilities Disputes," 61 Public Utilities Fortnightly 587 (1958) ; Sawyer, "Statement on Arbitration," Am. Transit Ass'n Proc. 91 (1947).

90 Kansas City Public Service Co., 8 Lab. Arb. Rep. 149, 169-70 (1947).

91 Simpson, note 1 *supra*, at 348.

92 McKenna, "CWA Policy toward Regulatory Commissions," 62 Public Utilities Fortnightly 236 (1958) ; Nash, "Impact of Labor Disturbances on Public Utilities," 38 P.U. Fort. 399, 400 (1946).

93 McCarthy, "Statement on Arbitration," Am. Transit Ass'n Proc. 95 (1947). See also Percival, "Strikes and the Cost of Living," 37 P.U. Fort. 415 (1946). See

At present, many labor disputes in the utilities industry are regularly submitted to boards of arbitration.[94] Usually these are selected by the appointment of one arbitrator by the company, one by the union, and a neutral selected by these two or appointed by some designated outside agency such as a federal judge, the American Arbitration Association, the Federal Mediation and Conciliation Service, or another. The arbitration board when organized spends much time taking testimony as to the equities of the workers as indicated by cost-of-living and wage rate and working condition comparisons, *i.e.,* the bases upon which they are demanding increased compensation. The arbitrators then ordinarily hear evidence offered by the utility company concerning its inability to meet the demands from a financial standpoint and the fairness of its working rules, as compared to those of similar employers. The arbitration board, largely dominated by the "neutral" chairman, who may know much or very little of the utility industry, will then proceed to tell the utility company what wages and working conditions it must concede.[95] The pressures which constrained the employer to agree to arbitration are likely to cause its performance of the award, no matter how extreme it may be.[96]

It is emphasized that such an arbitration board has no authority whatsoever in respect to the service rates to be charged by the utility company, and ordinarily its chairman can have but an estimate concerning the effect of an increase in public utility rates upon the gross income of the company.[97] Nor has the board any reliable means of ascertaining whether the rates already charged by the company are probably the maximum that will be paid by the public at that time and place.[98] Moreover a board of arbitration has no secure basis upon which to judge whether an increase of rates will

---

also Herrman, "Can Regulation Make Utility Investment Attractive?," 39 P.U. Fort. 536 (1947) and U. S. Const. Amend. V and XIV: Phelps v. United States, 274 U. S. 341 (1927). See 59 Harv. L. Rev. 1002 (1946) for a discussion of the failure of New Jersey's governmental seizure statute to afford "due process."

[94] Dana, "Report on Labor Policy Committee," Am. Transit Ass'n Proc. 99 (1947); Nurick, "Compulsory Arbitration of Labor Disputes affecting Public Utilities," 54 Dickinson Law Review 127 (1950). A good bibliography follows this article.

[95] McCarthy, The Evils of Labor Arbitration Affecting Public Utilities (1947), originally presented as an address before the New York State Motor Bus Ass'n, Inc.

[96] McCarthy, "Arbitration Doesn't Settle Anything," 43 Mass Trans. 465 (1947).

[97] McCarthy, *op. cit.,* note 57 *supra.*

[98] *Ibid.*

be futile because it will bring into play the law of diminishing returns, if it considers the matter at all.[99]

Hence arbitration proceeds under the pressure of evidence pertaining to a "round" of wage increases that may then be sweeping the country.[100] The board is likely to advance the wage rates to maintain a parity between the workers concerned and workers in private industry. It is almost sure to lack that background of technical information and experience that would be brought to bear upon the situation if it were submitted to a commission to regulate utilities.[101] Having heard and considered the evidence to the best of its abilities and, perhaps, having done its best to rise above its handicap of lack of technical knowledge of important factors in the public utilities field, the board makes its award. It is then free to dissolve and to leave to management the perplexing, if not impossible, task of reconciling a greatly increased cost of operations with a rate schedule that may not be changed until approved by a public utility commission or other regulating body.[102] When, as the almost inevitable next step in the matter, the rate-regulating commission is confronted with the utility's request for a service rate increase, it, according to long established habit and tradition, will likely first address its thought to preservation of the service to the public as against utility corporate welfare.[103] Confronted with the financially impossible situation of the utility company, the commission may or may not authorize some increases. If they are allowed, the law of diminishing returns may promptly operate so that the situation of the utility management will become perilous if not hopeless.

Whether there is a solution for this situation is uncertain. The United States Supreme Court said in the *Hope Natural Gas Com-*

---

99 "Higher fares will only be a palliative. Higher than basic 10 cents threatens to invoke the law of diminishing returns." Schram, "Labor and Its Handling," 43 Mass Trans. 308, 309 (1947).

100 Kansas City Public Service Co., 8 L.A. 149, 157 (1947).

101 Ames, "Should State Commissions Regulate Utility Labor Relations?", 39 P.U. Fort. 352, 355 (1947); Doreau, "Regulatory Licensing to Curb Utility Strikes," summarized in 39 P.U. Fort. 578, 579 (1947).

102 See "Regulation by Crisis — The Pittsburgh Railways Case," 60 Public Utilities Fortnightly 877 (1957). Editorial, "Arbitration Award Puts K. C. in Red," 43 Mass Trans. 480 (1947).

103 Hammer, "Trends in Regulation," 37 P.U. Fort. 289 (1946). See also Report of Committee on Progress in the Regulation of Transportation Agencies to Convention of National Association of Railroad and Utilities Commissioners in Miami Beach, Fla. (1945).

pany case that "Rates which enable the company to operate successfully, to maintain its financial integrity, to attract capital, and to
compensate its investors for the risks assumed certainly cannot be
condemned as invalid, even though they might produce only a
meager return on the so-called 'fair value' rate base." [104]

By implication, this emphasizes the duty of the state public utility commission to give consideration to operating expenses. Such
bodies have, on numerous previous occasions, asserted authority
to consider and to place restrictions upon salaries that they thought
were out of line.[105] While, as a rule, these have been payments to
executives, thought of as being unduly high and perhaps intended
to siphon off net earnings under the name of "salary" rather than
under some more properly applicable name, such as "dividend,"
their examination by the commission furnishes some foundation
for commission consideration of all salaries and wages, insofar as
they may constitute material factors bearing upon the public interest. It is therefore arguable that the entire wage structures of
some public utilities are wholly within the jurisdiction of regulatory bodies under broadly drawn, existing statutes.

Compulsory Arbitration — Within the area of state jurisdiction,
either as it now is under the preemption doctrine and the cession
of "no man's land" authority back to the states, or under an act
similar to that proposed by Senator Holland, it is obvious that the
foregoing proposal suggests some examination of the question
whether, in the effort to maintain uninterrupted public utility
service, compulsory arbitration may be constitutionally imposed
upon a utility employer and a labor organization representing its
employees.[106] Both aspects of this query require some examination.
Moreover, thought should be given to the inquiry whether, even
though compulsory arbitration might be constitutionally imposed
in the situation, it is likely that more satisfactory results might be

---

[104] FPC v. Hope Natural Gas Co., 320 U. S. 591, 605 (1944); for discussion of
the Hope opinion, see Updegraff, "Present Value" the Iowa Rate Base for Public
Utilities, *supra* note 88.

[105] Ross v. Burkhardt Mill & Elec. Power Co. 5 Wis. R.C.R. 139 (1911); Janesville v. Janesville Water Co., 5 Wis. R.C.R. 628 (1911).

[106] See Labor-Management Reporting and Disclosure Act of 1959, Sec. 701 adding subsection (c) to Section 15 of the NLRA Wilson v. New, 243 U. S. 332 (1917);
recognized that Congress had authority to enact the Adamson Act, which imposed
what amounted to compulsory arbitration. But *cf.* Wolff Packing Co. v. Industrial
Court, 262 U. S. 522 (1923).

reached by avoiding strictly compulsory arbitration, except in extreme or emergency situations, and providing a substantial "cooling-off" period during which investigation and conciliation efforts would be given a maximum opportunity to find a solution of issues between such parties.[107]

One long-influential objection to compulsory arbitration in the United States is that it denies freedom of contract. Another is that it may in ultimate effect result in a taking of property without due process.[108] Public utilities, however, are "impressed with a public interest," [109] their properties are in a large degree dedicated to the public service, and hence utility companies are, under long-established legal tradition, subject to regulation in the public interest.[110] They may be required to improve and in some degree to extend service to serve the public convenience.[111] Their service charges are subject to public regulation, though rates so imposed may not be confiscatory,[112] *i.e.,* officially imposed schedules of charges for services should be constructed so as to result in a gross income sufficient to cover operating expenses and a fair return.[113]

As is commonly known, the sovereign powers have many times, under authority to regulate, required expensive improvements of public utility services of many kinds, including construction and extension of physical properties to be used by utilities in discharg-

---

107 For further discussion, see Tobriner and Goldsmith, " 'Cooling-Off' and Mediation Statutes in the States," 20 So. Calif. L. Rev. 264 (1947).

108 See Cahill, "Do We Need Labor Courts?," 31 Marq. L. Rev. 1, 8-15 (1947), for an excellent discussion of how interpretation of freedom of contract under the due process clause of the Fourteenth Amendment (under which constitutional prohibition compulsory arbitration of labor disputes had been denied by the Wolff Packing Co. case, *supra* note 106) has been modified.

109 "A public utility implies a public use of an article, product or service, carrying with it the duty of the producer or manufacturer . . . to serve the public and treat all persons alike, without discrimination." Highland Dairy Farms v. Helvetia Condensing Co., 308 Ill. 294, 300, 139 N.E. 418, 420 (1923).

110 See Munsell, "An Executive's Advice to a Utility Union," 55 Public Utilities Fortnightly 102 (1955); Munn v. Illinois, 94 U. S. 113 (1876); Hall, Concept of Public Business 7 (1940), and Hamilton, "Affectation With a Public Interest," 39 Yale L. J. 1089, 1095 (1930).

111 Consumers Co., Ltd. v. Hatch, 224 U. S. 148 (1912).

112 State v. Fairchild, 224 U. S. 510 (1912); Schiller Piano Co. v. Illinois No. Util. Co., 288 Ill. 580, 123 N.E. 631 (1919).

113 FPC v. Hope Natural Gas Co., 320 U. S. 591 (1944); Waukesha Gas & Elec. Co. v. Wisconsin R. R. Comm'n, 181 Wis. 281, 194 N.W. 846 (1923); State Pub. Util. Comm'n v. Springfield Gas & Elec. Co. 291 Ill. 209, 125 N.E. 891 (1919).

ing the public services that they have undertaken.[114] It has long been established that public utilities may not, generally speaking, withdraw from the public service, in whole or in part, without obtaining permission to do so. This view, that such permission must be officially obtained, has been sustained even where the utility company has established that it has been operating under circumstances in which it was unable to earn a "fair return."[115] In some such instances, there have been involved financial difficulties which arose from contract rates;[116] in others, the unfortunate situation of the utility appears to have been simply the result of adverse economic circumstances.[117]

With these specific matters and the traditionally established character of the public utility in mind, it seems that there is a constitutional warrant for legislative action declaring that the public interest requires public utility services to be continuous and unbroken by work stoppages or lockouts and hence that utility companies and unions are required to arbitrate labor disputes where peaceful settlements are not reached. Certainly, there is little, if any, greater restriction put upon a utility company by officially and authoritatively stating what it shall pay employees than there is in fixing maximum rates it may charge patrons. As above indicated, utility concerns have long been subject to public regulations pertaining to fixing of executives' salaries and many other details concerning costs of operation since these, being deductions from gross income to ascertain "fair return," are essential factors to be considered in fixing rates and ascertaining whether the rates when established will be constitutionally sound or confiscatory.[118] In this connection, commissions have asserted authority in fixing rates even to disregard prices paid for equipment when there is evidence

114 State *ex. rel.* Alton R.R. v. Public Serv. Comm'n, 334 Mo. 1001, 70 S.W. 2d 61 (1934), holding that a state may order improvements necessary for public safety regardless of effect upon the railroad's financial condition.

115 State v. Kansas Postal-Telegraph-Cable Co., 96 Kan. 298, 150 Pac. 544 (1915). But *see* Bullock v. Florida, 254 U. S. 513 (1921), holding that in the absence of statute or contract a utility will be permitted to discontinue operation if there is no reasonable prospect of profitable operation in the future; Transit Comm'n of N.Y. v. United States, 284 U. S. 360 (1932); Updegraff, Regulation of Public Utilities in Iowa 141 (1932).

116 Southern Util. Co. v. Palatka, 268 U. S. 232 (1925); Collier, Franchise Contracts and Utility Regulation, 1 Geo. Wash. L. Rev. 172, 299 (1933).

117 See cases cited in note 115 *supra*.

118 See cases cited in note 105 *supra*.

to support the belief that the transaction was designed to cover up net earnings or unduly to transfer them to a holding company or to an unregulated co-subsidiary supply or equipment company.[119]

It seems apparent that the same considerations that might persuade a court to hold that compulsory arbitration may be constitutionally applied to a utility company might support a conclusion that it would be valid to impose arbitration upon organizations of utility company employees if accompanied by an absolute prohibition against strikes or other economic pressures.[120] It is arguable that while individual workers for public utility companies should and must be at all times free to quit work as individuals and so avoid involuntary servitude, any labor union that purports to speak for such men collectively may also be held subject to certain public duties and responsibilities.[121] It is readily apparent that an organization of public utility employees, through its officers, may be regarded as being fully cognizant of the fact that interruptions of services of a public utility may bring discomfort to many and even public disaster. Hence, it could be concluded that while labor union organizations dealing with nonutility employers have the right to strike, such right of work stoppage is terminable by statute in the utility field because of the public interest involved. The law has many adjustments to make in the balancing of social interests. Under the police power, asserted also in the public interest, the law has many times restricted individual and group

---

[119] Smith v. Illinois Bell Tel. Co., 282 U. S. 133 (1930). See also Columbus Gas & Fuel Co. v. Public Util. Comm'n of Ohio, 292 U. S. 398 (1934); Dayton Power & Light Co. v. Public Util. Comm'n of Ohio, 292 U. S. 290 (1934); Western Distrib. Co. v. Public Serv. Comm'n of Kansas, 285 U. S. 119 (1932).

[120] "Neither the common law, nor the Fourteenth Amendment, confers the absolute right to strike." Dorchy v. Kansas, 272 U. S. 306, 311 (1926). In a dissent to Duplex Co. v. Deering, 254 U. S. 443, 488 (1921), Mr. Justice Brandeis said: "Because I have come to the conclusion that both the common law of a State and a statute of the United States declare the right of industrial combatants to push their struggle to the limits of the justification of self-interest, I do not wish to be understood as attaching any constitutional or moral sanction to that right. All rights are derived from the purposes of the society in which they exist; above all rights rises duty to the community. The conditions developed in industry may be such that those engaged in it cannot continue their struggle without danger to the community."

[121] The argument as applied to management has been that when an owner voluntarily places his property in control of the state, he cannot complain because it becomes subject to the regulatory powers of the state. State v. Florida East Coast Ry., 69 Fla. 480, 68 So. 729 (1915). The argument appears to be equally applicable to labor. See Nash, Impact of Labor Disturbances on Public Utilities, 38 P.U. Fort. 399 (1946).

rights that have been regarded for a time as existing under the general heading of freedom of contract.[122]

There is reason to believe, therefore, that should federal impediments to state statutes be removed and state acts be provided to impose compulsory arbitration upon public utility employers and the unions that bargain collectively with them, such acts should be held constitutional even though similar laws might fail if sought to be applied in nonpublic utility industries. The question should be considered, however, whether it would be expedient to compel arbitration or whether the public would be better served by statutes providing substantial "cooling-off" periods with investigation and mediation steps to precede an election by the parties to arbitrate or to engage in a test of economic strength (strike or lockout) if agreement is not reached by the end of the required waiting period.

Compulsory arbitration seems to be at the present time equally unpalatable to employers[123] and employees.[124] Considerable resistance can be expected to extend to it in the future. Employers can be expected to contend in litigation that wage rates resulting from compulsory arbitration will result in confiscation of their property, a taking without due process.[125] Employees will probably urge with equal insistence that compulsory arbitration will rob them of freedom of contract and result in involuntary servitude.[126] If the em-

---

122 Mr. Justice Holmes, dissenting in Adkins v. Children's Hospital, 261 U. S. 525, 568 (1923) , said: "But in the present instance the only objection that can be urged is found within the vague contours of the Fifth Amendment, prohibiting the depriving of any person of liberty or property without due process of law. To that I turn. The earlier decisions upon the same words in the Fourteenth Amendment began within our memory and went no farther than an unpretentious assertion of the liberty to follow the ordinary callings. Later that innocuous generality was expanded into the dogma, Liberty of Contract. Contract is not specially mentioned in the text that we have to construe. It is merely an example of doing what you want to do, embodied in the word liberty. But pretty much all law consists in forbidding man to do some things they want to do, and contract is no more exempt from law than other acts." The Adkins case was overruled by West Coast Hotel Co. v. Parrish, 300 U. S. 379, 1 LRRM 754 (1937) . As to the especial right to regulate where public good is concerned, see United States v. Associated Press, 326 U. S. 1 (1945) , citing Nebbia v. People of New York, 291 U. S. 502 (1933) .
123 Fitzpatrick, "The Settlement of Contract Negotiation Disputes: A Business Viewpoint," 12 Law and Contemp. Prob. 346 (1947) .
124 Shiskin, "The Settlement of Contract Negotiation Disputes: A Labor Viewpoint," 12 Law & Contemp. Prob. 357 (1947) .
125 Fitzpatrick, note 123 supra.
126 See notes 120, 121, and 124 supra.

ployees, despite such a statute, should strike, they could be subjected to penalties and possible loss of collective bargaining rights because of "unfair labor practices," but these legal retaliatory steps would not insure the practical objective of legislation to prevent the interruption of service.

Local Emergency Powers — Just as the Taft-Hartley Act recognizes and makes special provision for "national emergency" disputes,[127] a state statute, once the federal preemption objection is overcome, might equally recognize the critical need for unbroken utility services in thickly populated areas and make special provision to avoid city, town, or community emergencies that might result from interruption of electricity, gas, water, or another utility service. In this connection, the public utility laws, or state labor statutes, should designate certain businesses to be deemed "public utilities" for all the purposes of the act.[128] The act could further provide that no slowdown, strike, or lockout would be permitted in respect to any such business until after a notice given a substantial period in advance of the intent to bring about the same had been served upon the opposing party, the chairman of the public utilities commission of the state, and perhaps the governor. Further procedure might in some degree parallel that set up in the Taft-Hartley Act, with a conclusion that if the parties have failed to find a solution for the dispute at the end of the first notice or waiting period, extended not to exceed an additional specific period, either party would be free to bring economic pressure upon the other. Provision might be made that at any stage in the dispute the parties may settle their differences by submitting the controversy to the public utility commission for arbitration either by it directly or before arbitrators or referees appointed by it. Possibly also before application of economic pressures, employees should determine by election whether or not to accept the employer's last offer.

In cases where the public interest is extreme or great public hardship or possible disaster may result from interruption of service, the act should provide that operation of the utility might be

---

127 61 Stat. 136 (1947), 29 U.S.C.A. Sections 176-80 (Supp. 1947).
128 Ames, No Strikes for Utilities, 39 P.U. Fort. 687, 689 (1947).

taken over by public authority as expressed by the governor.[129] In such case, the utility would continue in operation and the parties would be offered the opportunity to arbitrate before the state public service commission or its appointees. The commission or arbitrators should consider not only the wage rates or working rules or other matters in dispute between the parties directly but also the financial structure and rate schedule of the employer utility insofar as the same might be affected by, or be likely to be affected by, or concerned in results which might flow from any decision on any phase of the dispute.

This type of state legislation should ultimately prove acceptable to public utility companies, since it insures their receiving consideration of the service rate structure by a commission with authority to modify it in direct connection with the consideration of any wage issue that must necessarily be so related to the service rate structure that a wage determination overnight may make the service rate inadequate or for another reason require its modification. Labor unions' collective bargaining rights and ultimate privilege to impose economic pressures in general would be preserved by such statutes. True, union contentions for increases in compensation might in some instances require consideration in relation to service rate structures. It would seem that this would at times lead to prompt and extensive increases in wage rates in circumstances in which management could feel the same comfortably might be paid. In such cases, of course, labor representatives would suffer no inconvenience. No doubt in other cases, labor unions would feel that their demands for increases had been resisted or curbed because of administrative refusal to adapt the service rate structure to meet higher wages as an augmented operating cost. In such cases, necessarily, the paramount public interest will have been served through prevention of the interruption of service. The broad, public interest will have overweighed the narrower employee group interest just as it has for so many decades overridden the investor group interest.

---

129 The governor is enabled to take this type of action by the present New Jersey and Missouri statutes when other methods have failed. N.J. Rev. Stat., tit. 34, c. 13B (Supp. 1945-46) ; Mo. Rev. Stat. Ann. Sec. 10178.119 (Supp. 1947). See Tuck, "How a Governor Stopped a Threatened Utility Strike," 38 P.U. Fort. 267 (1946).

In this connection, the general comment is ventured that consideration of expenses of utility companies should be undertaken with a view toward attaining justice for three groups of parties, *employees, patrons, and investors.*[130] That which is just cannot be overly generous to one group and grossly unfair to any other. The true course of justice would require a search for a course that may offer relative fairness to all in the light of all surrounding circumstances. This may result in some disappointment to all from time to time. The probabilities of a generally satisfactory result, however, would appear to be practically much greater when the interests of all three vitally interested groups are before the same tribunal than when conflicting interests are separately considered.

To refer again to the words quoted above from the *Hope Natural Gas Company* case,[131] it would seem to be futile to talk about fixing a service rate that will "attract capital" unless in attempting to fix such a rate the utility commission shall have authority in respect to every expense factor that could prevent the realization of any net income applicable to compensate for the use of capital. To be sure, this proposal will involve some overlapping of authorities, or at least some cooperation between the public utility commissions and the state labor commissions (or labor relations boards), but it cannot reasonably be expected that public utilities can operate on a sound financial basis, whether publicly or privately owned, unless such authoritative action is possible.[132]

As above stated, some state statutes seem to contemplate that public authorities will take over and operate any public utility that gets into a labor dispute that threatens to result in an interruption of the public service.[133] After a utility company has been taken over for temporary public operation under such statutes, such operation continues until representatives of management and labor have worked their way into some kind of contract. Another type of statute merely provides for continuous operation and

---

130 Loomis, "Rights, Responsibilities and Relationships of Labor, Capital and Management," 14 I.C.C. Pract. J. 921 (1947); Whiting, Investor, Indispensable Man, 41 P.U. Fort. 267 (1948).
131 FPC v. Hope Natural Gas Co., 320 U. S. 591 (1944).
132 Ames, note 101 *supra.*
133 See note 129 *supra.*

compulsory arbitration.[134] These plans appear to be only a rather restrained gesture toward discharging the entire legislative duty to the public. They meet only a minor part of the issue actually presented. Most of these state laws are of doubtful validity at present and will so remain until Congress clears the preemption ruling from their clear legality and enforceability. Whether the essential regular operation of any public service is jeopardized by a threat of capital to close down and lockout or a labor demand coupled with a strike threat, some board with competent authority should have power to work out all aspects of the entire problem as presented, including the adjustment of service rates, almost invariably needed to provide for any substantial increase added to operating costs by wage increases or changes in "working conditions." Forward-looking legislation should not require that management and labor reach an impasse before government aid may be invoked. In other words, it seems that public utility commissions should become *wage regulating* commissions for the public utilities as well as *rate regulating* bodies, or as above intimated, the actual labor arbitration should be delegated by proper legislation to especially created labor arbitration or mediation boards after the pattern of the Federal Railway Labor Act.

As above noted, the Federal Government has preempted virtually the entire field of regulating labor relations. Congress has moved to eliminate the no man's land left by the *Guss Case*, but it should not leave the fashioning of laws to the courts as indicated in the *Lincoln Mills* case. The courts' law-making is too slow, piecemeal, and uncertain for modern society. The legislative method of confronting the problem, studying fully and designing a suitable remedy, is much the better. It is highly desirable that Congress soon take some further remedial steps in relation to public utility labor problems.

---

134 These have been of two types: the labor court type with the court having power to order changes in working conditions, wages, etc., which was abandoned in Kansas after the decision in the Wolff Packing Co. case, 262 U. S. 522 (1923), and the mediation board type utilized in the Railway Labor Act, 44 Stat. 577 (1926), 45 U.S.C. Section 151 *et seq.* (1940).

Chapter VI

THE LEGAL RULES OF EVIDENCE – THEIR FUNCTION IN RELATION TO ARBITRATION

SECTION 1

The Legal Rules of Evidence — Their Nature and Purpose

"Evidence" refers to the means by which any disputed matter of fact may be established or disproved. In a broad sense, legal rules of evidence are all rules of exclusion. In other words, all relevant and probative information offered to a court or other tribunal will be received unless some specific rule or principal of evidence requires that it be excluded. Obviously, no evidential rules of exclusion would be likely to develop and to survive through the decades and centuries unless founded upon good reason. It may be assumed, therefore, that information that is relevant, competent, material, and has such probative value that it may be deemed to be reasonably reliable, would not be excluded by any court, nor denied to a jury by a court.[1]

In brief, the evidential rules of exclusion under which courts refuse admission to certain papers, types of statements, and to certain words of would-be witnesses day after day, are applied because such excluded materials are deemed to be of no value or perhaps to be downright misleading. Such rules have an inherent validity that requires everyone undertaking to act as a trier of fact to study them, to respect them, and, if able to do so, to apply them as bearing upon credibility if not admissibility.

In general, arbitrators receive virtually any and all kinds of supposed information offered to them by all parties coming before

---

[1] For a valuable discussion of rules of evidence and the labor arbitrational process, see Chapters IV to XII in Problems of Proof in Arbitration, Proceedings of the Nineteenth Annual Meeeting, National Academy of Arbitrators (Washington: BNA Books, Incorporated, 1967) ; Amalgamated Asso. of S.E.R. v. Connecticut Co., 142 Conn. 186, 112 A. 2d 501, 24 LA 107 (1955) ; American Almond Products Co. v. Consol. Pecan Sales Co., 144 F. 2d 448 (C.C.A. 2d, 1944) .

them. Innumerable writings and oral statements daily offered to arbitrators would not be admissible as evidence in a court of law. Having received such materials, however, the arbitrator should ponder them and consider them while alert to the fact that they are wanting in some qualities and characteristics that would make them admissible in a court. Again, it sometimes happens that a person offered as a "witness" to an arbitrational hearing has no first-hand information at all and would not be allowed in court to present one word of the "evidence" he is permitted to put in by the arbitrator. It will be a dubious arbitrator, indeed, who will be unaware of the type witness he has heard and who will ascribe undeserved weight to such so-called "testimony."

From time to time, the parties during arbitration will stipulate facts or submit a question for arbitral decision on briefs only. The arbitrator in such cases is expected to study the briefs, and in cases of apparent inconsistencies of the information supplied, to consider all statements in their entirety, the agreement between the parties, their relationship, the character of the industry, and all other surrounding factors and to decide the facts, the law, and the interpretation of the contract on the basis of the limited materials so supplied. When the parties have agreed to this type of proceeding in advance, neither is in a position thereafter to challenge the course of decision and the conclusion of the arbitrator that in such a case must perforce be rested upon the limited materials with which he was supplied.

In some labor arbitrations, the principal spokesmen of the parties apparently do not deem it necessary nor desirable to bring to the arbitrational hearing the witnesses who can and would, if present, give to the arbitrator first-hand testimony as to matters in dispute. Labor arbitrators are familiar with the situation in which a personnel manager and other supervisory officers will recite what they deem to be the facts as they have previously been given them by a foreman or by some other representative of management who was on the job at the time when the question arose. Management may not care to call the true witness into the hearing because he is working on a different shift and is home asleep or there may be some other reason why his words are submitted second-hand to the arbitrator. It also frequently happens that a

labor union will bring to the hearing only a bargaining committee and the department steward as witnesses and will not produce at the hearing the party to the actual grievances who may
well be the only one in the union who has first-hand knowledge
and who would be competent to testify if the matter were in
court. When the parties are satisfied to proceed on the basis of
such information and when no formal objection or challenge is
stated in the record, it seems incumbent upon the arbitrator, as
a rule, to proceed as the parties apparently mutually desire. However, if either of the principal spokesmen raises the objection
that there is no evidence of competent nature before the arbitrator
and all that is offered is hearsay, the arbitrator should be cautious
indeed about proceeding further and probably would be wise to
urge the parties to bring in first-hand testimony.[2] The arbitrator
should be aware that the rule against hearsay testimony rests on
the right of a party to be confronted with adverse witnesses and
have the privilege of cross-examining them. But he should be
aware that the hearsay rule has numerous exceptions. Some of
these are briefly described in section seven and following in this
chapter. The arbitrator should consider all hearsay evidence with
these in mind.

Courts have commonly held that an award to be valid and binding on the parties must rest upon legally sound evidence unless
the parties have indicated otherwise.[3] This does not mean that a
reviewing court will require that it be satisfied that the conclusion reached by the arbitrator was supported by a preponderance
of the evidence, but it is likely to require a showing that there
was some relevant, competent, and material legal evidence tend-

---

[2] An excellent treatise on Evidence is that of Wigmore. For a brief or "reminder"
use, Wigmore's Code of Evidence, is recommended. Published by Little, Brown &
Company, Boston.

See Section 7 *infra*, this chapter, and see Bernhardt v. Polygraphic Co., 350 U. S.
198, 76 S.Ct. 273, 25 LA 693 (1956) .

[3] See 5 Am. Jur. 2d "Arbitration and Award," §§ 122 (1962) and following. Here
the text is, "In the absence of an agreement to the contrary, the requirement that
the arbitrators must meet and hear the parties implies that relevant evidence if
offered, shall be received and considered." . . . "But if the evidence is clearly necessary to a party's case opportunity should be afforded to obtain and produce it,
however distant the scene of the transaction may be."

See Frantz v. Inter-Insurance Exchange, 229 Cal. App. 2d 269, 40 Cal. Reptr 218
(1964) and other cases cited in Am. Jur.

ing to support the finding of facts ultimately relied on by the arbitrator.[4]

All of the foregoing appears to make it essential that even though the rules of evidence, as they are known and commonly applied in the courts as rules of exclusion are not recommended for wide adoption for use in the same way in arbitration hearings, a brief treatment of them should be included in this book. It is intended and hoped that arbitrators making use of this work will read the following brief treatment of the legal rules of evidence and by such review be advised of the weight that should, and should not, be given to the "evidence" and other materials tendered at hearings. A comprehensive treatise on the law of evidence may extend into a considerable number of volumes. All that is attempted here is a brief summary.

SECTION 2

Burden of Proof — Weight and Sufficiency of Evidence

The phrase "burden of proof" concerns the relative duties of parties in respect to the initial production of evidence. Primarily it refers to the duty of presenting proof that is logically cast upon any party to establish the basic facts it asserts as a basis of claiming relief. It often is said that this duty requires proof by "a preponderance of the evidence."[5] In criminal cases the prosecution is required to prove the guilt of the accused by proof that establishes guilt "beyond a reasonable doubt."[6] The party having the burden of proof is ordinarily given the right to open and close. This right, however, may be waived.

Sometimes the term "burden of proof" is used to denote the obligation of a party to meet with evidence a *prima facie* case that has been made against it.[7] In this sense, the "burden of

---

4 See Section 2 *infra*, this chapter.

5 See "Burden of Proof in Labor Arbitration," 3 Duke Bar Journal 127 (1953); Gorske, "Burden of Proof in Grievance Arbitration," 43 Marquette Law Review 135 (1959); McCloskey v. Kopler, 329 Mo. 527, 46 S.W. 2d 557, 92 A.L.R. 641 (1932); Celotex Corp. 24 LA 369 (1955).

6 E.g., Cartlon v. People, 150 Ill. 181, 37 N.E. 244 (1894); State v. Lapointe, 81 N.H. 227, 123 A. 692, 31 A.L.R. 1212 (1924); Marlin Rockwell Company, 24 LA 728 (1955).

7 Commonwealth v. Palmer, 222 Pa. 299, 71 A. 100, 19 L.R.A. (N.S.) 483, 128 Am. St. Rep. 809 (1908).

proof" may appear to shift during a hearing from one side to the other.[8]

To illustrate the uses of the two concepts designated by the words "burden of proof," suppose the employer, "E," has discharged grievance-claimant, "G," for deliberate destruction of materials while working on a forming press. Assume that the contract between the employer and the union provides that no man will be "unjustly" discharged. It commonly is ruled that the "burden of proof" after the foregoing issues are set will rest upon the employer to establish that the discharge was not unjust because (1) "G" was guilty, and (2) that for the type of guilt involved, discharge was not so unduly severe a penalty as to be unjust. Throughout the hearing the "burden of proof" to establish guilt in such a sense, and the justice of the company action, will remain upon the company. However, if after the company has made a *prima facie* case, that is, such a case as will justify decision in favor of its contentions unless the same is controverted, "G" and the union supporting him, take the position that he was guilty of no sabotage of materials. They contend that the metal sheets furnished for stamping by the company at the time of his, "G's," wrongdoings were brittle and not of the type or standard metal on which the job was originally designed. Hence, they assert the loss and breakage of materials was not the fault of "G" but rather that of the party responsible for the change of the material in the sheets offered for stamping. The burden of establishing this contention, in the sense that the burden of proof shifts from one side to the other will be upon "G" and the union. If strong evidence supporting this contention is offered, then the burden of going forward with proof would appear to be again upon the company to prove, if possible, that the materials furnished during the period in dispute were actually within proper standards. Such evidence would put the burden of further proof back upon "G."

It is the common practice of labor arbitrators to receive virtually all types of oral statements, written testimony, and other

---

8 Southern Bell Tel. Co., 25 LA 85 (1955); First Nat. Bank v. Ford, 30 Wyo. 110, 216 Pac., 691, 31 A.L.R. 1441 (1923). Technically speaking, the burden of proof does not shift — it is the "risk of non-persuasion" or burden of going forward with evidence to rebut the prima facie case that shifts. See Kohlsaat v. Parkersburg and Marine Sand Co., 266 Fed. 283, 11 A.L.R. 686 (1920); Smith v. Hill, 260 U. S. 592, 67 L.Ed. 419, 43 S.Ct. 219 (1923).

evidence offered. However, when a definite challenge is made in court as to the validity of an award on the ground that the conclusions of fact upon which it rests were supported by no evidence and amounted merely to unsupported arbitrary assumptions showing bias or misconduct of the arbitrator, the amount and character of the evidence comes under the review and scrutiny of a court.[9] Generally speaking, in such proceedings the courts require that the conclusions of fact by the arbitrator be supported by some legal evidence, or, at least, by some stipulation of the parties or by some type of showing that the parties waived legal evidence and mutually agreed to proceed to final award upon the basis of hearsay or other statements not amounting to legal evidence.[10] It is important to remember then that when legal evidence is critically required, the so-called "evidence" that is often received in arbitration hearings is technically insufficient and therefore is, as far as the operation of law is concerned, no evidence at all.[11]

In line with the foregoing, it becomes important for parties preparing to present testimony in arbitration hearings to use the best evidence of a transaction available. That is to say, if documentary evidence is available, it should be presented.[12] If firsthand, eye-witness testimony is available, it should be offered.[13] Many employers prefer not to call union members to testify on

---

[9] This is important when one party claims, in court, that the arbitrator misconstrued the submission agreement and excluded evidence that should have been admitted. Halstead v. Seaman, 82 N.Y. 27, 37 Am. Rep. 536 (1880); Hartford Fire Ins. Co. v. Bonner Mercantile Co., 44 Fed. 151 (1890), mod. in 56 Fed. 378 (1893).

[10] In some arbitrations, questions to be decided are submitted without a hearing and "on briefs." It can hardly be disputed in such cases that both parties have waived their rights to have the questions decided on the basis of true legal evidence. See Puget Sound Bridge Etc. Co. v. Lake Wash. Shipyards, 1 Wash. 2d 401, 96 P. 2d 257 (1939).

[11] Fitzgerald v. Southern R. Co., 141 N.C. 530, 54 S.E. 391, 6 L.R.A. (N.S.) 337 (1906). An award will not be set aside unless there has been fraud, misconduct, an error as to authority, or the arbitrator has acted under the influence of mistake or bias. A purported conclusion of fact wholly unsupported by legal evidence where such evidence was or should have been required or followed would normally be proof of bias or misconduct of the arbitrator. See Note 9 *supra;* Laidlaw v. Sage, 158, N.Y. 73, 52 N.E. 679 (1899); Roberts v. Consumers' Can Co., 102 Md. 362, 62 A. 585 (1905), and, 11 L.R.A. 626; People v. Galbo, 218 N.Y. 283, 112 N.E. 1041 (1916); Beckemeier v. Baessler, (Mo. Ct. of Appeals), 270 S.W. 2d 782 (1954).

[12] T. H. Symmington Co. v. National Malleable Steel Castings Co., 250 U. S. 383, 63 L.Ed. 1045 (1919); Probst v. Board of Domestic Missions, 129 U. S. 182 (1888); Estey Organ Co. v. Lehman, 132 Wis. 144, 111 N.W. 1097 (1907).

[13] Hetzel v. Baltimore & O. Ry. Co., 169 U. S. 26 (1897); Continental Casualty Co. v. Paul, 209 Ala. 166, 95 So. 814 (1923); Eibel Process Co. v. Minnesota and O. Paper Co., 261 U. S. 45, 67 L.Ed. 523 (1923).

behalf of the company's contentions. They explain this by saying it may get the man "in bad" with his fellow union members. Moreover, they indicate, the party may refuse to testify or may evade or falsify as to the facts in dispute. Labor unions sometimes avoid calling foremen or others from management for the same reason. Both of these positions are commendable, but it must not be overlooked that there are extreme instances in which the witness from the opposing side should be called on to give evidence and even possibly cross-examined as a hostile witness. At times arbitrators are called on to advise such witnesses that it is their duty to testify and to do so truthfully. In some jurisdictions where statutes authorize arbitrators to subpoena witnesses and to require them to take oaths to testify truthfully, this method of conducting a case may be decisive.[14]

Labor dispute arbitrators are often confronted with situations in which both parties, "to avoid interruption of production," attempt to prove their opposing contentions by use of "witnesses" who have only hearsay information on the dispute while persons with first-hand information are at work in an adjoining building. If there is a clear understanding between the parties that they want the arbitrator to proceed only upon secondary and limited information so offered at the hearing and that each side waives the nonpresence of witnesses with first-hand knowledge, the arbitrator may be safe in proceeding accordingly.[15] He will be wise, however, to advise the parties that the proceedings would be much more satisfactory and proper if the witnesses with first-hand knowledge were brought in and their own words offered directly into the record. Of course, no award safely may rest upon testimony which is obviously untrue, or incredible.[16] In a recent instance one party to an arbitration urged that the other had agreed to a contract so completely destructive of all its legitimate interests that such conduct, if true, must have been called mistaken or corrupt. Another interpretation was available and more logical. Had the arbitrator rested his award upon the first contention, it surely must have been set aside by any reviewing court.

---

14 See Chap. II, Sec. 3 and Chap. VI, Sec. 2.

15 Notes 10 and 11 *supra.*

16 See note 9 *supra,* and Miller v. Service & Sales Co., 149 Ore. 11, 38 P. 2d 995 (1934) ; Com. L. Ins. Co. v. Pendleton, 231 Ky. 591, 21 S.W. 2d 985 (1929) ; Cluck v. Abe, 328 Mo. 81, 40 S.W. 2d 558 (1931) ; People v. Galbo, 218 N.Y. 283, 112 N.E. 1041 (1916) .

One point that may be emphasized here is that the number of witnesses called does not necessarily establish the truth of a party's contentions.[17] When a considerable number of witnesses are testifying repetitively, it is within the discretion of the arbitrator or the power of the court to limit the number to be heard.[18] Ordinarily it is within the authority of the trier of facts, if he so desires, to believe the lesser number of witnesses and disbelieve the greater number, provided the testimony upon which he relies is legally sound and persuasive.[19]

Expert opinion testimony may be believed or disbelieved by the arbitrator just as is the case with ordinary testimony. This is true even though the expert testimony has not been contradicted by other expert testimony of equivalent nature. But the trier of fact should disregard this expert testimony only in the light of the possible bias of the witness, the process of reasoning with which he has testified, his ability and character, etc.[20]

The term "preponderance of the evidence" is synonymous with "greater weight of evidence." [21] It may be said to mean the more valuable and persuasive force of the aggregate evidence on both sides. Sometimes the preponderance of evidence has been said to be the more credible or probable evidence. To create a preponderance of evidence the testimony offered must be adequate to overcome opposing presumptions and evidence.[22] It is, therefore, necessary in a closely controverted case for the arbitrator to be aware of all presumptions that may be relied upon by one of the parties and to weigh carefully the evidence on both sides as he proceeds to his conclusion. Where there is a direct conflict of evidence, however, and it seems to be very evenly balanced, the arbitrator must make his choice. In doing so, he will do well to explain at

---

17 Pawnee Farmers' Elevator & Supply Co. v. Powell, 76 Colo. 1, 227 P. 836 (1924) . See Ann. Cases 1913 D, 676.

18 Garver v. Garver, 52 Colo. 227, 121 P. 165 (1912) . See Amer. Jur. title "Trial."

19 Note 17 *supra.*

20 Dayton Power & Lt. Co. v. Public Utilities Comm. 292 U. S. 290 (1934) ; People v. Harvey, 286 Ill. 593, 122 N.E. 138 (1919) ; Bratt v. Western Airlines, 155 F. 2d 850, *cert. den.* 329 U. S. 735 (1946) .

21 Cincinnati Butchers' Supply Co. v. Conoly, 204 N.C. 677, 169 S.E. 415 (1933) ; Lampe v. Franklin American Trust Co., 339 Mo. 361, 96 S.W. 2d 710 (1936) .

22 Howland v. Blake, 97 U. S. 624 (1878) ; First Nat. Bank v. Ford, 30 Wyo. 110, 216 P. 691 (1923) .

Proof consistent with both opposing contentions supports neither. Blackhawk Hotels Co. v. Bonfoey, 227 F. 2d 232 (1955) .

least briefly in his opinion the reason why he has found the ultimate facts to be in favor of the successful party.

Much interest has been generated recently with regard to the admissibility into arbitration hearings of the results of lie detector polygraph tests. Such results have overwhelmingly been adjudged to be inadmissible by arbitrators on the ground that such tests are unreliable and inaccurate.

Similarly, an employee's refusal to take a lie detector test is not insubordination such as to warrant a discharge. This is true, stated one arbitrator, because since lie detector results would be inadmissible in evidence anyway, an employee cannot be required to perform "what is essentially a useless action." [23]

One author has concluded that the scientific unreliability of the polygraph stems from three problems: The value of the findings depends wholly on the experience, qualifications, or inexperience of the operator of the machine; the emotional state of a sensitive person may render the tests useless; the machine itself is not free from error.[24]

SECTION 3

Presumptions

In the hearing of many disputed matters, a party may be aided in establishing his contentions by the operation of a presumption.[25] He is given the assistance of the probative value that is attached to certain specific, undisputed, or established facts. For example, it is always presumed that a statute is constitutional and that those who signed a contract knew its terms.[26] The phrase "presumption of law" is sometimes used to describe or refer to

---

[23] Lag Drug Co., 39 LA 1121 (Dec. 20, 1962), 63-1 Arb. ¶ 8106. Also 1965 Proceedings of ABA Section on Labor Relations Law, p. 292 et seq.

[24] Lee M. Burkey, "Lie Detectors in Labor Relations," in The Arbitration Journal, Vol. 19, No. 4 (1964). The author also predicts that the emphasis of inadmissibility of polygraph results on grounds of scientific unreliability will shift to inadmissibility on grounds of violation of civil rghts, i.e., the employee's right to privacy and his right against self-incrimination. See also p. 204, Problems of Proof in Arbitration, Proceedings of the Nineteenth Annual Meeting, National Academy of Arbitrators (Washington: BNA Books, 1967), op. cit. in note 1 supra.

[25] Hinds v. Dept. of Labor and Industries, 150 Wash. 230, 272 P. 734 (1928); Conklin v. Silver, 187 Iowa 819, 174 N.W. 573 (1919).

[26] Vol. 11 Amer. Jurisprudence, title "Constitutional Law," S 128-133. As to contracts see, Butler Candy Co. v. Springfield F. & M. Ins. Co., 296 Pa. 552, 146 A. 135 (1929); Bixler v. Wright, 116 Me. 133, 100 A. 467 (1917).

an actual rule of law or an established legal fiction.[27] A presumption of fact, however, is one that involves an inference made from certain other facts that when disputed may be rebutted by other evidence.[28]

An arbitrator sometimes is confronted with a ruling of a state official on some matter of workmen's compensation, unemployment compensation, or other law applying to the rights of parties involved in arbitration. In the same way, he will occasionally encounter rulings from the National Labor Relations Board, the Wage and Hour Division, or other officials having to do with various federal labor statutes. When the evidence of such action is clear, the proper course for the arbitrator is to presume that the public officer has properly performed the duties of his office and to act upon that assumption unless clear evidence to the contrary is received to displace the presumption.[29]

SECTION 4
Judicial Notice

While generally speaking parties making contentions at hearings are required to present full proof of the same, many facts may be "judicially noticed" by the court, jury, or other trier of the issue and need not be proved.[30] Where judicial notice is properly taken, it may be said to take the place of proof. In general, matters of which judicial notice are taken are matters of such common knowledge or matters of such notoriety and public concern that they are known generally by all well-informed persons. Judicial notice will always be taken of the laws of the federal government and those of the state in which the hearing is held. Laws of other states, however, must be proved as matters of fact.[31]

27 State v. Wells, 35 Utah 400, 100 P. 681 (1909).
28 Ausmus v. People, 47 Colo. 167, 107 P. 204 (1910); Simpson v. Simpson, 162 Va. 621, 175 S.E. 320 (1934). Certiorari denied 295 U. S. 735.
29 U. S. v. Chemical Foundation, 272 U. S. 1 (1926); Hamilton v. Erie R. Co., 219 N.Y. 343, 114 N.E. 399 (1916).
30 Wilson v. Shaw, 204 U. S. 24 (1907); Ricaud v. American Metal Co., 246 U. S. 304 (1918). It is clear that the arbitrator may draw on his personal knowledge in reaching his conclusions and award. Springs Cotton Mills v. Buster Boy Suit Co., 88 N.Y.S. 2d. 295, 300 N.Y. 586, 89 N.E. 2d 877 (1949).
31 Mills v. Greene, 159 U. S. 651 (1895); Dillon v. Gloss, 256 U. S. 368 (1921); Lloyd v. Matthews, 155 U. S. 222 (1894); Summer v. Mitchell, 29 Fla. 179, 10 So. 562 (1892); People ex rel. Stephens v. Fidelity & G. Co., 153 Ill. 25, 38 N.E. 752 (1894).

Where judicial notice is properly taken, it serves convenience, time, trouble, and expense in establishing well-known facts. A few examples of subjects of judicial notice are: the sequence of the months; the order of days of the week; legal holidays; and legislative, historical, geographical, economic, and social factors that are not open to dispute and are subjects of common knowledge.[32] Many other matters of common knowledge are topics of which courts will take judicial notice.

Arbitrators in practice take judicial notice in much the same way as do the judges of courts. In addition arbitrators have and apply substantial expert knowledge of labor law, labor law history, labor economics, and union and employer practices. Judges and arbitrators may refresh their information as to matters within judicial notice by using commonly distributed books and information such as encyclopedias, dictionaries, and the like. In doing so, however, they are permitted only to refresh their information in the areas of common knowledge.[33] Specialized encyclopedic information not in "common knowledge," though printed in a widely distributed work, should not be sought by judge or arbitrator and relied on as within the area of judicial notice.

SECTION 5
Best-Evidence Rule

The best-evidence rule requires that the best evidence that it is possible to produce be presented as proof of disputed facts.[34] Secondary evidence is receivable only when the primary evidence is unavailable because it has been lost or destroyed, is beyond the jurisdiction of the tribunal, or is in the hands of the opponent.[35] This rule is applicable where the evidence offered is clearly a substitution or is testimony upon a point on which better evidence for some reason has been withheld. Of course, if one of the parties

---

[32] Jacobson v. Massachusetts, 197 U. S. 11 (1905); Varcoe v. Lee, 180 Cal. 338, 181 P. 223 (1919); see annotation 89 Am. Dec. 663.

[33] Werk v. Parker, 249 U. S. 130 (1919); Bowser v. State, 136 Md. 342, 110 A. 854 (1920).

[34] Chesapeake & Potomac Tel. Co., 21 LA 367 (1953); Slater v. Mexican Nat. R. Co., 194 U. S. 120 (1904); State v. Rockich, 66 Wash. 390, 119 P. 843 (1911); see annotation 11 Eng. Ruling Cases 505.

[35] People v. Dennis, 4 Mich. 609 (1857); Higgins v. Reed, 8 Iowa 298 (1859); Goodrich v. Weston, 102 Mass. 362 (1869).

wishes to jeopardize its chance for success by offering uncertain evidence rather than the best available, it normally is permitted to do so with possibly an admonition from the arbitrator or judge to call attention to what it is doing.[36] Suppose, for example, in a situation where it is contended that a certain man was absent without excuse on a given date, the company persists in using as its witness only a foreman who states that he did not see the employee at work on that date. It refuses to produce its payroll records, production records, and other evidence that might speak more positively and certainly as to the attendance in dispute. Some inference could be drawn as to why this usually better, regular, written record was withheld. In such an instance, the employer would be entitled to explain its use of what appears to be more dubious evidence by offering testimony that the time card, payroll, and production records had been falsified. In the absence of such a showing, the use of the secondary evidence would properly raise doubts as to credibility.[37]

Usually the best evidence of anything recorded in writing is the writing itself.[38] Other evidence is secondary, and offer of the same instead of the best evidence ought to be explained. Check stubs have at times been held inadmissible because the best evidence of payment would be the cancelled vouchers or checks themselves.[39] On the other hand, if the stubs are offered in a disputed payroll matter, they would be normally admissible as "original entries kept in the usual course of business."[40]

Enacted laws of other states should be proven by a duly authenticated copy.[41] If court decisions of other states are involved, the official reports of the same or expert witnesses qualified to testify in relation to them should be offered.[42] Copies of original writings

---

[36] See Thomson-Houston Elect. Co. v. Palmer, 52 Minn. 174, 53 N.W. 1137 (1893) ; see annotation L.R.A. 1917 D, pp. 542 et seq.

[37] American Tel. & Tel. Co., 6 LA 31 (1946) ; Probst v. Presbyterian Church, 129 U. S. 182 (1889) ; Estey Organ Co. v. Lehman, 132 Wis. 144, 111 N.W. 1097 (1907).

[38] Tayloe v. Riggs, 1 Pet. (U. S.) 591 (1828) ; Herman and Ben Marks v. Hass, 166 Iowa 340, 147 N.W. 740 (1913).

[39] Nall v. Brennan, 324 Mo. 565, 23 S.W. 2d 1053 (1929) ; Simons v. Hoagland, 205 N.Y. 171, 98 N.E. 395 (1912).

[40] See annotation at 68 A.L.R. 695 Laning's Estate, 241 Pa. 98, 88 A. 289 (1913).

[41] Nashua Sav. Bank v. Anglo-Amer. Agency, 189 U.S. 221 (1903) ; also annotations 25 L.R.A. 449 and 113 Am. St. Rep. 868.

[42] Pierce v. Idseth, 106 U.S. 546 (1882) ; Newsom v. Adams, 2 La. 153 (1831).

are secondary evidence and arbitrators should require the production of the originals or have the nonproduction satisfactorily explained.[43] However, it is not uncommon practice for the arbitrator to observe the original and, having compared it with a copy, to retain the copy for evidential and review use, returning the original to its normal place in the party's records.

SECTION 6

Relevancy, Materiality, and Competency

The tender of any statement or testimony at any hearing should be based upon the belief that the evidence bears upon the issue in dispute and will tend to prove or disprove something in relation to it.[44] If statements or materials are offered that do not have these characteristics, they have no logical place in the hearing at all. Hence, it is obvious that even the broad-minded arbitrator, who is tolerant enough to receive even related statements in the nature of hearsay and otherwise, may at times call a halt and check with the parties whether "testimony" being offered him has any relevance or probative value in relation to the issues in the arbitration. If it has not, the taking of such information should be terminated on the simple and logical ground that it is sheer waste of time of all parties at the hearing,[45] and, in addition, may cause them unnecessary expense.

Moreover, if parties may introduce evidence of facts not logically connected with the matter in dispute, the point in issue may be totally submerged in a flood of irrelevancies. Although an orderly presentation of the matter in dispute may be altered to provide a forum for "letting off steam," the arbitrator should be careful not to use such evidence as a foundation for his decision on the point in issue.

Each fragment of testimony should be relevant. Sometimes a party will begin offering testimony that at first blush appears to have no relationship to the issue in dispute. In such case, the

---

43 Note 36 *supra*.

44 Bird v. United States, 180 U.S. 356 (1901); Whiteman v. State, 119 Ohio St. 285, 164 N.E. 51 (1928).

45 United States v. Corwin, 129 U.S. 381 (1889); People v. C.M. & St. P.R. Co., 306 Ill. 486, 138 N.E. 155 (1923).

arbitrator may find it expedient to inquire directly of the party entering the evidence as to just why he feels the evidence should be considered. The arbitrator, however, should always be slow to exclude testimony that any party confidently asserts will ultimately affect the issue when all of his testimony is in the record. If, at the close of the hearing, the arbitrator has refused to receive evidence that a reviewing court finds to be relevant and material and has awarded adversely to the party proffering it, it is likely that the court would set the award aside.[46]

In general, where the issue of relevancy or materiality is "doubtful" in the arbitrator's mind, the evidence should be admitted for the purpose stated by the party.

For example, it is common practice for an arbitrator to consider an employee's past conduct or his prior work record, and such evidence is considered relevant and admissible since it serves to aid the arbitrator in reaching a decision on the merits of the matter in dispute at the hearing.[47]

"Past practice" relates to a much-repeated course of conduct regularly engaged in over a very substantial period of time by parties who can reasonably be presumed to be aware of such conduct. This may refer to innumerable courses of action by either the union or the employer or both. Hence, proof of a pattern of conduct that has existed over an extended period should be admitted. A few casual incidents do not establish a true "past practice." Proper proof of long-standing repetition with full knowledge on both sides justifies a conclusion that the practice should not be changed without mutual agreement, unless it is of such nature that in the normal course of industrial relations it is regarded as a matter that lies entirely within the rights and discretion of one party. Proof in this area is important since a clearly established "past practice" should be sustained just as if it were written in the contract.[48]

---

46 Halstead v. Seaman, 82 N.Y. 27 (1880); Hartford F. Ins. Co. v. Bonner Mercantile Co., 44 Fed. 151; modified in 56 Fed. 378 (1893); see annotation 11 L.R.A. 626; 8 Ann. Cas. 510.

See Sec. 2, this chapter and cases there cited.

47 Int'l. Brotherhood of Pulp, Sulphite, and Paper Mill Workers, Local 874 v. St. Regis Paper Co., 362 F. 2d 711 (5th Cir., 1966).

48 See Chap. IX, Sec. 4, infra.

SECTION 7

The Hearsay Rule

Hearsay evidence usually is not admissible in a court hearing. The basis for its exclusion is that normally it is not subject to the tests that can be applied to ascertain the truth of firsthand testimony.[49] For one thing, the witness may safely make an oath that some absent third person stated a certain thing to be a fact.[50] Thus the witness is not confronted with the responsibility of asserting the truth of the testimony which he gives to prove the disputed fact. Moreover, the witness who would state only hearsay, while himself subject to cross-examination, cannot respond to searching questions bearing upon the ultimate truth of the matters that he states were affirmed to him.[51] Again, even in a civil case a party is entitled to be confronted by the witnesses who testify against his interests. This rule requiring or permitting confrontation is violated by the receipt of secondhand or hearsay testimony. It is the general rule that when hearsay testimony is admitted without timely objection, however, the objection is waived and the court, jury, arbitrator, or other trier of facts will be permitted to proceed, in part at least, on the basis of the same.

In arbitrational hearings, hearsay testimony is very freely received. Indeed, in many instances the record seems to consist of little else. Much of this stems from the reluctance of employers to bring more than the minimum of employees from their duties to the hearing and from the efforts of union officers and spokesmen to proceed without the evidence of men and women who would prefer to be earning their usual income in the usual way and who may dislike participating in a controversy. However, there is a widespread feeling that the employer should not call union members to testify against union contentions and that the union should avoid use of management people as witnesses. As a result, many efforts are made to prove contentions by secondary

[49] See Bower Roller Bearing Co., 22 LA 320 (1954) and Maguire, "Evidence, Common Lease and Common Law," p. 11 et seq., The Foundation Press, Brooklyn. Llewellyn v. Electric Reduction Co., 275 U.S. 243 (1927); Donnelly v. United States, 228 U.S. 243 (1913). Potter v. Baker, 162 Ohio St. 488, 124 N.E. 2d 140 (1955).

[50] Ibid. And see Marshall v. Chicago, etc. R. Co., 48 Ill. 475 (1868); State v. Crean, 43 Mont. 47, 114 P. 603 (1912).

[51] Spiller v. Atchison T. & S.F. R. Co., 253 U. S. 117 (1920); Barlow v. Verrill, 88 N.H. 25, 183 A. 857 (1936). See Chap. VII, Sec. 1., infra.

evidence or hearsay. The arbitrator should be aware of this and at times should question the opposing parties as to knowledge of facts that would appear to be within their possession and not available to the other.

Having freely received the hearsay, the arbitrator should be aware of its character and of its deficiencies when he is reviewing the record and reasoning to his conclusions. Hearsay evidence is not necessarily confined to oral testimony. Statements within various documents, printed papers, books, and otherwise are open to the same objection.[52] Exceptions to the hearsay rule are considerable in number. Some of these are set forth briefly in the following sections of this chapter.

An arbitrator can lend a great service to the parties if he informs them that the evidence they are offering is hearsay, when that is true. He might well remind them that direct evidence will be given more weight than hearsay. In some instances he should indicate the applicability of one of the exceptions to the hearsay rule. This is not to suggest that the arbitrator become technical in his rulings on admissibility, but only that he should act to get the most reliable evidence into the record. This is what the arbitrator will have to rely on as the support of his conclusions.

SECTION 8

Admissions Against Interest

Admissions or declarations made by a party against his own interest are frequently brought into a hearing as hearsay statements,[53] and their use involves an exception to the hearsay rule.[54] They are statements or admissions, adverse to the claims of the speaker, to some person other than the witness who has been offered to give them in evidence. A statement of a party inconsistent with his claim in a law suit or arbitration is an admission and may be used as proof against him. It will not be excluded even in court as ordi-

---

[52] Lacy v. Meador, 170 Ala. 482, 54 So. 161 (1910); see Ann. Cases 1912 D 787, 792.

[53] Caswell v. Maplewood Garage, 84 N.H. 241, 149 A. 746 (1930); Aldred v. Ray, 54 Okla. 154, 153 P. 664 (1915).

[54] *Idem* and Casey v. Burns, 7 Ill. App. 2d 316, 129 N.E. 2d 440 (1955).

nary hearsay.[55] Any statement made by a party against his own interests in a legal controversy that would tend to establish or disprove his material contentions may be used as evidence against him in a hearing on that issue. Admissions or statements against interest may be admitted whether written or oral, but are subject to the requirement that the entire statement must be considered, including portions both favorable and unfavorable to the party offering the evidence.[56]

Relevant to numerous disputes that appear in arbitration is the rule that offers of compromise, though possibly logically implying admissions against interest, are not admissible regardless of whether the offer was made orally or in writing, or whether it was made directly to the opposing party or his agent.[57] This view is sustained on the basis of public policy that encourages settlement of disputes between the parties and out of court. Offers of settlement of grievances appear to fall within this rule.[58]

Statements of agents within the scope of their employment, with the actual or apparent authority of the principal, are binding upon the latter.[59] In this connection, the statement of a business agent, international representative, or union officer, other than an offer to compromise, may often be binding upon the union represented as well as upon individual members of the union for whom the union officer may be appearing as representative in a grievance matter at any stage.[60] The same would be true of statements made by officers and other representatives of management within the scope of their employment and the areas of their responsibilities.[61]

---

[55] Donnelly v. United States, 228 U. S. 243 (1913); Hines v. Comm., 136 Va. 728, 117 S.E. 843 (1923).

[56] Mutual Bel. L. Ins. Co. v. Newton, 22 Wall (U. S.) 32 (1874); Granger v. Farrant, 179 Mich. 19, 146 N.W. 218 (1914).

[57] West v. Smith, 101 U. S. (1879); Olshove v. Pere Marquette R. Co., 263 Mich. 579, 248 N.W. 906 (1933).

[58] See cases cited in Elkouri, How Arbitration Works, (Washington: BNA Books, 1960).

[59] Hitchman Coal & Coke Co. v. Mitchell, 245 U. S. 229 (1917); State v. Sweeney, 180 Minn. 450, 231 N.W. 225 (1930). Howell v. J. Mandelbaum & Sons, 160 Iowa 119, 140 N.W. 397 (1913).

[60] See Flintkote Co., 9 LA 976 (1948) and Jarecki Mach. & Tool Co., 12 LA 161 (1949), but care must be observed to be sure such actions are adequately authorized to make them binding on the union.

[61] Kempsmith Machine Co., 5 LA 520, 530 (1946); Pope and Talbot, Inc., 1 ALAA par. 67, 157, p. 67, 324 (1942).

SECTION 9

Confessions

From time to time in disciplinary and discharge matters, arbitrators are confronted with evidence that the accused party has confessed. Evidence of confessions is generally accepted as an exception to the hearsay rule provided they have been made voluntarily and without improper inducements that might tempt the accused to falsify.[62]

In a discharge case where an employee was given his job back on condition of confession of wrongdoing and soon thereafter was discharged again on a different charge, the earlier confession should not be heard against him. The fact that it was induced by the promise of rehiring would seem to invalidate it.[63]

In some jurisdictions confessions are admissible only after the accused has been warned that his statement may be used against him. It must be emphasized that the confession, to be admissible, must be free and voluntary.[64] Obviously, a confession of theft from the employer obtained by the police from an employee by any third degree or "sweat box" would be inadmissible in a criminal prosecution and should be disregarded in an arbitration.[65]

SECTION 10

Former Testimony

The statement or testimony given by one of the witnesses at a prior hearing is often needed in evidence.[66] The proper procedure it to present the same witness who testified in the first place to appear and to testify again. Evidence of his statements at the former trial, if given by a third person, is hearsay.[67]

---

[62] Kroger Co., 12 LA 1065 (1949); State v. Royce, 38 Wash. Ill, 80 p. 268 (1905). See 18 L.R.A. (N.S.) 771 and 50 L.R.A. (N.S.) 1077.

[63] W. T. Washer v. Bullitt County, 110 U. S. 574 (1883); State v. German, 54 Mo. 526 (1874); People v. Kennedy, 159 N.Y. 346, 54 N.E. 51 (1899).

[64] See Maki v. State, 18 Wyo. 481, 112 p. 334 (1911), 33 L.R.A. (N.S.) 465.

[65] Wilson v. United States, 162 U. S. 613 (1896); State v. Storms, 113 Iowa 385, 85 N.W. 610 (1901). See 50 L.R.A. (N.S.) 1077.

[66] St. Joseph v. Union R. Co., 116 Mo. 636, 22 S.W. 794 (1893); New York Cent. R. Co. v. Stevens, 126 Ohio St. 395, 185 N.E. 542 (1933).

[67] Bower Roller Bearing Co., 22 LA 320 (1954). See Annotation 91 Am. St. Rep. 197.

At times arbitrators are confronted by offers in evidence of notes or minutes that purport to be statements of bargaining representatives made in conferences leading up to a contract. This testimony should not be received as proving facts that serve or sustain the contentions of the party offering the testimony. On the other hand, such testimony may well qualify for consideration when it amounts to an admission against interest and, as such, is offered against the opposing party.[68] Here again, however, the arbitrator should bear in mind the best evidence rule and should remind the party offering the evidence of the importance of using firsthand evidence if it can be found available.

In this connection, however, it should be noted that the testimony of a person since deceased is ordinarily admissible where such witness was cross-examined or there was an opportunity for cross-examination.[69] This, of course, would not operate to render admissible statements made in the relatively informal, early steps of the ordinary grievance procedure or in contract negotiations. But some of these might be admissible as admissions against interest.

SECTION 11

Res Gestae

The use of evidence of *res gestae* is an exception to the hearsay rule.[70] *Res gestae* is thought of as incidental to the main fact and explanatory thereof. Usually *res gestae* is so closely related to the principal fact in dispute that it has been brought out as a spontaneous or instinctive statement or reaction in which forethought or fabrication would seem to be highly unlikely or impossible. The very term *res gestae* suggests that the uncontemplated or instinctive words and facts speak for themselves.[71] The surrounding circumstances are eloquent to sustain the veracity of the words or acts constituting the so-called *res gestae*.

---

68 See Sec. 8 *supra*, this chapter.

69 Washington Gaslight Co. v. Dist. of Col., 161 U. S. 316 (1896); Davis v. Kline, 96 Mo. 401, 9 S.W. 724 (1888).

70 Winchester & P. Mfg. Co. v. Creary, 116 U. S. 161 (1885); Boyer Chem. Lab. v. Industrial Comm., 366 Ill. 635, 10 N.E. 2d 389 (1937).

71 Beal-Doyle Dry Goods Co. v. Carr, 85 Ark. 479, 108 S.W. 1053 (1908); Sparks Bus Line v. Spears, 276 Ky. 600, 124 S.W. 2d 1031 (1939). Annotation at 42 L.R.A. (N.S.) 918.

Sometimes *res gestae* statements are similar to admissions against interest in that they are verbal acts contrary to the interest of the speaking party.[72] Where evidence is offered to a tribunal as *res gestae,* however, the party tendering it must be ready to establish the act itself before the accompanying declarations may be put in evidence.[73] While usually *res gestae* statements are oral, a written statement is sometimes held to be so admissible.[74] The rule is that to be admissible the *res gestae* statement must have been impulsive, uncontemplated, and virtually contemporaneous in that sense, with the event established as the principal act. It should spring from the act without any interval or opportunity for deliberation or fabrication of the statement.[75]

SECTION 12

Statements of Deceased Persons

There are statutes in a number of jurisdictions that provide that declarations of deceased persons may be received as evidence.[76] Here again is a hearsay exception. One type of such statute permits only the admission of such testimony against the personal representative of the deceased in matters pertaining to his estate. Another type is broader and permits receiving of evidence of such declarations by deceased persons in all types of actions.[77] The latter statutes, however, require the party wishing to rely on such testimony to establish that the declaration of the deceased person is offered in good faith.[78] In some states it is required that the statement must have been made before the commencement of the action.[79] However, the act may limit the statement of the deceased person to statements of facts within his personal knowledge. Obviously a hearsay statement by a person now deceased may borrow no credibility from his death that it did not have in his lifetime.[80]

---

[72] Murray v. Boston & Me. R. Co., 72 N.H. 32, 54 A. 289 (1903).

[73] Bankers Life Co. v. Nelson, 56 Wyo. 513, 111 P. 2d (1941). See Annotation 95 Am. Dec. 66.

[74] Starr Jobbing House v. May Hosiery Mills, 207 Ala. 620, 93 So. 572 (1922); McGoon v. Irvin, 1 Pinney (Wis.) 526 (1845).

[75] Alabama G.S.R. Co. v. Hill, 90 Ala. 71, 8 So. 90 (1890); Sample v. Consol. Light & R. Co., 50 W. Va. 472, 40 S.E. 597 (1901).

[76] See Annotation, 96 A.L.R. 686-703.

[77] See also 20 Am. Jur., Title, "Evidence," S 613.

[78] Idem. and see Rich v. Finley, 325 Mass. 99, 89 N.E. 2d 213 (1949).

[79] Note 74 *supra,* and see Walter v. Sperry, 86 Conn. 474, 85 A. 739 (1913).

[80] Dorchester Trust Co. v. Casey, 268 Mass. 494, 176 N.E. 178 (1929).

The statement of a deceased person made reportedly to another deceased person will ordinarily be inadmissible. "The dead cannot thus be made to speak through the dead." [81]

SECTION 13

Real Evidence

This type of testimony includes all of the proof presented directly to the senses of the arbitrator, judge, or jury, such as objects brought into the hearing room.[82] It may consist of materials, instruments, and devices used in connection with work. Included are those numerous and various things that with some frequency arbitrators are requested to observe when invited to visit the scene of work and to look at manufacturing and assembling processes. Like the judge, the arbitrator must always be alert to discover whether he is being offered a fair example of machinery, working conditions, materials, locale, or otherwise. It is true, however, that it is not always necessary to insist upon conditions identical to those that existed at the time the grievance occurred.[83] That is to say, it is at times helpful to visit the scene of an incident so that testimony of witnesses concerning what transpired at a given time may be, by the mind of the arbitrator, projected upon an accurate understanding of the surrounding machinery, building, mine, or other area that may have been involved in the dispute.[84]

The value of this type of evidence is illustrated by these examples:

(1) It was contended that two workers had identical skill, but when two finished pieces separately made by them were compared, it was demonstrated that one was far more skillful than the other.

(2) An invitation to visit a mine to see a "stone ceiling" declared to be incapable of caving in brought forth vivid truth when a part of the ceiling came down during the visit.

---

81 Annotation, 96 A.L.R. 702.

82 Githins v. Great Amer. Ins. Co., 201 Iowa 266, 207 N.W. 243 (1926); Logan v. Empire Dist. Elec. Co., 99 Kan. 381, 161 P. 659 (1917).

83 Bonnet v. Foote, 47 Colo. 282, 107 P. 252 (1910).

84 People v. Pfanschmidt, 262 Ill. 411, 104 N.E. 804 (1914); Clancy v. State, 93 Tex. Crim. Appeals 380, 247 S.W. 865 (1923).

No doubt, most experienced arbitrators are familiar with the bringing of finished and unfinished parts of manufactured items to a hearing for the purpose of showing the work steps to be done upon them in the process of earning incentive pay.

Photographs are real evidence and should be looked at critically with an eye to discover whether they were taken at a time when, and in circumstances in which they can be relied on to present a true impression.[85]

Experiments are sometimes offered to prove contentions concerning working conditions, possibilities of production, and other matters of controversy. Here again, the arbitrator must always be alert to be sure that the conditions are identical with those existing when the issue in dispute arose. He should not be misled by a so-called experiment offered under different conditions.[86]

SECTION 14

Opinion and Expert Testimony

The ordinary witness normally is required to confine his testimony to statements concerning his actual knowledge.[87] He should not be asked questions calling for his opinion or conclusion upon facts that are to be determined by the arbitrator.[88] His testimony should state his information concerning facts; the opinion as to the significance of such facts is to be drawn by the trier of the facts. This rule is a familiar one regularly invoked in all hearings to exclude statements indicating the opinion of a witness on matters requiring no special knowledge or training and capable of being described so that the arbitrator, court, or jury, with adequate understanding, may draw proper inferences therefrom.

It is to be recognized, however, that where it is not possible to enable the formulation of an intelligent conclusion, witnesses who have had means of full observation of the same are properly permitted to put before the trier of the facts all of the details and cir-

---

85 Brownlie v. Brownlie, 357 Ill. 117, 191 N.E. 268 (1934); Kingsley v. Delaware Lackawanna & W. R. Co., 81 N.J.L. 536, 80 A. 327 (1911).

86 Note 82 *supra*, and see Annotations at 85 A.L.R. 480 and 15 L.R.A. 221.

87 Girson v. U. S., 88 F. 2d 358 (1937); Kerr v. Lunsford, 31 W.Va. 659, 8 S.E. 493 (1888).

88 Mah See v. No. Amer. Accident Ins. Co., 190 Cal. 421, 213 P. 42 (1923); Graney v. St. Louis I. M. & S.R. Co., 157 Mo. 666, 57 S.W. 276 (1900).

cumstances to state their opinions and impressions.[89] The trier of facts, however, should give no weight to such an opinion unless it is accompanied by sufficient evidence as to the facts upon which it is based to furnish at least strong corroboration of the trustworthiness of the opinion or inference.[90]

In this area, expert or skilled witnesses are frequently offered where the dispute concerns a subject requiring scientific or specialized knowledge and experience and cannot be determined intelligently merely from the deductions made and inferences drawn on the bases of ordinary knowledge, common sense, and experience.[91] In the area of subjects often covered by expert testimony are such matters as the knowledge of chemists, physicists, electronic engineers, surgeons, and medical specialists generally.

Where the matter in dispute is one justifying the receipt of expert testimony, this fact should be made clear by ordinary evidence. The expert then should be called and fully qualified as an expert capable of giving worthwhile testimony upon the matter in dispute.[92] He should be permitted to testify on the basis of suitable hypothetical questions framed to enable the arbitrator to proceed with his conclusions of fact.[93] Sometimes experts, having been qualified, will refer to scientific books and read from them. This is not considered introduction of the books in evidence.[94] The books are treated as merely being the witness' offer of corroboration of his own conclusions. He is ordinarily freely allowed to use and to refer to standard scientific works.[95]

---

[89] Shiver v. Tift, 143 Ga. 791, 85 S.E. 1031 (1915); Kunst v. Grafton, 67 W.Va. 20, 67 S.E. 74 (1910).

[90] See Annotation L.R.A. 1918 A. 665, Va. R. & Pwr. Co. v. Burr, 145 Va. 338, 133 S.E. 776 (1926).

[91] Metrop. Ice Cream Co. v. Union Mut. Fire Ins. Co., 358 Mo. 727, 216 S.W. 2d 464 (1949); Jackson v. Schine Lexington Corp., 305 Ky. 823, 205 S.W. 2d 1013 (1947).

[92] Union Ins. Co. v. Smith, 124 U. S. 405 (1888); Spears v. Stone & W. Engineering Corp., 161 So. 351 (La. App., 1935).

[93] Bram v. U. S., 168 U. S. 532 (1897); Green v. Ashland Water Co., 101 Wis. 258, 77 N.W. 722 (1898).

[94] Fidelity & Casualty Co. v. Meyer, 106 Ark. 91, 152 S.W. 995 (1912).

[95] Western Assur. Co. v. J. H. Mohlman Co., 83 F. 811 (1897). See annotation in 40 L.R.A. 561.

SECTION 15

Written Proof — Documents and Records

Legal evidence includes all sorts of writings, documents, and records roughly designated as "documentary evidence."[96] In this area the document itself is the witness, hence, the arbitrator should be astute to be sure that the writings he relies on were relevant, competent, and material to the issue.[97] The document that is hearsay is no better than the human witness who can give nothing but hearsay testimony.[98] Official records that public officers are required to keep or make by statute or by the nature of their office should be received as evidence and given *prima facie* approval. Labor arbitrators often are confronted with official state and federal documents, reports, or rulings of one sort or another. Ordinarily these should be received in evidence and given *prima facie* credit for their contents and the direction the ruling followed unless there is clear evidence to invalidate it by showing its inapplicability.[99] Private writings such as union or company records that contain valuable and useful evidence material to the issue should not be excluded because they also contain other statements. From time to time, employers offer records or minutes of bargaining or grievance step meetings as indicating the previous history of the grievance before the arbitrator.[100] In such cases, the documents offered should be received and all of the contents considered together with all evidence offered by the opposing party tending to invalidate or contradict the effect of the writing. As a rule, if a part of a writing is offered in evidence, the entire writing should be made available and all of it considered if this is requested by an interested party.[101]

---

[96] American Tel. & Tel. Co., 6 LA 31 (1946); Curtis v. Bradley, 65 L.R.A. 143 (1895).

[97] Arnold v. Pawtuxet Valley Water Co., 18 R.I. 189, 26 A. 55, 19 L.R.A. 602 (1893).

[98] Salinger v. United States, 272 U. S. 542 (1926); Mattingly v. Shortell, 120 Ky. 52, 85 S.W. 215 (1905).

[99] Chesapeake & D. Canal Co. v. United States, 240 F. 907, affd. 250 U. S. 123 (1919); Lummus Cotton Co. v. Arnold, 151 Tenn. 540, 269 S.W. 706 (1925). See also Rule 44b, Federal Rules of Civil Procedure.

[100] See Bower Roller Bearing Co., 22 LA 320 (1954); Bell Aircraft Corp., 18 LA 374 (1952); R.P.M. Mfg. Co., 19 LA 151 (1952).

[101] State v. McKee, 73 Conn. 18, 46 A. 409, 49 L.R.A. 542 (1900); 7 Wigmore on Evidence, 3d ed. § 2102.

In this connection, it is worthy of note that it has become common practice for labor unions to demand certain documentary information or records from the employer bearing upon wages, earnings, attendance at work, and other matters. Under the spur of National Labor Relations Board rulings that the refusal of this information is an unfair labor practice and a refusal to bargain collectively in good faith, it has become the practice of companies to open such records rather widely to labor unions and employees.[102] Hence, much of this evidence is likely to come before an arbitrator. On the whole, this is probably a desirable development. It tends to bring the records of the employer to the hearing promptly and with directness. These are ordinarily accurately kept and may be relied upon concerning matters of attendance, production, seniority, overtime, layoffs, and the like. Such evidence, of course, should always be studied in the atmosphere of its surroundings and with an effort to be sure that the documents have been regularly and correctly made and produced in evidence. While the arbitrator should reasonably assist either party in getting information from the opponent, he should likewise be always alert to prevent either party from merely "fishing" into the records of private information of the other.[103]

SECTION 16

Parol Evidence Rule

The evidential rules pertaining to parol and extrinsic evidence concerning writings affects every area of the law.[104] Probably every labor arbitrator of substantial experience has at one time or another been offered oral testimony that certain specific language, though written into the labor agreement and executed on behalf of the parties, was not intended to be effective as literally indicated, or was subject to unilateral change or to some unwritten

---

102 NLRB v. Dixie Mfg. Co., 180 F. 2d 173, 25 LRRM 2528 (1950); NLRB v. F. W. Woolworth Co., 352 U. S. 938, 39 LRRM 2151 (1956). Westinghouse Elect. Supply Co. v. NLRB, 196 F. 2d 1012, 30 LRRM 2169 (1952).
103 I. Hirst Enterprises, Inc., 24 LA 44 (1954); *Ex Parte* Clark, 126 Cal. 235, 58 P. 546 (1899); Mank v. So. Kansas Stage Lines, 143 Kan. 642, 56 P. 2d 71 (1936); Lester v. People, 150 Ill. 408, 23 N.E. 387 (1890).
104 As a subheading the words "Parol Evidence Rule" appear in the law digests and encyclopedias generally under all titles that commonly involve documentary proof.

242 ARBITRATION AND LABOR RELATIONS

understanding that it was not to be effective at all.[105] The so-called
parol evidence rule operates to exclude all evidence of prior or
contemporaneous oral agreements offered to alter the effect of the
written contract.[106] This rule, of course, is assumed to operate in
the case of an existing, valid, written agreement. Hence, if the oral
testimony attacks the legality or the existence of the contract, it
is not excluded. In other words oral evidence should be received
if intended to show illegality or fraud going to the existence of the
contract, or mistake, undue influence, or other ground for invalidity.[107] Moreover, after a written contract has been clearly executed
and agreed on by the parties, it is always subject to a subsequent
agreement on their part to amend or rescind it, or it may become
affected by conduct amounting to waiver.[108] The doctrine of estoppel may also operate to prevent enforcement of claims under a
written agreement.[109] Evidence establishing any of these should be
readily received, as also should evidence tending to establish a mutual interpretation or practice under the contract if it is relied on
as giving meaning to its terms.[110] In the latter case, however, clear
and definite meaning of a contract should not be held to give way
to oral testimony, but any ambiguity requiring interpretation may
well turn upon oral testimony of mutual interpretation or even
interpretation or practice by one party apparently understood and
concurred in substantially by the other.[111]

Where the contract is silent on an issue, the question is one of
justifiable inferences to be drawn by the arbitrator from the silence. For example, where the contract is silent on the question of

105 See Textron, Inc., 12 LA 475 (1949); Union R.R. Co., 20 LA 219 (1953);
Hercules Steel Products Corp., 12 LA 281 (1949); Jarecki Machine & Tool Co.,
12 LA 161 (1949).
106 Northern Assur. Co. v. Grand View Assn., 183 U. S. 308 (1901); Cherry v.
Joyce, 168 Kan. 475, 213 P. 2d 1010 (1950); Des Moines v. W. Des Moines, 244
Iowa 310, 56 N.W. 2d 904 (1953).
107 See Graham v. Savage, 110 Minn. 510, 126 N.W. 394 (1910); Coffman v.
Malone, 981 Neb. 819, 154 N.W. 726 (1917); Annotation L.R.A. 1917 B 264. See
also "American Jurisprudence" titles "Fraud and Deceit" and "Mistake."
108 See Chap. IV, Sec. 8, supra and 12 Am. Jur. title "Contracts," pp. 1006-12.
Baltimore Pearl Hominy Co. v. Linthicum, 112 Ind. 27, 75 A. 737 (1910); Jones v.
New York Guaranty and Indem. Co., 101 U. S. 622, 25 L. Ed. 1030 (1879).
109 Ibid. Knickerbocker L. Ins. Co. v. Norton, 96 U. S. 234 (1877). See also
25 Ruling Case Law, p. 433, § 1.
110 Lowry v. Hawaii, 206 U. S. 206 (1906); Mobile v. Louisville & N.R. Co., 84 Ala.
115, 4 So. 106 (1888); Powell v. Virginia Const. Co., 88 Tenn. 692, 13 S.W. 691
(1890).
111 See Chap. XIII, Sec. 3, infra.

"contracting out" work, arbitrators usually consider the negotiations of the parties, established past practices, customs, and other matters outside the written agreement to give light on the dispute.[112]

A party intending to make a definite point as to the invalidity of parol evidence in this connection should make a timely objection and ask the reporter or arbitrator to make a record that the objection was made. This may be decisive in some states if the matter ultimately reaches a review by a court.[113]

As would be assumed, this parol evidence rule does not exclude the introduction of a written statement against the party who now contends for an interpretation or meaning of the written contract that he waived or denied in the writing offered in evidence.[114]

To fix a specific date or period for performance or for filing a grievance by parol evidence when no date is specified in a writing is not permissible.[115] In such instances, the law supplies the requirement that the date or time for performance be such as would be "reasonable in all the circumstances." However, ambiguities and contradictions within the contract may be explained by parol evidence.[116] Technical terms are subject to definition by parol evidence but this is explained as not changing but merely as clarifying the terms of the writing.[117]

---

112 See Chap. IX, Sec. 13, *infra.*
113 Loomis v. N.Y., N.H. & H. R.R. Co., 203 N.Y. 359, 96 N.E. 748 (1911). See 92 A.L.R. 826.
114 Coffin v. Bradbury, 3 Idaho 770, 35 P. 715 (1894); Phelps v. James, 86 Iowa 398, 53 N.W. 274 (1892).
115 Cohn v. Dunn, 111 Conn. 342, 149 A. 851 (1930); Randall v. Tradewell Stores, 21 Wash. 2d 742, 153 P. 2d 286 (1944); annotation 31 L.R.A. (N.S.) 619.
116 Gisborn v. Charter Oak L. Ins. Co., 142 U. S. 326 (1891); Young v. Schriner, 190 Va. 374, 57 S.E. 2d 33 (1950); Capital Electric Pwr. Assoc. v. Hinson, 226 Miss. 450, 84 So. 2d 409 (1956).
117 Order of R. Conductors v. Swan, 329 U. S. 520, 19 LRRM 2180 (1946); Maurin v. Lyon, 69 Minn. 257, 72 N.W. 72 (1897); Levi v. Schwartz, 201 Md. 575, 95 A. 2d 322 (1915).

Chapter VII

PROCEDURE

SECTION 1

Responsibility of the Arbitrator — Requirement of Notice —
Selection of Meeting Place — Submission Agreement —
Method of Proceeding — Burden of Proof and Right to
Open and Close — Exclusion of Witnesses — Oath of
Arbitrator and Swearing the Witnesses — Introduction
of Evidence — Rulings on Evidence — Recesses and
Adjournments — Evidence Submitted After the Hearing —
Records

General — Responsibility of the Arbitrator — Whether the arbitration is before a single arbitrator or a board of three, five, or seven, the procedure will be much the same. The arbitrators appointed by the parties usually act merely as advocates, leaving the work of presiding over the hearing to the chairman of the board as fully as if he were the sole arbitrator. The responsibility for the conduct of the hearing is upon the impartial arbitrator, who almost invariably is expected to be the chairman. The most serious consequences — even to the impeachment of the award — may result from a failure properly to discharge that responsibility.

Despite the informal, voluntary, and usually very friendly character of the proceedings, it must be borne in mind that one or the other party may afterwards, in dissatisfaction with the award, seek to avoid compliance. There are certain formal procedural requirements that must be met if the award is to be immune from successful attack in the courts. Briefly stated, these are: (1) that all interested parties receive notice of the time and place of hearing, with an opportunity to attend; (2) that the parties be permitted to introduce evidence, both documentary and oral, without un-

reasonable restriction; (3) that they be permitted full cross-examination of the adverse witnesses; (4) that they be permitted to
make oral argument at the conclusion of the evidence; and (5)
that, if they so desire, they be given a reasonable opportunity to
file written briefs. These may all be summed up in one requirement: that the entire proceeding be conducted fairly and impartially.[1] These formal requirements may be complied with in such
an informal manner that the parties will not realize that any element of formality has been introduced. Ordinarily, the more informal the atmosphere can be kept, the less tension and restraint
will develop, and the more amicable the entire proceedings will
be. However, it should be remembered that a full and fair hearing must be held, even though this may require firm directions as
to behavior and order of proof.

Requirement of Notice — Usually, there are only two parties to
an industrial dispute — the company and the union. Since they
have requested the services of the arbitrator, either directly or
through some appointing agency, such as the American Arbitration Association or the Federal Mediation and Conciliation Service, the arbitrator will write to them suggesting a time and place
for the hearing. A very brief exchange of letters is usually sufficient to reach an agreement. When that agreement has been thus
reached by friendly letters, the formal requirement of "notice"
has been met without any realization by the parties that anything
formal has been done.[2] To follow up now with a formal notice,
"You will please take notice that," etc., would not merely be re-
dundant; it would in many cases serve, with the formal and perhaps technical language used, to create that very tension and combativeness that it should be the constant aim of the arbitrator to
avoid.

Sometimes the rights of a third person are involved, as where,
for example, the union is demanding that the company discharge
an employee. This situation most frequently arises in cases where
there is a union-shop or "maintenance-of-membership" agreement.

---

[1] Puget Sound Bridge and Dredging Co. v. Lake Washington Shipyards, 1 Wash.
2d 401, 96 P. 2d 257 (1939); Edmundson v. Wilson, 108 Ala. 118, 19 So. 367 (1896);
Hollingsworth v. Leiper, 1 Dall. 161, 1 L.Ed. 82 (1786); Bivans v. Utah Lake Land,
Water & Power Co., 53 Utah 601, 174 Pac. 1126 (1918).

[2] See Sapp v. Barenfeld, 34 Cal. 2d 515, 212 P. 2d 233 (1949); and Modern System
Bakery v. Salisbury, 215 Ky. 230, 284 S.W. 994 (1926).

In such case, the third party or parties must be given notice of the hearing so that they may attend if they desire. It would be impractical to attempt to consult their wishes as to time and place. But when the principals — the company and the union — have reached an agreement on those matters, a brief letter to the employees involved, notifying them of the time, place, and purpose of the meeting, with an invitation to attend and take part, should be sent. This is not absolutely essential, however, as verbal notice given by either the company or the union generally would suffice.[3]

Selection of Meeting Place — The arbitrator, particularly if he lives in a city other than that in which the hearing is to be held, will often leave it to the parties to arrange for a hearing room. Usually the parties will wish the hearing held in a hotel parlor, or, where they are accustomed to holding friendly conferences or conducting amicable negotiations in the company's offices, they may agree to meet there. But where the union is relatively new in the plant, its officers young and inexperienced, or relations between the parties have become strained, there is a psychological disadvantage to meeting on anything but neutral territory. If the union has lost argument after argument in the company's conference room, its representatives will come there for an arbitration hearing with a feeling of being at a disadvantage, which will tend to make them combative. And the company's representatives, sitting in their own chairs, in their own room, may unconsciously adopt the unbending attitude of the superior rather than the amiable role of one who has agreed with his equal to accept the decision of a neutral. To start the hearing in an atmosphere of tension or combativeness is to risk that the entire proceeding will develop a bitterness that will persist after the award has been rendered.

One further disadvantage sometimes results from the use of the company's office, particularly if it be a private office of the executive who presents the company's case. He may have agreed to the arbitration from necessity, and very grudgingly. If so, he will have a tendency to resent the intrusion of the arbitrator, even though he is there by reason of his invitation and not from choice. Such an executive is likely to take his accustomed seat behind his desk, leaving the arbitrator to make out as best he can at one end

---

3 Cf. Gannon v. McClannahan, 204 Ky. 67, 263 S.W. 770 (1924).

of the desk, and then to dominate, or attempt to dominate, the proceedings. Faced with such a situation, the arbitrator will need much tact, and may have to resort to firm words to gain control. The experienced arbitrator will sense what is impending before he starts a hearing in such circumstances, and will find a ready excuse, after a few preliminary remarks, to adjourn to another place later in the day.

In those rare cases in which there is considerable public interest in the dispute, the parties may have arranged for a hearing in a court room or other public place. Where they have been unable to agree, as for example where the company has insisted on meeting at its offices or the union has insisted on meeting at the union hall, the arbitrator may find it necessary to designate a neutral place. A hotel parlor or meeting room is usually satisfactory where one is available. Sometimes a room can be arranged for in the post office, court house, city hall, a school, or other public building.

Submission Agreement — After the preliminaries of getting acquainted with the parties, trying to create an easy atmosphere and dispel whatever tension or discomfort may be apparent, the first responsibility of the arbitrator will be to see that his authority is clearly defined. If the parties have been represented by attorneys, a clearly written submission agreement may have been executed. Most frequently it will be found not to have been. And even in those cases where it has been, the experienced arbitrator will examine it carefully, and question the parties to make sure that it accurately states the real issues in such manner that the award may definitely end the dispute.[4] For example, in a case where the employees were paid straight time and contend they should have received doubletime, the submission agreement may state the issue to be: "Should the employees have been paid doubletime for work done on Sunday, August 4th?" If a hearing is entered upon that issue, the union contending for doubletime and the company for straight time, an entire day may be taken up with evidence and argument, the parties may file briefs, and when the arbitrator has made a careful study of the contract, record, and briefs, he may conclude that the employees should have been paid at the rate of time and a half. In such event he can only answer the question sub-

---

4 See Chap. IV for full discussion of this subject.

mitted by an award that the employees should not have been paid at double time. A time-consuming and perhaps expensive proceeding will thus have proved abortive; nothing will have been decided; the parties will have to start over again. This could have been avoided if the arbitrator had suggested an amendment of the issue to make it read: "What was the proper basis of pay for Sunday, August 4th?" [5]

It may be noted in this connection again that the *Lincoln Mills* decision, discussed in Chapters I and II *supra,* now may be so applied as to make the agreement to arbitrate specifically enforceable without making a clear definition of the issue by the parties a prerequisite. It should be assumed, however, that in situations where a party contends that no issue to be arbitrated has been ascertained, the court having jurisdiction will direct that the arbitrator give necessary aid in arriving at the same, if such an issue exists. Without this, any procedure in arbitration would appear to be impossible. As stated below, it sometimes develops that a dispute exists as to facts underlying the filing of the grievance. In such cases, the parties may agree to submit the issue to be decided as, "Shall the grievance herein considered be sustained?"

The responsibility of the arbitrator to be sure there is a clearly defined issue to be decided either in a submission agreement, or

---

[5] See "Prehearing Arbitration Problems: A Panel Discussion," The Arbitrator, the NLRB, and the Courts, Proceedings of the Twentieth Annual Meeting, National Academy of Arbitrators (Washington: BNA Books, 1967) , Chap. IX. For valuable earlier materials see Matter of Smith & Wesson, Inc., Case No. 111-1262-D, decided by the National War Labor Board, July 30, 1943, where the Board had under consideration a dispute resulting from the refusal of the company to abide by an arbitrator's award. (The company had instituted proceedings in the state court to set aside certain portions of the award.) One of the issues set out in the submission agreement was: "Shall night stewards be permitted to attend Union activities?" The arbitrator's award on this issue read: "Night stewards shall be permitted to attend union meetings six hours a month with pay, provided, however, that they give the management twenty-four hours notice." The board modified this award by striking out the provision for pay on the ground that the arbitrator had exceeded his jurisdiction in passing upon a question not encompassed within the issue submitted. In a well-considered opinion, public member (later United States Senator) Wayne L. Morse said: "It is clear beyond dispute that the award exceeded the frame of reference when it was extended so as to include a provision requiring the company to compensate night stewards while in attendance at union activities. * * * We cannot torture the language of Issue No. 1 in such manner as to authorize the arbitrator to rule upon the question of compensation."

For further discussion of this case, see Freidin and Ulman, "Arbitration and the War Labor Board," 58 Harvard Law Review 309 (1944-45) .

See also Minneapolis Savings and Loan Assn. v. King, 198 Minn. 420, 270 N.W. 148 (1936) .

some court-declared equivalent thereof, or otherwise, cannot be overemphasized. It is true that, since the agreement is a private contract between the company and the union, it is primarily their responsibility to furnish understandable terms for it. If it is badly drawn, one or both of them will suffer the consequences. In a strictly legal sense the arbitrator is not concerned with its contents; he is engaged by the parties, or appointed by a court or other authority with the concurrence of the parties, to act under a contract that they have made and for which they are legally responsible. But in a moral sense he is responsible, for presumably he is experienced in a field where they are not. If the personnel manager of the company and the business agent of a local union have framed the issue, and the arbitrator sees that it does not properly cover the matter really in dispute, he will be derelict in his duty if he does not call their attention to it before proceeding. Even where the issue has been framed by experienced lawyers, unless their experience has been in the field of labor arbitrations, it may be found to be defective. Indeed it is not uncommon to find lawyers endeavoring to gain an advantage by framing an issue too narrowly, or too loosely, in which case the arbitrator owes a duty, being engaged by the parties jointly, to point out to them the dangers involved.

As shown in preceding chapters, the submission agreement should not be confused with a hastily drawn stipulation to arbitrate, and the latter should rarely if ever be permitted to take the place of the former — this for the reason that the stipulation to arbitrate is usually quite loosely drawn, with the issue left in the vaguest terms. It must be remembered that the submission agreement, whether it be in the form of a formal written contract, an informal stipulation, or a mere verbal agreement, is the basis of the arbitrator's authority. It defines his powers, fixes their limits. Where any complexity is involved, this matter of prime importance should not be left to verbal understandings or hastily drawn stipulations; it should be reduced, if possible, to a carefully thought-out formal statement. And the parties, whether represented by counsel or not, would be well advised to seek the advice of the experienced arbitrator in drawing it. The conscientious arbitrator would refuse to accept employment to arbitrate under a submission that he knew was unfairly worded with respect to one of the parties, or worded in such a manner that the arbitration might easily fail to settle the dispute — at least without first giving the parties full warning of the possible consequences.

Where the contract between the parties provides for arbitration of grievances, and the subject matter of the arbitration is a grievance, which is in writing and clearly stated, the submission agreement may be dispensed with.[6] If a submission agreement is entered into in such circumstances, the most satisfactory form of stating the issue is: "What disposition should be made of grievance number 7-G-3?" With the issue framed thus broadly, the arbitrator has a wide latitude, and may take into consideration all the factors, legal and equitable, that ought to produce a satisfactory result if one is possible.

Method of Proceeding — With the submission agreement executed or dispensed with, the hearing can get under way. An inquiry sometimes met at the outset of a hearing concerns the order and method of proceeding. The answer will be almost as varied as the number of classes of arbitrations. One great advantage of arbitration over litigation is the flexibility of its procedure to meet the necessities of the particular cases.

The most informal cases are those where there is no issue of fact but only one of law or of policy. For example, an issue arises from time to time concerning the right of the employer to subject employees to physical examinations. The determination of such a question depends on the specific provisions of the contract, if there are any, and, if not, on general considerations of policy. In most cases very little formal evidence is required. The representatives of the parties at a hearing on this issue at times discuss the subject much as they would if no arbitrator were present. They cite contract provisions, they believe applicable, and make their arguments. While one side or the other may be asked to open the argument,

---

6 There is a certain danger, however, in entering upon an arbitration simply on the general agreement to submit contained in the contract, and without a new and specific submission agreement. This danger is illustrated in the case of Texoma Natural Gas Co. v. Oil Workers I. U. etc., 58 F.Supp. 132, affd., 146 F. 2d 62 (1944), where the court held that the subject of the arbitration was not properly arbitrable under the contract and that the arbitrators exceeded their jurisdiction. In effect the court performed the functions of the arbitrators and annulled the award because it disagreed with it. Such a result could hardly have ensued if a submission agreement had been executed, but even under the Lincoln Mills decision it is always an unfortunate possibility. See *ante* Chapter 1, Sections 3 and 4.

in all likelihood all pretense of formality soon disappears. Back-and-forth argument may take place until the subject is exhausted. Similar results may be encountered in any other type of case where the facts are not disputed and the parties are at odds over a matter of contract interpretation.

At the other extreme in respect of formality will be the discharge case, where possibly due to a strike inconveniencing the entire community, great public interest has been aroused and the parties are still feeling the bitterness of conflict. In such case the arbitrator may find that both parties are represented by skillful lawyers, a court room has been engaged for the hearing, and a large crowd of interested spectators is present. In a court room, seated behind the judge's bench, with lawyers ready to display their battling ability for their respective clients, there is little that an arbitrator can do, or should do, to create the atmosphere of informality that in other circumstances would be desirable. Perhaps the greater the formality and dignity, in these circumstances, the less will be the danger of the hearing becoming disorderly. With no bailiff to keep order and no power to punish for contempt such as a judge would have, the arbitrator must keep the proceedings orderly only by virtue of his own personal dignity and firmness. He will be wise to permit the lawyers to conduct the hearing precisely as if it were a trial in court.

Between the two extremes will be found the average case, and the procedure employed will be a mean between complete informality and strict formality. The hearing will be held perhaps in a company or union conference room or hotel parlor. Tables will have been arranged in the form of a T, liberally supplied with pitchers of water and ash trays. The arbitrator or arbitrators will take their places at the head, and the representatives of the parties will take their seats at the table facing each other. A number of curious observers and witnesses are likely to be seated along the walls.

Burden of Proof and Right to Open and Close — The atmosphere of ease and informality generated by this comfortable setting, enhanced perhaps by some friendly conversations encouraged by the arbitrator, may be quickly shattered by a suggestion from the company's attorney that since the burden of proof is on the union, it should proceed first with its evidence. This never fails to arouse the union's leaders to suspicious dissent, even though they intended to open the case. On the manner in which the arbitrator handles that first flash of conflict may depend the temper of the entire hearing. If a heated argument is permitted to develop, followed by a formal ruling that since the union presented the grievance it has the burden of proof and must proceed with its evidence, the hearing will probably be characterized by bickering throughout. Suspicions have been aroused, a "technicality" has been brought in, and the arbitrator has upheld the lawyer's technicality. The result may be more satisfactory if the arbitrator stops the argument at its inception with the statement that he will make no ruling at the time on burden of proof but will reserve it for future consideration, and gives an assurance that in 99 cases out of 100 it is utterly immaterial who has the "burden of proof." He may then suggest to the union spokesman in a friendly manner that perhaps the case could be developed most logically and understandably if the union would proceed first. In discipline or discharge cases, such request should be directed to the employer, if it has contracted not to take such actions without just cause. By such a simple, common-sense approach, suspicion is dissipated; the parties then know that technicalities will not influence the arbitrator.

Of course the doctrine of burden of proof has its place in arbitration hearings just as in law suits. Simply stated, that principle is that where the evidence is exactly balanced as between the proponent and opponent of a proposition, the proponent, or one who advanced the proposition, has failed to prove it. This is more fully set forth herein at Chapter V, Section 2.

If one side introduces evidence that exactly equals, and does not overbalance, the evidence of the other, the two parties are in the same position as if neither had introduced any evidence at all, and the one who advanced the proposition has failed to prove it — he has failed to meet the burden of proof. This is so sensible and logical a principle that no one, understanding it, would disagree. But it is in only a very small proportion of cases that it comes into play; seldom is the evidence so exactly equal that it becomes necessary to decide the question of burden of proof. To decide it unnecessarily at the outset of a hearing is to borrow trouble.

The right to put on one's evidence first is generally considered an advantage, and it is given to the party who carries the burden of proof partly to offset the disadvantages inherent in that burden, but partly also because the logical method of proceeding is for the one who has advanced a grievance to state it and prove it. Yet this will not always be the method best calculated to gain a quick understanding of the controversy or to bring the parties to the real issue of fact. Often in a discipline case, layoff or discharge, the union's spokesman will not know all the facts on which the company intends to justify the discipline imposed. If compelled to proceed first, the union might introduce a staggering amount of evidence in a more or less blind effort to prove a negative, namely that no sufficient cause for the discipline existed. When the company's evidence later comes in it may become apparent that most of the union's evidence was immaterial, and the time taken with examination and cross-examination of its witnesses largely wasted. In such case, the parties get down to the real issue only on the union's rebuttal. Where the arbitrator can see at the outset, or shortly after, that this is likely to be the situation, he should avoid it by requesting the company to open, and if necessary *requiring* it to open. Normally the fact the employer has taken the disciplinary or discharge action is undisputed; it is usually quite willing to give the reasons for such action and to assert its contention that in the circumstances the result is just and proper. Even though the company is represented by an attorney, no objection is likely to be raised to this if the purpose is properly explained and the assurance given that no ruling on burden of proof is involved. Many arbitrators have been inclined to hold and to state at the beginning of the hearing that a clause in the agreement binding the employer to avoid "unjust" (or some equivalent word or phrase) discipline or discharge, puts the burden of proof as to justice upon the employer. It is wise to avoid such a commitment if possible.

Exclusion of Witnesses From the Hearing — At times the request will be made by one of the parties that the witnesses be required to retire from the hearing room. Usually such request is not objected to by the opposing party, because the practice in courts of law, and the reason for it, is well known. If objection is made, it will quickly be withdrawn when the arbitrator suggests the folly of being maneuvered into a position where the other party can have ground for suspecting bad faith. If the objection is persisted in, it should be overruled. In this case, as in every case where the arbitrator is compelled to make a ruling, his guiding principle should be to convince both parties that he will insist on the proceedings being completely fair. To refuse to exclude the witnesses would amount to announcing that it was perfectly agreeable to the arbitrator for one witness to hear the other's testimony and vary his own accordingly. Neither party is prejudiced by the exclusion of the witnesses from the hearing; one party might conceivably be injured or might have reasonable ground for thinking he has been injured, by the refusal to exclude them.

When the witnesses are excluded, an exception should be made for the complaining witness, *i.e.*, the one whose grievance is being arbitrated, and also of those who intend to handle the case for the respective parties. When one who had not expected to be a witness remains in the hearing, and an unexpected occasion arises for using him as a witness, the decision as to whether to permit him to testify rests in the sound discretion of the arbitrator. Ordinarily he would be permitted to testify. His having heard the evidence given by others should go to the credibility or weight of his testimony, not its admissibility.

Oath of Arbitrator and Swearing the Witnesses — Where the proceeding is had under statute, an oath to be taken by the arbitrators is usually prescribed, and the form of oath to be administered to the witnesses is set out. But where the arbitration is at common law, no oath is required of either the arbitrator or the witnesses.[7] Frequently, however, even in a common-law proceeding, the arbitrator will swear the witnesses for the moral effect, and if he neglects to do so, one of the parties may request it. If, under the applicable statute, the arbitrator is without legal authority to administer an oath in such case, it will be without legal effect and no prosecution of perjury may be maintained by reason of it. Some arbitrators have thought to impart validity to the oath by having it administered by a notary public or other officer authorized by law to administer an oath. It is well settled, however, that this ex-

---

7 In a few states, however, statutes requiring oaths have been held applicable to both statutory and common-law arbitrations. *In re* Strassburger, 12 F.Supp. 420 (1935); Keppler v. Nessler, 232 N.Y.S. 232, 225 App. Div. 99 (1928); Rickman v. White, 266 S.W. 997 (Mo., 1924).

pedient is ineffective unless an applicable statute provides for its validity.[8]

Introduction of Evidence — While a certain degree of informality in the examination of witnesses is desirable, this cannot be carried so far as to interfere with the orderly presentation of the evidence. Frequently the arbitrator has succeeded so well in attaining a friendly atmosphere that a witness, asked a question to which he cannot at once recall the answer, will call across the room to one of the spectators to have his recollection refreshed, and the spectator will prompt him. Sometimes spectators venture to volunteer interruptions or even contradictions. The first time or two that this happens, it may be allowed to pass unnoticed, because the questions usually relate to merely formal matters; but it must be checked before all semblance of order is lost. Frequently, the spokesman for one party will interrupt the examination of a witness before his time for cross-examination has arrived. This should be checked before tempers are aroused.

The hearing will proceed most expeditiously, and with the least danger of rancor, if the order of proof prevailing in actions at law is rather closely followed. The party who opens calls his first witness and examines him. When he has completed his questioning, and not until then, is the other party permitted to cross-examine. Following that, the first party may question the witness again. Technical rules as to limiting the cross-examination to matters testified to in the examination-in-chief, or limiting the redirect examination to matters brought out on the cross, should be ignored. The parties must be made to feel that the arbitrator wants the facts, and all the facts, without regard to rules of procedure. The parties should be permitted to examine the witness by turns, without regard to the number of re-crosses or re-directs, until they have reached the point where the arbitrator can tactfully suggest that this witness has apparently told all he knows and is merely repeating.

Frequently where one of the parties is not represented by an attorney, or its case is being presented jointly by an attorney and a layman, the practice will develop of two or more taking turns at cross-examining a witness. As long as this occurs only in the form

---

8 U. S. v. Curtis, 107 U. S. 671, 2 S.Ct. 507, 27 L.Ed. 534 (1883).

of an occasional question, no notice should be taken of its impropriety, or an objection from the opposing party should be temporized with to avoid a ruling; but if it develops into time-wasting repetition, it should be firmly discouraged. Flat rulings are usually avoided in all cases where they can be avoided, but they should be made unhesitatingly where necessary to preserve an orderly procedure. In the great majority of arbitration hearings suggestions are accepted quite readily, and rulings are unnecessary.

When the party who opened the case has called all the witnesses he desires to call, he rests his case. Sometimes the arbitrator may shorten the proceedings by suggesting, when the complainant has made out a *prima facie* case, that he rest and reserve his other witnesses for rebuttal if required. The opposing party then puts on his witnesses, and rests. The first party then has an opportunity to offer rebuttal testimony. Within the limits of reason this process should continue until both sides are satisfied, though in rare cases it might become necessary to suggest to the parties that they have pretty thoroughly exhausted the case.

Rulings on Evidence — Arbitrators are not bound to apply the generally accepted rules of evidence, but within the bounds of reason may receive any evidence, regardless of the rules, that seems relevant and of probative force.[9] The most frequent objection made to evidence is that it is hearsay. Usually a ruling can be avoided by suggesting to the examiner that he postpone bringing out that evidence until he gets another witness on the stand who has first-hand knowledge of the facts. Where this is not possible, the usual practice, where the evidence sought to be elicited is clearly hearsay, is to rule that it will be admitted "for what it is worth." Such a ruling usually satisfies both parties: It satisfies the offerer of the testimony because he is getting the evidence in; it satisfies the objector because of the clear implication that the arbitrator knows the worthlessness, in most instances, of pure hearsay.

Often one party or the other will endeavor to introduce an affidavit in lieu of the testimony of a witness. Where this is objected to, most arbitrators will treat it as other hearsay, and receive it

[9] Sabin v. Angell, 44 Vt. 523 (1842); Liggett v. Torrington, 114 Conn. 425, 158 Atl. 917 (1932). In this connection see Chapter VI *supra*, for an extended discussion of "The Legal Rules of Evidence."

"for what it is worth."[10] In making these, and all other rulings on evidence, the arbitrator is making an effort to assure the parties that he wants to hear all they have to offer, good or bad; he wants to know just as much about the case as they do, that is relevant or even of doubtful relevancy. If they have confidence in him, they will be satisfied to rely on his ability to distinguish the important from the unimportant, and to base a decision on only those pertinent facts that are proved to his satisfaction as an intelligent man.

The above general observations on the receiving of evidence are of most importance where one or both parties are not represented by attorneys. If both parties are represented by attorneys and a rather formal type of hearing is involved, closer adherence to the most substantial and least technical rules of evidence may be desirable. In this as in all other matters arising in the course of a hearing, the arbitrator will be governed by the circumstances of the particular case. If a most flagrantly objectionable piece of evidence is offered in a hearing where lawyers are not taking part, the arbitrator may think it expedient to let it in, rather than to disregard it completely. But that same evidence offered by a lawyer and objected to by the opposing lawyer might well be rejected by the arbitrator, who would rather not risk the indignation of the objecting attorney. Even in such a case, however, the arbitrator may decide to receive such testimony, "for what it is worth."

Erroneous rulings on evidence will not be ground for attacking the validity of the award,[11] unless they are so flagrant as clearly to indicate bias and unfairness. For this reason the parties should limit their objections to matters of real importance. In a trial at law it often appears that the attorneys are chiefly concerned with keeping all possible facts from the jury; in an arbitration hearing there is no jury, and the arbitrator's knowledge of immaterial or

---

10 See Code of Ethics of American Arbitration Association and National Academy of Arbitrators, Part II, Section 4, e; Rule 28, Voluntary Labor Arbitration Rules, American Arbitration Association, provides "The arbitrator shall be the judge of the relevancy and materiality of the evidence offered and conformity to legal rules of evidence shall not be necessary * * * ." Rule 29 provides: "The arbitrator may receive and consider the evidence of witnesses by affidavit, but may give it only such weight as he deems it entitled to after consideration of any objection to its admission * * * ."

11 Whitney Co. v. Church, 91 Conn. 684, 101 Atl. 329 (1917); Koepke v. E. Liethen Grain Co., 205 Wis. 75, 236 N.W. 544 (1931); Hollingsworth v. Leiper, 1 Dall. 161, 1 L.Ed. 82 (1786). For further discussion of this matter see Chapter V, *supra*.

irrelevant facts is not likely to affect his decision. Objections some-times serve a useful purpose, however, particularly where the arbi-trator is a layman, in calling his attention to the lack of probative force of the evidence to which objection is taken.

Recesses and Adjournments — The great majority of arbitrations will be concluded in one day, with a recess for lunch and perhaps one for dinner. No formality is required in the taking of such re-cesses, and their length should be determined, where possible, by agreement. Despite the anxiety to finish, it is well to avoid too pro-tracted hearings, and especially to avoid proceeding through meal time. Tempers become shorter as men get tired, and headaches develop from empty stomachs. The desire of a business agent, a company lawyer, or the arbitrator to catch a certain train may be very great, but it is much more important that the parties be given a fair opportunity, and in an unhurried manner, fully to present their cases. If the losing party reflects afterward that he might have won if he had not been hurried, little good will have been done in the advancement of arbitration as a means of settling labor dis-putes.

Where the hearing cannot be concluded in one day, it is often a mistake to hold a night session. The arbitrator can adjourn the hearing to the following day, or to any day certain. No further no-tice will be required, if the time and place of the adjourned session is announced before adjournment. But of course, if the adjourn-ment is an indefinite one, the same requirements as to notice will have to be observed as for the initial hearing.[12]

Evidence to Be Submitted After the Hearing — It would be highly improper of course, and ground for impeachment of the award, if after the hearing the arbitrator should receive evidence from one side, *ex parte*. It frequently happens, however, during the hearing that certain facts, usually statistical data such as payroll figures, which the parties had not thought it necessary to produce, are desired by the arbitrator. In order to avoid an adjourned hear-ing or a prolonged recess for the assembling of such facts, the par-ties may agree that they will jointly prepare them and forward them to the arbitrator. Or, where the rates of pay in other plants are deemed important, the parties may agree that each will obtain

---

12 Inman v. Keil, 206 S.W. 403 (Mo. App., 1918).

them from independent sources, the company from the companies in question and the union from the unions in those plants. They would forward the results separately to the arbitrator. In such case, each party should be required to furnish the other with a copy of the material thus presented, and the arbitrator should require proof that this has been done. Such a procedure would not be violative of the fairness that must characterize the proceedings throughout, for the parties have by agreement waived the hearsay character of the testimony thus to be elicited, and have waived the right to cross-examination. Furthermore, they will still have the opportunity, if gross discrepancies are discovered before an award is rendered, to demand a further hearing for the purpose of resolving those discrepancies.

Transcripts and Records — Ordinarily, no official record is kept of the hearing, though of course the arbitrator will take notes of the important evidence, motions, and rulings made. It has come to be quite common, almost usual, for one party or both to have a court reporter present to make a verbatim record of the proceedings. The arbitrator should permit this to be done, at the expense of the party or parties desiring it, but with the understanding that it is no more official, or of presumptive accuracy, than would be the notes taken by one of the attorneys or agents. It should be understood, too, that if both parties desire a copy, they shall be entitled to them at the standard or an agreed price.

Exhibits introduced in evidence should be carefully labelled "Company's Exhibit 1," etc., and "Union's Exhibit 1," etc.; and the arbitrator should exercise considerable care to keep them together, available for use during the hearing, and safe from becoming mixed up with the many papers of the parties, and so becoming lost. It is common practice to substitute xerox or other copies for original records by consent of the parties.

SECTION 2

Effective Presentation of Case — Preparation — Attendance of Witnesses — Examination of Witnesses — Depositions and Affidavits — Closing Arguments — Briefs

Effective Presentation of Case — Whether or not to employ an attorney is the first question that will present itself to parties preparing to enter upon an arbitration. The answer to that question will depend upon many factors. Those companies, and there are many, that have earnestly sought to live in peace with the unions and therefore have sought to avoid even the appearance of opposition to the extent of conducting contract negotiations without legal assistance, will often go into an arbitration hearing unrepresented by counsel if they know that the union also will be so unrepresented. Some unions, even the larger locals who could financially well afford legal assistance, often look upon it as an expensive luxury to be dispensed with if possible. Both parties are likely to feel that since they have adopted the nonlegal procedure of arbitration in lieu of "going to court," lawyers are unnecessary. There has been a strong tendency, however, to increase the employment of attorneys for arbitrational work in recent years. Several of the larger unions have assigned carefully selected but nonlawyer representatives to specialize in arbitrations. Some of these men compare very favorably with experienced lawyers in their abilities to represent their unions and members.

In many cases the parties appear to be justified in avoiding legal details and leaving the issue to the arbitrator "as man to man to decide on a fair basis." Where an employee has been discharged because he feloniously and without provocation assaulted the superintendent, and the union has seen fit to carry the case to arbitration, the finest legal talent it could employ could make out no better case than would the business agent or chairman of the grievance committee. And the foremost lawyer practicing before the Supreme Court of the United States would be unable to strengthen the facts justifying the discharge, or to cite any law stronger than the common sense that the company's manager of industrial relations could cite.

But all arbitration cases are not so simple. Often a dispute that might well have gone to the National Labor Relations Board, involving difficult and disputed issues both of fact and law, and requiring the most careful analysis and presentation, will be the subject of an arbitration.[13] Difficult questions of contract construction, the correct determination of which may be of vital interest to the parties, are often presented. It is interesting to reflect that many

---

13 See Chapter I, Sections 2 and 4, *supra*, for various examples.

parties who a few years ago would not submit the most trivial of controversies to a court without representation by carefully chosen legal representation would proceed to arbitrate important questions without the aid of law-trained men. Many continue to be willing to present vital grievance matters to an arbitrator without counsel, but are reluctant to arbitrate disputes which arise in contract negotiations.

The increased and still increasing use of law-trained men in negotiations and arbitrations clearly arises from increased appreciation by the parties that contentions are not won or lost by reason of the lawyer's superior knowledge of those mysterious things known as writs, replications, demurrers, *injuria absque damnaum,* etc.; but by the ability of the lawyer to *present the facts* in such manner, and with such force and persuasiveness, as to convince the trier of the facts, and negotiators of the correctness of his contentions. It appears to be more appreciated now than formerly by unions that cases are most often won by those lawyers who have made careful study and preparation of the evidence *before the trial starts.* Misconceptions and lack of experience are disappearing, and, as above stated, lawyers are much more frequently encountered on both sides.

No argument should now be needed to convince anyone that the man who has devoted years of study and practice to acquiring proficiency in the preparation and presentation of facts to judges and juries is far better qualified than the most intelligent layman to win a meritorious case before an arbitrator. When an arbitration involves, in addition to such questions of proving facts, some doubtful point of law, the value of legal advice is even more apparent. It simply is not true that difficult or involved cases can be presented "man-to-man" to an arbitrator with the same assurance of a fair and just conclusion being reached as would be the case if competent lawyers were employed. It is quite true that the employment of counsel is expensive; but the result of failure to employ counsel may be vastly more expensive.

This subject might be left with the simple conclusion that lawyers should be employed in those cases which seem difficult, and dispensed with in those of a very simple character. But even this conclusion has the very obvious disadvantage of requiring the parties to determine what laymen are often unable to determine. What appears at the outset to be simple may in fact be most difficult and involved. The party having the right of a case might easily lose it through failure of analysis or through want of knowledge of a very simple principle of law. If the arbitrator is a lawyer, he may fairly be depended upon to apply the facts to the law that he knows; but he cannot be expected to know facts of which, through failure of the parties to realize their importance, he is kept in ignorance.

The safest rule would be to retain a lawyer in all cases, primarily to give advice as to whether the case should be handled by a lawyer, and secondarily to present the case to the arbitrator if he thinks it advisable. Those small unions that are financially unable to do this might well enter into reciprocal arrangements for sharing such expenses.

Preparation — Where lawyers have been retained, the parties will not have the problem of preparing their cases. Where such is not the case, the parties will have the responsibility of doing what takes the greater part of the time of the successful trial lawyer. Witnesses must be interviewed, and their statements taken down, so that their varying recollections or versions of the facts can, if possible, be reconciled or explained. Affidavits must be obtained where they are admissible in evidence, or where witnesses will not be able to be present in person and their affidavits, even though objectionable as hearsay, may be of some possible value. Wage data from other plants must be obtained if the issue is one of wages. Evidence as to workloads, or other working conditions, in similar plants must be obtained where the issue involves these matters.

Parties to an arbitration proceeding must bear in mind that they will win or lose their cases depending largely upon how well they prepare and present them. Too often they fail in understanding the fundamental function of the arbitrator. He is a judge, differing from the judge of a court of law only in that his office is created by act of the parties instead of by government sanction; he is not an investigator such as the examiners sent out by the National Labor Relations Board to investigate the facts where a charge has been filed with that Board. Such an examiner will take upon himself the burden of discovering the facts. An arbitrator will not, for if he did so he would lose his character as an impartial judge. Instead of judging he would be prosecuting. Of course he will ask such questions of the witnesses as he deems necessary, being careful not to exhibit any bias. He may even suggest that he would like to receive some particular kind of evidence bearing on some disputed issue, but he should not assume the burden of pursuing an investigation to discover that evidence.

When all the facts obtainable have been collected, a "trial brief," or outline of the case as the party plans to present it, should be prepared. A simple form of this would be a listing of the important facts, with subheadings of the evidence intended to prove those facts, and a notation of the names of the witnesses with knowledge of them. This may be followed by a brief outline of the legal argument to be made, if one is contemplated, with quotations from the contract, statutes, or of decisions of courts or of arbitrators in similar cases. The trial brief usually is not for presentation to the arbitrator, but for the guidance of the party during the hearing. Some parties, however, do prepare hearing briefs to give the arbitrator. This is a matter of individual choice of procedure.

Attendance of Witnesses — At common law there was no power in the arbitrator to compel the attendance of witnesses.[14] Usually no difficulty is presented here, however, as most of those having knowledge of the facts are entirely willing to aid in arriving at the truth in a friendly proceeding. Occasionally a man will express before the hearing an unwillingness to testify, either because he is afraid of incurring the ill will of someone or because what he knows would hurt the party with which he is allied. In either case he will seldom be pressed. If a witness should be called and refuse to testify, the arbitrator could do nothing but excuse him in the absence of statutory authority.

Usually the company and the union agree to a reciprocal arrangement, where it is necessary or advisable — the union to secure the presence of any of its members desired by the company who otherwise might be unavailable, the company to excuse from work any employees desired by the union. These matters seldom present any difficulty.

14 In several jurisdictions, by the terms of a statute such power is now conferred. The arbitrator when approached to sign and issue subpoenas will be wise to inform himself of all limitations upon his authority and of the objects and purposes of calling the witnesses concerned.

Examination of Witnesses — The witnesses are examined in much the same manner as in court, though usually with a little less formality. The party examining should bear constantly in mind, however, that the function of the witness is to state facts within his knowledge, not argument. Argument has its place in an arbitration hearing, but it should be reserved for the most part until the conclusion of the hearing when all the facts upon which the argument can be based have been developed. The essential thing is to develop the facts first. It is a complete waste of time to permit witnesses to depart from the facts relating to the issue in dispute, to air their grievances upon unrelated matters. Considerable tact is required on the part of arbitrators to prevent this.

Cross-examination should be limited to bringing out matters that the examiner knows he can make the witness admit, and the admission of which will weaken his testimony. Parties should bear in mind that they can seldom prove the facts as they want them to appear by cross-examination of adverse witnesses. A sound admonition is: "Prove your case by your own witnesses. Do not fish for your facts on cross-examination. The other party's witnesses are there to oppose you, not help you." Skilled lawyers have often lost cases by asking one question too many on cross-examination. It is common for skilled trial lawyers to say: "If a witness has not hurt you, let him alone." A tendency merely to engage the witness in disputation should be avoided by the examiner and discouraged by the arbitrator. Many hearings develop into time-wasting arguments because not firmly controlled in this respect.

Very little more that would be helpful to the layman can be said on the subject of examination and cross-examination of witnesses. It may be all summed up in the reminder that *the purpose is to bring out the facts.* Insofar as it departs from that purpose it will be useless.[15]

Depositions and Affidavits — In preparing their cases, parties should not rely on obtaining depositions and affidavits of witnesses

---

[15] For a full discussion, see Wellman's Art of Cross Examination (N.Y.: Macmillian, 1923). See also and study the summaries at the end of this chapter entitled, "Preparation for Arbitration and Hearing Procedure" and "Guidelines for Arbitration Witnesses." If a party plans to use as witnesses persons not accustomed so to appear, it may help them and all participants if they also are made aware of the proper conduct of those giving testimony in such matters.

who find it inconvenient to attend the hearing. Except in those cases where they would be admissible in evidence in court, which are rare, they are of little value in an arbitration. The reasons are obvious: The witness is not present where the arbitrator can observe his appearance and manner of testifying; the opposing party is deprived of the opportunity of weakening his testimony on cross-examination; and his written statements are likely to be vague and ambiguous. As pointed out in an earlier section, such affidavits, though they would be excluded as hearsay in an action at law, are usually received by the arbitrator "for what they are worth." And this is entirely proper in a proceeding not bound up with rules, for the arbitrator is presumably competent to judge the value of evidence and, in reaching his conclusions, to disregard matter which has no probative value.

Occasionally, in spite of its weakness as hearsay, an affidavit will throw valuable light on the facts. If it states matter that the opposing party admits to be true or inadvertently brings out facts that aid the case of the opposing party, all objection to it as hearsay disappears. But it should be used with great reluctance, for the very reason that it is likely to be either superfluous or dangerous. The only circumstances of frequent occurrence in which the arbitrator would be justified in giving weight to it in favor of the party offering it would be where (1) a really sufficient excuse for the nonattendance of the witness is offered; (2) the facts deposed, if untrue, could be quite readily disproved by the opposing party; and (3) it is quite clear the opposing party realizes the necessity of disproving those statements and remains silent.

Closing Arguments — In numerous hearings, the parties will be content, when they have concluded their evidence, to waive oral argument, relying entirely upon the arbitrator's understanding of the issues and evidence. In many cases, however, one or both of the parties will wish to sum up the case, putting the facts proved into logical sequence to establish the ultimate fact in issue, and applying the terms of the contract, or recognized practices where there is no contract, to those ultimate facts. Where the parties desire to do so, they have such a right. Where the facts are largely technical, as in an arbitration over workloads, an incentive system, or job classifications, and the arbitrator is not a technical man familiar with the industry, such summing up may be extremely valuable and important. In a case involving an interpretation of law, such as one requiring application of a wage and hour or factory statute, where the arbitrator is not a lawyer trained in the interpretation of legal instruments, a closing argument may make the difference between a correct and an incorrect decision.[16]

If the parties have prepared their cases properly before coming to the hearing, with an outline of the facts they expected to prove and of the evidence that they expected to introduce to prove them, and have made notes throughout the hearing of the evidence introduced both for and against them, a recess of a few minutes will enable them to assemble their notes to form the outline of a closing argument. Where the principal issue is one of fact, rather than of law, the summing up should emphasize the ultimate facts, reminding the arbitrator of those evidentiary facts that tend to prove the ultimate facts and of the weaknesses in the opposing testimony.[17] Too often the summing up of the evidence fails of its real purpose because the parties lose themselves in a rehashing of more or less immaterial evidence, forgetting to connect the evidence in such a way as to convince the arbitrator of the truth of their fact contentions. A skilled attorney will concentrate upon the weaknesses of the opposing evidence on matters of slight importance, in an effort to distract the arbitrator's attention from the strength of the evidence on matters of more importance. If the opposing side permits a red herring thus to be drawn across the trail, a meritorious case may be lost, particularly if the arbitrator is a layman unused to the tactics of skilled lawyers.

---

16 For an excellent discussion of the importance of the closing argument, its composition and delivery, see pages 204 *et sequitur*, Torrence, Tested Techniques in Labor Arbitration, Funk and Wagnalls, New York, 1948.

17 The distinction between ultimate facts and evidentiary facts, familiar to lawyers, may be best made clear by an example. In a discharge case the union will have to prove that the discharge was, under the circumstances, unjustified. That is the ultimate fact to be proved. Evidentiary facts tending to prove that ultimate fact may be: that a foreman had asserted shortly before that he would soon find an excuse to discharge him; that other employees had committed similar offenses without being penalized; that the discharged employee had been an unusually active union worker; etc. Evidentiary facts to disprove the ultimate fact may be: that the official who discharged the employee had not known that he was a member of the union; that the foreman in question had had no part in the discharge; that the company officials had not known of the offenses of the other employees; etc.

Briefs — Due process of hearing entitles either or both parties to have their briefs received and considered. Hence, if either party desires to file a posthearing brief, the arrangements should be made before adjournment of the hearing. Whether they will so desire will depend largely on their appraisal of the thoroughness of the arbitrator's understanding of the facts and the law. In the average case, the arbitrator makes up his mind when he has learned the facts. In doubtful or more complicated cases he may want to review his notes or the record, and give some thought to the legal problems involved. The arbitrator should request briefs if he believes they will help him to a correct decision.

If briefs are to be filed, the time for their filing should be agreed on at the hearing. Since one of the great advantages of arbitration over litigation is the speed with which vexing problems can be disposed of, the time should be strictly limited. It will, however, depend upon the amount of evidence that will have to be digested and the importance of the issues. Where one week should be ample for the preparation of briefs in a simple case that has taken only one day for the hearing, a month might not be unreasonable where the hearing has lasted several days, and the record will not be typed for perhaps a week. If the parties desire time for reply briefs, the time limit should be definitely set and thoroughly understood.

The form and length of the brief will depend entirely on the circumstances of the case. Ordinarily it will consist of a statement of the facts that the party thinks he has proved, with some reference, where desirable, to the particular evidence that supports those facts, followed by an argument on the legal effect of the facts. No particular form will be required. The brief is simply a written summary of the case in a last effort to inform and convince the arbitrator. In some instances the briefs have the composition and contents of quite informal letters. They may be of great value, particularly if the arbitrator has had little experience in the industry concerned.

SECTION 3
Conduct of Arbitrators

Upon the individual arbitrator today rests the responsibility of influencing, by his conduct, impartiality, and sound judgment, the course that industrial disputes will take during future years. Either the present tendency of industry and labor to resort to this method of settling their controversies in preference to strikes and lockouts will continue and be increased, or it will give way to the bitter and sometimes bloody methods of picket lines and strikebreakers with which the country has been familiar in the past. Progress has been slow, and sensational news is still made of strikes. But the machinery of arbitration is being adopted with increasing frequency both as a means of settling strikes and as a contract provision for their prevention. Many arbitrations during World War II were compulsory, ordered by the War Labor Board; many of the contract provisions for arbitration which appeared during that period were imposed by order of the War Labor Board and so lacked real contractual consent. But arbitration under them generally produced results satisfactory to both industry and labor and many contracts providing for arbitration that were entered into under compulsion have been since renewed from time to time to the present year. Whether arbitration will continue to produce such satisfactory results will depend entirely upon the character and intelligence of those who engage in it.[18]

The arbitrator should remember that when he is called in, the time for the give and take of negotiation and compromise is past. Conferences have failed, conciliation has failed, compromises have been rejected. Each party is firmly convinced that he is right and the other is wrong, and usually each would rather be told he is wrong than to receive a decision that merely represents "splitting the difference." If three issues are presented, and a party is wrong on all three, the arbitrator who gives it one decision on the principle of "throwing it a sop," is no more honest than the amateur umpire who calls a low pitch a strike because he has already called two balls. Just as the pitcher in such case would merely feel contempt for the umpire, so will the party dishonestly favored by an arbitrator feel toward the latter. Confidence in arbitration cannot be built on any foundation except that of respect. No arbitrator can build a reputation on any firmer ground than that of fearless impartiality.

---

18 See Updegraff, "Reflections of a Labor-Management Arbitrator," 9 Arbitration Journal (U. S.) 70 (1954).

Management has its legitimate functions and rights; the unions and employees have theirs. Each knows its proper sphere, but each at times will encroach on the other's if it can. If either party finds that it can win its cases on any basis other than that of sheer right, it will at once lose confidence in the arbitrator concerned because it will know that next time the opposite party may win for some reason other than sheer right. Confidence lost in one arbitrator is confidence lost in arbitration as a whole. Either party will forgive honest mistakes; neither will forgive decisions based on expediency or controlled by bias.

It is commonly agreed that an arbitrator should not render a decision that represents a compromise. By this is meant that, knowing what is right, he should not award any less than that in an effort partially to satisfy both parties. In many cases, however, the right lies somewhere between the contentions of the two parties; in a sense an award of the right in such case would be a compromise. Only in that meaning of the word is a compromise ever justified in an arbitration award. For example, in a case where the employees are contending for doubletime on a certain holiday, and the company is contending for straight time, if the correct interpretation of the contract requires the payment of time and a half, that should be the award; but if the arbitrator merely awards time and a half because he does not want to decide flatly against the party who is wrong, he will satisfy neither with that weak and intellectually dishonest decision. And worse, he will bring the entire process of arbitration into disrepute and contempt.[19]

---

19 A somewhat similar question has been much debated — namely whether the arbitrator should ever try to conciliate. This will of course depend on the circumstances of the case. If the dispute is such as cannot reasonably be determined on a right and wrong basis, as, for example, when the issue is whether certain clauses should be included in a contract then being negotiated, the arbitrator will be rendering a distinct service to the parties if he can encourage them to engage in "give and take" and so reach agreement. Such an issue, being not one by its nature subject to *decision* on a strictly right and wrong basis, but one on which the parties ought if possible to *agree*, offers an opportunity for conciliation. Also, where the arbitrator can see that future amicable relations between the parties may be greatly improved if the party that is wrong on an issue can be induced to concede it rather than to suffer what to that party would be a great hurt to its pride, an opportunity presents itself for the skilled conciliator. In certain areas arbitration is often resorted to before negotiation and conciliation have been exhausted, and the parties enter upon arbitration expecting conciliation. This again presents the opportunity. But apart from the exceptional cases the authors are of

In his conduct of the hearings the arbitrator should be scrupulously fair, not only in his actual rulings but in his entire attitude and demeanor. Carelessness even in such small matters as talking in a whisper to one of the parties, though he may only have been remarking on the heat of the day, may arouse suspicion on the other side of the table. In his every word and act he must remember that he is being observed for some indication of bias.

In the matter of granting recesses, fixing the time for meeting the following day, fixing time limits for briefs, and in every other decision that he is called on to make, he must make every effort to avoid any appearance of favoring one side over the other. If he has admitted a bit of hearsay evidence when offered by the union, because it apparently has some small value, and then later rejects an obviously worthless piece of hearsay when offered by the company, he has opened himself to possible criticism.

Whether he has to hold himself entirely aloof from the parties outside the hearing room[20] will depend upon the circumstances of the particular case, the personalities involved, and his own ability to impress the parties with his fairness. The wisest rule is to play safe.

Obviously he should not discuss the case separately with one party or the other, or listen to evidence or argument from either party after the hearing is concluded. Proof that he did so would be ground for impeaching and setting aside the award.

As a general rule it is well for the arbitrator to refrain from letting the parties know what his decision is to be, even when he has made up his mind at the hearing. Sometimes an arbitrator, when pressed, will facetiously tell the parties that he always gets safely out of town before announcing it. There is always the possibility that briefs may call his attention to something of more importance than he had realized, or that reflection may suggest factors entitled to more weight than he had originally given them. Snap judgments should be avoided on principle. But more im-

---

the opinion that the arbitrator is treading on dangerous ground when he attempts to step out of his role into another's role. Ordinarily, when the parties have reached the point of calling in an arbitrator they want a decision and will resent being cajoled into negotiation or compromise.

20 See Robinson v. Shanks, 20 N.E. 713, 118 Ind. 125 (1888); McGregor v. Sprott, 13 N.Y.S. 191 (1891).

portant, the arbitrator can seldom, in an oral opinion, convince a party that he was wrong. Quite often, after a lapse of a week or two, when the parties, as well as the arbitrator, have had a chance to reflect on the evidence, the losing party will realize that he deserved to lose, and the written decision will come as no surprise, particularly if it is full, sound, and convincing, as an oral opinion very seldom can be.

PREPARATION FOR ARBITRATION
AND HEARING PROCEDURE

A Summary of Advice and Information for
Company and Union Representatives

By Clarence M. Updegraff

It is believed that if the following suggestions are followed all matters of fact, contract interpretations and points of law relevant to labor disputes will in most cases be fully and properly presented at arbitrational hearings:

1. When selecting an impartial arbitrator or chairman look for intelligence, honesty, experience, and courage. The broader the arbitrator's background of knowledge, the more likely he is to understand your case fully and to decide it correctly.

2. Try to get, as early as possible, a complete understanding of the opposing parties' evidence and contentions. This may lead to a settlement. It will, at least, tend to prevent your being "surprised" at the hearing.

3. Avoid being so steeped and stubborn in your own feelings about the dispute that you cannot see the possible merits of your opponents' position. You can't defeat their contentions if you refuse to understand them.

4. Remember that fixing a time and place for hearing requires commitments for numerous people. Be as considerate of the others as they should be of you in adapting other work to arrange attendance at the hearing. After the date is fixed, do not try to change it.

5. Make a searching, full examination of the testimony of your own witnesses well before the hearing. Make a brief, logical summary of their evidence and write a preliminary statement of the contentions you will make at the hearing. This will aid you to plan a full, logically organized, and persuasive presentation of your position.

6. Be sure that all of the people who will be in your group at the hearing understand who will be the principal spokesman for your side, who the witnesses will be, and what will be the main substance of their testimony. This will contribute to making the hearing orderly and efficient.

7. Try to agree with the opposing party as to wording the exact question or questions to be submitted to the arbitrator and have a written memorandum stating the same signed by both parties prior to the date set for the hearing. Deliver a copy of this to the arbitrator as soon as it is ready, or offer it at the beginning of the hearing.

8. If there are several issues to be submitted, try to agree with all other parties in advance on the order in which they will be taken up at the hearing.

9. Prepare a brief, written prehearing summary of your contentions and deliver one copy of it to the arbitrator and one copy to your opponent at the beginning of the hearing or prior thereto. If possible, agree with the opposition for both parties to do this at the same time.

10. Have copies of all documents that you desire to present as evidence ready for delivery at the hearing. Have also at least one copy of each one for your opponent unless you know he has copies of the same.

11. If a view of a place, a machine, or an operation would seem to be helpful, have a picture, drawing, or blueprint of it ready for introduction in evidence or arrange in advance that it will be available for observation and for the arbitrator to go to see it during the hearing so that as little time as possible will be required.

12. Be on time, or early if at all possible, in arriving at the place set for hearing. Tardiness wastes the time of others, is discourteous, and creates a generally bad impression.

13. Do not shout or speak more loudly than necessary at the hearing. Never use provocative words or epithets. These actions create bad impressions of those guilty of them and in fact cloud rather than clarify issues.

14. During the hearing, do not mention or refer to old and long-settled former frictions or acts of misconduct by your opponent unless the matters brought up are clearly relevant to the issue at present in dispute.

15. Strive for clearness and coherence in your oral presentation and, as much as possible, avoid repetition; if one of your colleagues has stated facts or arguments, avoid restating the same matters.

16. Avoid mixing presentation of facts and arguments. The effect of this is confusing and may result in weakening your own case.

17. Do not interrupt statements of the opposing party or the presentation of its evidence. You will have full opportunity to cross-examine opposing witnesses. You and your witnesses will be protected from interruption. This is an arbitrational hearing, not an informal grievance committee meeting or bargaining conference.

18. If you intend to call witnesses, have them present in the room or in an adjacent room ready for call when the hearing starts. (If they are employed near the hearing room, they may remain at work, but they should be notified in advance that they may be called and should be requested not to leave, even though their work shift may end before they are needed as witnesses.)

19. Prove your case by your own witnesses. Do not try to establish it by evidence gleaned from people put on the stand by your opponent. They are there to oppose you, not help you.

20. If you cross-examine the other parties' witnesses, *make it short.* Do not unduly prolong cross-examination in attempts to get damaging admissions. The more questions you ask on cross-examination, the more opportunity you give a hostile witness to repeat the adverse testimony he came to give. Choose most carefully the inquiries you make of such parties. Make them as few as possible.

21. Each party has the right to ask leading questions when cross-examining hostile witnesses. Each party should save time by asking its own witnesses leading questions, excepting at points where disputed facts are involved. Testimony on controverted matters should be brought out by questions that do not suggest the answer, if possible.

22. Do not make captious, whimsical, or unnecessary objections to testimony or arguments of the other party. Such interruptions are likely to waste time and confuse issues. The arbitrator, no doubt, will realize without having the matter expressly mentioned more than once, when he is hearing weak testimony such as hearsay or immaterial and irrelevant statements.

23. If you have extraordinarily long or highly technical matters to present, or if you wish for any reason to preserve a reliable record of the hearing, make advance provision for the attendance at the hearing of an efficient public court reporter. This involves a moderate expense that in most cases is equally divided between the parties. It will tend to insure that when the arbitrator is working on the award and reviewing the evidence, he will have it all before him and will not be hampered by the frailties of human memory. Furthermore, it will furnish a reliable record of the actual words of witnesses, should a question arise concerning the same at a later time.

24. If one party requests the privilege of filing a posthearing brief, it must be granted, as part of a "fair hearing." Both parties, however, should be given equal time, which should be limited to a comparatively short period of a week or two after the hearing or after the reporter's transcript is received. If reply briefs are agreed upon, they should follow within three or four days after the delivery of the posthearing briefs. It is customary in these situations for the parties to mail briefs to the arbitrator and to opponents at the same time.

Many arbitrations are closed without posthearing briefs, but they are desirable if the written statement prepared for the arbitrator prior to the hearing was not full, or if, in the light of matters which developed at the hearing, it should be for any reason supplemented.

25. After you receive it, read the entire award, not merely the result. Try to give your constituents and associates a full, correct understanding of the arbitrator's reasoning. Only in this way can you get the full value of the decision whether it was in your favor or against you. The logic of the prior decision often indicates clearly whether the next dispute should be taken to arbitration because distinguishable, or dropped because it is similar to the previous one.

26. If there is any question in your mind as to the expenses of arbitration, ask the arbitrator about it at the earliest possible time.

It has been found helpful to advise inexperienced witnesses as follows:

GUIDELINES FOR ARBITRATION WITNESSES

1. *Dress sensibly* for the hearing. Don't try to be impressive in this respect.

2. *Tell the truth* in respect to *facts* and tell it as *clearly* and *briefly* as you can.

3. The witness is present to tell what *he knows of the facts*. It does not serve any purpose to have him present unless he makes his words understood — hence, *speak up clearly and distinctly*. Be sure the *arbitrator* and the *reporter*, if one is present, hear you.

4. *Listen to the questions* carefully so that you will not try to answer before you know what has been asked. *If you don't understand the question, ask that it be clarified for you.*

5. *Don't lose your temper* or show great personal feeling. You are at the hearing to give the arbitrator the facts, not emotional pressure.

6. *Don't be a "smart Alec."* If the questioner "gets smart with you," you will do your side the best service by remaining cool, clear, and in calm self-control.

7. Don't let the questioner *on either side lead you into statements of facts of which you do not have full knowledge.* Tell only the facts *you do know — don't be led into stating your inferences* from the facts. The arbitrator is required to draw his own inferences.

8. *Don't volunteer information* — just answer the question.

9. If you are asked if you have talked over your testimony with the attorney or other spokesman for your side, *answer truthfully. You are expected to do this.* This is the only proper way to decide whether to offer you as a witness or not.

10. *If you are asked if you are being paid for the time you are acting as a witness, tell the exact truth.* Such conduct is sound and proper, but it can be made to seem reprehensible, if falsely denied.

11. If an opposing attorney indicates he wants *time to state an objection, be polite;* keep still until he has spoken. To blurt out an answer in these circumstances is to invite suspicion of your good faith and reliability as a witness.

12. *Don't try to testify as to facts on a secondhand or "hearsay" basis.* If testimony expected of you is within an exception to the hearsay rule, wait, and the attorney on your side should lay a proper foundation for it. When you say, "I know John hit Bill first, because Jim said so," you are not the witness. Jim is. He should be called.

13. *Don't argue with the person questioning you.* It makes no difference which side he is on. Answer the questions and then be silent. If he asks, "Is there anything you would like to add?" either give more facts or say "No." Don't offer your inferences from the facts or opinions. These are not part of the witness' responsibility.

14. *If you don't know the answer* to a question when you are sure you understand it, say "I don't know." No other answer will do as well. Too many witnesses try to guess the answers they don't know. They involve themselves in rambling speculations and sometimes lose a good case for their organization.

15. Moreover, there are times when facts once well-known to an individual will partly or completely pass from his memory. Don't hesitate to say "I don't remember," if that is the truth. In many cases regularly kept records or other memoranda may be used to supplement or revive the memory. Your attorney should be ready with these, when they can be used.

16. *Don't write out a full statement of your expected testimony and plan to read it.* It never sounds convincing that way.

17. *Don't let a cross-examiner get you to make a "yes or no" answer unless it is correct.* If you are sure the answer must be qualified, put your reply accordingly, and respectfully but firmly indicate that you do not believe the "yes or no" will be a truthful statement.

18. *Don't talk to opposing parties before the hearing about your intended testimony.* This forewarns them and may, with or without justification, open you to the charge that as a witness you have contradicted the statements you made in the careless prehearing conversations.

19. *Be prompt in arriving at the place of hearing at the beginning and after each recess.* If you are working and your shift ends before you are called to testify, *don't leave the plant until you are assured that you will not be needed as a witness that day.*

CHAPTER VIII
AWARDS AND THEIR ENFORCEMENT
SECTION 1
Form and Validity

The award is the final ruling of the arbitrator or board of arbitration. It frequently is called the decision. Unless the proceeding has been conducted under statutory authority,[1] in which case the award would have to conform to the statutory requirements, no particular form is required.[2] Whether in such case the entire award, or only that portion which goes beyond the matter submitted, would be void, would depend upon whether the award is severable, the two subjects being fairly separate and distinct.

For example, suppose the question submitted was whether union stewards should be permitted to attend to union activities during working hours, and the award provided that they should be so permitted for not more than six hours a week and should be paid by the company for such time. The provision for pay would be outside the scope of the issue submitted and void; but being separable from the valid provision, the void part would not invalidate the balance of the award.[3] On the other hand,

---

[1] Unless required by statute or the submission agreement it need not even be in writing. Smith-Schultz-Hodo Realty Co. v. Henley-Spurgeon Realty Co., 224 Ala. 331, 140 So. 443 (1932). See Griffith Co. v. San Diego College for Women, 45 Cal. (2d) 501, 289 P. (2d) 476 (1955).

[2] Towne v. Jaquith, 6 Mass. 46, 4 Am. Dec. 84 (1809); Brescia Constr. Co. v. Walart Constr. Co., 264 N.Y. 260, 190 N.E. 484 (1934); 1 Teller, Labor Disputes and Collective Bargaining (1940), § 184; Goff v. Goff, 78 W.Va. 423, 89 S.E. 9, 11 (1916); De Groot v. United States, 5 Wall. 419 (U. S. 1866); Snead & Co. Iron Works v. Merchants' Loan & Trust Co., 225 Ill. 442, 80 N.E. 237, 241 (1907); Acme Cut Stone Co. v. New Center Development Corp., 281 Mich. 32, 274 N.W. 700 (1937); Geiger v. Caldwell, 184 N.C. 387, 114 S.E. 497, 499 (1922); Heggeberg v. New England Fish Co., 7 Wash. (2d) 509, 110 P. (2d) 182, 186 (1941); 6 Williston, Contracts (Rev. Ed. 1938) § 1929; St. Paul Fire & Marine Ins. Co. v. Tire Clearing House, 58 F. (2d) 610, 613 (C.C.A. 8th, 1932).

[3] Matter of Smith & Wesson, Inc., Case No. 111-1262-D, decided by the National War Labor Board, July 30, 1943; J. F. Fitzgerald Co. v. Southbridge Water S. Co., 304 Mass. 130, 23 N.E. (2d) 165, 167 (1939); Marchant v. Mead-Morrison Mfg. Co.,

where one of two participants in a fist fight was discharged and the question submitted was whether the discharge was justified, an award that the discharge was justified but that the other participant, being equally guilty, must also be discharged, would be void in its entirety because the valid and invalid portions are inseparable. It is apparent that the arbitrator would likely have held the discharge not justified if he had realized his lack of power to compel equal treatment by ordering the other discharge.[4]

The award need not state the evidence on which it is based, contain a finding of facts, or give the reasoning that led the arbitrator to his conclusion. Where it does so, it is usual to separate the award proper from the statement of facts and reasoning, calling the latter by the term "statement," "opinion," or "decision," and to denominate the entire paper by some such term as "opinion and award."

Whether to precede the award with an opinion should depend on the various factors involved in a particular situation. The arbitrator of a labor dispute should never lose sight of the importance of contributing, insofar as he can, to future amicable relations between the parties. Where there has been a particularly bitter controversy leading up to the arbitration, but tempers have cooled and relations improved and the parties seem willing to forget the past, it might be a great mistake to write an opinion detailing facts now all but forgotten.

In the usual case, however, it is felt by most arbitrators that the parties are entitled to know the basis on which the award rests. The participants in the dispute are usually content to accept a defeat with good sportsmanship, provided they are convinced that the arbitrator understood their positions and arguments and gave them fair consideration. The only way to convince them that this has been done is to write an opinion stating the evidence

---

252 N.Y. 284, 169 N.E. 386, 392 (1929) ; Harris v. The Social Mfg. Co., 8 R.I. 133, 5 Am. Rep. 549 (1864) ; Goff v. Goff, 78 W.Va. 423, 89 S.E. 9, 11 (1916) ; Bartlett v. Bartlett Co., 116 Wis. 450, 93 N.W. 473 (1903) ; McCormick v. Gray, 13 How. 26, 38 (U. S. 1851) ; De Groot v. United States, 5 Wall. 419, 430 (U. S. 1866) ; Rand v. Mather, 11 Cush. 1, 59 Am. Dec. 131 (Mass. 1853) ; Geiger v. Caldwell, 184 N.C. 387, 114 S.E. 497, 499 (1922) ; Lyle v. Rodgers, 5 Wheat. 394, 409 (U. S. 1820) .

4 See Coleman Co. v. International Union, United Auto., A. and A.I. Workers, 181 Kan. 969, 317 P. (2d) 831, 41 LRRM 2113, 29 LA 434 (1957) ; Donaldson v. Buhlman, 113 N.W. 638, 134 Wis. 117 (1908) , rehearing denied, 114 N.W. 431, 134 Wis. 117 (1908) .

and arguments, and the reasoning that led to the conclusion. Quite often, if the arbitrator is particularly persuasive, he will by this means convince the losing party that he was wrong. It is hardly necessary to state that when that result is accomplished, a distinct benefit results to future relations between the parties and to the advancement of arbitration as a means of settling disputes.

The award need not be in writing, unless required by statute or the terms of the submission agreement.[5] The advantages of a written over an oral award are so obvious, however, that the parties and the arbitrator should insist on it. In those cases where the parties have provided by contract that the decision must be rendered within a specific time, it must of course be rendered within that time;[6] otherwise it will be void.

Where the award is in writing it must be signed by all the arbitrators if a unanimous decision is required, or by those concurring in it if a majority decision is sufficient. It is a practice of parties to some labor arbitrations to provide in the submission agreement that in the event a unanimous decision cannot be reached, the neutral member, or umpire, shall render the decision.[7] In such case, of course, only his signature is required. But the award should specifically state the inability of the arbitrators to reach a unanimous decision.[8]

Inclusion in the opinion or award of the terms of the submission agreement, or a recitation of facts that notice was properly

---

[5] An exception to this statement exists in such cases as decide the title to land and certain other subjects within the statute of frauds, but such cases seldom arise in labor arbitrations.

[6] Such provisions are being frequently inserted in labor contracts, the usual period specified being 15 days. Doubtless the reason behind such a provision is the desire of the parties to insure against dilatoriness of the arbitrator. It is extremely doubtful, however, whether it would ever give such insurance. Sickness or accident to the arbitrator, or even the necessary delays of the parties in preparing briefs, might make an award within a specified time impossible. The result might be that the losing party would refuse to abide by the award because rendered a day late, which it would be legally justified in doing. It is submitted that such clauses in contracts are too fraught with danger to compensate for any benefit they might have. The best insurance of speed of decision is the same as that of soundness of decision, namely, care of the selection of the arbitrator.

[7] For a convincing argument for such a provision see Braun, The Settlement of Industrial Disputes, pp. 130, 131 (Philadelphia: Blakiston Co., 1944).

[8] Shepard v. Springfield Fire and Marine Ins. Co., 41 R.I. 403, 104 Atl. 18, 104 Atl. 635, 105 Atl. 576 (1918).

given all parties, that they attended and were given full opportunity to offer evidence, and other such formal matters, are unnecessary but desirable. They serve to round out a complete picture, and make of the decision a complete record of the case for the convenience of the parties.

It is essential to the validity of the award that it make final disposition of the matter submitted.[9] An award that leaves the dispute in any substantial aspect undecided fails to accomplish the very purpose of arbitration. This does not mean, however, that the award will be void merely because some matter with respect to compliance or enforcement is omitted.[10] Thus, where an employee is ordered reinstated with back pay for time lost by reason of an unjustified discharge, the determination of the amount due him rests merely in computation and its omission will not invalidate the award. Or an award that all employees who worked on July 4th be paid at the rate of doubletime is not rendered invalid for failure to name the employees or the several sums due them, unless required by the terms of the submission. Should a dispute afterwards develop as to whether a specific employee worked on that day, it would be a dispute arising from an alleged failure to comply, and as such would constitute a new dispute.

It has been generally held by the courts that since the award must be final, the arbitrators may not retain power to decide at a later time any matter that they should have decided in the award. The award must be entire. In the absence of express authority to do so contained in the submission agreement, arbitrators may not retain jurisdiction even to decide incidental difficulties that may arise in connection with compliance with the award, as for example, in the computation of back pay due a reinstated employee. The courts hold that the matter of enforcement is for the courts, and such an attempted reservation, being an effort to usurp judicial functions, would be void.

---

9 Pierce Steel Pile Corp. v. Flannery, 319 Pa. 332, 179 A. 558 (1935); McInnish v. Lanier, 215 Ala. 87, 109 So. 377 (1926).

10 McIntosh v. Hartford Fire Ins. Co., 106 Mont. 434, 78 P. (2d) 82 (1938); Smith-Schultz-Hodo Realty Co. v. Henley-Spurgeon Realty Co., 224 Ala. 331, 140 So. 443 (1932).

SECTION 2

Termination of Arbitrator's Jurisdiction — Motions for Rehearing — Interpretation of Awards

Termination of Arbitrator's Jurisdiction — To be valid, the award not only must be strictly confined to the issue submitted, but it also must be rendered during the time the arbitrator has jurisdiction. His power may be terminated in four ways: (1) by the withdrawal of one of the parties;[11] (2) by expiration of a time fixed in the submission or the contract;[12] (3) by rendition of a final award;[13] and (4) by operation of law.[14]

The courts look upon enforcement of an agreement to arbitrate as quite different from enforcement of an award. Until the award is rendered the agreement is executory; when the award is rendered it is executed. The state courts enforce compliance with an award because it is an executed contract, but in the absence of a statute to the contrary they have often refused in the past to compel parties to comply with an executory contract to arbitrate. This now disappearing view has been said to rest upon the basis that it is against public policy to deny to the parties the right to resort to the courts. Whether that is a sound basis for the rule or not, the rule itself was well settled prior to the general adoption of statutes.[15]

At common law, either party could at any time before the award was rendered withdraw from the arbitration and end the power of the arbitrator that rested solely on their mutual assent. Technically, this would amount to a breach of the contract to arbitrate, giving rise to a cause of action, but practically, in labor cases, prior to the *Lincoln Mills* decision, it would merely give rise to

---

11 Christenson v. Cudahy Packing Co., 198 Cal. 685, 247 Pac. 207 (1926); Ames Canning Co. v. Dexter Seed Co., 195 Ia. 1285, 190 N.W. 167 (1922); Jones v. Jones, 229 Ky. 71, 16 S.W. (2d) 503 (1929); Shafer v. Metro-Goldwyn-Mayer Distributing Corp., 36 Ohio App. 31, 172 N.E. 689 (1929).

12 Brotherhood of Railway and S.S. Clerks v. Norfolk Southern Ry. Co. (C.C.A. 4th) 143 F. (2d) 1015, 14 LRRM 905 (1944). But see 154 A.L.R. 1394 and 1403. 6 C.J.S. 193.

13 6 C.J.S. 192.

14 As by the death of the arbitrator, or the death or other disability of one of the parties. See 6 C.J.S. 177.

15 But see Chapter I *supra*, and Park Construction Co. v. Independent School District No. 32, 209 Minn. 182, 296 N.W. 475 (1941).

economic conflict. The effect of the decision of *Textile Workers Union* v. *Lincoln Mills of Alabama* has been treated herein at Chapter I, Sections 3 and 4 and in Chapter X.

Where the power to withdraw exists, it must be exercised by positive act to be effective. Mere failure to appear at a hearing, after receiving due notice, would not constitute such a withdrawal, nor would leaving the hearing while in progress, unless under such circumstances as clearly to indicate an intention by so doing put an end to the proceedings.

Since at common law the contract to arbitrate was not an executed one until the award was rendered, the power to withdraw could be exercised even after the hearings were concluded, if before the award was actually rendered. In those cases where the award was rendered orally at the conclusion of the hearing, the announcement of it by the arbitrator ended the power to withdraw. Where a written award was to be rendered, the power would ordinarily continue until the formal written award was executed. But if, in a case where a written award was contemplated, the arbitrator announced what his decision would be, it is doubtful whether a party could withdraw between the time of that announcement and the formal written rendition.[16] In such case the analogy of a judgment would probably be applied, where it is generally held that the oral announcement of the judge is the "rendition" of the judgment, though it must be followed by a formal written judgment.[17]

Where the submission agreement provides that the award must be made within a specified time, the power of the arbitrator cannot extend beyond that time unless the parties agree to an extension. Frequently labor contracts providing for arbitration stipulate that an award must be rendered within a fixed period. The submission agreement may in such case make no mention of that limitation, but the limitation will nonetheless be binding, because it will be presumed, where the arbitration is had under the terms of a general contract, that the parties did not intend to depart from it. A clear intention to relax the general provisions of

---

16 See Bernhardt v. Polygraphic Co., 350 U. S. 198, 76 S. Ct. 273, 25 LA 693 (1956) and Ernst v. McDowell, 11 Ohio N.P. (N.S.) 145 (1911).

17 Lanier v. Richardson, 72 Ala. 134 (1882).

the contract must be shown in the submission agreement, and since the submission would then effect an amendment to the contract, to be effective it would require the signatures of agents having authority from the company and the union to execute such an amendment.

A final award exhausts the power of the arbitrators, and thereafter no action that they take will have any validity unless the parties confer further power on them. What is the effect of a partial award is not so clear. Unless the submission agreement authorizes it, successive partial awards are not permissible, for the parties are assumed to have contemplated, in submitting the matter to arbitration, a single, final determination of it. A partial award, not being a final award, would not end the power of the arbitrators, but neither would it end the power of the parties, or either of them, to revoke the authority of the arbitrators. If a final award was afterwards rendered, without the power to revoke having been exercised, it would probably be held that the parties had waived the impropriety of making a partial award. Of course if the award purports to be final, but in fact is only partial because the arbitrators have neglected to decide an issue submitted without indicating in any way an intention to pass on such issue in a later award, the award will be considered final. But in such case it will be invalid and subject to impeachment.[18]

As pointed out in the preceding section, any attempt by the arbitrators, in a final award, to reserve jurisdiction would be obnoxious to the rule that the award must be entire, and so would be ineffective in the absence of express authority in the submission agreement. It is frequently desirable in labor arbitrations to reserve jurisdiction to settle disputes that may arise in interpretation or in matters of compliance, and arbitrators often do so. Usually this meets with the approval of the parties, and no question is raised. To guard against the possibility of such action precipitating a contest, however, it would be advisable to provide for it in the submission agreement or by an agreement of the parties at the close of the hearing.

---

18 See Albert v. Goor, 70 Ariz. 214, 218 P. (2d) 736 (1950), and Section 3, following.

Motions for Rehearing — It is the duty of the parties to produce all their evidence at the scheduled hearings. When both sides have rested, and the hearings are finally adjourned, it is too late for one of the parties to demand another opportunity. To permit it would often cause great inconvenience and added expense, and, moreover, would defeat one of the chief purposes of arbitration, which is to provide for speedy settlement of disputes.

But while a rehearing is not a matter of right, it is clear that until the power of the arbitrators has expired they may in their discretion grant a request for a further hearing. If objection is not made by the opposing party, a further hearing will usually be granted as a matter of course. But if objection is made, a very substantial showing should be required to justify the exercise of the arbitrator's discretion. If new and important evidence has been discovered that could not with reasonable diligence have been produced at the hearing, if a party has been prevented from making out a claim or defense by fraud, accident, or mistake without fault on his part, or if a similarly strong showing is made, the reasons of policy against prolonging the proceedings should give way to the demands of fair play and to the federal policy that favors arbitration of labor disputes.

When the final award has been rendered, however, all power of the arbitrators is exhausted, and any further action that they take will be utterly void unless the parties confer new authority upon them.[19] When it is apparent that an injustice has occurred through mistake, inadvertence, or neglect of the losing party to produce important evidence, the arbitrator may succeed in securing consent of both parties to reopen the case. If such consent is obtained, it amounts to a new submission, whether or not it is reduced to formal writing. Without such consent the arbitrator cannot rescind or modify the award. According to some cases, he can correct obvious mistakes apparent in the award, and can

---

[19] The cases are unanimous in supporting this principle. See Jannis v. Ellis, 149 Cal. App. (2d) 751, 308 P. (2d) 750 (1957); Hightower v. Ga. Fertilizer & Oil Co., 145 Ga. 780, 89 S.E. 827 (1916); Smith v. Smith, 28 Ill. 56 (1862); Indiana Cent. R. Co. v. Bradley, 7 Ind. 49 (1855); Inman v. Keil (Mo. App.) 206 S.W. 403 (1918); Ogden v. Baile, 73 Fla. 1103, 75 So. 794 (1917); Granette Products Co. v. Neumann & Co. 208 Ia. 24, 221 N. W. 197 (1929); Mecury Oil Refining Co. v. Oil Workers Int'l. Union, CIO C.A. Okla., 187 F. 2d 980 (1951); Librascope Inc. v. Precision Lodge #1600, I.A.M., AFL-CIO, 10 Cal. Rept. 795, 189 C.A. 2d 71 (1961).

correct clerical errors or errors in figures.[20] Even this limited power would not be conceded by all courts, however.[21] In theory, it would seem that the arbitrator should have this power, in analogy to the power of a court to amend a judgment *nunc pro tunc* even after expiration of the term.

Interpretation of Awards — Frequently arbitrators are called upon to clarify or interpret the award. Where both parties join in the request this also amounts to a new submission, and renews the arbitrator's power. But if only one party requests it, the clarification or interpretation, if made, will have no legal effect. It would be an attempt to amend an award by one who has no power of amendment. It might lead to serious consequences, for the party benefiting from the interpretation, if not aware of its invalidity at law, might think itself justified in taking drastic measures to enforce compliance.

Where a change of conditions caused an award to be ambiguous it was sent back to the arbitrator for clarification.[22] In another matter in which diverse interpretations caused collateral disputes, the awards were sent back to the arbitrators for re-study and re-wording.[23] In yet another case the court indicated belief that the intent of the arbitrator was clear and unambiguous, but the court furnished some supplemental terms further to clarify the award.[24]

Where the contract is of uncertain meaning, however, but the award of the arbitrator based on the contract is clear, it is not proper for the court, by reconstruing the contract, to alter the arbitrator's result.[25]

---

20 Hartley v. Henderson, 189 Pa. 277, 42 Atl. 198 (1899); Goodell v. Raymond, 27 Vt. 241 (1855); see also anno. 104 A.L.R. 710, 717; Code Civil Procedure § 1284, § 1286.6, and § 1286.8 (The Calif. Arbitration Law); N.Y. Civil Practice Law and Rules § 75N; 9 U.S.C.A. § 10 (United States Arbitration Act).

21 Dudley v. Thomas, 23 Cal. 365 (1914); 5 C.J. 81, note 95; Mole v. Queen Ins. Co. of America, 217 N.Y.S. 2d 330, 14 A.D. 2d 1 (1961).

22 Kennedy v. Continental Transp. Lines, Inc., 230 F. Supp. 760, 56 LRRM 2663 (W.D. Pa., 1964). The question was whether the arbitrator awarded "identical work" or "identical runs," and a definition was required by the court.

23 Transport Workers v. Philadelphia Trans. Co., 228 F. Supp. 423, 55 LRRM 3014 (E.D. Pa., 1964). The dispute was as to an award that did not specify which automobile trucks were to be "gassed" by the employees concerned.

24 UAW v. Fafnir Bearing Co., 151 Conn. 650, 201 A. 2d 656, 56 LRRM 2518 (1964).

25 Avco Corp. v. Mitchell, 336 F. 2d 289, 57 LRRM 2119 (6th Cir., 1964).

SECTION 3

Impeachment — Vacation or Modification

An award is neither a contract nor a judgment, but it partakes of the nature of both.[26] It is the result of a contract, the submission agreement, whereby the parties agreed to comply with the award. The award having been made, the parties are bound by their contract to abide by it; hence the award partakes of the nature of a contract, in that it is the act of the arbitrators, not of the parties themselves. It partakes of the nature of a judgment in that, if it is valid, it is binding upon the parties though imposed by an outside source. It is in fact an extra-judicial judgment of a tribunal selected by and given power by the act of the parties legally approved and enforceable.

Where the proceeding is had under authority of a statute and the statute is complied with, it is usually provided that the award may be filed in court and judgment entered on it. The procedure for converting an award into a judgment is often followed in commercial arbitrations, but is practically never used in labor arbitrations. The reasons are, first, that the parties are anxious to avoid the courts, and second, that labor disputes are usually of such a nature that no benefit would accrue from the securing of a judgment. For example, a judgment to the effect that a company had the right to discharge an employee would add nothing to the arbitrators' award to that effect. Even in cases where there might be some added legal benefit from a judgment, such as one converting an award of back pay into a money judgment, the benefit would be theoretical for the union would seldom resort to the courts for enforcement. If the company filed a suit to set the award or judgment aside, the very economic conflict that was sought to be avoided would ensue. Thus the question of judicial enforcement of awards is not an important one in most labor arbitration cases. The parties deliberately choose to arbitrate their grievances to avoid the time and expense of judicial proceedings, and the overwhelming majority of awards are promptly performed by the parties.

---

[26] Smith-Schultz-Hodo Realty Co. v. Henley-Spurgeon Realty Co., 224 Ala. 331, 140 So. 443 (1932).

Impeachment — In those rare[27] cases where one party or the other may desire to attack the award and risk the danger of strike or lockout, three methods are open: (1) The dissatisfied party may simply refuse to comply, and prepare to defend an action at law on the award; (2) it may commence a suit in equity to set the award aside; or (3) the party in whose favor the award was rendered may sue for specific performance. In any of these cases the principles determining the validity and enforceability of the award will be the same.

The most common reason for requesting judicial review of an arbitration award is that the arbitrator has exceeded his authority under the agreement to arbitrate or under the submission.

The labor dispute arbitrator derives his authority from the collective bargaining agreement, and it is limited to the powers conferred in that agreement. Here he must limit his consideration to the interpretation and application of the agreement, and his award "must draw its essence from the collective bargaining agreement."[28]

The question of the arbitrator's authority is subject to judicial review, and the reviewing court will not hesitate to refuse to enforce an award where it appears the arbitrator has derived his authority from sources outside the contract. Thus an arbitrator exceeded his authority in deciding that a collective bargaining agreement contained an implied provision, based on prior practice, that the employer would allow his employees paid voting time of one hour on election day.[29]

Back-pay awards have sometimes been reviewed, and, although arbitrators' decisions on this matter have been generally sustained, on some occasions the court has concluded that under the contract terms such an issue was not intended to be arbitrated or was

---

27 For some interesting statistics showing how very rarely are awards in labor arbitrations subjected to court review, see Freidin and Ulman, Arbitration and the War Labor Board, 58 H.L.R. 309, 316, note (1944-45).

28 United Steelworkers v. Enterprise Wheel and Car Corp., 363 U. S. 593, 80 S. Ct. 1358, 4 L.Ed. 2d 1424, 46 LRRM 2423 (1960).

29 Torrington Co. v. Metal Products Workers, 362 F. 2d 677, 62 LRRM 2495 (2d Cir., 1966). See also International Ass'n of Machinists v. Jeffrey Galion Co., 350 F. 2d 512, 60 LRRM 2108 (6th Cir., 1965).

expressly excluded.[30] In one case a federal appellate court held that an award of back pay exceeded an arbitrator's authority, where the only question submitted was the propriety of a layoff.[31]

In most instances, however, the judicial conclusion is that the arbitrators have not exceeded the authority given them in the agreement to arbitrate or in the submission.[32] Thus, an arbitrator could order reinstatement and back pay where he found that a layoff violated the contract.[33] Similarly, a court enforced an arbitration award directing a company to return machinery and equipment to a plant, and to reinstate all of the plant's employees with full back pay and without loss of seniority.[34]

The usual approach, in reliance on the *Enterprise Wheel and Car Corp.* case, is to refuse to set an award aside unless it can be shown that it did not draw its essence from the collective bargaining agreement. One recent case, indicative of such an approach, found the submission agreement sufficiently vague to encompass an award of back pay and reinstatement in the company's profit-sharing plan. The agreement stated that, in addition to ruling on the employer's refusal to extend the grievant's leave of absence, the arbitrator was authorized to "apply" the remaining provisions of the contract, which resulted in the severance of her employment.[35]

Where the employer did not know until the announcement of the arbitrator's decision that the arbitrator had determined issues

---

30 In re Hodges v. Atlantic Coast Line R.R., 238 F. Supp. 425, 59 LRRM 2792 (N.D. Ga., 1964); Oil Workers v. Mobil Oil Co., 350 F. 2d 708, 59 LRRM 2938 (7th Cir., 1965); IBEW v. Bally Case and Cooler, Inc., 232 F. Supp. 394, 56 LRRM 2831 (D.C. Pa., 1964).

31 Kansas City Luggage and Novelty Workers v. Neevel Luggage Manufacturing Co., 325 F. 2d 992, 55 LRRM 2153 (8th Cir., 1964).

32 In re Certain Carriers, 247 F. Supp. 176, 60 LRRM 2494 (D.D.C., 1965); American Bosch Arma Corp. v. International Union of Electrical Workers, 243 F. Supp. 493, 59 LRRM 2798 (N.D. Miss., 1965). (Award of pay enforced for day other than that claimed in grievance); Atchison, T. & S. F. Ry. v. Brotherhood of R. R. Trainmen, 229 Cal. App. 2d 607, 40 Cal. Rptr. 489 (1964) (award of extra pay for coupling air hose on cars for other crews within usage or "law of the shop").

33 Minute Maid Co. v. International Brotherhood of Teamsters, 331 F. 2d 28 (5th Cir., 1964).

34 Selb Manufacturing Co. v. International Assn. of Machinists, 305 F. 2d 177, 50 LRRM 2671 (8th Cir., 1962).

35 Kroger Co. v. Int'l. Brotherhood of Teamsters, 380 F. 2d 728, 65 LRRM 2573 (6th Cir., 1967). See also Local 77, Am. Federation of Musicians v. Philadelphia Orchestra Assn., 252 F. Supp. 787, 62 LRRM 2102 (E.D. Pa., 1966).

outside of his jurisdiction, the employer was not precluded from attacking the award as in excess of authority because he had participated in the arbitration with the union.[36] The court noted that had the employer known of the matter proposed to be arbitrated and participated therein with such knowledge,[37] or had he agreed to submit to the arbitrator the question of his jurisdiction, the result would have been different. A former case laid down the principle that a party, by proceeding to arbitration, waives its right to argue that the agreement did not provide for the arbitrability of the issue. It held that once a party participates in the selection of the arbitrator or in the proceedings, he may not move to vacate on the ground there was no contract to arbitrate or that the arbitrator exceeded his jurisdiction.[38]

The courts, on the other hand, have in recent opinions expressed an extreme reluctance to review the merits of an arbitrator's decision, and usually will refuse to overrule an award where it contains a reasonable or plausible analysis of the provisions of the collective agreement[39] and is not capricious or arbitrary.[40] This principle, enunciated by courts on numerous occasions, finds as its source the trilogy cases and the federal labor policy encouraging the use of arbitration to promote the peaceful settlement of industrial disputes.

The dual or anomalous nature of the award serves to explain the limited grounds on which it may be successfully impeached. Not every ground for attack upon a judgment will be good against an award; nor will every ground on which relief might be had against performance of a contract serve to relieve against an award. In general, it may be said that the ground urged must be such as would be good both for attack upon a judgment and for relief

---

36 Consolidated Carting Corp. and Local 282, Int'l. Brotherhood of Teamsters, 28 A.D. 2d 667, 280 N.Y.S. 2d 872, 65 LRRM 3069 (1967).

37 National Cash Register Co. v. Wilson, 8 N.Y. 2d 377, 208 N.Y.S. 2d 951, 171 N.E. 2d 302 (1960). (See 35 LA 646.)

38 Kessler v. National Casualty Co., 8 A.D. 2d 105, 185 N.Y.S. 2d 437 (1959).

39 Safeway Stores v. American Bakery and Confectionary Workers, 390 F. 2d 79, 67 LRRM 2646 (5th Cir., 1968).

40 International Bhd. of Pulp Workers, Local 874 v. St. Regis Paper Co., 362 F. 2d 711, 62 LRRM 2483 (5th Cir., 1966). Compare Metal Products Workers v. Torrington Co., 358 F. 2d 103, 62 LRRM 2011 (2d Cir., 1966), where the arbitrator said that the union's grievance was not arbitrable in spite of the latter's argument that national labor policy required that the grievance be arbitrated on the merits. The parties had agreed to submit the issue of arbitrability to the arbitrator.

against the terms of a contract. These are: (1) fraud on the part of the arbitrator; (2) fraud or misconduct of the parties affecting the result; (3) gross unfairness in the conduct of the proceeding; (4) want of jurisdiction in the arbitrator; (5) violation of public policy; and (6) want of entirety in the award.[41]

Positive dishonesty on the part of the arbitrator,[42] as, for example, the acceptance of a bribe, will, of course, invalidate the award, just as similar conduct on the part of a judge would lead to setting aside a judgment. Fraud on the part of one of the parties, as in fabricating evidence, or misconduct in bringing improper influence to bear on the arbitrator would have the same effect.[43] Gross unfairness in the conduct of the proceedings, such as prevented the parties from having a fair hearing, likewise would render the award subject to impeachment.[44] If the arbitrator exceeds the power conferred on him, or acts after his power has expired, his award is void.[45] Or if he requires a party to do or refrain from an act in violation of public policy, the award will not be enforced. For example, an award requiring an employer to recognize a closed shop in violation of present federal statutes obviously would be unenforceable. And finally, the award may be impeached if it violates the rule that it must be entire, that is, make final disposition of all issues submitted.[46]

All of these grounds of attack on an award would be good if the attack were against a judgment[47] or for relief against a con-

---

41 Statutes cited in 20 *supra*: Where there was no evidence of prejudice during the proceedings, the fact that the "impartial arbitrator" selected by two of the three parties was the owner of an engineering company that had done work for one of the parties did not constitute evident partiality within the meaning of the statute, and the motion to vacate was denied. Commonwealth Coatings Corp. v. Continental Casing Co., 382 F. 2d 1010 (2d Cir., 1967).

42 Smith v. Home Insurance Co., 183 S.E. 166, 170, 178 S.C. 436 (1936) ; 5 C.J. p. 189 note 39 (a) ; Ricomini v. Pierruci, 202 Pac. 344, 54 Cal. App. 606 (1942).

43 Woods v. Roberts, 57 N.E. 426, 185 Ill. 489 (1900) modifying 82 Ill. App. 630 (1898) ; Holt v. Williams, 240 S.W. 864, 210 Mo. App. 470 (1922) ; Monidah Trust v. Arctic Const. Co., 264 F. 303 (1920) ; Jacob v. Pacific Export Lumber Co., 297 Pac. 848, 136 Or. 622 (1931).

44 American Guaranty Co. v. Caldwell, 72 F. (2d) 353, 80 Utah 442 (1932).

45 DeGroot v. U. S., 5 Wall. 419 (1866) ; Acme Cut Stone Co. v. New Center Development Corp., 274 N.W. 700, 281 Mich. 32 (1937).

46 Niles-Bement-Pond Co. v. Amalgamated Local 405, United Automobile, Aircraft and Agricultural Implement Wkrs. of America, 140 Conn. 32, 97 A. (2d) 898, 20 LA 520 (1953) ; McInnish v. Lanier, 109 So. 377, 215 Ala. 87 (1926) ; American Trading Co. v. Steele, 274 F. 774 (C.C.A. China, 1921) ; Maw v. Kitzman, 214 N.W. 273, 55 N.D. 463 (1927).

47 To suggest just one example, in an action of detinue, a judgment for the

tract.[48] But certain other grounds that would be sufficient in an appeal from a judgment would not be grounds for impeaching an award for the reason that the contractual element is present in the award. Thus, the fact that the arbitrator made erroneous rulings during the hearing or reached erroneous findings of fact from the evidence is no ground for setting aside the award where the parties have agreed that he should be the judge of the facts.[49] Even his erroneous view of the law may be binding where the parties have agreed to accept the arbitrator's view of the law. Were it otherwise in these cases, arbitration would fail of its chief purpose; instead of being a substitute for litigation it would merely be the beginning of litigation.[50] Error of law renders the award void only when it would require the parties to commit a crime or otherwise to violate a positive mandate of the law.[51]

Vacation or Modification — Where the arbitration is held under a statute and is filed in court as provided by the statute, the court may vacate it for any of the reasons discussed above.[52] In the absence of express statutory authority it is generally held that the court is without authority to modify the award. Where the arbitration is at common law, the vacation of the award is accomplished simply by setting it aside in a suit in equity, by entering judgment for the defendant if an action has been brought on it,

---

chattel but not for its alternate value would be defective. See Kirkland v. Pilcher, 174 Ala. 170, 57 So. 46 (1911).

[48] By their submission agreement the parties have contracted to abide by a final entire award rendered within the terms of the submission by arbitrators who act honestly and fairly. An award which fails in any of these respects is not one they have contracted for and therefore it would not be binding upon them.

[49] Koepke v. E. Liethen Grain Co., 205 Wis. 75, 236 N.W. 544 (1931); Harvey Aluminum Corp. v. United Steelworkers, 263 F. Supp. 488, 64 LRRM 2580 (C.D. Calif., 1967).

[50] Burchell v. Marsh, 17 How. (U. S.) 344, 15 L.Ed. 96 (1854); Pierce Steel Pile Corp. v. Flannery, 319 Pa. 322, 179 A. 558 (1935); Putterman v. Schmidt, 245 N.W. 78, 209 Wis. 442 (1932); Bryson v. Higdon, 21 S.E. (2d) 836, 222 N.C. 17 (1942); Parry v. Bache, 125 F. (2d) 493 (1942).

[51] This distinction may perhaps be made a little clearer by example. If an arbitrator should fix a wage rate at less than the minimum fixed by the Fair Labor Standards Act, his award would be void. But if, through error of law in construing a contract, he should fix a wage rate for a job at a higher figure than was proper under the contract, his error would not invalidate the award.

[52] Code Civ. Pro. §§ 1280 - 1294.2 (The Calif. Arbitration Law); N.Y. Civil Practice Law and Rules §§ 7501 - 7514; 9 U.S.C.A. §§ I-M (United States Arbitration Act).

or by a proceeding under a state or federal declaratory judgment act.[53]

There have been few cases involving civil contempt in connection with the enforcement of an arbitration award. A federal appellate court affirmed a fine of $100,000 per day on a union for civil contempt of the order of a district court enforcing an arbitrator's award. The union contended that under 18 U.S.C. 3692 it was entitled to a trial by jury before it could be cited for contempt.

The court held that the order was not an injunction under that statute but an order within Section 301 . . . for specific performance of the collective bargaining agreement, which made the award final and binding. Originally there had been a labor dispute between the parties, but it had been settled by the arbitrator's award.[54]

It is not certain whether the successful party in a suit to affirm or vacate an arbitration award is ever entitled to attorney's fees and costs. In two suits to enforce an award, however, the courts denied them on the ground that federal labor law, which was controlling, did not provide for such fees.[55]

Courts have been devoting increasing attention to the question of the enforcement of arbitration awards as, in effect, injunctive remedies inconsistent with the Norris-LaGuardia Act. The Supreme Court in *Textile Workers Union* v. *Lincoln Mills*[56] held that the Norris-LaGuardia restrictions on injunctions in labor disputes were inapplicable to Section 301 suits to compel arbitration. In *Sinclair Refining Co.* v. *Atkinson*,[57] however, the Supreme Court said that Section 4 of Norris-LaGuardia 29 U.S.C. Section 104 precluded the federal courts from enjoining strikes in viola-

---

53 Jud. Code, Sec. 274d, 28 U.S.C.A., Sec. 400. See Texoma Natural Gas Co. v. Oil Workers I.U., 58 F. Supp. 132 (1943), aff'd 146 F. (2d) 62, 15 LRRM 668 (1944).

54 Philadelphia Marine Trade Ass'n. v. ILA, Local 1291, 368 F. 2d 932, 65 LRRM 2510 (3rd Cir., 1967).

55 Retail Clerks Int'l. Ass'n., Local 1207 v. Seattle Dept. Stores. Ass'n., 54 L.C. 11,405 (W.D. Wash., 1966); Lee Co. v. Printing Pressmen, Local 74, 255 F. Supp. 929 (D.C. Conn., 1966). The former opinion indicated it was following the rule of law for the Ninth Circuit established in Maier Brewing Co. v. Fleischman Distilling Co., 359 F. 2d 156 (9th Cir., 1966).

56 353 U. S. 448, 77 S. Ct. 912, 1 L.Ed. 2nd 972, 40 LRRM 2113 (1957).

57 370 U. S. 195, 82 S. Ct. 1328, 8 L.Ed. 2d., 50 LRRM 2420, (1962).

tion of a no-strike clause. The question which naturally follows is: Can the state and/or federal courts enforce a labor contract when these total up to the equivalent of an injunction?

The Third Circuit has held that Norris-LaGuardia's ban on injunctions in labor disputes is inapplicable to an order compelling a union to refrain from striking in compliance with an arbitration award. The district court had jurisdiction to enforce the award.[58]

The Fifth Circuit, in a later case,[59] similarly held that the federal courts can enforce an arbitration award ordering an end to work stoppages. It stated that *Sinclair* doesn't prevent injunctive relief, and distinguished that case by noting that it did not involve arbitration. "There is real difference," said the court, "between an ordinary injunction and an order enforcing the award of an arbitrator although the end result is the same."

The Norris-LaGuardia Act does not deprive the court of jurisdiction. It is limited to labor disputes, and the controversy in the instant case was outside the scope of a labor dispute. The opinion concluded that by agreeing to arbitrate their differences, the parties surrendered their right of self-help in a labor dispute even to the point of permitting the arbitrator to forbid a strike. Norris-LaGuardia and arbitration under Section 301 of Taft-Hartley should be construed in *pari materia*. The opinion adds, "The vitality of Norris-LaGuardia is in no wise diminished by the judicial enforcement of the award of an arbitrator made pursuant to a contract."

This strong authority favoring enforcement of arbitration awards prohibiting strikes has not been fully supported by other courts. In one case a district court held that Section 4 of Norris-LaGuardia prohibits federal courts from enforcing awards ordering unions to stop striking.[60] However, the judge added, "this

---

58 Philadelphia Marine Trade Ass'n. v. ILA, Local 1291, 365 F. 2d 295, 62 LRRM 2791 (3rd Cir., 1966), cert, granted 386 U. S. 907, 87 S. Ct. 860, 17 L.Ed. 2d 782 (1966).

59 New Orleans S.S. Ass'n. v. Gen. Longshore Workers, ILA, Local 1418, 389 F. 2d 369, 67 LRRM 2430 (5th Cir., 1968).

60 Tanker Service Comm., Inc. v. Masters, Mates and Pilots and Maritime Service Comm., Inc. v. Masters, Mates and Pilots, 269 F. Supp. 551, 65 LRRM 2848 (E.D. Pa., 1967).

does not mean the defendant is immune from all forms of judicial intervention to encourage compliance with the Arbitrator's award, and I conceive it to be the task of the court in this situation to attempt to fashion a remedy which ought to have that effect, without countering the Congressional mandate." Damages had been assessed by the arbitrator in the sum of $250,000. The judge entered a judgment for damages subject to its being vacated if the award was obeyed by a specified date. He indicated he would go further if refusal to comply with the award was maintained. This action was sufficiently effective so that the events that soon followed caused the dismissal of the appeal since all questions therein had become moot.[61] In *Avco,* however, as noted in the preface herein, the U. S. Supreme Court has taken the view that it is sound procedure for a federal court to remove a case from a state court and to dissolve an injunction against a strike in breach of contract.[62] Nothing was added in that opinion to indicate a belief that the courts should fashion some remedy calculated to bring about compliance with the terms of an award if an antistrike order was included in it.

---

[61] Tanker Service Committee v. International Organization of Masters, Mates and Pilots Local 14, 394 F. 2d 160, 68 LRRM 2457 (1968) .

[62] Avco Corporation v. Aero Lodge Number 735, International Association of Machinists and Aerospace Workers, 390 U. S. 557 (No. 445) , 67 LRRM 2881 (1968) .

CHAPTER IX

OBSERVATIONS CONCERNING SEVERAL OF THE TYPES OF DISPUTES COMMONLY ARBITRATED

SECTION 1

Purpose of the Present Chapter

There is, of course, no limit upon the types of disputes that may be arbitrated. Disputes range from the subject of the terms of a proposed contract to be executed by the parties down to the trivial claim of an employee for a few cents in wages alleged to have been wrongfully withheld. Where there is a labor agreement between the parties providing for arbitration, the question of what disputes are arbitrable under that contract depends largely upon its proper construction. That is often the first question the arbitrator must decide. But where the arbitration is the result of a submission agreement alone, the arbitrability of the question submitted is of course not in issue unless specifically put in issue by that agreement. Where there is a contract, but one party contends that the issue is not properly an arbitrable one, the submission agreement should specifically raise that question. If by their submission agreement the parties unconditionally submit a question, they will be held to have waived the issue of arbitrability.[1]

While it may be said that a considerable body of substantive law relating to industrial disputes has been built up by decisions of arbitrators, the National Labor Relations Board, and other government agencies, this statement is not literally true in the same sense that court decisions make up the common law. There is no

---

1 This might be done by wording the question as follows:
    (1) Is the demand of the union for the removal of a foreman arbitrable?
    (2) If so, should Foreman A. B. Jones be removed from his position?
See Chap. IV, Sec. 9 *supra*.

doctrine of *stare decisis* in arbitrations.[2] The arbitrator or board of arbitration decides each case on its own facts and merits. But obviously, previous, well-considered decisions, if presented, will be persuasive though not binding. Some labor contracts specifically provide that no arbitration decision shall be binding as a precedent in future disputes.

It is not the undertaking of this chapter to discuss exhaustively the issues and the better views concerning the several frequently arbitrated subject matters briefly treated below. The purpose is rather to round out the treatment of *Arbitration and Labor Relations* by setting forth the nature of some of the often-encountered issues and some of the contentions and conclusions expressed in relation to them. For that purpose some of such well-known types of disputes, with occasional indications of the considerations that frequently guide arbitrators in their conclusions, are discussed in the following sections.

SECTION 2

New Provisions to Be Included in Agreements — Wages and Other Compensation

An obvious and fundamental difference between arbitration of new contract clauses and arbitration of grievances appears in the fact that the former, but not the latter, are likely to be addressed almost entirely to the discretion and sense of economic and social propriety of the arbitrator. The latter are submitted to the arbitrator in most cases to find and to declare the rights of the grievance claimants under the terms of the applicable labor agreement and the law. In contract-clauses disputes, the unions will be seeking to improve the wages or working conditions of workers. The employers will be seeking to retain as much control as possible

---

2 The maxim is *Stare decisis, et non quieta movere.* Adhere to precedents; do not unsettle established rules.

Each decision of the court is assumed to constitute a rule for disposition of future similar matters. Hence, nonsimilar matters are not so controlled. In arbitrational matters, there are likely to be essential differences in contractual and other backgrounds. Moreover, the arbitrator has authority to decide only for the parties as authorized in the particular dispute between them. He is not authorized by public authority, like the judge, to declare the law as applicable to all men.

over the direction of labor and to avoid granting of concessions that will involve increasing wages or other costs of operation.[3]

In some contract arbitrations, each and every one of the terms of a new labor agreement between the parties are submitted to arbitration. In other cases, only one or two matters in dispute may be submitted. When undertaking to act in a case of this kind, whether the matter concerns a single issue of wages or a multiplicity of issues, the arbitrator must remain acutely aware that he has been selected as an impartial and neutral person. It will, therefore, ordinarily be his objective to put the agreement of the parties justly in line with the accepted standards or practices of the particular industry concerned in the particular time and place in which the decision is to be made. The arbitrator should not permit himself to be either a crusader to establish new and extensive rights and privileges of employees, or an ally of management to deny workers just rewards and working conditions in view of the condition of the industry, the area, and the relationships of the particular parties.

The ingredients of evidence with which the arbitrator is ordinarily required to work and on which he must base his decisions will usually consist of showings of economic conditions and comparative wage and contract structures and provisions.[4] These, of course, are the tools of collective bargaining. The arbitrator will be required to decide by his award issues which are properly within the scope of collective bargaining and upon which the parties have failed to reach an agreement.

Most completed contracts specifically exclude general wage questions from arbitration, but in negotiations for a new contract the parties frequently become deadlocked on this issue and agree to arbitrate it. During the World War II period, when government wage controls were in effect, the problems involved were, and to some extent remain, more complicated than in previous times. Here again, extreme care should be taken that the award be law-

---

[3] In some writings the issues as to new contract terms are designated "interests disputes" and the issues arising under an existing agreement as grievances are called "rights disputes." See Elkouri, How Arbitration Works (Washington: BNA Books, 1960).

[4] See Kansas City Public Service Co., 8 LA 149 (1947); Gary Railways, Inc., 8 LA 641 (1947).

ful, for the arbitrator's award would be no protection to a company against the penalties provided for violations of the Fair Labor Standards Act,[5] the Walsh-Healey Act,[6] or other applicable statutes.[7] When a wage demand is in issue, the submission agreement should specifically provide that any award as to wages that is required by law to be approved by any government agency shall be subject to such approval.

It is well settled that paid vacations, shift bonuses, pay for upkeep of uniforms, tools, etc., and all other matters that directly or indirectly affect the employee's income or expenditures form a part of wages and are subject to the orders of any government agency having power to fix wages. No change in these conditions will be valid unless clearly consistent with law. This is particularly true in relation to any government payroll. It is well known that there has been a great increase of collective bargaining and arbitration concerning government employees in recent years.

The considerations that will enter into determination of the rates of compensation issues will be, among others, such matters as: (1) wages for comparable jobs in other plants in the area; (2) wages for comparable jobs in other plants in the same industry; (3) changes in living costs; and (4) the financial condition of the company and its prospects for the future. These are the facts that are essential to a proper decision, but they are facts that too often the parties are unable or unwilling to furnish. The company will often give the figures on wages paid in other plants, but refuse to identify the plants because the facts were given in confidence. Evidence of that sort is quite obviously worthless. Seldom will a company give evidence of its financial position.[8] In some cases the arbitrator seems to be expected to make a blind guess without proper evidence to support factual findings. Arbitration in such circumstances is entirely unsatisfactory and tends to discredit the arbi-

---

5 52 U. S. Statutes 1060; 29 U. S. Code, § 201.

6 49 U.P. Statutes 2036-2039; 41 U. S. Code §§ 35-45.

7 See Davis-Bacon Act, 46 U.P. Statutes, 1494; 49 U.S. Statutes, 1011; 40 U.S. Code § 276a and "Anti-Kick-Back Law," 48 U. S. Statutes, 948, 40 U. S. Code §§ 276b and c. Numerous state statutes also bear upon this subject.

8 An employer may not be required to present evidence as to its financial standing unless it puts its own inability to pay into issue. NLRB v. Truitt Mfg. Co., 351 U. S. 149, 38 LRRM 2042 (1956); NLRB General Counsels Administrative Decision (1956) Case No. K-467, 38 LRRM 1076.

See Chap. V, Sec. 15 *supra.*

trational process. Such a situation will justify the arbitrator in suggesting an adjournment of the hearing until more clarifying and complete evidence is made ready for presentation. In these cases, perhaps more than in any others, the parties need the services of attorneys who realize that arbitration is essentially a judicial process, requiring competent proof of material facts.

Many contracts that do not provide for arbitration of general wage disputes nevertheless permit claims of individuals that they are wrongly classified and therefore improperly paid to go to arbitration. Disputes concerning the proper rate for a newly created job classification are also usually arbitrable. Changes in mechanical equipment, or the methods of performing jobs, frequently bring complaints that the piece rates require adjustment. These, and similar grievances, are usually subject to arbitration. The problems are varied, and call for technical study, rather than legal analysis.[9]

In this area it has come to be increasingly emphasized that interests of the public at large and of the nation as a whole must be borne in mind and that the decisions of arbitrators must not lose sight of, nor fail to observe such interests when possible and consistent with justice to the parties.[10]

SECTION 3

Interpretation of Existing Contract Terms —
Rules of Interpretation of Contracts

Only a few years ago the great majority of labor contracts were extremely brief and simple. Many of them hardly deserve to be

---

[9] See sections 7, 8 and 9, this Chapter *infra;* John Deere Des Moines Works, 23 LA 206 (1954) and Virginia-Carolina Chemical Corp., 23 LA 228 (1954).

[10] This is emphasized by the "National Emergency" provisions of the Taft-Hartley Act (Public Law 101, 80th Cong. 1st Sess. and Public Law 902, 80th Cong. 2nd Sess., 61 U. S. Statutes 136; 29 U. S. Code, Sec. 206-210).

See U.S. v. Intl. Longshoremen's Assn., 116 F. Supp. 262, 33 LRRM 2018 (1953); Youngstown Sheet and Tube Co. v. Sawyer, 343 U. S. 579, 30 LRRM 2172 (1952); Labor-Management Reporting, etc. Act of 1959.

Compare, Labor Unions and Public Policy, pp. 7-9 *et seq.,* Amer. Enterprise Assoc., Washington, D.C., 1958. The "Public Members" of the various tripartite boards during World War II were a recognition of the ever-present, legitimate public interest in labor controversies and adjustments. This interest should not be subordinated to segmentary interests of either management or labor.

called contracts. Having won the right under the Wagner Act[11] to bargain, the unions were content with any instrument called a contract that recognized them as bargaining agents. But today this situation no longer exists. The average labor contract contains many detailed provisions and covers many pages. These contracts are often entered into without a thorough understanding by either party of the meaning of the various articles, sections, and subsections. The national office of the union sends the local union "standard forms"; the company accepts many of these as written because on cursory examination they seem harmless. In a short time disputes arise because one party or both lacked a proper understanding of what the contract meant as applied to particular states of fact.[12] It is not uncommon, for example, to find in a contract provisions for seniority rights without a clear specification of whether it is plant-wide, by departments, by jobs, or as to how seniority is to be applied.[13] Neither is it uncommon to find that, though the parties have provided for departmental seniority, job seniority has always been practiced, and the parties had not realized the effect of what they had written.

A grievance filed by an employee may disclose the need for interpretation. The arbitration of such grievances requires a legal decision based upon recognized principles of the law of contracts and contract construction. Where the issue is a vital one to the parties, the arbitrator, like a judge, should have the benefit of the research and arguments of counsel. The rules of law for the construction of contracts are not, as the layman too often supposes, "mere technicalities"; they are the product of the best minds of lawyers, scholars, and judges through generations.

Very frequently in interpretation arbitrations, as well as others, strong arguments are made that the arbitrator should avoid legalism and that he should be guided by "common sense" and by considerations concerning social justice and the like. Sometimes these arguments come from the employer side and sometimes from the union. In each instance, the basic reason for the contention is

---

11 29 U.S.C.A. §§ 151-66.

12 Steed, "Rules of Contract Interpretation in Labor-Management Arbitration," 8 Arb. Journal (A.S.) 183 (1953).

13 See for examples Bethlehem Steel Co., 21 LA 598 (1953); Kennecott Copper Corp., 25 LA 37 (1955); Di Giorgio Wine Co., 28 LA 746 (1957); Aerojet-General Corp., 49 LA 1073 (1967).

likely to be the same — the party offering the contention would like to persuade the arbitrator to award it some condition or advantage to which it is not entitled under the terms of the agreement. If the contention is accompanied with evidence of fraud, sharp practice, or other impropriety of conduct of the party relying on the contract as written, this should be seriously considered. In the absence of such a showing, however, the proper course usually will be to follow the terms of the agreement. Ordinarily there is no clearer pathway of justice than to give the parties exactly what they are entitled to have as the result of their bargaining and of the writing which they signed to perpetuate it. If there are unfortunate terms in the agreement, the parties should correct these by collective bargaining when they negotiate their next contract. Complaints about law, legalism, and legalistic results are usually found to originate with those who have an axe to grind by denying either a union or an employer the legal rights to which it is entitled or with those who have no understanding of law and justice under the law.[14]

Sometimes a distinction between "strict" interpretation and "liberal" interpretation is attempted. This usually means that the one urging the "liberal" interpretation is undertaking to override the strict rights of one of the parties and express a "liberal interpretation" such as will excite pleasure and commendation. Certainly such an interpretation is to be avoided if it ignores the clear and definite meaning of words to be interpreted.

---

[14] "Good intention and common sense are not sufficient to make an arbitrator. Since he often has to apply the law, at least where rules of procedure have been laid down in laws or by precedent, and since his activities are similar to those of a judge in other respects; since, in short, he holds a post of a judicial nature, he needs not only economic, but also legal knowledge and experience. Thus, it seems desirable that at least the chairman of a board have all these qualifications. An insufficient knowledge of the particular economic conditions, deplorable as it would be, may be overcome by help of the expert members of the board or by the hearing of experts or the parties before the board. The information thus obtained should be sufficient to enable a skilled jurist to deal with the matter. In contrast, inexperience in conducting negotiations and hearings or ignorance of the substantive or procedural law cannot be similarly overcome." Braun, The Settlement of Industrial Disputes, pp. 140, 141 (Philadelphia: Blakiston Co., 1944).

For a similar, more recent statement by the same author see Braun, Labor Disputes and Their Settlement, pp. 203-206 (Baltimore: Johns Hopkins Press, 1955).

In fairness it should be added that some very good labor dispute arbitrators have not had formal law training, but these will be found to have trained themselves in the relevant areas of law.

A. "Primary rules of interpretation" may be briefly summarized as follows:[15]

1. The common or normal meaning of language will be ascribed to the provisions of a contract unless circumstances show a special meaning is justified.

2. Where technical words have been used, they will normally be given the intended technical meaning unless it clearly appears by local usage or otherwise that a different intention was mutually agreed by the parties.

3. The entire agreement should be read as a whole, and every part of it interpreted with reference to all other parts. It should be so interpreted as to give effect to its entire general purpose, if possible.

4. Consideration should be given to the circumstances under which the writing was negotiated or made.

B. Certain rules of interpretation which are commonly designated "secondary" may be put as follows:[16]

1. An interpretation that gives reasonable, lawful, and effective meaning to all manifestations in the writing is preferred to an interpretation that leaves a part of such a manifestation unreasonable, unlawful, or of no effect.

2. The principal apparent purpose of the parties is given great weight in determining the meaning to be given to each manifestation of intention or to any part thereof.

3. Where an inconsistency is found between general provisions and specific provisions, the latter ordinarily qualify the meaning of the general provisions.

4. Words or other manifestations of intention that bear more than one reasonable meaning shall be interpreted more strongly against the party by whom they were written unless their use by him was required by law.

5. Written provisions inconsistent with printed provisions in the same agreement are preferred over the printed.

6. If public interest is affected, an interpretation favoring the public is preferred.

---

15 3 Williston on Contracts (Revised Ed.) § 618.
16 Restatement of the Law of Contracts, § 236 *et seq.*

In this connection it will be well to remember that the parol-evidence rule, which is not only a rule of evidence but also a rule of construction and interpretation, must always be considered and applied in these cases.[17]

As previously stated, custom is permissible to explain and to assist in interpretation of the meaning of words used in a contract. When custom is relied on, the evidence should establish it in the very broad sense and must further establish that the party against whom it is to be operative understood it and contracted in the light of such knowledge.[18]

An arbitrator can frequently get great assistance from the interpreting statements made by the parties themselves or from their conduct in rendering or receiving performance of the provisions of the agreement. It is fundamental that where the parties have concurred in a clear and undisputed interpretation of a contract over a substantial period, this conduct strongly supports the conclusion that such mutual interpretation was the intended interpretation of the parties as they negotiated and closed their agreement.[19]

SECTION 4

Past Practice

Past practice or usage is often an important factor in interpreting or determining the scope and meaning of a labor agreement. To be determinative on the rights of contending parties, a usage or customary "past practice" must be proven to have been such a long-continued, well-known and mutually concurred-in course of conduct that it is logical to conclude the parties in making their labor agreement did so upon the tacit assumption that this practice would continue on into and through the life of the contract.[20] Thus, an occasional or a few detached incidents, apparently accept-

---

17 3 Williston on Contracts (Revised Ed.) § 631.
18 Corbin on Contracts, § 557.
19 *Ibid*, § 558.
20 See 3 Williston on Contracts (Revised Ed.), §§ 629, 657, 660; Corbin on Contracts, §§ 34, 556-557; Restatement of the Law of Contracts, §§ 245-249; Garment Workers' Union v. Nazareth Mills Co., 22 LA 862 (Pa. Ct. of Common Pleas, 1954) ; West Pittston Iron Works Inc., 3 LA 137 (1944) .
See Chap. VI, Sec. 16 *supra*.

able to both parties, do not constitute a "past practice" that will govern the rights of the parties.[21] Neither does conduct, though long maintained, over the protests or challenges of the other party fall into that designation.

The kind of practice or conduct held to be equitably enforceable under this heading must not be such as one or the other of the parties is recognized as having the undisputed right to change at will. That is to say, the past practice of manufacturing by a certain process would not bind the company to continue using that process since it is always assumed to be within the discretion of management to make changes in respect to processes. On the other hand, the fact that the union in the past had always permitted members to pay their dues at the office of the union and never collected on premises of the employer should not exclude them from collecting at reasonable times and places at the place of employment. It is well established that all past practices that are inconsistent with or modified by a subsequent express agreement between the parties must give way to the terms of the contract.[22]

Arbitrators are frequently perplexed by contentions of "past practice" that are sustained only by evidence of such sporadic or isolated instances of occurrence that they can hardly be called "practices" at all. Moreover, a contending party may point to a practice of the past that it asserts should be continued, while the opposing party asserts that the practice was sporadic or occasional or always wholly within the discretion of the particular party against whom the practice is urged.

The quicksands in this area for the arbitrator are in the difficulties in ascertainment whether there indeed has been a consistent mutually agreeable past practice, and whether it has been a practice of such nature that it can be said to support the assumption that it would continue during the full period of the last negotiated agreement. Some of the "past practices" that have not been

---

21 To be binding, the past practice must be "consistent" and of a very substantial duration. See Aaron, "The Uses of the Past in Arbitration," in Arbitration Today, Proceedings of the Eighth Annual Meeting, National Academy of Arbitrators (Washington: BNA Books, 1955), pp. 1 et seq.

22 John Deere Des Moines Works, 22 LA 628 (1954); Moore v. United States, 196 U. S. 157 (1905); Barkhaus v. Producers' Fruit Co., 192 Cal. 200, 219 P. 435 (1923); Bethlehem Steel Co., 33 LA 367 (1959).

subject to unilateral change because tacitly assumed to have been a basis for contracting are:

1. Certain lines for promotion open only to specified employees for a period of several years.

2. A method of recall to work upon which the employees had come to rely.

3. A method of selecting and posting periods of vacation.

4. A time, place, and method of payment of wages.

5. A practice of job posting and bidding not made the subject of contract.

Numerous other examples appear in *Labor Arbitration Reports.*

Needless to say each case in this category must stand on its own feet. Evidence must be brought in to establish the continuity of the practice for such length of time and with such common knowledge about it that it is reasonable to assume the parties contracted on the assumption that it would continue.[23]

SECTION 5

Seniority and Ability

One of the most prized assets of employees today is the right to have their seniority considered in relation to relative claims for promotions, recalls from layoffs, shift preferences, vacation-time choices, and the like. Such rights exist, of course, only where secured by contract.[24] Contract clauses on this subject have consid-

---

[23] The key question is whether the parties contracted with reference to the past practice or usage assuming it would continue through the life of the agreement. This depends not upon the expressed assent to the retention of the usage, but rather upon the question whether on the facts each party had a justifiable belief that the other was adopting it. As between an employer and a union this may be much affected by prior grievances and negotiations. See Restatement of Law of Contracts §§ 247, 248 and Carlsten-Williams Co. v. Marshall Oil Co., 187 Ia. 80, 173 N.W. 903 (1919).

Compare Cox, "Arbitration in the Light of the Lincoln Mills Case," at pp. 24, 44-46 in Arbitration and the Law, Proceedings of the Twelfth Annual Meeting, National Academy of Arbitrators (Washington: BNA Books, 1959).

[24] For good discussion see Elder v. N.Y. Central R.R. Co., 152 F. 2d 361, 17 LRRM 631 (1945) ; Wagner v. Puget Sound Pwr. & Lt. Co., 41 Wash. 2d 306, 248 P. 2d 1084, 31 LRRM 2035 (1952) ; Rose v. Great Northern Ry., 151 F. Supp. 806, 40 LRRM 2218 (1957) .

erable variations, and are the subjects of many disputes. Some contracts provide for plant-wide seniority, others for departmental seniority, others for job seniority, either within the departments or plant-wide or company-wide; some provide for seniority by shifts. Combinations and variations of these general classes are numerous.[25]

The dispute may relate to the proper legal construction of the provision as related to a certain state of facts, or it may be the result of a claim that an employee's seniority right was violated when he was passed over for a promotion or was laid off out of turn. The company's usual defense to such a claim is the employee's asserted inferiority in skill and ability as compared with that of the junior employee who was given preference.[26]

Such complaints present very difficult problems for the arbitrator, especially where the contract, as it often does, provides that seniority shall prevail only where skill and ability are relatively equal as between the several employees.[27] The union will usually insist that the arbitrator decide whether the senior employee has skill and ability relatively equal to the junior who was given preference; the company will contend that the determination of such matter is a function of management, and that no arbitrator may substitute his uninformed opinion for the considered judgment of the foreman or superintendent who made the decision.[28] Arbitrators quite generally adopt a middle ground and hold that the decision of such a matter is one primarily for management, subject to being set aside only upon satisfactory proof that the decision was not a *bona fide* exercise of judgment and discretion but was

25 G. W. Taylor, "Seniority Concepts," at p. 127 in Arbitration Today, Proceedings of the Eighth Annual Meeting, National Academy of Arbitrators (Washington: BNA Books, 1955); Yoder, Personnel Management and Industrial Relations, pp. 461-465.

26 Jas. J. Healy, "The Factor of Ability in Labor Relations," at p. 45 in Arbitration Today, Proceedings of the Eighth Annual Meeting, National Academy of Arbitrators (Washington: BNA Books, 1955); Wayne E. Howard, "The Interpretation of Ability by Labor-Management Arbitrators," 14 Arbitration Journal 117 (1959); Bethlehem Steel Corp., 48 LA 190 (1967); U. S. Plywood-Champion Papers, Inc., 50 LA 507 (1968); Reliance Universal, Inc., 50 LA 397 (1968).

27 See General Box Co., 48 LA 530 (1967); DeKalb-Ogle Telephone Co., 50 LA 445 (1968).

28 See the majority and the dissenting opinions of National War Labor Board in matter of Johns-Manville Co., Case No. 111-2526-D, decided Feb. 15, 1944.

the result of bias, favoritism, anti-union prejudice, or such like matter, or was the result of a clear mistake.[29]

Another sometimes perplexing problem is presented when the agreement is uncertain in its failure to indicate clearly whether the seniority shall be plant-wide or on a departmental or job basis. Here the character of the business may furnish a determining index. If there are several jobs involving greatly varying skills in a situation where there is great likelihood that people of one skill may be needed at times when others are not, the conclusion that the seniority was intended to be on a departmental or skill classification basis may be justified. On the contrary, if there is virtually no work usually classified as skilled within the plant, the conclusion may well be that seniority should be recognized as on a plant-wide basis.[30] The intention of the parties is the controlling factor, and the terms of the agreement if reasonably clear should control. Otherwise, the nature of the business and past practice may furnish the guiding lights.

SECTION 6

Discipline and Discharge Cases

Perhaps the greatest single cause of disputes is the imposition of discipline — discharge or layoff.[31] The union may contend that the employee was not guilty, or that he was discriminated against in being disciplined when similar offenses by others went unnoticed, or that his punishment was more severe than justified.

Where the issue is guilt or innocence, the arbitrator will be faced with conflicting theories of his functions similar to those commented upon in connection with seniority. The union will insist that the arbitrator judge guilt or innocence as a judge or jury would do; the company will contend that the decision of manage-

---

29 James C. Hill, "Summary," at p. 44 in Management Rights and the Arbitration Process, Proceedings of the Ninth Annual Meeting, National Academy of Arbitrators (Washington: BNA Books, 1956).

30 See Bureau of Labor Statistics, Union Agreement Provisions, Bulletin 686, pp. 118, 120 (1942) and Bureau of Labor Statistics, Collective Bargaining Provisions etc., Bulletin 908-7, pp. 58-59 (1948).

31 This is recorded to be true by the American Arbitration Association's Annual Reports in 1966-1968. The same result is sustained by the Annual Reports of the Federal Mediation and Conciliation Service for the same years.

ment should not be disturbed in any case if made in good faith because such decisions are the function of management.[32]

Whether the arbitrator should substitute his judgment for that of management or should limit his inquiry to whether management acted honestly, without bias or prejudice, and without discrimination may well depend upon the nature of the case and the opportunities that the arbitrator has of obtaining the facts.[33] It may also be governed by the terms of the agreement of the parties. For example, if an employee has been discharged for stealing, and the evidence discloses that there is no dispute as to the essential facts, and those undisputed facts are such as would not in law justify conviction, most arbitrators would set the discharge aside no matter how great the good faith of the foreman or superintendent who had reached an unjustified conclusion from insufficient evidence.[34] On the other hand, if a craneman has smashed into a machine and been discharged for negligence, and the facts were investigated at once, the crane and machine examined on the spot, the witnesses immediately interviewed, and a decision made from first-hand knowledge thus gained, an arbitrator would risk doing a great injustice if he substituted his judgment, weeks or months later, for that of the foreman. He does not have the opportunity to judge the facts that the foreman had. Some evidence that the foreman had been guilty of prejudice, had not made a fair and complete investigation, or had made a very clear mistake, should be necessary in such case to justify a reversal. No rule or principle applicable to all cases can be laid down.[35]

Where guilt is admitted and the issue is as to the severity of the punishment, the guide to a correct decision will often be the proof of the penalty imposed in similar cases.[36]

---

[32] A. Howard Myers, "Concepts of Industrial Discipline" at pp. 59-83 in Management Rights and the Arbitration Process, Proceedings of the Ninth Annual Meeting, National Academy of Arbitrators (Washington: BNA Books, 1956).

[33] See Roland P. Wilder, Jr., "Discharge in the 'Law' of Arbitration," 20 Vanderbilt Law Rev., Dec. 1966, pp. 81-139, for a discussion of the factors used by the arbitrator in deciding a discharge case.

[34] See Owens-Corning Fiberglas Corp., 48 LA 1089 (1967); Thrifty Drug Stores Co., 50 LA 1253 (1968); Spartan Printing Co., 50 LA 1263 (1968).

[35] J. Fred Holly, "The Arbitration of Discharge Cases" at pp. 1-20 in Critical Issues in Labor Arbitration, Proceedings of the Tenth Annual Meeting, National Academy of Arbitrators (Washington: BNA Books, 1957).

[36] See Reynolds Electrical & Engineering Co., Inc., 50 LA 760 (1968); Eaton, Yale & Towne, Inc., 50 LA 517 (1968).

The practice, unfortunately rather prevalent, of rendering a decision that represents a compromise, should be avoided. Compromise has its place in negotiation and conciliation. But when the parties have exhausted those means and resort to arbitration, they want an honest decision, not a compromise.[37] If the facts disclose a case justifying discharge, a decision changing the discharge to a two-week layoff in an effort partially to satisfy one party without offending the other too greatly is not an honest award. And if the facts disclose that no penalty was called for, a decision to "save face" for management by a similar compromise is equally improper. A penalty should be modified only where the facts justify it — never for the purpose of compromise.[38] But where the evidence clearly indicates that justice requires a modification the arbitrator should not hesitate to award accordingly.[39]

SECTION 7

Working Conditions, Employee Classifications, Job Descriptions, and Job Rights

Workloads, rest periods, safety precautions, and similar working conditions form the subject of grievances that frequently go to arbitration.[40] They constitute collectively a most sensitive area of labor-management relations. Arbitration of the problems encompassed in this field at times requires a measure of technical knowledge of the industry concerned. Where the nature of the dispute

---

[37] "The principle of compromise has absolutely no place in an arbitration hearing. The moment an arbitrator compromises one of the issues involved in a case that moment he disqualifies himself as an arbitrator." — Senator Wayne Morse, in an address delivered April 6, 1940, before the Third Annual Convention of District 1, ILWU, at North Bend, Ore.

[38] Occasionally, however, the arbitrator will sense that the parties would be agreeable to a compromise in the interest of improving future relations. Discreet inquiry may then result in conciliation. Even so the parties may want the agreed-upon settlement put in the form of an award, with no suggestion in the formal opinion that it is an agreed-upon settlement.

[39] Note 35 *supra* and see Arthur M. Ross, "The Arbitration of Discharge Cases: What Happens after Reinstatement," at pp. 21-56 in Critical Issues in Labor Arbitration, Proceedings of the Tenth Annual Meeting, National Academy of Arbitrators (Washington: BNA Books, 1957).

[40] See James C. Phelps, "Management's Reserved Rights: An Industry View" and Arthur J. Goldberg, "Management's Reserved Rights: a Labor View" at pp. 102-148 in Management Rights and the Arbitration Process, Proceedings of the Ninth Annual Meeting, National Academy of Arbitrators (Washington: BNA Books, 1956).

and interests involved seemed to justify it, it is common practice today to bring in witnesses qualified by education and experience to testify upon such matters when they are in dispute. Experienced arbitrators have no difficulty with these questions when such evidence is supplied. In fact there has been such a volume of these issues in recent years that virtually all of the active labor arbitrators have valuable backgrounds of experience and knowledge concerning them.[41] If the contract does not so provide and the arbitrator feels it may be helpful in reaching a proper decision, he may well suggest that the parties incorporate into the submission agreement a provision authorizing him, if after examination of the evidence he deems it desirable, to call in a technician to make a study and advise him.[42]

In a great many industries, employees are divided into classifications usually designated by types of job names that relate those in such classifications to activities in certain skilled, semiskilled, or unskilled groups. For the purpose of arranging compensation on equitable levels, the jobs themselves (not the employees) are analyzed and evaluated and descriptions are written to indicate the general scope of duties required of those who will be assigned to do the designated jobs. Various systems or means have been used to survey, evaluate, and describe jobs. It is beyond the scope of this book to review these. One familiar method readily supplies all the illustration required here.

Under this well-known method, jobs are evaluated and "point rated." Thereafter, labor grades are assigned to jobs on the basis of the required characteristics and total points, and the employees are classified and paid accordingly.[43] In this process of job rating, certain weights or points are assigned to variations of required skill or experience, judgment, physical effort, responsibility, and working conditions. Sometimes other characteristics suitable to the particular industry are included. The measure of experience

---

41 This is attested by the statistics of the American Arbitration Association and Federal Mediation and Conciliation Service, see note 31 *supra*.

42 On use of experts and expert testimony, see Chap. VI, Section 14 *supra*, and on stipulation and waiver of direct evidence see Chap. VI, Sections 1 and 2.

43 An excellent and easy-to-read description of this method is "A Simplified Evaluation Plan for Manual Type Jobs," published by the Associated Industries of Missouri. See also Yoder on Personnel Management and Industrial Relations, pp. 101-129, 409-476.

required is carefully estimated or surveyed and points allotted according to predetermined skill-group patterns. The same process is followed in ascertaining points for the judgment factor. Here again four or five subdivision patterns of various point ratings are employed. The physical effort factor is observed and several grades or degrees are established to aid in determining whether little or very much physical effort is required. Again, points are assigned accordingly. The process is further followed in respect to the responsibility factor and the working-conditions factor. Job description sheets are worked out, points are ascribed to the various factors and when the points are totalled, the labor grade in which the job falls is designated by the total points and the compensation will be paid on the basis of the rate range applicable to the labor grade.

Disputes that arise in this area may involve a question in respect to any of the factors studied in respect to the job.[44] Evidence may be taken, for example, as to whether the physical-effort factor was correctly appraised in assigning points. At times an entire job description is attacked and in the light of all the evidence applicable the arbitrator must arrive at a conclusion whether additional points should be allowed.[45]

There are an increasing number of disputes involving fully automated or partially automated jobs that provide the arbitrator with various problems. A piece of automated equipment may be completely automatic in operation but require more extensive set-up work than the equipment it replaces. One job classification may be eliminated while the duties assigned to another classification are increased. The arbitrator may have to decide whether the change in duties caused by automation justifies an increase in the wage rate applied to a particular classification.[46] Sometimes an entirely new job classification is established that includes duties previously assigned to an eliminated classification. A dispute may arise over the amount of weight given to these duties in rating the

---

44 See Bethlehem Steel Corp., 49 LA 1014 (1967), where the ratings given seven factors in one job description were in dispute.

45 See Moloney Electric Co., 50 LA 927 (1967), where the union demanded revision of the entire job description, claiming the job had changed.

46 See Addressograph-Multigraph Corp., 46 LA 1189 (1966); Phoenix Closures, Inc., 49 LA 874 (1967).

new classification.[47] Whether or not a new job classification is within the bargaining unit has been a question for arbitration where automated equipment has caused the creation of a new job combining work associated with exempt technical personnel with functions previously performed by bargaining unit personnel.[48] If the collective bargaining agreement contains provisions relating to technological change, the arbitrator may be faced with a determination such as whether a new machine is within a provision that requires the employer to negotiate with the union over new wage rates when a new machine is installed that performs differently and has characteristics significantly different from machines in existing wage rate classifications.[49] Where there is similar automated equipment for which jobs have been rated, the arbitrator may be able to make a job-to-job comparison to determine whether a new job classification is required.[50]

The application of existing job evaluation plans designed for manual jobs to automated jobs present the arbitrator with special problems.[51] Automated jobs are frequently tension producing and require high degrees of attentiveness and alertness. The existing plan may not provide factors for measuring these parts of job content. Such jobs usually provide good working conditions, demand little physical effort and a relatively low degree of skill. Application of a plan placing emphasis on these latter factors can result in an unacceptably low rating for the automated job. On the other hand, automated equipment is usually expensive to acquire and repair and has a high production rate. These characteristics justify giving heavy weight to the responsibility factor. The operator of automated equipment may be required to intervene and control when something goes wrong, rather than merely to monitor. This possibility should be taken into consideration in assigning weight to the skill factor. The ultimate solution to these problems in job evaluation is the development of plans with special factors for automated equipment, but that is not the arbitrator's function. In

---

47 See Diamond Power Specialty Corp., 46 LA 295 (1966).
48 See Thompson Grinder Co., 50 LA 157 (1967).
49 See Lockheed-Georgia Co., 48 LA 518 (1967).
50 See E. W. Bliss Co., 50 LA 823 (1968).
51 See S. Herbert Unterberger, "Automation and Job Evaluation Techniques," at pp. 238 et seq., Labor Arbitration and Industrial Change, Proceedings of the Sixteenth Annual Meeting, National Academy of Arbitrators (Washington: BNA Books, 1963).

seeking an equitable result to a dispute in this area he must limit himself to an enlightened interpretation of the factors in the existing plan.

After a job name has been written and included in the list of jobs and a job description and job evaluation worked out, some unions and employees have contended that, on the basis of their contracts and traditional relationships with management and with each other, no man should be directed to do any work outside his own job description,[52] nor should he at any time be denied the right of doing all of the work within his job description even if that involves a callback for overtime.[53] These contentions are at times perplexing. If the contract is clear and definite that the claimant or claimants have the sole and exclusive right to render all the services within the scope of the classification or job description of the duties concerned, the decision will be free from difficulty.[54] Such easy matters, however, are not arbitrated. At times claims are made that certain work that the skilled or semiskilled worker himself associates with his job has been wrongfully or improperly done by a person in another classification. If the agreement is not specific as to the respective rights of the employer and of various workers, a perplexing issue may be presented.

In these cases, the arbitrator must study carefully the evidence as to past relationships and usages of the parties and the terms of the contract applicable between them. On the basis of such testimony, he must ascertain whether there has been an invasion of any employee's rights by having another employee do the work or some of the work the grievant usually has done. If this is found to be the case, an award should be made accordingly.[55] However, it should not be overlooked that in many situations job descriptions and job duties tend to overlap so that a job duty frequently done

---

52 See Lehigh Portland Cement Co., 47 LA 840 (1966).

53 See Carbide and Carbon Chemicals Co., 25 LA 857 (1956); Corn Products Refining Co., 21 LA 105 (1953); Nebraska Consol. Mills Co., Inc., 22 LA 785 (1954); National Rejectors, Inc., 48 LA 941 (1967); Adams Packing Assn., Inc., 50 LA 818 (1968).

54 See Fruehauf Corp., 46 LA 62 (1966); McCall Corp., 49 LA 183 (1967).

55 See as examples Bethlehem Steel Co., 21 LA 283 (1952); International Minerals and Chemical Corp., 22 LA 446 (1954); Continental Can Co., 22 LA 880 (1954); Kennecott Copper Corp., 25 LA 263 (1955).

by one man may well lie also in the job description of another.[56] It is regarded as clear, as indicated by books upon the subject and numerous decisions, that job descriptions as a rule are not intended to set forth complete and exhaustive listings of all job details and duties. They are intended only to mention enough of the characteristics of the job to identify in a general way the duties of the employee and the job to which he is assigned. Thus, he should usually expect to do at least some work not mentioned in his job description but which is incidental to it. On the other hand, there will ordinarily be a considerable number of duties indicated in the worker's job description that he will seldom, if ever, be required to perform.[57] Some job details or specific duties may appear on several different job descriptions or be necessarily incident to two or more jobs. Again, some details of skilled tradesmen's work is now done by "helpers" or other semiskilled or unskilled men. The propriety of all this will require full study of the agreement and past practices of the parties.

As above indicated, arbitration issues in this area involve contract interpretation, evidence as to correct and just surveys, job descriptions, and proof of usages in relation to job details and duties. The evidence on all these matters is sometimes rather voluminous. The parties should see that their contentions are well supported in detail by competent witnesses. The more information supplied to the arbitrator in cases in this category, the more likely he is to arrive at a correct conclusion.

SECTION 8

Incentive Systems

Much has been stated and written concerning arbitration of disputes that arise in relation to incentive plans and earnings. Incentive systems are numerous and varied. Among the more prominent may be mentioned the Taylor Differential Plan, the Halsey 50-Percent Premium Plan, the Rowan Premium Plan, the Gantt Task

---

56 See Dow Chemical Co., 22 LA 336 (1954); United States Steel Corp., 22 LA 157 (1953); Marblehead Lime Co., 48 LA 310 (1966); and Yoder, *op. cit.* pp. 107 *et seq.*

57 John Deere, Des Moines Works, 23 LA 206 (1954); Pilot Freight Carriers, 23 LA 520 (1954); Jones & Laughlin Steel Corp., 24 LA 650 (1955); Reynolds Metals Co., 25 LA 44 (1955); Victor Mfg. & Gasket Co., 48 LA 957 (1967).

and Bonus Plan, the Emerson Efficiency Plan, the Barth Premium Plan, the Knoeppel Bonus Plan, the Bedeaux Plan, the Merrick Piece-Rate Plan, the Ficker Plan, and the Baum Plan.[58] These are constructed upon five fundamental types of wage incentive plans that may be designated:

(1) Straight piecework.

(2) The 50-50 premium bonus plan (Halsey).

(3) The point plans (*e.g.*, the Bedeaux System).

(4) The hour-for-hour or 100-percent bonus plan.

(5) The measured-day work plan.

There are numerous variations and adaptations of these. If there is anything upon which the exponents of piecework plans appear to agree upon, it is that any such plan, to be successful, must be simple enough and clearly enough applied so that it can be fully and readily understood by the worker.[59] Certainly it may be concluded that all of the plans are readily understandable by reasonably qualified and experienced arbitrators who have had experience with various types of bonus and piecework systems.

The most frequently occurring dispute concerns whether the incentive plan has been fairly and properly applied to produce a fair and proper compensation rate for the job in dispute.[60] It may be contended that timing of certain elements has been omitted or that some elements have been mistimed. It may be argued that the basic timing was done while only exceptional or high-speed workers were on the job. Or it may be argued that, though the timing was done while ordinary workers were on the job, their efforts during the time study were discounted improperly, the true timing ignored, and a higher or "tight" timing set.[61]

---

58 For brief descriptions see Bloomfield, Financial Incentives, pp. 6, 32 *et seq.* and Louden, Wage Incentives, pp. 29, 46.

59 *Ibid.* See also Yoder, *op. cit.* at pp. 379-384, 390-401.

60 See Square D Co., 47 LA 383 (1966); Borg-Warner Corp., 49 LA 321 (1967).

61 See W. W. Waite, "Problems in the Arbitration of Wage Incentives," at pp. 25-44, in Arbitration Today, Proceedings of the Eighth Annual Meeting, National Academy of Arbitrators (Washington: BNA Books, 1955); also "Arbitration of Disputes Involving Incentive Problems," "An Industry View," by Owen Fairweather and "A Labor View," by Wm. Gomberg in Critical Issues in Labor Arbitration, Proceedings of the Tenth Annual Meeting, National Academy of Arbitrators (Washington: BNA Books, 1957).

After an incentive rate has been in effect for some time, a dispute may arise based on the claim that management has made one or more changes in the methods, machines, or materials to be used and that this has significantly changed the effort or speed of production required of the worker.[62] Again, it may be contended that the methods required by the company have never been properly described and timed on the basis understood by employees or employee representatives. Moreover, it may be argued in some instances that management has for a long time permitted a "short-cut" method of production that it now contends injures quality, and that it wishes now to reassert, inequitably to the workers, a slower method of production. In this case, the employer may claim that it was never aware the "short cut" had started until just before it was prohibited. Numerous other types of disputes will occur, prominent among which are the claims that management has changed the materials on which the work is to be done or has transferred the same to a less efficient machine.[63]

When any of the foregoing charges are made, the company's position will naturally be to contend that proper timing and proper standards were applied in calculating the rates to be paid and the materials are standard and have not been in any sense changed adversely to the operators. In a considerable number of instances, employee time-study representatives as well as those of the employer will have timed the work and the only difference in their results may be found to be on the basis of effort rating. If the company has given the effort rating a low figure, it likely will contend that when being timed the worker on the job was deliberately producing at a slow rate so as to bring about publication of an unduly high piecework rate. The union's time-study man and witness will probably contradict this. It will then be up to the arbitrator to consider the respective time studies and to weigh them in the light of all the evidence, such as similar production on similar machines in the factory or in other factories of the same company or some other company.[64] While this is a somewhat perplexing

---

62 See United States Steel Corp., 46 LA 660 (1966); Carrollton Manufacturing Co., 47 LA 1157 (1966).

63 See Waite, *op. cit.*; Fairweather, *op. cit.*; and Gomberg, *op. cit.*

64 See Brown & Sharpe Mfg. Co., 11 LA 228 (1948); Bethlehem Steel Co., 21 LA 378 (1953); Dayton Steel Foundry Co., 22 LA 450 (1954); Kaiser Steel Corp., 31 LA 447 (1958).

question, the arbitrator is seldom expected to take a stopwatch and make his own independent time study. The fact that in this direct conflict of evidence there may appear some difficulties in decision is not material. This is a familiar situation to any trier of facts, and it is up to him to reach his conclusion on the basis of the direct evidence and on the collateral factors on which he may rest his reasoning. At times a neutral expert is called in to make a study and to testify. This may be helpful, but the arbitrator must still weigh the evidence and bear the responsibility for the decision.[65]

It is not within the purpose of this book to set forth the characteristic details of the various piecework plans or systems. It should suffice to say that the ones mentioned in the foregoing have come to be well-known in American industry. They are all relatively familiar to all who have been arbitrators for any considerable time. On the whole, they are readily explainable and understandable so as to enable an experienced arbitrator to proceed with a proper decision on the evidence bearing upon them.[66]

SECTION 9
Distribution of Overtime Work

The Walsh-Healey Act,[67] which applies to work done under government supply contracts, requires premium pay at the rate of one and one-half times the basic rate for all work over eight hours in a day or 40 hours in a week, whichever is greater. The Fair Labor Standards Act[68] requires such premium for all work over 40 hours in any workweek. In addition many labor contracts provide premium pay for overtime work and for premium pay for work done on cer-

---

[65] See Discussion pp. 82-84 in Critical Issues in Labor Arbitration, Proceedings of the Tenth Annual Meeting, National Academy of Arbitrators (Washington: BNA Books, 1957).

[66] The Chairman of the Department of Business Economics and Industrial Engineering of the Illinois Institute of Technology, who is also an extensively experienced and qualified labor arbitrator, wrote, "Because of the foregoing facts, I suggest that management not include in their arbitration clauses the frequently encountered provision requiring that the arbitrator of incentive grievances be a qualified industrial engineer. Avoid the resultant search that leads round and round to nowhere." Pearce Davis at p. 83 *ibid.*

[67] 4 U.S.C.A. §§ 34-45.

[68] 29 U.S.C.A. §§ 201-219; see also 40 U.S.C. §§ 276a, *et seq.*, §§ 270 *et seq.* and §§ 321 *et seq.*

tain specified holidays. Many contracts also require that premium pay, time and a half or doubletime, be paid for work done on Saturdays and Sundays.[69] A tremendous number of disputes have arisen over the proper interpretation of these laws and contract provisions. An attempt to indicate in full the principles involved in these disputes in a work of this scope would be more misleading than helpful. It is sufficient to say that these controversies call for the highest type of legal analysis for their proper solution. For if an arbitrator should, through mistake of law, decide that a company need not pay the overtime wages required by the Fair Labor Standards Act, and the company should act upon that award, it would subject itself to severe penalties. The arbitrator's award would be no protection to it.[70]

It will be recalled that the basic theory on which "penalty pay" or "extra pay for overtime" was first rationalized was that it was intended to deter the employer from requiring employees to work undesirably long hours or on undesirable days. Without doubt, however, the 40-hour week of the Fair Labor Standards Act (Wage and Hour Act) was intended to shorten the workweek at the regular rate of pay and to exert pressure upon employers to put on swing shifts and to employ more people. In other words, it was at least in part a "make-work" provision passed when jobs were few and unemployment was great.[71]

Inconsistent with this basic theory concerning penalty overtime pay, numerous unions now are demanding that overtime work opportunities be equally divided among employees in a given department or a given classification. The theory seems to be not that the overtime is unwelcome and should be imposed equally among employees for that reason but, on the contrary, that the overtime-work opportunities are desirable and valuable and that each man should have his fair chance to get some of the extra earnings. In situations of this kind, there appear from time to time disputes as

---

69 See Seyfarth, Shaw, Fairweather and Geraldson, "Labor Relations and the Law in the United Kingdom and the United States," University of Michigan: Ann Arbor 1968, Chapter 20, and Collective Bargaining, Negotiations and Contracts (Washington: The Bureau of National Affairs, Inc.) .

70 See Fair Labor Standards Act, supra, §§ 15-17; Bay Ridge Operating Co. v. Aaron, et al., 334 U. S. 446, 8 W.H. Cases 20 (1948) .

71 See findings of Congress or preamble to the Fair Labor Standards Act, supra § 2.

to the liability of the employer for unworked overtime where the grievant-claimant was not called to take his overtime turn or for some other reason claims to have been denied his equal share of the premium overtime pay.[72]

The arbitrator's solution of these questions normally will lie in the past practice and in careful interpretation of the exact type of the labor agreement of the parties. Very few, if any, labor agreements state that overtime-work opportunities shall be equalized over definite and specific periods and that, failing this, the employer shall pay enough premium or penalty pay to those who did not get their share of overtime work during such periods as liquidated damages to equalize their pay with that of those who did. Again, few, if any, contracts clearly provide that, upon failure of the employer to equalize overtime, he shall be liable at any specified time for such payments as may be awarded by an arbitrator in the last step of the grievance machinery. In the absence of such provisions, the arbitrator must look to see whether there has been intentional or deliberate discrimination against men entitled to receive their share of overtime earnings, or whether they have been unfairly or negligently assigned to tasks that, by their operation, have caused them to lose permanently the special earnings in question so that they cannot be made up or equalized within a reasonable time.[73] An old aphorism is that: "The law abhors penalties." Courts generally refuse to enforce penalties between contracting parties even where contracts clearly provide for them.[74] However, if a "penalty" can be interpreted to mean liquidated damages, it will be enforced by the courts, but only to the extent of actual damages.[75]

---

[72] Auto-Lite Battery Corp., 21 LA 288 (1953); Celanese Corp. of America, 24 LA 168 (1954); Linde Air Products Co., 25 LA 799 (1956); Paragon Bridge & Steel Co., 48 LA 995 (1967); Sundstrand Corp., 48 LA 1022 (1967); Copper-Bessemer Corp., 50 LA 642 (1968).

[73] See Refinery Employees' Union of Lake Charles v. Continental Oil Co., 268 F. 2d 447, 44 LRRM 2388, 32 LA 813 (1959); Celanese Corp. of America, 24 LA 168 (1954); but see Eagle-Picher Co., 24 LA 196 (1955) and Food Machinery and Chemical Corp., 24 LA 717 (1955); Laughoff Grain Co., 46 LA 138 (1966); Mead Corp., 46 LA 641 (1966).

[74] See United States v. Bethlehem Steel Co., 205 U. S. 105 (1907); May v. Young, 125 Coun. 1, 2 A 2d 385 (1938); Stevenson v. Stoufer, 237 Iowa 513, 21 N.W. 2d 287 (1946); McMurray v. Faust, 224 Iowa 50, 276 N.W. 95 (1937) and 15 American Jurisp., Title "Damages," §§ 245-255.

[75] Ibid. See p. 17 McCormick on Damages, where that author suggests that "any wide disparity" between an arbitrator's award of damages and legal damages might cause a court to set the award aside.

In solving these overtime cases, the arbitrator must be watchful that he does not make a penalty award simply upon the theory that, unless he does so, there appears to be no immediate other relief available to the man who was not given his turn for overtime. Moreover, he should be sure there were actual damages. In a number of such cases, it has been held that the employee is entitled only to a later opportunity at overtime work to enable him to equalize his earnings with the other men in his group.[76] In other cases, arbitrators have required the employer to pay damages to equalize the earnings.[77] It is to be assumed that the usages and the contracts concerned in these cases were such that the arbitrators reasonably concluded that (1) they had the authority to award damages for the failure to call the employee in his turn or to give him his aliquot share of the overtime-work opportunities, (2) the pay so awarded did not exceed proper damages, and (3) the award did not amount to a penalty.[78]

SECTION 10
Paid Holidays and Paid Vacations

While a considerable number of disputes involving paid holidays and paid vacations go to arbitration, they nearly all turn on contract interpretations.

Holiday pay is often conditioned upon the employee's having been employed a certain length of time and also upon his having worked one or a certain number of consecutive work days prior to and after the holiday. Grievances in this area usually present a question of whether the employee worked the days in question

---

76 Supra, n. 73 and Robertshaw-Fulton Controls Co., 22 LA 144 (1953). Or the arbitrator may have concluded there were no actual damages suffered. A. O. Smith Corp., 33 LA 365 (1959); Evans Products Co., 48 LA 47 (1966).

77 Ingersoll-Rand Co., 7 LA 564, 570 (1947); Firestone Tire & Rubber Co., 9 LA 518 (1948); International Harvester Co., 9 LA 894 (1947); U. S. Rubber Co., 13 LA 839 (1949); Trailmobile Inc., 20 LA 488 (1953); Mississippi Aluminum Corp., 27 LA 625 (1956); International Paper Co., 31 LA 494 (1958); Sundstrand Corp., 48 LA 1022 (1967); Copper-Bessemer Corp., 50 LA 642 (1968).

78 Note 73 supra, Refinery Employees' Union of Lake Charles Area v. Continental Oil Co. This opinion would seem to limit the award of the arbitrator to not more than reasonable, liquidated damages where he is authorized to decide the damages question and exclude any damages award unless clearly within an arbitrational agreement. Petition for writ of certiorari denied on Nov. 16, 1959, 45 LRRM 2131.

and, if not, whether he had an excuse that is sufficiently meritorious that the failure to work should not operate against him.[79] Some employers take the position that no excuse should be accepted in these cases.[80] If the contract is sufficiently positive and specific that working a certain number of consecutive work days prior to the holiday is indispensably required to entitle one to holiday pay and that no excuses shall be acceptable for absences during such days, this must be the ruling of the arbitrator.[81] However, most contracts leave the arbitrator some margin of discretion in cases of this kind.[82] This he must exercise in the light of the evidence concerning the employer's past practice, and possibly testimony showing the industry and community practice, if it is thought to be relevant in the particular case.[83]

Vacation pay is another "fringe compensation." If an employee is otherwise qualified for vacation pay, he is normally entitled to it or a proportional share of it when, without his fault, and by action of the employer, he is deprived of the opportunity of working the necessary time to qualify for the entire pay.[84] However, where the contract is sufficiently definite and specific that no holiday pay shall be deemed earned or payable unless a minimum number of days have been worked during a specified year, the arbitrator must so hold.[85] If this appears to be somewhat unfortunate to the employee, it must be noted that the union can avoid this by bargaining away from such specific provisions of the contract and

---

79 American Chain & Cable Co., 21 LA 15 (1953); Crucible Steel Co., 21 LA 686 (1953); ITT Cannon Electric, 50 LA 861 (1968); Femco Inc., 50 LA 1146 (1968).

80 *Ibid.* See also Bethlehem Steel Co., 25 LA 680 (1955); American Can Co., 11 LA 405 (1948); Ford Motor Co., 11 LA 1181 (1948).

81 *Ibid.*

82 See Lake City Malleable, Inc., 25 LA 753 (1956); Bemis Bro. Bag Co., 25 LA 429 (1955).

83 Price-Pfister Brass Mfg. Co., 25 LA 398 (1955); Connecticut Valley Mfg. Co., 23 LA 476 (1954); ITT Cannon Electric, 50 LA 861 (1968).

84 American Zinc Co. of Illinois, 23 LA 86 (1954); Bachman Uxbridge Worsted Corp., 23 LA 596 (1954); Phelps Dodge Refining Corp., 25 LA 503 (1955) and Wauregan Mills, Inc., 31 LA 522 (1958). Where a contract provided for loss of vacation pay in case of justifiable discharge, the employees were held entitled to their earned vacation pay after the permanent closing of the factory since they were not terminated for cause due to fault on their part. Globe Corporation, 23 LA 298 (1954); Bachman Uxbridge Worsted Corp., *supra;* Matter of Rattray and Co., Inc., 144 N.Y.L.J. 17 (1960).

85 Chrysler Corp., 11 LA 1058 (1948); Lewis Knitting Co., 11 LA 1124 (1948); see also Martin Machine and Foundry Co., 23 LA 186 (1954).

by seeing to it that provision is made to protect proportional parts of vacation pay.[86]

SECTION 11

Retirement and Pensions

Until some 25 years ago, matters of retirement and pensions were largely dominated by unilateral decisions of employers. Many extensive retirement plans were set up by employers for the purpose of stabilizing employee groups. Some of these were without established reserves and were otherwise of dubious value.

Various statutory provisions now seek to establish security and stability for such plans and to require adequate reserves and suitable protection for them.[87] The great majority of pension programs are now the subject of collective bargaining agreements. Hence decisions in this area now are largely matters of new pension terms in labor agreements or interpretation of pension provisions agreed to by the employer and the union. In respect to the former, the awards show a tendency to "go along" with the practice of the industry in the particular time and place.[88] Some awards, however, have denied the demand for a retirement and pension plan, finding that the employer was not in a suitable financial condition to allow one.[89]

When a clear agreement is reached as to retirement, the employer apparently is entitled to enforce compulsory retirement unless the contract sets up a retirement board or some criteria to be applied as the result of medical examination or otherwise which will entitle the employee who has reached retirement age, but is still vigorous and physically able, to continue his employ-

---

[86] See Rib Mountain Granite Co., 21 LA 219 (1953) ; and American Zinc Co. of Illinois, note 84 *supra.*

[87] See Labor-Management Reporting and Disclosure Act of 1959, Sec. 2 (Act of Sept. 14, 1959, **P.L.** 86-257, 86th Congress, 1st Session), also see section 302 (c) (5) of Labor Management Relations Act, 1947 (Taft-Hartley) and Inland Steel Co. v. NLRB, 170 F. 2d 247, 22 LRRM 2506 (1948).

[88] Third Ave. Transit Corp. *et al.,* 1 LA 321 (1946) ; N.Y. City Omnibus Corp. *et al.,* 7 LA 794 (1947) ; Atlas Raincoat Mfg. Co., 25 LA 54 (1955) and Railroads v. Non-Operating Unions, 22 LA 392 (1954).

[89] Bay Cities Transit Co., 11 LA 747 (1948) ; Felters Co., 13 LA 702 (1949) ; and Bell Aircraft Corp., 13 LA 813 (1950).

ment.[90] It is clear beyond question that the layoff and discharge provisions of the contract do not apply to retirement.[91]

In this connection, the parties should bear in mind that the employer's traditional authority to terminate or retire employees continues to inhere in management unless modified by statute or by a contract. Hence, if the union would defeat a compulsory retirement, it must discover in the contract a clear and definite provision against the action of management.[92]

The employer, however, must follow a consistent policy regarding retirement.[93] If, for example, there has been a past practice of allowing employees to continue in employment beyond the age of 65 as long as physically able, and the employer announces that age 65 shall thereafter be the compulsory retirement age and that it will be retroactively applied to all employees above that age, this might be decided to be the introduction of a new condition of employment, i.e., a violation of a binding past practice.[94] Such result would be particularly true in a case where an employer should undertake to compel retirement of an employee who lacked only a short time of remaining service for qualifying for a company pension. A showing that other employees had been allowed to work to a similar or greater age and to qualify for the pension would usually be decisive against the employer.[95] Obviously, compelling retirement of an active and aggressive union officer, while permitting other employees of the same age and physical condition to continue working, would appear to be an unlawful discrimination.

---

[90] Lamon v. Georgia Southern and Florida Ry. Co., 212 Ga. 63, 90 S.E. 2d 658, 37 LRRM 2115 (1955) ; U. S. Steel Corp. v. Nichols, 229 F. 2d 396, 37 LRRM 2420 (1956) and General Aniline and Film Corp., 25 LA 50 (1955).

[91] International Minerals and Chemical Corp., 22 LA 732 (1954) and S. H. Kress & Co., 25 LA 77 (1955).

[92] Note 91 supra; Cook & Brown Lime Co., 50 LA 597 (1968).

[93] In re International Harvester Co., 24 LA 274 (1955) ; Hercules Powder Co., 23 LA 214 (1954) ; Pan American Airways, Inc., 13 LA 326 (1949) and Ohio Steel Foundry Co., 14 LA 490 (1950).

[94] Ford Motor Co., 20 LA 13 (1952), and see West Pittston Iron Works, Inc., 3 LA 137 (1944) ; Vulcan Radiator Co., 50 LA 90 (1968) ; Herman Nelson Div., 50 LA 1177 (1968).

[95] Notes 93 and 94 supra; Pullman Standard Car Mfg. Co., 24 LA 779 (1955).

SECTION 12

Jurisdictional Disputes

The words "jurisdictional dispute" have been used to refer to two situations: (1) where two unions or members of two unions are making rival claims for certain work, and (2) where two unions are seeking recognition for collective bargaining rights.[96] Where work alone is in dispute between members of two unions employed by the same employer, a likely result, prior to the Taft-Hartley Act, would have been a work stoppage and picketing by the union denied the work. At times, this picketing kept all men from the job and shut down entire plants or construction jobs.[97] The Taft-Hartley Act added to the National Labor Relations Act Section 8 (b) (4) (D),[98] making such jurisdictional strikes an unfair labor practice, and Section 10 (k),[99] directing the National Labor Relations Board "to hear and determine the dispute out of which such unfair labor practice shall have arisen, unless . . . the parties to such dispute submit to the Board satisfactory evidence that they have adjusted or agreed upon methods for the voluntary adjustment of, the dispute." In the *Plumbers and Pipefitters'* case[100] the Third Circuit construed Section 10 (k) as requiring the Board to make a final determination of which of the two unions is entitled to do the disputed work. The Second and Seventh Circuits construed the section the same way,[101] while the Fifth Circuit[102] accepted the Board's view that it had no duty under Section 10 (k) to make an affirmative award of the work between the employees of the competing unions. The U. S. Su-

---

96 See Gregory, "Labor and the Law," pp. 410-412 and John T. Dunlop, "The Arbitration of Jurisdictional Disputes in the Building Industry," pp. 161-165 in Arbitration Today, Proceedings of the Eighth Annual Meeting, National Academy of Arbitrators (Washington: BNA Books, 1955).

97 Irving Kovarsky, "The Jurisdictional Dispute," 42 Iowa Law Review 509 (1957); H. H. Rains, "Jurisdictional Dispute Settlements in the Building Trades," 8 Labor Law Journal 385 (1957).

98 29 U.S.C. § 158 (b) (4) (D). The National Labor Relations Act as amended deals with representation rivalries in § 8 (b) (4) (C), 29 U.S.C. § 158 (b) (4) (C).

99 29 U.S.C. § 160 (k).

100 NLRB v. United Assn. of Plumbers and Pipefitters, AFL, 242 F.2d 722 (1957); 5 U.C.L.A. Law Review 349 (1948) and 33 N.Y.U. Law Review 619 (1958).

101 NLRB v. Radio & Television Broadcast Engineers, 272 F.2d 713 (1959); NLRB v. United Brotherhood of Carpenters, 261 F.2d 166 (1958).

102 NLRB v. Local 450, International Union of Operating Engineers, 275 F.2d 413 (1960).

preme Court granted certiorari to the Second Circuit in *NLRB v. Radio and Television Broadcast Engineers*[103] and held that under Section 10 (k) "... it is the Board's responsibility and duty to decide which of two or more employee groups claiming the right to perform certain work tasks is right and then specifically to award such tasks in accordance with its decision."

Prior to their merger in 1955, both the AFL and the CIO had established certain "no-raiding" rules that were relatively successful in limiting jurisdictional conflicts. Among the objectives of that organization, as now consolidated, are (1) to prevent "raiding" by the affiliated organizations in situations where one union is seeking to replace another that has been recognized by the employer or certified by the National Labor Relations Board; (2) to prevent or settle disputes as to which of two or more unions is the appropriate one in an organizing situation; and (3) to maintain jurisdictional lines as established in union charters or by customs in the assignment of work, etc.[104] Since the AFL-CIO consolidation, raiding appears to have been reduced among the affiliated unions. A certain amount of competition, however, would seem to be inevitable among unions, some of which regard themselves as primarily craft unions and others of which are industrial organizations and hence include skilled craft members.[105]

The U. S. Supreme Court has supported arbitration as a method for the voluntary adjustment of work assignment disputes. In *Carey* v. *Westinghouse Corp.*[106] the Court held that an employer must arbitrate a work assignment dispute if requested to do so by one of the unions involved. Though recognizing that for the

---

[103] NLRB v. Radio and Television Broadcast Engineers, 364 U. S. 573, 81 S.Ct. 330, 47 LRRM 2332 (1961); James B. Atleson, "The NLRB and Jurisdictional Disputes: The Aftermath of CBS," 53 Georgetown Law Journal 93 (1964).

[104] See as to the period prior to 1955, Cole, "Arbitration of Jurisdictional Disputes," at pp. 149-151 in Arbitration Today, Proceedings of the Eighth Annual Meeting, National Academy of Arbitrators (Washington: BNA Books, 1955); also Feinsinger at pp. 156 *et seq.*; see for examples under the AFL-CIO Internal Disputes Plan; Electrical Workers, IBEW v. Machinists, 49 LA 1210 (1967); Retail Clerks v. Meat Cutters, 49 LA 707 (1967); IBEW v. Communication Workers, 50 LA 777 (1968).

[105] See John Hutchinson, "The Constitution and Government of the AFL-CIO," 46 Cal. Law Rev. 739, 758 (1958) and Upholsterers' Union v. Furniture Workers, 33 LA 376 (1959).

[106] Carey v. Westinghouse Corp., 375 U. S. 261, 84 S.Ct. 401, 55 LRRM 2042 (1964).

arbitrator's determination to be final the second union might have to intervene or be joined, the Court stated:

> "Yet the arbitration may as a practical matter end the controversy or put into movement forces that will resolve it. . . . since § 10 (k) not only tolerates but actively encourages voluntary settlements of work assignment controversies between unions, we conclude that grievance procedures pursued to arbitration further the policies of the Act."

The evidence to be observed by the arbitrator in cases of this kind should cover fully the nature and character of the two competing unions and the history or past practice of both unions in relation to the work and the interested employer. It should also fully show the business of the factory, warehouse, or store of the employer and all details concerning the nature of the disputed work.[107]

Section 704 (c) of the Labor-Management Reporting and Disclosure Act of 1959 added to the National Labor Relations Act a new Section 8 (b) (7) , making it, under specified circumstances, an unfair labor practice to picket with the object of forcing an employer to recognize or the employees to select the picketing organization as their bargaining representative unless currently certified as such. It seems possible that these provisions, coupled with the continued existence of several strong international craft- and industrial-type unions seeking members in the same or closely related areas of employment, may result in arbitration where competition for recognition rises as between AFL-CIO affiliates in the future.[108]

SECTION 13

"Subcontracting" or "Contracting Out"

"Subcontracting" or "contracting out" as used synonymously in labor relations means making an agreement to have another person (human or corporate) do construction, perform service,

---

107 Stewart Warner Corp., 22 LA 547 (1954) and Pennsylvania R.R. Co., 25 LA 352 (1955) .

108 The arbitration procedures for jurisdictional disputes which functioned for some time in both the AFL and the CIO before the 1955 consolidation seem to have pointed the way to this end. See pp. 149-165, Arbitration Today, Proceedings of the National Academy of Arbitrators (Washington: BNA Books, 1955) .

or manufacture or assemble products that could be performed by payroll, unit employees. The terms are at times misleadingly used to cover transferring work from unit to nonunit employees or to another plant of the employer. Strictly speaking, these last two meanings or uses of the term are inaccurate, but since the changes to which they apply have the effect of taking work from one group of employees and giving it to others, they are included in the area under discussion. Some awards have been made resting on the conclusion that such work was improperly taken from one worker or group and given to another.

Claims that work that should have been done by unit employees has been improperly subcontracted in violation of their rights have been urged when the labor agreement was in fact silent on the matter. These are, at times, rested on the contention that the employer has by recognizing the union (certified or otherwise) impliedly agreed that all normal, usual or regular work of the bargaining unit shall be done by members of the same. At times this contention has the support of a "joint-agreement" clause in which the employer has agreed it will change no work assignments without a "joint agreement" with the union. In some instances the contention is made that job descriptions and employee classifications are tantamount to an employer's undertaking that all work in such job descriptions shall be done only by unit employees. In some instances clauses intended only to exclude supervisory personnel from unit work have been unclearly stated so as to appear to exclude all people other than unit employees from work they have ordinarily done in the past. Such uncertainties, of course, require the reception of evidence to resolve ambiguity as to the mutual intention of the parties at the time the contract was made. This is, of course, consistent with the parol-evidence rule.

When the employer and the union have directly and clearly considered the question of "contracting out" they tend to agree along some four main classifications. These are:[109]

1. The company will *inform* the union of work contemplated

---

[109] Donald A. Crawford, "The Arbitration of Labor Disputes over Subcontracting," Challenges to Arbitration, Proceedings of the Thirteenth Annual Meeting, National Academy of Arbitrators (Washington: BNA Books, 1960) p. 51.

to be contracted out and *discuss* it with the union prior to completing the agreement concerning it.

2. The company agrees that, "no regular work shall be done
by any employee not covered by the contract except in emergencies or when work must be performed for which regular employees are not qualified."

3. The company will make "every reasonable effort" to use its
own working force and agents to avoid giving its work to outside
contractors, or "the company will use its own employees whenever possible."

4. The company will not contract out unit work when its own
employees are on layoff or when layoff or demotion of any of its
employees would result from the same.

Obviously these clauses do not free the disputed instances of
contracting out from problems. Facts must be found as to what
is included in "regular work," whether there was an emergency,
and whether employees claiming the work were qualified to do it.
These clauses also may at times demand some study of "reasonable effort," whether it was "possible" to use the regular working
force on the disputed work and whether they are entitled to do
it on the overtime-pay basis, if they cannot do it on straight time.[110]

Arbitrator Dash's opinion and award in *Celanese Corporation
of America and District 50*[111] contains a very interesting study and
effort to gain light by classifying and comparing the arbitrational
decisions in this area prior to that time (1960). The arbitrator
in that case observed that the "majority of courts" had ruled that
contracting out issues were nonarbitrable where there was no
express language to the contrary. He also declared that arbitrators
leaned strongly in favor of arbitrability in such cases where the
language was not clear. These attitudes, which no doubt affect
basic approaches, do not, without more, furnish complete bases

---

[110] A brief examination of the numerous subcontracting cases in the indices of
the Labor Arbitration Reports (The Bureau of National Affairs, Inc., Washington)
under "Job Protection," "Subcontracting" #117.38 and "Subjects for Arbitration,"
#94.166, will indicate the great variety of the contracting out clauses and requires
the conclusion that awards concerning them will have minimal value as precedents
or supporting authorities in other cases. They differ so greatly in phrasing and
facts that the "all fours" case seems nonexistent. Of course, some cases with useful
similarities can be found.

[111] Arbitrator Dash, 33 LA 925 (1960).

for decisions. Nor does the approval or disapproval of the residuum or reserved-rights theory.[112] Obviously, the application of the latter will lead to an interpretation of the agreement favoring management unless some provision against contracting out can be clearly found in it. On the other hand, it has been much contended by union spokesmen in numerous cases that the very existence of the collectively bargained agreement, from recognition clause to listing work classifications and job descriptions, is pregnant with implication that all production, maintenance, or even construction work needed by the employer in or around the plant concerned during the term of the contract shall be done by the unit employees. Arbitrators have been inclined to hold that work should not be so contracted out that the remaining portion of it, to be done by unit employees, shall be "arbitrarily or unreasonably" reduced.[113]

After the treatment of the subject of this chapter was presented in *Challenges to Arbitration*,[114] the *"Steelworkers' trilogy"* appeared on June 20, 1960.[115] Four years later *Fibreboard*[116] gave substantial treatment to the subject of subcontracting in connection with an NLRB decision on an unfair labor practice complaint. In the light of those factors, it now seems sound to conclude that the *Warrior and Gulf* decision of the trilogy appears to make almost any union claim against an employer's contracting out work potentially arbitrable. Subcontracting was arguably excluded from arbitration by the agreement in that case by the words "matters which are strictly a function of management shall not be subject to arbitration." However, questions concerning "con-

---

112 See James C. Phelps, "Managements Reserved Rights; an Industry View" from Management Rights and the Arbitration Process, Proceedings of the Ninth Annual Meeting, National Academy of Arbitrators (Washington: BNA Books, 1956), p. 106.

113 See Challenges to Arbitration, note 109 *supra*, at pp. 60-68. Several awards are here cited and in part quoted. See the quotations there from Arbitrator Milton Schmidt in Continental Can Co. and United Steelworkers of America, 7 B S A 4975 (1958) and compare A. B. Chance Company award, 38 LA 769 (1958) by Arbitrator Clarence Updegraff.

114 Note 109 *supra*.

115 United Steelworkers of America v. America Mfg. Co., 363 U.S. 564, 80 S.Ct. 1343, 46 LRRM 2414 (1960); United Steelworkers of America v. Warrior & Gulf Navigation Co., 363 U.S. 574, 80 S.Ct. 1347, 46 LRRM 2416 (1960); United Steelworkers of America v. Enterprise Wheel & Car Corp., 363 U.S. 593; 80 S.Ct. 1358, 46 LRRM 2423 (1960).

116 379 U.S. 203; 57 LRRM 2609 (1964).

tracting out" were then, with numerous other matters, swept wholesale into the area of arbitration and the range of arbitrators' awards by a provision in the agreement that if "any local trouble of any kind" shall arise, it shall be subject to grievance procedure. The breadth of this provision was expressly relied on for the conclusion of the Court.

Fibreboard indicates that when to attain economy, an employer contracts out work that has been done by unit employees, terminates employees, thus reducing payroll and fringe benefit expenses, and evades or refuses to bargain on the matter with the union, such conduct amounts to an unfair labor practice. In this opinion the U. S. Supreme Court quoted from *Warrior and Gulf* to the effect that "Contracting out work is the basis of many grievances; and that type of claim is grist in the mills of the arbitrators." [117]

The employer company was required to restore the work to the payroll unit, to rehire the terminated employees, and to pay their lost wages.

From *Fibreboard*,[118] therefore, it appears that when work that has been for a time regularly done by unit employees is considered for "contracting out" the subject is a "condition of employment." Since it is such, the parties must recognize it as a mandatory subject for collective bargaining. However, even though that is true, it is not required that the parties bargain or arbitrate concerning it during the term of an agreement if they have discussed it and rejected it or included it in some way during the bargaining that led to the unexpired agreement.[119] In such case the parties are not required to arbitrate any phase of such subject during the current agreement unless it is included in the grievance-arbitration provision of the then contract. However, it should not be forgotten that in *Warrior and Gulf Navigation Company*[120] the U. S. Supreme Court held that "contracting out" was arbitrable under the general provision that the parties would apply the

---

[117] Steelworkers v. Warrior & Gulf Navigation Co., 363 U.S. 574, 80 S.Ct. 1347, 46 LRRM 2416 (1960).

[118] Note 116 *supra*.

[119] See Westinghouse Salaried Employees Assoc. v. Westinghouse Electric Corp., 217 F. Supp. 622, 53 LRRM 2204 (D.C. Pa., 1963); and NLRB v. Jacobs Mfg. Co., 196 F.2d 680, 30 LRRM 2098 (1952). Compare Independent Petroleum Workers of America v. American Oil Co., 324 F.2d 903, 52 LRRM 2678 (C.A. 7, 1963).

[120] Note 115 *supra*.

contract grievance procedure to "any local trouble of any kind." Hence, it may be inferred that even during the period of a collective agreement when the parties are not expressly bound to bargain concerning "contracting out," if the subject arises within the terms of a broad grievance and arbitration provision, it would seem to be arbitrable and call for the utmost care of the arbitrator to be sure he is informed on all relevant facts bearing upon his award.

We thus are confronted with several clear guidance factors for the arbitrator. Those may be expressed briefly thus:

1. The arbitrator, at all events, must stay within the authority given him by the mutual action of the parties.

2. He must be aware that the union is legitimately seeking to protect jobs of its members by a logical contention that a contract with employees, assuming obvious consequences of their bargaining rights, implies an obligation to employ them for the "regular" or "usual" work then in contemplation of the union and the employer representatives. Hence, any subcontracting which unreasonably reduces such available employment should not be approved without clear authority for it.

3. The arbitrator must bear in mind that the employer must have the necessary managerial discretion to operate the business with reasonable chances of success, and to deny it necessary and reasonable subcontracting rights will be impractical as well as probably uncontemplated at the time of contracting. Contracts are usually held to be binding only in respect to matters in contemplation of the parties when the contract is made.

4. An award of all-inclusive type, either for or against contracting out, will be unrealistic. Hence, the exact subject and nature of the contracting out work clearly before the arbitrator must be considered and decided.

5. The award should not unreasonably reduce the workload available to the unit nor unreasonably constrict managerial discretion unless one of such courses is necessary and there is clear authority for such an award.

6. As bearing upon factor 5 above, the arbitrator must consider: the terms and implications of the contract; the nature and customs of the business; the past practice (if any gives light on the issue); and the foreseeable consequences of the decision, whether reasonable or unreasonable, in their impact upon either party. If the parties do not offer evidence upon these subjects, the arbitrator should ask for it and explain its importance.

If possible the arbitrator should be sure that his award will not unreasonably impair any essential purpose of the labor agreement. The work-protection clauses in labor agreements are almost infinite in the variety of their wording. To the extent these have bearing upon the claims of the parties and the resulting authority of the arbitrator, they must be studied and respected. These cases are of great importance to the parties, as is evidenced by their inherent nature and by the great number of them that have occurred in recent years.

CHAPTER X

JUDICIAL ENFORCEMENT OF CONTRACTS TO ARBITRATE

SECTION 1

Background — Aftermath of *Textile Workers* v. *Lincoln Mills*

It was generally recognized under common law and in the absence of statutes, that an agreement to arbitrate was not enforceable by the courts until completed by a valid award.[1] The party revoking was simply liable in damages to the other party to the extent that damages could be proved.[2] The substantial rights and liabilities of the parties respecting present or prospective questions in dispute were not affected. The courts would take jurisdiction of the matter in dispute irrespective of the agreement to arbitrate. This was true both in the law courts and in equity, and in the latter specific performance of the contract to arbirate would not be decreed.[3] Courts have at times decided that where a preliminary question of fact is, by agreement of the parties, to be submitted to arbitration prior to suit, the courts would not entertain an action upon the main contract until the arbitration or appraisal, as the case may be, had been completed.[4]

---

[1] W. H. Blodgett Co. v. Bebe Co., 190 Cal. 665, 214 Pac. 38 (1923); Oskaloosa Sav. Bank v. Mahaska County State Bank, 205 Iowa 1351, 219 N.W. 530 (1928); Continental Ins. Co. v. Vallandingham, 116 Ky. 287, 76 S.W. 22, 105 Am. St. Rep. 218 (1903); Re Lower Baraboo River Drainage Dist., 199 Wis. 230, 225 N.W. 331 (1929); United Electrical, Radio and Machine Workers v. Allen-Bradley Co., 259 Wis. 609, 49 N.W. (2d) 720, 17 LA 429 (1951).

[2] Red Cross Line v. Atlantic Fruit Co., 264 U.S. 109, 68 L. Ed. 582, 44 S. Ct. 274 (1924); Goerke Kirch Co. v. Goerke Kirch Holding Co., 118 N.J. Eq. 1, 176 A. 902 (1935); Mentz v. Armenia Fire Ins. Co., 79 Pa. 478, 21 Am. Rep. 80 (1875); Martin v. Vansant, 99 Wash. 106, 168 Pac. 990 (1917).

[3] Goerke Kirch Co. v. Goerke Kirch Holding Co., 118 N.J. Eq. 1, 176 A. 902 (1935); People ex rel. Union Ins. Co. v. Nash, 111 N.Y. 310, 18 N.E. 630, 7 Am. St. Rep. 747 (1888); Kaufmann v. Liggett, 209 Pa. 87, 58 A. 129, 103 Am. St. Rep. 988 (1904).

[4] W. H. Blodgett Co. v. Bebe Co., 190 Cal. 665, 214 Pac. 38 (1923); Dunton v. Westchester Fire Ins. Co., 104 Me. 372, 71 A. 1037 (1909); Hutchinson v. Liverpool & London & Globe Ins. Co., 153 Mass. 143, 26 N.E. 439 (1891); Chadwick v. Phoenix Acci. & Sick Ben. Assoc., 143 Mich. 481, 106 N.W. 1122 (1906).

This might well apply to certain types of labor contracts. For example, it might be agreed that disputed classifications of certain men are by a grievance to be made the subject of arbitration. If an effort then was made in court to establish that the same workmen were improperly classified and therefore underpaid, and a judgment sought for the alleged underpayment, the same process of reasoning might be expected to lead the court to rule that the matter of personnel classification would have to go to arbitration before the court would proceed. Except under statute, however, state courts do not ordinarily decree specific performance of arbitrational agreements. Nor will they refuse to proceed prior to arbitration where the agreement to arbitrate is purely collateral and cannot be construed as a condition precedent to the right to maintain an action.[5] This has been held to be true in the federal as well as in the state courts.[6] If the parties are proceeding in arbitration as the result of an order or rule of court, however, the submission agreement is enforceable and they are generally required to proceed to the attainment of an award which will bind them, despite the effort of one party to avoid it and to appeal directly for a court judgment.

Much fluidity in respect to what formerly might have been considered the settled law set forth in this chapter has been injected by the much-discussed United States Supreme Court decision of *Textile Workers Union* v. *Lincoln Mills Inc. of Alabama* and the expanding importance of the preemption doctrine as applied to federal labor legislation. These are discussed in Chapter I, Section 3, and Chapter II, Section 2, *supra*. The *Lincoln Mills* decision held that the undertaking to arbitrate disputes affecting commerce that might in the future arise under a labor agreement is specifically enforceable when such a dispute arises. This conclusion was rested upon the view that the union and employees have agreed not to strike during the term of the agreement and hence must be held entitled to enforce the alternative

---

5 Hamilton v. Home Ins. Co., 137 U. S. 370, 34 L. Ed. 708, 11 S. Ct. 133 (1890); Crescent Stave Co. v. Brown, 181 Ky. 787, 205 S.W. 937 (1918); Fox Film Co. v. Ogden Theatre Co., 82 Utah 279, 17 Pac. (2d) 294 (1933); Kohlsaat v. Main Island Creek Coal Co., 90 W.V. 656, 112 S.E. 213 (1922).

6 Shanferoke Coal & Supply Corp. v. Westchester Serv. Corp., 293 U. S. 449, 79 L.Ed. 583, 55 S.Ct. 313 (1935); Marine Transit Corp. v. Dreyfus, 284 U. S. 263, 76 L. Ed. 282, 52 S. Ct. 166 (1932); Red Cross Line v. Atlantic Fruit Co., 264 U. S. 109, 68 L. Ed. 582, 44 S. Ct. 274 (1924).

method of resolving disputes, *i.e.,* arbitration. The Court indicated it approved and accepted a mandate from Congress to fashion the necessary rules of law to implement this authority, which it inferred from Section 301 of the Taft-Hartley Act.

It is important to reemphasize here the words of the Court quoted from *American Manufacturing Company* in Chapter I, Section 3, to the effect that the function of a court on a question of enforcing an arbitrational agreement is to ascertain whether the contract *prima facie* includes for arbitration the claim for which that procedure is sought. It must *not* undertake to decide whether the claimant's contract interpretation is correct or otherwise. That opinion clearly states that the court must not, by undertaking decision on such question, deprive the moving party of an arbitrational judgment for which both parties to the controversy bargained and agreed should be final.

This decision and many which followed in its wake have all but cancelled the effect which the *"Cutler-Hammer* doctrine" once threatened to have. Indeed that decision has been clearly abrogated by statute in the state where it was decided.[7] Recent decisions have "lined up" with this view. If the parties have agreed to arbitrate a question, the conclusions concerning it and the award must come from an arbitrator and should not be made by a judge no matter how little merit he may believe the contentions of one party may have.

Many court decisions of both state and federal courts have directed parties to proceed to and through arbitration. These have been mentioned with the *Avco* decision herein in the Preface of this edition and in Chapter II, Section 3 hereof. As those comments indicated, it remains to be learned from future decisions whether agreements to arbitrate, with an implied[8] or express agreement against strikes and lockouts, may be enforced or whether a petition and prayer for obedience to an agreement to arbitrate since *Avco* must be presented without a request for relief by injunction in deference to the Norris-LaGuardia Act. (See note herein in Preface to Third Edition and in Chapter II, Section 2,

---

7 McKinney's Consol. Laws of New York, Book 7B, Civil Practice Law and Rules § 7501.

8 Local 174 Teamsters v. Lucas Flour Co., 369 U. S. 95, 49 LRRM 2717 (1965).

at note 153.) Aside from the conclusion that section 301 of the LMRA did not by implication modify Norris-LaGuardia so as to validate injunctions against strikes in breach of contracts, the view seems to be established that both state and federal courts may decree that parties who have agreed to arbitrate are required to do so.

It is interesting to reflect in view of the later *Avco* (1968) decision that the U. S. Supreme Court has held that a serious breach of a no-strike clause does not extinguish a union's right to arbitration of the discharge of the strikers.[9] Thus the no-strike clause is largely denuded of worth to the employer. It seems paradoxical to say now that the union surrendered its right to strike to gain arbitrational rights (*Textile* case, etc.) yet may enjoy the arbitrational rights despite breach of the no-strike covenant.

Moving of plants and corporate mergers do not necessarily terminate or keep alive the obligation to arbitrate.[10] But this result may follow where the merging companies have collective bargaining relations with different unions.[11] Broad arbitration clauses should be avoided lest at times startling results may follow in the form of an equally broad order to proceed to arbitration upon some question not in contemplation of both parties when they executed their contract. An arbitrator has been authorized to write a health and welfare trust plan.[12] A subcontracting dispute has been ordered to arbitration where the contract contained no restriction against it but did state that it settled all bargainable issues.[13] In other cases, subcontracting issues were held nonarbitrable where the parties had agreed to arbitrate "alleged violations of the terms of this agreement" and the agreement was silent on

[9] Packinghouse Workers, Local 721 v. Needham Packing Co., 376 U. S. 247, 84 S.Ct. 773, 55 LRRM 2580 (1964).

[10] Wiley & Sons v. Livingston, 376 U.S. 543, 84 S.Ct. 909, 55 LRRM 2769 (1964); Steelworkers v. Reliance Universal Inc., 335 F. 2d 891, 56 LRRM 2046 (CA 3, 1964); Carpenters' Local 2549 v. Kimball Co., 379 U. S. 357, 85 S.Ct. 441, 57 LRRM 2628 (1964).

[11] McGuire v. Humble Oil & Refining Co., 335 F. 2d 352, 61 LRRM 2410 (CA 2, 1966), *cert. den.* 384 U. S. 988, 62 LRRM 2339 (1966).

[12] Builders Assn. of Kansas City v. Hod Carriers, 326 F. 2d 867, 55 LRRM 2199 (CA 8, 1964), *cert. den.* 377 U. S. 917, 56 LRRM 2289 (1964).

[13] Electrical, Radio & Machine Workers v. General Electric Co., 332 F. 2d 485, 56 LRRM 2289 (CA 2, 1964).

the subject of contracting out work.[14] A court has refused to order arbitration of a new contract under an arbitration clause of one which had expired.[15] But it has been held that a union that has lost an election was entitled to complete arbitration of a grievance filed before the election.[16]

An order to proceed to arbitration has been made despite the fact unfair labor practice charges were pending on the same subject.[17] But it has been held that after a trial examiner had ruled against it on an unfair labor practice charge, a union was not entitled to arbitration.[18]

But in another case, where the matter arose before there was a decision on a complaint, the Board dismissed the complaint on the ground that the issue presented was within the arbitrational agreement of the parties and no effort had been made by the union to apply it before filing the charge. It was clearly indicated that where arbitration has been agreed on and there is no reason to believe such procedure will not be just and fair, it should be pursued instead of adding another unnecessary dispute to the crowded docket of the Board. The decision and order stated in that case:[19]

> . . ."the contract established grievance and arbitration machinery to handle matters involving, as this did, interpretation and administration of the contract. In this instance, however, the Union made no attempt to utilize such grievance and arbitration machinery, but instead filed the charge upon which the complaint herein is based. . . ."In view of this background of a peaceful and what appears to be a wholly salutary employer-employee relationship, we are reluctant to issue a remedial collective bargaining order as a result of the

---

14 Assn. of Westinghouse Salaried Employees v. Westinghouse Electric Corp., 217 F. Supp. 622, 53 LRRM 2204 (D.C. Pa., 1963); and Independent Petroleum Workers v. American Oil Co., 324 F. 2d 903, 54 LRRM 2598 (CA 7, 1963).

15 Mo., Kans. & Okla. Transit Lines v. Street, Elect. Ry. and Motor Coach Employees, Division 892, 319 F. 2d 488, 53 LRRM 2662, cert. den. 375 U. S. 944, 54 LRRM 2715 (1963).

16 United Electrical Workers (U.E.) v. Star Expansion Industries, Inc., 246 F. Supp. 400, 56 LRRM 2286 (D.C. N.Y., 1964).

17 Steelworkers v. American International Aluminum Corp., 334 F. 2d 147, 56 LRRM 2682 (1964), cert. den., 379 U. S. 991, 85 S.Ct. 702, 58 LRRM 2256 (1965).

18 Kentile v. Rubber Workers, Local 457, 228 F. Supp. 541, 55 LRRM 3011 (D.C. N.Y., 1964).

See excellent articles in The Arbitrator, the NLRB, and the Courts, Proceedings of the Twentieth Annual Meeting, National Academy of Arbitrators (Washington: BNA Books, 1967).

19 Crown Zellerbach Corporation and International Woodworkers of America, 95 NLRB 753, 28 LRRM 1357 (1951).

Respondent's isolated unilateral action. Particularly is this so since the parties have failed to utilize the contractual procedures established for bargaining concerning the interpretation and administration of their contract, and where there is apparently no serious obstacle to an amicable settlement of the issue through bargaining within the framework provided in that contract. Indeed, the Board has frequently stated that the stability of labor relations which the statute seeks to accomplish through the encouragement of the collective bargaining process ultimately depends upon the channelization of the collective bargaining relationship within the procedures of a collective bargaining agreement. By encouraging the utilization of such procedures in this case, we believe that statutory policy will best be effectuated. Affirmative Board action would on the other hand put the Board in the position of policing collective bargaining agreements, a role we are unwilling to assume. Accordingly, we shall dismiss the complaint without determining whether the Respondent's conduct would, under other circumstances, warrant the issuance of a remedial order."

It is the practice of the NLRB to study the type of dispute, evidence, and award in matters which come before it and to honor the award if it appears to be consistent with federal policy as applied by the Board and to reject it otherwise.[20]

A suit of an individual union member against an employer was sustained where the employer had obtained a stay in a suit to compel arbitration then (apparently with concurrence of the union) had refused to arbitrate.[21]

Courts have recognized the legal propriety of arbitration in work-assignment matters. But it is clear that where the NLRB has jurisdiction in such a dispute, it has authority to decide and to exclude an arbitrational decision.[22] The availability of an ordinary action or suit arising out of an alleged breach of contract to arbitrate unfair labor practice conduct cannot be used to ex-

---

20 See Marlboro Cotton Mills, 53 NLRB 965, 13 LRRM 142 (1943); Midland Broadcasting Co., 93 NLRB 455, 27 LRRM 1404 (1951); Honolulu Star-Bulletin, Ltd., 123 NLRB 395, 43 LRRM 1449 (1959); Howard Electric Co., 166 NLRB 62, 65 LRRM 1577 (1967). The Spielberg Mfg. Co. case, 112 NLRB 1080, 36 LRRM 1152 (1955) is frequently referred to and the criteria for valid awards therein set forth and applied. Numerous other Board decisions apply this policy.

21 Zuber v. Commodore Pharmacy, 262 N.Y.S. (2d) 155, 60 LRRM 2007 (N.Y. S. Ct., App. Div., 1965).

22 New Orleans Typographical Union v. NLRB, 368 F. 2d 755, 63 LRRM 2467 (CA 5, 1966); Carey v. Westinghouse Elect. Corp., 375 U. S. 261, 84 Sup. Ct. 401, 55 LRRM 2042 (1964).

clude such charges from coming before the NLRB.[23] But an arbitrational award properly issued on a seniority question does bar an employee's damage suit against the employer for alleged disregard of seniority rights.[24]

The historic technical legal view that the agreement to arbitrate a future dispute was against public policy, discussed herein at Chapter I, Section 1, has little or no modern practical effect. It has given way to modern statutes that recognize arbitration as a sound, legitimate way of resolving disputes. In any case where interstate commerce is concerned, the federal statutes and decisions assure enforcement of legitimate claims for arbitrational procedure. In the rare cases where interstate commerce is not involved it seems unlikely that the courts of any state would all lack authority, under present statutes and decisions, to decree specific performance of the arbitrational agreement. (See Appendix herein for citations to state statutes.)

Indeed the great number of arbitrational clauses in collectively bargained labor agreements, and the proven suitability of the arbitrational process for solving labor disputes, give strong support to the conclusion that when arbitration is refused in breach of contract in this age, it very likely can be and will be specifically enforced by a court.

The crowded dockets of the courts have made arbitration to them a welcome form of relief where suitable. It remains, however, to note that the breadth and scope of arbitrators' decisional authority is controlled by the terms of the contract to arbitrate and the submission agreement. Consequently a damage suit may be stayed when the defendant insists on its right to arbitrate.[25] Of course, a stay will be refused if arbitration is legally unsuitable either because of the fact the arbitration agreement does not include the matter in dispute, damages for breach of no-strike clause, or because the subject is one for which the court does not have jurisdiction under the applicable statute.[26]

---

[23] Machinists Lodge #743 v. United Aircraft Corp., 332 F. 2d 784, 56 LRRM 2416 (CA 2, 1964), cert. den. 380 U. S. 910, 58 LRRM 2496 (1965).

[24] Panza v. Armco Steel Corp., 316 F. 2d 69, 52 LRRM 2749 (CA 3, 1963), cert. den. 375 U. S. 897, 54 LRRM 2393 (1963).

[25] Wilson Bros. v. Textile Workers, TWUA, 132 F. Supp. 163, 35 LRRM 2508 (D.C. N.Y., 1954).

[26] United Electrical Radio and Machine Workers of America Local 146 v. Miller Metal Products, Inc., 215 F. 2d 221, 34 LRRM 2731 (CA 4, 1954).

In respect to the issue of arbitrability, the parties are at times at odds as to whether one party is not seeking to obtain by means of arbitration some concession previously discussed by them at the last bargaining period and by mutual agreement left out of the agreement at that time. Such a matter is excluded from bargaining until the then present contract comes to an end.[27] On this type of issue the bargaining history may be very helpful if not indeed decisive. The parol-evidence rule may require disregard of evidence as to any prior or contemporaneous agreement urged as modifying the integrated agreement, but if there is found to exist an ambiguity in the agreement to arbitrate, (or deceit or mutual mistake in the bargaining) the legitimate conclusion may be that the parties omitted coverage of the issue in dispute in their agreement because they intended to reserve it for arbitration as one party now contends.[28]

To some degree, with some details yet to be determined, Section 701 of the Labor-Management Reporting and Disclosures Act of 1959 has returned an area of jurisdiction over labor disputes affecting commerce to the states. This consists of disputes rejected by the National Labor Relations Board under its jurisdictional standards in effect on August 1, 1959, as shown in Chapter II, Section 3, note 162. In respect to disputes concerning any matters so returned to the jurisdiction of state courts, the state rules concerning enforceability and nonenforceability of contracts to arbitrate may be expected to continue, at least for some time, with much the same effects as in the immediate past. The practical truth is that in an overwhelmingly great number of cases the parties now proceed unhesitatingly to arbitration. Consequently the remaining cases are few in number, though, of course, some of them are very important. The *Lincoln Mills* decision does not

---

27 NLRB v. Jacobs Manufacturing Co., 196 F. 2d 680, 30 LRRM 2098 (1952).

28 Holding such evidence admissible are Pacific N.W. Bell Tel. Co. v. Communications Workers of America, 310 F. 2d 244, 51 LRRM 2405 (CA 9, 1962); Independent Petroleum Workers of America v. American Oil Co., 324 F. 2d 903, 54 LRRM 2598 (CA 7, 1963), *affd.* 379 U. S. 130, 57 LRRM 2512 (1964). Genl. Teamsters, Chauffeurs and Helpers Union v. Blue Cab Co., 353 F. 2d 687, 60 LRRM 2491 (CA 7, 1965).

Excluding such evidence were Electrical, Radio & Machine Workers v. General Electric Co., 332 F. 2d 485, 56 LRRM 2289 (CA 2, 1964) and Assn. of Westinghouse Salaried Employees v. Westinghouse Elect. Corp., 283 F. 2d 93, 46 LRRM 3084 (CA 3, 1960); A. S. Abell Co. v. Baltimore Typographical Union No. 12, 338 F. 2d 190, 57 LRRM 2480 (CA 4, 1964).

eliminate the importance of the states as to enforcement of arbitration, but it has clearly furnished a strong impetus of acceptability and enforceability as far as the numerous matters within the federal jurisdiction are concerned.

SECTION 2

Law Applicable to Determine Validity

Arbitration agreements generally have been held to deal with remedies rather than with substantive rights. The validity of and any other question in respect to the agreement therefore, have been dealt with under the law of the state of the court having jurisdiction over any law suit that may arise therefrom.[29] These determinations are not governed by the law of the state in which the contract was made. Nor is the law of the state in which the contract is or was to have been performed applicable. It may be said, therefore, that if a contract to arbitrate is enforced by any court when the agreement was to arbitrate in another jurisdiction, it is because the law of the state in which the court is sitting, that is to say, the "law of the forum," is held to be applicable. The law of the forum, however, may be so applied as to result in an order that the arbitration proceed in another state prior to the completion of litigation started in the court so ordering.[30] This is done only where the law of the state of the court making the order does not recognize any "public policy" opposing the requirement that the arbitrational proceeding be carried out, and on principles of comity gives recognition to the law of the other jurisdiction as also suitable for application between the parties and likely to lead to just and fair results.[31] Generally speaking, the party opposing a court action on the ground that arbitration should first be com-

---

29 Theofano Maritime Co. v. 9,551 Long Tons of Chrome Ore (D.C., Ind.) 122 F. Supp. 853 (1954) ; Pioneer Trust & Sav. Bank v. Screw Machine Prod. Co. (D.C., Wis.) 73 F. Supp. 578 (1947) ; California Prune & Apricot Growers' Assoc. v. Catz American Co., 60 F. (2d) 788 (1932) ; United States Asphalt Ref. Co. v. Trinidad Lake Petroleum Co., 222 F. 1006 (1915) ; In re California Packing Corp., 121 Misc. 212, 201 N.Y.S. 158 (1923) .

30 Gilbert v. Burnstine, 255 N.Y. 348, 174 N.E. 706 (1931) ; Nippon Ki-Ito Kaisha v. Ewing-Thomas Corp., 313 Pa. 442, 170 A. 286 (1934) .

31 Marine Transit Corp. v. Dreyfus, 284 U. S. 263, 76 L. Ed. 282, 52 S. Ct. 166 (1932) ; Mittenthal v. Mascagni, 183 Mass. 19, 66 N.E. 425, 97 Am. St. Rep. 204 (1903) .

pleted is entitled to a stay of proceedings in the court until such arbitrational agreement is performed.[32] Such orders have been made even by courts that usually have refused to order specific performance of arbitrational agreements.[33]

If the law of the forum state does not approve a general agreement to arbitrate, the fact that the contract between the parties contains a provision for arbitration prior to court action will not necessarily move the court to refuse jurisdiction of a suit brought by a party that fails to participate in arbitration. This is true even though the contract to do so was valid where made and where it was to have been performed.[34] On the other hand, if the contract has provided that arbitration of certain fact questions shall be a condition precedent to suit, and the law of the forum and the law of the place where the contract was made both approve such agreement, the court in which suit is brought will ordinarily stay proceedings until the arbitration has been completed.[35] Some courts have proceeded even further where the law of the forum approves such an arbitrational condition, and the law of the place where the contract was made (*lex loci contractus*) does not fully approve the condition, by enforcing arbitration according to the law of the forum as a condition precedent to maintenance of the suit in court.[36] It has at times been pointed out that the place

---

[32] Under Section 3 of the United States Arbitration Act, it is settled that a stay of a suit in a court of the United States is to be allowed only where the arbitration agreement is of the kind specified in Section 2 of that Act. Bernhardt v. Polygraphic Co. of America, 350 U. S. 198, 76 S. Ct. 273, 25 LA 693 (1956). It must be a maritime transaction or a transaction in interstate or foreign commerce. See also discussion of Lincoln Mills Case, Sec. 1, *supra*, this chapter and Shanferoke Coal & Supply Corp. v. Westchester Serv. Corp., 293 U. S. 449, 79 L. Ed. 583, 55 S. Ct. 313 (1935); Danielsen v. Entre Rios Railroad Co., 22 F. (2d) 326 (1927); Re Inter-Ocean Food Products, 206 App. Div. 426, 201 N.Y.S. 536 (1923).

[33] Shanferoke Coal & Supply Corp. v. Westchester Serv. Corp., 293 U. S. 449, 79 L. Ed. 583, 55 S. Ct. 313 (1934); Danielsen v. Entre Rios Railroad Co., 22 F. (2d) 326 (1927); Kelvin Engineering Co. v. Blanco, 125 Misc. 728, 210 N.Y.S. 10 (1926).

[34] Fisher v. Merchants Ins. Co., 95 Me. 486 (1901); Miles v. Schmidt, 168 Mass. 339 (1897); Meacham v. Jamestown, Franklin & Clearfield Railroad Co., 211 N.Y. 346, 105 N.E. 653 (1914).

[35] Hamilton v. Home Ins. Co., 137 U. S. 370, 34 L. Ed. 708, 11 S. Ct. 133 (1890); W. H. Blodgett Co. v. Bebe Co., 190 Cal. 665, 214 Pac. 38 (1923); Continental Ins. Co. v. Vallandingham, 116 Ky. 287, 76 S.W. 22, 105 Am. St. Rep. 218 (1903); Hutchinson v. Liverpool & London & Globe Ins. Co., 153 Mass. 143, 26 N.E. 439 (1891).

[36] California Prune & Apricot Growers' Assoc. v. Catz American Co. (C.C.A. 9th), 60 F. (2d) 788 (1932); Lappe v. Wilcox, 14 F. (2d) 861 (1926); Berkowitz v. Arbib & Houlberg, 230 N.Y. 261, 130 N.E. 288 (1921).

where the contract was to have been performed is not necessarily the place where the parties may have contemplated that they would seek judicial relief for breach of the contract. Therefore, even if the law where the contract was made or was to have been performed does not fully support the condition based upon arbitration, the court may apply the law of the forum and enforce the condition.[37]

Since in labor relations in the United States, through the operations of many unions and employers in several states, the various state courts as well as the federal courts may be open to the parties, the above rules seem to result in some complexities. The law formerly seemed settled that arbitrational clauses were procedural and pertained to remedies rather than to substantive rights under the contracts.

The federal courts have traditionally indicated a similar understanding of the U. S. Arbitration Act. It has been said to deal primarily with remedies rather than with substantive rights.[38] Like the state statutes it was taken to have supplemented rather than to have repealed the common law as to arbitration.[39] It is evident that if arbitrational rules and policies are purely procedural, the court of the forum may disregard the law of the place of contracting and apply the law of the forum.[40]

In 1956, however, the United States Supreme Court was confronted with the contention that the laws of a state entitled the plaintiff to ignore an agreement to arbitrate and to take a dis-

---

[37] California Prune & Apricot Growers' Assoc. v. Catz American Co. (C.C.A. 9th), 60 F. (2d) 788 (1932); United States Asphalt Ref. Co. v. Trinidad Lake Petroleum Co., 222 F. 1006 (1915); Berkowitz v. Arbib & Houlberg, 230 N.Y. 261, 130 N.E. 288 (1921).

[38] But Bernhardt v. Polygraphic Co., 350 U. S. 198, 76 S. Ct. 273, 25 LA 693 (1956) where the majority ascribes substantive significance to state arbitration laws. Cf. Marine Transit Corp. v. Dreyfus, 284 U. S. 263, 76 L. Ed. 282, 52 S. Ct. 166 (1932); Red Cross Line v. Atlantic Fruit Co., 264 U. S. 109, 68 L. Ed. 582, 44 S. Ct. 274 (1924); Marchant v. Mead-Morrison Mfg. Co., 29 F. 2d 40 (1928); Berkovitz v. Arbib & Houlberg, 230 N.Y. 261, 130 N.E. 288 (1921).

[39] See note 10 *supra,* and Marine Transit Corp. v. Dreyfus, 284 U. S. 263, 76 L. Ed. 282, 52 S. Ct. 166 (1931); Red Cross Line v. Atlantic Fruit Co., 264 U. S. 109, 68 L. Ed. 582, 44 S. Ct. 274 (1923); California Prune & Apricot Growers' Ass'n v. Catz American Co. (C.C.A. 9th), 60 F. 2d 788 (1932).

[40] See note 10 *supra,* and Red Cross Line v. Atlantic Fruit Co., 264 U. S. 109, 68 L. Ed. 582, 44 S. Ct. 274 (1923); Aktieselskabet Korn-Og Foderstof Kompagniet v. Rederiaktiebolaget Atlanten (C.C.A. 2d) 250 F. 935 (1918); California Prune & Apricot Growers' Ass'n v. Catz American Co. (C.C.A. 9th), 60 F. 2d 788 (1932).

pute directly to court under the U. S. Arbitration Act. It held that the latter Act did not apply to the type of issue concerned and that the applicable state laws should be ascertained and applied by the district court to which the matter was remanded.[41]

SECTION 3
Actions at Law

The refusal by one party to proceed with an agreed arbitration left the other party without remedy except for breach of contract at common law.[42] This view continues to have some respect as historically valid in a few states though the old basic views have been much amended or entirely modernized by statutes. It is to be remembered that the strict legal remedy for refusal to arbitrate in breach of contract, in the absence of statute, was a judgment for damages. Equity traditionally acts where there is no adequate remedy at law. For this reason the system or equity developed the remedies of specific performance, and injunction. Hence equity had the means, at a much earlier time than the passage of the arbitration statutes, to direct the parties to proceed with arbitration and punish for contempt any party who refused to obey the decree. This procedure, however, was very little used. It is well known, of course, that modern statutes have now largely merged the jurisdictions of the two systems and in some states one set of courts dispenses justice in either the pattern of law of or of equity as the particular case may require. For clear understanding, however, it seems well here, as elsewhere, to start discussion from pre-statutory views and practices.

An early practice was for the parties to make efforts to establish the security of the arbitration agreement by the exchange of bonds. This is still done in a few instances. While the bonding

---

41 See note 16 *supra,* and Bernhardt v. Polygraphic Co., 350 U. S. 198, 76 S. Ct. 273, 25 LA 693 (1956); Home Ins. Co. v. Morse, 20 Wall. (U. S.) 445, 22 L. Ed. 365 (1874); Dickson Mfg. Co. v. American Locomotive Co., 119 F. 488 (1902); Continental Ins. Co. v. Vallandingham, 116 Ky. 287, 76 S.W. 22, 105 Am. St. Rep. 218 (1903); and Mittenthal v. Mascagni, 183 Mass. 19, 66 N.E. 425, 97 Am. St. Rep. 404 (1903). A good note appears in 100 L. Ed. 211 (1956).

42 Red Cross Line v. Atlantic Fruit Co., 264 U. S. 109, 68 L. Ed. 582, 44 S. Ct. 274 (1924); Goerke Kirch Co. v. Goerke Kirch Holding Co., 118 N.J. Eq. 1, 176 A. 902 (1935); Jones v. Enoree Power Co., 922 S. C. 263, 75 S.E. 452 (1912); Martin v. Vansant, 99 Wash. 106, 168 P. 990 (1917).

practice would seem to give some stability to the transaction, it has not worked out satisfactorily, in every respect, nor can it be expected to do so. The amount of the penalty in the bond, even though it may recite itself as being "liquidated damages," will not be the measure of plaintiff's recovery for the defendant's refusal to arbitrate unless the plaintiff can establish actual damages to such an extent that they may be said to be reasonably measured by the agreed "liquidated damages." In other words, the penalty, if it is indeed such, is unenforceable in the courts. Thus, while there is a rather strong moral suasion to arbitrate rather than to become liable upon the bond, there is in most cases no substantially greater pressure from fear of liability where a bond is given than where none exists.[43] Nevertheless, where the relationships between a union and an employer organization are somewhat uncertain, the added stability given to an arbitrational agreement involved in giving a bond to perform the agreement might perhaps be recommended to the parties in some situations. The existence of the bond will not be effective to prevent a revocation, as far as common law or state law is concerned. Its main value lies in its furnishing an added pressure in the direction of carrying the arbitrational agreement through to an award and observing it. In such cases, perhaps the bond should be conditioned to secure the parties from the losses due to a strike or lockout should such pressure be substituted by one of the parties for arbitration in case of a controversy.

Where arbitration of certain factual questions specifically has been made a condition precedent to suit on a contract, the courts today generally have authority to order a stay of proceedings until that condition precedent is performed.[44] In such situations, it is said to be incumbent on the plaintiff to plead and prove his performance of all conditions including that of arbitration, or by proper allegations to establish a valid excuse for his nonperform-

---

[43] Bozeman v. Gilbert, 1 Ala. 90 (1840); Blaisdell v. Blaisdell, 14 N.H. 78 (1843); Union Ins. Co. v. Central Trust Co., 157 N.Y. 633, 52 N.E. 671 (1899); Grady v. Home Fire and Marine Ins. Co., 27 R.I. 435, 63 A. 173 (1906); Mead v. Owen, 83 Vt. 132, 74 A. 1058 (1910); Riley v. Jarvis, 43 W.Va. 43. 26 S.E. 366 (1896).

[44] Shanferoke Coal & Supply Corp. v. Westchester Serv. Corp. (C.C.A. 2d), 70 F. (2d) 297 (1934); Pacific Indemnity Co. v. Insurance Co. of North America, (C.C.A. 9th), 25 F. (2d) 930 (1928).

ance.[45] This is consistent with the ordinary rule concerning conditional undertakings.[46] The courts have frequently held, however, that if the arbitration is not of the essence of the contract, they will proceed, and the party who sets up the failure to arbitrate must show that the opponent has agreed to arbitrate in a certain contingency, that the actual contingency or occurrence of the arbitrable question did arise, and that the other party failed or refused to participate in such proceeding.[47] Unless the refusal to arbitrate is properly set up in the pleadings in due time, it is deemed abandoned or waived.[48] Some courts have required the defendant to plead that it made good-faith efforts to bring about arbitration, and that such efforts were defeated by the action or inaction of the plaintiff.[49] It is ordinarily sufficient as a defense, however, simply to set up the agreement to arbitrate and its nonperformance where arbitration is a condition precedent to suit. In some older cases, the courts proceeded to final judgment despite the arbitration agreement and failure to arbitrate.[50] The decision was rested on the ground that the arbitration was concerned only with the ascertainment of facts, not with ultimate liability, that these facts could be ascertained through customary procedures of the court, and that the courts should not be ousted from their jurisdiction.[51] Such courts declared that the award, while evidence of the facts, would not be indispensable so long as the evidence upon which the award itself would be based in case of arbitration is available to the court.[52]

---

45 Dunton v. Westchester Fire Ins. Co., 104 Me. 372, 71 A. 1037 (1909); Fisher v. Merchants Ins. Co., 95 Me. 486, 50 A. 282, 85 Am. St. Rep. 428 (1901); Thorndike v. Wells Memorial Assoc., 146 Mass. 619, 16 N.E. 747 (1888).

46 Carroll v. Girard Fire Ins. Co., 72 Cal. 297, 13 Pac. 863 (1887); Vernon Ins. & Trust Co. v. Maitlen, 158 Ind. 393, 63 N.E. 755 (1902); Mosness v. German-American Fire Ins. Co., 50 Minn. 341, 52 N.W. 932 (1892).

47 Low v. Fisher, 27 F. 542 (1886); Carroll v. Girard Fire Ins. Co., 72 Cal. 297, 13 Pac. 863 (1887); Cupples v. Alamo Irrig. & Mfg. Co., 7 Kan. App. 692, 51 Pac. 920 (1898).

48 Hudmon v. Cuyas, 57 F. 355 (1893); Bergman v. Commercial Union Ins. Co., 12 Ky. Law Reporter 942 (1891); Dyer v. Piscataqua Fire & Marine Ins. Co., 53 Me. 118 (1865).

49 Concordia Fire Ins. Co. v. Bowen, 121 Ill. App. 35 (1905); Bergman v. Commercial Union Ins. Co., 12 Ky. Law Reporter 942 (1891); Jones v. Enoree Power Co., 92 S.C. 263, 75 S.E. 452 (1912).

50 See Martin v. Vansant, 99 Wash. 106, 168 P. 990, Ann. Cas. 1918D 1147 (1918); 8 Am. St. Rep. 921; 47 L.R.A. (N.S.) 388.

51 Ibid.

52 Second Soc. of Universalists v. Royal Ins. Co., 221 Mass. 518, 109 N.E. 384 (1915); Soars v. Home Ins. Co., 140 Mass. 343, 5 N.E. 149 (1885); Billmyer v. Hamburg-Bremen Fire Ins. Co., 57 W.Va. 42, 49 S.E. 901 (1906).

SECTION 4

Suits in Equity

Before passage of the arbitration acts, unperformed contracts to arbitrate were generally held not specifically enforceable by a court of equity.[53] But in many jurisdictions this view has been changed by the statutes.[54] Furthermore, in the absence of any statute, a party who refused to perform an agreement to arbitrate could become a plaintiff in a court of equity and his refusal to arbitrate would not bar pursuit of his remedy therein by becoming the basis for a stay of proceedings.[55] If the agreement to arbitrate, however, was supported by an order of court, it was in most jurisdictions, when unperformed, treated as a ground for a stay of proceedings since it was already a matter of court action by reason of the order.[56] The refusal of earlier courts of equity to take steps toward enforcement of arbitration agreements covered almost every conceivable type of remedy which a litigant might request. The courts would not require appointment of arbitrators nor coerce consent to arbitrators appointed by the other party.[57] Agreements to arbitrate were not generally thought to be specifically enforceable[58]

---

53 Caldwell v. Caldwell, 157 Ala. 119, 47 So. 268 (1908); Kennedy v. Monarch Mfg. Co., 123 Iowa 344, 98 N.W. 796 (1904); Pepin v. Societe St. Jean Baptiste, 23 R.I. 81, 49 A. 387, 91 Am. St. Rep. 620 (1901); Schneider v. Reed, 123 Wis. 488, 101 N.W. 682 (1905).

54 As previously discussed in Chapter 1, Sections 2, 3, and 4, the United States Supreme Court did enter such a decree under Section 301 of the National Labor Relations Act in Textile Workers' Union of America v. Lincoln Mills of Alabama, 353 U. S. 448, 77 S. Ct. 912, 40 LRRM 2113, 28 LA 519 (1957). See Shanferoke Coal & Supply Corp. v. Westchester Serv. Corp., 293 U. S. 449, 79 L. Ed. 583, 55 S. Ct. 313 (1935); Marine Transit Corp. v. Dreyfus, 284 U. S. 263, 76 L. Ed. 282, 52 S. Ct. 166 (1932); Glidden Co. v. Retail Hardware Mut. Fire Ins. Co., 181 Minn. 518, 233 N.W. 310 (1930); Nippon Ki-Ito Kaisha v. Ewing-Thomas Corp., 313 Pa. 442, 170 A. 286 (1934).

55 Red Cross Line v. Atlantic Fruit Co., 264 U. S. 109, 68 L. Ed. 582, 44 S. Ct. 274 (1924); Hamilton v. Home Ins. Co., 137 U. S. 370, 34 L. Ed. 708, 11 S. Ct. 133 (1890); Western Assur. Co. v. Hall, 120 Ala. 547, 24 So. 936, 74 Am. St. Rep. 48 (1898); Continental Ins. Co. v. Vallandingham, 116 Ky. 287, 76 S.W. 22, 105 Am. St. Rep. 218 (1903).

56 Hecker v. Fowler, 2 Wall. (U. S.) 123, 17 L. Ed. 759 (1864); Alexandria Canal Co. v. Swann, 5 How. (U. S.) 83, 12 L. Ed. 60 (1847); Murphy v. Greenberg, 246 Pa. 387, 92 A. 511 (1914).

57 Tobey Furniture Co. v. Rowe, 18 Ill. App. 293 (1886); Saint v. Martel, 127 La. 73, 53 So. 432 (1910); Biddle v. Ramsey, 52 Mo. 153 (1873); Corbin v. Adams, 76 Va. 58 (1881).

58 Payton v. Hurst Eye, Ear, Nose and Throat Hospital, Texas Civil Appeals, 318 S.W. 2d 726 (1958). Prior to adoption of the Federal Arbitration Act courts generally did not favor arbitration agreements and often indicated that public policy denied them specific performance. See Petition of Pahlberg, D.C.N.Y. 43 Fed. Sup.

and moreover courts would not compel submission to the jurisdiction of the arbitrators by disclosure of evidence nor would they require arbitrators, if appointed, to act either in the holding of a hearing or in the making of an award.[59]

Courts of equity favored requiring performance of preliminary arbitrations and appraisals, where such performance was expressly agreed upon as a condition precedent to a suit.[60] But it was not until statutes were enacted expressly providing for arbitrations that the courts and judges sitting in equity began to give effective support to arbitrational proceedings.[61] In virtually all jurisdictions today, an arbitrational proceeding may be under a statute, or if the statute has not been complied with, it may be a common-law proceeding, under the older rules and principles, merely supplemented by the statute.[62] In the latter case, it remains uncertain whether state courts of equity will give any aid or relief toward the actual furtherance of the arbitration, or whether on the other hand, they will refuse aid and leave the disappointed party to his action for damages.[63] The tendency developed *under statutes* for courts of equity to refuse to consider a case or controversy on its merits where the plaintiff who has entered into a valid agreement to arbitrate as a remedy or procedure prior to litigation, has refused to proceed with the arbitration, and has attempted to enter the

---

761 (1942). Appeal dismissed, C.C.A. 131 Fed. 2d 968 (1942). See also Local 205 United Electrical, Radio and Machine Wkrs. of America v. General Electric Co., C. A. Mass., 233 F. 2d. 85, 38 LRRM 2019 (1956), affd. 353 U. S. 547, 1 L.Ed. 2d 1028, 77 S.Ct. 921 (1957).

59 McGunn v. Hanlin, 29 Mich. 476 (1874); Woodruff v. Woodruff, 44 N.J. Eq. 349, 16 A. 4 (1888); Rison v. Moon, 91 Va. 384, 22 S.E. 165 (1895); Schneider v. Reed, 123 Wis. 488, 101 N.W. 682 (1905).

60 Holmes v. Richet, 56 Cal. 307, 38 Am. Rep. 54 (1880); Goerke Kirch Co. v. Goerke Kirch Holding Co., 118 N.J. Eq. 1, 176 A. 902 (1935); Bristol v. Bristol & Warren Waterworks, 19 R.I. 413, 34 A. 359 (1896).

61 American Bakery and Confectionery Workers of America AFL CIO v. National Biscuit Co., D.C., N.J., 252 Fed. Supp. 768, Affd. C.A., 378 F. 2d 918 (1967); Shop 'N Save Corp., et al. v. Retail Food Clerks' Union, (Calif. Super. Ct. 1940); Marine Transit Corp. v. Dreyfus, 284 U. S. 263, 76 L.Ed. 282, 52 S.Ct. 166 (1932); Gilbert v. Burnstine, 255 N.Y. 348, 174 N.E. 706 (1931); Nippon Ki-Ito Kaisha v. Ewing-Thomas Corp., 313 Pa. 442, 170 A. 286 (1934).

62 Lilley v. Tuttle, 52 Colo. 121, 117 Pac. 898 (1911); Modern System Bakery v. Salisburg, 215 Ky. 230, 284 S.W. 994 (1926); Bunnell v. Reynolds, 205 Mo. App. 653, 226 S.W. 614 (1920).

63 Saint v. Martel, 127 La. 73, 53 So. 432 (1910); Reed v. Washington Fire & Marine Ins. Co., 138 Mass. 572 (1885); Schneider v. Reed, 123 Wis. 488, 101 N.W. 682 (1905); See 15 L.R.A. 142.

courts directly and without the arbitration.[64] The judges of courts of equity have shown a strong tendency to assume a wide discretionary jurisdiction in such matters and have at times decreed relief based directly on the contract where, in the opinion of the court, it would have been inequitable to impose pressure upon a party by compelling arbitration.[65]

In the exceptional cases prior to the modern arbitrational statutes when equity virtually did enforce arbitration, the court decisions stressed that the parties had clearly agreed upon arbitration or appraisal as a basis of ascertaining some subordinate fact as a condition to precede any suit.[66] From this the courts were led to the conclusion that to refuse enforcement of arbitration would be to force upon the parties a contract other than that to which they had agreed.[67] Nevertheless, if the arbitrational or appraisal matter was merely collateral to the main contract, courts of equity were inclined to grant enforcement of the main contract, even though the appraisal or arbitration remained unperformed.[68] In other words, if the arbitrational provisions of the contract are independent or collateral, and not an essential or substantial part of the principal contract, as a rule the latter could be enforced without performance of the arbitration prior to the modern statutes.[69] This was particularly true in cases where the main contract had

---

[64] See Trubowitch v. Riverbank Canning Co., 30 Cal. (2d) 335, 182 P. (2d) 182 (1947); Holmes v. Richet, 56 Cal. 307, 38 Am. Rep. 54 (1880); Goerke Kirch Co. v. Goerke Kirch Holding Co., 118 N.J. Eq. 1, 176 A. 902 (1935); Mutual Life Ins. Co. v. Stephens, 214 N.Y. 488, 108 N.E. 856 (1915).

[65] See Fernandez v. Golodety (C.C.A. 2d N.Y.) 148 F. (2d) 625, (1945); Pacific Indemnity Co. v. Insurance Co. of North America, (C.C.A. 9th) 25 F. (2d) 930 (1928); Ezell v. Rocky Mountain Bean & Elevator Co., 76 Colo. 409, 232 Pac. 680 (1925); White Eagle Laundry Co. v. Slawek, 296 Ill. 240, 129 N.E. 753 (1920); Gilbert v. Burnstine, 255 N.Y. 348, 174 N.E. 706 (1931).

In Underhill v. Deckoff the New York Supreme Court decreed specific performance of an award reinstating an employee. 105 N.Y.L.J. 98 (1941).

[66] Lake Shore Power Co. v. Edgerton, 43 Ohio App. 545, 184 N.E. 37 (1932); Kaufmann v. Liggett, 209 Pa. 87, 58 A. 129, 103 Am. St. Rep. 988 (1904); Cooke v. Miller, 25 R.I. 92, 54 A. 927 (1903); Martin v. Vansant, 99 Wash. 106, 168 Pac. 990 (1917).

[67] Goerke Kirch Co. v. Goerke Kirch Holding Co., 118 N.J. Eq. 1, 176 A. 902 (1935); Mutual Life Ins. Co. v. Stephens, 214 N.Y. 488, 108 N.E. 856 (1915); Bristol v. Bristol & Warren Waterworks, 19 R.I. 413, 34 A. 359 (1896).

[68] Fisher v. Merchants Ins. Co., 95 Me. 486, 85 Am. St. Rep. 428 (1901); Hunn v. Pennsylvania Institution for Blind, 221 Pa. 403, 70 A. 812 (1908); Grady v. Home Fire & Marine Ins. Co., 27 R.I. 435, 63 A. 173 (1906).

[69] March v. Eastern Railroad Co., 40 N.H. 548, 77 Am. Dec. 732 (1860); Goerke Kirch Co. v. Goerke Kirch Holding Co., 118 N.J. Eq. 1, 176 A. 902 (1935); Lake Shore Power Co. v. Edgerton, 43 Ohio App. 545, 184 N.E. 37 (1932).

been performed in part.[70] There can be no doubt that since *Textile Workers* v. *Lincoln Mills* the state courts, at least in labor dispute cases, have much more readily decreed proceeding with arbitration than was formerly the case. This is an obvious consequence of the declaration that in cases concerning interstate commerce the state laws must be regarded as having given way to federal policy and federal law.

The modern application of these principles to an annual labor contract, including an arbitrational provision, would seem to be altogether applicable in theory to a situation in which the parties, though not fully complying with present legislation on arbitration, have agreed and entered into performance of a contract fixing hours, wages, seniority rights, and holiday or vacation privileges, subject to certain arbitration in respect to the fixation of wage levels for some classification. On such facts an effort to recover because of alleged inadequacies in the wages paid, on the ground that they have not met the terms of the general agreement or have not satisfied statutory minimum wage levels, might well be met with a stay of proceedings in a state court. It is quite likely that under the influence of the *Steelworkers' trilogy*, particularly *American Manufacturing*, a decree ordering specific performance of the arbitration under the state arbitration statute would be allowed if the agreement satisfied the law. After such a ruling, the court should refuse to act further until the arbitrational proceeding concluded and the wages properly payable determined by an award. In such a case as this in the federal area of jurisdiction, the agreement to arbitrate would, no doubt, be specifically enforced today under the *Lincoln Mills* decision.

As previously indicated a court of equity may adopt a somewhat different attitude toward a contract partially performed than toward a contract that is wholly unperformed, or, as sometimes called, "executory."[71] In respect to the partially performed contract, where one party will suffer undue and unjust hardship by reason of fail-

---

70 Lake Shore Power Co. v. Edgerton, 43 Ohio App. 545, 184 N.E. 37 (1932); Kaufmann v. Liggett, 209 Pa. 87, 58 A. 129, 103 Am. St. Rep. 988 (1904); Cooke v. Miller, 25 R.I. 92, 54 A. 927 (1903); Martin v. Vansant, 99 Wash. 106, 168 Pac. 990 (1917).

71 Cooke v. Miller, 25 R.I. 92, 54 A. 927 (1903); Cogswell v. Cogswell, 70 Wash. 178, 126 Pac. 431 (1912); Hopkins v. Gilman, 22 Wis. 476 (1868).

ure of the other party to participate in arbitrational proceedings, the court may either order the arbitration completed or virtually complete the same itself by appointing an officer of the court, such as an appraiser or an arbitrator, to complete the same under the auspices or order of the court.[72] The maxims, "He who comes into equity, must come with clean hands," and "He who asks equity must do equity," are both frequently invoked in principle to indicate that relief will be readily granted to a party who in good faith has tried to carry out an agreed arbitration, but has been frustrated by the other party, while on the other hand, one who has refused to perform an agreement to arbitrate, or has otherwise prevented the carrying on of the same, may discover he is not qualified for equitable relief and will be met by a stay of proceedings or possibly a decree ordering specific performance of the arbitrational agreement.[73] Whether the latter will be allowed is likely to depend upon whether the complaining party will be subjected to an unconscionable or irreparable handicap or disability by non-arbitration in violation of the agreement of the parties.

SECTION 5

Practice Under Arbitration Statutes

If an arbitration agreement complies with the applicable statute and indicates that the parties have contemplated a statutory arbitration, the intended proceeding is usually enforceable under the act, either in a suit in equity or in an action of law. If the matter at issue is not suitable for arbitration under the contract of the parties, it will likely be given a court hearing and decision.[74]

---

72 Castle Creek Water Co. v. Aspen, (C.C.A. 8th) 146 F. 8 (1906); Mutual Life Ins. Co. v. Stephens, 214 N.Y. 488, 108 N.E. 856 (1915); Kaufmann v. Liggett 209 Pa. 87, 58 A. 129, 103 Am. St. Rep. 988 (1904); Martin v. Vansant, 99 Wash. 106 168 Pac. 990 (1917).

73 See Livingston v. John Wiley & Sons Inc., 313 F. 2d 52, affd. 84 S.Ct. 909, 376 U. S. 543, 11 L.Ed. 2d 898, 52 LRRM 2223 (CA 2, 1964); Hotel & Restaurant Employees' Alliance, et al. v. Wisconsin Employment Relations Board, 6 LRRM 1136 (Wis. Cir. Ct., 1940); Coles v. Peck, 96 Ind. 333, 49 Am. Rep. 161 (1884); Kaufmann v. Liggett, 209 Pa. 87, 58 A. 129, 103 Am. St. Rep. 988 (1904); William H. Low Estate Co. v. Lederer Realty Corp., 35 R.I. 352, 86 A. 881 (1913).

74 International Union of Automobile Wkrs. v. Benton Harbor Malleable Industries, (C.A. Mich.) 242 F. 2d 536, cert. den. 355 U. S. 814 (1957); NLRB v. Columbian Enameling & Stamping Co., 96 F. (2d) 948, 2 LRRM 727 (1938); California Academy of Sciences v. Fletcher, 99 Cal. 207, 33 Pac. 855 (1893); Holdridge v. Stowell, 39 Minn. 360, 40 N.W. 259 (1888); Stiringer v. Toy, 33 W.Va. 86, 10 S.E. 26 (1889).

In some jurisdictions, the statute expressly takes away the common-law right of revocation of the arbitration agreement, and if it is wilfully unperformed by either party, his conduct will bar him from maintaining a suit in respect to the controversy. In some states, the statute provides that the agreement to arbitrate may be the subject of a rule of court.[75] In such cases, the arbitration procedure is enforceable on the same terms as a submission resulting from an order or ruling of court independent of the arbitrational statutes.[76] Once the parties have entered into a statutory submission of a pending action by reason of a rule or order of court, they are bound to complete it. The defendant cannot avoid completing the arbitration, nor may the plaintiff dismiss suit after the proceedings have started.[77]

The statutes of several of the states, like the United States Arbitration Act (which applies to commerce and maritime transactions) declare agreements to arbitrate existing or prospective differences to be valid and irrevocable if set forth in writing.[78] Many of the statutes authorize enforcement by courts of equity either through the grant of a stay of proceedings or a decree of specific performance of the arbitration agreement.[79] Some statutes even provide for appointment of arbitrators by the court, and direct that an *ex parte* arbitration may be carried through where one party fails or refuses to participate in the hearing or other proceedings.[80]

---

[75] Marine Transit Corp. v. Dreyfus, 284 U. S. 263, 76 L.Ed. 282, 52 S.Ct. 166 (U. S. Arbitration Act) (1932) ; Murphy v. Greenberg, 246 Pa. 387, 92 A. 511 (1914) ; Zehner v. Lehigh Coal & Navigation Co., 187 Pa. 487, 41 A. 464, 67 Am. St. Rep. 586 (1898) .

[76] Murphy v. Greenberg, 246 Pa. 387, 92 A. 511 (1914) ; Zehner v. Lehigh Coal & Navigation Co., 187 Pa. 487, 41 A. 464, 67 Am. St. Rep. 586 (1898) ; see 42 A.L.R. 735.

[77] Amsterdam Dispatch, Inc. v. Devery, 278 N.Y. 688, 16 N.E. (2d) 403 (1938) ; Davis v. Forshee, 34 Ala. 107 (1859) ; *In re* Silliman, 159 Cal. 155, 113 Pac. 135 (1911) ; Zehner v. Lehigh Coal & Navigation Co., 187 Pa. 487, 41 A. 464, 67 Am. St. Rep. 586 (1898) .

[78] Goerke Kirch Co. v. Goerke Kirch Holding Co., 118 N.J. Eq. 1, 176 A. 902 (1935) ; Gilbert v. Burnstine, 255 N.Y. 348, 174 N.E. 706 (1931) ; Nippon Ki-Ito Kaisha v. Ewing-Thomas Corp., 313 Pa. 442, 170 A. 286 (1934) .

[79] Marine Transit Co. v. Dreyfus, 284 U. S. 263, 76 L.Ed. 282, 52 S.Ct. 166 (1932) ; California Prune & Apricot Growers' Assoc. v. Catz American Co., (C.C.A. 9th) 60 F. (2d) 788 (1932) ; Gilbert v. Burnstine, 255 N.Y. 384, 174 N.E. 706 (1931) .

[80] Red Cross Line v. Atlantic Fruit Co., 264 U. S. 109, 68 L.Ed. 582, 44 S.Ct. 274 (1924) ; Finsilver, Still & Moss v. Goldberg, Mass & Co., 253 N.Y. 382, 171 N.E. 579 (1930) ; Nippon Ki-Ito Kaisha v. Ewing-Thomas Corp., 313 Pa. 442, 170 A. 286 (1934) ; see 199 Cornell Law Quarterly, 222 *et seq.* (1934) .

While these statutes substantially change the common-law rules, many courts have held they refer to remedies rather than to the substantive rights of the parties.[81] They have been applied in some instances to contracts made before their enactment.[82] Under the statutes, arbitration agreements have been held to be proper proceedings through which to enforce a mechanic's lien even though enforcement was also available under a statute in a direct action upon the contract of employment.[83] It appears to be clear, however, that power to order a stay of proceedings is not necessarily conditioned upon the existence of statutory authority of the court to compel arbitration.[84] For example, the latter power under the United States Arbitration Act apparently would be limited to commerce and maritime transactions and arbitration agreements included within the same so far as the statute is concerned, but the power of the federal courts is clearly broader than that provided by that statute.[85] The *Lincoln Mills* decision, making virtually all labor contracts in the federal jurisdiction specifically enforceable, clearly asserts this. (See Chapter I, Sections 3 and 4.)

Arbitration statutes usually provide procedures, additional to common-law remedies, to enforce awards of arbitrators.[86] The procedure to be followed generally is specifically set forth and should

---

[81] But see notes 16 and 19, *supra*, and cf. Marine Transit Corp. v. Dreyfus, 284 U. S. 263, 76 L.Ed. 282, 52 S.Ct. 166 (1932); California Prune & Apricot Growers' Assoc. v. Catz American Co., (C.C.A. 9th) 60 F. (2d) 788 (1932); Gilbert v. Burnstine, 255 N.Y. 348, 174 N.E. 706 (1931).

[82] California Prune & Apricot Growers' Assoc. v. Catz American Co., (C.C.A. 9th) 60 F. (2d) 788 (1932); Pacific Indemnity Co. v. Insurance Co. of North America, 25 F. (2d) 930 (1928); Berkovitz et al. v. Arbib & Houlberg, 230 N.Y. 261, 130 N.E. 288 (1921).

[83] Brescia Constr. Co. v. Walart Constr. Co., 264 N.Y. 260, 190 N.E. 484 (1934); see 93 A.L.R. 1151 *et seq.*

[84] See Bernhardt v. Polygraphic Co. of America, herein at notes 10 and 16 *supra*; and Shanferoke Coal & Supply Corp. v. Westchester Serv. Corp. 293 U. S. 449, 79 L.Ed. 583, 55 S.Ct. 313 (1935); Marine Transit Corp. v. Dreyfus, 284 U. S. 263, 76 L.Ed. 282, 52 S.Ct. 166 (1932); Finsilver, Still & Moss v. Goldberg, Maas & Co., 253 N.Y. 382, 171 N.E. 579 (1930).

[85] Sanferoke Coal & Supply Corp. v. Westchester Serv. Corp., (C.C.A. 2d) 70 F. (2d) 297, affirmed in 293 U. S. 449, 79 L.Ed. 583, 55 S.Ct. 313 (1935); Krauss Bros. Lumber Co. v. Louis Bossert & Sons, (C.C.A. 2d) 62 F. (2d) 1004 (1933); California Prune & Apricot Growers' Assoc. v. Catz American Co., (C.C.A. 9th) 60 F. (2d) 788 (1932).

[86] Black v. Woodruff, 193 Ala. 327, 69 So. 97 (1915); Modern System Bakery v. Salisburg, 215 Ky. 230, 284 S.W. 994 (1926); Bunnell v. Reynolds, 205 Mo. App. 653, 226 S.W. 614 (1920); *Re* Lower Baraboo River Drainage Dist., 199 Wis. 230, 225 N.W. 331 (1929).

be carefully observed.[87] Under some acts, the courts are given power to provide procedural rules where suits are brought on arbitrational awards. But the usual rules of procedure of the court will ordinarily govern where no specific or special ones are set up by the statute.[88] On the other hand, where the statute itself provides procedural steps, they are usually similar to those followed in the courts in respect to other matters, and are subject to interpretation by the courts, which generally apply them so that in effect they conform as nearly as possible to ordinary procedure in the jurisdiction.[89]

Under the state statutes, the courts are usually directed to enforce arbitration agreements in all cases where they have jurisdiction over the parties or over the subject matter.[90] If the parties stipulate that their agreement to arbitrate is irrevocable, it is usually declared by the Act to be an equitable defense that the arbitration agreement was not performed.[91] Ordinarily, it is expressly provided that the court may make an order staying litigation upon a contract until an award of arbitrators as provided in the agreement shall be made.[92] This is frequently brought about by means of a motion.[93] Such motion is equivalent to an application for an

---

[87] Shanferoke Coal & Supply Corp. v. Westchester Serv. Corp., 293 U. S. 449, 79 L.Ed. 583, 55 S.Ct. 313 (1935) ; Finsilver, Still & Moss v. Goldberg, Maas & Co., 253 N.Y. 382, 171 N.E. 579 (1930) ; Nippon Ki-Ito Kaisha v. Ewing-Thomas Corp., 313 Pa. 442, 170 A. 286 (1934) .

[88] Schoenamsgruber v. Hamburg-American Line, 294 U. S. 454, 79 L.Ed. 989, 55 S.Ct. 475 (1935) ; Marine Transit Corp. v. Dreyfus, 284 U. S. 263, 76 L.Ed. 282, 52 S.Ct. 166 (1932) ; California Prune & Apricot Growers' Assoc. v. Catz American Co., (C.C.A. 9th) 60 F. (2d) 788 (1932) ; Nippon Ki-Ito Kaisha v. Ewing-Thomas Corp., 313 Pa. 442, 170 A. 286 (1934) .

[89] Shanferoke Coal & Supply Corp. v. Westchester Serv. Corp., 293 U. S. 449, 79 L.Ed. 583, 55 S.Ct. 313 (1935) ; Marine Transit Corp. v. Dreyfus, 284 U. S. 263, 76 L.Ed. 282, 52 S.Ct. 166 (1932) ; Finsilver, Still & Moss v. Goldberg, Maas & Co., 253 N.Y. 382, 171 N.E. 579 (1930) .

[90] See American Airlines Inc. v. Louisville and Jefferson County Air Board, (C.A. Ky.) , 269 F. 2d 811 (1959) ; Gilbert v. Burnstine, 255 N.Y. 348, 174 N.E. 706 (1931) ; Nippon Ki-Ito Kaisha v. Ewing-Thomas Corp., 313 Pa. 442, 170 A. 286 (1934) ; see 93 A.L.R. 1073 et seq.

[91] Schoenamsgruber v. Hamburg-American Line, 294 U. S. 454, 79 L.Ed. 989, 55 S.Ct. 475 (1935) ; Shanferoke Coal & Supply Corp. v. Westchester Serv. Corp., 293 U. S. 449, 79 L.Ed. 583, 55 S.Ct. 313 (1935) ; Red Cross Line v. Atlantic Fruit Co., 264 U. S. 109, 68 L.Ed. 582, 44 S.Ct. 274 (1924) .

[92] Shanferoke Coal & Supply Corp. v. Westchester Serv. Corp., 293 U. S. 449, 79 L.Ed. 583, 55 S.Ct. 313 (1935) ; Marine Transit Corp. v. Dreyfus, 284 U. S. 263, 76 L.Ed. 282, 52 S.Ct. 166 (1932) ; Pacific Indemnity Co. v. Insurance Co. of North America, (C.C.A. 9th) 25 F. (2d) 930 (1928) .

[93] Shanferoke Coal & Supply Corp. v. Westchester Serv. Corp., 293 U. S. 449, 79 L.Ed. 583, 55 S.Ct. 313 (1935) ; Marine Transit Corp. v. Dreyfus, 284 U. S. 263, 76 L.Ed. 282, 52 S.Ct. 166 (1932) ; see 93 A.L.R. 1080.

interlocutory injunction, based upon a special defense.[94] Its approval by the court obviously is not the equivalent of a final judgment. It is more in effect like the grant of a temporary injunction.[95] Where a court grants an application for an order directing arbitration to proceed, the action is often, in form, a ruling on a motion, but under some statutes the courts have treated such a ruling as, in effect, the grant of specific performance of the contract to arbitrate.[96] Under some statutes, the powers of the court have been held broad enough to authorize a decree of specific performance even though the Act itself did not in terms provide for such relief.[97] It is to be borne in mind that the court should not consider the merits of the grievance but only decide whether the parties have agreed it is to be settled by arbitration.[98]

If the party opposing the arbitration takes the position that the contract alleged to include that proceeding does not exist or is wholly void for any reason, that question may be tried independent of the special relief by which the arbitration may be enforced. If the court ultimately decides that the contract is valid and that the arbitrational provisions should be enforced, it will make an order accordingly and defer further proceedings in court until the arbitration has been completed.[99] Some statutes provide for a jury trial of the question whether the contract was ever legally agreed

---

[94] Schoenamsgruber v. Hamburg-American Line, 294 U. S. 454, 79 L.Ed. 989, 55 S.Ct. 475 (1935); Shanferoke Coal & Supply Corp. v. Westchester Serv. Corp., 293 U. S. 449, 79 L.Ed. 583, 55 S.Ct. 313 (1935); Enelow v. New York Life Ins. Co., 293 U. S. 379 (1935).

[95] Schoenamsgruber v. Hamburg-American Line, 294 U. S. 454, 79 L.Ed. 989, 55 S.Ct. 475 (1935); Shanferoke Coal & Supply Corp. v. Westchester Serv. Corp., 293 U. S. 449, 79 L.Ed. 583, 55 S.Ct. 313 (1935); Enelow v. New York Life Ins. Co., 293 U. S. 379 (1935); General Electric Co. v. Marvel Co., 287 U. S. 430 (1932).

[96] Red Cross Line v. Atlantic Fruit Co., 264 U. S. 109, 68 L.Ed. 582, 44 S.Ct. 274 (1924); California Prune & Apricot Growers' Assoc. v. Catz American Co., (C.C.A. 9th) 60 F. (2d) 788 (1932); Nippon Ki-Ito Kaisha v. Ewing-Thomas Corp., 313 Pa. 442, 170 A. 286 (1934).

[97] Red Cross Line v. Atlantic Fruit Co., 264 U. S. 109, 68 L.Ed. 582, 44 S.Ct. 274 (1924); Nippon Ki-Ito Kaisha v. Ewing-Thomas Corp., 313 Pa. 442, 170 A. 286 (1934); see 93 A.L.R. 1074 et seq.

[98] United Steelworkers of America v. American Manufacturing Co., 363 U. S. 564, 46 LRRM 2414 (1960); Potoker v. Brooklyn Eagle Inc., 2 N.Y. 2d 553, 161 N.Y. Supp. 2d 609, cert. den. 355 U. S. 883 (1957).

[99] Marine Transit Corp. v. Dreyfus, 284 U. S. 263, 76 L.Ed. 282, 52 S.Ct. 166 (1932); California Prune & Apricot Growers' Assoc. v. Catz American Co., (C.C.A. 9th) 60 F. (2d) 788 (1932); Finsilver, Still & Moss v. Goldberg, Maas & Co., 253 N.Y. 382, 171 N.E. 579 (1930).

to by the parties.[100] Where an arbitration statute sets up a purely equitable type of remedy, however, the right to a jury trial may be held nonexistent. If the question whether a contract exists is raised, it is heard by a court sitting in equity.[101]

It is altogether likely that the near future will witness a much greater tendency toward uniformity of statutes and decisions dealing with arbitration than have the decades just past. Legislatures in recent years have shown a tendency to borrow more from each other and to pass uniform laws. The entire labor field has been receiving growing attention from lawmakers. The net result should be desirable in its elimination of apparently arbitrary differences as state lines are crossed and in its stimulation of confidence in the minds of employers and employees that what is "good law" in one state is "good law" in many.[102] It is an accepted truism today that where the interstate features of any concerned business requires it, federal law or state law compatible with federal law, will govern. The words of the U. S. Supreme Court in *Textile Workers* v. *Lincoln Mills* are:

> "The question then is, what is the substantive law to be applied in suits under § 301 (a)? We conclude that the substantive law to apply in suits under § 301 (a) is federal law, which the courts must fashion from the policy of our national labor laws. See Mendelsohn, Enforceability of Arbitration Agreements Under Taft-Hartley Section 301, 66 Yale L. J. 167. The Labor Management Relations Act expressly furnishes some substantive law. It points out what the parties may or may not do in certain situations. Other problems will lie in the penumbra of express statutory mandates. Some will lack express statutory sanction but will be solved by looking at the policy of the legislation and fashioning a remedy that will effectuate that policy. The range of judicial inventiveness will be determined by the nature of the problem. See *Board of Commissioners* v. *United States*, 308 U. S. 343, 351. Federal interpretation of the Federal law will govern, not state law. Cf. *Jerome* v. *United States*, 318 U. S. 101, 104. But state law, if compatible with the purpose of § 301, may be

---

100 Marine Transit Corp. v. Dreyfus, 284 U. S. 263, 76 L.Ed. 282, 52 S.Ct. 166 (1932); The Eagle, 8 Wall. (U. S.) 15 (1868); The Genesee Chief, 12 How. (U. S.) 443 (1851); Finsilver, Still & Moss v. Goldberg, Maas & Co., 253 N.Y. 382, 171 N.E. 579 (1930).

101 Marine Transit Corp. v. Dreyfus, 284 U. S. 263, 76 L.Ed. 282, 52 S.Ct. 166 (1932); California Prune & Apricot Growers' Assoc. v. Catz American Co., (C.C.A. 9th) 60 F. (2d) 788 (1932); Finsilver, Still & Moss v. Goldberg, Maas & Co., 253 N.Y. 382, 171 N.E. 579 (1930).

102 For full citations to present state arbitration statutes, see Appendix D.

resorted to in order to find the rule that will best effectuate the federal policy. See *Board of Commissioners* v. *United States, supra,* at 351-352. Any state law applied, however, will be absorbed as federal law and will not be an independent source of private rights."

Thus preemption and federal supremacy are introduced as powerful factors operating toward uniformity of approach to enforcement of agreements to arbitrate labor disputes. Possibly this may furnish a unifying influence in respect to arbitrations generally.

SECTION 6

Federal Statutes and Proposed Federal Legislation

The United States Arbitration Act,[103] which became law on July 30, 1947, is an arbitration agreement enforcement statute; however, it is limited by its terms to "maritime transactions" and to contracts "evidencing a transaction involving commerce." It expressly states that the word "commerce" means commerce "among the several states or with foreign nations." It adds that "nothing herein contained shall apply to contracts of seamen, railroad employees or any other class of workers engaged in foreign or interstate commerce."

Section 3 of the Act provides for a stay of proceedings where the issue upon which suit has been brought is referable to arbitration. The United States court having jurisdiction of any such suit has authority to order and compel arbitration and to designate the arbitrators if the parties fail to do so consistently with their agreement. Arbitrators are given authority to subpoena witnesses, and fees are provided to be the same as witnesses before masters in the United States courts. Provision is made for entry of judgments on awards where parties have agreed to such procedure. Awards may be set aside for corruption, fraud, or other improper procedure and rehearing may be ordered in such cases. The Act contains provisions that awards may be modified or corrected where there has been a miscalculation of figures, where the arbitrators have undertaken to award upon a matter not submitted to them, and where the award is imperfect in form not affecting the merits of the controversy.

---

[103] 61 Statutes at Large 669; U. S. Code Annotated, Title 9, Sections 1-14.

Both the majority and the minority of the United States Supreme Court in the case of *Textile Workers Union* v. *Lincoln Mills of Alabama*[104] assumed the inapplicability of the United States Arbitration Act to the ordinary type of labor dispute. As discussed earlier,[105] the majority of the Court concluded that Section 301 (a) of the Labor Management Relations Act was applicable and enforced the contract to arbitrate under that very vague and general section. In the majority opinion, the Court indicates its approval and acceptance of a mandate to "fashion" federal laws to be applied as Section 301 is enforced. The judicial technique of declaring or making law is to establish only as much at a time as may be required by the issues of the case before it. Thus the development of a full, reliable, coherent, and workable system of law for arbitration agreement enforcement, if left to the piecemeal, fortuitous, catch-as-catch-can possibilities of judicial development may require decades if not centuries. Even granted it sometime may attain a relative completeness, it would be most unlikely to have workable unity and clearness. Development of law in this important area requires promptness and full, careful thinking — in other words, a well-worked-out act of Congress.

There have been suggestions from time to time that the United States Arbitration Act could be readily amended and should be amended to apply to labor disputes. There would appear to be a strong preference, however, for a very different type of act as advocated by the National Academy of Arbitrators and its active committee on legislation. The committee has observed that the *Lincoln Mills* decision makes arbitration agreements enforceable in the federal courts where there is the necessary relationship to interstate commerce, and that by judicial decisions a body of federal law is to be developed and applied to enforcement of arbitration. Hence, the Academy committee has concluded it should urge the passage by Congress of a carefully worked-out federal labor arbitration act to be applicable to disputes affecting interstate commerce. Its proposal would require the respective arbitrators to decide virtually all preliminary controversies or questions unless the parties expressly contract that such an issue as that of arbitrability

---

104 353 U. S. 448, 1 L.Ed. 2d 972, 77 Sup. Ct. 912, 40 LRRM 2113, 28 LA 519 (1957) and compare Bernhardt v. Polygraphic Co. of America, notes 10, 16 and 19 *supra*.
105 Chapter 1, Sections 3 and 4, *supra*.

itself is to be preliminarily decided by the court. Thus, it would leave to the court in prearbitration proceedings only the determination of the existence and validity of the arbitration agreement. The bill proposed by the Academy would require the courts to make use of the list of qualified arbitrators maintained by the Federal Mediation and Conciliation Service when they are required to appoint arbitrators. The proposal briefly requires only that the arbitration procedure, "shall provide for a fair hearing." Thus, it would leave much discretion in this area to the arbitrator. Details of time for completing and filing an award, fees, expenses, etc. are covered in the proposed act, a copy of which is found in Appendix C.

It must be recognized that the full, joint effect of *Textile Workers* v. *Lincoln Mills*,[106] the *Steelworkers'* trilogy cases[107] and the numerous other decisions which have followed in their wake has been to reserve to and require of labor arbitrators the exercise of full arbitrational authority. This is consistent with the rather obvious observation that when parties agree to arbitrate, they are generally undertaking to contract themselves out of a court procedure. If their agreement to arbitrate is distorted by any statutory enactment into a vehicle to bring them into court and to subject the issues they have agreed to arbitrate to court procedure and court decision, the effect of the statute will be to give them exactly what they do not want. In the delicate area of employer-labor relations, this may be not only harmful to the relationship itself but also so slow in solving issues that may arise that the whole purpose of the parties in contracting for arbitration will be defeated. The lack of a well-fashioned and complete federal labor arbitration act will be constantly apparent until one is supplied.

---

106 Textile Workers v. Lincoln Mills, 353 U. S. 448, 40 LRRM 2113 (1957).

107 United Steelworkers of America v. American Mfg. Co., 363 U. S. 564, 80 S.Ct. 1343, 46 LRRM 2414 (1960); United Steelworkers of America v. Enterprise Wheel and Car Corp., 363 U. S. 593, 80 S.Ct. 1358, 46 LRRM 2423 (1960); United Steelworkers of America v. Warrior and Gulf Navigation Co., 363 U. S. 574, 80 S.Ct. 1347, 46 LRRM 2416 (1960).

Specimen Forms of Contract Clauses
Covering Arbitration

Of the following specimen contract clauses covering arbitration, the first two represent composites of the better features of a number of contract clauses actually in effect. The others are taken verbatim from various contracts.

SPECIMEN 1.
(For Single Arbitrator)

In the event that a mutually satisfactory settlement of any grievance is not reached within five days after the meeting of the Grievance Committee and Management, either party may request the . . . .
. . . . to appoint an arbitrator, and both parties shall be bound to accept the arbitrator so appointed. A hearing shall be held before such arbitrator as soon as reasonably possible, and his decision shall be final and binding. The expense of such arbitrator, if any, shall be borne one-half by the union and one-half by the company.

In lieu of the last sentence above, the following may be substituted:

The arbitrator's fee and expenses shall be borne by the parties in such proportions as such arbitrator shall determine. In making such determination the arbitrator shall be guided by the factors which ordinarily guide a judge of a court of equity in taxing court cases, namely, the relative fault of the parties on the merits of the controversy, the fault, if any, of failure to reach a settlement, etc. It is contemplated that ordinarily the fee and expenses will be divided equally.

The following additional or alternate clauses may be added, or substituted, where appropriate:

A. If the issue be of a technical nature, such as workloads, job evaluation, etc., the arbitrator may seek expert opinion outside the hearing, and give such opinion such weight as he sees fit.

B. The arbitrator's decision shall not be binding as a precedent in later disputes, but may be offered in evidence at later arbitrations for what it is worth.

C. No award of back pay may be made in a discipline case unless written grievance was filed with the company within five days of the imposition of the discipline.

D. The arbitrator may issue successive partial awards where in his judgment that course seems desirable, and may in his decision reserve jurisdiction to decide disputes that may arise over the interpretation or application of his decision.

E. Where the issue is of a technical nature, and the arbitrator feels that a factual study and report by a disinterested technician would be of value, he may request the Technical Division of the Federal Mediation and Conciliation Service to make such study and report, and may in his discretion either hold a further hearing after receipt of such report or proceed to render his decision without further hearing.

F. Either party may request the Director of the Federal Mediation and Conciliation Service to furnish a list of five arbitrators, and the arbitrator shall be selected from such list by the parties alternately striking, the party to strike first being determined by tossing a coin.

SPECIMEN 2.
(For Board of Arbitration)

In the event that any grievance or dispute arising out of the interpretation or application of any clause of this contract, or any other grievance, remains unsettled after the steps provided by the grievance machinery have been taken, either party may require the other to submit the dispute or grievance to arbitration. The party requesting arbitration shall appoint two arbitrators, and furnish the other with the names of those so selected, and within three days thereafter the other party shall appoint two arbitrators and give similar notification. The four arbitrators so appointed shall meet within three days and endeavor to agree upon an umpire to act as the fifth member of the Board of Arbitration. In the event of failure of the four arbitrators to so agree within three days, either party may request the .... to name the umpire.

The Board of Arbitration so chosen shall meet upon call of the umpire, shall hold a hearing, and render a written decision. In the event the parties are unable to agree upon the wording of a Submission Agreement the grievance itself shall be submitted. A decision by a majority of such board shall be final and binding on the parties. In the event the umpire shall determine that a majority decision cannot be reached, the decision shall be rendered solely by said umpire, and his decision shall be final and binding. Neither the board nor the umpire shall have the power to alter any term of this contract.

The board or umpire, as the case may be, shall have the power to render successive partial awards, and may in any decision reserve jurisdiction to decide matters which may arise in connection with the interpretation or application of the award.

Each party shall bear the costs incurred incident to the services of the arbitrators appointed by it. The joint and several liability of the parties incident to the services of the umpire shall be borne in equal shares by the company and the union.

In lieu of the last paragraph, above, the following may be substituted:

Each party shall bear the cost, if any, of furnishing the arbitrator or arbitrators appointed by it. The fee and expenses of the umpire shall be borne by the parties in such proportions as he shall determine. In making such determination the arbitrator shall be guided by the factors which ordinarily guide a judge of a court of equity in taxing court costs, namely, the relative fault of the parties on the merits of the controversy, the fault, if any, of failure to reach a settlement, etc. It is contemplated that ordinarily the fee and expenses will be divided equally.

The additional or alternate clauses following Specimen 1 above, with some modification to fit them to a board, may be added or substituted where appropriate.

SPECIMEN 3.
(For Permanent Umpire)

In the event of failure to adjust the case at this point, it may be appealed to the impartial umpire, providing it is the type of case on which the umpire is authorized to rule.   *   *   *

The impartial umpire shall have only the functions set forth herein and shall serve for one year from date of appointment provided he continues to be acceptable to both parties.   *   *   *

It shall be the function of the umpire, after due investigation and within 30 days after submission of the case to him, to make a decision in all claims of discrimination for union activity or membership and in all cases of alleged violation of the terms of the following sections of this agreement, and written local or national supplementary agreements on the same subjects: Recognition; representation; grievance procedure; seniority; disciplinary layoffs and discharges; call-in pay; working hours; leaves of absence; union bulletin boards; strikes, stoppages and lockouts; wages; general provisions; upgradings; trainees; procedures on production standards; employment of laid-off employees; and of any alleged violations of written local or national wage agreements. The umpire shall have no power to add to or subtract from or modify any of the terms of this agreement or any agreements made supplementary hereto; nor to establish or change any wage; nor to rule on any dispute arising regarding production standards. Any case appealed to the umpire on which he has no power to rule shall be referred back to the parties without decision.

The corporation delegates to the umpire full discretion in cases of violation of shop rules, and in cases of violation of the Strikes, Stoppages, and Lockouts section of the agreement the umpire shall have no power to order back pay, but if the penalty imposed by the corporation is two weeks' layoff or more, the grievance machinery must be expedited so that the umpire's decision will come within two weeks of the written filing of the grievance.   *   *   *

No decision of the umpire or of the management in one case shall create a basis for a retroactive adjustment in any other case prior to the date of written filing of each such specific claim.   *   *   *

There shall be no appeal from the umpire's decision, which will be final and binding on the union and its members, the employee or employees involved, and the corporation. The union will discourage any attempt of its members, and will not encourage or cooperate with any of its members, in any appeal to any court or labor board from a decision of the umpire.   *   *   *

Any issue involving the interpretation and/or the application of any term of this agreement may be initiated by either party directly with the other party. Upon failure of the parties to agree with respect to the correct interpretation or application of the agreement to the issue, it may then be appealed directly to the umpire.   *   *   *

SPECIMEN 4.

Should any difference arise between the employer and the union or any employee, the union agrees that there shall be no slowing up or stoppage of work on account of such condition. Both parties agree that in such case an earnest effort shall be made to settle such difference immediately in the following manner: *   *   *

After a grievance, whether with respect to a wage matter or any other grievance, has gone through the procedure laid down in the local agreement and has not been settled thereunder, the local union may refer it to the international union. If within 20 days after the international union has filed this grievance with the management of the company the grievance has not been satisfactorily settled, the international union may then ask that the matter be finally settled by arbitration. It shall thereupon be the duty of the management to meet forthwith with the designated representatives of the union, and endeavor to agree upon an arbitrator or arbitrators. If within three days no such agreement has been reached, either party may certify the matter to the Director of the Federal Mediation and Conciliation Service, who shall be requested to appoint an arbitrator or arbitrators whose decision shall be final and binding. The expense of any such arbitrator shall be borne one-half by the union and one-half by the company.

SPECIMEN 5.

Alleged grievances said to arise out of the operation or interpretation of this contract or concerning wages, hours, or conditions of employment not otherwise disposed of as herein provided shall be settled in the following manner: *   *   *

If either party desires, it can notify the other party in writing at this meeting [between national union and company representatives] or within 24 hours following this meeting that it wants the matter referred to arbitration, and name its arbiter. The other party must name its arbiter within 24 hours of receipt of this notification. The arbiters so selected shall meet within seven days after the notification of the appointment of the second arbiter, and endeavor to adjust the matter. If unable to reach an agreement, they shall name a third arbiter who shall be umpire. If the two arbiters cannot agree upon the third arbiter within three days, either party may request the Director of the Federal Mediation and Conciliation Service to name promptly such third arbiter. The board of arbitration shall thereupon immediately make such investigation, hear such statements, and consider such matters as may be material, and as promptly as possible reach and announce its decision. The decision of any two members of the board of arbitration shall be binding on the parties hereto.   *   *   *

SPECIMEN 6.

Should differences arise between the company and the union as to the meaning and application of the provisions of this agreement or as to any question relating to the wages, hours of work, and other conditions of employment of any employee, there shall be no interruption or impeding of the work, work stoppages, strikes, or lockouts on account of such differences, but an earnest effort shall be made to settle the matter promptly in the manner hereinafter outlined.   *   *   *.

Whenever either party concludes that further conferences cannot contribute to settlement of the grievance, such grievance may be appealed by either party to an impartial umpire to be appointed by mutual agreement of the parties hereto within 15 days following receipt by either party of a written request for such appointment. The decision of the umpire shall be final. The expense and salary incident to the services of the umpire shall be shared equally by the company and the union. Awards of settlement of grievances may or may not be retroactive as the equities of each case (discharge cases excepted) may demand, but in no event shall any award be retroactive beyond the date on which the grievance was first presented in written form.

An umpire to whom any grievance shall be submitted in accordance with the provisions of this section shall have jurisdiction and authority to interpret and apply the provisions of this agreement insofar as shall be necessary to the determination of such grievance, but he shall not have jurisdiction or authority to alter in any way the provisions of this agreement. * * *

SPECIMEN 7.
(For International Board)
EXHIBIT A
INDIVIDUAL ARBITRATION AGREEMENT

It is agreed between ...., Proprietor of the ...., party of the first part, and ...., Union No. .... of ...., party of the second part, by its president duly authorized to act in its behalf, as follows:

Section 1.   In the event of any difference arising between the parties to this contract which cannot be adjusted by conciliation, such difference shall be submitted to arbitration under the Code of Procedure provided by the International Arbitration Agreement, effective January 1, 1958, between the American Newspaper Publishers Association and the International Printing Pressmen and Assistants' Union of North America.*

Section 2.   This contract shall cover any contract between the parties of the first and second parts whether the same is in writing or an oral understanding, subject to the conditions expressed in the International Arbitration Agreement, effective January 1, 1958, between the American Newspaper Publishers Association and the International Printing Pressmen and Assistants' Union of North America.*

Section 3.   It is expressly understood and agreed that the International Arbitration Agreement and the Code of Procedure, both hereunto attached, between the American Newspaper Publishers Association and the International Printing Pressmen and Assistants' Union of North America shall be integral parts of this contract and shall have the same force and effect as though set forth in the contract itself.*

Section 4.   The parties hereto specifically authorize the Board of Directors of the International Printing Pressmen and Assistants' Union of North America and the Special Standing Committee of the American Newspaper Publishers Association to give public disavowal to any failure to comply with this contract as provided in Section 13 of the International Arbitration Agreement.*

This contract shall be in full force and effect on the .... day of ...., 19......., and continue until the .... day of ...., ..., inclusive.

In Witness Whereof the undersigned proprietor of the said newspaper, and the president of the ....
Union No. ...., have hereunto affixed their respective signatures this .... day of ...., 19 ....

....

....
Witness as to Proprietor   Proprietor

                                              ....Union No. ......

....
Witness as to President   President

                                              ....
                                                       Secretary

The American Newspaper Publishers Association, by the Chairman of its Special Standing Committee, duly authorized to act in its behalf, hereby underwrites the obligations assumed by the party of the first part under this agreement and guarantees their fulfillment.

                              ....
                              Chairman, Special Standing Committee,
                              American Newspaper Publishers Association.

....

The International Printing Pressmen and Assistants' Union of North America, by its President, duly authorized to act in its behalf, hereby underwrites the obligations assumed by the party of the second part under this agreement, and guarantees their fulfillment.
Witness as to President:

                              ....
                              President, International Printing Pressmen
                              and Assistants' Union of North America.

....

---

* The agreement and Code of Procedure provide for arbitration of virtually all types of disputes, exclude all other means of solution, and set forth full and detailed procedures for selection of arbitrators and hearing procedure.

APPENDIX B

Specimen Forms of Submission Agreements

1. FORM OF SUBMISSION AGREEMENT
FOR BOARD OF ARBITRATION

The following form of Submission Agreement is adapted to a Board of three or five members:

The Apex Company and the United Steelworkers of America having been unable satisfactorily to adjust certain grievances it is agreed that the same be submitted to arbitration as provided in Article ..... of the agreement between parties. The Company has named ....
its arbitrator, the Union has named .... its arbitrator, and upon request for the appointment of a third and neutral arbitrator or umpire the .... has appointed
....

It is agreed that the following issues be submitted to the Board of Arbitration above named:

1. Is John Smith properly classified as Machinist, 2nd Class?

2. If not, what is his proper classification and rate of pay, and as of what effective date?

3. What disposition should be made of the grievance of the Union numbered .....?

It is agreed that if the Board is unable to reach a unanimous decision the decision shall be rendered solely by the said ....
as Umpire. And the decision, whether of the full Board or of the said
.... shall be final and binding, and the parties agree faithfully to abide by it.

Done this 1st day of ...., 19......

> Apex Company
> by ....
> United Steelworkers of America
> By ....

To the above may also be added any additional clauses, such as those suggested in the contract forms found in Appendix A, to make the Submission Agreement conform to the provisions of the contract.

2. FORM OF SUBMISSION AGREEMENT FOR
SINGLE ARBITRATOR OR UMPIRE

The Apex Company and the United Steelworkers of America, Local No. ......, having agreed to submit certain disputes to the Impartial Umpire, ..., as provided in the contract between the parties,

It is agreed that the following questions be submitted to said .... :

1. Does the union have a right at this time to demand a general wage increase?

2. If so, what wage increase, if any, should be put into effect, and as of what effective date?

It is agreed that the umpire may render separate awards on the two questions, if he deems it desirable, and may hold additional hearings after having rendered an award on the first issue if he deems it expedient. It is further agreed that he may if he desires call upon any outside agency to make a survey of the wage structure in the plant of this company as compared to that in other companies, and may consider the report of such survey in reaching his determination of the issues. His decision shall be in writing, and shall be final and binding on the parties.

Dated ...., 19......

Apex Company
By ....

United Steelworkers of America
By ....

To this form, also, additional clauses such as those suggested in the forms in Appendix A may be added.

Proposed U. S. Labor Arbitration Act
and
Proposed Uniform State Act

A UNITED STATES LABOR ARBITRATION ACT AS
PROPOSED BY THE LAW AND LEGISLATIVE
COMMITTEE OF THE
NATIONAL ACADEMY OF ARBITRATORS
(NOVEMBER 1959)

AN ACT to provide for the judicial enforcement of agreements to arbitrate labor disputes arising in industries affecting commerce and to define the jurisdiction of the courts with reference to the arbitration of such disputes.

SECTION 1, Be it enacted, etc., that

(a) This Act may be cited as the "United States Labor Arbitration Act."

(b) The Congress hereby finds that the refusal by employers or labor organizations in industries affecting commerce to abide by the terms of agreements to arbitrate labor disputes or to honor awards made pursuant thereto burdens commerce and the free flow of goods in commerce and leads to labor disputes burdening and obstructing commerce and the free flow of goods in commerce.

The Congress hereby finds further that the voluntary arbitration of disputes between employers and labor organizations, particularly disputes arising under collective bargaining agreements, is an accepted and approved method of settling such disputes. Such method, being voluntary and, itself, the result of collective bargaining, should be encouraged and supported. In view of the wide variety of collectively negotiated kinds of arbitration procedures in use, the parties to collective bargaining agreements should continue to have the greatest degree of freedom to shape their arbitration procedures to suit their needs and desires, subject only to limitations which are essential to preserve the integrity of the process, to provide safeguards against improper usurpation of authority by the arbitrator, and to insure the opportunity for full and fair consideration of the issues involved. Judicial intervention in the process should be minimized, but should be available, where necessary, to enforce compliance with agreements to arbitrate, to prevent the assumption of arbitral jurisdiction where a valid agreement to arbitrate does not exist, to enforce awards, and to provide for limited judicial review of awards.

(c) It is the purpose and policy of this Act, in order to promote the free flow of commerce and to remove burdens and obstructions thereto, to provide for the judicial enforcement of agreements to arbitrate labor disputes in industries affecting commerce and to define the jurisdiction of the courts with reference to the arbitration of such disputes.

SECTION 2. As used, in this Act,

(a) The term "employer" includes any person acting as an agent of an employer, directly or indirectly, but shall not include the United States or any wholly owned Government corporation, or any Federal Reserve Bank, or any state or political subdivision thereof, or any corporation or association operating a hospital, if no part of the net earnings inures to the benefit of any private shareholder or individual, or any person subject to the Railway Labor Act, as amended from time to time, or any labor organization (other than when acting as an employer), or anyone acting in the capacity of officer or agent of such labor organization.

(b) The term "employee" shall include individuals employed as supervisors, but shall not include any individual employed by an employer subject to the Railway Labor Act, as amended from time to time, or by any other person who is not an employer as herein defined.

(c) The term "labor organization" means any organization of any kind, or any agency or employee representation committee or plan, in which employees participate and which exists for the purpose, in whole or in part, of dealing with employers concerning grievances, labor disputes, wages, rates of pay, hours of employment, or conditions of work.

(d) The term "commerce" means trade, traffic, commerce, transportation or communication among the several States, or between the District of Columbia or any Territory of the United States and any State or other Territory, or the District of Columbia, or within the District of Columbia or any Territory, or between points in the same State but through any other State or any Territory or the District of Columbia or any foreign country.

(e) The term "affecting commerce" means in commerce, or burdening or obstructing commerce, or having led or tending to lead to a labor dispute burdening or obstructing commerce or the free flow of commerce.

(f) The term "agreement to arbitrate" means a written agreement between a labor organization or organizations and an employer or employers or an association or group of employers, in an industry affecting commerce, to submit to arbitration an existing dispute, or a collective bargaining agreement providing for the arbitration of any or all future disputes.

(g) The term "collective bargaining agreement" means a written agreement between a labor organization or organizations and an employer or employers or an association or group of employers, in an industry affecting commerce, concerning rates of pay, wages, hours or other terms and conditions of employment.

(h) The term "district court" means United States District Court.

(i) The term "arbitrator" means the arbitrator or arbitrators designated pursuant to the agreement to arbitrate or under this Act.

NOTE

The above provision incorporates the following changes from § 2 of the second draft:

(1) The terms "employer" and "labor organization" are expressly defined in the same manner as in the NLRA, rather than by reference as in the second draft. The purpose of this change is to insure that, even if the NLRA were amended so as to exclude some categories of employers and labor organizations from the coverage of the act, the arbitration act would still have as broad an application as possible.

(2) A definition of the term "employee" is added [as sub-section (b)] in order to insure that the act would apply to arbitration agreements between employers and organizations representing supervisory employees.

(3) In subsection (f) a slight change is made so as to make it clear that "an agreement to arbitrate" is either a specific arbitration submission agreement, or a collective bargaining agreement containing an arbitration clause.

SECTION 3. *Validity and enforceability of agreement to arbitrate.*

An agreement to arbitrate shall be valid, irrevocable and enforceable, save upon such grounds as exist at law or in equity for the revocation of any contract.

NOTE

Academy Committee opinion has been divided on the question whether a statute should be applicable unless the parties specifically agree otherwise, or, on the other hand, should be inapplicable (except for the provision making arbitration agreements enforceable) unless the parties agree to accept the statute. This is the so-called "contracting out" problem.

The recently decided *Lincoln Mills* case (353 U. S. 448) makes arbitration agreements enforceable in the federal courts in all cases where there is the necessary relationship to interstate commerce, and holds that the federal courts are to develop, from all available sources, a body of federal law to be applied in the resolution of substantive and procedural problems in the enforcement of such agreements. To incorporate a "contracting in or out" provision in a proposed federal statute would border on the ridiculous, for it would invite Congress on the one hand to pass a law resolving problems or arbitration procedure and substance, and, on the other hand, permit the parties, by force of their own disavowal of the statute, to require the federal courts to proceed to develop rules as if the statute did not exist.

For this reason the act, as proposed, omits any "contracting in or out" provision. A majority of the Committee members who have made comments approve this omission.

SECTION 4. *Jurisdiction of the arbitrator.*

The arbitrator's authority to determine any controversy shall, unless the parties by their agreement have expressly provided for prior judicial determination, include the authority initially to determine any issue raised regarding his jurisdiction, subject to judicial stay, review or intervention only on the grounds provided in Sections 5, 13 and 14 of this Act; provided, however, that if the agreement to arbitrate specifically provides that the question of the arbitrator's jurisdiction shall be subject to prior judicial determination, such provision shall be controlling. The participation by a party in an arbitration proceeding subject to this Act shall not be deemed a waiver of any claim of lack of jurisdiction or authority of the arbitrator if such claim is made during the proceeding and is not thereafter expressly waived.

NOTE

The foregoing preserves the substance of § 4 of the second draft. The only change of substance is the recognition of "General Electric" type contract provisions expressly providing for judicial determination of the arbitrability of a claim, prior to the arbitration hearing if a party claims lack of arbitrability. Otherwise, the basic intent is to establish that the arbitrator has jurisdiction to determine, in the first instance, any question of "arbitrability" which may be raised, subject, of course, to judicial review as provided later in the act.

SECTION 5. *Proceedings to compel or stay arbitration.*

(a) If a party fails or refuses to proceed to arbitration under an agreement to arbitrate, the other party may apply to the appropriate district court for an order directing the parties to proceed with arbitration. The court, except as provided in subsection (e) of this section, shall order arbitration unless the opposing party denies the existence or validity of an agreement to arbitrate, or denies his failure to comply therewith. If either such issue is raised, the court shall take proof and determine the issue in summary proceedings. Upon finding that there is no valid agreement to arbitrate, or that there is no default thereunder, the proceedings shall be dismissed. Upon finding that a valid agreement to arbitrate exists, and that a party has failed or refused to proceed thereunder, the court shall direct the parties to proceed with arbitration in accordance with the agreement to arbitrate.

(b) A party against whom an arbitration proceeding has been commenced or threatened, and who denies the existence or validity of an agreement to arbitrate, may apply to the appropriate district court for an order staying an arbitration commenced or threatened. If the opposing party asserts the existence or validity of an agreement to arbitrate, the court shall take proof and determine the issue in summary proceedings. Upon finding that a valid agreement to arbitrate does not exist, the court shall enter an order staying the arbitration. Upon finding that a valid agreement to arbitrate does exist, the court shall, except as provided in subsection (e) of this section, direct the parties to proceed with arbitration in accordance with the agreement to arbitrate.

(c) An action or proceeding in any court involving an issue subject to arbitration under an agreement to arbitrate shall be stayed, except as provided in subsection (e) of this section, if an order for arbitration or an application therefor has been made under subsection (a) of this section, or if an application for a stay of arbitration has been made under subsection (b) of this section. If the issue is severable, the stay of such action or proceeding may be with respect to the severable issue only. Such stay shall remain in effect until the application for arbitration, or for the stay of arbitration, is disposed of, and shall become permanent if the application to proceed to arbitration is granted or the application to stay arbitration is denied.

(d) The court shall not have power to stay arbitration, or to refuse to order arbitration, if a valid agreement to arbitrate exists. If such agreement exists, but a party raises a question concerning the jurisdiction of the arbitrator under the agreement to arbitrate, the court shall not decide the issue, but shall, except as provided in subsection (e) of this section, refer the question to be decided by the arbitrator in the first instance subject to review as provided in Sections 13 and 14 of this Act.

(e) If the agreement to arbitrate provides expressly for a judicial determination, prior to the arbitration hearing, of a question raised concerning the arbitrability of the claim or claims made by the party demanding arbitration, the court shall, upon application of a party raising such question, take proof and determine the issue in summary proceedings. Upon finding that any such claim is arbitrable, the court shall direct the parties to proceed with the arbitration of such claim in accordance with the agreement to arbitrate. Upon finding that any such claim is not arbitrable, the court shall enter an order staying the arbitration of such claim.

NOTE

Section 5 incorporates these principles: (1) That, except where the arbitration agreement provides expressly for judicial determination of an issue of arbitrability prior to the arbitration hearing, the role of the court in pre-arbitration proceedings should be confined to the determination of the existence and validity of the underlying arbitration agreement, or the question of default thereunder; (2) that summary proceedings should be available both to compel and stay arbitration and to determine any question of arbitrability where the contract provides for judicial determination thereof prior to the arbitration hearing; and (3) that if a valid agreement to arbitrate exists, and a party is in default thereunder, the court should remand any question of arbitrability to the arbitrator for decision in the first instance (unless the contract expressly provides otherwise) subject to the standards of judicial review set forth later in the statute.

The section thus rejects the premise of the Uniform Act that courts should have pre-arbitral jurisdiction not only to determine the existence of an agreement to arbitrate, and the question of default thereunder, but also, subject to the criterion of *bona fides,* to determine a claim of non-arbitrability. A majority of the Committee believes that it is preferable, for the purpose of giving proper scope to the arbitration process, to permit the arbitrator himself to make the initial determination of issues of arbitrability (except where the contract expressly provides otherwise) so that, if judicial review follows at a later stage, the reviewing court will have the benefit of the arbitrator's reasoning on any such issue.

Section 5 (e) in the second draft provided juridiction in the district courts to stay state court proceedings under certain circumstances. It was decided to transfer this provision to a later point in the statute and to deal with the subject of state court jurisdiction somewhat more broadly. The new subsection (e) deals with the case where the agreement to arbitrate provides expressly for judicial determination, prior to the arbitration hearing, of questions of arbitrability.

Section 6. *Appointment of arbitrators.*

If the agreement to arbitrate provides a method of appointment of arbitrators, this method shall be followed. In the absence of such provision, or if the agreed method fails or for any reason cannot be followed, or when an arbitrator appointed fails or is unable to act and his successor has not been duly and promptly appointed, the appropriate district court on application of a party shall appoint a sole arbitrator to hear and determine the controversy. In making such appointment the court shall obtain from the Federal Mediation and Conciliation Service a list of nine (9) persons from the panel of arbitrators of the Service and shall make the appointment of the arbitrator from such list. An arbitrator so appointed shall proceed to hear and determine the controversy with all the powers he would have had if designated by the parties.

NOTE

This section departs from the substance of the Uniform Act only in requiring the court to make use of the FMCS in the appointment of a substitute arbitrator. Deleted from the second draft was the provision requiring the court to mail to the parties the FMCS list and the provision permitting each party to strike three names. In addition, the number of persons to be included on the list was raised from seven to nine.

Section 7. *Majority action by arbitrators.*

The powers of the arbitrators, if there be more than one, may be exercised by a majority unless otherwise provided by the agreement to arbitrate or by this Act.

NOTE

This section omits the provision in the first draft concerning the contingency that an arbitrator may cease to act. The first draft provided that the remaining arbitrator or arbitrators, if appointed as neutrals, could continue with the case. Such provision seems unnecessary in view of the appointment provisions of Section 6.

Section 8. *Arbitration procedure.*

The arbitration shall be conducted in accordance with rules and procedures agreed upon by the parties or, in the absence of such agreement, by rules and procedures determined by the arbitrator. Such rules and procedures shall provide for a fair hearing.

NOTE

This section constitutes a radical departure from the corresponding section of the second draft. The change consists of the deletion of the specification of the details concerning hearing procedure, and the substitution of a simple provision leaving it to the parties or the arbitrator to prescribe rules of procedure subject only to the statutory requirement that the hearing be "fair."

This change was decided upon by the sub-committee for several reasons. For one thing, § 8 of the second draft made the procedural standards set forth in subsection (b) subject to an agreement of the parties on procedure. Thus, they were not mandatory in any case, and it seemed, upon reflection, pointless to specify them. (The obvious reason for not making them mandatory in all cases is that the arbitration process should remain flexible in the matter of procedures, as it now is.) Moreover, it was felt that the specification of some of these procedural requirements would tend to invite litigation directed solely to the alleged failure to meet the statutory requirements. Finally, it was recognized that procedural standards are being evolved by the FMCS, AAA, and the NAA, and that these will probably provide sufficient guidance so that precatory provisions in the statute are unnecessary.

(SECTION 9. *Witnesses, subpoenas.*)

NOTE

A majority of the Committee members who have submitted comments favor omitting altogether this section of the first draft. This constitutes a departure from the Uniform Act, which would grant subpoena power to the arbitrator and provide for witness fees. The power of subpoena is really unnecessary, as experience shows, and to introduce it would be to invite irritating difficulties in the form of an attempt by parties to involve unwilling or adverse persons as witnesses, or to harass an opponent by "fishing" for documents. Any provision for witness fees is likewise inappropriate for labor dispute arbitrations.

SECTION 9. *Award.*

(a) The award shall be in writing and signed by the arbitrator. The arbitrator shall cause a signed copy to be delivered to each party personally or by registered or certified mail or as provided by agreement of the parties.

(b) An award shall be made within the time fixed therefor in the agreement to arbitrate or at the hearing, or, if not so fixed, within a reasonable time. A party waives the objection that an award was not timely made unless he notifies the arbitrator and the other party of his objection prior to the delivery of the award.

NOTE

Subsection (b) deletes from the comparable provision in the second draft the specification that the award shall be filed within thirty days following the closing of the hearing where the parties have not fixed some other time. The provision that the parties may extend the time is likewise deleted. The thirty-day provision, upon further reflection, was thought to be too rigid, and it seems unnecessary to provide in the statute that the parties may stipulate for an extension of time.

SECTION 10. *Change of award by arbitrator.*

On application of a party or, if an application to the district court is pending under Sections 12, 13 or 14, on submission to the arbitrator by the court under such conditions as the court may order, the arbitrator may modify or correct the award where:

(1) There was an evident miscalculation of figures or an evident mistake in the description of any person, thing or property referred to in the award;

(2) The award is imperfect in a matter of form, not affecting the merits of the controversy; or

(3) For the purpose of clarifying the award.

The application shall be made within twenty (20) days after delivery of the award to the applicant. Written notice thereof shall be given forthwith to the opposing party, stating he must serve his objections thereto, if any, within ten (10) days from the notice. The award so modified or corrected is subject to the provisions of Sections 12, 13 and 14 of this Act.

NOTE

This section conforms in substance with the corresponding section of the Uniform Act.

SECTION 11. *Fees and expenses of arbitration.*

Unless otherwise provided by agreement of the parties, the arbitrator's expenses and fee shall be divided equally between the parties.

NOTE

This section differs from the corresponding section in the second draft in two respects, *viz:* (1) The words "or by this Act" appearing in the second draft, page 16, line 18, are omitted in view of the fact that the present draft omits any provision with respect to transcripts and the apportionment of the cost thereof; (2) the words "together with other expenses, not including counsel fees," appearing at page 17, lines 1 and 2, of the second draft, are omitted on the ground that they simply introduced a needless ambiguity.

SECTION 12. *Confirmation of the award.*

Upon application of a party, the district court of the district in which the arbitration was held shall confirm an award unless within the time limits hereinafter imposed grounds are urged for vacating or modifying or correcting the award, in which case the court shall proceed as provided in Sections 13 and 14.

NOTE

This section conforms with the corresponding section of the Uniform Act.

SECTION 13. *Vacating an award.*

(a) Upon application of a party, the district court of the district in which the arbitration was held shall vacate the award:

(1) Where the award was procured by corruption, fraud, or other undue means;

(2) Where there was no agreement to arbitrate and the party claim-

ing the absence of such agreement made such claim in the arbitration proceeding and did not expressly waive it thereafter;

(3) To the extent that the award is affected by the arbitrator's determination of an issue which he had no jurisdiction to determine, and the parties have not expressly agreed to be bound by the arbitrator's determination of his jurisdiction. The award shall not be vacated if there was a reasonable basis for the arbitrator's determination, express or implicit, of his jurisdiction. The fact that the award orders relief of a kind which might not be granted by a court of law or equity is not ground for vacating the award;

(4) To the extent that the award directs a party to commit an act or engage in conduct prohibited by state or federal law;

(5) Where the arbitrator so conducted the hearing, contrary to provisions of Section 8, as to prejudice substantially the rights of a party.

(b) An application under this section shall be made within thirty (30) days after delivery of a copy of the award to the applicant, except that, if predicated upon corruption, fraud or other undue means, it shall be made within thirty (30) days after such grounds are known or should have been known.

(c) In vacating the award on grounds other than stated in clause (2) of subsection (a) the court may order a rehearing before another arbitrator chosen as provided in the agreement to arbitrate, or in the absence of such provision, by the court in accordance with Section 6 of this Act, or, if the award is vacated on grounds set forth in clauses (3) and (5) of subsection (a), the court may order a rehearing before the arbitrator who made the award or his successor appointed in accordance with Section 6. The time within which the agreement to arbitrate requires the award to be made is applicable to the rehearing and commences from the date of the rehearing or from such date as is determined by the court.

(d) If the application to vacate is denied and no motion to modify or correct the award is pending, the court shall confirm the award.

NOTE

This section incorporates two changes of substance from the comparable section of the second draft.

In subsection (a) (2) the language appearing in the second draft at page 17, lines 18 and 19, was omitted as being unnecessary. It is believed that, if a court has determined, in a proceeding under Section 5, that there was an agreement to arbitrate, such determination would be *res judicata*.

Subsection (a) (3) has been completely recast. It was thought that this subsection of the second draft, although intended to deal primarily with the review of issues of arbitrability, actually would permit a review, subject to the stated limitation, of error in the interpretation of the collective agreement. It was thought that this problem might be met by restating the basis for review in such a way as to omit any reference to "excess of powers," and substitute what is in clause (3) of the present draft. Thus recast, the only basis for review under this clause is that the arbitrator determined an issue which he had no jurisdiction to determine.

SECTION 14. *Modification or correction of award.*

(a) Upon application made within thirty (30) days after delivery of a copy of the award to the applicant, the district court of the district in which the hearing was held shall modify or correct the award where:

(1) There was an evident miscalculation of figures or an evident mistake in the description of any person, thing or property referred to in the award;

(2) The award is imperfect in a matter of form, not affecting the merits of the controversy.

(b) If the application is granted, the district court shall modify and correct the award so as to effect its intent and shall confirm the award as so modified and corrected. Otherwise, the district court shall confirm the award as made.

(c) An application to modify or correct an award may be joined in the alternative with an application to vacate the award.

NOTE

This section differs from the corresponding section of the second draft only in the deletion of subsection (a) (2) of that draft. This deletion was thought desirable since Section 13 deals adequately with the subject matter.

SECTION 15. *Judgment or decree on award.*

Upon the granting of an order confirming, modifying or correcting an award, judgment or decree shall be entered in conformity therewith and be enforced and docketed as any other judgment or decree. Costs of the application and of the proceedings subsequent thereto, and disbursements may be awarded by the court.

SECTION 16. *Applications to court.*

Except as otherwise provided, an application to the appropriate district court under this Act shall be by motion and shall be heard in the manner and upon the notice provided by law or rule of court for the making and hearing of motions. Unless the parties have agreed otherwise, notice of an initial application for an order shall be served in the manner provided by law for the service of a summons in an action, provided, that the process of the district court shall extend to and be valid when served in any judicial district.

SECTION 17. *Venue.*

Except as otherwise provided herein, an initial application shall be made to the district court of the district in which, under the agreement to arbitrate, the arbitration hearing shall be held. If the agreement to arbitrate makes no provision for the place of hearing, such application shall be made to the district court of the district in which the dispute arose, or in the event that the dispute arose in more than one district the application shall be made to the district court for the district in which is located the employer's principal place of business. All subsequent applications shall be made to the court hearing the initial application unless the court otherwise directs.

SECTION 18. *State court jurisdiction.*

(a) Nothing in this Act shall be deemed to preclude the assumption by a state court of jurisdiction with respect to an agreement to arbitrate provided its action is consistent with the provisions of this Act;

(b) The appropriate district court may, upon application of a party to an agreement to arbitrate, stay the prosecution of a state court proceeding to stay arbitration or to set aside an arbitration award in any case in which state court action is sought upon a ground which would not be a proper ground for the requested relief under this Act;

(c) A proceeding in a state court to compel or stay arbitration, or to set aside or enforce an arbitration award, in which an alleged agreement to arbitrate is the basis for or involved in the proceeding, may be removed to an appropriate district court, without regard to the citizenship or residence of the parties, in the manner provided by law.

NOTE

In the second draft, Section 5 (e) gave the federal courts jurisdiction to stay proceedings in state courts, "involving issues the decision of which may subvert the purposes and policies of this Act." It was considered desirable to deal with the subject of state court jurisdiction somewhat more comprehensively, and in a separate section. The intended effect of Section 18 is to insure, if a party so desires, that state court jurisdiction shall not be assumed to accomplish an objective which could not be accomplished under the federal act.

SECTION 19. *Appeals.*

(a) An appeal may be taken from:

(1) An order denying an application to compel arbitration made under Section 5;

(2) An order granting an application to stay arbitration made under Section 5;

(3) An order confirming or denying confirmation of an award;

(4) An order modifying or correcting an award;

(5) An order vacating an award without directing a rehearing;

(6) A judgment or decree entered pursuant to the provisions of this Act; or

(7) An order made under Section 18 staying the prosecution of a state court proceeding.

(b) The appeal shall be taken in the manner and to the same extent as from orders or judgments in a civil action.

NOTE

This section includes what was in Section 18 of the second draft, and adds only clause (7) to subsection (a).

SECTION 20. *Constitutionality.*

If any provision of this Act or the application thereof to any person or circumstance is held invalid, the invalidity shall not affect other provisions or applications of the Act which can be given effect without the invalid provision or application, and to this end the provisions of this Act are severable.

SECTION 21. *Repeal.*

All acts or parts of acts which are inconsistent with the provisions of this Act are hereby repealed.

SECTION 22. *Time of taking effect.*

This Act shall take effect ....

A PROPOSED ACT RELATING TO ARBITRATION AND TO MAKE UNIFORM THE LAW WITH REFERENCE THERETO

Adopted by the National Conference of the Commissioners on Uniform States Laws, August 20, 1955, as amended August 24, 1956. Approved by the House of Delegates of the American Bar Association, August 26, 1955, and August 30, 1956.

SECTION 1. *(Validity of Arbitration Agreement.)*

A written agreement to submit any existing controversy to arbitration or a provision in a written contract to submit to arbitration any controversy thereafter arising between the parties is valid, enforceable and irrevocable, save upon such grounds as exist at law or in equity for the revocation of any contract. This act also applies to arbitration agreements between employers and employees or between their respective representatives (unless otherwise provided in the agreement).

SECTION 2. *(Proceedings to Compel or Stay Arbitration.)*

(a) On application of a party showing an agreement described in Section 1, and the opposing party's refusal to arbitrate, the Court shall order the parties to proceed with arbitration, but if the opposing party denies the existence of the agreement to arbitrate, the Court shall proceed summarily to the determination of the issue so raised and shall order arbitration if found for the moving party, otherwise, the application shall be denied.

(b) On application, the court may stay an arbitration proceeding commenced or threatened on a showing that there is no agreement to arbitrate. Such an issue, when in substantial and bona fide dispute, shall be forthwith and summarily tried and the stay ordered if found for the moving party. If found for the opposing party, the court shall order the parties to proceed to arbitration.

(c) If an issue referable to arbitration under the alleged agreement is involved in an action or proceeding pending in a court having jurisdiction to hear applications under subdivision (a) of this Section, the application shall be made therein. Otherwise and subject to Section 18, the application may be made in any court of competent jurisdiction.

(d) Any action or proceeding involving an issue subject to arbitration shall be stayed only if an order for arbitration or an application therefor has been made under this section or, if the issue is severable, the stay may be with respect thereto only. When the application is made in such action or proceeding, the order for arbitration shall include such stay.

(e) An order for arbitration shall not be refused on the ground that the claim in issue lacks merit or bona fides or because any fault or grounds for the claim sought to be arbitrated have not been shown.

SECTION 3. *(Appointment of Arbitrators by Court.)*

If the arbitration agreement provides a method of appointment of arbitrators, this method shall be followed. In the absence thereof, or if the agreed method fails or for any reason cannot be followed, or when an arbitrator appointed fails or is unable to act and his successor has not been duly appointed, the court on application of a party shall appoint one or more arbitrators. An arbitrator so appointed has all the powers of one specifically named in the agreement.

SECTION 4. *(Majority Action by Arbitrators.)*

The powers of the arbitrators may be exercised by a majority unless otherwise provided by the agreement or by this act.

SECTION 5. *(Hearing.)*

Unless otherwise provided by the agreement:

(a) The arbitrators shall appoint a time and place for the hearing and cause notification to the parties to be served personally or by registered mail not less than five days before the hearing. Appearance at the hearing waives such notice. The arbitrators may adjourn the hearing from time to time as necessary and, on request of a party and for good cause, or upon their own motion may postpone the hearing to a time not later than the date fixed by the agreement for making the award unless the parties consent to a later date. The arbitrators may hear and determine the controversy upon the evidence produced notwithstanding the failure of a party duly notified to appear. The court on application may direct the arbitrators to proceed promptly with the hearing and determination of the controversy.

(b) The parties are entitled to be heard, to present evidence material to the controversy and to cross-examine witnesses appearing at the hearing.

(c) The hearing shall be conducted by all the arbitrators but a majority may determine any question and render a final award. If, during the course of the hearing, an arbitrator for any reason ceases to act, the remaining arbitrator or arbitrators appointed to act as neutrals may continue with the hearing and determination of the controversy.

SECTION 6. *(Representation by Attorney.)*

A party has the right to be represented by an attorney at any proceeding or hearing under this act. A waiver thereof prior to the proceeding or hearing is ineffective.

SECTION 7. *(Witnesses, Subpoenas, Depositions.)*

(a) The arbitrators may issue (cause to be issued) subpoenas for the attendance of witnesses and for the production of books, records, documents and other evidence, and shall have the power to administer oaths. Subpoenas so issued shall be served, and upon application to the Court by a party or by the arbitrators, enforced, in the manner provided by law for the service and enforcement of subpoenas in a civil action.

(b) On application of a party and for use as evidence, the arbitrators may permit a deposition to be taken, in the manner and upon the terms designated by the arbitrators, of a witness who cannot be subpoenaed or is unable to attend the hearing.

(c) All provisions of law compelling a person under subpoena to testify are applicable.

(d) Fees for attendance as a witness shall be the same as for a witness in the .... Court.

SECTION 8. *(Award.)*

(a) The award shall be in writing and signed by the arbitrators joining in the award. The arbitrators shall deliver a copy to each party personally or by registered mail, or as provided in the agreement.

(b) An award shall be made within the time fixed therefor by the agreement or, if not so fixed, within such time as the court orders on application of a party. The parties may extend the time in writing either before or after the expiration thereof. A party waives the objection that an award was not made within the time required unless he notifies the arbitrators of his objection prior to the delivery of the award to him.

SECTION 9. *(Change of Award by Arbitrators.)*

On application of a party or, if an application to the court is pending under Sections 11, 12 or 13, on submission to the arbitrators by the court under such conditions as the court may order, the arbitrators may modify or correct the award upon the grounds stated in paragraphs (1) and (3) of subdivision (a) of Section 13, or for the purpose of clarifying the award. The application shall be made within twenty days after delivery of the award to the applicant. Written notice thereof shall be given forthwith to the opposing party, stating he must serve his objections thereto, if any, within ten days from the notice. The award so modified or corrected is subject to the provisions of Sections 11, 12 and 13.

SECTION 10. *(Fees and Expenses of Arbitration.)*

Unless otherwise provided in the agreement to arbitrate, the arbitrators' expenses and fees, together with other expenses, not including counsel fees, incurred in the conduct of the arbitration, shall be paid as provided in the award.

SECTION 11. *(Confirmation of an Award.)*

Upon application of a party, the Court shall confirm an award, unless within the time limits hereinafter imposed grounds are urged for vacating or modifying or correcting the award, in which case the court shall proceed as provided in Sections 12 and 13.

SECTION 12. *(Vacating an Award.)*

(a) Upon application of a party, the court shall vacate an award where:

(1) The award was procured by corruption, fraud or other undue means;

(2) There was evidence of partiality by an arbitrator appointed as a neutral or corruption in any of the arbitrators or misconduct prejudicing the rights of any party;

(3) The arbitrators exceeded their powers;

(4) The arbitrators refused to postpone the hearing upon sufficient cause being shown therefor or refused to hear evidence material to the controversy or otherwise so conducted the hearing, contrary to the provisions of Section 5, as to prejudice substantially the rights of a party; or

(5) There was no arbitration agreement and the issue was not adversely determined in proceedings under Section 2 and the party did

not participate in the arbitration hearing without raising the objection;

But the fact that the relief was such that it could not or would not be granted by a court of law or equity is not ground for vacating or refusing to confirm the award.

(b) An application under this Section shall be made within ninety days after delivery of a copy of the award to the applicant, except that, if predicated upon corruption, fraud or other undue means, it shall be made within ninety days after such grounds are known or should have been known.

(c) In vacating the award on grounds other than stated in clause (5) of Subsection (a) the court may order a rehearing before new arbitrators chosen as provided in the agreement, or in the absence thereof, by the court in accordance with Section 3, or, if the award is vacated on grounds set forth in clauses (3), and (4) of Subsection (a) the court may order a rehearing before the arbitrators who made the award or their successors appointed in accordance with Section 3. The time within which the agreement requires the award to be made is applicable to the rehearing and commences from the date of the order.

(d) If the application to vacate is denied and no motion to modify or correct the award is pending, the court shall confirm the award.

SECTION 13. *(Modification or Correction of Award.)*

(a) Upon application made within ninety days after delivery of a copy of the award to the applicant, the court shall modify or correct the award where:

(1) There was an evident miscalculation of figures or an evident mistake in the description of any person, thing or property referred to in the award;

(2) The arbitrators have awarded upon a matter not submitted to them and the award may be corrected without affecting the merits of the decision upon the issues submitted; or

(3) The award is imperfect in a matter of form, not affecting the merits of the controversy.

(b) If the application is granted, the court shall modify and correct the award so as to effect its intent and shall confirm the award as so modified and corrected. Otherwise, the court shall confirm the award as made.

(c) An application to modify or correct an award may be joined in the alternative with an application to vacate the award.

SECTION 14. *(Judgment or Decree on Award.)*

Upon the granting of an order confirming, modifying or correcting an award, judgment or decree shall be entered in conformity therewith and be enforced as any other judgment or decree. Costs of the application and of the proceedings subsequent thereto, and disbursements may be awarded by the court.

[SECTION 15. *(Judgment Roll, Docketing.)*

(a) On entry of judgment or decree, the clerk shall prepare the judgment roll consisting, to the extent filed, of the following:

(1) The agreement and each written extension of the time within which to make the award;

(2) The award;

(3) A copy of the order confirming, modifying or correcting the award; and

(4) A copy of the judgment or decree.

(b) The judgment or decree may be docketed as if rendered in an action.]

SECTION 16. *(Applications to Court.)*

Except as otherwise provided, an application to the court under this act shall be by motion and shall be heard in the manner and upon the notice provided by law or rule of court for the making and hearing of motions. Unless the parties have agreed otherwise, notice of an initial application for an order shall be served in the manner provided by law for the service of a summons in an action.

SECTION 17. *(Court, Jurisdiction.)*

The term "court" means any court of competent jurisdiction of this State. The making of an agreement described in Section 1 providing for arbitration in this State confers jurisdiction on the court to enforce the agreement under this Act and to enter judgment on an award thereunder.

SECTION 18. *(Venue.)*

An initial application shall be made to the court of the (county) in which the agreement provides the arbitration hearing shall be held or, if the hearing has been held, in the county in which it was held. Otherwise the application shall be made in the (county) where the adverse party resides or has a place of business or, if he has no residence or place of business in this State, to the court of any (county). All subsequent applications shall be made to the court hearing the initial application unless the court otherwise directs.

SECTION 19. *(Appeals.)*

(a) An appeal may be taken from:

(1) An order denying an application to compel arbitration under Section 2;

(2) An order granting an application to stay arbitration made under Section 2 (b) ;

(3) An order confirming or denying confirmation of an award;

(4) An order modifying or correcting an award;

(5) An order vacating an award without directing a rehearing; or

(6) A judgment or decree entered pursuant to the provisions of this act.

(b) The appeal shall be taken in the manner and to the same extent as from orders or judgments in a civil action.

SECTION 20. *(Act Not Retroactive.)*

This act applies only to agreements made subsequent to the taking effect of this act.

SECTION 21. *(Uniformity of Interpretation.)*

This act shall be so construed as to effectuate its general purpose to make uniform the law of those states which enact it.

SECTION 22. *(Constitutionality.)*

If any provision of this act or the application thereof to any person or circumstance is invalid, the invalidity shall not affect other provisions or applications of the act which can be given without the invalid provision or application, and to this end the provisions of this act are severable.

SECTION 23. *(Short Title.)*

This act may be cited as the Uniform Arbitration Act.

SECTION 24. *(Repeal.)*

All acts or parts of acts which are inconsistent with the provisions of this act are hereby repealed.

SECTION 25. *(Time of Taking Effect.)*

This act shall take effect ....

Brackets and parenthesis enclose language which the commissioners suggest may be used by those states desiring to do so.

Appendix D

Citations to State Arbitration Statutes

STATE STATUTES ESTABLISHING PERMANENT AGENCIES FOR LABOR ARBITRATION

ARIZONA — Ariz. Rev. Stat. Ann. § 23-107 (1969) (SLL 12:101).

COLORADO — Colo. Rev. Stat. Ann. § 80-2-5 (1953) (SLL 15:262).

CONNECTICUT — Conn. Gen. Stat. §§ 31-91; 31-101-111, (1958) (SLL 16:227-233, 16:265).

ILLINOIS — Ill. Rev. Stat. ch. 10, § 20 (1959) (SLL 23:245).

KENTUCKY — Ky. Rev. Stat. § 336.150 (1958) (SLL 27:102).

LOUISIANA — La. Rev. Stat. § 23:863 (1950) (SLL 28:246).

MAINE — Me. Rev. Stat. Ann. tit. 26 § 911 (1964) (SLL 29:229).

MARYLAND — Md. Code Ann. art. 89, §§ 3-13 (1968) (SLL 30:251).

MASSACHUSETTS — Mass. Gen. Laws Ann. ch. 23, § 7 (1956) (SLL 31:101).

MICHIGAN — Mich. Comp. Laws § 423.3 (1948) (SLL 32:245).

MONTANA — Mont. Rev. Codes Ann. § 41-901 (1947) (SLL 36:225).

NEW HAMPSHIRE — N.H. Rev. Stat. Ann. § 273:12 (1955) (SLL 39:203).

NEW JERSEY — N.J. Rev. Stat. § 34:13A-4 (1958) (SLL 40:246).

OKLAHOMA — Okla. Stat. tit. 40, § 4 (1951) (SLL 46:101).

PUERTO RICO — P.R. Laws Ann. tit. 3, § 321 (1955) (SLL 49:102).

RHODE ISLAND — R.I. Gen. Laws Ann. § 28-10-1 (1956) (SLL 50:101).

WASHINGTON — Wash. Rev. Code § 43.20.260 (1927) (SLL 58:101).

WYOMING — Wyo. Const. art. 19, § 5 (SLL 61:225).

OTHER STATE LAWS DEALING WITH LABOR ARBITRATION

ALABAMA — Ala. Code tit. 26 §§ 338-342 (1940) (SLL 10:202).

ALASKA — Alaska Comp. Laws Ann. 90.43.010 to 120 (1968) (SLL 11:222a).

ARIZONA — Ariz. Rev. Stat. Ann. §§ 12-1501 to 12-1517 (1962) (SLL 12:255).

ARKANSAS — Ark. Stat. Ann. § 81-107 (1947) (SLL 13:101).

CALIFORNIA — Cal. Civ. Proc. Code § 1280-1294; Cal. Civil Code 3390; Cal. Labor Code 1700.45.

CONNECTICUT — Conn. Gen. Stat. § 31-117 (1958).

COLORADO — Col. Rules of Civil Porc., Rule 109 (1963); Col. Rev. Stat. Ann. §§ 80-4-11 to 80-4-22; 80-5-10 to 11 (1963) (SLL 15:231-246; 15:261).

DELAWARE — Del. Code Ann. tit. 19, § 121 (1961) (SLL 17:106).

HAWAII — Hawaii Rev. Laws § 90B-1 (1963).

ILLINOIS — Ill. Rev. Stat. ch. 10, §§ 20-30 (1959) (SLL 23:245).

INDIANA — Ind. Ann. Stat. §§ 40-2401 to -2415 (1952) (SLL 24:158).

IOWA — Iowa Code ch. 90 (1958) (SLL 25:146).

KANSAS — Kan. Gen. Stat. Ann. §§ 44-603 to 626; 44-817 (1949) (SLL 26:219).

KENTUCKY — Ky. Rev. Stat. §§ 336.140, 336.150 (1958) (SLL 27:102).

LOUISIANA — La. Rev. Stat. §§ 23:861-23:876 (1950) (SLL 28:245).

MAINE — Me. Rev. Stat. Ann. tit. 26 §§ 881-922 (1964) (SLL 29:229).

MARYLAND —Md. Ann. Code art. 89, §§ 3-24; (1957) (SLL 30:251-30: 254).

MASSACHUSETTS — Mass. Gen. Laws Ann. ch. 150, §§ 1-11 (1956) (SLL 31:251).

MICHIGAN—Mich. Comp. Laws §§ 423.1-423.311 (1948) (SLL 32:245).

MINNESOTA—Minn. Stat. § 179.09 (1947) (SLL 33:225).

MONTANA—Mont. Rev. Codes Ann. §§ 41-901 to -909 (1947) (SLL 36:225).

NEVADA—Nev. Rev. Stat. §§ 614.010-.080 (1959) (SLL 38:235).

NEW HAMPSHIRE—N.H. Rev. Stat. Ann. §§ 273:12-27 (1955) (SLL 39:203).

NEW JERSEY—N.J. Rev. Stat. §§ 34:13, 13A, and 13B (Public Utilities) (1958) (SLL 40:243; 40:245; 40: 221).

NEW YORK—McKinney's Consolidated Laws of N.Y., Labor Law: §§ 751-760 (SLL 42:253).

NORTH CAROLINA—N.C. Gen. Stat. §§ 95-36.1 to -36.9 (1958) (SLL 43:217).

NORTH DAKOTA—N.D. Rev. Code, §§ 34-10-04 to 06 (1953) (SLL 44:226).

OHIO—Ohio Rev. Code Ann. §§ 4129.01-.12 (1954) (SLL 45:215).

OREGON—Ore. Rev. Stat. §§ 662.405-.455 (1957) (SLL 47:258) .

PENNSYLVANIA—Pa. Stat. Ann. tit. 43, §§ 211.31-.39 (1958) (SLL 48:241).

PUERTO RICO—P.R. Laws Ann. tit. 29, § 70(2) (c) (1955) (SLL 49:222).

RHODE ISLAND—R.I. Gen. Laws Ann. §§ 28-9-1 to -16 (1956) (SLL 50:255).

SOUTH CAROLINA—S.C. Code §§ 40-301 to -307 (1952) (except railroads and express companies) (SLL 51:221).

TEXAS—Tex. Rev. Civ. Stat. Ann. art. 239 to 249 (1959) (SLL 54:221).

UTAH—Utah Const. Art. XVI § 2; Utah Code Ann. § 35-1-16 (1953) (SLL 55:101).

VERMONT—Vt. Stat. Ann. tit. 21, §§ 501-513 (1959) (SLL 56:202).
WASHINGTON—Wash. Rev. Code § 49.08 (1958) (SLL 58:245).
WISCONSIN—Wis. Stat. §§ 111.10, 111.11 (1957) (SLL 60:225).

GENERAL ARBITRATION STATUTES APPARENTLY APPLICABLE TO BOTH COMMERCIAL AND LABOR DISPUTES

ALABAMA—Ala. Code tit. 7 §§ 829-844 (1940).
ARIZONA—Ariz. Rev. Stat. Ann. §§ 12-1501 to -1511, except 12-1509 (1956) (SLL 12:255).
ARKANSAS—Ark. Stat. Ann. §§ 34-501 to -510 (1947) (SLL 13:235).
CALIFORNIA—Cal. Civ. Proc. Code §§ 1280 to 1293 (1959) (SLL 14:249).
CONNECTICUT—Conn. Gen. Stat. § 52-408 (1958) (SLL 16:271).
DELAWARE—Del. Code Ann. tit. 10, §§ 5701-5706 (1953) (SLL 17: 129).
DISTRICT OF COLUMBIA—D.C. Code Ann. §§ 11-804, 16-701 to -1719 (1951) (SLL 18:232).
FLORIDA—Fla. Stat. tit. 6, ch. 57 (1943) (SLL 19:225).
GEORGIA—Ga. Code Ann. ch. 7. §§ 101-111; 201-224 (1935) (20:217).
HAWAII—Hawaii Rev. Laws 90B-1 to 90B-14 (1963).
IDAHO—Idaho Code Ann. §§ 7-901 to -910 (1947) (SLL 22:235).
ILLINOIS—Ill. Rev. Stat. ch. 10, §§ 1-17 (1959) (SLL 23:245).
INDIANA—Ind. Ann. Stat. §§ 3-201 to -226 (1946) (SLL 24:155).
IOWA—Iowa Code ch. 679 (1958) (SLL 25:145).
KANSAS—Kan. Gen. Stat. Ann. §§ 5-201 to -213 (1949) (SLL 26:251).
KENTUCKY—Ky. Rev. Stat. §§ 417.010-.040 (1958) (SLL 27:221).
LOUISIANA—La. Rev. Stat. §§ 9:4201-4217 (1950).
MAINE—Me. Rev. Stat. Ann. tit. 14, 1151-1155 (1964).
MASSACHUSETTS—Mass. Gen. Laws Ann. ch. 251, §§ 1-22 (1956).
MICHIGAN—Mich. Comp. Laws 600.5001 to 5031 (1963).
MINNESOTA—Minn. Stat. §§ 572.07 to 572.30 (1963) (SLL 33:251).
MISSISSIPPI—Miss. Code Ann. §§ 279-297 (1942) (SLL 34:222).
MISSOURI—Mo. Ann. Stat. §§ 435.010-.280 (1952) (SLL 35:220).
MONTANA—Mont. Rev. Codes Ann. §§ 93-201-1 to -10 (1947) (SLL 36:227).
NEBRASKA—Neb. Rev. Stat. §§ 25-2103 to 2120 (1943) (SLL 35:225). 35:225).
NEVADA—Nev. Rev. Stat. §§ 510-543 (1959) (SLL 38:237).
NEW HAMPSHIRE—N.H. Rev. Stat. Ann. ch. 542 (1955) (SLL 39: 202f).
NEW JERSEY—N.J. Rev. Stat. §§ 2A:24-1 to -11 (1958) (SLL 40:241).
NEW MEXICO—N.M. Stat. Ann. ch. 22, art. 3 (1953) (SLL 41: 213).
NEW YORK—N.Y. Civ. Prac. Act §§ 7501-7514 (SLL 42:256).

NORTH CAROLINA—N.C. Gen. Stat. §§ 1-544 to -567 (1953) (SLL 43:219).
NORTH DAKOTA—N.D. Rev. Code §§ 32-2901 to -2921 (1943) (SLL 44:226).
OHIO—Ohio Rev. Code Ann. §§ 2711.01-2711.15 (1954) (SLL 45:218).
OREGON—Ore. Rev. Stat. Ch. 122 §§ 1-4 (1957) (SLL 47:255).
PENNSYLVANIA—Pa. Stat. Ann. tit. 5 (1958) (SLL 48:242).
SOUTH CAROLINA—S.C. Const. Art. 6, § 1; S.C. Code §§ 10-1901 to 1904 (1952) (SLL 51:221).
TENNESSEE—Tenn. Code Ann. §§ 23-501 to -519 (1956) (SLL 53: 221).
TEXAS—Tex. Rev. Civ. Stat. Ann. art. 224 to 239 (1959).
UTAH—Utah Code Ann. §§ 78-31-1 to -22 (1953) (SLL 55:231).
VIRGINIA—Va. Code Ann. §§ 8-503 to -507 (1950) (SLL 57:215).
WEST VIRGINIA—W. Va. Code ch. 55, art. 10, §§ 1-7 (1955) (SLL 59:211).
WISCONSIN—Wisc. Stat. §§ 298.01-298.15 (1951) (SLL 60:245).
WYOMING—Wyo. Stat. §§ 1-1025 to -1048 (1957) (SLL 61:221).

GENERAL ARBITRATION STATE STATUTES
EXPRESSLY EXCLUDING LABOR DISPUTES

MICHIGAN—Mich. Comp. Laws § 600.5001 (1963).
OREGON—Ore. Rev. Stat. §§ 33.210-.340 (1957) (SLL 47:255).
PUERTO RICO—P.R. Laws Ann. tit. 32, §§ 3201-3229; tit. 31, § 4841 (1955) (SLL 49:245).
RHODE ISLAND—R.I.Gen . Laws Ann. §§ 10-3-2 to -20 (1956).
WASHINGTON—Wash. Rev. Code § 7.04 (1958) (SLL 58:245).
WISCONSIN—Wis. Stat. §§ 298.01-.18 (60:245).

Appendix E

Arbitration Policies, Functions, and Procedures of the Federal Mediation and Conciliation Service; Voluntary Labor Arbitration Rules of the American Arbitration Association; and Code of Ethics for Arbitrators, Procedural Standards for Arbitrators, and Conduct and Behavior of Parties

SECTION 1

Arbitration Policies, Functions, and Procedures
of the Federal Mediation and Conciliation Service

Text of Regulations Part 1404, dealing with arbitration policies, functions, and procedures, as last revised by the Director of the Federal Mediation and Conciliation Service, effective October 21, 1968. Notice of proposed rule changes was published in the FEDERAL REGISTER June 21, 1968 (68 F.R. 7358).

SECTION 1404.1 *Arbitration.*

The labor policy of the U. S. Government is designed to foster and promote free collective bargaining. Voluntary arbitration is encouraged by public policy and is in fact almost universally utilized by the parties to resolve disputes involving the interpretation or application of collective bargaining agreements. Also, in appropriate cases, voluntary arbitration or factfinding are tools of free collective bargaining and may be desirable alternatives to economic strife in determining terms of a collective bargaining agreement. The parties assume broad responsibilities for the success of the private juridical system they have chosen. The Service will assist the parties in their selection of arbitrators.

SECTION 1404.2 *Composition of roster maintained by the Service.*

(a) It is the policy of the Service to maintain on its roster only those arbitrators who are qualified and acceptable, and who adhere to ethical standards.

(b) Applicants for inclusion on its roster must not only be well-grounded in the field of labor-management relations, but, also, usually possess experience in the labor arbitration field or its equivalent. After a careful screening and evaluation of the applicant's experience, the Service contacts representatives of both labor and management since arbitrators must be generally acceptable to those who utilize its arbitration facilities. The responses to such inquires are carefully weighed before an otherwise qualified arbitrator is included on the Service's roster. Persons employed full time as representatives of management, labor, or the Federal Government are not included on the Service's roster.

(c) The arbitrators on the roster are expected to keep the Service informed of changes in address, occupation or availability, and of any business connections with or of concern to labor or management. The Service reserves the right to remove names from the active roster or to take other appropriate action where there is good reason to believe that an arbitrator is not adhering to these regulations and related policy.

SECTION 1404.3 *Security status.*

The arbitrators on the Service's roster are not employees of the Federal Government, and, because of this status, the Service does not investigate their security status. Moreover, when an arbitrator is selected by the parties, he is retained by them and, accordingly, they must assume complete responsibility for the arbitrator's security status.

SECTION 1404.4 *Procedures; how to request arbitration services.*

The Service prefers to act upon a joint request which should be addressed to the Director of the Federal Mediation and Conciliation Service, Washington, D.C. 20427. In the event that the request is made by only one party, the Service may act if the parties have agreed that either of them may seek a panel of arbitrators, either by specific ad hoc agreement or by specific language in the applicable collective bargaining agreement. A brief statement of the nature of the issues in dispute should accompany the request, to enable the Service to submit the names of arbitrators qualified for the issues involved. The request should also include a copy of the collective bargaining agreement or stipulation. In the event that the entire agreement is not available, a verbatim copy of the provisions relating to arbitration should accompany the request.

SECTION 1404.5 *Arbitrability.*

Where either party claims that a dispute is not subject to arbitration, the Service will not decide the merits of such claim. The submission of a panel should not be construed as anything more than compliance with a request.

SECTION 1404.6 *Nominations of arbitrators.*

(a) When the parties have been unable to agree on an arbitrator, the Service will submit to the parties the names of seven arbitrators unless the applicable collective bargaining agreement provides for a different number, or unless the parties themselves request a different number. Together with the submission of a panel of suggested arbitrators, the Service furnishes a short statement of the background, qualifications, experience and per diem fee of each of the nominees.

(b) In selecting names for inclusion on a panel, the Service considers many factors, but the desires of the parties are, of course, the foremost consideration. If at any time both the company and the union suggest that a name or names be omitted from a panel, such name or names will be omitted. If one party only (a company or a union) suggests that a name or names be omitted from a panel, such name or names will generally be omitted, subject to the following qualifications: (1) If the suggested omissions are excessive in number or otherwise appear to lack careful consideration, they will not be considered; (2) all such suggested omissions should be reviewed after the passage of a reasonable period of time. The Service will not place names on a panel at the request of one party unless the other party has knowledge of such request and has no objection thereto, or unless both parties join in such request. If the issue described in the request appears to require special technical experience or qualifications, arbitrators who possess such qualifications will, where possible, be included in the list submitted to the parties. Where the parties expressly request that the list be composed entirely of technicians, or that it be all local or nonlocal, such request will be honored, if qualified arbitrators are available.

(c) Two possible methods of selection from a panel are — (1) at a joint meeting, alternately striking names from the submitted panel until one remains, and (2) each party separately advising the Service of its order of preference by numbering each name on the panel. In almost all cases, an arbitrator is chosen from one panel of names. However, if a request for another panel is made, the Service will comply with the request, providing that additional panels are permissible under the terms of the agreement or the parties so stipulate.

(d) Subsequent adjustment of disputes is not precluded by the submission of a panel or an appointment. A substantial number of issues are being settled by the parties themselves after the initial request for a panel and after selection of the arbitrator. Notice of such settlement should be sent promptly to the arbitrator and to the Service.

(e) The arbitrator is entitled to be compensated whenever he receives insufficient notice of settlement to enable him to rearrange his schedule of arbitration hearings or working hours. In other situations, when an arbitrator spends an unusually large amount of time in arranging or rearranging hearing dates, it may be appropriate for him to make an administrative charge to the parties in the event the case is settled before hearing.

SECTION 1404.7 *Appointment of arbitrators.*

(a) After the parties notify the Service of their selection, the arbitrator is appointed by the Director. If any party fails to notify the Service within 15 days after the date of mailing the panel, all persons named therein may be deemed acceptable to such party. The Service will make a direct appointment of an arbitrator based upon a joint request, or upon a unilateral request when the applicable collective bargaining agreement so authorizes.

(b) The arbitrator, upon appointment notification, is requested to communicate with the parties immediately to arrange for preliminary matters such as date and place of hearing.

SECTION 1404.8 *Status of arbitrators after appointment.*

After appointment, the legal relationship of arbitrators is with the parties rather than the Service, though the Service does have a continuing interest in the proceedings. Industrial peace and good labor relations are enhanced by arbitrators who function justly, expeditiously and impartially so as to obtain and retain the respect, esteem and confidence of all participants in the arbitration proceedings. The conduct of the arbitration proceeding is under the arbitrator's jurisdiction and control, subject to such rules of procedure as the parties may jointly prescribe. He is to make his own decisions based on the record in the proceedings. The arbitrator may, unless prohibited by law, proceed in the absence of any party who, after due notice, fails to be present or to obtain a postponement. The award, however, must be supported by evidence.

SECTION 1404.9 *Prompt decision.*

(a) Early hearing and decision of industrial disputes is desirable in the interest of good labor relations. The parties should inform the Service whenever a decision is unduly delayed. The Service expects to be notified by the arbitrator if and when (1) he cannot schedule, hear and determine issues promptly, and (2) he is advised that a dispute has been settled by the parties prior to arbitration.

(b) The award shall be made not later than 30 days from the date of the closing of the hearing, or the receipt of a transcript and any post-hearing briefs, or if oral hearings have been waived, then from the date of receipt of the final statements and proof by the arbitrator, unless otherwise agreed upon by the parties or specified by law. However, a failure to make such an award within 30 days shall not invalidate an award.

SECTION 1404.10 *Arbitrator's award and report.*

(a) At the conclusion of the hearing and after the award has been submitted to the parties, each arbitrator is required to file a copy with the Service. The arbitrator is further required to submit a report showing a breakdown of his fees and expense charges so that the Service may be in a position to check conformance with its fee policies. Cooperation in filing both award and report within 15 days after handing down the award is expected of all arbitrators.

(b) It is the policy of the Service not to release arbitration decisions for publication without the consent of both parties. Furthermore, the Service expects the arbitrators it has nominated or appointed not to give publicity to awards they may issue, except in a manner agreeable to both parties.

Section 1404.11 *Fees of arbitrators.*

(a) No administrative or filing fee is charged by the Service. The current policy of the Service permits each of its nominees or appointees to charge a per diem fee for his services, the amount of which is certified in advance by him to the Service. Each arbitrator's maximum per diem fee is set forth on his biographical sketch which is sent to the parties at such time as his name is submitted to them for consideration. The arbitrator shall not change his per diem fee without giving at least 90 days advance notice to the Service of his intention to do so.

(b) In those rare instances where arbitrators fix wages or other important terms of a new contract, the maximum fee noted above may be exceeded by the arbitrator after agreement by the parties. Conversely, an arbitrator may give due consideration to the financial condition of the parties and charge less than his usual fee in appropriate cases.

Section 1404.12 *Conduct of hearings.*

The Service does not prescribe detailed or specific rules of procedure for the conduct of an arbitration proceeding because it favors flexibility in labor relations. Questions such as hearing rooms, submission of prehearing or posthearing briefs, and recording of testimony, are left to the discretion of the individual arbitrator and to the parties. The Service does, however, expect its arbitrators and the parties to conform to applicable laws, and to be guided by ethical and procedural standards as codified by appropriate professional organizations and generally accepted by the industrial community and experienced arbitrators.

In cities where the Service maintains offices, the parties are welcome upon request to the Service to use its conference rooms when they are available.

SECTION 2

Voluntary Labor Arbitration Rules
as Amended and in Effect February 1, 1965

1. *Agreement of Parties*—The parties shall be deemed to have made these Rules a part of their arbitration agreement whenever, in a col-

lective bargaining agreement or submission, they have provided for arbitration by the American Arbitration Association (hereinafter AAA) or under its Rules. These Rules shall apply in the form obtaining at the time the arbitration is initiated.

2. *Name of Tribunal*—Any Tribunal constituted by the parties under these Rules shall be called the Voluntary Labor Arbitration Tribunal.

and an arbitration is instituted thereunder, they thereby authorize the AAA to administer the arbitration. The authority and obligations of the Administrator are as provided in the agreement of the parties 3. *Administrator*—When parties agree to arbitrate under these Rules and in these Rules.

4. *Delegation of Duties*—The duties of the AAA may be carried out through such representatives or committees as the AAA may direct.

5. *National Panel of Labor Arbitrators*—The AAA shall establish and maintain a National Panel of Labor Arbitrators and shall appoint

6. *Office of Tribunal*—The general office of the Labor Arbitration arbitrators therefrom, as hereinafter provided.
Tribunal is the headquarters of the AAA, which may, however, assign the administration of an arbitration to any of its Regional Offices.

7. *Initiation Under an Arbitration Clause in a Collective Bargaining Agreement*—Arbitration under an arbitration clause in a collective bargaining agreement under these Rules may be initiated by either party in the following manner:

(a) By giving written notice to the other party of intention to arbitrate (Demand), which notice shall contain a statement setting forth the nature of the dispute and the remedy sought, and

(b) By filing at any Regional Office of the AAA two copies of said notice, together with a copy of the collective bargaining agreement, or such parts thereof as relate to the dispute, including the arbitration provisions. After the Arbitrator is appointed, no new or different claim may be submitted to him except with the consent of the Arbitrator and all other parties.

8. *Answer*—The party upon whom the demand for arbitration is made may file an answering statement with the AAA within seven days after notice from the AAA, in which event he shall simultaneously send a copy of his answer to the other party. If no answer is filed within the stated time, it will be assumed that the claim is denied. Failure to file an answer shall not operate to delay the arbitration.

9. *Initiation under a Submission*—Parties to any collective bargaining agreement may initiate an arbitration under these Rules by filing at any Regional Office of the AAA two copies of a written agreement to arbitrate under these Rules (Submission), signed by the parties and setting forth the nature of the dispute and the remedy sought.

10. *Fixing of Locale*—The parties may mutually agree upon the locale where the arbitration is to be held. If the locale is not designated in the collective bargaining agreement or submission, and if there is a dispute as to the appropriate locale, the AAA shall have the power to determine the locale and its decision shall be binding.

11. *Qualifications of Arbitrator*—No person shall serve as a neutral Arbitrator in any arbitration in which he has any financial or personal interest in the result of the arbitration, unless the parties, in writing, waive such disqualification.

12. *Appointment from Panel*—If the parties have not appointed an Arbitrator and have not provided any other method of appointment, the Arbitrator shall be appointed in the following manner: Immediately after the filing of the Demand or Submission, the AAA shall submit simultaneously to each party an identical list of names of persons chosen from the Labor Panel. Each party shall have seven days from the mailing date in which to cross off any names to which he objects, number the remaining names indicating the order of his preference, and return the list to the AAA. If a party does not return the list within the time specified, all persons named therein shall be deemed acceptable. From among the persons who have been approved on both lists, and in accordance with the designated order of mutual preference, the AAA shall invite the acceptance of an Arbitrator to serve. If the parties fail to agree upon any of the persons named or if those named decline or are unable to act, or if for any other reason the appointment cannot be made from the submitted lists, the Administrator shall have power to make the appointment from other members of the Panel without the submission of any additional lists.

13. *Direct Appointment by Parties*—If the agreement of the parties names an Arbitrator or specifies a method of appointing an Arbitrator, that designation or method shall be followed. The notice of appointment, with the name and address of such Arbitrator, shall be filed with the AAA by the appointing party.

If the agreement specifies a period of time within which an Arbitrator shall be appointed, and any party fails to make such appointment within that period, the AAA may make the appointment.

If no period of time is specified in the agreement, the AAA shall notify the parties to make the appointment and if within seven days thereafter such Arbitrator has not been so appointed, the AAA shall make the appointment.

14. *Appointment of Neutral Arbitrator by Party-Appointed Arbitrators*—If the parties have appointed their Arbitrators, or if either or both of them have been appointed as provided in Section 13, and have authorized such Arbitrators to appoint a neutral Arbitrator within a specified time and no appointment is made within such time or any

agreed extension thereof, the AAA may appoint a neutral Arbitrator, who shall act as Chairman.

If no period of time is specified for appointment of the neutral Arbitrator and the parties do not make the appointment within seven days from the date of the appointment of the last party-appointed Arbitrator, the AAA shall appoint such neutral Arbitrator, who shall act as Chairman.

If the parties have agreed that the Arbitrators shall appoint the neutral Arbitrator from the Panel, the AAA shall furnish to the party-appointed Arbitrators, in the manner prescribed in Section 12, a list selected from the Panel, and the appointment of the neutral Arbitrator shall be made as prescribed in such Section.

15. *Number of Arbitrators*—If the arbitration agreement does not specify the number of Arbitrators, the dispute shall be heard and determined by one Arbitrator, unless the parties otherwise agree.

16. *Notice to Arbitrator of His Appointment*—Notice of the appointment of the neutral Arbitrator shall be mailed to the Arbitrator by the AAA and the signed acceptance of the Arbitrator shall be filed with the AAA prior to the opening of the first hearing.

17. *Disclosure by Arbitrator of Disqualification*—Prior to accepting his appointment, the prospective neutral Arbitrator shall disclose any circumstances likely to create a presumption of bias or which he believes might disqualify him as an impartial Arbitrator. Upon receipt of such information, the AAA shall immediately disclose it to the parties. If either party declines to waive the presumptive disqualification, the vacancy thus created shall be filled in accordance with the applicable provisions of these Rules.

18. *Vacancies*—If any Arbitrator should resign, die, withdraw, refuse or be unable or disqualified to perform the duties of his office, the AAA shall, on proof satisfactory to it, declare the office vacant. Vacancies shall be filled in the same manner as that governing the making of the original appointment, and the matter shall be reheard by the new Arbitrator.

19. *Time and Place of Hearing*—The Arbitrator shall fix the time and place for each hearing. At least five days prior thereto the AAA shall mail notice of the time and place of hearing to each party, unless the parties otherwise agree.

20. *Representation by Counsel*—Any party may be represented at the hearing by counsel or by other authorized representative.

21. *Stenographic Record*—Whenever a stenographic record is requested by one or more parties, the AAA will arrange for a stenographer. The total cost of the record shall be shared equally among parties ordering copies, unless they agree otherwise.

22. *Attendance at Hearings*—Persons having a direct interest in the arbitration are entitled to attend hearings. The Arbitrator shall have the power to require the retirement of any witness or witnesses during the testimony of other witnesses. It shall be discretionary with the Arbitrator to determine the propriety of the attendance of any other persons.

23. *Adjournments*—The Arbitrator for good cause shown may adjourn the hearing upon the request of a party or upon his own initiative, and shall adjourn when all the parties agree thereto.

24. *Oaths*—Before proceeding with the first hearing, each Arbitrator may take an Oath of Office, and if required by law, shall do so. The Arbitrator may, in his discretion, require witnesses to testify under oath administered by any duly qualified person, and if required by law or requested by either party, shall do so.

25. *Majority Decision*—Whenever there is more than one Arbitrator, all decisions of the Arbitrators shall be by majority vote. The award shall also be made by majority vote unless the concurrence of all is expressly required.

26. *Order of Proceedings*—A hearing shall be opened by the filing of the oath of the Arbitrator, where required, and by the recording of the place, time and date of hearing, the presence of the Arbitrator and parties, and counsel if any, and the receipt by the Arbitrator of the Demand and answer, if any, or the Submission.

Exhibits, when offered by either party, may be received in evidence by the Arbitrator. The names and addresses of all witnesses and exhibits in order received shall be made a part of the record.

The Arbitrator may, in his discretion, vary the normal procedure under which the initiating party first presents his claim, but in any case shall afford full and equal opportunity to all parties for presentation of relevant proofs.

27. *Arbitration in the Absence of a Party*—Unless the law provides to the contrary, the arbitration may proceed in the absence of any party, who, after due notice, fails to be present or fails to obtain an adjournment. An award shall not be made solely on the default of a party. The Arbitrator shall require the other party to submit such evidence as he may require for the making of an award.

28. *Evidence*—The parties may offer such evidence as they desire and shall produce such additional evidence as the Arbitrator may deem necessary to an understanding and determination of the dispute. When the Arbitrator is authorized by law to subpoena witnesses and documents, he may do so upon his own initiative or upon the request of any party. The Arbitrator shall be the judge of the relevancy and materiality of the evidence offered and conformity to legal rules of evidence shall not be necessary. All evidence shall be taken in the

presence of all of the Arbitrators and all of the parties except where any of the parties is absent in default or has waived his right to be present.

29. *Evidence by Affidavit and Filing of Documents*—The Arbitrator may receive and consider the evidence of witnesses by affidavit, but shall give it only such weight as he deems proper after consideration of any objections made to its admission.

All documents not filed with the Arbitrator at the hearing but which are arranged at the hearing or subsequently by agreement of the parties to be submitted, shall be filed with the AAA for transmission to the Arbitrator. All parties shall be afforded opportunity to examine such documents.

30. *Inspection*—Whenever the Arbitrator deems it necessary, he may make an inspection in connection with the subject matter of the dispute after written notice to the parties who may, if they so desire, be present at such inspection.

31. *Closing of Hearings*—The Arbitrator shall inquire of all parties whether they have any further proofs to offer or witnesses to be heard. Upon receiving negative replies, the Arbitrator shall declare the hearings closed and a minute thereof shall be recorded. If briefs or other documents are to be filed, the hearings shall be declared closed as of the final date set by the Arbitrator for filing with the AAA. The time limit within which the Arbitrator is required to make his award shall commence to run, in the absence of other agreement by the parties, upon the closing of the hearings.

32. *Reopening of Hearings*—The hearings may be reopened by the Arbitrator on his own motion, or on the motion of either party, for good cause shown, at any time before the award is made, but if the reopening of the hearing would prevent the making of the award within the specific time agreed upon by the parties in the contract out of which the controversy has arisen, the matter may not be reopened, unless both parties agree upon the extension of such time limit. When no specific date is fixed in the contract, the Arbitrator may reopen the hearings, and the Arbitrator shall have 30 days from the closing of the reopened hearings within which to make an award.

33. *Waiver of Rules*—Any party who proceeds with the arbitration after knowledge that any provision or requirement of these Rules has not been complied with and who fails to state his objection thereto in writing, shall be deemed to have waived his right to object.

34. *Waiver of Oral Hearing*—The parties may provide, by written agreement, for the waiver of oral hearings. If the parties are unable to agree as to the procedure, the AAA shall specify a fair and equitable procedure.

35. *Extensions of Time*—The parties may modify any period of time by mutual agreement. The AAA for good cause may extend any period of time established by these Rules, except the time for making the award. The AAA shall notify the parties of any such extension of time and its reason therefor.

36. *Serving of Notices*—Each party to a Submission or other agreement which provides for arbitration under these Rules shall be deemed to have consented and shall consent that any papers, notices or process necessary or proper for the initiation or continuation of an arbitration under these Rules and for any court action in connection therewith or the entry of judgment on an award made thereunder, may be served upon such party (a) by mail addressed to such party or his attorney at his last known address, or (b) by personal service, within or without the state wherein the arbitration is to be held.

37. *Time of Award*—The award shall be rendered promptly by the Arbitrator and, unless otherwise agreed by the parties, or specified by the law, not later than thirty days from the date of closing the hearings, or if oral hearings have been waived, then from the date of transmitting the final statements and proofs to the Arbitrator.

38. *Form of Award*—The award shall be in writing and shall be signed either by the neutral Arbitrator or by a concurring majority if there be more than one Arbitrator. The parties shall advise the AAA whenever they do not require the Arbitrator to accompany the award with an opinion.

39. *Award Upon Settlement*—If the parties settle their dispute during the course of the arbitration, the Arbitrator, upon their request, may set forth the terms of the agreed settlement in an award.

40. *Delivery of Award to Parties*—Parties shall accept as legal delivery of the award the placing of the award or a true copy thereof in the mail by the AAA, addressed to such party at his last known address or to his attorney, or personal service of the award, or the filing of the award in any manner which may be prescribed by law.

41. *Release of Documents for Judicial Proceedings*—The AAA shall, upon the written request of a party, furnish to such party at his expense certified facsimiles of any papers in the AAA's possession that may be required in judicial proceedings relating to the arbitration.

42. *Judicial Proceedings*—The AAA is not a necessary party in judicial proceedings relating to the arbitration.

43. *Administrative Fee*—As a nonprofit organization, the AAA shall prescribe an administrative fee schedule to compensate it for the cost of providing administrative services. The schedule in effect at the time of filing shall be applicable.

44. *Expenses*—The expenses of witnesses for either side shall be paid by the party producing such witnesses.

Expenses of the arbitration, other than the cost of the stenographic record, including required traveling and other expenses of the Arbitrator and of AAA representatives, and the expenses of any witnesses or the cost of any proofs produced at the direct request of the Arbitrator, shall be borne equally by the parties unless they agree otherwise, or unless the Arbitrator in his award assesses such expenses or any part thereof against any specified party or parties.

45. *Communication with Arbitrator*—There shall be no communication between the parties and a neutral Arbitrator other than at oral hearings. Any other oral or written communications from the parties to the Arbitrator shall be directed to the AAA for transmittal to the Arbitrator.

46. *Interpretation and Application of Rules*—The Arbitrator shall interpret and apply these Rules insofar as they relate to his powers and duties. When there is more than one Arbitrator and a difference arises among them concerning the meaning or application of any such Rules, it shall be decided by majority vote. If that is unobtainable, either Arbitrator or party may refer the question to the AAA for final decision. All other Rules shall be interpreted and applied by the AAA.

SECTION 3

Code of Ethics for Arbitrators, Procedural Standards for Arbitrators, and Conduct and Behavior of Parties*

PART I

CODE OF ETHICS FOR ARBITRATORS

I. *Character of the Office*

The function of an arbitrator is to decide disputes. He should, therefore, adhere to such general standards of adjudicatory bodies as require a full, impartial and orderly consideration of evidence and argument, in accordance with applicable arbitration law and the rules or general understandings or practices of the parties.

The parties in dispute, in referring a matter to arbitration, have indicated their desire not to resort to litigation or to economic conflict. They have delegated to the arbitrator power to settle their differences. It follows that the assumption of the office of arbitrator places upon the incumbent solemn duties and responsibilities. Every person who acts in this capacity should uphold the traditional honor, dignity, integrity and prestige of the office.

---

* Reprinted with the permission of the American Arbitration Association.

II. *The Tri-Partite Board*

Where tri-partite boards serve in labor arbitrations, it is the duty of the parties' nominees to make every reasonable effort to promote fair and objective conduct of the proceedings, to aid the arbitration board in its deliberations and to bring about a just and harmonious disposition of the controversy. It is recognized, however, that the parties frequently expect their appointees to serve also as representatives of their respective points of view. In such cases, the rules of ethics in this Code, insofar as they relate to the obligations of strict impartiality, are to be taken as applying only to the third or neutral arbitrator.

Such representatives, however, unless the parties agree otherwise, should refrain from conveying to the parties who appointed them, the discussions which take place in executive session and any information concerning the deliberations of the board. No information concerning the decision should be given in advance of its delivery simultaneously to both parties.

III. *Qualification for Office*

Any person whom the parties or the appointing agency choose to regard as qualified to determine their dispute is entitled to act as their arbitrator. It is, however, incumbent upon the arbitrator at the time of his selection to disclose to the parties any cricumstances, associations or relationships that might reasonably raise any doubt as to his impartiality or his technical qualification for the particular case.

IV. *Essential Conduct*

a) The arbitrator should be conscientious, considerate and patient in the discharge of his functions. There should be no doubt as to his complete impartiality. He should be fearless of public clamor and indifferent to private, political or partisan influences.

b) The arbitrator should not undertake or incur obligations to either party which may interfere with his impartial determination of the issue submitted to him.

V. *Duty to the Parties*

The arbitrator's duty is to determine the matters in dispute, which may involve differences over the interpretation of existing provisions or terms and conditions of a new contract. In either event, the arbitrator shall be governed by the wishes of the parties, which may be expressed in their agreement, arbitration submission or in any other form of understanding. He should not undertake to induce a settlement of the dispute against the wishes of either party. If, however, an atmosphere is created or the issues are so simplified or reduced as to lead to a voluntary settlement by the parties, a function of his office has been fulfilled.

VI. *Acceptance, Refusal or Withdrawal from Office*

The arbitrator, being appointed by voluntary act of the parties, may accept or decline the appointment. When he accepts he should continue in office until the matter submitted to him is finally determined. When there are circumstances which, in his judgment, compel his withdrawal, the parties are entitled to prompt notice and explanation.

VII. *Oath of Office*

When an oath of office is taken it should serve as the arbitrator's guide. When an oath is not required or is waived by the parties, the arbitrator should nevertheless observe the standards which the oath imposes.

VIII. *Privacy of the Arbitration*

a) An arbitrator should not, without the approval of the parties, disclose to third persons any evidence, argument or discussions pertaining to the arbitration.

b) There should be no disclosure of the terms of an award by any arbitrator until after it is delivered simultanteously to all of the parties and publication or public disclosure should be only with the parties' consent.

Discussions within an arbitration board should be held in confidence. Dissenting opinions may be filed, however, but they should be based on the arbitrators' views on the evidence and controlling principles, and not on the discussions which took place in the executive sessions of the board.

IX. *Advertising and Solicitation*

Advertising by an arbitrator and soliciting of cases is improper and not in accordance with the dignity of the office. No arbitrator should suggest to any party that future cases be referred to him.

PART II

PROCEDURAL STANDARDS

FOR ARBITRATORS

The standards set forth in the following sections are intended only as general guides to arbitrators and to parties in arbitration proceedings. It is not intended that they will be literally adhered to in every particular, nor are they intended to supplant contrary practices which in particular cases have been established or accepted by the parties. These standards are meant to be equally applicable to partisan and neutral members of arbitration boards.

These standards of procedure are not to be deemed mandatory precepts or controlling rules which will furnish a basis for attacking awards or enlarging the grounds prescribed by law for the impeachment of awards.

I. *Compensation and Expenses of the Arbitrator*

a) Arbitrators serving in labor-management disputes generally receive compensation. The position of an arbitrator, whether compensated or not, is an honorary one and is accepted as an opportunity for public service.

b) Compensation for arbitrators' services should be reasonable and consistent with the nature of the case and the circumstances of the parties. A fee previously fixed by the parties, or by schedule, should not be altered during the proceeding or after the award is delivered.

c) It is commonly understood that necessary expenses, including travel, communications and maintenance, may be incurred by the arbitrator and that such expenses are reimbursable. The arbitrator should be prepared to render a statement of his expenses if the parties desire it.

II. *Hearing Arrangements*

a) The arbitrator should consult the convenience of the parties in fixing the time and place for the hearing but should not allow one party to delay unduly the fixing of a date for the hearing. Written and timely notice of the date, time and place of the hearing should be given.

b) Whenever the law permits, the arbitrator in his discretion may issue subpoenas.

III. *Oath of Office*

The following is the general form of oath which the law of certain states requires the arbitrator to take:

.... being duly sworn deposes and says that he will faithfully and fairly hear and examine the matters in controversy between the above named Parties, and that he will make a just award according to the best of his understanding.

IV. *The Hearing*

a) The arbitrator should be prompt in his attendance at the hearing and should so conduct the proceeding as to reflect the importance and seriousness of the issue before him. The orderly conduct of the proceeding is under his jurisdiction and control, subject to such rules of procedure as the parties may prescribe. He should proceed promptly with the hearing and determination of the dispute. He should countenance no unnecessary delays in the examination of witnesses or in the presentation of evidence. Where the law requires it, witnesses must be sworn unless the parties duly waive this requirement.

b) The arbitrator may participate in the examination of parties or witnesses in order to clarify the issues and bring to light all relevant facts necessary to a fair and informed decision of the issues submitted to him. However, he should bear in mind that undue interference or emphasis upon his own knowledge or view may tend to prevent the proper presentation of the case by a party. Examinations should be fair and courteous and directed toward encouraging a full presentation of the case. The arbitrator should avoid assuming a controversial attitude toward witnesses, parties or other arbitrators. He should avoid expressing a premature opinion.

c) The informality of the hearings should not be allowed to affect decorum and the orderly presentation of proof. The arbitrator should seek to prevent any argument or conduct at the hearings which would tend to cause bitterness or acrimony.

d) Unless the parties approve, the arbitrator should not, in the absence of or without notice to one party, hold interviews with, or consider arguments or communciations from the other party. If any such communications be received, their contents should be disclosed to all parties and an opportunity afforded to comment thereon.

e) The arbitrator should allow a fair hearing, with full opportunity to the parties to offer all evidence which they deem reasonably material. He may, however, exclude evidence which is clearly immaterial. He may receive and consider affidavits, giving them such weight as the circumstances warrant, but in so doing, he should afford the other side an opportunity to cross-examine the persons making the affidavits or to take their depositions or otherwise interrogate them.

f) The arbitrator is expected to exercise his own best judgment. He is not required except by specific agreement of the parties to follow precedent. He should not, however, prevent the parties from presenting the decisions of other arbitrators in support of their positions. When the parties have selected a continuing arbitrator, it is generally recognized that he may establish or follow precedents for the same parties.

V. *The Award*

a) The arbitrator should render his award promptly and must render his award within the time prescribed, if any. The award should be definite, certain and final, and should dispose of all matters submitted. It should reserve no future duties to the arbitrator except by agreement of the parties.

b) The award should be stated separately from the opinion, if an opinion is rendered.

c) It is discretionary with the arbitrator, upon the request of all parties, to give the terms of their voluntary settlement the status of an award.

d) The award should be personally signed by the arbitrator and delivered simultaneously to all parties. The arbitrator should exercise extreme care to see that the contractual or legal requirements for making and delivering the award are met.

e) It is discretionary with the arbitrator to state reasons for his decision or to accompany the award with an opinion. Opinions should not contain gratuitous advice or comments not related or necessary to the determination of the issues. If either party requests the arbitrator to prepare an opinion, such request should be followed.

f) After the award has been rendered, the arbitrator should not issue any clarification or interpretation thereof, or comments thereon, except at the request of both parties, unless the agreement provides therefor.

VI. *Privacy of Proceeding and Award*

The arbitrator should not publish or publicly comment on the proceedings or the award against the wishes of the parties.

PART III

CONDUCT AND BEHAVIOR OF PARTIES

I. *General*

Arbitration is predicated on the voluntary agreement of the parties to submit a dispute to a disinterested third party for final determination. It implies not only the willingness to arbitrate but the willingness to attend a hearing, submit evidence, submit to cross-examination and to abide by the decision of the arbitrator.

II. *Scope*

The power of the arbitrator depends upon the agreement of the parties. Accordingly, the contract or the submission agreement should define his powers. In initiating an arbitration—whether under a clause in a collective bargaining agreement or under a submission agreement or a stipulation — it is the duty of the parties to set forth the nature of the controversy, the claim asserted and the remedy sought. The initiating party has the duty of setting forth its claim and the defending party the right to outline its position.

III. *Selection of Arbitrator*

The parties should select the arbitrator, in accordance with their agreement, to determine the controversy existing between them and his designation should be based on his integrity, knowledge and judgment. A party should not seek to obtain the appointment of an arbitrator in the belief that he will favor that party and thereby give him an advantage over his adversary.

In keeping with the desire for complete impartiality, parties should reject as arbitrators persons who solicit cases.

IV. *The Tri-Partite Board*

When parties select members of tri-partite boards, it is recognized that generally each will select a representative rather than an impartial arbitrator, but in making such appointment parties should select persons who will join with the impartial arbitrator in a full and fair discussion and consideration of the merits of the question to be determined.

V. *Essential Conduct*

Parties should approach arbitration in a spirit of cooperation with the arbitrator and should seek to aid him in the performance of his duties.

Having selected an arbitrator, the parties are under a duty not to subject him to improper pressures or influences which may tend to prejudice his judgment. They should neither give nor offer favors of any kind to the arbitrator. As a general rule they should not communicate with him privately; and if it becomes necessary to communicate with him, it should be done in writing and a copy thereof should be simultaneously delivered to the other party.

Parties should respect the office of the arbitrator and recognize his essential right to control the conduct of the arbitration and should abide by whatever rulings he may make.

When an arbitrator elects to withdraw from a proceeding and gives the parties his reasons, they should respect his right to do so in the interest of good arbitration.

VI. *The Hearing*

Parties should not unduly delay the fixing of a date for the hearing nor the completion of the hearing. They should be prepared to proceed expeditiously with their evidence and their witnesses, have their exhibits ready and cooperate with the arbitrator in furnishing whatever additional information he may deem necessary.

They should be prompt in attendance at the hearing.

Parties should be fair and courteous in their examination of witnesses and in their presentation of facts. Concealment of necessary facts or the use of exaggeration is not conducive to a good or sound determination of the differences between the parties. Acrimonious, bitter or ill-mannered conduct is harmful to the cause of good arbitration.

When hearings are concluded, parties should not attempt to communicate any additional information to the arbitrator. If new evidence becomes available, written application for the re-opening of the proceeding with the reasons therefor should be made to the arbitrator and a copy transmitted simultaneously to the other party.

When it has been agreed that briefs will be submitted, they should be filed promptly on the date arranged and no new matter should be included in the briefs. Briefs should be a summarization of the evidence presented at the hearing, together with the arguments of the parties and their comments on the evidence.

VII. *Privacy of the Arbitration*

The parties should consider whether the subject matter of the arbitration is of such public interest as to warrant publicity concerning the proceeding and publication of the award and opinion, if any; and should advise the arbitrator accordingly on the record or in writing.

VIII. *Arbitrators' Executive Meetings*

Meetings of the arbitrators and discussions in executive sessions by members of boards of arbitration are private and confidential and parties should not seek to obtain information concerning such meetings either from the third arbitrator or from their nominees. Parties should likewise refrain from attempting to secure in advance from the arbitrator or their nominees information concerning the award but should wait until the award is received in the regular course by both parties.

IX. *The Award*

Parties, having agreed to arbitration, should accept and abide by the award.

After an award has been rendered, neither party should unilaterally request a clarification or interpretation of the award from the arbitrator. If one is necessary, it should be requested jointly by both parties.

X. *Settlements*

If the parties reach a settlement of their dispute but desire nevertheless to have an award made, they should give the arbitrator a full explanation of the reasons therefor in order that he may judge whether he desires to make or join in such an award.

XI. *Compensation of the Arbitrator*

Parties should agree in advance of the hearing with the arbitrator on his compensation or the basis upon which it will be determined, but such arrangements should be made only in the presence of both parties. If the parties do not agree with one another as to the compensation, they should discuss the matter in the absence of the arbitrator in order that there be no intimation or suggestion that one party is willing to pay more compensation than the other and thereby raise the possibility of a question thereafter as to partiality on the part of the arbitrator.

Having agreed on the compensation for an arbitrator's services or to the reimbursement of his necessary expenses, parties should remit promptly and under no circumstances should such payment be withheld because of displeasure over the award.

TOPICAL INDEX

A

Abridgement of the Law, Statham   6
Affidavits
—in lieu of testimony   257 (see footnote)
—Voluntary Labor Arbitration Rules   257 (see footnote)
—witnesses unable to be present, value of affidavits in preparing cases   264
Agreement to arbitrate   82, 120
—amending agreements, method of   152
—bad faith or fraud during original negotiation as making contract voidable at option of other party   161
—breach of agreement, damages resulting from, party opposing revocation, right of action for   154
—contracts *uberrimae fidei*   163
—interpretation of agreements   150
—legal submission to arbitration, award as taking place of original claim   159
—legislation to provide written agreements to submit existing disputes to arbitration as bar to suits pending arbitration   155
—partnerships, all partners as signatories to agreement   135
—revocation (see Revocation of agreement to arbitrate)
—state and federal courts, applicable laws construed so as to broaden effects of certain classes of agreements   155
Air transport industry
—Railway Labor Act, coverage under   194
American Arbitration Association
—case load, 1948–1968   10
—submission of dispute to party named by AAA   34
Anti-injunction laws
—Norris-LaGuardia Act   13 (see footnote), 26, 32, 46, 66
Antitrust laws
—state enforcement of   68
Arbitrability, determination of
—(see also Arbitration, subhead: sub-

jects of)
—arbitrability as arbitrable issue   34
—combined criminal and civil-action questions   8
—common law as unreceptive toward arbitration   32
—courts v. arbitrators   31–38
—criminal matters   121
—Cutler-Hammer Doctrine   33
——criticism of   36
—disputes raising legal rights of action   82 et seq.
—Supreme Court of U.S. rulings   31 et seq.
Arbitration
—(see also specific subject heads)
—advantages over litigation   21
—automated jobs, partially or fully, increasing numbers   309
—bias, prejudice   107, 161, 257
—capacity of parties to enter into arbitration agreements   127
—commercial case, arbitration as substitute for litigation   37
—compulsory binding arbitration, legislative approval   188
—contract terms concerning   150
—control of process   131
—corporations as parties to   135
—court action, termination as result of parties entering into arbitration agreement   149
—disputes arising in the future, unperformed agreement as void in some states   144
—effective support to arbitrational proceedings   346
—fashioning of federal law by Supreme Court, effect   72
—fees of arbitrators, liability of the parties   119
—functional field of   19
—future controversies, agreement to arbitrate   124, 144
—grievances and new contract clauses, arbitration of differences between   294
—historical backgrounds   4
—human element, failure to take into account   109

Evidence—Contd.
—records of employers   228, 259
—rehearing, new evidence   282
—relevancy, materiality,
    competency   229
—*res gestae*   235
—review by courts   220
—right to open and close   251
—rulings by government agencies   226
—rulings on   256
—scientific or technical books   239
—settlement offers   232
—subpoena   116
—testimony of witnesses   220, 234,
    244, 254, 263, 264
—ultimate facts   266 (see footnote)
—under oath   254
—vacation   289
—weight and sufficiency of   220
—witnesses, use of   223
—written evidence, arbitrator's author-
    ity to order production of   116
Ex parte proceedings, arbitrator's au-
    thority   155, 258
Executory contract   144

F

Fair Labor Standards Act
—as limiting arbitral awards   122
—historical background   49, 66
—Sec. 1 provision   26
Federal laws
—Congressional policy   63
—Lincoln Mills decision, issues raised
    by, solution of   32
Federal Mediation & Conciliation
Service
—arbitration policies, functions, and
    procedures of   389
—case load
——by industry, 1968   180
——1948–1968   10
—notification requirement   27
—submission of dispute to party named
    by FMCS   34
Federal preemption
—(see Federal-state jurisdiction)
Federal-state jurisdiction   64 et seq.
—(see also Jurisdiction of courts; Na-
    tional Labor Relations Board)
—arbitration, suits to enjoin   78
—federal-preemption doctrine
——exceptions to   202
——implementation of, resume   64 et
    seq.
—individual union member or non-
    member, absence of fair representa-

tion in arbitration, relief under Secs.
    9 or 301, LMRA   131
—interstate, intrastate, and local com-
    merce   65, 91
—labor arbitration, U.S. Supreme
    Court holding   72
—libel suit brought by campaigners for
    one union against another union,
    state jurisdiction   90
—Lincoln Mills decision, effect of   126
—LMRA, Sec. 8 (b) (4), 1959 amend-
    ments as widening potential scope
    of federal action against union unfair
    labor practices   83
—NLRB refusal to take jurisdiction,
    state jurisdiction, provision for   100
—"no man's land"   56, 71, 91, 100,
    101, 201, 208
—piggy-back case   94
—preemption, states' authority   80, 84
—public utilities
——application of   201
——compulsory arbitration   208
——state courts' co-jurisdiction with
    NLRB   66
—termination by retirement of em-
    ployees between ages 60 and 65 as
    consistant with agreement   79
—unfair-labor-practice disputes under
    Sec. 8 (b) decided by NLRB   83
—union-shop agreement in right-to-
    work-law state   95
—unions, suits by and against, Sec.
    301, LMRA   76
Fiduciaries   133 et seq.
Findings of fact   112
Formal requisites   140
Forum, law of   339 et seq.
Frankfurter, Mr. Justice   29, 30, 84,
87, 200

G

Government contracts
—Walsh-Healey Act requirements   44
Grievance procedure   137
—awards as precedent   140
—charges and responses as compared
    with pleadings   139
—compliance as condition to
    arbitration   157
—employee's consent to
    settlement   130
—flexibility, provision by contract be-
    tween parties   137
—grievance as submission agree-
    ment   138, 250
—individual presentation under Taft-
    Hartley Act   51

TABLE OF CASES CITED

A

Abell, A. S. Co. v. Baltimore Typographical Union No. 12, 338 F. 2d 190, 57 LRRM 2480 (CA 4, 1964) 338

Acme Cut Stone Co. v. New Center Development Corp., 281 Mich. 32, 274 N.W. 700, (1937) 275

Adair; U.S. v., 208 U.S. 161, 28 S.Ct. 277 (1908) 42, 47, 65

Addeo v. Dairymen's League, 262 N.Y.S. 2d 771, 47 Misc. 2d 426, 60 LRRM 2235 (1965) 76

Addressograph-Multigraph Corp., 46 LA 1189 (1966) 309

Adinolfi v. Hazlett, 242 Pa. 25, 88 A. 869 (1913) 24

Adkins v. Children's Hospital, 261 U.S. 525, 568, 43 S.Ct. 394 (1923) 49, 212

Aerojet-General Corp., 49 LA 1073 (1967) 298

Aetna Indemnity Co. v. Waters, 110 Md. 673, 73 A. 712 (1909) 152

Aetna Ins. Co.
—v. Jester, 37 Okla. 413, 132 Pac. 130 (1913) 165
—v. McLead, 57 Kans. 95, 45 P. 73, 57 Am. St. Rep. 320 (1896) 156

Agostini Bros. Bldg. Corp. v. U.S. etc. 142 Fed. (2d) 854 (1944) 26

Aktieselskabet Korn-Og Foderstof Kompagniet v. Rederiaktiebolaget Atlanten (C.C.A. 2d) 250 F. 935 (1918) 341

Alabama G.S.R. Co. v. Hill, 90 Ala. 71, 8 So. 90 (1890) 236

Alameda County Water Dist. v. Spring Valley Dist., 67 Cal. App. 533, 227 Pac. 953 (1924) 149

Albert
—v. Albert, 391 S.W. 2d 186 (Tex. Ct. of Civ. App., 1965) 159, 160
—v. Goor, 70 Ariz. 214, 218 P. (2d) 736 (1950) 281

Alcoa v. Local 760, Electrical Workers, 203 Tenn. 12, 308 S.W. 2d 477 (1957) 186

Alexander v. Fletcher, 175 S.W. (2nd) 196 (1944) 15

Alexandria Canal Co. v. Swann, 5 How. (U.S.) 83, 12 L.Ed. 60 (1847) 154, 160, 177, 345

Algoma Net Co.; NLRB v., 124 F. (2d) 730, 9 LRRM 531 (1941) 123

Allen-Bradley Co. v. Anderson & Nelson Distilleries Co., 99 Ky. 311, 35 S.W. 1123 (1896) 105

Althen v. Tarbox, 48 Minn. 18, 50 N.W. 1018, 31 Am. St. Rep. 616 (1892) 133

Alton R.R., State ex. rel. v. Public Service Comm., 334 Mo. 1001, 70 S.W. 2d 61 (1934) 210

American Airlines Inc. v. Louisville & Jefferson County Air Board, (C.A. Ky.), 269 F. 2d 811 (1959) 352

American Almond Products Co. v. Consol. Pecan Sales Co., 144 F. 2d 448 (C.C.A. 2d, 1944) 217

American Bakery & Confectionery Workers (AFL-CIO) v. National Biscuit Co., D.C. N.J. 252 Fed. Supp. 768, Affd. C.A., 378 F. 2d 918 (1967) 346

American Bosch Arma Corp. v. Electrical Workers, IUE, 243 F. Supp. 493, 59 LRRM 2798 (N.D. Miss., 1965) 286

American Can Co., 11 LA 405 (1948) 319

American Cent. Ins. Co.
—v. Bass Bros., 90 Tex. 380, 38 S.W. 1119 (1897) 162
—v. District Ct., 125 Minn. 374, 147 N.W. 242 (1914) 111

American Chain & Cable Co., 21 LA 15 (1953) 319

American Federation of Labor
—v. Buck's Stove & Range Co., 219 U.S. 581, L.Ed. 345, 31 S.Ct. 472 (1910) 23
—v. Swing, 312 U.S. 321, 326, 7 LRRM 307 (1941) 86, 87

American Fire Ins. Co. v. Bell, 33 Tex. Civ. App. 11, 75 S.W. 319 (1903) 165

423

H

Kennedy
—v. Bell Telephone Co., 52 CCH Lab.
Cas. ¶ 16,639 (S.D.Cal., 1965)   76
—v. Continental Transp. Lines, Inc.,
230 F. Supp. 760, 56 LRRM 2663
(W.D. Pa., 1964)   283
—v. Monarch Mfg. Co., 123 Iowa 344,
98 N.W. 796 (1904)   345
—People v., 159 N.Y. 346, 54 N.E.
51 (1899)   234
—v. UAW, 52 CCH Lab. Cas. ¶ 16,
578 (1965)   75
Kentile, Inc. v. Rubber Workers, Local
457, 228 F. Supp. 541, 55 LRRM 3011
(E.D.N.Y. 1964)   78, 335
Keppler v. Nessler, 232 N.Y.S. 232,
225 App. Div. 99 (1928)   254
Kerr v. Lunsford, 31 W.Va. 659, 8
S.E. 493 (1888)   238
Kessler v. National Casualty Co., 8
A.D. 2d 105, 185 N.Y.S. 2d 437
(1959)   287
Key v. Norrod, 124 Tenn. 146, 136
S.W. 991 (1910)   175
King
—v. Beale, 198 Va. 802, 96 S.E. 2d
765 (1957)   148, 174
—v. Cook, 1 T.U.P. Charit, (Ga.) 286,
4 Am. Dec. 715 (1810)   149
—v. Delaware Lackawanna & W.R.
Co., 81 N.J.L. 536, 80 A. 327
(1911)   238
Kinkead v. Hartley, 161 Iowa 613, 143
N.W. 591 (1913)   134
Kinney v. Baltimore & Ohio Em-
ployees' Relief Assn., 35 W.Va. 385,
14 S.E. 8 (1891)   142
Kirch (see Goerke Kirch)
Kirk
—v. Hamilton, 102 U.S. 68, 26 L.Ed.
79 (1880)   162
—v. Pilcher, 174 Ala. 170, 57 So. 46
(1911)   289
Kitchens v. Doe, 172 So. 2d 896; (Fla.,
1965)   87
Klinger, Victor, et al. and J. S. Krum,
Inc., 19 N.Y. S. (2d) 193 (1940)   124
Knaus v. Jenkins, 40 N.J.L. 288, 29
Am. Rep. 237 (1878)   116, 123, 173,
174
Knickerbocker L. Ins. Co. v. Norton,
96 U.S. 234 (1877)   242
Kociuba v. Stubnitz Greene Corp., 52
CCH Lab. Cas. ¶ 51,388 (Pa. C.P.,
1964)   75
Koepke v. E. Liethen Grain Co., 205
Wis. 75, 236 N.W. 544 (1931)   257,
289
Kohl v. Beach, 107 Wis. 409, 83 N.W.
657 (1900)   134

Kohlsaat
—v. Main Island Creek Coal Co., 90
W.Va. 656, 112 S.E. 213
(1922)   146
—v. Parkersburg & Marrietta Co., 266
Fed. 283, 11 A.L.R. 686
(1920)   221
Kohn v. Wagner, 52 CCH Lab. Cas.
¶ 51,354 (N.Y. Sup. Ct., 1965)   85
Konigmacher v. Kimmel, 1 Penrose &
W. (Pa.) 207, 21 Am. Dec. 374
(1829)   20, 134
Kracoff v. Retail Clerks, 244 F. Supp.
38, 59 LRRM 2942, (E.D. Pa.,
1965)   79
Kramer & Uchitelle, Inc., 288 N.Y.
467, 43 N.E. 2d 493 (1942)   125
Kress, S. H. & Co., 25 LA 77
(1955)   321
Kroger Co.
—v. Teamsters, 380 F. 2d 728, 65
LRRM 2573 (CA 6, 1967)   286
—12 LA 1065 (1949)   234
—25 LA 906 (1955)   122
Kunst v. Grafton, 67 W. Va. 20, 67
S.E. 74 (1910)   239

L

Labor Board (see name of opposing
party)
Labor Relations Board (see name of
opposing party)
Lacy v. Meador, 170 Ala. 482, 54 So.
161 (1910); see Ann. Cases 1912 D
787, 792   232
Ladies Garment Workers (see Garment
Workers, ILGWU)
Lag Drug Co., 39 LA 1121 (Dec. 20,
1962), 63-1 Arb. ¶ 8106   225
Laidlaw v. Sage, 158 N.Y. 73, 52 N.E.
679 (1899)   222, 223
Lake City Malleable, Inc., 25 LA 753
(1956)   319
Lake Shore Power Co. v. Edgerton,
43 Ohio App. 545, 184 N.E. 37
(1932)   176, 347, 348
Lammonds v. Aleo Mfg. Co., 26 LA
351 (N.Car. Sup.Ct., 1956)   131
Lamon v. Georgia Southern & Florida
Ry. Co., 212 Ga. 63, 90 S.E. 2d 658,
37 LRRM 2115 (1955)   321
Lampe v. Franklin American Trust Co.,
339 Mo. 361, 96 S.W. 2d 710
(1936)   224
Lanier v. Richardson, 72 Ala. 134
(1882)   280
Laning's Estate, 241 Pa. 98, 88 A.
289 (1913); see annotation at 68
A.L.R. 695   228